D1320697

WE, THE NATION

WE, THE NATION

The Conservative Party
and the Pursuit of Power

—◆—

A. J. Davies

LITTLE, BROWN AND COMPANY

A *Little, Brown* Book

First published in Great Britain in 1995
by Little, Brown and Company

Copyright © Andrew Davies 1995

The moral right of the author has been asserted.

A CIP catalogue record for this book
is available from the British Library.

ISBN 0 316 91445 2

Typeset by Palimpsest Book Production Limited,
Polmont, Stirlingshire
Printed and bound in Great Britain by
Clays Ltd, St Ives plc

Little, Brown and Company (UK)
Brettenham House
Lancaster Place
London WC2E 7EN

Acknowledgements

My biggest debt is to the hundreds of people who have so readily talked to me about the Conservative Party over the last ten years. Family, friends and brief acquaintances have sometimes found the conversation not very skilfully steered into political paths. These contacts have ranged from Cabinet ministers, MPs, agents and 'rank and file' Conservatives to downright opponents of the Party and all its doings.

In particular I want to thank the members of various adult education classes who generously criticised, discussed and got excited about many of the ideas and arguments which now appear in *We, The Nation*. This tradition of adult education – University Extra-Mural Departments, the Open University, the Workers' Educational Association (WEA) and many others – is one of Britain's finest twentieth-century achievements. It would take another book to list everyone concerned, and many never gave me their names: so a big and generalised thank you.

Also, thank you to the staffs of the various libraries who have been so helpful: the Public Records Office at Kew, the House of Lords Records Office, the staffs at the Westminster, Islington and Marylebone Libraries, the Essex Records Office in Chelmsford, the British Library, Cambridge University Library, Cambridge Public Library, Norwich Public Library, the Marx Memorial Library, the London Library, the British Library Manuscript Collections and finally Dr Martin Maw, the Conservative Party Archivist at the Bodleian.

I would also like to thank the copyright holders of unpublished material for giving me permission to quote. In particular, I would like to thank Alistair Cooke of the Conservative Political Centre for permission to quote from the Conservative Party Archive held at the Bodleian Library, Oxford. All unpublished material is clearly indicated and referenced in the Notes.

Thank you to everyone at Little, Brown for their faith in the book and their hard work: Alan Samson, Andrew Gordon, Janet Ravenscroft and Linda Silverman.

Finally, one or two individuals. My parents, staunch but not unthinking Conservatives who embody all that is best in the Tory story – tolerance, humour, patience and a sense of proportion. Andrew Lownie, my agent and friend, who is himself much involved in the Conservative Party and who has provided ideas, contacts and encouragement.

Margaret Jordan has looked after me and cheerfully provided cups of tea and coffee at 4 in the morning despite my being glued wordlessly to the word processor. She even remained good humoured and full of love when I couldn't locate that elusive reference and was once again turning over the flat.

Finally, Jean Collingsworth has once again toiled away on successive versions of the book. Not content with editing the manuscript, her stimulus, love and support were and are invaluable and incomparable. Thank you.

'We have to remember that the Conservative Party is not a debating society. It is not indulging in internal discussion for some sort of literary purpose. Politics is about power.'

Defence Secretary Malcolm Rifkind
BBC1's *On the Record*, 18 December 1994

Contents

WE, THE NATION

1

The Tory Story
An introduction

'We have our agreements in public and our disagreements in private.'

> John Major at the Conservative Party conference,
> October 1993

'The Royal Society for the Protection of Birds . . . has more members than the Labour, Conservative and Liberal Democrat Parties combined.'

> *The Economist*, 13 August 1994

In the midst of election riots at Tamworth, Staffordshire, in 1818, the Conservative candidate Robert Peel received a letter from his father Sir Robert, who was himself a Tory MP: 'I think you will find it in our interest to have the town sobered by inactivity . . .'

'Sober inactivity' has for decades served the world's most successful political party well. With an unbroken existence going back over 150 years, the Conservative Party in terms of electoral success, power and influence clearly leaves its rivals here in Britain, and its Christian Democrat counterparts on the Continent, standing.

When asked to explain the Conservative Party's formidable record, most commentators reach for words such as loyalty, unity, resilience. These words, all true as far as they go, tend to reinforce the image of sober inactivity. But in fact if one begins to dig below the surface of 'public agreement' then underlying tensions and arguments quickly come to light. The Conservative Party is not the natural party of government as it would often wish us to believe – no party is – and in reality its long-standing dominance has inevitably been the result of struggle and conflict.

The official Tory story is one of sweetness and light, worthy but a little dull. Unofficially, however, the story contains hidden details and meanings which are much more intriguing and revealing than the sanitised version. Why is it that so many critics and observers have happily taken the Conservative Party at its own valuation?

For one thing, Conservatives themselves have a vested interest in claiming the Party's record to be one of unity, loyalty and unblemished virtue. They know full well that no political party with pretensions to power benefits from being seen by the electorate as divided and fractious.

It is no accident, therefore, that most Conservative philosophers discourage activity or inquiry, preferring to argue that people should simply accept their fate. Too much analysis or agitation might upset the natural order of things. The Conservative historian Sir Keith Feiling put it best in his book *Toryism* (1913): 'We do not trust human reason.' Or, in Benjamin Disraeli's words, 'Man was made to adore and obey.'

Meanwhile, from the other end of the political spectrum, many socialists and Marxists have offered lazy caricatures of the Conservative Party. Such clumping generalities as 'ruling class this' and 'Colonel Blimp that' completely ignore the nuanced and many-layered history of the Party, its members and supporters. If the Party is a conspiracy directed against the public, then most of the public seem only too happy to join in.

The Conservative Party has also been anxious to reinforce the idea that politics happens only at the Houses of Parliament. This simplification obscures the fact that much of the Party's strength derives from powerful interests such as the press and business which generally operate well away from Westminster.

The veil of secrecy that sometimes conceals the workings of British society similarly hinders any frank reappraisal of the Party. We have no Freedom of Information Act and no written constitution. Many government agencies, securely cocooned by the paraphernalia of Official Secrets Acts and 'D notices', are inadequately supervised. The public's right to know is very limited indeed.

These powerful silences are unlikely to be pierced by a press which generally rallies to the Conservative Party and, at the same time, often trivialises and personalises political issues. We know rather more about the private lives of certain politicians than we do about the workings of British government. Stringent libel laws and the inordinate cost of litigation have largely strangled any British investigative tradition, with the honourable exception of occasional features in the 'serious' newspapers or magazines. That Robert Maxwell was able to get away with his crimes is a sad reflection on the state of the British press.

Too many political reports in newspapers contain the words 'as a senior Cabinet minister said to me' or 'senior sources confirmed today'. These conveniently anonymous and unverifiable phrases prompt one to ask who is using whom and for what purpose. The autobiography of the long-time editor of the *Sunday Express*, Sir John Junor, shows how some politicians and members of the press collude in this game. Politics is reduced to one long round of cosy lunches, convenient leaks and mutual congratulation – a process which Aneurin Bevan once memorably described as 'gastronomic pimping'.

Other branches of the media are rarely braver than the press. Government pressure on the BBC's licence fee and on the franchises of commercial television, together with the dictates of ratings figures, does not encourage investigative reporting. Greg Dyke, former chief executive of London Weekend Television, warned in 1994 that broadcasters were in danger of losing their independence: 'With broadcasters [the BBC and commercial companies] constantly wanting favour and legislative action from government, it gives the Government far too much power in the relationship.'

In any case, all political parties – and not just the Conservatives – now come fully armed with a battery of 'spin doctors' and media advisers who are adept at 'playing' the media.

In the world of books and academia too, the Tory story has

been neglected. Publishers have traditionally regarded titles about the Left as being more commercial than those about the Right. Likewise, Conservatism and the Conservative Party have always been unfashionable academic subjects. Brian Harrison has ascribed this to age: when young, historians are not attracted by movements which delay change; when middle-aged, 'they lack the time and enthusiasm required for doing justice to the subject'.

The task of delving into the Conservative Party is made even more daunting by the prospect of all those mountainous self-serving memoirs to be read. There are Harold Macmillan's six hefty volumes, Anthony Eden's three and the tomes of Thatcher, Lawson, Baker, Ridley, Young, Fowler, Parkinson, Tebbit, Whitelaw, Hailsham – with only an occasional Alan Clark or Julian Critchley to lighten the load. The private papers of former Prime Minister Arthur Balfour weigh nearly half a ton, a fraction of the Churchill collection which breaks the scales at fifteen tons. Even the papers of Selwyn Lloyd, an important but hardly world-famous Conservative politician, fill up 495 boxes.

Perhaps mesmerised by the quantity of such material, most observers have tended to produce straightforward narrative accounts in which the detail is all, the argument nothing. Although this approach may be justified when writing biographies, it does not lend itself readily to discussion or analysis and as a result many uncomfortable questions relating to the Conservatives' past have been avoided.

Historians are understandably devoted to the printed word. Fine, but in the case of the Conservative Party such devotion may lead them to miss much. Professor John Vincent put it well:

> The way to study Conservatives is to meet Conservatives; and here Leftist writers are at a loss. They resemble early Victorian anthropologists, whose willingness to pronounce on the nature of man bore no relation to their readiness to commune with natives by sleeping in straw huts. Naturally, self-imprisoned in their intellectual ghetto, Leftists concentrate on printed texts which, in Tory terms, means the ephemeral, the tangential, and the epiphenomenal.

I have certainly met Conservatives (being brought up in a Conservative household and experiencing a public school and Oxbridge education), but I have also slogged through 'ephemeral' printed texts; not just the conventional material of Public Record Office, party records and private papers, but more diverse sources ranging from newspapers and novels to films and cartoons.

My use of such catholic and wide-ranging material in preparing this book has meant that *We, The Nation* is not a traditional political history. The Conservative Party is a diverse and octopus-like creature: to focus exclusively on the 'high politics' of Cabinet papers or *The Times* is to miss the charm, humour and personal touch that have been integral to the Party's success.

The Royal Society for the Protection of Birds (RSPB) has more members than the three main political parties combined. It seems to me that a healthy dose of scepticism is therefore in order when faced with the self-important posturing of some politicians and commentators.

For example, many political books are written solely for insiders and 'those in the know'. One recent academic work carries the potentially revealing title *Back from Westminster* and is in part an interesting study of British MPs and their constituents. But few people in their right minds would try to decipher tables of statistics devoted to Cross-Party Factor Solution (Unrotated Factor Loadings) and Regression Coefficients for Conservative and Labour ICVC. (As is generally known, ICVC stands for 'Incumbent Constituency-specific Vote Change'.)

Tattooed on the forehead of every political historian should be the words of the veteran *Sunday Times* journalist James Margach: 'Politics is about power. Power is about people. People are personalities.'

In part, this book is an attempt to penetrate some of those veils and evasions which have cloaked chapters of our past, hiding the unofficial faces of the Conservative Party. One of my favourite quotations comes from the radical philosopher and thinker Thomas Paine, contained in his *Examination of the Prophecies* (1806):

In writing upon this, as upon every subject, I speak a language full and intelligible. I deal not in hints and intimations. I have several reasons for this: first, that I may be clearly understood. Secondly, that it may be seen that I am in earnest; and thirdly, because it is an affront to truth to treat falsehood with complaisance.

This is the ideal that I have tried to emulate.

We, The Nation covers a great deal of ground, but it is impossible to understand the workings of the Conservative Party unless one tries to view the organisation in its entirety, teasing out the connecting threads and strands. Specialised studies and monographs are invaluable, but sometimes an overall map is required to make sense of the detail.

We, The Nation adopts a thematic approach, but has been designed to be read straight through if the reader wishes. Chapter 2 offers a brief history of the Party, which is then followed by a discussion of Conservatism as a body of ideas. The next three chapters explore Conservative leaders, their followers in the House of Commons and the Party outside Westminster in the constituencies.

Chapter 7 looks at exactly how the Conservative Party is financed, after which there is a study of the Party's electoral record and two separate examinations of dirty tricks directed against both external and internal opponents. The following two chapters scrutinise the record of Conservative governments on the economy and welfare.

Chapter 13 considers the Party's relationship with the Establishment and a further chapter explores the Conservative sense of national identity and what that has meant to the Party. Chapter 15 traces the careers of a number of Tory rebels and mavericks. The next two chapters consider how the Conservative Party has been portrayed by Conservatives, historians and in the wider media. The book ends by pulling together some of the most important themes.

We, The Nation contains footnotes, but they are designed in such a way that the text is not disfigured by an array of numbers. Key words provide the source of the reference which is duly provided in the notes at the end of the book. Chapter 17, which deals with images of the Conservative Party, contains what is in effect an essay on further reading.

In a complex and complicated society it is vital for our well-being that we subject those who govern on our behalf to unrelenting scrutiny — even if such attention may disturb their sober inactivity.

A Question of Terminology

Conservative politicians have an annoying habit of changing their names. Probably the all-time record is held by Sir Alec Douglas-Home. He began his political career as a young Conservative MP called Lord Dunglass. Upon inheriting his father's title he became the 14th Earl of Home. When he renounced his title on becoming Prime Minister in October 1963, he turned into Sir Alec Douglas-Home. On retirement he re-entered the House of Lords as Lord Home of the Hirsel. It is not surprising that his wife once complained about the frequency with which they had to change their headed note-paper.

Quintin Hogg is another Tory politician who is also well-known as Lord Hailsham. And of course distinguished figures change their names when entering the House of Lords; thus Mrs Margaret Thatcher is now Baroness Thatcher of Kesteven and Nigel Lawson is Lord Lawson of Blaby.

In general, I have called each person by the name under which they were known at the time of my reference.

Terminological uncertainty extends to the very name of the Conservative Party itself. Today its official title is the Conservative and Unionist Party. From 1886 to 1925 it was officially known just as the Unionist Party in order to signal its opposition to the powerful Home Rule movement in Ireland.

So where does the label 'Tory' come from? In the eighteenth and early nineteenth centuries, the two British political parties were referred to as Tories and Whigs. Broadly, the Tories represented the 'throne and altar' spectrum of opinion, the Whigs spoke for the reforming commercial and professional interests. Both terms had originally been ones of abuse. A 'toiridhe' was an Irish bog-trotter, a 'whiggamore' a Scottish cattle-rustler.

In the first decades of the nineteenth century, British politics was transformed by the onset of industrialisation, by migration from the countryside to the cities and, in 1832, by the passage of the first Reform Act which increased the number of people eligible to vote.

The old Tories, as we shall see, faced a major problem. How were they to react to this hated brave new world? Would they retreat into their shell and maintain a marginal existence as dyed-in-the-wool reactionaries, or would they accept change? Under Sir Robert Peel the second option was taken, and many historians dignify the decision by introducing the label Conservative Party.

But, of course, the name Tory lives on. Some people like its connotations of ancient privilege and patrician qualities; perhaps, too, its concern with social issues. On the other hand, numerous critics of the Party find the word Tory effective as a word of abuse. The banners and posters of, say, the Socialist Workers' party lambast the Tories and never the Conservatives – and not just because the word Tory is shorter, easier, and cheaper to print.

I have decided for the sake of consistency to use the word Conservative, relying on Tory as a second best and with a specific meaning only if it is made clear in the context.

Finally, a word needs to be said about money values. A rough guide is to multiply sums before the First World War by a figure of fifty in order to get an approximation to current values. In other words, the pound of 1914 is now worth two pence. Much of this devaluation took place after 1945.

To give an example: tycoon Sir John Ellerman's contribution of £5,000 a year to party funds in the 1920s would now be in excess of £200,000 a year.

Old Dog, New Tricks

A brief history of the Conservative Party

'Damn your principles! Stick to your party.'
　　Benjamin Disraeli to his friend Edward Bulwer Lytton

'In their most true blue moments, Conservatives feel that it is contrary to the natural order of things for them to be out of power.'
　　　　　　　　　　　　Sir Ian Gilmour, *The Body Politic* (1971)

'The Tory Party is, above all, a party dedicated to being in office and to that end has always looked for talent from any quarter.'
　　　　　　　　　　Norman Tebbit, *Sunday Telegraph*, 16 May 1993

The Conservative Cabinet of 1895 was led by a marquess and contained a duke, an earl, a viscount, three barons, two baronets, another marquess, the son of a duke, the brother-in-law of a duke and just six 'commoners', all of whom were prosperous and well-connected.

The name is the same, but the Conservative Cabinet one hundred years later in 1995 has a rather different composition. The titled landed aristocracy has been elbowed out by career politicians from middle-class backgrounds.

The contrast between old and new is most striking when one

compares the careers of Lord Salisbury, Conservative Prime Minister in 1895, and John Major, Conservative Prime Minister in 1995. Educated at Eton and Cambridge, Salisbury lived in the majestic Hatfield House and his family's involvement with public affairs stretched back to the days of Elizabeth I. Salisbury's self-confidence and assurance were fully exhibited when he remarked, 'There are only two positions of any importance in Britain, Prime Minister and Foreign Secretary, and I hold both of them.'

John Major, of course, experienced a rather less privileged upbringing. A patchy formal education ended at sixteen and was followed by a brief spell of unemployment. Both men immersed themselves in politics at an early age – at twenty-five Salisbury was an MP and Major a Lambeth councillor – but there the similarity ends. Lord Salisbury emphasised the importance of authority, hierarchy and tradition. John Major, in contrast, has declared, 'If you wanted to boil my political views down to a single sentence, it would be that I don't believe anybody should know their place.'

The fact that both Salisbury, Major and their respective Cabinets would have unhesitatingly claimed the Conservative label, under-lines the way in which the British Conservative Party has managed to adapt and accommodate itself to different circumstances. Its success is shown by the prominent role the Party has played in British society over nearly two centuries. It has supplied Prime Ministers and governments, its activists run councils and its supporters are embedded in institutions from the judiciary to the Civil Service. Membership of the Party has always been numbered in hundreds of thousands and today the 1,350 Conservative Clubs up and down the country offer irrefutable evidence of its presence in the community.

Proud of itself as a political organisation which is not very interested in politics, the Conservative Party has carefully projected an image of stability and moderation. Commentators have obligingly taken this cue and reach for words such as gradual, durable or evolutionary in order to describe the development of the Party. Unsurprisingly therefore, textbook histories of the Conservative Party tend to be rather dull. Just as the Whigs in the nineteenth century produced a Whig theory of history, which supposedly showed the inevitability of their party's triumph, in the twentieth century many Conservatives seem to believe that political success is theirs by right.

In fact it is just as valid, and much more revealing, to view the history of the Party as one of upheaval, conflict and change. In order to survive, the British Conservative Party has continually recreated itself by accommodating new demands and circumstances. It has been successful in this struggle because, like the Catholic Church, it has learnt how to manage change. In particular, the Party has always tried to ensure that change takes place within a framework of continuity and tradition so that, in many cases, it is hardly noticeable until it takes effect.

Dedicated to the pursuit of power, the Conservative Party is fully aware that the methods needed to win or retain power are always changing. The Party has always appreciated the force of Francis Bacon's words: 'He who will not apply new remedies must expect new evils for time is the greatest innovator.'

On the face of it, therefore, the British Conservative Party appears to be like a swan, gliding gracefully along, serene and self-confident. Hidden below the surface, however, the feet are churning and working hard in order to power such apparently untroubled progress.

It is instructive to contrast the Conservatives' acceptance of change with the behaviour of the British Labour Party. Supposedly a radical and innovative body, the Labour Party has generally been characterised by the defensiveness and ponderous attitudes of its trade union creators.

This tension between continuity and discontinuity in the Conservative Party's history is demonstrated by the periodic attempts made to change its name. This usually happens when the Party is in trouble. Following the catastrophic split over Sir Robert Peel's repeal of the Corn Laws in 1846, for instance, some Conservatives wanted the Party to be renamed the Country Party or the Protectionists. In the 1870s, party leader Lord Salisbury preferred the name Constitutional Party, but his colleagues disapproved of the idea.

After the First World War, the rise of the labour movement alarmed many thoughtful Conservatives. The influential Alderman Salvidge of Liverpool agitated for the Party to be renamed the Constitutional Reform Party, and F.E. Smith and others planned to position the Party as the basis of a new centre party, to be called variously the National Party, the Constitutional Party or the People's Party. Similarly, after the traumatic election defeat of 1945, party chairman Lord Woolton advocated the new name of the Union Party, whilst Harold Macmillan recommended the New Democratic Party label.

Today, some supporters contend that the Scottish Conservatives should be renamed the Scottish Unionists in order to distance themselves from the unpopular Conservative tag. In the European Parliament the Conservatives are affiliated to the European People's Party.

In fact the Conservative Party has sometimes changed its title, most notably in 1886 when it renamed itself the Unionist Party as a sign of its hostility to the idea of Home Rule for Ireland. However the Conservative tag was still widely used, which often made matters rather complicated. In June 1923, for example, the Party's agents had to ask Central Office to print posters and literature 'with the words "Unionist", "Conservative and Unionist" and "Conservative" to suit the requirements and wishes of the various constituencies.' After the partition of Ireland the Unionist label was subsequently downgraded in favour of Conservative.

In Scotland the Party was called the Scottish Unionist Association between 1912 and 1965. In local politics, too, Conservatives traditionally sailed under a variety of flags of convenience such as Independent, the Ratepayers' Association or the Municipal Association.

Uncertainty and argument over something as fundamental as the name of the Party demonstrates how strenuously the Conservatives have had to struggle in order to survive. There was never any cast–iron guarantee that the Conservative Party would in fact endure. After all, comparable throne and altar parties established on the Continent 150 years ago have long been dead and buried. But in Britain the Conservatives have managed to surmount each of the major crises that have threatened their existence and hold on to power: regrouping, consolidating and then continuing.

Few Conservative politicians have ever matched the rectitude, self-confidence and grandeur of the 1st Duke of Wellington. This internationally renowned conqueror of Napoleon was given a grand house, known simply as 'No 1, London', by a grateful nation. Followed by admiring crowds as he walked through the capital's streets, the Duke was an active and influential member of Lord Liverpool's Tory government in the 1820s.

But not even the charisma of 'the Iron Duke' could withstand the economic and social forces which were transforming his Britain. Cocooned as he was in his own haughty world, Wellington knew little about the arrival of industrialisation, the enclosure of common land or the quickening migration from the country to the city. But despite the Duke's ignorance it was these forces that were inexorably undermining the *ancien régime* with which he had grown up. Politics for him was a matter of a tightly restricted electorate, personal allegiance and royal patronage.

It was not that the Duke was opposed to all change – he had helped push through the Catholic Emancipation Act in 1829 that allowed Catholics the right to vote – but he was hostile to attempts to widen the political process by extending the franchise. For him, the Constitution was perfect and not to be altered in any way.

By 1830, however, popular agitation for electoral reform was growing apace. Neither the Tories nor their opponents the Whigs wanted change, but whereas the Whigs could see that it was better to concede something, the Tories under the Duke's promptings were categorically hostile to any measure whatsoever.

In 1831 popular feeling ran so high at the Tory government's hostility towards parliamentary reform that Derby prison was stormed, Nottingham castle was set alight and there were riots in Bristol. As for the Duke himself, for so long the popular hero, he was jostled and physically threatened in the street, and the windows of No 1, London, were smashed to bits by a cursing mob.

The Whigs subsequently passed a Reform Act which doubled

the electorate so that approximately one in five adult males could vote. At the following general election, the Tories were reduced to a rump of just 185 seats. For the Duke and his fellow die-hards, it was better to make a principled stand against reform, even if that meant defeat and disaster, than to give in to change.

The events of 1832 represented the first major crisis in the Party's history. If the Party had adopted the Duke's way of thinking, it would have remained a small, grumbling, disaffected and utterly impotent minority – as was the fate of several other throne and altar parties on the Continent. The Tories would have merited at most a footnote in British history.

In fact, there was an alternative. One of the Duke's Cabinet colleagues in the 1820s had been the young Home Secretary, Sir Robert Peel. His background was rather different from the Duke's. Not only was he a Northerner who always retained traces of his northern accent, for which he was ridiculed by some of his colleagues, but the fortunes of the Peel family had been built upon the new cotton textile industries. Despite his privileged education at Harrow and Oxford, Peel knew that there were other and equally influential worlds miles away from Westminster.

After the 1832 general election Peel assumed the leadership of the Tory Party and he began gently to guide the Party away from the insularity of the Duke of Wellington towards more mainstream positions. The change was symbolised by the message that Peel issued to all 555 voters in his constituency of Tamworth, Staffordshire, in 1834.

This document, which became known as the Tamworth Manifesto, was significant less for what it said than for its very existence. Very cautiously, Peel was signalling to the country that the Conservative Party would no longer be opposed to all change but would accept reform if, but only if, an irrefutable case had been made in its favour:

> . . . if the spirit of the Reform Bill implies merely a careful review of institutions, civil and ecclesiastical, undertaken in a friendly temper, combining with the firm maintenance of established rights the correction of proved abuses and the redress of real

grievances – in that case I can for myself and my colleagues undertake to act in such a spirit and with such intentions.

The hesitant and tortuous language suggests how carefully Peel was feeling his way. More adventurous was the fact that Peel, after discussing the document first with his Cabinet, actually sent the 'manifesto' to the national press for publication.

This decision, abhorred by the Duke, demonstrated Peel's understanding that the world of politics was changing and that the Party had to change too. Harold Macmillan always claimed that Peel was the first modern politician because he understood the importance and value of image. At the same time, in recognition of these Peel-induced changes, the name Conservative Party began to supersede that of the Tory Party.

As for the Duke of Wellington, he lived on until 1852, a not always happy inhabitant of a world rather different from the one he had known as a young man. Although he eventually regained favour as a popular hero, his temporary fall from grace had shaken him. When he was cheered as he returned home to No 1, London, the Duke would simply point to the iron blinds which he had installed to protect his windows after their destruction in 1831, make a sarcastic bow and then pass inside without a word: a grand Tory gesture acknowledging the fickleness of the popular mood.

If it was Sir Robert Peel who was primarily responsible for the Conservative Party overcoming the first crisis in its history, it was Peel himself who bears most responsibility for the creation of the second.

Like the Duke, Peel placed a very high importance on the interests of the nation, as he saw them. Correspondingly, he had little regard for the interests of Party, perhaps because he himself had spent only a short time on the backbenches because of his early promotion to office. His contempt for his own backbenchers was unmatched until the days of Edward Heath. Like Heath, Peel's sense of personal integrity meant that he disdained to hand out honours to his followers as sweeteners. He was therefore respected rather than liked.

This high-minded approach was fine when things were going well, as they did after 1841 when Peel, as Prime Minister, inched the British economy towards policies of laissez-faire and the dismantling of trade tariffs, introducing income tax in 1842 in order to finance expenditure. But when things started to go wrong, as for example when he changed his mind about the advisability of retaining the Corn Laws, then he needed the enthusiastic support of his own backbenchers – and it was not forthcoming.

The Corn Laws were re-introduced in 1815 in the wake of the Napoleonic Wars in order to guarantee the price of corn and reassure the landed interest of their central importance in British life. This landed interest formed the backbone of the old Tory Party and was deeply suspicious of Peel's determination to widen the appeal of the new Conservative Party in the 1830s. Heartened by Peel's pledge at the 1841 election to retain the Corn Laws, they were correspondingly furious at his decision, in 1846, to repeal them.

Peel is credited with changing his mind because of the effects of the Irish famine and the belief that the Corn Laws were preventing food from reaching the starving Irish peasants. In fact, the peasants were too poor to afford the food whatever the price. It seems just as likely that, intellectually, Peel had now convinced himself that the Corn Laws were an unnecessary and divisive piece of 'class legislation' which threatened the representation of the Conservatives as a national party.

The Corn Laws were repealed but the measure passed through the House of Commons only with the support of the Whigs. Almost immediately, the disaffected Conservative backbenchers, led by Benjamin Disraeli, combined with the Whigs to vote Peel out of office on an issue to do with Ireland. Peel's feelings of relief at his dismissal were clear. As he wrote in a letter of August 1846: 'Thank God, I am relieved for ever from the trammels of such a party!'

Despite loudly voiced fears, repeal of the Corn Laws in fact made little difference to the agricultural interest, which continued to prosper until the depression of the 1870s. But, as a result of Peel's downfall, the Conservative Party itself was now split in two. In one camp were the Peelites, who included most of the Party's leading lights and emerging talents. In the other camp were the Protectionists, led by the Earl of Derby and the inexperienced Disraeli.

This second major crisis for the Conservative Party was easily the most prolonged of them all. Between 1846 and 1874, for example, the Party held office briefly on just three occasions. The mid-Victorian period proved to be the age of the Whigs who, by widening their appeal to new interests in British society such as the middle classes and nonconformists, transformed themselves into the Liberals. It looked as if the Conservatives would remain permanently out of office.

This lengthy period of impotence taught Conservatives many painful and never-to-be-forgotten lessons. First of all, they realised the futility of being shackled to deeply unpopular policies such as that of Protection in an age of free trade. This policy had to be, and was, discreetly jettisoned.

Secondly, the wilderness years brought the understanding that the British public valued stability, and stability came about as a result of unity. In turn, unity was best achieved by loyalty; no matter how vehemently conflicting views might be expressed behind closed doors, members were ultimately prepared to toe the line. As early as the 1830s a Whig MP, Sir James Mackintosh, had shrewdly observed that 'a Tory is more influenced by loyalty, and a Whig by the love of liberty'. The Party had to be bigger than any one individual's conscience or principles if it was to be effective.

Thirdly, the Conservatives had to learn and appreciate the importance of 'Party', a factor which Peel for one had refused to recognise. From the 1860s, therefore, the Conservatives began, slowly and hesitatingly, to organise themselves as a recognisably modern political body. In 1867 the National Union of Conservative and Constitutional Associations was formed in order to help organise the Party outside of Westminster. Three years later, Conservative Central Office was set up in order to provide a central base. A national agent was appointed and the Party made a concerted attempt to fight as many parliamentary seats as it could. Political success could only be rooted in effective organisation.

Finally, the Party recognised that it was vital to offer a positive vision of Britain and of the Conservatives' place within it. The Party had to convince people that it possessed a sense of identity. Without a popular base it would be impossible to defend the existing order, and this support had to be attracted by something more than negative attacks on political opponents.

Benjamin Disraeli played the leading role in educating his own party to accept these changes. Views on just how acutely he understood the situation and tried to deal with it have varied. After his death in 1881, Disraeli was virtually canonised by Conservatives as the saviour of his Party. More recently, however, historians have begun to chip away at the legend and to argue that he was less perceptive and more opportunist than his admirers claimed.

What is clear is that Disraeli gave the Conservative Party a sense of cohesion and identity during the difficult years when it was excluded from power. His showmanship and display demonstrated his instinctive understanding of the public relations side of politics. He was bored by the nuts and bolts of administration and expected his appointees simply to get on with it.

Disraeli was much more interested in the intellectual content of Conservatism. In his novels Disraeli had derided Peel's negative Toryism and instead he set out to emphasise the Party's national appeal. Unlike Peel, he tried to ensure that the interests of the Party and the interests of the country were regarded as identical. Horrified by the divisiveness of class politics, he knew how important it was that the Conservative Party should not be regarded as the spokesman of an elite or a minority: that way lay electoral disaster.

Disraeli grasped, too, that modern politics was as much about show as about substance. The growth of the electorate and the granting of the vote to the less educated and literate created a need for gestures and showmanship. The Party manifesto or policy statement was never likely to capture the popular imagination: simple but powerful slogans, appealing in large part to the emotions, were therefore crucial. Just look at this passage from his famous speech at the Crystal Palace in 1872:

The Tory Party, unless it is a national party, is nothing. It is not a confederacy of nobles, it is not a democratic multitude; it is a party formed from all the numerous classes in the realm – classes alike and equal before the law, but whose different conditions and different aims give vigour and variety to our national life.

This need to attract the 'democratic multitude' meant that the Party had to include some commitment to social reform. Just as Disraeli had outflanked the Liberals over the Second Reform Act in 1867, he effectively took away the card of social reform, at least temporarily, from the Liberals.

'Who made ten thousand people owners of the soil and the rest of us trespassers in the land of our birth?' This ringing question from David Lloyd George, Liberal Chancellor of the Exchequer in 1909, indicated just how dramatically the inter-party consensus which had held for much of the nineteenth century was beginning to break up. Here was a Chancellor of the Exchequer no less, a politician from outside the traditional political class who had not been at public school or Oxbridge and didn't care that he hadn't, challenging the whole basis of England's landed society by asking why a minority of the population owned the majority of the land.

The bravura and self-confidence of Lloyd George together with the dynamism of the Liberal Government in introducing sweeping social reforms and, more worryingly, their ability to win general elections, represented the next crisis for the Conservative Party.

After Disraeli's death in 1881, the Party continued to enjoy solid and unspectacular success under his successor Lord Salisbury. The founding of the Primrose League in November 1883, supposedly in honour of Disraeli's favourite flower, brought hundreds of thousands of 'non-political' individuals within the orbit of the Party, providing an army of volunteers and canvassers at election time. Although not formally affiliated to the Conservative Party until just before the First World War, the grassroots activities of the Primrose League ensured that the Conservatives would always be a so-called mass party with a very visible presence throughout Britain.

The Party was also helped by its links with various important interests which tacitly, if not overtly, favoured the Conservatives.

The glitz and show of the Empire and of Victoria's Jubilees; the arrival of the popular press with Lord Northcliffe's *Daily Mail* in 1896; the links with powerful financial lobbies such as the brewers and finally the influence of such activities as organised sport and the music hall – these all tended to help the Conservative Party.

In political terms, the Party continued under the firm, world-weary leadership of Lord Salisbury. His approach was rooted in the belief that any party of reform, in this case the Liberals, would by reason of their interfering and galvanising activities inevitably alienate important sections of public opinion. The Conservatives could and should exist simply as the Party of resistance. In any case, the reformers would sooner or later fall out amongst themselves. This, of course, they did in the middle of the 1880s when the Liberal Party split over Gladstone's conversion to Home Rule for Ireland.

As Salisbury no doubt also fully realised, despite all their huffing and puffing the Liberals broadly believed in the same things as the Conservatives. As long ago as the 1850s, *The Times* newspaper claimed that England had learnt how to confine the spirit of party politics within limits, rendering it harmless 'to the amenities of social life and the welfare of the nation'.

Forty years later, Arthur Balfour, who was shortly to succeed his uncle Salisbury as the leader of the Conservatives, complacently wrote in similar vein: 'Our alternating Cabinets, though belonging to different parties, have never differed about the foundations of society.'

But by the early years of the twentieth century this consensus was proving to be less self-evident. The spirit of laissez-faire was giving way to public demands that, as on the Continent, the government should play a much greater role in providing social services and facilities. The shock of the Boer War, when so many of the would-be conscripts had to be rejected on health grounds, was exacerbated by the findings of Charles Booth and Seebohm Rowntree whose researches in London and York painted a depressing picture of the low standard of life experienced by the urban majority. Their findings showed that poverty was less a matter of character defect than of harsh circumstance, which any amount of individual effort and self-help could barely touch.

It was not surprising, therefore, that for the first time influential politicians such as Lloyd George began to question the very foundations of the existing order. Disraeli and Gladstone might have detested each other personally, but they had at least agreed on the fundamentals of British politics. Now, however, the growth of the trade unions and their political wing, the Labour Party, was undermining the old consensus while the vociferous campaigns of the suffragettes and the Home Rule movement in Ireland made a point of flouting traditional proprieties.

Important interests within the Conservative Party were also under attack. The political power of the landed aristocracy, as represented in the House of Lords, was severely curtailed by the passage of the Parliament Act in 1911. This reform reflected the continued decline of British agriculture since the 'Great Depression' in the 1880s when cheap imported corn from America flooded the market.

The effect of these external threats was aggravated by internal conflict within the Party; conflict which was not hidden away from the public view. The crushing election defeat of 1906 duly confirmed how ossified the Conservative Party had become under the 'hands-off' control of 'Hotel Cecil', the name given to the Salisbury clan.

Three years before, the leadership had been fiercely assailed by the Chamberlain dynasty from Birmingham. The issue on which the Chamberlains chose to challenge the Party hierarchy was tariff reform, arguing that free trade was outdated and in fact harmful to the country. Instead the British economy should be rebuilt behind a wall of tariffs. The ferocious energy and organising skills of Joseph Chamberlain ensured that within eighteen months, the Tariff Reform League had 235 branches up and down the country.

The Conservative Party could easily have fragmented as the two factions fought bitterly for control, particularly after the election rout in 1906, using every possible forum to advance their interests. By 1911 it was clear to all that Balfour's casual leadership was only making matters worse and he was replaced by the virtually anonymous figure of Andrew Bonar Law.

Bonar Law is perhaps the least known of this century's Prime Ministers – his biographer called him the unknown Prime Minister – and he held office for just 209 days until ill-health forced his resignation in May 1923. Yet Bonar Law is amongst the most important leaders of the Conservative Party, simply because he managed to hold the Party together during a particularly traumatic period.

In defiance of one of the most hallowed of party tenets, both free trade and tariff reform Conservatives argued their case in full view of the public. Bonar Law carefully steered a middle path between the two camps, making sure that the Party was not captured by one section within it. He also carried the Party into the Coalition Government of the dynamic Lloyd George during the First World War and brought it out again intact – unlike the Liberals themselves who disastrously split into two groups. Bonar Law and the Conservatives had clearly learnt full well the damaging effects of the disunity which followed Peel's downfall in 1846.

That Bonar Law became Prime Minister in 1922 at the head of a united Conservative Government, except for a handful of dissenting voices who were soon compelled to make their peace, was a tribute to his powers of dogged determination and integrity. Bonar Law's leadership was never spectacular but in terms of the survival of the Party as a political force, it was much more valuable than the actions of other more ostentatious leaders and enabled the Conservatives to retain their identity.

'A man of the utmost insignificance.' This was Lord Curzon's apparently crushing verdict on the opponent who beat him to the leadership of the Party in 1923. That man was Stanley Baldwin but, just as the seemingly unpromising Bonar Law proved to be a success, so the same could be said of the man who had once been Law's political secretary. Baldwin proved to be one of the most successful leaders of the Conservative Party and a statesman remembered long after the demise of Curzon.

An ironmaster from Worcestershire, Baldwin's elevation shows how attuned the Conservatives had now become to the popular mood. For example, when the Party was restructured after 1918, new rules confirmed the importance of women by stipulating that they were to be allocated a minimum of one-third of the places available on representative bodies both centrally and in the local associations.

Similarly, Baldwin's accession to the leadership was a recognition that the Conservatives could only prosper by responding to new social forces. In the recent past, Salisbury and his nephew Balfour had represented 'Hotel Cecil', namely the self-confident assumption by the landed aristocracy that political leadership was theirs by right. This sense of superiority was well displayed in a letter which Balfour sent to Salisbury in 1891, discussing the suitability of a colleague for a ministerial position: 'He has great tact and judgement – middle-class tact and judgement I admit, but good of their kind.'

The inter-war years were in fact dominated by precisely such representatives of the middle classes: Bonar Law was an iron merchant from Glasgow, Baldwin another iron merchant from Worcestershire, and the prosperity of the half-brothers Austen and Neville Chamberlain was based upon the family's screw-making business in Birmingham. These politicians had earned rather than inherited their wealth.

The fourth Conservative crisis revolved around the apparently unstoppable rise and rise of the Labour Party. Founded only in 1906, it grew alongside the trade union movement and by the 1920s had already replaced the divided Liberals as the main opposition party. Labour represented the arrival of class politics, the phenomenon which Lord Salisbury had always hated and feared because it struck at the Conservative claim to be a national party, explicitly questioning their apolitical and nonpartisan image.

It is difficult nowadays to understand the fears and anxieties provoked in the governing class by the rise of the Labour Party. Today, we know that the Labour Party has in fact turned out to be a model of propriety and decorum. The monarchy, for instance, existed quite happily under successive Labour admin-istrations without paying income tax. But in the 1920s, in the aftermath of the Russian Revolution, of industrial turmoil fol-lowing the First World War and the General Strike of May

1926, this comforting state of affairs was rather less clear to Conservatives.

Baldwin decided to tame the Labour Party, allowing a minority Labour government to take office in 1924. He also adopted a relatively emollient stance during the General Strike. Hostile to the squalid methods of Lloyd George in raising money from the sale of honours, Baldwin and his lieutenant, party chairman J.C.C. Davidson, secured the Conservatives' financial basis by turning to the City of London and business for donations. However, Baldwin was enough of a Conservative to relish power at almost any price, even if that meant turning a blind eye to the activities of Davidson and his henchman Joseph Ball. These activities included the publication of the so-called 'Zinoviev letter' in 1924 and were rather more sinister than anything Lloyd George had carried out.

Baldwin also tried to widen the social appeal of the Conservative Party and passed the Reform Act of 1928 which finally granted the vote to all men and women over the age of twenty-one. Like Benjamin Disraeli who had presided over the Reform Act of 1867, he preferred to implement Lord Randolph Churchill's cry of 'Trust the people'. Nevertheless, he sometimes had misgivings: 'Can we educate them in time?' he once asked.

Die-hard Tories fought against this measure. The *Daily Mail*, for instance, worried about the 'risks from the voting of impulsive and politically ignorant girls [influenced by] the foolish Communistic sentiments of their boyfriends', but in fact much of the Con-servatives' electoral success since 1928 can be attributed to the 'women's vote'.

By lowering the political temperature – the sober inactivity praised by Sir Robert Peel senior – Baldwin ensured that controversy and dissension was shuffled off into the wings and that the Conservative Party came to be seen as the epitomy of mainstream Britain. He also made sure that former Liberals deserting the sinking Liberal ship were made welcome. The Tories have always been astute in mopping up other political groupings, whether it be the Liberal Unionists or the National Liberals. Crucial to this process was the Carlton Club in London; as Sir Charles Petrie vividly put it, 'For many decades the Carlton Club served as the depot where the new recruits to the Conservative Party learned their drill.'

The journalist Virginia Cowles observed that Conservative candidates fighting the 1945 general election were sent into battle with little more than a photograph of Winston Churchill. Just as the Duke of Wellington's international reputation in the 1820s had not forestalled demands for change, Churchill's fame as a war leader proved to be insufficient for electoral victory.

The Conservative Party's preference for a quiet life has often led to a kind of inertia. Thus their initial response to unemployment and the rise of Fascism in Europe in the 1930s was to do as little as possible. Nevertheless, the electorate returned the Conservatives at the 1935 general election and the rudimentary opinion polls suggested that they would probably have won at the 1940 general election, if it had been held; it was cancelled because of the Second World War.

The war had shaken up and radicalised large sections of the community, primarily because calls for equality of sacrifice and the consequences of what was called total war revealed much that had been hidden from the public gaze. This meant that the do-nothing approach of the 1930s seemed, in retrospect, even more reprehensible.

Before the war, opponents of the Conservatives had argued in vain for a more dynamic government role. During the conflict, however, the failings of the private sector were vividly exposed. Again and again, it was the Government which had to step in to rectify the inadequacies of health, transport, education and housing provision.

At the general election in July 1945, Churchill's Conservative Party was trounced by Attlee's Labour Party. Winston Churchill himself was shocked by the unexpected result, asking of one senior Tory: 'What was it that enabled Stanley Baldwin to win elections while I always lose them?'

Beaten and bewildered Conservatives cast around for possible reasons for their humiliation. It was suggested that the Conservatives alone of the major parties had patriotically run down their constituency organisations when their agents and voluntary workers went off to enlist. Others blamed the left-wing publications of Penguin Books and Victor Gollancz or even the army educational service for spreading subversive ideas. Rather less attention was paid to the fact that the 1945 election was the first and only time that the national press had been equally divided in its allegiance between the two major parties.

Even more important was the simple fact that the popular mood was unsympathetic to Conservatism, just as it had been in 1831–2 and 1905–6 when the Party had suffered similarly crushing election defeats. Despite the efforts of a few young Conservatives banded together in the Tory Reform Committee, the Party proved unable to create an alternative to the ideal of the Welfare State proposed by Sir William Beveridge in his Report of 1942. All three parties' manifestos for the 1945 election had in fact been broadly similar – and Beveridge himself was a Liberal – but it was the Labour Party that was judged to be serious about implementing the new policies because the Liberals were likely to have too small a parliamentary presence.

Viewed from certain angles, the defeat of the Conservatives was not as shattering as it first seemed. The Labour Party had benefited unduly from the vagaries of the electoral system: their 48 per cent share of the votes gave them 62 per cent of the seats. But it did look to some observers as if the Labour Party was set to dominate the political scene for years to come.

The Conservative response to this crisis had very little to do with Party leader Winston Churchill who virtually retired from active politics in order to concentrate on writing his war memoirs. Instead the drastic overhaul of the Party was left in large part to two men who, although personally antipathetic to each other, instituted the sweeping changes which were required: Lord Woolton and R.A. Butler.

Woolton's contribution as chairman of the Party was to reorganise its administration. He placed it on a sound financial basis, successfully launching an appeal for the immense sum of £1 million as well as trying to attract parliamentary candidates with a wider social background than in the past. He also expanded enormously the individual membership of the Conservative Party which reached levels not seen since the heady days of the Primrose League. Accurate figures were never kept but it seems that individual party membership rose to the two million mark.

Butler was largely responsible for the intellectual transformation of the Party. As a politician in the 'One Nation' mould, adamant that the Party should be seen as a national organisation concerned for the welfare of all, he published a series of policy documents or charters which seemed to draw a line between the inter-war and post-war Party. The charters were less important for their turgid content than for their very existence; like Sir Robert Peel's Tamworth Manifesto, they signalled to the electorate that the past was past and that the new Conservative Party would endeavour to be more responsive to popular feeling.

There was undoubtedly much stage management in this supposed transformation of the Party. Despite Lord Woolton's trumpetings, for instance, the restricted background of Conservative MPs barely altered, whilst the charters themselves were more referred to than read. But, as Benjamin Disraeli had known full well, image is often as important as reality.

The effectiveness of the Conservative response is shown by the fact that whereas crushing election defeats in the 1840s and 1906 led to years out of power, by 1951 the Conservative Party was safely back in office. The Labour Party had to console itself with the knowledge that it had at least drastically changed the Conservative Party, just as in the 1980s the actions and policies of the Conservative Party played a major part in transforming the Labour Party.

Similar powers of recuperation and renewal were displayed by the Party yet again a few years later after the Suez crisis of 1956 had split the country. The Conservative leader Sir Anthony Eden was eased out and under his successor Harold Macmillan the Party won yet another resounding electoral victory in 1959.

In his diary entry for October 1963, Prime Minister Harold Macmillan wrote gloomily that 'All our policies at home and abroad are in ruins.'

This despairing attitude was not one usually associated with the unflappable 'Supermac' who prided himself on his sagacity and wisdom. And indeed his administrations seemed to have much to be proud of: virtually full employment, low inflation, steady if unspectacular economic growth, a stable and tranquil consumer society and, not least, continued Conservative election wins.

Despite the superficial successes, however, Macmillan was aware of more long-term problems. The economies of war-ravaged Germany, France and Italy were already overtaking that of Britain. Some party critics argued that the high level of public spending was injecting a potentially lethal dose of inflation into the economic system. These dissenting voices – most notably Macmillan's own treasury team of Thorneycroft, Birch and Powell – resigned en bloc in 1958. Four years later in the infamous 'Night of the Long Knives', Macmillan, fearful of internal party conspiracies, sacked one-third of his Cabinet in a display of blood-letting that took place in full public glare.

Uncertainty was increased by the weakening of the special relationship with the United States, which had been strained by the Suez fiasco in 1956. Furthermore, whilst divesting itself of its colonial interests, the Conservative administration was also losing its self-confidence. As the Common Market grew in size and influence, Britain's casual attitude towards its development – and Macmillan had often been more dismissive than most – was turning out to be an increasingly short-sighted mistake. An application to join was humiliatingly vetoed by General de Gaulle in 1963; hence Macmillan's despairing diary entry.

From this point onwards, the history of the modern Conservative Party is a catalogue of responses to continuing British economic failure and loss of influence. Such crises have been particularly damaging because it is the Conservative Party that has generally been the Party in office. Much damage limitation has been necessary. Since the 1960s it is the Conservative Party which has invariably been the radical and questioning Party and the Labour Party that has seemed to be the Party of consolidation and continuity.

Between the wars, the Conservative response to crisis brought about a change in the background of its leaders. The same thing happened in the 1960s, 1970s and 1990s. After the 'industrial' careers of Bonar Law, Baldwin and Chamberlain, the Conservative Party had reverted to something close to type with the succession of Churchill, Sir Anthony Eden, Harold Macmillan, Sir Alec Douglas-Home. The last three men were Old Etonians, whilst Churchill's grandfather was the Duke of Marlborough.

By the 1960s this elitism was felt to be a handicap and the procedure for the choice of a leader was changed. Instead of informal discussions amongst Tory grandees which resulted in the 'emergence' of a leader rather like the selection of a Pope, a more democratic and open system was instituted. Conservative MPs were now balloted on their preference. Under the new rules the successive leaders of the Party have been Heath, Thatcher and Major – none of whom could have expected to fill that post before the 1960s. Such a bloodless revolution further emphasises that the Conservative Party's main objective is power. As Norman Tebbit once observed, the Conservative Party is willing to enlist talent from whatever source in its pursuit of power. This pursuit can sometimes result in iconoclastic and radical measures.

The Conservative Party had been built on the foundations of economic growth and a confident national identity, but by the 1960s and 1970s these were beginning to disintegrate. Economic growth, for example, had allowed the Party to retain the privileges of its supporters whilst professing concern, and sometimes indeed doing something, about the worst-off members of society. Since Disraeli the Party had happily traded on its nationalism and a sense of identity rooted in 'Britishness', but the decline of the Church of England, uncertainty over institutions such as the monarchy, the Civil Service, the legal system and the City, fierce argument over Europe, political apathy and cultural diversity meant that the Conservative Party was inevitably becoming less sure of its place and role in British society.

The policies drawn up by Heath and his advisers during the late 1960s represented a reversal of the generous and inclusive 'One Nation' Tory tradition favoured by Conservative administrations since the Second World War. Instead the continuing failures of the economy were to be solved by a re-invigoration of British capitalism. Government expenditure would be reined back and loss-making 'lame duck' industries would no longer be propped up by tax-payers' money, whatever the cost in unemployment. New industrial legislation would seek to curtail the unofficial strikes which had been prevalent since the 1950s and which Harold Wilson's government had tried and failed to deal with in 1969.

To most commentators' surprise Heath won the 1970 election and took office in propitious circumstances. As one senior civil servant has since pointed out, his was the only government since the war to take office without the handicap of a balance of payments crisis or severe industrial relations problems. Yet despite, or perhaps because of, the detailed research and policy making carried out when the Party was in opposition, the technocratic Heath failed to communicate any vision of where he thought Britain should be going.

He also lacked the political will and obstinacy to continue with his policies in the face of public discontent. Opposition to his economic policies quickly mounted, leading to a series of humiliating 'U-turns' over the proposed closure of loss-making concerns such as the Upper Clyde Shipbuilders. The trade union legislation provoked marches and demonstrations whilst the new Industrial Relations Court proved to be a non-starter because the unions refused to co-operate. In his search for modernisation, Heath appeared to have little respect for traditional continuities; for example the local government reforms of 1972 led to the imposition of bureaucratic and alien super-councils which attracted the loyalty of none.

The gathering sense of crisis that dogged the Heath administration was compounded by international events outside the government's control, such as the quadrupling by the oil-producing countries of the price of oil. At home, there was no let-up in the opposition to Heath's policies and industrial disputes resulted in the imposition of no fewer than five states of emergency. Conflict with the miners led to power cuts and even the introduction of a three-day working week. The election of February 1974 was fought on the question of 'Who rules Britain?' After four years of turmoil and confusion, the electorate decided that it certainly was not the Heath government.

Further election defeat in October 1974 signalled the end for Heath. A party which places such a high premium on electoral success was never likely to rest happy with a leader who had lost three elections out of four. Heath's poor handling of his Conservative parliamentary colleagues also alienated important sections of his party. In 1975 he was deposed by a virtually unknown challenger, Mrs Margaret Thatcher.

The one lasting consequence of Heath's administration was British entry into the Common Market. This was in itself further evidence of the severe challenges facing Britain and amounted to a desperate hope that entry would provide a fresh start. It didn't, and in the years to come the European issue was to be the source of much dispute and conflict within the Party.

'A leader must lead, must lead firmly, have firm convictions, and see that those convictions are reflected in every piece of policy.' Both the nature of Mrs Thatcher's views and, just as importantly, the forcefulness with which they were expressed, signalled her break from the recent Tory past. Unlike Edward Heath, Margaret Thatcher certainly had a vision of Britain and this vision was the source of her energy and dynamism. Her activism was rather different from the laid-back style favoured by some former leaders such as Baldwin and Macmillan.

It was inconceivable that in the past the Conservative Party could ever have elected a woman as its leader, and although Mrs Thatcher had risen up the ranks by hugging the inside track and not rocking the boat, her background and her gender meant that she inevitably retained a sense of being an outsider. Her election was one more indication of the gathering crisis facing the Party which had only been exacerbated by the Heath years. It was as if the Party was prepared to try almost anything to recover itself.

Margaret Thatcher was provided with a raft of ideas by various independent think-tanks such as the Institute of Economic Affairs, many of which gleefully challenged conventional wisdom. Their publications seemed to confirm Mrs Thatcher's belief that the massive expansion in government activity since the Second World

War was strangling both initiative and enterprise and that market forces were much to be preferred over the choices of bureaucrats sitting in Whitehall. In particular, the pernicious effects of trade union power were deplored.

There were several ironies about this new situation. Both Mrs Thatcher and her intellectual mentor Sir Keith Joseph had been big spenders when in office under Heath and it was actually Denis Healey as Chancellor of the Exchequer in the Labour governments of 1974 to 1979 who had first introduced a monetarist approach. Critics of what was soon dubbed Thatcherism also failed to recognise that her approach represented a return to the traditional hands-off policies pursued by Conservative administrations before 1940 rather than a revolutionary new philosophy.

What made the situation unprecedented were the suicidal actions of the trade unions which had paralysed the country under the Labour government of 1974–9 and appeared to support Mrs Thatcher's diagnosis that over-mighty unions were at the heart of Britain's economic malaise. A further novelty was the almost Messianic zeal with which she led the Party. In the past, Conservatives had prided themselves on their inclusive character: it was tacitly assumed that 'those not against us are with us'. Under Mrs Thatcher, this attitude was reversed: those not completely with us are most definitely against us. Conviction replaced consensus because, in one of her favourite sayings, 'there is no alternative'.

This forthright stance appealed to a new Conservatism of achievers and the self-made who were impatient with British lethargy and acceptance. It was understandably less popular amongst traditional 'One Nation' Tories. Harold Macmillan, for one, snobbishly lamented the way in which a national party had been turned into a suburban rump.

After her election as Prime Minister in 1979, Mrs Thatcher was fully prepared to push through her policies in the face of widespread public criticism. In this, she was braver than Edward Heath. Unemployment mounted, the economy went into recession, riots broke out in inner-city areas but still Mrs Thatcher and her Chancellor, Sir Geoffrey Howe, refused to reflate the economy. Inflation had to be beaten. A series of union laws democratised the trade unions, introducing the idea of ballots and accountability to members. And in 1982 came the Falklands War with Argentina, just in time to turn Margaret Thatcher into a sort of latter-day Britannia as she fought to make Britain 'Great' again.

Living standards for those in work – the majority – went up and it was expected that the 'haves' would always be likely to out-vote the 'have-nots' at general elections. The Party won again in 1983 and the Government proceeded to abolish councils such as the Greater London Council, some of whose actions were heaven-sent propaganda for the Conservatives. Then came a year-long dispute with the miners led by Arthur Scargill. Mrs Thatcher was fortunate that bitter internal fighting within the Labour Party and its adoption of unilateralist and anti-Europe views suggested to voters that there really was no alternative to her administrations.

She was also fortunate in having two heaven-sent gifts. First of all, there was North Sea oil whose £100 billion windfall during the 1980s effectively financed the unemployment benefits of the large numbers out of work, and secondly the implementation of 'privatisation' under which public industries were sold back to the public and the proceeds went to the Government.

There were, however, limitations to Mrs Thatcher's radicalism. True, the Conservatives under Heath and then Thatcher had snatched from Labour's grasp the 'modernisation' card briefly held by Harold Wilson in the mid-1960s. But Mrs Thatcher was careful not to tread on the toes of her committed supporters: mortgage tax relief, for instance, remained even though it weakened the economy. Likewise, the Government's economic policies often favoured the short-term interests of the City over the interest of manufacturing. Service industries were meant to fill the employment gap, but these jobs proved to be ephemeral and low-paid: hardly the basis on which to challenge Britain's overseas competitors or generate lasting wealth creation.

Another election was won in 1987, but an election-induced boom under Chancellor Nigel Lawson soon ran out of steam and for the second time in the 1980s the economy plunged into recession. This time the prime sufferers were supposedly 'natural' Conservative supporters who had been encouraged to over-expand both their businesses and their home-owning capabilities. But still the thrust of the zealous and radical Conservative administrations swept on, turning their attention to methods of paying for local government. The poll tax replaced the old system of rates and satisfied virtually no one.

Even more important was the fact that Mrs Thatcher was impaled on the horns of her nationalist rhetoric. Her distrust of foreigners in general and of the European Community in particular, which for her symbolised the evils of profligate bureaucracy and feather-bedding so painfully extirpated in Britain, was always evident. Some of her most important business supporters, however, were happy to widen their horizons.

In addition to the problems of unemployment, the recession, the poll tax and Europe – a formidable catalogue in itself – Mrs Thatcher's aggressive style of government was systematically alienating friend and foe alike. When believers such as Nigel Lawson and Sir Geoffrey Howe were allowed to fall by the wayside, it became obvious that Mrs Thatcher was rapidly running out of supporters. Lawson has claimed that she treated Howe 'as something halfway between a punchbag and a doormat'. Even her generous distribution of honours to parliamentary colleagues and her cheer-leaders in the press were insufficient to rally sustained support. In the end, there were simply too many of 'them' and not enough of 'us'.

In 1990 she was challenged for the leadership by Michael Heseltine, one of her opponents who had resigned from the government four years before. Most Conservative MPs, concerned less with ideology and 'rolling back the state' than with the retention of their own parliamentary seats, clearly felt that Mrs Thatcher, whatever her past unbeaten record, was not going to win the next election. Mrs Thatcher recorded more votes than Heseltine in the first ballot but not enough to win an overall victory.

It was now that Mrs Thatcher showed she was a Conservative first and a radical second. Instead of fighting on for her ideals, she was brought to recognise that no leader, not even she, was bigger than the Party. With reluctance, Margaret Thatcher fell on her sword. The smooth accession to power of John Major exemplified what political commentator Matthew Parris, himself a former Tory MP, termed the Party's 'instinct to survive'.

Few Conservative leaders have ever endured such a barrage of public abuse as John Major. Of course leaders in the past such as Balfour, Baldwin and Eden have been criticised and excoriated, but they always had the consolation of knowing that their Fleet Street supporters would generally rally to their cause.

Despite the prophecies of commentators and opinion polls, the Conservatives under John Major won the 1992 general election, thus seeming to validate the decision of Conservative MPs to oust Mrs Thatcher in 1990. But from this high point, everything began to unravel. The recession continued undiminished, even though Government supporters continually detected a recovery just around the next corner. The arguments over Europe became more fierce as anti-Europe rebels were able to hold the Government's small parliamentary majority to ransom. Massive Government spending before the election had to be reined back as the deficit became starkly clear and the pledge not to raise taxes – a stick wielded hard and often against Labour proposals in the 1992 election campaign – was looking increasingly foolhardy.

Tory disunity and disarray were paraded in public in a way traditionally characteristic of the Labour Party – and not in fact seen within the Conservative Party since the acrimonious debates over tariff reform at the start of the century. In November 1994, eight Conservative MPs were deprived of the Party whip, an unprecedented move and one which plunged the government into yet deeper trouble.

Pulled this way and that, John Major naturally found it difficult to establish his presence and to articulate a Conservative vision of Britain. At one point he dabbled in visions of a classless society but could not countenance some of the measures which this might entail, such as the phasing out of the so-called public schools. Falling party membership and growing public apathy about politics in general were not helpful, nor was the sense of a Party which had been too long in office for its own or the country's good.

The Conservative Party was running out of options and therefore the leader, as the visible representative of the Party, was bearing the brunt of difficult and long-term problems. Just as Mrs Thatcher was sacrificed for the greater good of the Party, so too did his critics call for the head of John Major. Name-calling and personal abuse was much easier than serious analysis of a difficult situation.

In the past, the Conservative Party has always reassured itself with the knowledge that it was by some way the country's most formidable electioneering machine. In 1950, for instance, the Party's shrewd exploitation of the new postal voting gained it at least ten, crucial, seats in that year's general election. The Party has always ensured that, where possible, the redistribution of seats by the Boundary Commission has been favourable. Finally, in the general election of 1992 it is thought that the expatriate vote may well have well won the Conservatives two extra seats.

But such expertise in itself is not always sufficient to get the Party out of holes. The latest crisis in the history of the Conservative Party shows no sign of such painless resolution, particularly as the issue of Europe is not susceptible to the traditional methods of obfuscation and smoothing over. It is not easy to spot any convenient middle ground which would satisfy Euro-sceptic and Euro-enthusiast alike.

So what does this brief outline of the British Conservative Party's history reveal? First of all, and most obviously, that the organisation is a great survivor. The Duke of Wellington and Sir Robert Peel begin the chapter; Mrs Thatcher and John Major end it. Their assumptions and activities are so profoundly different that it is remarkable they should all have belonged to the same Party.

Secondly, the Conservative Party has done rather more than just survive; it has often succeeded, particularly in this century. Since the Disraeli government in 1874, the Conservatives have been in power for virtually all of the period from 1874 until 1905, between 1916 and 1945, 1951 to 1964 and finally from 1979 up to today. Commentators used to talk about the pendulum of British politics: first one party would have a spell in office, soon to be followed by their opponents. The pendulum shows a distinct preference to swing to one side rather than the other.

This success was by no means pre-ordained and has been achieved and maintained by means of argument, debate and disagreement. In particular, the Conservative Party has managed to deal with all of the crises outlined above and yet still retain its presence and influence. The history of the Right on the Continent is one of continual splits, disintegration and failure. In Britain, the Conservative Party has, so far at least, always found an answer to each challenge.

Marxists were once fond of arguing that only permanent revolution would ensure the triumph of socialism. How ironic, then, that the Communist Party of the Soviet Union already lies dead and buried after just eighty years. In contrast, after 150 years, the Conservative Party sails serenely along, living testimony to a series of continuous revolutions which belie its name. It has survived the transition from a Britain where few could vote and the landed aristocracy ruled supreme, to the astonishingly different world of computers, Welfare State and multinationals.

These extraordinary powers of self-renewal show how responsive and flexible the Conservative Party has been in adapting to new circumstances, whether it be the extension of the vote or the rise of the Labour Party. The Conservative Party has its roots embedded deep within British society and it is impossible, therefore, to look at the history of the Conservative Party in a vacuum. These roots have provided the Party with a fundamental sense of continuity.

But in itself that is not enough. As all successful businesses know, continuity must go hand-in-hand with change. And here the Party has excelled at responding to change, but, just as importantly, it has learnt to manage change with one aim in sight: namely, the acquisition of power.

Conservatives know full well that politics is about power, not about posture. This realisation was confirmed by the Tory 'wilderness years' in the middle of the nineteenth century when the Party was almost permanently excluded from office. And in pursuit of power, virtually anything is acceptable.

This is the governing idea, often unspoken because it is taken for granted, that has yoked together the disparate elements within the coalition of interests which makes up the Conservative Party. No wonder the Party stresses the value of loyalty and of unity in public: no army expects to triumph with dissent in the ranks. As one young Conservative candidate put it in 1903: 'After all, the question of tactics should be left to the generals. It is not for the common soldier to assert himself whatever his private opinions on the question of tactics may be.'

Similarly, it is foolish for officers to waste too much time on theoretical debates and terminological quibbles. Ideological baggage is cumbersome; doctrinal purity is admirable but usually powerless.

It is hardly surprising, too, that the Conservative Party shows such admirable powers of recuperation and resilience: no fighting force defeated in battle – or in this case in an election – spends too much time feeling sorry for itself. Better to regroup, consolidate and be ready for the next time. As Sir Ian Gilmour once observed, 'in English politics, the prizes go to the Party that does not split'.

Essential to the continued success of the Party is its potent representation of itself as a national party. Whatever its accuracy in practice, this claim helps explain why the history of the Conservative Party is so fascinating and multi-layered. As a coalition, the Party simply cannot afford to let itself be seen as the prisoner of any single interest whether it be that of industrialists, farmers or small businessmen. The history of the British Conservative Party is more complex than might, at first, be assumed. Any crass generalisations about the Party, its members and its supporters should be scrutinised with care.

And yet there is no compelling reason which lays down that the Conservative Party, however successful it may have been in the past, will continue to be so in the future. In fact, if one simply numbers the crises discussed above – although of course not all of them have been of the same magnitude – then the recent history of the Party seems to be a catalogue of almost continuous crisis. The Conservative Party has no divine right to rule.

Sir Robert Peel and his colleagues had to decide how best to respond to the Reform Act in 1832 and Benjamin Disraeli to deal with the fragmentation of the Party after 1846. This century, the

Party has had to cope with the onslaught of a triumphant liberalism under Lloyd George, rapidly followed by the rise of the Labour Party. In 1945, the Party was badly defeated at the general election. And since the 1960s there have been the differing reactions of the Heath, Thatcher and Major administrations towards economic decline, the European question, a rapidly changing society and much else threatening the so-called natural (Tory) order of things.

Thus six of the eight major crises to confront the Conservative Party have occurred this century, and four of them have happened since the Second World War. Even more worryingly for the Party, the reactive policies of Conservative governments since the early 1970s have had, at best, only partial success. They have effected some short-term damage limitation without addressing, let alone solving, profound long-term difficulties.

In recent years, it is almost as if the Party has come to accept crisis as normal. Even in the supposedly 'lotus years' of the 1980s, the two recessions at the beginning and end of the decade outnumbered the boom years before and after the 1987 election. In this crisis culture, leaders are regularly assailed or ejected in an attempt to find a solution to what may turn out to be insoluble problems.

It is this development and history of the Conservative Party which is explored in the rest of *We, The Nation*, a pursuit which has made the Party such a formidable beast. It is a story of people, promises, achievements and mistakes – above all, a story which continually confounds prejudices and stereotypes.

Why Are We Here?

Conservative thinkers and their thoughts

'Nothing matters.'
>A frequently expressed remark of Lord Salisbury

'Tory philosophy is a discussion of the length of chain needed to tether the slave to the oar.'
>Professor John Vincent, 1970

'Leave talking about politics to the Left. They have nothing better to do.'
>Professor Michael Oakeshott (quoted in the *Daily Telegraph*
>by Peregrine Worsthorne, 1990)

Dashing through the countryside in his blue MG sports car, a lover of wine, women and tobacco, blessed with an army of devoted friends, indifferent to worldly success and the academic round of conferences and committees, Michael Oakeshott did not fit the stereotype of a professor of philosophy. In 1936 he published a book called *Guide to the Classics* and its title encouraged many schools to order copies for their Latin and Greek classes. There must have been much surprise and disappointment when they arrived: the book's alternative title was 'How to Pick the Derby Winner'.

Despite his disregard for the opinions of his peers, Oakeshott's obituary notice in the *Daily Telegraph* on 21 December 1990 began with the fulsome claim that he was 'the greatest political philosopher in the Anglo-Saxon tradition since Mill – or even Burke'.

Michael Oakeshott was Professor of Political Science at the London School of Economics from 1951. Yet despite the eminence of his position, Oakeshott's writings are distinguished by their withering contempt for politics as being 'vulgar', 'bogus' and 'callous', characterised above all by 'the false simplification of human life implied in even the best of its purposes'. He condemned both rationalism because of its attempt to solve problems and rationalists for their desire to get things done. 'I vote – if I have to vote – for the Party which is likely to do least harm. To that extent I am a Tory.'

Oakeshott argued that politics should be akin to polite conversation, offering an example of civility and good manners rather than of argument and disputation. Seductive though this model may be, Oakeshott had nothing to say about the hard choices which continually confront politicians and administrators on welfare or rights or liberty or other everyday issues. If, as has been argued by Eugen Weber, 'The great decisions of politics are still about who pays, who gets, and who decides this' – then Oakeshott's other-worldliness has little to contribute.

Once, having chaired a meeting devoted to British entry into the European Community, Oakeshott was asked where he stood on the matter. 'I do not find it necessary to hold opinions on such matters,' he replied loftily. For him, the role of government was simply to maintain order and to cherish tradition – even though every society contains a variety of often conflicting traditions. Instead the problem of choice is submerged beneath appeals to eternity:

> In political activity, then, men sail a boundless and bottomless sea; there is neither harbour for shelter nor floor for anchorage, neither starting-place nor appointed destination. The enterprise is to keep afloat on an even keel . . .

Keeping afloat and not doing harm – this limited ambition exemplifies the restraint and caution of Conservative philosophy. British Conservatism has always been more interested in power than ideas. As Lord Hailsham once put it, 'An ounce of practice is worth a ton of theory.' The Left, on the other hand, generally excluded from office and effective action, have rather more time to devote to theory. When in opposition Labour leaders usually feel impelled to publish some statement of their political philosophy, even the severely down-to-earth Clement Attlee whose *The Will and the Way to Socialism* was as pedestrian and unexciting as its title.

Conservative lack of interest in abstract theory has led some commentators to dismiss it as, in John Stuart Mill's words, 'the stupid party'. This is of course a gross simplification: for a start five of the men who have explored the nature of Conservatism, Lords Halifax and Hailsham, Sir Keith Joseph, William Waldegrave and John Redwood, have all been Fellows of All Souls, Oxford, a bastion of intellectual superiority.

Yet one Conservative response to the 'stupid' label has been, in effect, to wear it with pride. That self-styled personification of 'Englishness', Stanley Baldwin, once told the young Conservative MP, R.A. Butler, that the sin of intellectualism was worse than death, and even Harold Macmillan, proud of his Oxford First, claimed that 'the clever people in a nation at any given moment are nearly always wrong. Distrust the clever man.'

Similarly, Iain Macleod declared on the hustings that 'The Labour Party may dream their dreams and Liberals scheme their schemes, but we have work to do.' How ironic, then, that Macleod himself should once be dismissed by Lord Salisbury as 'too clever by half'. A disdain for 'thinkers' as opposed to 'doers' is frequently voiced by Conservatives.

A different Conservative reaction to the 'stupid' tag has been to assert that the educated Englishman's genius lies in his instinct for personal relationships rather than for doctrine. Yet another reply is to forestall the discussion by simply asserting that Conservatism is 'the very breath of English history' and leave it at that.

But perhaps the most powerful retort has been to stress the value of experience; as early as July 1763 that grand Tory, Samuel Johnson, assured Boswell that 'human experience, which was constantly contradicting theory, was the great test of truth'. This emphasis on Experience, on Tradition and Authority, is a feature of British Conservative thought, even though it does not address the question of which Experiences, Traditions or Authority are to take priority. Nor does it answer the question: 'Why be a Conservative in the first place?'

How have Conservative thinkers in the past tried to define Conservatism and how successful have they been? Can one uncover a distinctive Conservative philosophy or is Conservatism just 'all things to all men'; a convenient garb to cloak self-interest and the Party's voracious appetite for power and office? Some of the most stimulating responses are contained in the writings of Edmund Burke, the eighteenth-century 'Irish Adventurer' who was an MP, journalist and thinker.

Born in Dublin in 1729, Burke was educated at Trinity College before coming to London where he qualified as a barrister. At the age of thirty-five he was elected an MP and his place in high society was assured by his purchase of Gregories, a substantial estate just outside Beaconsfield – even though it is still unclear how he was able to afford such a property. His intellect and force of personality were such that he was one of the few people to debate and argue on equal terms with Samuel Johnson: 'His stream of mind is perpetual . . . Take up whatever topic you please, he [Burke] is ready to meet you . . .'

Burke was to sit as the Member of Parliament for Wendover and then for Bristol, where he issued his famous plea that MPs should be free to vote and act according to their own conscience rather than be a delegate carrying out the mandate of their constituents. Ironically, Burke's much-quoted appeal would be systematically undermined over the next two centuries as MPs found their power diminished by the growing hold of party machines and more particularly by the role of the whips in Parliament.

Although Burke called himself a Whig, he was definitely a conservative with a small 'c'. As a result, his ideas have been appropriated by Conservatives both here and abroad, and over a period of thirty years Burke furnished a formidable array of arguments and propositions which are still drawn upon today.

Reacting against the spirit of progress and rationalism engendered by the Enlightenment in the last half of the eighteenth century, he fashioned a distinctive body of political thought. This was not a systematic theory – like all Conservative thinkers he considered all systems to be pernicious – but a number of themes do emerge clearly from his writings.

First of all, there is Burke's call for balance or, to use his own word, 'equipoise'. In a rapidly changing world, he wanted to ensure the maintenance of continuity and stability. Support for the status quo was buttressed by a rather nebulous appeal to 'History' and by his emphasis on the value of the civil associations within British society. Like many Conservatives after him, Burke was keen to play down the importance of politics as an activity.

As a result of his reverence for the 'natural' or 'proper' order, Burke was implacably hostile to any suggestion of parliamentary reform, arguing that if the constitution was in a state of 'equipoise' then there was no need to change it.

But we should remember what this natural parliamentary order actually meant in practice. One has only to look at William Hogarth's four *Election* paintings of 1754 for a graphic portrayal of an eighteenth-century election; bribery, corruption, mob riot are all present. In any case, only a small minority of the population was allowed to vote.

Burke's satisfaction with this state of affairs displays the anti-democratic strand which has always run through Conservative thought. On one famous occasion he referred to the majority of Britons as 'the swinish multitude', a remark which launched a range of satirical publications glorying in his phrase.

Burke was also adamant that Conservatism should revere the particular and the everyday rather than the abstract: 'Circumstances (which with some gentlemen pass for nothing) give, in reality, to every political principle its distinguishing colour and discriminating effect. The circumstances are what render every civil and political scheme beneficial or obnoxious to mankind.' This undogmatic adherence to freedom of action is one of the abiding features of British Conservatism. In effect, pragmatism is more important than principle.

Burke understood that ideas in themselves are insufficient; in order to be fully effective they must be expressed collectively through political parties. In turn these parties need to establish standards of organisation, unity and loyalty. It took Conservatives some decades to understand fully what was entailed, but in this century the Conservative Party can justifiably claim to be the world's most successful political body.

So far one could describe Burke's approach as one of what we have we (organised as a party) hold. But there is more to Burke than this rigidity: on occasion his honesty and integrity caused him to peer over the precipice at worlds about which his colleagues knew little. Take this moving passage from his *Vindication of Natural Society* which is usually excluded from the anthologies compiled by Conservative commentators. Apart from anything else it displays the literary qualities evident in Conservative thought from Burke to Oakeshott:

> There are in Great Britain upwards of a hundred thousand people employed in lead, tin, iron, copper, and coal mines; these unhappy wretches scarce ever see the light of the sun; they are buried in the bowels of the earth; there they work at a severe and dismal task, without the least prospect of being delivered from it; they subsist upon the coarsest and worst sort of fare; they have their health miserably impaired, and their lives cut short, by being perpetually confined in the close vapour of these malignant minerals. A hundred thousand more at least are tortured without remission by the suffocating smoke, intense fires, and constant drudgery, necessary in refining and managing the products of those mines. If any man informed us that two hundred thousand innocent persons were condemned to so intolerable slavery, how should we pity the unhappy sufferers, and how great would be our just indignation against those who inflicted so cruel and ignominious a punishment!

Yet despite his periodic glances at the iniquities of servile labour, Burke always pushed aside the implications of what he saw. A firm advocate of the abolition of the slavery abroad, he was unwilling to do anything about this 'intolerable slavery' at home. Instead he evaded the issue by claiming that the poor should be satisfied with the prospect of future consolation in the Kingdom of Heaven. The bulk of people must labour 'to obtain what by labour can be obtained; and when they find, as they commonly do, the success disproportioned to the endeavour, they must be taught their consolation in the final proportions of eternal justice'.

There is a certain authoritarian menace in the phrase 'they must be taught' just as there is in Burke's assertion that 'men have no right to what is not reasonable and to what is not for their benefit'. Left unstated but clearly detectable is the assumption that it is Burke and his peers who will decide what is reasonable and beneficial.

This last remark of Burke's comes from his most famous work, *Reflections on the Revolution in France*, written to express his horror and disgust at the events of the French Revolution. In language reminiscent of twentieth-century denunciations of Bolshevism and 'the communist menace', Burke excoriated the French Revolution and all those associated with it. His 'just indignation' had now indeed found full vent.

The problem with his rhetoric was that, as even his sympathetic Victorian biographer John Morley pointed out, Burke simply did not know what he was talking about. His knowledge of social and economic conditions in France was minimal and he therefore never asked himself whether the revolution might not in part have been caused by 'intolerable slavery' similar to that which he had observed in his own country. It was a failure of human understanding and sympathy.

Despite this drawback, however, Burke did provide a forceful and eloquent challenge to the dangers of totalitarianism. His most recent biographer, Conor Cruise O'Brien, justifiably claims that his writings attacking the French Revolution were 'the first great act of intellectual resistance to the first great experiment in totalitarian innovation'. In a century which has witnessed the twin terrors of Fascism and communism, Burke's warnings should still be read and heeded.

Towards the end of his life Edmund Burke was nearly ennobled as Lord Beaconsfield. Tragically, however, his only son died of tuberculosis and, in the moving words of one observer, 'There ended Burke's whole share of earthly happiness. There ended all his dreams of earthly grandeur. Thenceforth a Coronet was to him a worthless bauble which he must decline to wear.'

Ironically, the politician who was eventually awarded that 'worthless bauble' of the title of Lord Beaconsfield was Benjamin Disraeli, another thinker who contributed to the philosophy of Conservatism.

Although he flourished in drawing rooms and at fashionable soirées, Disraeli's rackety early life with his repeated failures as a novelist, businessman and journalist seems to have widened his sympathies. In his *A Vindication of the English Constitution* (1835), Disraeli argued that 'The Tory Party in this country is the national party' and should therefore champion the interests of the common people. He attacked utilitarianism which in its doctrinaire quest for 'the greatest happiness of the greatest number', seemed to elevate self-interest above any notion of community.

He explored these themes more thoroughly in his two novels *Coningsby* (1844) and *Sybil* (1845). In *Coningsby* Disraeli castigates Peel's Conservative Party for being unprincipled, for failing to educate public opinion and for being unable to answer the question 'what will you conserve?' In *Sybil* he intensifies his attack on Peel and sketches out his own conception of Conservatism. As with Burke, there is an appeal to History and, in addition, Disraeli rather tediously identifies a line of Tories which to him embody the Party's history.

More interestingly, the novel is subtitled 'The Two Nations' and Disraeli depicts vividly the 'constant degradation of the people' and the divisions opening up between rich and poor. Following on from *Vindication* he argues that Toryism should announce that power has only one duty — to secure the social welfare of the people.

This is Disraeli's legacy to Tory thought: the exhortation that the Conservatives should represent 'One Nation' by always bearing in mind the common people. Like the majority of Tory thinkers, Disraeli was clear about the limits of individualism. The credo of each for him or herself undermined any claim that the Conservatives were a national party. He wanted to remind his readers that man was a social being, a member of a community which was patterned by mutual duties and responsibilities rather than the selfish individual associated with liberalism.

However, these collective obligations and commitments had no connection with the idea of class. This potentially divisive concept, which first appeared in the 1820s as industrialisation transformed British society, finds no place in Tory philosophy. Any talk of class politics is condemned outright. Instead, refuge is taken in other more nebulous and vague concepts which usually come complete with capital letters: Nation, Church, Monarchy, Family, Authority, the Rule of Law (Justice is less in evidence), Order, Hierarchy, Deference, Community and so forth.

After his death in 1881, Disraeli's legacy of socially concerned 'One Nation' Toryism was promoted as a counter-weight to the powerful presence of the Liberal, William Gladstone. It was also exploited by ambitious politicians such as Lord Randolph Churchill who were anxious to make their way in the Party.

Some Conservatives have always been a little uneasy about the collectivist and paternal implications of Disraeli's One Nation approach. In the 1970s and 1980s, for instance, a number of academics associated with Mrs Thatcher argued that Disraeli's legacy had been exaggerated and it was another Victorian grand Tory, Lord Salisbury, who was in fact 'the giant of Conservative doctrine' and the key exponent of Conservatism. They dutifully called their journal the *Salisbury Review*.

Disinherited by his father who disapproved of his choice of wife, Salisbury took up a career as a journalist. He contributed a series of thirty-two unsigned articles to the *Quarterly Review* between 1860 and 1873 which formulated his conception of Conservatism. Like Burke, Salisbury also despised abstraction and thought that 'there are no absolute truths or principles in politics'.

Salisbury's philosophy was more passive than Disraeli's. He perceived that 'the Party of movement [that is, the Liberals] lives upon discontent' and his aim was to smother possible discontent in a smog of inactivity. It was up to the Liberals and their allies to make the case for change because the Tories were happy with the status quo. One of Salisbury's Tory contemporaries, Lord George

Hamilton, described a Conservative as being a person who was 'more or less contented or happy with his condition'.

He also exhibited another prejudice common to most Conservative thinkers, namely the distrust of experts who consider themselves superior to the wisdom of 'common sense'. Just as Edmund Burke had scorned 'short-sighted coxcombs of philosophy', Salisbury was similarly scathing:

> No lesson seems to be so deeply inculcated by the experience of life as that you should never trust experts. If you believe the doctors, nothing is wholesome. If you believe the theologians, nothing is innocent. If you believe the soldiers, nothing is safe. They all require to have their strong wine diluted by a large mixture of common sense.

Typically, Salisbury fails to ask the question whose common sense? The common sense of one group of people may well be the height of stupidity to another. And how does common sense change? It may well have been taken for granted and 'commonsensical' in the nineteenth century that women should not have the vote; common sense today decrees otherwise. Thus common sense becomes another rather vague concept behind which Conservatives can shelter at times of trouble or stress – a 'Back to Basics' which means all things to all people.

Salisbury's nephew, Arthur Balfour, who was highly regarded as a philosopher, was once asked what his political principles entailed. 'I suppose the principles of common sense,' he replied before continuing, 'to do what seems to be the right thing in a given case.' Not a very illuminating answer.

Salisbury's fatalistic strain was most apparent in his famous essay of 1883 which he called 'Disintegration'. In it he argued that the country had been going to the dogs ever since the Reform Act of 1867. Balfour took an even more long-term view of decline; his book *The Foundations of Belief* (1905) contains this profoundly gloomy passage: 'We survey the past, and see that its history is of blood and tears, of helpless blundering, of wild revolt, of stupid acquiescence, of empty aspirations.'

If Salisbury influenced his nephew, he clearly influenced his sons too. One of them, Lord Hugh Cecil, took his father's defence of the status quo to the highest degree. His book *Conservatism* (1912) seemed to oppose any form of social change whatsoever: 'Why change? It is wiser to let it alone.' The view from the drawing room at Hatfield House might well have seemed idyllic and should on no account have been disturbed, but of course it was a view which was enjoyed by only a handful of people.

Burke, Disraeli, Salisbury and Cecil were all self-confident members of the governing class, sure of themselves and their place in society. Apart from the doctrine of utilitarianism, their ideas went relatively unchallenged because the Victorian age produced so few intellectuals critical of their own society. The prosperity of Victorian life for the educated dulled the radical and dissenting spirit. Lord Annan has suggested that this was because of the tendency of the intellectual families – the Trevelyans, Wedgwoods and so on – to intermarry.

The only radical thinker who rejected the entire ordering of society was Karl Marx, and the obscurity of his work, written originally in German and published mainly after his death in 1883, meant that its impact was initially limited. His habit of viewing the world through stark and melodramatic glasses – black-hearted bosses versus virtuous workers, the inevitability of struggle, the climax of revolution – was also not attractive to the more cautious and tentative English frame of mind.

The one attempt to establish an explicitly intellectual Conservatism came with the founding of the magazine *National Review* in 1883. It was created with the express purpose of refuting Mill's 'stupid' tag. One of the writers associated with it, W.H. Mallock, although little read today, was in some ways a pioneer of the ideas now labelled as Thatcherism.

Mallock thought that the most effective way to salve social sores was to preside over a thriving economy. If the cake was growing for all, then arguments as to who should have which share were easier to deflect because everyone would have more. Mallock was more interested in the creation of wealth brought about by 'the directive ability of the few' than in the traditional Tory concern for an organic and ordered society.

But this more market-oriented brand of Conservatism made little headway. In particular, it ran against the grain of Conservative paternalism which preferred to glorify the rural image of England as a garden and denigrate the industrial and commercial workshop. The most powerful exponent of this creed was undoubtedly Stanley Baldwin, Prime Minister on three separate occasions between the wars, whose 'non-political' speeches ran to no fewer than five volumes.

Baldwin chose to present himself as 'Farmer Stan', the avuncular father figure whose native shrewdness and common sense were infinitely preferable to mere 'brains'. His writings, some of which were supplied by his cousin Rudyard Kipling, are replete with cosy nostalgia for a mythical time when everyone knew their place, masters were kind and never sacked anyone, and the workforce touched their forelocks and never went on strike. He once described the old family firm:

> It was a place where I knew, and had known from childhood, every man on the ground; a place where I was able to talk with the men not only about their troubles in the works, but troubles at home and their wives. It was a place where the fathers and grandfathers of the men then working there had worked, and where their sons went automatically into the business. It was also a place where nobody ever 'got the sack'.

It was no coincidence that the family's iron foundry at Wilden was run on semi-feudal lines with a strong tradition of paternalism, nor that Baldwin was fond of referring to English people as 'stock'.

Another senior Conservative favouring this paternalist tradition was Lord Halifax, a big land owner in Yorkshire who was to become Viceroy of India and Neville Chamberlain's Foreign Secretary. He too idealised the past, as his first biographer shrewdly noted: 'He proclaims a vision of a Merrie England with subsidies which as an ideal and a symbol is the British counterpart of Gandhi's spinning-wheel.'

The potency of this rural imagery is shown by the instinctive way in which Conservative politicians at times of crisis reach for 'greenery'; during the Suez episode in 1956 Harold Macmillan spoke of his determination to keep 'the lawns of England green' for his grandchildren. And, notwithstanding Mrs Thatcher's enthusiasm for economic growth and market forces, the Party rallies during her 1987 election campaign invariably began with a rendition of Blake's 'Jerusalem' with its idealisation of a green and pleasant land.

It is clear that what we are talking about here is England and rarely Britain; Scotland, Wales and Ireland are often conspicuously absent from these rural panegyrics.

This 'naturalist' tradition of Toryism was well aware of the unsettling, dynamic effects of capitalism with its proclivity for change; Lord Hailsham in *The Case for Conservatism* explicity dwelt on the venerable Conservative tradition which criticised capitalism as 'an ungodly and rapacious scramble for ill-gotten gains, in the course of which the rich appeared to get richer and the poor poorer'.

To assuage these anxieties, some Conservatives have argued that it is Christianity which provides the social bonds and framework within which Conservatism must be placed. Edmund Burke, for example, regarded 'the laws of commerce' as being 'the laws of nature, and consequently the laws of God'. Disraeli, too, claimed that: 'Religion gives politics its meaning and dignity. Without the Church there can be no state.' And finally, Lord Hugh Cecil thought that 'The championship of religion is therefore the most important of the functions of Conservatism.'

This century, Christian Conservatism has been conspicuous in the writings of Lords Halifax and Hailsham who both claimed that Christianity does not in fact carry any political message. Despite a few perfunctory asides exhorting people to remember the less advantaged, the status quo was quite good enough to be going along with. If pressed, Conservatives would buttress their position by arguing that mankind was inherently wicked: 'Conservatism is the creed of original sin and the politics of imperfection,' maintained Nigel Lawson in 1980.

The Conservative Party, by and large, favoured the Church of England, whilst the Labour Party owed as much to Methodism as Marxism and perhaps even more to the Christian Socialism of influential figures such as George Lansbury who was its leader in the 1930s. Perhaps the best representative of this strand was the radical Archbishop of Canterbury during the Second World War, William Temple. In his book *Christianity and Social Order* (1942), Temple argued that Christians should follow Christ's example and devote their efforts to improving the lot of the poor and downtrodden. Clearly these interpretations of the social and political implications of Christianity are rather more active and radical than those of Halifax and Hailsham.

Sometimes Christian Conservatism has adopted a triumphal note, as it did during the Cold War when communism and communists were regularly lambasted. In February 1949, even Harold Macmillan was to be heard calling for a Crusade directed against this twentieth-century 'invasion of the Goths': 'We must make active inroads for ourselves into the enemy's own territory. With spiritual as well as material instruments we must seek the reconversion of the world.' In 1963 it was Macmillan's own Cabinet which discussed plans to link up with the Catholic Church in a propaganda offensive against the atheistic Soviet Union.

There were and are, however, differences between Christian Conservatism in Britain and Catholic Christian Democracy on the Continent. The latter, to take one clear example, strongly favours legislation to protect the weaker members of society and therefore their political representatives all favour the passage of the 'social charter'. British Conservatives, on the other hand, argue that such legislation will fetter the powers of the wealth creators in whom lies the best bet for improved social conditions for all.

Perhaps the most elegant exponent of old-style traditional Conservatism since the war has been Sir Ian Gilmour, Old Etonian, member of the Guards, barrister and distinguished historian. Gilmour rejoices in traditional One Nation themes and stresses the value of diversity, the inevitability of human imperfection and the need for social conscience: 'So far as philosophy or doctrine is concerned, the wise Conservative travels light.' 'Balance and moderation are integral to Toryism,' he declared in his book *Inside Right*.

Sadly for Gilmour, his brand of Conservatism was scornfully

dismissed in the late-1970s and the 1980s. He himself was sacked from Mrs Thatcher's Cabinet in 1981 during a purge of the 'wets'. Gilmour's account of the Thatcher years was simply titled *Dancing with Dogma*. His critics were equally scathing; Oxford academic John Gray's review of *Dogma*, published under the dogmatic headline 'Thatcherism is as British as Gaullism is French', was short and to the point: 'The chief significance of Gilmour's book may be in its exemplification of a certain turn of mind in British conservatism, which contents itself with deploring realities it does not begin to understand.'

The vituperation of Gray's review was characteristic of the often personal arguments of Thatcherism and of its blunt rejection of the gentlemanly old-style Tory philosophy. Conservative thinkers in the past had never shown any great urgency over their task, preferring to muse gently over the after-dinner port. Ideas themselves were potentially dangerous and unsettling and therefore Tories needed to handle them with careful detachment. This attitude was to change dramatically.

'We must have an ideology. The other side have got an ideology they can test their policies against. We must have one as well.' So Mrs Thatcher is reported to have said shortly after being elected leader of the Conservative Party in 1975. Left-wing critics were soon happily analysing something they dubbed 'Thatcherism'. It was the first time that any British Conservative leader had spawned an '-ism' or an '-ology': Baldwin, Churchill or Macmillan would have frowned upon any such personal phenomenon.

It is in fact difficult to know just how interested Mrs Thatcher really was in ideas except in so far as they reinforced her moral instincts and her access to power. Mrs Thatcher's memoirs of her years in office, for instance, barely mention the names of those intellectual mentors – Paul Johnson, Ralph Harris, Alfred Sherman, Maurice Cowling, Hugh Thomas – whose arguments were thought by some to underpin her approach.

A recent book which charts the progress of various free market think-tanks recounts the story of Mrs Thatcher at a Conservative meeting in 1975 purportedly discussing 'Family Policy'. The ideas on offer were all apparently 'wishy washy'. Mrs Thatcher pulled out a copy of a book by free-marketeer Frederick von Hayek and, banging it down on the table, stated 'This is what we believe!'

In fact, Hayek's work *Constitution of Liberty* contains virtually nothing on the family. Force of personality and fierce conviction seem rather more apparent in this story than any great interest in ideology or doctrine. One analyst of Thatcherism, Shirley Robin Letwin, is certain that the phenomenon was, above all, a process rather than a theory. One might go further and call it a messianic complex, particularly as Mrs Thatcher herself often talked in biblical terms. Of her downfall in 1990, she has said, 'My trouble was that the believers had fallen away.'

The situation was muddied by the use of a shorthand tag 'the New Right'. Under this heading were yoked together a variety of different ideas and thinkers who were in reality united by little more than a detestation of socialism and the supposedly 'pinkish' tendencies of the post-war Conservative Party.

But the fact that think-tanks such as the Institute of Economic Affairs (IEA) and the Centre for Policy Studies (CPS) or the Economic Dining Club formed by Nicholas Ridley were indeed effective was in large part because the Conservative Party lacked any formalised method of policy making. The Conservative Political Centre (CPC), founded by Rab Butler after the Second World War, encouraged political discussion within the Party yet not in such a way that it ever became acrimonious or disruptive.

Within the Labour Party, on the other hand, policy was conscientiously debated and agreed upon after dull debates at Party conferences. In the early 1980s in particular, relatively abstruse arguments led to public bickering and helped fuel the perception that the Labour Party was divided. The Conservative Party had and has no such procedure for adapting the ideas of its activists. Its abiding principle of 'all power to the leader' meant that if that leader was content to draw upon the ideas of the think-tanks – and Mrs Thatcher had helped to set up the Centre for Policy Studies in the first place – then those ideas automatically became influential.

Not that the doctrines which constituted Thatcherism were

entirely unprecedented within Conservatism. For example, the Conservative Party manifesto of 1979, which embodied much of the 'new' approach, was very similar to that on which Edward Heath's Conservatives had fought the general election in 1970, just nine years before. The central theme – the strict control of public spending – was one with which Sir Robert Peel and Neville Chamberlain amongst previous Conservative Prime Ministers would have sympathised. Admittedly it had been a minority and muted stance within the party since the Second World War when the emphasis had instead been placed on the benefits of government expenditure, but it had never been extinguished entirely.

However the ideas of the New Right may come to be judged, it is impossible not to admire the tenacity and perseverance with which they had kept arguing their corner in deeply unsympathetic circumstances. The Institute of Economic Affairs, for instance, was founded as long ago as 1957, with the aim of trying 'to teach the virtues of the free economy'. Its short and punchy pamphlets were written in deliberately concise and clear language, unlike the turgid output which the Left seemed to think was compulsory. Financed privately – of course – the IEA had no difficulty in raising over over a half million pounds a year through personal contacts.

It was clear that the body of ideas which began to be called Thatcherism represented a reversal of the old One Nation tradition in favour of a more market-oriented approach in which every aspect of government – except for the maintenance of law and order and defence – was questioned and had to be accounted for. Mrs Thatcher accompanied her policies with fanfares calling for 'the rolling back of the frontiers of the state'.

So far, Tory philosophy might be summed up as the attempt to reconcile the two strands of paternalist One Nation Conservatism and of free market individualism. Or, to put it more succinctly, the traditional versus the libertarian. What was novel about Thatcherism was its explicit abandonment of any attempt to reconcile the two strands and its determination to tilt the balance strongly towards one side. The genie of individualism, with its potentially destructive and unsettling impact on traditional Tory verities, was now out of its bottle.

She and her colleagues were happy to use most 'un-Tory' words such as 'revolution' and 'radical' to describe their approach. In her memoirs, for instance, Mrs Thatcher says of the 1983 election victory that 'There was a revolution still to be made, but too few revolutionaries', whilst Nigel Lawson happily subtitled his book 'Memoirs Of A Tory Radical'. Lord Salisbury for one would have found such language most disturbing.

Thatcherism also explicitly rejected traditional Conservative hesitations about materialism. It had no time for Lord Halifax's tacit approval of Gandhi's spinning wheel, let alone the patrician fastidiousness of an R.A. Butler who in 1976 was to be found worrying that the Tory Party might be identified with the 'vulgar' kind of profits currently being made by some City businessmen, 'Driving around in those vast cars and eating those enormous lunches . . .'

Hostile not only to the world-weary 'let it be' approach of many Tories in the past, Thatcherism was simply not interested in any notion of community, preferring instead to emphasise the virtues of aggressive private enterprise. Mrs Thatcher notoriously remarked that there was no such thing as society, only individuals and their families.

Traditionally, Conservatives had mused about ideas in private, which meant there was little danger of public disunity or controversy. The deliberations of Tory dining clubs remained private; the ruminations of the socialist gatherings hosted by playwright Harold Pinter and historian Lady Antonia Fraser at their home in London's Campden Hill Square inevitably ended up in the newspapers.

Unusually, however, one of the characteristics of Thatcherism was a seeming delight in taking on opponents in public. Its cut-and-dried view of the world was exemplified by the division of Conservative colleagues into the categories 'wet' and 'dry'. This belligerence is perhaps explained by the fact that several members of Thatcher's entourage, such as Paul Johnson, Alfred Sherman and Woodrow Wyatt, had once belonged to the Left and therefore brought with them an ideological fervour and disputatiousness usually absent from Tory circles.

But Thatcherism was always an uneasy mix of elements. It

contained both the Traditionalists or Authoritarians who favoured controls, harsher laws and more severe punishments but also the Libertarians; at its most extreme, the latter's 'power to the people' stance favoured the legalisation of drugs on the grounds that if people wished to take them, then that was their business. This conflict prevented Thatcherism from developing any 'moral right' or 'moral majority' slant. Nor was it easy for Mrs Thatcher to reconcile her devotion to market forces with her equally obvious devotion to nationalism and national sovereignty.

Mrs Thatcher's attitude to hereditary titles is a telling example of this confusion. The theoretical Thatcherite position seemed to be that people must make their own way in a classless world, yet in practice she awarded an hereditary title to Willie Whitelaw and a baronetcy to her husband. As a result Mark Thatcher, her son, will automatically become Sir Mark Thatcher no matter what his achievements or failings. 'Isn't my mother wonderful,' Mark Thatcher was quoted as saying ingenuously in the *Mail on Sunday*, 'Doing this for me and my son.'

For good or for bad, Mrs Thatcher always remained a politician rather than a philosopher: it was the quest for power rather than ideas in themselves that fuelled her dynamism. As early as 1983, some of her devotees at the IEA were turning against the Prime Minister because of her unwillingness to dismantle the Welfare State, the kind of project which looked fine on paper but was simply not practical politics for the Conservative Party. Similarly, one of the writers who had most influenced her, the journalist T.E. Utley, observed that although Mrs Thatcher was personally in favour of educational vouchers, the instincts of the professional politician ruled out such a radical policy.

The practical impact of Thatcherism on the Conservative Party, the economy and much more is discussed elsewhere in this book, but in terms of philosophy it seemingly discredited the old paternalist strain of Toryism whilst putting little in its place. This vacuum becomes embarrassingly clear when the present Prime Minister, John Major, has a stab at philosophising: 'Fifty years from now, Britain will still be the country of long shadows on county grounds, warm beer, invincible green suburbs, dog lovers, and – as George

Orwell said – old maids bicycling to Holy Communion through the morning mist.'

Somehow these Baldwinesque sentiments seem rather silly and desperately out of place in the 1990s. The rootlessness and loss of direction is evident too in the memoirs produced by those who were members of Mrs Thatcher's Cabinets in the 1980s. Few of them rise above tedious narrative and simplistic claims about making Britain 'Great' again.

Some Conservative thinkers, once fervent supporters of Mrs Thatcher, are now desperately backpedalling and arguing that market forces must be reconciled with traditional notions of community and social obligation. Following on from Edmund Burke, for instance, John Gray currently stresses the importance of civil society, namely the world of families, clubs, churches and voluntary associations which give a sense of meaning and belonging to our lives.

David Green, a member of the staff at the free-market Institute of Economic Affairs, similarly argues in his *Reinventing Civil Society* (1993) that voluntary societies and associations should be nurtured and encouraged, even though it was the free-market philosophy which, as we will see in Chapter 13, helped to promote such a marked loss of confidence in those same societies and associations during the 1980s. Likewise, Conservative MP David Willetts calls for a 'civic conservatism'. Rather belatedly perhaps, right-wing ideologues have begun to recognise that the full-blooded expression of market forces requires some form of institutional framework or foundation.

In other words, Edmund Burke's 'little platoons' are today back on parade, even though it is not easy to see how they can withstand the bracing effects of competition and the market. In the context of global free trade, the increasing dominance of multinationals such as, say, Hollywood, Coca-Cola and Rupert Murdoch's News International, mean that the little platoons are always likely to be outgunned.

The attempt to recreate a sense of community and to revive respect for the idea of the public rather than the private may perhaps be too little, too late. Like Humpty Dumpty, it is not easy to stick back together again notions of society which have taken such a battering.

Thatcherism had been like a blowtorch, scorching old shibboleths and assumptions, rooting out reactionary habits and attitudes of mind: better defined by what it was against rather than what it was for. In particular, its disapproval of anything public or of any notion of the common good handicapped and continues to hinder Conservatives in their attempt to fashion a guiding philosophy or vision for the next century.

But if Conservatism is in turmoil, then the Left in Britain and Europe is equally unclear about where it stands. Now that high taxation and public ownership have apparently been discarded as electoral albatrosses, it is almost impossible to identify what socialism stands for or advocates.

All over the world, systems of state control and public welfare are under attack. Indeed the very word 'socialism' is distrusted by some on 'the Left' – the inverted commas testify to the overall uncertainty. The views of Tony Blair, eminently well-meaning and generous though they are, have not as yet clarified matters.

An analysis of Conservative thought throws up several striking features. Firstly, and most evident, all the thinkers discussed above have been men, with the exception of Mrs Thatcher who was in any case a 'doer' rather than a 'thinker'. The pages of the *Salisbury Review* are virtually a woman-free zone. One Conservative intellectual of the 1920s, F.C.C. Hearnshaw, even went to the lengths of tracing the doctrine of original sin right back to Eve's misbehaviour in the Garden of Eden. It is a marvellously revealing passage which deserves to be quoted in full:

In that visionary abode of bliss Adam was the person who rep-resented the conservative qualities of contentment and stability. Eve was the innnovator, eager for novelty, ready for reckless experiment, liable to be led away by any such seductive slogan as 'Eat more Fruit,' or 'Free Fig Leaves for all'. As to the devil who, in the form of a serpent, tempted Eve, I suppose that he was the nearest approximation possible, before the Christian era, to the idea of Karl Marx. As to the fact that Adam became involved in the tragic fate of Eve, is it not a warning against the lamentable consequences likely to accrue when the conservative adopts the radical programme?

Hearnshaw clearly felt that Eve's bad behaviour justified the anti-feminist strand within Conservatism. Still, Conservatives are not alone in this; most published socialist thinkers have been men too.

A second characteristic is that all the men whose ideas have been looked at in this chapter have been wealthy and well-connected. It is generally thought to be bad form to mention this obvious fact – most historians of ideas like to pretend that various concepts spring fully formed from the minds of philosophers who are somehow detached members of society, able to rise majestically above its petty concerns and influences.

But of course ideas do not exist in a vacuum and it is therefore hardly surprising that Conservative thinkers have inevitably stressed the importance of property and of maintaining the status quo and the rule of law. They have a great deal to lose: 'what we have we hold'. No Conservative thinker has so far argued in favour of a massive redistribution of wealth and income. If he did, he would not be regarded as a Conservative in the first place. Conservatism is not the voice of the dispossessed or of the have-nots. Edmund Burke once 'beseeched the Government':

Manfully to resist the very first idea, speculative or practical, that it is within the competence of Government, taken as Government, or even of the rich, to supply to the poor, those necessaries which it has pleased the Divine Providence for a while to with-hold from them. We, the people, ought to be made sensible, that it is not in breaking the laws of commerce, which are the laws of nature, and consequently the laws of God, that we are to place our hope of softening the divine displeasure to remove any calamity under which we suffer, or which hangs over us . . .

Fine, but the claim that as members of 'We, The Nation' we are all in 'it' together is rendered a little less convincing when one realises that some people have a rather greater share of 'it' than others. Likewise the argument that members of the public must be free to exercise choice and liberty – an opinion often deployed by those eager to dismantle public services – is challenged by reality: 'Nothing, let us forget, sets a stronger limit on the liberty [or choice] of the citizen than a total absence of money', observed J.K. Galbraith.

Clearly it would be electoral suicide if arguments for the legitimacy of the present order were presented in too blunt and elitist terms. Sometimes, however, Conservative thinkers have with commendable honesty let the cat out of the bag. Peregrine Worsthorne, for instance, for many years the editor of the High Tory *Sunday Telegraph*, has never hidden his fondness for an elite: 'The principal purpose of politics [is] the evolution and maintenance of a securely established ruling class with a justified sense of its own honourable superiority.'

Even more bluntly, Professor Roger Scruton maintains that 'in all healthy societies, it must be the needs and values of the strong which should . . . dominate'. No namby-pamby stuff here about protecting the weak or powerless.

Worsthorne and Scruton apart, Conservative thinkers have generally preferred to couch their arguments in rather more gentle terms, stressing that certain values and traditions are paramount: monarchy, religion and so on are summoned up in support but never, as we saw, divisive concepts such as class.

Sometimes refuge is sought in vague concepts like 'decency' or 'common sense' which allow the Party to present a supposedly non-political and public face of unanimity. Lord Salisbury did it one hundred years ago and today one of the most influential of young Conservative MPs, David Willetts, continues in this manner. In his book *Modern Conservatism* (1992), Willetts argues that 'In Britain at its best, that common sense is so deep and powerful as to become true wisdom.'

Excellent words indeed but inclined to fall apart after a little probing. What is the 'true wisdom' commended here? Almost certainly it has to do with monarchy, religion and so on. But in a society which is multi-racial and multi-ethnic, containing an enormous and stimulating variety of religions, faiths and cultures, the unspoken assumptions surrounding this so-called common sense have become meaningless. The ill-fated Back to Basics campaign launched by John Major sounded so simple, yet was damaged by just such uncertainties and equivocations. What and whose 'basics' were being singled out for emulation?

By taking refuge in eternal 'verities' such as crown, Church, family and so on, Conservative philisophy has for a long time been able to conceal that it is concerned above all with the maintenance of an existing and unequal social order. Hand in hand with this goes the marginalisation of any intellectual challenge to the status quo.

To put it in rather more comprehensible and less brutal language, the Liberal politician Lord Morley – a Cabinet colleague of both Gladstone and Lloyd George – once shrewdly remarked: 'When I hear a man say that he has no particular politics, I know that he is going to vote Conservative.'

Ironically, Conservatives have always looked askance at politics. Why? Because political activity and inquiry always carry the threat of public disagreement or argument which might in turn disturb the existing order. Anyone interested in politics is probably a troublemaker. At the time of controversy over the poll tax, backbench Tory MPs anxiously reported that people were now actually discussing politics in pubs.

Of course politics is not the be-all and end-all of human life, but it is too easy to use this reflection as a convenient get-out clause and retreat to the importance of family and friends. After all, a family is shaped and influenced by the type of schooling its members receive, the house and neighbourhood in which the family live, the jobs which its members have or don't have, the health care available to it. And so here we are, back in the arena of political choices and priorities which Conservative thinkers such as Michael Oakeshott prefer to ignore.

Conservatives have often found it easier to define themselves in terms of what they are against rather than what they stand for. The threat of Soviet communism or 'Bolshevism' came in very useful.

It was relatively easy for any Conservative when challenged to argue that whilst the British way of life and government had drawbacks and failings, these deficits were as nothing compared with the barbarities of what was going on behind the 'Iron Curtain'. This was indeed true and justifiable but, in the 1990s, the end of the Cold War has left Conservatives with an undoubted sense of loss.

Another characteristic of Conservative thought is its promiscuity; its readiness to borrow from all and sundry. It is not, though, quite so promiscuous as Kenneth Baker in his recent anthology of Conservatism seems to imagine. The inclusion of George Bernard Shaw and George Orwell as exponents of the Tory viewpoint seems rather peculiar. It is interesting to speculate what Shaw and Orwell themselves would have had to say about it.

But the Conservative Party's fondness for travelling light with a minimum of ideological baggage does of course serve another purpose. As Professor G.W. Jones points out: 'The Party's long history offers a varied repertoire of rhetoric to justify any position judged electorally expedient. Its intellectual promiscuity is no electoral liability.'

In other words, by being all things to all men, Conservatism has given no hostages to fortune. Principle must never be allowed to get in the way of power. Doctrine must not inhibit freedom of manoeuvre. But whether this vacuum is sustainable in a Britain which is better educated and more given to questioning than in the past is not so clear.

Conservatism's lack of focus and coherence since the impact of Thatcherism destroyed the old paternalist Tory tradition, lies at the root of its current troubles. Without a clear and identifiable public philosophy, the Conservative Party will continue to have problems of identity.

All Power To The Leader?

'Leading the Party is like driving pigs to market.'
Stanley Baldwin, 1924

'The loyalties which centre upon number one are enormous.
If he trips he must be sustained. If he makes mistakes they
must be covered. If he sleeps he must not be wantonly
disturbed. If he is no good, he must be pole-axed.'
Winston Churchill,
quoted in Sir Nigel Fisher *The Tory Leaders* (1977)

'. . . there are very few exceptions indeed to the rule that
the fortunes and misfortunes in private lives markedly shape,
distort and affect the public ones.'
Sir Robert Rhodes James *Bob Boothby* (1991)

The Conservative Party does not exist in law. In a tax dispute in
1981 the High Court ruled that the Party was neither a charity,
a club, an association nor a corporation. The Party therefore
had no legal existence and simply amounted to a private part
of the leader's office. The accurate way to refer to the world's
oldest political organisation is in fact 'John Major, trading as the
Conservative Party'.

This legal fiction emphasises the pre-eminent position held by the
leader of the Conservative Party. Unlike the Labour leader, he or
she selects the Cabinet when in office, the shadow Cabinet when

out of office (the Labour Party elect theirs) and also appoints the Party chairman who runs Central Office in Smith Square, London, as the leader's personal fiefdom.

The role of the Party leader has in any case been enhanced by the creeping Americanisation of British politics during which the leader is becoming more of a presidential figure: less 'first among equals' than the focus of the Party, the recipient of enormous media coverage, the guest at international summits, the centre of electoral campaigns and the subject of a thousand photo-opportunities. And the electoral success of the Conservatives this century has ensured that their leader becomes Prime Minister: of the sixteen leaders of the Conservative Party since Sir Robert Peel only one, Austen Chamberlain, has failed to reach 10 Downing Street.

In theory, therefore, the Conservative leader is virtually a dictator. In practice, of course, it works out rather differently. The power of the leader ultimately depends upon the consent of the led, whether the electorate or party colleagues, and when that disappears then power goes with it. No matter that Winston Churchill was a world-famous statesman in 1945 – the electorate didn't vote for him in that year's general election and he was therefore no longer Prime Minister. No matter that Mrs Thatcher had won three elections in a row and was an international figure – her fellow Conservative MPs didn't vote for her in sufficient numbers in 1990 to allow her to continue as Prime Minister and leader.

Professor Bob McKenzie once summed up the 'now you see it, now you don't' nature of Conservative leadership: 'When appointed, the leader leads and the Party follows, except when the Party decides not to follow – then the leader ceases to be leader.'

One of the most striking passages in Alan Clark's *Diaries* tells of a meeting during the election contest of 1990 when Mrs Thatcher was still Prime Minister but was clearly on the way out. A number of senior Conservatives met to discuss life post-Thatcher: 'The really sickening thing, though, was the urgent and unanimous abandonment of the Lady. Except for William [Waldegrave]'s little opening tribute she was never mentioned again.'

The Conservative Party's overriding objective is electoral victory and therefore defeat, or the prospect of it, inevitably renders the leader vulnerable. To adapt McKenzie's phrase, the Party decides most surely not to follow the leader when faced with electoral calamity. As Alan Clark wrote of Mrs Thatcher in March 1990, 'Her "constituency" in this place [Westminster] depends solely on her proven ability to win General Elections. But now this is in jeopardy she has no real Praetorian Guard to fall back on.'

Labour leaders by contrast are more secure in their tenure even when elections are lost. Generally they resign when they want to (Clement Attlee, Harold Wilson, Jim Callaghan, Neil Kinnock) or else die in office (Hugh Gaitskell). Only George Lansbury and Michael Foot were under pressure to depart and both men, at the end of lengthy political careers, were only too glad to leave.

In the nineteenth century, Tory leaders had enjoyed a similar security of tenure: there were only four (Peel, Derby, Disraeli, Salisbury) in seventy years. But this century the casualty rate amongst Conservative leaders has been dramatically high. Balfour was under severe pressure to resign in 1911; Austen Chamberlain was deposed; Baldwin narrowly survived moves to ditch him on several occasions; Chamberlain was ejected from the premiership in 1940; Churchill went unwillingly in 1955; Eden and Macmillan's health problems masked their exits in 1957 and 1963; Heath was removed in 1975 and, most spectacularly of all, Mrs Thatcher was ousted in 1990.

The leader does however have some weapons in the armoury. The most potent and therefore frequently used is the appeal to party unity – the plea that this is not the time to rock the boat (although there has yet to be a good time to rock it). Every leader under pressure plays this card and it usually, but not always, proves to be a trump. Electoral defeat can sometimes overtrump it.

This contrast between the possession of enormous power and its sudden loss makes analysis of the Conservative Party leadership peculiarly fascinating. An examination of past Conservative leaders is also a study of personality because the character of each leader has crucially influenced their record in office.

So how do Conservative leaders ever reach what Disraeli famously called 'the top of the greasy pole'? How are they elected or, as was the case in the past before the Party held formal elections, how did they 'emerge'?

★   ★   ★

'The King is Dead, Long Live the King.' This traditional cry articulated the continuity of the medieval monarchy. The institution itself was more important than any single occupant of the throne; however distinguished the dead king, subjects were expected to transfer their loyalty with no regrets.

Well aware that nothing damages the prospect of power more effectively than party disunity, the Conservative Party has always sought to ensure that the replacement of its leaders takes place with the minimum of fuss and damage. They have shied away from potentially divisive leadership contests. In one much-used word, leaders 'emerged' to general acclamation. Peel, Derby, Disraeli, Salisbury – the four Conservative leaders of the nineteenth century – stood head and shoulders above their colleagues in terms of ability and experience and were virtually the only possible choices as leader. The accession of each was taken for granted amongst the governing circles of the Party.

They were not always popular: Disraeli in particular was 'the Jew boy' to his enemies, but after the retirement of Derby in 1868 he was the only possible successor. Similarly Peel, despite his personal aloofness, was certain to succeed Lord Liverpool.

By the early twentieth century the appearance of a more transparently ambitious breed of politician, represented above all by the figure of Joseph Chamberlain, meant that there would invariably be several rivals for the post of leader. The dilemma was how to end up with the best candidate without endangering party unity? Drawing up rules would invite debate, argument and then disagreement. The test came in 1911 when Arthur Balfour stepped down and for the first time the succession was not clear cut.

There were two rival claimants: Sir Walter Long and Austen Chamberlain, son of Joseph who was himself out of the running because of a serious stroke suffered several years before. Neither were especially suited to the post. Both men lacked energy and charisma and were identified with particular factions within the quarrelling party.

In a masterpiece of political legerdemain a third, compromise, candidate emerged in the form of Andrew Bonar Law, a Glaswegian ironmaster without public profile or ministerial experience. Crucially, however, he offered the possibility of avoiding internal and perhaps public dissent; he might well be able to keep the Party together. Bonar Law himself had doubts about his own fitness for the role. As he was going to the crucial meeting at the Carlton Club his confidant Max Aitken said to him 'You are a great man now. You must talk like a great man, behave like a great man.' 'If I am a great man,' replied Bonar Law, 'then a good many great men must have been frauds.'

Aitken (the future Lord Beaverbrook) knew that this meeting would conclude with the unanimous approval of Bonar Law. Both Chamberlain and Long had sacrificed their personal ambition to the interests of the Party and withdrawn from the contest, setting a precedent which was often followed in years to come. One observer noted of Long's withdrawal speech: 'He spoke and evidently felt strongly of the degradation that it would have been to the Party to have elected a leader by secret ballot.'

That this Carlton meeting was attended solely by MPs was another foretaste of the future. The Conservative Party outside Westminster played no part in the proceedings. MPs argued that, as it was they who would be working most closely in Parliament with the new leader, they and they alone should have the determining choice. Less widely voiced was their conviction that wider consultations might well lead to public friction which must be avoided at all costs.

In fact the real choice in 1911 had been made less by the MPs, who were presented with a *fait accompli*, than by a tight circle of men within the upper echelons of the Party who could be sure their deliberations would remain private. That most of the Party concurred with this way of doing things was shown by the words of backbench MP Ernest Pretyman.

It was Pretyman who in 1921 moved the resolution inviting Austen Chamberlain to become Conservative leader after Bonar Law's temporary resignation due to sickness: 'I think it will be a bad day [when we] have solemnly to meet to elect a leader. The leader is there, and we all know it when he is there.' Pretyman was echoing the sentiments of Sir Walter Long, expressed ten years before. Just as the new Pope was suddenly there, so too it seemed were Conservative leaders.

In 1923 the sudden resignation of Bonar Law because of ill-health together with his unwillingness to recommend a successor meant that the Party was faced with the prospect of conflict. Moreover, since the Conservative Party was in office they were choosing not just a leader but also a Prime Minister.

Austen Chamberlain ruled himself out of the running, but again there remained two seemingly unsuitable candidates. Lord Curzon, a former Viceroy of India ensconced in the House of Lords, was faced by the little-known Stanley Baldwin who had been Bonar Law's private secretary and a not very successful Chancellor of the Exchequer. Baldwin had only tasted ministerial office the year before and many agreed with Curzon's contemptuous dismissal of him as 'a man of the utmost insignificance'.

He may have been then, but there was also a feeling that it was no longer acceptable for the Conservative leader to sit in the House of Lords – particularly as the main opposition party, Labour, had no representatives in that Chamber. After much to-ing and fro-ing Baldwin was elected leader. It is very revealing that despite his confidence that he himself would be the Party's choice, Curzon still managed to swallow his pride and put party unity first. He proposed Baldwin's name at the meeting where he knew Baldwin would be chosen unanimously.

The choice of the next three Conservative Party leaders represented a return to the nineteenth-century system under which the obvious candidate was simply confirmed to party acclamation. Neville Chamberlain was the only successor to Baldwin; Winston Churchill, as wartime Prime Minister, naturally slipped into the post of Conservative Party leader and Eden had been the heir apparent to Churchill for years. Because all three men were certainties, it was safe for them to be nominated and confirmed at Party meetings attended by more than just MPs.

The rapid demise of Eden in 1957 after the Suez debacle, however, led to a less certain succession. The obvious choice was R.A. Butler who had been a loyal member of the Conservative

Party and of various governments since the 1930s. A national figure because of his part in the Education Act of 1944 and a successful Chancellor of the Exchequer in the early 1950s, Butler had taken charge of the Government in the summer of 1953 when both Churchill and Eden were incapacitated because of illness.

For some important sections in the Conservative Party, however, he was tainted by his enthusiasm for the policies of appeasement in the 1930s. His rival was Harold Macmillan, Eden's Chancellor of the Exchequer. The contest between the two men provides a clear example of the role of personality in politics. The principled but less than dynamic Butler – all too like his surname – was no match for the vigorous Macmillan who knew that the Party was looking for forceful and unapologetic leadership in the aftermath of Suez.

There is a wonderful cameo of both men addressing a meeting of the 1922 Committee, the powerful group of backbench MPs. Butler gave a clear, concise and deeply uninspiring speech. Macmillan, the showman, launched into a bravura performance with gestures so sweeping that he nearly knocked Butler off the platform.

In fact the MPs present at that 1922 meeting had little say in this matter; the crucial choice had been made by the 'magic circle' of senior Conservatives as they were dubbed or, later still, 'the men in suits'. Soundings taken amongst the Cabinet almost certainly showed that Butler was favoured over Macmillan, but such an informal procedure naturally depends on who takes the soundings and how they represent what they find. Unfortunately for Butler the most influential of the 'sounder-outs' was Lord Salisbury, an inveterate opponent of his.

Instead of kicking up a fuss, the defeated candidate did the decent thing. Butler accepted what had happened and stoically proposed Macmillan's name at the Party meeting where he was duly and unanimously elected to replace Eden.

Six years later, in 1963, Butler had a second opportunity to become leader when Macmillan's ill-health prompted him to step down. But Macmillan was determined that Butler would not succeed him. He kept his departure a secret whilst working out his strategy. The prime difficulty was that Butler was much better qualified than any other candidate. Moreover, two potential rivals, Lord Hailsham and Lord Home, were both in the House of Lords and thus posed no immediate threat to him although the possibility now existed of their renouncing their peerages.

Macmillan seems to have embarked upon a high risk strategy, putting off the announcement of his departure until he could best bring forward a candidate who was not Butler. When he did resign in October 1963 the search for his successor therefore took place in the full glare of the Party conference held at Blackpool. Private disunity became public conflict – the very opposite of traditional Conservative practice. Critics and participants alike referred disparagingly to 'The Blackpool Follies of 1963'.

The highly charged proceedings went to some candidates' heads. One of (Quintin) Hailsham's supporters, Randolph Churchill, was to be found at Blackpool handing out badges with 'Q' on them. Typically, the badges lacked pins and were therefore useless. Hailsham damaged his chances further with a poorly judged conference speech. Another possible candidate, Reginald Maudling, fared no better at the rostrum and neither did Butler himself.

As luck would have it, that year's chairman was Lord Home and in the absence of Macmillan it was Home's task to read out the intended speech of the recently departed Prime Minister. Home was able to present himself as being above the wrangling and thus a possible compromise candidate. Macmillan had now decided that Home was best suited for the job and may well have artificially boosted the chances of Hailsham as an alternative to Butler, in order to allow Home to come through as if breaking a deadlock.

Such a manipulation could not have succeeded, however, without Butler's failure to press his case forcefully – as no doubt Macmillan foresaw would happen. The inner circles of the Party helped Home by misrepresenting their 'soundings', just as they had done in 1957. The Lord Chancellor, Lord Dilhorne, reported that an overwhelming majority of the Cabinet were in favour of Home, even though this was not true. Simple arithmetic showed that at least nine members of the twenty-man Cabinet were in favour of Butler. Yet Butler was hamstrung by his paralysing loyalty to the Party; one of his most fervent supporters who was indeed prepared to rock the boat on 'Rab''s behalf, Enoch Powell, has put it best:

'We handed him a loaded revolver and told him all he had to do was to pull the trigger. He asked if it would make a noise and we said "That is in the nature of guns, Rab." He asked if it would hurt and we said, "That too is in the nature of guns, Rab," and he said, "I don't think I will. D'you mind?"'

The election of Home proved to be a Pyrrhic victory for the old Tory grandees. Initially they must have thought that they had got away with it, but it was not to be. Randolph Churchill, Winston's son and always a loose cannon within the Tory Party, worked as a journalist and he hastily assembled an account of the leadership contest which detailed the manoeuvres and machinations that had occurred. It was not so much the book itself which caused damage but rather the review by ex-Cabinet minister Iain Macleod, a Butler supporter, in the weekly *Spectator*.

In his disgust at the proceedings, Macleod had subsequently refused to serve under Home – thereby irreparably damaging his own future leadership prospects – and his article exposed to public glare the inner workings of the Party hierarchy. In particular he pointed to the existence of the magic circle of old Etonians: eight of the nine senior Conservatives consulted over the leadership had been at Eton.

Reaction to Macleod's revelations was bitter and hostile: not because his account was inaccurate but because he had made the internal struggles public. Cut dead by his party colleagues when he ventured into the House of Commons smoking room, Macleod was so upset that he even contemplated giving up politics altogether.

Yet Macleod was not alone in his perception that the undemocratic method of emergence was bringing the Party into disrepute. In 1962, for instance, a senior Tory had been memorably quoted in Anthony Sampson's *Anatomy of Britain*: 'The Tory Party is run by about five people, and they all treat their followers with disdain; they're mostly Etonians, and Eton is good for disdain.'

In particular, the Party's informal method of selection compared very unfavourably with leadership elections in the Labour Party under which MPs voted by means of a secret ballot on a one-MP one-vote basis. Conservative backbencher Humphry Berkeley wrote to *The Times* in October 1963 and his letter summed up the failings of the traditional methods: 'The essence of the system was secrecy of consultation, the absence of openly competing candidates, and, where there was no heir-apparent, such speed of action that the matter was settled and over before the rank-and-file of the Party was aware what had happened.'

Bowing to the weight of pressure, the Conservative Party leadership agreed to draw up a formal process for future election contests. What Sir Walter Long had called, fifty years before, the 'degradation' of electing a leader by secret ballot had now to be accepted.

These rules were needed within two years when Home decided to resign after the loss of the 1964 general election. Even though Home himself remained in favour of emergence – in his memoirs, he wrote that 'the "magic circle" of selectors had almost every-thing to be said for it' – he drew up the new procedure. The 'Douglas-Home rules' confirmed that Conservative MPs were to be the sole electoral college for any election. They were expected to take soundings from their constituency parties – but, as was seen in 1957 and 1963, there are soundings and soundings.

The election process was to proceed in stages. To win the first ballot the successful candidate had to secure a majority of votes of the Conservative parliamentary party. In effect this ballot operated as a referendum on the merits of the existing leader because he or she would almost certainly be standing. If no overall majority was obtained then a second ballot would take place, allowing other candidates to enter the contest. Here, a simple majority was sufficient. If that was still not achieved then a third contest was to be held at which MPs would express a second preference.

In the 1965 election, Edward Heath defeated Reginald Maudling by a comfortable majority but did not secure outright victory on the first ballot. Both Maudling and the other candidate Enoch Powell voluntarily withdrew and Heath was acclaimed as leader. The fact that the system had been used at all and produced a leader from a less privileged background reflected how the Party was changing. It emphasised too the role of each candidate's campaign managers in persuading fellow MPs to vote for their choice. Heath's team was led by the efficient and able Peter Walker.

The rules did not in fact provide for the re-election of a leader, let alone any method of ousting him should he prove unpopular or unsuccessful. After the loss of both elections in 1974 however – which meant that he had now lost three out of four elections as leader, not the sort of record likely to satisfy the Party – a groundswell of discontent with Heath grew amongst MPs at Westminster, exacerbated by his disdain and lack of courtesy towards backbenchers. In order to retain his position Heath needed to lance the boil and face down his antagonists.

The elder statesman Lord Home was once more called upon to draw up additional rules allowing an annual challenge directed at the sitting incumbent. Again, the electoral college was restricted to MPs solely, even though there had been moves to include some peers and area chairmen in the process.

Heath was challenged in January 1975 by the relatively unknown Mrs Thatcher, for whom Airey Neave played the part taken by Peter Walker ten years before. Mrs Thatcher decisively defeated Heath in the first ballot, although consultation of the constituency associations showed a big majority in favour of his continuance in office. Heath dropped out and an unstoppable momentum propelled Mrs Thatcher to victory in the second ballot over an assortment of new runners, including Willie Whitelaw, whose loyalty to Heath had prevented him from standing against his old boss in the first ballot.

Under the old system of soundings by men in suits, there is no possibility that Mrs Thatcher could ever have been leader of the Conservative Party. Her election demonstrated the ability of the Party to recreate itself, to disguise far-reaching change within a framework of continuity.

Few Conservatives had ever considered the possibility of a challenge to the leader of the Party when that leader was actually Prime Minister. But in 1989, after ten years in Downing Street, this is precisely what happened. The hostility of some sections of the Party towards Mrs Thatcher was compounded by the thwarted ambitions of those MPs she had passed over for office and by unease about her chances of winning yet another general election.

Under the Home rules, Sir Anthony Meyer, an old-school Tory

wet, stood against Mrs Thatcher in the autumn of 1989. She won by an overwhelming margin but the very fact that there was a challenge at all signalled the end of Mrs Thatcher's dominance of the Party. Thirty-three MPs voted for Meyer and a further twenty-seven abstained. Mrs Thatcher's leadership had been called into question before – but from this point onwards her opponents began to see a real possibility of removing her from office.

Continuing unpopularity and fears about the poll tax reinforced the fears of many Conservative MPs that Mrs Thatcher was unlikely to win the next election. And that, as we have seen again and again, is the bottom line for the Conservative Party: power. Mrs Thatcher's victories at three successive elections mattered little – that was history. Who cared that she enjoyed an international reputation unmatched by a British Prime Minister since Churchill? Foreigners don't vote in general elections. A Conservative leader is only as good as the outcome of the next election.

In November 1990, after much hesitation but finally spurred on by Geoffrey Howe's powerful resignation speech, Michael Heseltine challenged Mrs Thatcher. As Heath had found before her, it was difficult for the incumbent to know what approach to adopt. Should one canvass in person and possibly appear undignified, as if desperate for votes; or is it better to remain serenely above the fray and not stoop to electioneering? Mrs Thatcher adopted the latter stance and the inadequacies of her campaign team proved to be crucial. She won the first ballot but fell four votes short of the majority needed for outright victory.

Mrs Thatcher resigned when she felt that her continuation in office was damaging Party unity. And that, as Austen Chamberlain, Walter Long, Lord Curzon and others had likewise realised before her, was the paramount issue. In the end Conservative leaders are prepared to fall on their swords even if a few, such as Winston Churchill in the 1950s, need rather a lot of encouragement.

The Home procedure for electing a leader had stipulated that MPs should consult their constituency parties and also take into the account the opinions of Conservative members of the House of Lords. The worthlessness of these provisions is clearly demonstrated by the fact that in 1975 the vast bulk of local party opinion favoured

Heath over Mrs Thatcher and, in 1990, wanted the retention of Mrs Thatcher herself. It is also notable that, despite his assiduous courting of the local parties after his resignation from the Cabinet in 1986, Michael Heseltine failed to become leader in 1990.

The formal election process had the merit of containing dissent; when John Major was elected leader, both his rivals – Douglas Hurd and Michael Heseltine – were prepared to accept office under him. The entire process clearly displayed yet again, in the words of political commentator Matthew Parris, the Conservative Party's 'instinct to survive'.

The 'ticking bomb' was the provision for an annual challenge to the leader, a stipulation which has proved immensely destabilising and leaves any Conservative Prime Minister vulnerable to opinion polls and anxieties about a forthcoming election.

The rules were modified in July 1991: currently the leader can only be challenged within fourteen days of the opening of the annual parliamentary session and by a minimum of ten per cent of the parliamentary party. This alteration was meant to reduce the chance of rogue maverick challenges.

Some argue that the system itself should not be used to challenge a Conservative leader who is also Prime Minister. As Lady Thatcher has recently expressed it: 'Being Prime Minister is something much bigger than being leader of a party. It's being Prime Minister of a nation.'

Despite the vagaries of the procedures used since Peel, overall they have served the Conservative Party reasonably well, allowing relative outsiders to become leader (Disraeli, Heath, Thatcher, Major) and accurately mirroring the changing composition of the Party itself. Between the wars, for instance, the manufacturing and industrial background of Bonar Law, Baldwin and Chamberlain was dominant and since the 1960s it has been the turn of the 'less privileged' trio of Heath, Thatcher and Major.

Only the Conservative Party has ever had a Jew (Disraeli), a bachelor (in fact two, Balfour and Heath), a Canadian (Bonar Law) and a woman (Mrs Thatcher) as its leader. When power is the name of the game then the background of its leaders becomes of minimal importance. This does not mean, however, that sections of the Party do not resent those they see as outsiders: Peel was mocked by some Tory colleagues because of his northern accent; Lord Londonderry dismissed Neville Chamberlain as being 'a Birmingham tradesman'; Heath, Thatcher and Major have all been subject to some unpleasant snobbery and patronising put-downs by those Mrs Thatcher calls the Tory Party grandees.

Duellist, friend of Byron, passionate husband, fervent art collector and a man who burst into tears when told of an assassination attempt on Queen Victoria – it is hard to believe that this is a description of Sir Robert Peel, the first leader of the modern Conservative Party and a man whose public image was one of haughty aloofness. His fellow duellist, the Irish leader Daniel O'Connell, famously compared Peel's smile to 'the silver plate on a coffin'.

After his premature death in 1850, Peel was much revered by the Victorians because of his statesmanlike qualities, but in this century he has been neglected. There is one standard biography of him but no memorial lectures or copious quotation from his speeches by aspiring Conservative politicians. He was respected and admired perhaps, but never loved.

This century, influential Tories have always mistrusted Peel; as R.A. Butler once said, 'The story of Sir Robert Peel splitting the Tory Party was for me the supremely unforgettable political lesson of history. It made an absolutely indelible impression. I could never do the same thing in the twentieth century, under any circumstances whatever.' A divided party inevitably diminishes the Conservative hold on power.

Peel's family background demonstrates how some individuals in Britain flourished with the onset of industrialisation. His grandfather was initially a pedlar who hawked knick-knacks around Lancashire. His father became one of the first great cotton magnates, amassing a fortune which was valued at £1.5 million on his death in 1830. Himself a Tory MP, this Sir Robert Peel initiated some early factory legislation.

His son Robert, who inherited the family baronetcy, was educated at Harrow and then at Oxford, becoming an MP at just twenty-one. His obvious talents led to his appointment as Home Secretary in 1821 aged thirty-three. A formidably hard worker, Peel was responsible for the abolition of the death penalty for over a hundred offences, for prison reform and also for the creation of the Metropolitan Police Force.

Peel's first clash with his own Party came when he changed his mind on the issue of Catholic Emancipation and argued that Catholics should have the vote. This volte-face angered die-hard sections of his Party and relations with his own father were strained. It was not so much that Peel was considered wrong to change his opinions, or that he was wrong to do so on this issue. What galled many colleagues was the sanctimoniousness which accompanied this reversal – an attitude which was later to be exemplified by Peel's follower William Gladstone.

Peel was the natural leader of the Conservatives in the 1830s and it was his so-called Tamworth Manifesto of 1834, addressed to his constituents, which heralded the emergence of the Party into the modern world. Briefly Prime Minister in 1834–5 at the head of a minority government, Peel was returned to power with a substantial majority after the general election of 1841.

The government led by Peel between 1841 and 1846 – 'the ministry of all the talents' – is regarded as one of the finest of the nineteenth century. Spurred on by the formidable administrative and financial talents of Peel himself, it laid the foundations of the Victorian free trade system which brought unparalleled prosperity to Britain. In order to reduce import duties Peel reintroduced income tax in 1842. This method of taxation had first been levied by Pitt the younger during the Napoleonic Wars but had then been abolished in 1815. Imposed at a rate of seven pence in the pound on all incomes of over £150 a year, its implementation shifted the burden from the trader to the ordinary citizen and helped stimulate economic growth.

But for all his intelligence, Peel either did not see or was indifferent to the rise of modern political parties and the delicate relationships between leader and led. He was a poor manager of people who had spent much of his political career in office, rarely bothering to disguise his contempt for his own backbenchers. Like

Edward Heath, his sense of integrity led him to scorn the use of the honours system in order to buy loyalty.

None of this would have mattered so much except that Peel had pledged to retain the Corn Laws which artificially maintained the price of corn, protecting the landed interest that formed the backbone of the old Tory Party. Having emerged from a commercial and industrial background himself, Peel felt no abiding loyalty to the landed aristocracy. The disastrous famine in Ireland in 1845 finally caused him to advocate an end to the Corn Laws.

His change of mind left him dangerously exposed and in 1846, after forcing through the repeal of the Corn Laws only with the help of Whig MPs, he was defeated on a motion which allowed an unholy alliance of anti-Peel Tories and Whigs to gang up against him. He left office, never to return. Peel's sense of relief was palpable: 'Thank God,' he wrote in a letter of August 1846, 'I am relieved for ever from the trammels of such a party!'

Peel's indifference to fellow human beings outside his own family indirectly caused his early death in 1850. His groom was so scared of his master that he did not dare tell Peel that the horse he was preparing to ride along Constitution Hill was a bad-tempered animal. Peel was thrown off and subsequently died of his injuries.

The departure of Peel and his followers left the Conservative Party bereft of talent. The only possible successor to Peel was the Earl of Derby, the representative of a staunchly Conservative family. In any case the dominance of the Whigs over the next thirty years meant that the Tories only formed governments when their opponents fell out amongst themselves; when the Whigs made it up, the Tories were rejected. It meant that Derby was twice Prime Minister – in 1852 and 1858 – but only briefly.

Derby's attitude to politics was one of noblesse oblige, a feeling that the well-born such as himself were under a duty to become involved in public affairs. In this he was very different from the man who succeeded him, Benjamin Disraeli.

Many non-Conservatives have a soft spot for Disraeli – Michael Foot even called his dog Dizzy. There is something enormously appealing about the outsider overcoming adversity, much of it of his own making, and becoming the leader of such an 'exclusive' body as the Conservative Party.

Disraeli's early career was full of failure and financial embarrassment and it took him five contests to get into Parliament. Once there, his maiden speech proved to be a disaster. He was relentlessly taunted by the sneer of 'Jew boy' from his own colleagues. An incompetent Chancellor of the Exchequer whose budgets were ridiculed by his opponent William Gladstone, Disraeli was hardly more successful as a party leader, losing six elections in all – a record which nowadays would lead to a swift poleaxing.

Yet today Disraeli is one of the most revered members of the Conservative pantheon. He was a typical Conservative in preferring flexibility to principle; once asked what electoral programme he was standing on, he replied simply 'on my head'. He was also careful to change his mind – as he did over such crucial issues as protection and parliamentary reform – in such a way that few held it against him. Disraeli's volte-faces took place behind a smokescreen of elegant but vacuous phrases.

Always there was his flamboyance and witticisms: 'When I want to read a novel, I write one', he declared. Likewise his remark on being ennobled and moving to the House of Lords: 'I am dead, dead but in the Elysian fields.' There was his tender relationship with his wife Mary Anne, the daffy but warm and generous woman who was never able to remember who came first, the Greeks or the Romans. And the sheer cheek which allowed him, after the crushing election defeat of 1880, to accept the huge advance of £10,000 in order to write a novel.

Disraeli was also a deeply manipulative politician; in his early career he deliberately cultivated an image of eccentricity in order to stand out from the crowd. His Tory democrat credentials hid his indifference to public opinion, particularly when it was unfavourable to himself. He took unconcealed pleasure in exercising patronage. When a senior ecclesiastical post fell vacant he remarked to his secretary: 'Another Deanery! The Lord of Hosts is with us!' Yet there was also, sometimes, a stand on an issue of principle, notably his support for the admission of Jews into Parliament despite the virulent hostility of elements within his Party.

One influential Conservative who opposed this measure and subsequently resigned from the Cabinet when Disraeli introduced the Second Reform Act was his successor as leader, Lord Salisbury. Photographs show Salisbury as the pillar of rectitude, looking down from his full height of six-foot-four and sporting a thick beard similar to those favoured by Karl Marx, William Morris and Old Testament prophets. Unlike most prophets, Salisbury had a sense of humour. He bought a paper-knife with which he prodded himself in order to keep awake during dull meetings.

A dry, gallows humour emerged when he was discussing the suitability of two candidates for the post of Home Secretary in 1877: 'I doubt his making a good Home Secretary. He is so amiable, he would hang nobody.' But of the rival for the post, 'He would make a very good Home Secretary: and would hang everybody.' Unlike Disraeli, Salisbury hated the sordid business of patronage: 'I believe they [bishops] die to spite me.'

Bullied at Eton 'from morning to night without ceasing', he avoided the main streets of London during the holidays in case he bumped into a schoolfellow – although it didn't stop him sending all his own sons to his place of torment. Salisbury was cut off by his father because of his choice of wife and had to earn his living as a journalist.

The death of his invalid older brother meant that he became Lord Salisbury and inherited Hatfield House whose extensive grounds he would negotiate on a tricycle with a servant perched precariously behind. He also built a scientific laboratory, using the nearby River Lea to provide energy for one of the country's first electric light systems.

After Disraeli's retirement in 1880 Salisbury initially shared the Party leadership with Northcote because of his place in the House of Lords, but force of character soon meant that he was recognised as the sole leader. At the same time as being Prime Minister he was also Foreign Secretary and presided over the expansion of the empire.

Never one for mincing his words, a 'salisbury' became a synonym for a political imprudence. He once wrote, 'My epitaph must be: "Died of writing inane answers to empty-headed Conservative associations."' Salisbury's realism doubtless contributed to his knowledge of the whereabouts of the political jugular. He easily saw off challengers, routing Lord Randolph Churchill when the latter launched a campaign for power in the 1880s.

Although Salisbury's tenets can be summed up as 'I am against' and his whole instinct seems to have been to conserve the status quo, he was enough of a realist not to oppose all change. As one newspaper noted on his resignation from office in 1902: 'What closes today with Lord Salisbury's departure is a whole historic era. It is ironic that what he hands on is a democratized, imperialized, colonialized and vulgarized England – everything that is antithetic to the Toryism, the aristocratic tradition and the High Church that he stood for.'

Salisbury was succeeded by his nephew Arthur Balfour, whose nonchalant and casual approach reflected his indecisive nature. As a young man Balfour was one of the leading lights in the circle known as the 'Souls', which preferred intellectual debate to the more vigorous pursuits of the Prince of Wales' Marlborough House set. His first book was called *In Defence of Philosophic Doubt* (1879), not on the face of it a title one would expect from a Conservative, and his derisive early nicknames drew attention to his effeminate streak: 'Prince Charming', 'Miss Balfour' and 'Pretty Fanny'.

As Secretary of State for Ireland in the 1880s, he achieved notoriety when the forcible suppression of a riot and the subsequent death of two rioters earned him the title 'Bloody Balfour'. His domestic reputation was boosted when he pushed through the Education Act of 1902 which reorganised the system of secondary education, but his habitual boredom with the world around him became more pronounced and he proved no match for the vigour of the Liberal government powered by Asquith, Lloyd George and Churchill. Balfour himself once claimed that he was 'utterly unsuited to the kind of work [politics] into which I have been dragged . . .' and he gets excited writing to his mistress Lady Elcho only when describing a game of golf.

Internal party friction was too acrimonious and unsettling for Balfour – his manoeuvres prompted one observer to liken him to 'an eel in a bucket of soft soap' – and he stepped down in 1911 to be replaced by Andrew Bonar Law, the unknown Prime

Minister. Canadian-born but raised in Scotland, Bonar Law was dour, shrewd, teetotal, a chainsmoker and an excellent chess player with a phenomenal memory.

His life was full of personal tragedy – the early death of his wife and the loss of two sons in the First World War – and he seems to have expected little. Lloyd George once asked Bonar Law what he enjoyed most in life: music, pictures, women, theatre, politics? 'After a pause he gave me a sweet sad smile and said "I rather like a game of bridge."'

No one ever impugned Bonar Law's integrity. In 1916 he actually turned down the chance of being Prime Minister because he thought Lloyd George was better suited to the job. He had a wry sense of realities. Once when dining in splendour at a time of industrial unrest his twittering hostess asked what on earth the strikers wanted. Bonar Law looked around at the opulent surroundings and murmured, 'Perhaps they want just a little of this.'

It is difficult to know what emotions Bonar Law hid behind his austere manner. His colleague Austen Chamberlain claims that Law once said to members of the press: 'You make a great mistake about me. You think I am a modest man with no ambition. I am really very ambitious.' But whether he was or not, ill-health meant that Bonar Law was only briefly Prime Minister in 1922–3 after the resignation of Lloyd George, He was forced to resign after only 209 days because of the cancer that eventually killed him. His main achievement as party leader was to keep the Conservative Party together during testing circumstances which included fierce internal rows over free trade and the First World War.

For much of his early political career Stanley Baldwin languished on the backbenches but after a spell as Bonar Law's private secretary, he became an unexpected and undistinguished Chancellor of the Exchequer. Despite these reversals he rose swiftly to the leadership in 1923, a contradiction typical of one of the most enigmatic of all modern politicians.

Like Harold Macmillan after him, Baldwin cultivated an air of serenity and calm but in fact he used to panic before major speeches just as Macmillan was sick before his. Again like Macmillan, he appreciated the power of image, in his case as Farmer Stan who was everyone's friend and announced, 'I want to be a healer.' 'I am not a clever man', he said, and posed as an amateur in a world of wily opportunists even though his speeches and broadcasts were a model of professionalism.

'The main ambition of my life is to prevent the class war becoming a reality', Baldwin declared, and he succeeded: on the Continent the class war led to revolution, coups and riots. In Britain, apart from the General Strike of May 1926 which was adeptly handled by Baldwin, the labour movement was peacefully integrated into the body politic.

He also handled the abdication with skill, introduced the India reforms which initiated decolonialisation and ensured that the challenge of the press barons Lords Rothermere and Beaverbrook's New Empire Party was still-born. Unlike several other party leaders, Baldwin always made sure he kept in touch with backbench opinion.

Long summer holidays and a short working week also seemed to be a vital part of Baldwin's recipe for success; his colleague J.C.C. Davidson used to turn down Saturday speaking engagements for the Prime Minister: '. . . very much doubts whether Mr Baldwin will be able to attend, more especially as he likes to keep his week-ends free as far as possible, for purposes of rest'.

Baldwin happily displayed a sense of generosity towards political friends and opponents alike. He always maintained that one of the least enjoyable duties of a Conservative leader was to have to listen to lectures on the laziness of the working class from men whose idea of a hard day's work was to spend an hour blowing greenfly off their roses with the smoke of a cigar.

And yet talking of the Clydeside Labour MPs who represented a militant brand of socialism, Baldwin remarked that 'They are wrong-headed but not black-hearted.' His successor, Neville Chamberlain, was notable for his disdain for political opponents, treating them – as Stanley Baldwin once pointed out to him – 'like dirt'. The unabashed Chamberlain went on to remark, 'The fact is that intellectually, with a few exceptions, they *are* dirt.'

Chamberlain embodied one of the least attractive strands within modern Conservatism. He was a punctilious pedant who excelled at handling the minutiae of administration but was devoid of any spark or flair or sense that administration is but the means to a greater end. Lloyd George called him 'a man of rigid competency' and went on to write that 'Such men have their uses in conventional times or in conventional positions, and are indispensable for filling subordinate posts at all times. But they are lost in an emergency or in creative tasks at any times.'

His father was the very formidable Joseph Chamberlain who had transformed Birmingham and then helped split the Liberal Party over the question of Home Rule for Ireland. Joe's intended political heir was his eldest son Austen, Neville's half-brother, but he lacked the metal to take him to the very top. As Churchill once observed, Austen 'always played the game and always lost it'.

Neville was a stronger personality, hardened perhaps by business failure in the Bahamas when a young man. He rose quickly through a relatively talentless Conservative Party, driven on by the same fierce ambition which had possessed his father. For instance, when the Conservative Research Department was set up in 1930, its initial task was to provide ideas for the Party at large. Chamberlain made sure he retained control of what became, in the 1930s, almost a private fiefdom.

His career as Prime Minister was dogged by problems of foreign policy, about which he was ignorant: his notorious dismissal of Czechoslovakia as a faraway country about which we know little was in reality a judgement on himself. As a fanatical anti-communist in the 1930s, his methods of news management relied on alternately browbeating and sucking up to proprietors and editors. Chamberlain was also prepared, like his father, to use dirty tricks against opponents; his underling and devoted supporter Sir Joseph Ball bugged the phones and blackened the reputations of the opponents of appeasement.

No one doubted Chamberlain's energy as he tried to negotiate with Hitler; one historian has pointed out that 'He virtually invented shuttle diplomacy.' His horror of war sprang from personal sorrow: the only book which he ever published was a tribute to his cousin Norman who was killed in the First World War.

Perhaps the key to Neville Chamberlain's character, as it had been to his father Joseph's, was identified by his colleague Leo Amery:

'[Neville] knew his own mind and saw to it that he had his own way. An autocrat with all the courage of his convictions right or wrong.' Often these convictions proved to be wrong; the twin albatrosses of appeasement and 1930s unemployment hung around the Tory neck for decades to come.

Churchill was inevitably an uneasy Conservative because he was always an uneasy Party man. Originally a Conservative, then a Liberal, then an Independent, then a Constitutionalist and finally a Conservative again, he had given many hostages to fortune. In October 1903 for instance, he candidly declared, 'I hate the Tory Party, their men, their words and their methods.' In his biography of Lord Randolph he noted how unpopular his father had been with the hierarchies of both parties. No doubt his animus towards party politics was aggravated by his own poor record as a candidate at general and by-elections before the 1930s.

In Churchill's one and only novel *Savrola*, published in 1900, the hero defiantly declares that 'I will never resign my independence . . . if they are not pleased, they can find someone else to discharge their public business.' Perhaps in keeping with this attitude, Churchill increasingly saw himself as above party politics – the Conservative Party manifesto in 1945 was simply called *Mr Churchill's Declaration of Policy to the Electors*. After 1945 his interest in domestic policy was minimal and instead he concentrated on his literary output and on foreign affairs, as well as discoursing generally; Harold Macmillan once said that meetings with Churchill were like continually having tea with Dr Johnson.

What never dimmed was Churchill's hankering for power; despite old age and chronic ill-health at the close of his career he only resigned after repeated postponements. Nor did he ever lose the endearing personal touches which make him so intensely human.

Whatever else may be said of Joseph Stalin, he was a shrewd judge of character. During the course of the Second World War when he frequently met Churchill and Eden, Stalin habitually ignored Eden as if he simply wasn't there. He had soon realised that film-star looks and early promotion – Eden had been Foreign Secretary at the age of thirty-eight – were no guarantee of political weight.

It is difficult not to see Eden's life in psychological terms. He had to cope with a domineering and difficult father, an adoring mother, a wife who ran off with another man and the towering figure of Churchill who kept him hanging on as his heir-apparent. Surely all this helps explain his petulance and vanity.

Eden's understanding of and interest in domestic policy was patchy, but his record when it came to foreign affairs is not much better. His preoccupation with the so-called special relationship with America and his failure to see that Britain could no longer stand alone meant that he was always hostile towards the European Community.

Eden also blundered into the Suez crisis where, typically, he got the worst of both worlds: sending in the troops but then pulling them out halfway through the military expedition. A run on the pound dealt the final blow to his short-lived premiership. Eden's duplicity over the extent of Anglo-French collusion with the Israelis was maintained by the highly selective memoirs he published in retirement.

Ironically the man who opposed the Suez venture, R.A. Butler, lost out to the man who was – at first – belligerently behind it, Harold Macmillan. This quickfooted knack of triumphing over adversity was typical of Macmillan and makes estimation of him so difficult. It is still not easy to know whether there was more or less to him than met the eye; was he really 'Supermac' or simply, as the younger Tory MPs preferred, the 'Old Poser'?

Two main influences shaped him as both man and politician. First there was his wife Dorothy's long-standing relationship with fellow Tory MP Bob Boothby, a liaison which caused Macmillan much anguish and led him to immerse himself in politics. It also strengthened his character, as though he now had something to prove to himself. Twice he did down the happily married and less ambitious Rab Butler.

Secondly, as the MP for the terribly deprived constituency of Stockton-on-Tees, Macmillan never forgot the searing effects of mass unemployment in the 1930s, and in fact he nearly joined the Labour Party. According to Clement Attlee: 'If it hadn't been for the war Macmillan would have joined the Labour Party. Approaches and talks were going on . . . I approved. If that had happened d'ye know the state of play? Macmillan would have been Labour's Prime Minister – and not me.'

Macmillan clawed his way to the top of the greasy pole after the Second World War, claiming much credit as Minister of Housing for the number of houses built, and surviving the Suez crisis when he was notoriously 'first in, first out' in his attitude towards military intervention. He seems to have manipulated the crisis, giving bogus figures about the effect of the run on the pound which further weakened Eden's grip on the Cabinet. Three years older than Eden, Macmillan had almost certainly assumed that the leadership would never be his, but when the opportunity presented itself he grasped it ruthlessly.

Once in office, Macmillan set out to master the new medium of television as well as shrewdly cultivate an image of imperturbability: a notice pinned on the door of the Cabinet Room claimed that 'Quiet, calm deliberation disentangles every knot.' In reality, however, this shy individual found public occasions a terrible strain on the nerves. As Prime Minister, he obsessively totted up in his diaries the size of his government's majorities after important divisions in the House of Commons.

This fundamental lack of confidence spawned a ruthlessness which he hid behind a mask of typically English understatement; a junior minister was dispatched from office with economy: 'I am appointing my Ministers. We cannot all play. I must ask you to go and sit in the pavilion.'

Macmillan's horror at memories of the 1930s ensured that for him economic growth, full employment and rising levels of consumer spending were paramount. By the end of the 1950s most British people were indeed enjoying unparalleled prosperity. Ironically, from today's perspective it seems that these growing living standards were not entirely a good thing.

Was this hire-purchase, premium-bond society created at the expense of investment and long-term economic growth? Was Macmillan in fact the unwitting architect of post-war British economic decline? Did he perhaps realise this when, although not himself an enthusiast for Europe, he vigorously pushed forward a British application to join the Common Market in 1963. It was vetoed by de Gaulle.

Even though colleagues such as Dr Charles Hill were adamant that Macmillan dominated his Cabinet 'by sheer superiority of mind and of judgement', he was damaged by the Profumo scandal and by a growing sense of personal failure. In 1963, Macmillan resigned on medical advice.

Today memories of his administrations are mixed; for Enoch Powell, 'Macmillan was such a double-crosser that when he hadn't got anyone to double-cross he would double-cross himself to keep in practice.' Others look back on his period in office as a halcyon time: there was virtually full employment, modest but sustained economic growth, low inflation and a stable and tranquil society.

The subsequent leadership contest produced a most unlikely leader of a political party for the 1960s: Lord Home. Like R.A. Butler, Home had been a minor architect of appeasement in the 1930s but in his case memories were short and his vehemently anti-communist stance had assuaged the doubters. He might almost be called the reluctant Prime Minister. During the leadership shenanigans in 1963 he remarked to journalist James Margach, 'Even if they can't agree on Rab or Quintin there must be somebody else. But please, please not me!'

Despite his personal integrity and honesty, Home was no match for the ebullient Labour leader Harold Wilson, then brimming with enthusiasm for the 'white heat of technological revolution'. Wilson was able to characterise his opponent as a gentleman amateur more at home on the grouse moors, out of step with the modern world, and Home obligingly seemed to confirm this when he remarked that he used matchsticks to help him with his mathematical calculations. Macmillan later came to believe that Butler would, after all, have been a better choice as leader than Home.

Edward Heath succeeded Home in July 1965, the carpenter's son who by sheer will-power and determination had forced his way to Oxford and then up through the Conservative Party. His attention to detail and long working hours, uncluttered by wife and family, suited his administrative talents. Some observers have argued that Heath would have made a better civil servant than politician. Other than his devotion to the European ideal, it has never been clear what vision or programme drives him on.

As Chief Whip, he held the Party together after the Suez debacle and was rewarded with a series of posts including the supervision of Britain's failed application to the Common Market in 1963. Two years later he defeated Reginald Maudling in the Conservative Party's first public leadership contest.

Although presented as the Tory Harold Wilson, Heath's humourless and pedestrian style contrasted poorly with that of the energetic Labour Prime Minister, even though doggedness eventually prevailed at the 1970 election. But despite its detailed plans drawn up when in Opposition, the Heath government was soon bogged down in an industrial and economic quagmire largely of its own making, although aggravated by the unexpected oil crisis in 1973–4.

Like Peel, Heath was not prepared to use patronage to smooth his path and he completely lacked Macmillan's ability to transform U-turns and defeats into victories. His presidential style could not conceal the fact that the Government, buffeted by a series of miners' strikes, was not in control. The decision to hold an early general election in February 1974 backfired and it was Wilson's Labour government which returned to office.

A further election loss in October 1974 and Heath's unconcealed contempt for most of his colleagues – one supporter pithily observed that Heath finds 'the small change of social life difficult' and another remarked on his tendency to talk at rather than to people – led to a challenge and his subsequent defeat by Mrs Thatcher in 1975. It was particularly galling that as a solitary bachelor not noted for his tactful handling of women he should eventually have been defeated by one. His graceless behaviour towards his successor contrasted all too sadly with that of his predecessor as leader, Sir Alec Douglas-Home, who was content to serve with dignity under Heath.

It is still difficult to believe that it was the British Conservative Party which first elected a woman as its leader. The male chauvinist remarks of some Conservative contemporaries – Enoch Powell's scorn for 'that dreadful voice, and those frightful hats' is typical – confirm that Mrs Thatcher had much to put up with from those she was expected to lead. Forever an outsider, she could never be fully absorbed into the masculine club-like ethos of the Party.

This sense of alienation fuelled her determination to ignore the old Tory Party grandees whom she blamed in part for the post-war decline of Britain. As a result, her hardest fights throughout her fifteen years as leader were with members of her own Party rather than with the Opposition. She is reported to have declared that 'There is no consensus. I call them [Conservative opponents] quislings and traitors.' No doubt this sense of being permanently on guard was reinforced by the murders of her colleagues Airey Neave and Ian Gow and her own near-death in the Brighton bombing in October 1984.

Mrs Thatcher made much of her background as a grocer's daughter in Grantham and she seems to have been convinced that she expressed the gut feelings of an important stratum within the Party on whom the Conservatives relied for votes but otherwise ignored. Her populist instincts were to the fore in her fierce attacks both on the Soviet Union and on over-mighty 'trade union barons'. Unlike any previous Conservative leader she was also prepared to dabble with the 'race card'; during a television interview in October 1977 she had referred to the fears of some Britons that they were in danger of being 'swamped' by immigrants.

Her views matched those of significant sections of the public – views also represented by Rupert Murdoch's *Sun* newspaper and by the emblematic 'Essex man'. But it was typical of her professionalism that her targets were not chosen at random. For instance, the seemingly off-the-cuff remark remark about swamping was uttered only after extensive private polling by the Party had shown that a strong anti-immigration stance might well prove to be an electoral bonus.

Mrs Thatcher could not accept the way in which the traditional establishment seemed happy to collude in the orderly and civilised management of British decline. She rejected the preoccupation of post-war Labour and Conservative governments with full employment and government intervention. Instead she explicity endorsed the potency of market forces, based on a simple view of capitalism as extending choice and prosperity whilst at the same time generating a trickle down of wealth from the haves to the have-nots.

Tory grandees such as James Prior complacently thought that this reversal of the One Nation tradition could not possibly be serious or sustained. They should have been warned by the bluntness of the sentiments which she expressed in February 1979 before she even reached Downing Street: 'I'm not a consensus politician or a pragmatic politician. I'm a conviction politician.'

She was immeasurably helped by the poor quality of the Opposition throughout much of the 1980s. In defiance of public opinion the Labour Party lurched to the Left and duly split. Those who departed, such as David Owen and Shirley Williams, formed the new Social Democratic Party which significantly divided the anti-Tory vote during much of the decade.

Other convenient Thatcher bogeymen were General Galtieri of Argentina, Ken Livingstone of the Greater London Council, the Militant leaders of Liverpool and Arthur Scargill of the National Union of Mineworkers. Mrs Thatcher's contempt for her opponents, summed up by her description of the striking miners as 'the enemy within', was reminiscent of abrasive Neville Chamberlain rather than emollient Stanley Baldwin.

In many ways the hostility and anger which Mrs Thatcher aroused in so many on the Left seems to have enfeebled their brains. Usually sane commentators like Eric Hobsbawm likened Britain in the 1980s to the state of bombed Germany in 1945, whilst Mary Warnock and others sneered at Mrs Thatcher's clothes and style.

The drawback to Mrs Thatcher's messianic stance was that the only disciples prepared to go to the end of the road with her proved to be 'non-politicians' such as Woodrow Wyatt and Paul Johnson. Conservative MPs and ministers invariably had one eye on their future political prospects. She demanded just six good men and true and claims that she never got them. Even believers like Sir Geoffrey Howe and Nigel Lawson eventually fell by the wayside, partly because her treatment of Howe in particular was thoroughly demeaning. This worm finally turned with devastating effect when his resignation speech in the House of Commons set off the leadership contest which was to topple her from office.

Increasingly Mrs Thatcher had leant heavily on her unelected but carefully selected entourage which included press secretary Bernard Ingham, Charles Powell in foreign affairs, Alan Walters an economics specialist, and her media advisers Sir Gordon Reece and Tim Bell. This coterie reinforced Mrs Thatcher's isolation from her Cabinet colleagues and the rest of the parliamentary party on whom her continued position ultimately depended, particularly after the resignation through ill-health of Willie Whitelaw, one of the Party's shrewdest 'fixers'.

A glance at the fate of her predecessors Sir Robert Peel and Edward Heath should have warned her that a semi-presidential style will always, in time, lead to defeat because over a prolonged period the enemies simply mount up. This was doubly certain in Mrs Thatcher's case because she systematically challenged so many British institutions from the Church of England, the Civil Service and the brewers to the health service, education and the commercial television companies.

Mrs Thatcher's 'poor but honest' background was something she was not above exploiting. In fact, however, this grounding must have been drastically modified by her privileged experience of education at Oxford, a professional life as a barrister and marriage to a wealthy businessman. Her successor John Major had more exposure to the less exalted aspects of British life with his patchy education, parents' financial problems, election as a Brixton councillor and a spell on the dole. However, he made less fuss about it.

Major has always been ambitious as a politician. One biography reports that as early as 1986 Major told a political colleague that he was determined to remain unidentified with any particular faction within the Party. This paid off in November 1990 when he was elected leader, but the drawbacks of this approach are now clear. Major was chosen for negative reasons – he was not Mrs Thatcher, nor was he Michael Heseltine, both of whom had vociferous pro- and anti-factions within the parliamentary party. He seemed to be all things to most Conservative MPs.

His election allowed the Conservative Party to avoid the threatening prospect of disunity after Mrs Thatcher's deposition. It is clear that John Major, whose unique selling point seems to be his apparent ordinariness, lacks a clear vision, well-meaning as his talk of the classless society and Back to Basics appears to be. He seems unable to offer any real solution as the foundations of the Conservative Party begin to crumble.

Growing fears that under his leadership the next general election will be lost – and the results at local, European and by-elections could hardly be worse – have provoked strong and continuing calls that he should be replaced. As Mrs Thatcher found out, a Tory leader is only as good as the result of the forthcoming election. The difficulty with ousting John Major is that he shows no signs whatsoever of going without a fight. Furthermore, internal dissension over the European issue means that no alternative candidate will be able to satisfy every faction within the Party.

Clearly the problems facing the Party go much deeper than the question of the leadership alone but, as always within the Conservative Party, it is the leader who acts as the lightning conductor for change and discontent. Tory leaders have in theory, and partly in practice, unfettered powers – unlike their Labour counterpart. The penalty for this power is that the electoral buck stops with them.

'The two most fascinating things in life are love and power. Love can endure: power cannot.' This is how the former Conservative Cabinet minister Reginald Bevins began his autobiography *The Greasy Pole*, published in 1965.

In other words, the politician's career is inevitably one of final disappointment and frustration. Many enter the political race, few actually make it into Parliament, fewer still into the Cabinet and only a handful can become leader of the Party and Prime Minister.

Worse still are the demands and requirements seemingly inseparable from a political life – 'There is no friendship at the top', as Lloyd George is supposed to have remarked – and the severe toll it can exact of an MP's family. One needs only to look at the difficult private lives of the children of both Winston Churchill and Harold Macmillan to see that the pressures of political life go far beyond the politician himself.

Austen Chamberlain once wrote in a letter to his step-mother: 'What are politics to a man who is happily, most happily married and has two delightful children and a very united, very loveable family circle?' But it was precisely this level-headedness and ordinary human qualities which explain in large part why Austen Chamberlain was one of 'the nearly men' of modern Conservative politics, unable to thrust himself forward when the chance came.

Exactly the same can be said of R.A. Butler, who could not stand up to Harold Macmillan. Butler's father, a distinguished civil servant, quickly seems to have made his assessment of his son's character: 'He thought that it was not in my line to take strong personal executive decisions. My forte was to be friends with all, impartial and diplomatic.' Rab called these views 'very strange', but, as is often the case, it was the parent who had the shrewder judgement.

Nevertheless all politicians possess, to a greater or lesser degree, the desire for power, Conservative leaders in particular. Stanley Baldwin sacrificed his chairman of the Party, J.C.C. Davidson, in 1930 when his own position was under threat, even though Baldwin was perhaps the best friend of Davidson and his wife Joan. Generally the more ruthless Baldwins and Macmillans win out over the more 'ordinary' Austen Chamberlains and Rab Butlers. Once power has been achieved, there is often, unsurprisingly, a reluctance to let it go; not just because of the trappings of office but because it has become accepted as normal.

Perhaps the most notorious example of a man clinging on doggedly is Winston Churchill. Many colleagues thought he would retire from leadership of the Conservative Party after the general election defeat of 1945. Indeed, the heir apparent, Sir Anthony Eden, was poised to take over. But no, Churchill made it clear that he intended to carry on. In 1947 some of his colleagues deputed the Chief Whip, James Stuart, to suggest he might care to set a date for his retirement. Churchill would have none of it, angrily thumping his stick on the floor.

After 1951 Churchill was again Prime Minister and once more hinting to Eden that his retirement was at hand, but somehow he never got round to specifying a date. As Churchill's eightieth birthday loomed, it was hardly surprising that his health began to deteriorate and his powers of concentration were limited. Meetings of the Cabinet were dominated by Churchill's reminiscences and often never got past the first item on the agenda. The Executive of the 1922 Committee once went to see him about the question of members' pay: 'After very few minutes had elapsed the Executive was regaled instead with a graphic account of the Battle of Omdurman! The Fuzzy-Wuzzies were soon whirling in our imaginations. Lances and swords were being discarded in favour of the pistol; dust was everywhere; the din was appalling; but – almost as though by the exertions of our raconteur alone – the Battle was won.'

The Executive departed; the issue of MPs' salaries had to wait for another day.

Churchill's health continued to decline and in 1952 he collapsed at a dinner. His doctor Lord Moran and his closest colleagues kept the severity of his illness hidden from the public until he had recovered; in fact Lord Moran's account of Churchill is one of almost continual ill-health. But still Churchill managed to return to Downing Street and held on for three more years, much to the exasperation of his Cabinet colleagues. Eventually he stepped down, unwillingly, in April 1955, aged eighty.

Inevitably the question of power is bound up with the issue of vanity. There is a thesis waiting to be written on how some British Prime Ministers (and the present Queen) have tried not to wear glasses in public in case it suggests human frailty and weakness: Eden, Macmillan and Thatcher. Eden was inordinately proud of his film-star good looks, whilst Mrs Thatcher almost remodelled herself during the 1980s as is clear if one compares photographs of her in 1979 when she took office and in 1990 when she left.

Any review of the career of Tory Party leaders suggests that prospective candidates must be very ambitious, willing to make huge sacrifices on behalf of both themselves and their families, keen to spend inordinately long hours wading through a mountain of paperwork, and impervious to the envy and criticisms of rivals and opponents. Not a very attractive prospect, but there is never any shortage of applicants. The moral seems to be that the desire for power can in itself be an immensely powerful force – without it, no one can climb far up the greasy pole.

Perhaps the second moral to be drawn is that, having reached the top, it is important for the leader to stay in touch with his or her colleagues, particularly today when there is the possibility of an annual challenge to the leadership. Arguably, Stanley Baldwin excelled at this art of personal communication but Sir Robert Peel and Edward Heath did not and, after ten years in office, Mrs Thatcher was surrounded by a Praetorian Guard who restricted access to her. A fervent Thatcherite MP, Theresa Gorman, commented that Mrs Thatcher would not have known her from the tea-lady. Power may or may not corrupt but it certainly isolates.

The third moral suggests that the leader's longevity depends on how much power he or she can actually provide for the Party. In order to maintain or extend its power, the Conservative Party will even set aside its supposed tribal loyalties and welcome back straying sheep into the fold. Winston Churchill, for instance, was a notorious party-hopper, Sir Anthony Eden resigned office and, according to one biographer, actually contemplated setting up a new party, whilst Harold Macmillan resigned the Party whip in June 1936.

No matter: all three men won general elections, and for that virtue much could be forgiven them. On the other hand, Edward Heath never strayed from the mainstream of the Party but his loyal orthodoxy proved no defence against electoral failure.

Perhaps the final ingredient is the one which makes politics so unpredictable, namely the role played by luck and chance. Napoleon famously asked of his generals only whether they were lucky and the history of the Conservative Party, like that of any organisation, is littered with might have beens.

Of course, bad luck is always someone else's good luck: Bonar Law's swift demise due to cancer meant that Stanley Baldwin unexpectedly became Prime Minister. Oliver Stanley died comparatively young, aged fifty-one, in 1950. If he had lived, he rather than Macmillan would probably have succeeded Eden. Similarly, Eden's botched bile duct operation provided a chance for Macmillan whilst the medical advice that Macmillan himself should retire in 1963, which he prematurely took and regretted for the rest of his life, opened the way for Sir Alec Douglas-Home.

Perhaps the saddest question is: what do former leaders and former premiers do when they no longer occupy high office? In only three cases has the departed Tory leader swallowed his pride and been prepared to accept a lesser office under his successors – but then politics never was the be-all and end-all for Arthur Balfour, Austen Chamberlain and Alec Douglas-Home.

In some cases the former leader seems to have dreams of being triumphantly recalled by a grateful nation: just as General de Gaulle retired to Colombey-les-Deux-Eglises and emerged as the country's saviour. Eden always hoped to return and, more than twenty years after his retirement, Harold Macmillan still harboured hopes of another innings. At one point Eden (by then Lord Avon) and Macmillan even mooted plans of setting up a national government: old men's talk.

Some play the elder statesman, cutting a dignified figure on state occasions and devoting themselves to their memoirs, as did Churchill, or to novel-writing, as did Disraeli. Others, however, refuse to retire gracefully or, indeed, at all. Edward Heath was only fifty-eight when he lost the party leadership in February 1975. There is still disagreement today as to whether Mrs Thatcher offered him any kind of job, but whether she did or not Heath chose to retire to the backbenches from where he waged unremitting war on the Thatcher regime.

Gratifyingly for Heath, he lived to see its downfall and has now, as his biographer John Campbell points out, emerged as a Major loyalist. This position happily allows him to denigrate Lady Thatcher, her supporters and all Euro-sceptics for being rebels and malcontents.

Nor has Lady Thatcher retired from the fray; she continues to make her opinions over the European issue very clear. Unlike Heath, however, she was prepared to depart from the House of Commons and set up the Thatcher Foundation. Modelled on the lines of the organisations established by former presidents of America, the Foundation exists to propagate her ideas and currently has offices in London and three other cities overseas. She has also devoted much effort to her memoirs, which have paid off a few old scores.

Somehow, however, one feels that Enoch Powell is right: 'All political lives, unless they are cut off in midstream at a happy juncture, end in failure, because that is the nature of politics and of human affairs.'

5

The Led

Conservative MPs, Cabinet ministers and peers

'I returned to the House of Commons in a gay and happy mood, almost enchanted to get back to this club which I adore, this smelly, tawny, male paradise.'

Chips Channon's *Diaries*, 24 May 1937

'We do not wish to interview any Jews, Catholics or those dreadful pansy creatures.'

Chairman of a Conservative selection committee in the late 1940s

'Young man, it does not do to appear clever: advancement in this man's party is due entirely to alcoholic stupidity.'

The advice of Dr Charles Hill, one of the Party's elders, to Conservative MP Julian Critchley when he found him reading a book in the Smoking Room of the House of Commons

Opponents of the Conservative Party have always delighted in making uncomplimentary remarks about its supporters in Parliament. Early this century, David Lloyd George lambasted Conservative peers for being aristocratic wastrels, taunting these 'five hundred men, chosen at random from among the ranks of the unemployed'.

Between the wars, Communist MP Willie Gallacher thought that Tory MPs exemplified the 'real hard-faced type of big business man, drawing tribute from all parts of the globe'. In the 1980s it was writer John Mortimer's turn to describe the new breed of Conservative MPs under Mrs Thatcher as 'upstarts, vulgar cads, besotted with materialism'.

The abuse has sometimes come from Conservatives themselves. Harold Macmillan complained that too many of his parliamentary colleagues in the 1930s were 'second-class brewers and company promoters', whilst more recently Alan Clark observed that his fellow Tory MPs were 'just into tax avoidance and gossip columns'.

Clearly, Conservative MPs and peers never are what they were, but have they changed over the years? Are the stereotypes of the landed buffoon, the hard-faced businessman and the estate agent-cum-accountant still accurate today?

Before 1858 property qualifications ensured that only the wealthy could stand for Parliament; indeed, until 1911 MPs were unpaid. It was therefore inevitable that almost all aspiring politicians were men of substantial independent means. Not only did they have to finance themselves as MPs but they also bore the cost of actually fighting the elections by which they gained their seat in the first place.

So expensive were these contests that in the 1860s more than three hundred seats were simply not fought at general elections. Outgoings could be enormous: for instance, many candidates had an arrangement with the local pub to pay for whatever drinks were served during the election campaign.

In 1864 *The Economist* magazine estimated that no more than five thousand individuals in Britain could possibly sustain the expense of a political career. It is therefore hardly surprising that both Conservative and Whigs MPs were drawn predominantly from the landed class – three-quarters of all MPs were patricians. Only they could afford to satisfy notions of public duty and noblesse oblige. Would-be Conservative candidates had to pass muster at the

Carlton Club which became, in the words of one contemporary, 'a sort of electoral labour exchange'.

It was the crippling cost of the 1880 election which finally prompted both political parties to support the introduction of legal restrictions on election spending. Few candidates could view with unconcern the expenditure of between £10,000 to £20,000 (in the region of half a million pounds at today's values) needed to fight some seats. The Corrupt and Illegal Practices Act of 1883 severely curtailed the sums of money which candidates could spend on their campaigns. To employ the services of professional workers became out of the question and instead political parties had to rely on unpaid volunteers. This was particularly the case in the urban constituencies which, with the extension of the franchise, were now vital to parties seeking power.

This widening of the social base of late Victorian political parties was compounded by the agricultural slump which damaged the landed interest and thus weakened the Tory heartlands. For some time, however, this made no appreciable difference to the composition of the parliamentary party. The landed classes continued to supply about 40 per cent of Conservative MPs between 1885 and 1905. There were two reasons for this: firstly, it always takes time for social changes to percolate through. Secondly, many constituency parties were clearly biased towards the well-connected and preferably titled candidate.

Just look at how one young man, later to be Earl Winterton, was chosen for the safe Conservative seat of Horsham and Worthing in 1904:

At the beginning of October 1904 I went up to Oxford to begin the third year of a University career which had brought me many friendships and much fun in the saddle, hunting in the winter with the Bicester, Heythrop and South Oxfordshire Hounds, and, in summer, playing polo in Port Meadow; unfortunately, my two years at the University had been barren of intellectual achievement of any value, for which the fault lay wholly with me. Early in October the Conservative Member for the Horsham Division, Mr Heywood Johnstone, died, and on Wednesday,

October 19th, I was proposed as Conservative candidate at the Selection Committee of the local Conservative Association. Thanks mainly to the support of Lord Leconsfield ... I was chosen, at the age of twenty-one and six months, to be the Conservative candidate in an important by-election.

Conservative Party managers and their Liberal opponents were fully aware of this constituency bias. Attempts were sometimes made to overcome it by bribing associations to put up working-class candidates, but to no avail. The enormous difficulties which faced less well-off Conservatives who might otherwise have stood for Parliament is summed up by the fate of J.H. Pettifer.

Pettifer was a popular figure within Conservative circles at the end of the nineteenth century who travelled around the country speaking at massively well-attended Party meetings. Yet there was never any prospect of a local Conservative association running Pettifer as a candidate because he could not afford to pay his election expenses, support himself as an MP or contribute to local funds. On the whole, Conservative Central Office discouraged working-class candidates from standing because they felt sure that many Tories would not vote for them.

Businessmen, on the other hand, were much more acceptable and it is estimated that ninety of them were Conservative MPs by 1906. One example of this type was Waldorf Astor, the fantastically wealthy entrepreneur and newspaper proprietor who was to be elected in 1910. Ironically this new breed had, in some ways, less knowledge of the common people than the old landed classes. There is a touching story that Astor refused to stand for Parliament until he felt that he had more experience of politics. Given his stately pile at Cliveden with its fifty gardeners and footmen with powdered hair, this cannot have been easy to achieve.

The Conservative MPs elected in 1918 on a coalition ticket were notorious as 'the hard-faced men who looked as if they had done well out of the war', a remark attributed variously to Churchill, Lloyd George and Baldwin. They embodied the continuing replacement of the landed classes by business and commercial interests, a process which was evident in the careers of the three leaders of the Conservative Party between the wars. Bonar Law had been an ironmaster from Glasgow, Baldwin an ironmaster from Worcestershire and Neville Chamberlain an industrialist from Birmingham.

The inter-war Conservative MPs have been criticised for their poor quality and many were indeed military men chosen more for their 'sound' character than for their political acumen. They did however include some formidable characters: there was Sir Frederick Banbury, most right-wing of the die-hard or reactionary faction who always attended the House dressed in a top hat and frock coat. Guy Gaunt was a former adventurer and explorer who became an admiral, whilst John Buchan was better known for his novels and historical biographies.

No more than fifty or sixty MPs entering Parliament in the 1920s and 1930s were what we would now call career politicians with their sights set on ministerial office and power. The majority were loyal amateurs 'on their way from the Brigade of Guards to the House of Lords'. Some were critical of their colleagues. Harold Macmillan, in particular, was scathing about the Conservative Party in general and his parliamentary counterparts in particular, arguing in June 1936 that the 'Casino Capitalism' of a Party dominated by money and the City was 'not likely to represent anybody but itself'. A familiar complaint!

Macmillan was married to Lady Dorothy, a daughter of the 9th Duke of Devonshire who had himself been a Tory MP and Cabinet minister like his father, the 8th Duke of Devonshire. Lady Dorothy's uncle had been a Conservative MP whilst her mother was the daughter of another Cabinet minister. And on it went.

A study of the Conservative Party, published in 1939, pointed up its hereditary bias: 145 of its MPs were linked together in a web of family relationships, comprising what was sometimes called the 'Cousinhood'.

Two charts contained in the book *Tory M.P.* show the political clout of two of the most influential Tory families, the Cavendishes and the Derbys, from the early nineteenth century up to the outbreak of the Second World War. These political family trees reveal the close and interlocking relationships which once sustained the governing circles within the Conservative Party: a network which was later to be dubbed the magic circle.

Candidates lacking these aristocratic connections had to have funds. MPs' salaries rose from £400 to £600 a year in 1937, but prospective Conservative candidates were still expected to pay their own election expenses and to contribute generously to association funds. The deputy chairman of the Party conceded in 1930 that the safest constituencies were effectively on sale to the highest bidder.

Biographies and memoirs confirm the importance of money. The Conservative grande dame Lady Astor complained that the first question associations generally asked of any aspiring candidate was: 'How much money have you got?' The young R.A. Butler, for example, was fortunate that his wife was a member of the wealthy Courtauld family who gave him an allowance of £5,000 a year and an election fund of £1,000 in order to help retain his Saffron Walden seat.

For those hopefuls who were neither well-connected nor well-off, the parliamentary path was hazardous. Quintin Hogg, the future Lord Hailsham, found it difficult to find a seat in the 1930s because constituencies expected candidates to disgorge at least £400 a year. Another ambitious young Tory, Ian Harvey, complained that candidates able to contribute just £100 a year or less to the local association's funds had virtually no chance of finding a seat. £200 was the minimum expected.

Sometimes the largesse could be provided in non-monetary form: Ronald Cartland, brother of romantic novelist Barbara Cartland whose novels had originally paid for his election expenses, was helped out by his supporter Lord Carlow who each year gave two tons of beef to Cartland's poorest constituents.

It is worth bearing in mind the size of the sums in question: the average wage in the 1930s was £2 a week or little more than £100 a year. In other words, Conservative hopefuls unable to donate up to twice the average annual income were not considered suitable as parliamentary candidates. Today, the average income is around £15,000 a year; double that figure was the amount which hopeful candidates were expected to lavish on their seats. The Conservative MP Duff Cooper wittily summed up: 'It as difficult for a poor man, if he be a Conservative, to get into the House of Commons as it is for a camel to get through the eye of a needle. This is not to say that it is impossible, any more than it is impossible, we hope, for a rich man to get into the Kingdom of Heaven, but in both cases entrance is attended with difficulty.'

Duff Cooper knew full well what he was talking about. After he had sensationally won a by-election in Westminster in March 1931, his association's finance committee met to discuss his expected level of contribution. The committee's resolution allowed no room for haggling: 'At the Committee request General Cooper undertook to see Mr Duff Cooper regarding a contribution to the funds of the Association. It was considered that £50 this year and £100 next year and annually thereafter would be reasonable.'

It should be stressed, however, that many affluent Tory MPs worked hard to retain their constituency's support; for instance, the socialite Chips Channon, despite a hectic social life, made sure he kept in touch with the constituents of his Southend seat – although he did not go so far as to live there.

The crushing election defeat in 1945 confirmed that much of the Conservative Party needed overhauling, not least its method of choosing candidates. At that year's conference a motion was discussed and remitted for further action which read: 'This meeting regards the almost complete lack of Wage-Earners and Trades Unionists in the ranks of Conservative Members of Parliament as detrimental to the future prospects of the Party.'

The chairman of the Party, Lord Woolton, was disturbed by the fossilisation of some associations: 'I noticed that the organization of the Party was weakest in those places where a wealthy candidate had made it unnecessary for the members to trouble to collect small subscriptions.'

A committee was appointed under the lawyer Sir David Maxwell-Fyfe which recommended that parliamentary candidates should be chosen on grounds of merit and suitability, not because of payment to local association funds. No candidate should subscribe more than £25 a year and no sitting MP more than £50, whilst the cost of fighting the election was to be borne solely by the association. The burden of organising and financing political activity was therefore thrust onto the constituencies themselves.

The choice of candidate remained solely in the hands of the local associations who fiercely resisted any outside interference from Central Office in London. This autonomy explains why the landed interest remained so powerful within the Conservative Party a hundred years after its economic dominance had been undermined – many constituences were delighted if their candidate had such a background, particularly if he also had local links.

Naturally Conservative associations strongly favoured married men with dutiful wives and a certain number of legitimate children. Until the 1940s, candidates had to state their religion on Central Office's forms. This meant that Jews and Roman Catholics, if not absolutely ruled out, faced an uphill struggle. Sexual unconventionality was an absolute bar, unless it could be kept hidden – homosexuality was of course illegal until 1967. Anyone found out could expect, in the title of the autobiography of one who was, Ian Harvey, 'to fall like Lucifer'.

A survey of Conservative MPs up to 1974, conducted by the eminent academic David Butler, found that overall there had been little change in their background since 1918: 'The absence of working-class representatives and dominance of the upper-middle-class in the senior Conservative ranks, both in parliament and in the constituencies, is nearly as marked today as it was in the late-1940s when the Maxwell-Fyfe proposals were introduced. Moreover, there have been few broad changes since the period after the First World War.'

In all the years since the Maxwell-Fyfe reforms, there had only been two working-class Tory MPs. One of them, the former electrician and member of the Electrical Trades Union, Ray Mawby, represented Totnes in Devon from 1955. His neighbouring Conservative MP for Torquay, Old Etonian Charles Williams, was unhappy: 'Devon and Cornwall should be the preserve of gentlemen, and trade unionists should not be selected'. Williams and others were perfectly happy for working-class supporters (and trade unionists) to vote Conservative and to supply many of the Party's volunteer workers, but MPs had to be 'gentlemen'.

The fact that J.H. Pettifer would still have had little chance of being adopted as a candidate in the late twentieth century suggests that social prejudice and not money was the real barrier. It is revealing to compare how some well-known Conservative figures were chosen as parliamentary candidates. Willie Whitelaw, with an impeccable Winchester, Cambridge and landowning background, was selected as candidate for Penrith in May 1954 after a friend had suggested he put his name forward: 'The Chairman, Colonel Fetherstonhaugh, later Sir Timothy Fetherstonhaugh, a determined figure and a powerful Chairman, had heard about me and decided that I was his man. He ensured that his selection committee shared his view.'

This demonstration of personal influence in a rural seat provides a graphic portrayal of the old Conservative Party at work. Everyone belonged to the same clubs, either the Carlton or Pratt's, and therefore knew about everyone else. The test was less competitive than an assessment of one's character and experience. Similarly, Jim Prior was driving a tractor when he was approached to stand as Tory candidate for Lowestoft by the local chairman who simply declared, 'You're a young man; you're just the type of person we want.'

It is illuminating to compare the experiences of Whitelaw and Prior with that of Norman Tebbit several years later at Epping in 1969. This was by no means a safe seat, yet more than 250 applicants put in for the nomination. Tebbit was finally chosen after a gruelling series of speeches, interviews and meetings. Wives were a part of the procedure too, though not, of course, in a speaking role: 'Margaret had been invited, perhaps required is the better word, to come with me although not to speak nor answer questions.'

There were a few minor changes in the composition of the parliamentary party after the Second World War: the 1945 election defeat precipitated a clear-out of many of the old ex-military stalwarts from the 1914–18 war but there were still strong cohorts of businessmen, lawyers and Old Etonians. Chief Whip James Stuart noted that many Conservative MPs were City stockbrokers in the mornings and MPs in the afternoons. It was noticeable that these businessmen MPs usually had a City rather than an industrial or manufacturing background.

The 1940s had also seen the squeezing out of the independents. Until 1948 twelve MPs, including A.P. Herbert, had represented University seats and were often genuine lone voices. But the Party machines, both Labour and Conservative, found such independence a dangerous irritant and the seats were abolished.

Sir Robert Rhodes James, a Clerk at the House of Commons and later himself a Conservative MP, has noted that in the 1950s there were still pronounced differences between Conservative and Labour MPs: 'When I first entered the House of Commons in 1955, politics was very much a heavy drinking profession, and it was a topic of dispute among us division clerks whether it was worse to take the Tories in the ten o'clock vote, reeking of port, brandy and cigars, or Labour, where the preference was for beer, whisky and cigarettes.' Rhodes James also claims that in the 1950s 'the worst thing you could say about a colleague was that he was "ambitious", ie. a cad, not to be trusted an inch'.

Since David Butler's survey, however, the 1980s have brought a few further modifications. The old social order, which centred on the top public schools and Oxbridge, is no longer quite so dominant. The 'knights of the Shires' and the Tory squirearchy have virtually disappeared and Old Etonians look set to join them – one of Mrs Thatcher's advisers has commented that she always felt 'there were too many Old Etonians around'. After the 1992 election only 60 per cent of Conservative MPs proved to have been educated at a public school, well down on the post-war average of 75 per cent.

Social observer Hugh Montgomery-Massingberd has bemoaned the fact that only a handful of Tory MPs are countrymen and not 'townees' and that the Conservative Party in the Thatcher era 'has become irredeemably middle-class'. More cutting was Harold Macmillan's snobbish observation about Mrs Thatcher's Conservatives that 'a great national party [has] become reduced to a suburban rump'.

Some of these shifts have indeed been due to the more populist Conservatism associated with Mrs Thatcher. For instance her loyal lieutenant, Norman Tebbit, argued that the so-called C1s and C2s were natural Conservatives and therefore the Party should speak their language. Likewise, Mrs Thatcher's emphasis on hard work, thrift and making one's own way in society was not a message that many Conservative MPs in the past would have found appealing, at least for themselves. Mrs Thatcher was not known for her cultural interests – it is no surprise that a 1994 survey of Conservative MPs' reading preferences concluded: 'Real Tories don't read books.'

Just contrast the views of Margaret Thatcher and Jim Prior on the diminishing band of middle-of-the-road, backbench and 'apolitical' Tory MPs who prided themselves on their breadth of interests. Prior praises the loyalty of these knights of the Shires, extolling the fact that they were pragmatists to a man (if never woman). In her memoirs, on the other hand, Thatcher was scathing about Tory MPs like Prior: 'I call such figures "the false squires". They have all the outward show of a John Bull – ruddy face, white hair, bluff manner – but inwardly they are political calculators who see the task of Conservatives as one of retreating gracefully before the Left's inevitable advance.'

Equally important has been the rise of the career politician: a type which has appeared in all parties, not merely the Conservative. Having set out to make a career in politics, these 'professional politicians' often have little experience of non-political work. Peter Riddell in his recent study of the career politician found that only 41 per cent of the 1992 intake of new MPs had ever had 'proper jobs', compared with 71 per cent in 1964 and 80 per cent in 1951. 'The proportion of full-time politicians among new MPs has risen from a tenth in 1951 to nearly a third in 1992.' Many MPs had once been local councillors or political research assistants.

In some ways this change has been inevitable simply because of the huge demands now made of MPs. One Conservative MP at the beginning of this century used to receive about twelve letters a year from his constituents. His son, a Conservative MP in the 1920s, received about two to three thousand letters a year. Today an MP receives, on average, thirty-three letters each day; almost ten thousand a year. Moreover, today's letters are increasingly technical and demand much more effort when replying.

MPs are also expected to hold regular surgeries for their constituents and to live in the area. Until recently many Conservative MPs – and Labour too – had very little to do with their constituency, particularly if they were national figures. The donkey work was left to their agent. In some memoirs the name of their seat is barely mentioned: you have to be sharp-eyed, for instance, to spot that Oliver Lyttelton, later Viscount Chandos, represented the safe seat of Aldershot.

The punishing and ridiculous hours at the House of Commons – often from early in the afternoon to early in the morning – mean that few businessmen can now combine two careers: the ninety Conservative businessmen MPs of 1906 had dwindled to sixteen by 1970. One recent study found that not only were British MPs amongst the worst paid in Europe but they 'currently work over 60 hours a week and collectively they keep the longest and latest hours of any Western Parliament; they seldom have a free weekend, and see little of their families'.

On the other hand, the demise of the part-time MP who regarded Parliament as a second job is not necessarily to be regretted. Certainly the gruelling weekends held by the Conservative Party Parliamentary Selection Board, at which would-be candidates are vigorously put through their paces, discourage the frivolous and uncommitted.

Winston Churchill, for one, would probably have supported such procedures, believing as he did that politics was and should be an all-consuming passion (even though he himself found the time to be protean in his achievements). His doctor, Lord Moran, reported one discussion in which Churchill 'built a theory that politics was a whole-time job to which men should devote their lives. It was a priesthood, a profession. He, Winston, felt vaguely that there should be some test which members of the House of Commons must pass before taking their seats.'

In summary, therefore, one could say that the parliamentary Conservative Party which was once the preserve of the hereditary landed class and was then seasoned by ex-military officers and City businessmen is today dominated by middle-class professional career politicians, often with a legal or accountancy background and experience of local government. The Cavendishes and the Derbys now prefer to run their stately homes as a business than to endure the mundane demands of a political career.

The likes and dislikes of Tory MPs have also clearly changed. In 1911, after his unexpected selection as leader of the Conservative Party, Andrew Bonar Law was given some solemn advice by one backbench MP: 'You're not very well known to our fellows, and you must get yourself popular. What you want to do is to drink a bottle of Champagne a day, and look as if you did.' Bonar Law was in fact a teetotaller. It seems unlikely that any backbench MP gave John Major such advice after his unexpected election in November 1990.

In several crucial respects, however, the background and interests of Conservative MPs have barely changed at all this century. The first and most obvious continuity is that we are talking almost exclusively about male Conservative MPs. In the 1992 election, for instance, only sixty-three out of well over six hundred Conservative candidates were women and few of those were adopted for safe seats – just twenty were actually elected. The Labour Party fielded 138 women candidates, of whom thirty-seven were elected: a little better if hardly earth-shattering.

Conservative constituency associations have always felt that if a woman candidate is married then she should be at home, and if she isn't married then there is something wrong with her. Some women feel it necessary to lop a few years off their age, as Theresa Gorman did when she was nominated for Billericay in 1983.

Even if a woman does get into Parliament then she has to combat the clubby male atmosphere and chauvinistic attitudes. The worst bigotry Nancy Astor faced when she became the first woman MP to take up her seat on winning Plymouth in 1918 was from her own Conservative colleagues. There has never been, for instance, a female whip, a post which nowadays often marks the first step on the ladder to ministerial office.

The second continuity is that parliamentary candidates still need to be reasonably wealthy. Lord Woolton was complacent about the success of the Maxwell-Fyfe proposals in the 1940s which restricted the sums that Conservative candidates could contribute to association funds: 'The change was revolutionary and, in my view, did more than any single factor to save the Conservative

Party . . . The way was clear for men and women of ability to seek election to Westminster.'

In practice, the successful candidate, however able, has to 'nurse' a constituency before the election. Margaret Thatcher always freely acknowledged the advantage of being married to a wealthy business-man – 'It was Denis's money that helped me on my way' – whilst a young John Major was told in 1967 that he would need to spend at least £500 on a seat in the form of contributions, fund-raising and so on. More recently one Conservative candidate claimed to be spending £5,000 a year in the attempt just to secure a winnable seat: money spent on travelling, attending conferences and training weekends, and staying away for interviews.

The third area in which the background of Conservative MPs has barely altered is that they continue to represent a wide range of outside business interests, whether as directors of companies or as paid lobbyists and spokesmen. In 1939 Simon Haxey in his detailed book *Tory M.P.* analysed the business affiliations of Conservative Members of Parliament and found that nearly half were company directors. A more recent study published in 1991 revealed that 384 MPs held a total of 522 directorships and 452 consultancies, the vast majority of which were claimed by Conservative Members of Parliament.

In the summer of 1994, the *Sunday Times* published the names of two backbench Tory MPs allegedly prepared to accept money in return for tabling questions in the Commons, and it later transpired that other MPs were only too happy to accept free gifts and holidays in return for their professional services. A poll published in the *Daily Telegraph* on 4 November 1994 revealed that substantial majorities thought that most MPs 'make a lot of money by using public office improperly' and care too much about special interests. In 1985, 42 per cent of a poll felt that most MPs had 'a high personal code'; by 1994, that figure had dropped to 26 per cent.

Clearly, therefore, the rise of the professional career politician does not mean Conservative MPs are unable to find the time to represent interests other than those of their constituents. One observer has pointedly asked whether 'elected public servants [should] also be the paid advocates of outside organisations?'

It is clear, too, that the influence of political lobbyists such as the fifty-strong Ian Greer Associates is much greater than that wielded by democratically elected backbenchers. Douglas Hurd once graphically compared political lobbyists to 'serpents, constantly emerging from the sea', strangling democratic processes and adding 'to the difficulty of reaching decisions in the general interest'.

In other words, comparatively minor changes in the background of Conservative MPs should not obscure the fact that as a body of individuals they remain thoroughly unrepresentative of the population as a whole. Sixty per cent of Tory MPs were educated at public school, compared with less than 4 per cent of the British population; 60 per cent of Tory MPs went to Oxford or Cambridge, compared with 2 per cent of the population. Eight per cent of Tory MPs are women; more than 50 per cent of the nation are women.

The fact that Conservative MPs have, by and large, been drawn from a narrow social range has inevitably meant they shared the same values and assumptions. These tribal loyalties or unspoken codes of conduct have in the past allowed Conservatives to enjoy a less strict party discipline than the tough regime imposed upon the parliamentary Labour Party. Bagehot memorably called Tory backbenchers of the nineteenth century 'the finest brute voting force in Europe'. What were these loyalties and values, how did they work and have they changed?

'My Party, right or wrong' – this has always been the cry of Conservative MPs aware that disunity and indiscipline jeopardise the Party's pursuit of power. In the past, the parliamentary party was prepared to swallow any misgivings members might have had in favour of the greater good of the Party itself. This obedience was clearly demonstrated in the 1930s over appeasement and the 1950s during the Suez crisis.

Neville Chamberlain's policies of appeasement towards Hitler and Mussolini divided the country but not the parliamentary party. The few dissenting voices at Westminster were drowned out by the bulk of the Party. One of Winston Churchill's supporters, Brendan Bracken, claimed that Conservative Central Office had secured backing for Chamberlain's policies by helping to pay the election expenses of no fewer than 170 MPs.

The Munich agreement in 1938 was greeted with almost unanimous acclaim by Conservative MPs. Defenders of Chamberlain's actions claim that only a handful of MPs opposed the agreement – but of course we will never really know how big that handful in fact was. How many MPs, torn by the struggle between individual conscience and Party loyalty, kept their fears to themselves, fully aware that the deadliest Tory sin is to dissent in public? Take, for example, the case of Harry Crookshank.

Crookshank was a junior minister in the Chamberlain Government; after the Second World War he was to become a leading Cabinet minister under Churchill and Eden and finally end up as Viscount Crookshank. In his diary entries for 1938, he records his growing alarm at Chamberlain's policies of appeasement. Crookshank nearly resigned in February 1938, along with Foreign Secretary Sir Anthony Eden, but accepted the Prime Minister's word that there had been in fact no change in policy.

In October 1938, after Duff Cooper had resigned, Crookshank plucked up enough courage to hand in his own resignation – but Chamberlain refused to accept it. Crookshank then went to see Chamberlain in Downing Street and, after the Prime Minister promised to take back his words 'peace in our time', Crookshank told him to burn his letter of resignation. From now on, Crookshank confided to his diary, 'my reservations would be mental not vocal'. He simply lacked the courage or conviction to rock rather than gently disturb the boat.

With critics as timid as Crookshank, it was hardly surprising that the outbreak of war in September 1939, followed by further examples of government incompetence, still produced no organised rebellion. Not until the fiasco of the Norwegian campaign in May 1940 did a mere thirty-five Conservative MPs feel emboldened enough to vote against Chamberlain; over three hundred and fifty (including Crookshank) still voted for him. If the bulk of Tory MPs had got their way, Winston Churchill would not have become Prime Minister.

In the 1950s the Suez campaign divided the country but hardly the parliamentary party. Although it has been estimated that between twenty-five and thirty Conservative MPs doubted the advisability of military action against Colonel Nasser's Egyptian regime, at the end of the crucial debate on 8 November 1956 there were just eight abstentions. Of the eight only three survived politically, two – Robert Boothby and Sir Edward Boyle – because of their enormous popularity as constituency MPs and the third, William Yates, just managed to retain his seat. The others, including writer Nigel Nicolson, were either deselected by their local parties or jumped before they were pushed.

And yet six months later, in May 1957, the parliamentary party obediently and overwhelmingly supported the government as it jettisoned its strong anti–Nasser line. This time there were just fourteen Conservative abstentions from the right of the Party. One commentator noted at the time: 'The Suez adventure may have been right or it may have been wrong, but the vast majority of Conservatives was willing to vote for going into Suez one day and for coming out a few days afterwards, for asserting that we should never allow the [Suez] Canal to be under the sole control of Nasser and for allowing it to remain under the sole control of Nasser.'

Rather different from these textbook examples of discipline and obedience has been the recent furore over the passage of the Maastricht bill. In her account of this particular struggle, one of the Euro-rebels, Theresa Gorman, has detailed some of the techniques used by the Party whips to try and force the dissenters back into line. These methods ranged from the witholding of perks such as foreign trips to the threat of boundary changes and deselection.

Initially, party discipline during the nineteenth century was comparatively lax. The whips – the term comes from the whippers-in of the hunt – had few means of ensuring obedience, if only because many MPs were simply not interested in political office. The private means enjoyed by all MPs gave them an enormous degree of independence.

Towards the end of the nineteenth century, however, the rise of party placed an increasing premium on discipline and loyalty. It was not long before Conservative backbenchers realised that they needed some form of organisation which would represent their interests in the face of the Party managers. The 1922 election returned a clutch of young, enthusiastic Conservatives to Parliament. In the words of one of them, Sir Gervais Rentoul: 'Flushed with triumph, they came to Westminster from their constituencies filled with an excusable sense of their own importance, and fully prepared to create a new Heaven and a new Earth. But they were speedily disillusioned.'

These new MPs found themselves to be merely insignificant backbenchers ignored by all and sundry. Rentoul decided to set up a committee which would at least allow them to channel their opinions to the whips. Its purpose was suitably vague: 'To render every assistance to the government and the Party whips in their efforts to carry on the affairs of the nation upon the sound basis of Conservative principles.'

And so the 'Conservative Private Members (1922) Committee', the most famous of all internal Conservative bodies, was formed. Initially the leadership regarded the 1922 as a nuisance, but Chief Whip Eyre Monsell soon realised that it was better for party discipline if the enthusiasm of the MPs could be harnessed and used. It offered a useful platform for the loyalist moderate majority and, in time-honoured Conservative fashion, diminished the possibility of internal dissent or the formation of factions.

Although it was restricted at first to newly elected MPs, the 1922 Committee soon expanded to include all Conservative members who were not members of the Government. A weekly meeting is held at 6 p.m. every Thursday. When the Conservatives are in office no ministers may attend the meetings, but a whip is always present in order to convey to the leader any worries or anxieties that backbenchers may have.

Regarding itself as the conscience of the Party, the 1922 Committee is in reality concerned with ensuring that the Conservative Party remains in power. In particular, it tries to surmount the problem which bedevils so many leaders, namely loss of contact with their own supporters. The work of the 1922 rarely extends actually to discussing policy, as opposed to people – very much a Tory characteristic. Even the Committee's historian, former Conservative MP Sir Philip Goodhart, admits that more time has been spent discussing MPs' pay than anything else.

This lack of interest accurately mirrors the decidedly 'non-political' character of many Conservative MPs, preoccupied in the past with their other careers and extensive outside interests. In any case most Conservative MPs would robustly maintain that family, sport, country, religion, pleasure and much else are more important than politics. Their credo was once declared by Lord Hailsham: 'The man who puts politics first is not fit to be called a civilized being, let alone a Christian.'

This did not mean that they failed to appreciate the virtues of loyalty, unity and character − they were Conservatives after all. But life was regarded as too short for much time to be wasted on political debate and the organising of factions. Many Tory MPs were simply not interested in the tedium and long hours necessitated by a ministerial career and preferred, like the hugely moustached Sir Gerald Nabarro, to enjoy life to its flamboyant full.

Nevertheless, for want of anything better, the 1922 Committee has been the formal custodian of the Party's leadership contests since the 1960s. After the turmoil of finding a successor to Harold Macmillan in 1963, it was clear that the days of the magic circle were numbered. The power of election was instead delegated to the parliamentary party − not a development of which the Cavendishes or Derbys would have approved − but the least harmful alternative to carrying out an election in too public an arena. The men in suits, as the 1922 Executive are sometimes labelled, can be relied upon to act with discretion: Mrs Thatcher, for instance, was ushered off the political stage in November 1990 with a minimum of fuss.

It is also clear that if the 1922 takes against a particular minister or even a leader, then the latter is in trouble. 1922 chairman W.S. Morrison is supposed to have ended R.A. Butler's hopes for the leadership by simply murmuring, 'the chaps won't have you'. In the early 1970s the chairman of the 1922 was Edward du Cann, an inveterate opponent of Edward Heath who played no small part in his downfall in 1975. More recently, the fate of aberrant ministers such as Lord Carrington over the invasion of the Falklands, Leon Brittan and Westland, Edwina Currie and salmonella in eggs, and finally David Mellor and Tim Yeo as regards their private lives was sealed by the 1922.

If the 1922 represents the interests of the backbenchers, then the Party leadership relies on the the whips' office to make sure that the parliamentary party stays in line. Unanimity of vote not conscience or scruple is the benchmark. The fourteen whips, or 'school prefects' as Theresa Gorman has called them, are responsible for keeping an eye on their colleagues, watching out for signs of disobedience, which are handled with a judicious mixture of threat and promise.

The whips, for instance, know more about potentially recalcitrant MPs than they would care to have known publicly – this, of course, represents the stick. The carrot is the power of patronage which the whips wield, rewarding pliant backbenchers with trips abroad, membership of important parliamentary committees and the hope of ministerial office. Today the vast majority of new MPs are hoping for a government post, and it takes a brave individual to defy the whips and as a result have nothing more to look forward to than a career becalmed on the backbenches.

Few dissident Conservative MPs, therefore, dare to carry through their rebellion against the Party machine, particularly in conjunction with others. The group Centre Forward, spearheaded by Francis Pym after his dismissal by Mrs Thatcher, quickly and ignominiously collapsed. In the words of Sir Anthony Meyer, the backbencher who stood against Mrs Thatcher for the Party leadership in 1989: 'For a Tory MP to vote against the Government might be condoned; but to organise others to do so was more what you might expect from shop stewards and their ilk; it is not the sort of thing that any decent Tory would do.'

According to Meyer, the most effective pressure the whips could bring to bear on a dissident MP was to stir up trouble in his or her constituency. He faced enormous troubles with his own association and had to work overtime to try and put things right. 'The price of liberty, for an independent-minded MP, is eternal coffee mornings,' Meyer noted in his autobiography.

The powers of the Chief Whip can indeed be formidable. At the end of the last century the activity of Aretas Akers-Douglas was crucial in underpinning the position and influence of party leader Lord Salisbury. Apparently freed by an unhappy marriage from the temptation of spending convivial evenings at home, Akers-Douglas devoted himself to the smooth and efficient running of the parliamentary party.

In the 1930s Captain David Margesson was instrumental in ensuring that the parliamentary party obediently acquiesced in the appeasement policies of Prime Minister Chamberlain. According to one MP, Margesson 'treated dissenters personally as defaulters on parade'. Another Tory once voted against the government and found that Margesson did not speak to him for seven years. Perhaps the most effective Chief Whip in recent times was Edward Heath who managed to hold the parliamentary party together during the Suez crisis in 1956–7.

Another successful Chief Whip was Willie Whitelaw who in his memoirs laid down the credo of both the whips and the Party in general: 'the more a party, through loyalty and discipline, manages to conduct its disagreements in private, the more successful its Government will be and, perhaps even more important, the more likely that party is to gain power and retain it.'

The way in which the character of the whips has changed demonstrates the more ambitious nature of the current parliamentary party. In the past, as Alan Clark has put it, they were predominantly Old Etonians, whereas today the whips' office is the nursery of aspiring careerists.

Despite the pushing and prodding of the 1922 on one side and the whips on the other, the bulk of the Conservative parliamentary party has always favoured the middle of the road. This almost instinctive sense of balance of course represents one of the Party's major strengths, giving it – to use an old-fashioned word once favoured by Tory MPs – 'bottom'.

In other words, they were content to support the Party leadership until, to adapt Bob McKenzie's phrase in the last chapter, they decide no longer to do so. Commentator Noel Malcolm has referred to 'the deepest need of Tory backbenchers of all ideological persuasions: the need to retain one's seat at a general election'.

This apolitical stance was even maintained during the more

fervently ideological years under Mrs Thatcher in the 1980s. One analysis of the 356 Tory MPs returned after the 1987 election concluded that 72 of them could be termed 'Thatcherites', 27 were 'wets' or anti-Thatcherities, 40 were 'damps' or mildly anti-Thatcher – but no fewer than 217 Conservative MPs, in other words nearly twice the number of zealots, were most accurately classified as 'Party Faithful'. Mrs Thatcher therefore failed to craft a parliamentary party in her own image and when it looked as if she might well lose the next election then the Party faithful, without fuss or ideological rancour, simply failed to support her.

Despite this preference for the unexciting middle ground, it is clear that the traditional unwritten codes and assumptions which formerly bound together the parliamentary party are starting to dissolve. In the words of Lord Rawlinson, a member of the Heath administration, there has been 'a loss of ballast'. Or as Bernard Levin has put it rather more tartly, 'Many new Tory MPs look, sound and behave like used-car salesmen.'

In part this simply illustrates how wider social changes such as the loss of deference and a decline in respect for long-established institutions have affected even Conservatives. But it reflects too the arrival at Westminster of increasingly ambitious young Conservative MPs concerned more with their own career than with embodying a spirit of social duty and noblesse oblige on the backbenches. The narrow social background which once typified most Tory MPs and generated its own sense of loyalties is now less apparent. In the recent past no Conservative MP ever carried a Christian name like Steve, Jerry or Gary.

Moreover, although Mrs Thatcher might have been ousted by the parliamentary party, the impact of her ideas and her years in office shook it from top to bottom. Her barely concealed contempt for the Tory grandees and their One Nation leanings undermined the old coherence and sense of identity. So much that originally had been taken for granted within the Conservative Party was now up for debate.

This new sense of unease and lost bearings was clearly demonstrated during the 1990 leadership contest. After Mrs Thatcher's withdrawal, the fight was between Michael Heseltine, Douglas

Hurd and John Major. Heseltine was distrusted by the more patrician elements within the Party as a parvenu, the kind of man who, the ultimate insult, combed his hair in public. The old school was represented by Douglas Hurd, a suitably distinguished Old Etonian, Cambridge and Foreign Office man. John Major's background was less exalted.

Yet instead of standing unapologetically on his credentials, Hurd allowed himself to be drawn into an extraordinary game of what journalist Alan Watkins called 'lowlier than thou'. He even began to describe his father, who had been a peer, as a tenant farmer and pleaded that he himself was essentially a self-made man. It was a game which Hurd simply could not win, but it was revealing that he felt obliged to play it at all. In the not so distant past, Hurd's background would have been considered an important asset by almost all Tory MPs. His dilemma illuminates the conflict which exists between the grammar school Conservatives and the Tory toffs.

Further evidence of a loss of cohesion is shown by the rash of internal groupings which have sprung up in the last few years and are fully prepared to go 'public'. The dining clubs once patronised by Conservatives made sure that their deliberations remained private. Not so today: the 92 Group, No Turning Back, Conservative Way Forward, the Bow Group, the Lollards, the One Nation Group, Blue Chip, Fresh Start, European Reform Group and others are eager to make their thoughts known. It used to be the far Left which excelled at faction-fighting.

This fractiousness has also been on public show throughout the debates over Europe. Back-bench dissidents have not been afraid to argue their case in defiance of their own government in public. Compare this with the blanket wall of silence throughout the Suez saga. The final step, which the rebels have so far spurned, is actually to run rival candidates at elections and by-elections. Even if this does not happen, it seems unlikely that the Conservative Party in Parliament will ever again demonstrate the unthinking obedience that it did in the past. Whether this is a good thing or a bad, it certainly has serious implications for the future of the Party generally.

★   ★   ★

'When the call came to me to form a Government, one of my first thoughts was that it should be a Government of which Harrow should not be ashamed.' On such a basis did Old Harrovian Stanley Baldwin form his first administration in 1923. Naturally, the best way to ensure that Harrow would not be ashamed was to follow in the tradition of aristocratic Cabinet-making. Between 1801 and 1924 306 people held Cabinet office of whom no fewer than 182, well over half, were aristocrats. The greasy pole was rather less greasy if one had the right family connections.

Ironically enough, despite Baldwin's solicitude for Harrow he had in fact hated his time there after he had been flogged at sixteen for possession of 'juvenile pornography'. In later life he rarely ever wore his Old Harrovian tie. On the other hand an Old Etonian like Harold Macmillan adopted a slightly different approach. In 1958 it was estimated that thirty-five members of his eighty-five strong government were related to him by marriage: clearly a government of which Macmillans themselves were not ashamed.

Few politicians now enter Parliament without the ambition to become a government minister, and the inexorable growth of government means that there is a good chance that they will succeed. Today, one in every three Conservative MPs is either a minister, a whip or a parliamentary private secretary (PPS) and therefore part of the 'payroll' vote.

Sir Humphrey Appleby described this initial process of selection cynically but accurately in an early episode of *Yes, Minister*: 'there are only 630 MPs and a party with just over 300 MPs forms a government – and of these 300, 100 are too old and silly to be ministers, and 100 too young and too callow. Therefore there are about 100 MPs to fill 100 government posts. Effectively no choice at all.'

The first step of advancement is either to the whips' office or to be appointed a PPS. The latter is essentially a minister's baghandler or general dogsbody but the job does at least offer the chance to mix with more powerful individuals, to listen, learn and discreetly to advertise one's talents.

The next step is to be appointed a junior minister, and now the workload becomes dramatically more onerous. There is simply no time to indulge one's conscience: one supports the Government come what may unless a speedy return to the backbenches is desired. Expert knowledge offers no certainty of promotion, if only because British governments pride themselves on their amateur stance.

For one thing, ministers have to be drawn from the available pool of sitting MPs – only rarely does a Prime Minister bring in an outsider, as Harold Wilson did with trade unionist Frank Cousins or Mrs Thatcher with businessman David Young – and often they are put in charge of huge departments about which they know little. Just as they are getting on top of the job, external political considerations will provoke the Prime Minister into a reshuffle and the minister is moved. Under Mrs Thatcher, for instance, there were no fewer than twelve different Ministers of Trade and Industry.

From being a junior minister, the next crucial step is promotion into the Cabinet itself, a twenty-plus inner elite which forms the top table of power. It is here that the important decisions are supposedly made. In fact, Prime Ministers have increasingly ensured that they get their way by forming smaller Cabinet committees whose decisions are then brought to full Cabinet simply for ratification. Under pressure of business Mrs Thatcher, for example, cut down the twice-weekly meetings to once a week, preferring to work through smaller and more pliable committees. Her supporter Kenneth Baker has noted, too, Mrs Thatcher's fondness for starting a meeting by summing up.

She was also prepared to announce government policy in interviews before it had been discussed by her Cabinet. She freely confessed as much in her memoirs: 'As I often did in government, I was using public statements to advance the arguments and to push reluctant colleagues further than they would otherwise have gone.'

If this technique invariably allowed her to get her own way, it also diminished what Lord Hailsham has called the collegiate atmosphere of the Cabinet. In the end such a change contributed to her downfall when, in November 1990, her own Cabinet ministers did not rally around her as she expected. Another way of trying to ensure unanimity is to appoint one's relations to the Cabinet: at one stage, seven of Macmillan's nineteen ministers were related to him.

The conduct of the Cabinet clearly depends largely on the personality and style of the Prime Minister. In the 1950s the ageing Churchill preferred reminscence to the nitty-gritty of everyday politics. Cabinet meetings used to terminate in a haze of nostalgia, but without having completed the first item on the agenda.

In the final resort it is the Prime Minister who retains the ultimate power of appointment and dismissal: in July 1962 during the so-called 'Night of the Long Knives' Harold Macmillan dismissed one-third of his Cabinet. The easy come, easy go attitude was illustrated by Macmillan's treatment of Lord Chancellor Kilmuir. When Kilmuir complained that he was being dismissed as if he were a cook, Macmillan cruelly replied that good cooks were harder to come by than Lord Chancellors.

A further indication of the more ambitious nature of British Conservatism today is that Cabinet ministers simply do not resign. In the past, ministers accepted that the actions of their departments were ultimately their responsibility; even if they had no personal knowledge of the misconduct or mistakes of one of their juniors, they occasionally had to go. Lord Carrington, for instance, felt honour-bound to resign as Foreign Secretary in 1982 – with a little help from his 'friends' on the 1922 Committee – when the Falkland Islands were unexpectedly invaded by Argentina.

Since then, however, certain ministers have been guilty of more serious misjudgements; over membership of the European Exchange Rate Mechanism, for instance, or the 'arms for Iraq' scandal but no one has felt the need to resign. Political honour counts for less than political ambition. And if you do resign, then you are out of the game.

Just as the workload of MPs has grown inexorably, so has that of Cabinet ministers. When the gifted amateur painter Lord Thorneycroft was a minister in the 1950s, he used to tell his civil servants that he would be otherwise engaged on Tuesdays and Thursdays between 6 p.m. and 9 p.m., drawing in the life class at Chelsea School of Art. No minister today could find time in his diary to set aside such precious hours. In 1990, for example, ministers dealt with no fewer than 250,000 letters, mostly from MPs. It is not surprising that Norman Fowler claimed his weekend never began before 4 p.m. on Sunday.

In his recently published memoirs, Geoffrey Howe calculated that during his six years as Foreign Secretary he took home as overnight work no less than twenty-four tons of paper – that is, three red boxes a night, six nights a week, forty weeks a year. Howe simply had to learn to function on four hours of sleep a night. No wonder Lord (Peter) Rawlinson called politics 'a form of madness' and titled his memoirs *A Price Too High* – or that tired politicians make mistakes.

Nevertheless, the rewards for some years of intensive ministerial activity can be great: a probable peerage, the opportunity to publish some self-justifying memoirs showing how one was right all along, and a clutch of lucrative directorships in business and the City. A survey of thirty-one former Cabinet ministers who held office between 1979 and 1990 shows that nineteen of them had secured a grand total of fifty-nine company directorships.

A Cabinet salary stands at £63,000 a year, but when the *Sunday Times* looked at the earnings of former Cabinet ministers it found that office in Britain is not financially attractive: Lord (David) Young is estimated to earn £1 million a year, Sir John Nott £400,000, Lord (John) Moore £350,000, Lord (Jim) Prior £300,000, and so on. No doubt this helps compensate for the departure from the corridors of power and the disorientating effect which this loss of office can cause. R.A. Butler, for instance, after many years in government, was bereft without the chauffeur driven cars and an attentive staff to take care of mundane matters.

The popular stereotype of the Tory peer has hardly changed at all: P.G. Wodehouse's slightly dotty Lord Emsworth, pottering up to London in order to lunch at his club, briefly dropping into the House for a little afternoon nap, being woken up to be told how to vote, followed by a leisurely return to the ancestral home of Blandings Castle.

Nevertheless, the distinguishing characteristic of the English aristocracy, rather like the Conservative Party itself, is actually its extraordinary ability to survive in modern Britain. No other country in the world allows a body which numerically is still dominated by hereditary individuals – peers not because of any merit of their own, but because of their father's birth – to have a say in popular legislation that affects us all.

Again like the Conservative Party, the secret is to know how far to go. This instinctive and apparently inbred knowledge comes from very long experience of government, not necessarily at Westminster but also in local government and affairs; many peers are or have been Lord Lieutenants, councillors and Justices of the Peace. The best example of this restraint came with the peers versus people controversy in 1909–11 when the House of Lords attempted to thwart the financial measures of the elected House of Commons.

The Chancellor of the Exchequer, David Lloyd George, introduced a budget in 1909 which seemingly hit at the landed aristocracy. It was the first explicit attempt to redistribute wealth in Britain by means of taxation. The tactics of the Liberal government were astute. By framing the debate as one about the basic democratic issue of elected or non-elected power, they made sure that public opinion was by and large on their side. Prime Minister Asquith also came up with the ingenious strategem of extracting from the King a promise that if necessary he would create enough new peers to swamp the reactionary rump within the Lords.

In response, Conservative peers roughly divided into two camps, nicknamed the 'hedgers' and the 'ditchers'; the hedgers were prepared in the ultimate resort to give way, whilst the ditchers were adamant that they would go down fighting, in the last ditch if necessary.

Here was a classic example of the Conservative Party, its back against the wall, having to decide where its best interests lay: it was a dilemma which the Duke of Wellington, Sir Robert Peel and many other Tories then and since have faced. Most of the peers had never recognised the right of the electorate to decide crucial issues for themselves, particularly where the aristocracy's own affairs were concerned.

The Conservative Party had long depended on that attitude,

secure in the expectation that, should any legislation dangerous to its members' interests actually make it through the House of Commons, it would certainly be extinguished in the House of Lords. Only three years before, in 1906, party leader Arthur Balfour had boasted that whether 'in office or out', the Party would 'continue to control the destinies of this great empire' from the impregnable citadel in the House of Lords.

In the end, enough Conservative peers either abstained or voted to pass the measure – but only just, by 131 votes to 114 – and a final confrontation between Commons and Lords was avoided. The peers versus people episode represented a classic demonstration of the Conservative art of fighting hard against reform but then giving way when reform proves inevitable and it is better to shape and limit its effects.

In any case, whatever the constitutional reduction of their actual legislative powers, the Conservative Party had the satisfaction of knowing that its supporters would continue to fill the Lords' benches. In the 1930s, for instance, 60 per cent of all peers had been educated at Eton and in 1941 no fewer than nine members of the Cecil family or near relatives were members of the House of Lords.

After the Second World War and the proclaimed intention of most Governments to create a modern and democratic Britain, it was clear that the hereditary principle would come under increasing fire. It became more and more difficult to maintain that accident of birth alone should give unelected individuals a vital say in amending and passing legislation which affected everyone else.

In the end, it was a Conservative Government which, in 1958, came up with the idea of creating life rather than hereditary peers. Not only did this reform successfully deflect criticism by introducing a meritocratic element, but the creation of life peers also allowed the elevation of non-Conservatives who could give the House of Lords a less lopsided political look – even if the Conservatives remained in a strong majority because of the political views of the hereditary peers.

In a poignant touch, the first list of peers created by Harold Macmillan included the name of Robert Boothby, the rebellious backbench Tory MP who for many years had enjoyed an affair with Macmillan's own wife, Lady Dorothy.

Like that of the Conservative Party in the House of Commons, the character of the Lords has changed. In the not-so-distant past, many peers were fully aware of the requirements of noblesse oblige. As late as 1960, according to Jeremy Paxman, no fewer than four dukes, one marquess, nine earls, four viscounts, five viscountesses, twenty-seven barons, thirty-four baronets, fifty-two knights and fifteen titled wives sat on English county councils. By 1990, however, they had all but vanished, concentrating instead on the commercial demands of managing their own estates.

From time to time, both the Liberal and Labour Parties come up with plans to replace the House of Lords with an alternative elected second chamber; but, apart from being only rarely in office and thus in no position to do anything constructive anyway, their range of conflicting views and ideas tend to cancel each other out. Rather like the abolition of the monarchy, no one can agree what, if anything, should replace it. For instance, how could one stop an elected body from becoming in some way a rival to the House of Commons?

Defenders of the Lords often argue that in the 1980s it was they who led the opposition to Mrs Thatcher. In fact, this opposition was muted. Commentator Peter Riddell summed up: 'Their lordships, whose virtues and independence have been more trumpeted than real, have inflicted regular, generally minor, defeats on Mrs Thatcher's legislation. The Government lost more than 120 times between 1979 and the end of the 1987–8 session. But most of these have been fairly minor, detailed, provisions rather than central clauses.'

To take one specific case. In July 1988 the House of Lords rejected the imposition of charges for eye tests by a vote of 120 to 94. The Government simply called on the support of its titled backwoodsmen and put the matter to the vote yet again. This time they won by 257 votes to 207. At the end of the day, the Conservatives retain an in-built majority in Balfour's 'citadel'.

What is undeniable, though, is that, free of the rancour of party spirit and political advancement, some excellent debates do sometimes take place in the House of Lords. Over the passage of the Maastricht bill, for example, the Chamber rang with the passionately held views of Lady Thatcher, Lord Tebbit, Lord Howe and Lord Whitelaw amongst others. Interested less in preferment than principle, the quality of the debate was much higher than in the Commons where ferocious 'whipping' ensured a spurious political consensus.

And, yet another reminder that the Conservative Party continually confounds lazy generalisations, it was Mrs Thatcher who, in 1990, created Britain's first female Asian peer, Lady Flather. Before that, Shreela Flather had been the first Asian female councillor in Britain and the first female Asian magistrate. The cynical might well mutter 'tokenism', but the process of integrating minority groups into public life has to start somewhere and it is revealing that it should be a Conservative who has started that process.

6

Now Is The Time For All Good Men (and Women) . . .

The Conservative Party in the country

'You can pass resolutions from now till 5 o'clock on these matters, and if we do not agree with them, they will never be carried out.'

Principal agent Sir Herbert Blain speaking to the council meeting of Conservative Party agents, 1925

'Conservatives do not believe that political struggle is the most important thing in life, the simplest among them prefer fox-hunting – the wisest religion.'

Quintin Hogg (Lord Hailsham), *The Case for Conservatism* (1947)

'Tories should be well turned out on all public occasions.'

Rupert Morris, *Tories* (1991)

Two men of Jewish origin died within a few years of each other in the early 1880s; both left a political legacy. Twenty years after Karl Marx's death in 1883 the Social Democratic Federation boasted a total membership of fewer than three thousand. In marked contrast the Primrose League, set up in honour of Benjamin Disraeli and called after what was supposedly his favourite flower, numbered its membership in hundreds of thousands, thus ensuring that it was

Conservatism rather than Marxism which played a central role in British life.

The Conservative Party has always been coy about the size of its membership, partly because no central records have ever been kept of members' names. Local associations prefer to retain such information themselves, a graphic illustration of the tension between the centre and those on the ground. At its peak in 1952 the Party claimed a membership of just under three million people which, outside of communist countries where political membership was often compulsory, meant that it was probably the largest political organisation of all time.

Since then its membership has dwindled, as has that of all political parties, but it still fluctuates around the half a million mark. Moreover the Party's presence is massively evident in local government, in its local associations and in Conservative Clubs.

It is this physical dimension which gives the Party a grassroots commitment that is particularly evident at election times when an army of canvassers and envelope-lickers suddenly materialises overnight. It generates, too, a loyalty and continuity which newer political organisations struggle to achieve. As the Social Democratic Party (SDP) discovered in the 1980s, political parties can quickly wither and die without well-established emotional and physical ties.

The Conservative Party has always prided itself on being a broad church. But in fact how broad is it? Does that broadness include minority groups? Are there regional differences? How powerful were the old party bosses? What is the relationship between Conservative Central Office, which is based in Smith Square in London, and the local associations out in the country which are linked together in the National Union of Conservative and Unionist Associations? How significant is the annual party conference? What is the future for political parties in general and the Conservative Party in particular?

Originally there was no need for grassroots organisation at all. The small size of the electorate and the nature of politics as personal allegiance meant that no political parties existed as we know them before the nineteenth century. The first recognisably modern political machine was in fact Irish. Daniel O'Connell's Catholic Association campaigned in the 1820s for Catholic Emancipation and the awarding of the vote to Catholics. Before the Act of 1829 Catholics had been excluded from much of British political life: they were not allowed to vote, or go to Oxford and Cambridge, nor could they be magistrates, or hold senior posts in the army and other areas of public life.

O'Connell's genius was to see that small subscriptions from many would add up to a substantial income and by 1825 the Association was raising up to £1,000 a week, a huge sum in the nineteenth century. He also understood the dramatic and emotional strength which could be gained from holding massive rallies or 'monster meetings'; one meeting in 1843 was reputedly attended by nearly three-quarters of a million people. Gatherings on such a vast scale gave members a sense of shared loyalty and commitment.

The early forms of political organisation on the mainland were a response to the passage of the first Reform Act in 1832. This statute stipulated that members of the electorate had to register their names with the authorities in order to be eligible to vote. Both the Conservative and Whig party realised the advantages of safely registering their own supporters whilst challenging the registration of their opponents. 'The battle of the constitution must be fought in the registration courts', claimed Sir Robert Peel in 1841.

By and large the Conservatives were quicker off the mark than their rivals, setting up what were called Conservative Operative Societies – in effect workingmen's clubs – and also 150 Conservative women's associations by 1874. Neither workingmen nor women had the vote, but these societies and associations were vital in canvassing support.

More formal attempts made by the Party to organise support in the community, however, were paralysed by a fear of seeming to challenge the parliamentary party at Westminster. In 1867 the National Union of Conservative and Constitutional Associations (NUCCA) was finally established in order to bring together local parties in some kind of formal network. Numbers rose satisfactorily

– 289 associations belonged by 1870, 475 by 1875 – but NUCCA was dogged by apathy. At its first conference in 1868 only six members and the chairman actually turned up. Political parties remained Westminster-based.

What transformed this situation was the evident success of the local Liberals in Birmingham, a city which after the 1867 Reform Act was scheduled to return three MPs to Parliament. The leaders of the Birmingham Liberal Association realised that if they organised and then allocated their votes correctly, they could ensure that all three MPs were theirs. This 'caucus', as it came to be called, was the forerunner of the modern mass political party which grew up in the late nineteenth century.

Thoughtful Conservatives could see that these Birmingham methods had to be emulated and the impetus to change was speeded up by the shock of the 1880 general election defeat and the recognition that their party organisation, such as it was, had been allowed to decay. Further impetus to renewal was provided by the Corrupt and Illegal Practices Act of 1883 which proved to be one of the most influential of all Victorian statutes.

Before 1883 the only limit on a candidate's election expenditure was the depth of his pockets. Inevitably, lack of regulation led to bribery, corruption and the buying of votes. Take this description of the vigorously contested election at Horsham in Sussex in 1847 when just 319 votes were at stake: 'Cash bribes of £40 and £50 were offered and taken; the public-houses ran up bills (which the candidates paid) to as much as £800; for the six weeks preceding the poll most of the men in the town were frequently, and some of them continuously, drunk; even schoolboys were reported to be going to their lessons in a state of intoxication.'

At Blackburn in 1868 drunken crowds fought in the streets, the committee rooms of each candidate were destroyed and the town's schools had to be turned into hospitals in order to accommodate the injured. In all, at least seventy-one separate incidents of serious disorder were recorded during election campaigns between 1865 and 1885.

The introduction of the secret ballot in 1872 was an important first step towards reform but the real breakthrough came after the

1880 election which everyone, Tory and Liberal alike, agreed was expensive and corrupt. The Liberal candidate for Taunton, Sir Henry James, was nearly unseated because of the £3,000 in gold sent by Conservative Central Office for the use of his opponents. As a result, he introduced the legislation which eventually became the Corrupt and Illegal Practices Act of 1883.

The 1883 Act imposed drastic restrictions on the amount of money which candidates could spend during elections. In order not to breach these rules, candidates had no alternative but to dispense with paid helpers and to rely on voluntary workers – and the more of them the better.

It was this far-reaching change which led directly to the creation of modern political parties as we still know them today; organisations which have individual membership, subscriptions and local branches that initiate a range of activities in order to attract enthusiastic volunteers. Once the Conservatives realised how essential it was to create an esprit de corps outside Westminster, they shamelessly imitated many of the techniques first pioneered in Birmingham.

The organisation which proved most successful at creating this spirit was the Primrose League. Although not formally tied to the Conservative Party until 1913, in effect the League supplied the Party with an army of voluntary workers. Many of them were women, and the Primrose League was undoubtedly one of the most successful of all British political bodies, adept at mobilising support for Conservative candidates at elections.

It is unclear who, if anyone, can claim to be the creator of the Primrose League. The idea was first mooted after Disraeli's death in 1881. Lord Randolph Churchill was alive to the possibility of harnessing grassroots support in his campaign against the Party hierarchy in the 1880s, and his wife Jennie was certainly an early driving force behind the League's formation. Initially membership cost an expensive guinea, but an associate membership of one shilling was quickly introduced to ensure grassroots support for the rather fragile blossom.

Members signed a Declaration of Faith: 'I declare on my honour and faith that I will devote my best ability to the maintenance of Religion, of the Estates of the Realm, and of the Imperial

Ascendancy of the British Empire . . .' These vague and imprecise sentiments echoed the set of values trumpeted by the Conservative Party in the later nineteenth century, and were intended to transcend material differences and to unite rich and poor. Queen, Country, Church, Empire were concepts which inspired far more loyalty than the radical appeal to class.

The archaic phrase 'the Estates of the Realm' had not been chosen at random, but reflected the medieval mystique with which the League was imbued. Members were organised not into branches but into 'habitations'; the grander sort of member was titled knight or dame; and ordinary members were able to purchase an elaborate range of knicknacks. The Jubilee Grand Star, for instance, was instituted in 1887 and its five points supposedly represented the empire in the five continents of the world. In turn the star itself was graded into five divisions which came at different prices and with different ribbons attached.

The key to the League's success was the range of social activities which it offered members in an attempt to make politics enjoyable; the League's historian has described their meetings as having 'the combined character of a music hall, a harvest supper and a women's institute'. Music, dances, teas, cycling corps, magic lantern shows, waxworks and much else were provided under the League's auspices. It was also an opportunity for boy to meet girl and its critics sneeringly called it a matrimonial agency, which no doubt increased membership still further.

The League and its habitations reflected the culture of each area. In Scotland, for instance, some habitations took on such colourful names as the 'Sir William Wallace' in Larbert or the 'Robert the Bruce' in Lochmaben. Some frowned upon the kind of activities commonplace in England. A Kincardineshire habitation which boasted a thousand members held strictly teetotal meetings and dourly decreed: 'dancing has been considered inadmissible as there is no need for it'.

Very quickly the League's membership extended far beyond the parsons and landlords who had traditionally made up the local Conservative Party associations. By 1891 it claimed to have enrolled one million members and to have distributed two million leaflets, a fantastic achievement before the days of mass communications. Two million individuals had enrolled by 1910.

The League was formidably hierarchical in its organisation. Its higher echelons were crammed with titled aristocrats and double-barrelled names and the bulk of the membership was suitably deferential. This has prompted some historians to be a little sniffy: 'The League remains most notable as a characteristic if extraordinary manifestation of the more occult depths of the English class system.'

Perhaps, but the League was rather more than an English eccentricity. Particularly significant was its appeal to women, who formed nearly half of its membership and welcomed the social life generated by the habitations. The League was also effective in attracting non-voters and thereby giving Conservatism the kind of popular base which Disraeli himself had advocated. It also pioneered techniques which the Conservative Party later successfully adopted: namely the idea of a low entrance fee which would allow a mass membership. Finally, the League supplied an army of volunteer workers who could be called upon at election times yet did not break the provisions of the Act of 1883. It even had a group of 'mobile skirmishers' for use at particularly rowdy elections.

The Liberal Party alternatively derided and envied the League. They scoffed at the way the League virtually canonised General Gordon after his murder in 1885 and were utterly hostile to the Home Rule movement for Ireland. Nevertheless the League's opponents envied the high level of participation of what they contemptuously called 'a League of farm labourers and servant girls'. Liberal attempts to emulate the League with a Progress League and a Lily League failed miserably.

To the charge of vulgarity, the League's leaders happily pleaded guilty. 'Vulgar?' replied Lady Salisbury, 'Of course, it is vulgar! But that is why we have got on so well.'

The Primrose League's associated organisations also notched up impressive numbers: 70,000 in the 'Jimps' or Junior Imperial and Constitutional League by 1911, 65,000 enrolled in the Juvenile Branch and so on. These were figures which left those of the radical groups of the time a long way behind and show how successful the League became through treating the broad mass of the population as being worthy of attention.

Another example of Conservatism's ability to put down roots country-wide was the growth of the Conservative Clubs, which were powerful enough to be formed into an association in 1894. The radical clubs of the time have received rather more attention from historians, but it was the Conservative bodies that, in terms of numbers and political activity, were much more important.

The earliest such organisation was the Carlton Club, established in fashionable St James's, London, in 1830. It was the first time that like-minded political partisans had gathered themselves together into an organisation. But the Carlton was, and still is, formidably exclusive and patrician – until the arrival of Mrs Thatcher women were not allowed to use the main staircase – and it was soon joined by a variety of other bodies whose subscription fees were less astronomic. Like the Primrose League, they had a flair for staging entertainments and their enthusiastic provision of alcohol helped to establish strong and enduring links between the brewers and the Conservative Party. Intriguingly, the Liberal Party's ties were with the grocers – Mrs Thatcher would not have approved.

The Association of Conservative Clubs fostered their members' political education by means of a lending library, provided advice and organised sports competitions. The clubs also supplied an army of volunteers at election times and the final crowning touch, according to historian Peter Marsh, was the formation of cycling clubs which trained dispatch riders for use on election day. Conservative club cyclists were even fitted out with a uniform which comprised tunic, knickerbockers, hat, and silver badge.

This growth of the Conservative Party in the country did not of course take place without friction and argument. The bone of contention was the relationship between the Party at large in the country and the parliamentary party at Westminster. The Party leaders had to perform a balancing act: eager for the services of the local associations and volunteers, particularly during elections, they were nevertheless determined not to be fettered in any way by the demands they might make. This tension was most apparent between NUCCA, that is the National Union which represented the grassroots, and Conservative Central Office, the private office of the leader.

Matters were not helped by the tendency of ambitious politicians to make use of the Party outside Westminster to further their own interests. Lord Randolph Churchill, for instance, made much of what he called Tory democracy: 'Trust the people!' he cried. When pressed on the matter Churchill admitted that he had little idea what this slogan meant, but he had no scruples about using the extra-parliamentary organisations in order to strengthen his campaign against party leader Lord Salisbury in the 1880s. Churchill was easily bought off, however, with a more senior position within the Party.

Conservative leaders did not want to cede too much power to external bodies, although each clearly needed the other. Just because sections of the working class now had the vote, that did not give them the right to an organisational voice within the Party. In fact, Disraeli set up Conservative Central Office in 1870 precisely to keep a check on the possible pretensions of the National Union. The annual party conference held by NUCCA was something of a safety valve which senior politicians rarely attended. However, it was tactful and diplomatic to pay lipservice to its importance and not to remark, as A.J. Balfour once did, that he paid more attention to his valet than to the conference itself.

In fact, Balfour's dismissive comment masked the fact that the success of the Party in the last decades of the nineteenth century owed much to its growth in the country at large, well away from the hot-house atmosphere of Westminster. And few did more to foster this growth than the Party's principal agent from 1885, Richard or 'Skipper' Middleton.

The grandson of an admiral, Middleton had entered the navy at fifteen and although he never rose higher than the rank of Lieutenant he was always referred to as 'Captain'. His grounding in Tory politics was earned through his post as secretary of a large suburban Conservative club. Middleton was convinced that the Liberal Party's organisational skills had to be met and matched, particularly after the further extension of the franchise in 1884 and the redistribution of seats the next year which increased the number of urban seats at the expense of those of rural MPs.

Originally it had been solicitors who had handled each association's affairs but, after the restrictions imposed in 1883 on local spending during election campaigns, their fees proved prohibitively expensive. Middleton's achievement lay in creating an extensive network of trained, full-time and professional agents. In 1891 a National Society of Conservative Agents was founded and by the end of the century full-time agents were employed in at least half the constituencies. It was the Conservatives and not the Liberals who first instituted a qualifying examination for prospective agents together with a monthly magazine and a pension fund.

As the Conservative Party expanded in the country, so inevitably did the character of the Party vary from region to region. Perhaps the most loyal of all Conservative cities was Liverpool: of its nine seats only one regularly returned a Liberal and even in its solidly working-class districts no Labour MP was elected until 1923. The Conservatives enjoyed uninterrrupted control of Liverpool for no less than a hundred years.

It was the Liberal Chamberlain family in Birmingham which had first shown how a city could be moulded into a political force by establishing a powerful caucus. In Liverpool, the main political influence was derived from the city's proximity to Ulster which gave areas of the city a distinct 'Orange' flavour and turned it into a stronghold of Conservatism. Religous differences were eagerly displayed and one onlooker, later Lord Woolton and a very influential figure within the Conservative Party, has provided a graphic picture of Liverpool life at the turn of the century:

We lived on the border between the Roman Catholic and the Protestant district in Liverpool. On the anniversary of the Battle of the Boyne, both in the north end and the south end of Liverpool, pandemonium reigned. The girls would wear orange or green hair-ribbons according to their religious adherence, flaunting their allegiance, be it said, rather than their belief, and they were not at all surprised when attacks were made on them by others, who attempted to cut off their hair with the offending ribbons. Bands of the Orange Lodges paraded the streets, singing songs about the Battle of the Boyne, and effigies of the Pope were carried – either as a demonstration of faith or as a provocation to the enemy: and far into the night in the Protestant area which was immediately adjacent to the Settlement people sat on their doorsteps and sang 'patriotic' songs. Then, quite suddenly, some ugly incident would arise and the battle would begin, ending for many either in the hospital or the police cell.

As in Belfast, the Catholics were often a persecuted minority who fought back physically, with the result that most elections were infamously rowdy affairs. In the 1860s the so-called 'Murphy Riots', named after a notorious anti-Catholic agitator Patrick Murphy who regaled his audiences with stories of weird Catholic sexual practices, convulsed Lancashire. Murphy himself came to a violent end: he was kicked to death by Irish Catholics in 1871. At times of religious controversy, churches were forcibly stormed and individuals beaten to death in the streets.

The Protestant majority in Liverpool spawned a form of populist Conservatism or Tory democracy which was hammered into shape by a succession of city bosses. The first of them was the very formidable Alderman Archibald Salvidge.

Learning from Daniel O'Connell, Salvidge fully understood the importance of 'the numbers game'. In 1892 he was elected chairman of the Liverpool Workingmen's Association and proceeded to remodel it entirely, setting up twenty-six new clubs and branches. Himself the son of a brewer, Salvidge was unusually sensitive to claims that the association was no more than a glorified drinking club. He therefore ensured that the Liverpool clubs were alchohol-free. Extending his hold first to the Liverpool Constitutional Association (local Tories sometimes preferred this less partisan word to that of 'Conservative') and then to the City Council itself, 'Boss Salvidge' as he was dubbed by friend and enemy alike kept a firm grip on political and religious affairs.

One of the stated objects of the Liverpool Workingmen's Association was 'to unite in maintaining Protestantism'. Any proposed legislation thought to pander to Catholicism or the High Church movement was met by implacable opposition from Salvidge and his supporters, an opposition which naturally included fights and riots.

Occasionally a handful of Liverpool Conservative MPs tried to break away from Salvidge's dominance, but if they valued their parliamentary careers they soon backed down. In 1927 seven Tory MPs raised the standard of revolt but withdrew it smartly.

Courted by national politicians, Salvidge was knighted in 1916 and made a Privy Councillor in 1922 but he preferred to stay in Liverpool and remain the biggest fish in a large local pond. It would be wrong, however, to dismiss 'the Dictator' simply as an uncouth reactionary or 'Tammany Boss'. Not only was the wife of this supposedly fanatical Protestant a Catholic but Salvidge favoured votes for women, raised money for strikers' families during a quarry strike in 1901, and ten years later in the face of Conservative opposition he secured the reinstatement of the railwaymen dismissed after another strike.

In 1921 Salvidge showed that in the last resort his loyalty was to the Conservative Party nationally when, despite intense Liverpool Protestant feeling, he argued in favour of accepting the division of Ireland. The die-hards or extreme right-wing Tories made him wonder 'whether the lunatic asylum should not be their place of abode'. For Salvidge, like many Conservatives, deals came before ideals.

The power of Conservatism in Lancashire also owed much to the political interests of the Derbys, an immensely wealthy landed family. The first Earl of Derby had played a decisive part at the Battle of Bosworth in 1485 which brought down Richard III and put Henry Tudor on the throne. His reward was to be granted all the estates in the North forfeited by Richard III's supporters. The Derby political tree clearly shows how large a part the family played in national politics, but they also made sure that their local base remained solid. The 17th Earl of Derby, for instance, had a rent-roll of £300,000 a year early this century – multiply that sum by fifty to get some idea of present-day values, and then remember that the standard rate of income tax at that time was one shilling in the pound.

Popularly known as the King of Lancashire, Derby's power and influence within the Conservative Party locally and nationally was formidable. His biographer, Randolph Churchill, noted that the Earl 'long held the view which, with a few exceptions, he successfully sustained throughout his life, that all patronage in Lancashire should pass through his hand'. Derby's machinations prompted opponents to call him the 'genial Judas'.

Derby always worked hand in hand with Alderman Salvidge. After Salvidge's death in 1928, the Derby patronage continued to be crucial in supporting Liverpool City bosses: Salvidge was succeeded by ex-cabin boy Sir Tom White, who eventually gave way to Sir Alfred Shennan, who in due course was replaced by Sir Ernest Stacey. One perk of the job was the automatic accession to the post of managing director of the local Bents Brewery (now Bass). Liverpool Conservatism long remained a closed society impervious to outsiders. When the young W.F. Deedes went to report on the local party for his newspaper in the mid-1930s, he found that 'It would have been easier to unravel Al Capone's affairs.'

Like Liverpool, Glasgow's politics also split on religious lines: Protestant Tories versus Catholic Liberals, later Labour. Both the Liverpool and Glasgow versions of Conservatism prided themselves on their rough, tough and steadfastly anti-Catholic character, so different from the genteel brand of Conservatism on offer in the Home Counties. The genius of the Conservative Party lay in its ability happily to embrace both strands.

The other major cities in the country also had their own formidable forms of Conservative organisation which were known as 'city associations'. These bodies once wielded immense power both in terms of local politics and the Conservative Party nationally. Some indication of their organisational strength is given by a study of Birmingham undertaken just after the Second World War. Each of the thirteen local associations had its own full-time agent together with secretarial assistance and the association could afford to employ more than thirty 'missioners', the name sometimes given to paid canvassers and subscription collectors. No fewer than a hundred people were on the Birmingham Conservative Party payroll in 1949.

Such powerful local control was not of course confined to the

Conservative Party: Herbert Morrison's London Labour Party was a stronghold of a different political persuasion, entrenched in County Hall across the river from Parliament. In the Conservative Party, however, local dominance was aided by the tradition of autonomy from the central party based in London. Funded by local businessmen, the City associations carefully excluded the area agents appointed by Conservative Central Office. Some City Conservatives helped their chances of election by standing not as Tories but as Municipal Association candidates; this bland flag of convenience meant that they could always accuse their Liberal and Labour opponents of unnecessarily bringing party politics into local affairs.

The roots of the strong Conservative Party presence in Liverpool and Glasgow grew out of both cities' religious identification. The weakening of this identity spelled long-term danger for the Party. The decline both of Protestantism and the influence of the kirk in Scotland since the 1950s was bound up with the collapse of manual labour. In 1955 there were thirty-six Scottish Tory MPs and the Party actually obtained a majority of the vote at that year's election; by 1992 the Conservative share of the vote had halved and they now have just eleven MPs.

After the Second World War, the city associations also started to wither away. In the past, continued success at elections had provided the most effective justification for their activities. The Conservatives won all twelve Birmingham seats at the 1935 general election, but in 1945 nine of the twelve were won by the Labour Party. By the 1960s the Birmingham city association had been reduced to just six paid employees. As for Liverpool, although one commentator in 1964 could still describe it as the 'last feudal fief' in the Conservative Party, a momentous event had in fact taken place nine years earlier when Labour won control of the council.

The *coup de grâce* for the associations was delivered by poor results in the 1964 and 1966 general elections. By the 1970s the city associations had been integrated into the national Conservative machine and the 'Municipal' label was also dropped. There would be no more talk of Al Capones or Chicago city bosses.

Instead a number of Labour council leaders were granted

mythic status by the media because of their alleged militancy: Ken Livingstone in London and Derek Hatton in Liverpool. Ironically, Hatton and Militant were merely copying some of the techniques which would have been familiar to Alderman Salvidge's Liverpool Conservatives.

More recently, however, a reminder of the past has surfaced in the shape of another Conservative 'city boss'. Dame Shirley Porter's control of Westminster council, one of the flagship councils in Britain, was always controversial but in January 1994 the Westminster district auditor published a report accusing Porter and several colleagues and officials of 'disgraceful, improper and illegal' behaviour in selling council homes at large discounts.

This policy had allegedly been carried out in such a way that the sales were directed at potential Conservative voters, particularly in eight marginal key wards, with the aim of protecting the Conservative majority at the then forthcoming elections in 1990. Similar allegations began to be levelled against other Conservative councils in London such as Wandsworth. No doubt this matter will rumble on through the law courts for several years, but it provided a reminder of old-style Tory city boss methods.

In general, however, the 1980s saw a weakening of local government inflicted by the Conservatives themselves – 85 per cent of local finance now originates nationally. Taken in conjuction with the contracting out of privatised services, few areas remain in which local councillors can exercise control and today's ambitious politician inevitably looks not to the town hall but to Westminster and Brussels.

The most visible of all the Party activities is the annual conference organised by the National Union of Conservative and Unionist Associations. Each year hundreds of delegates, commentators and voyeurs descend on either Blackpool or Brighton as Cabinet ministers try to woo the faithful with fresh policies announced first to them and not in Parliament. Fringe meetings are charged with passion and argument, but party managers try to ensure public agreement at the conference, particularly when the television cameras are switched on.

Many critics have been eager to dismiss the Conservative Party conference as either a rally for the simple-minded or a political beauty contest which stays well away from political discussion. Certainly the Conservative conference is a rather different creature from Labour's conference where policy is cobbled together by an arcane system of 'compositing' and trade union leaders cast millions of block votes on behalf of their members, many of whom in fact vote Conservative. Not a single ballot was held at the end of any debate at a Tory Party conference between 1950 and 1967.

Conservative conferences are less concerned with explicit policy: the motions are shorter and fewer than the Labour Party's resolutions and in any case, as we have seen, Conservatives prefer to embrace pragmatism and not give hostages to fortune. As with British Conservatism generally, the real power-broking takes place away from the public glare and therefore Tory conferences are more a matter of mood and impression; of informal personal contacts rather than printed words on the page. The historian of Conservative conferences, Richard Kelly, has noted that this model of a listening leadership rather than a voting membership reduces the possibility of factions and in-fighting.

The Conservative instinct for public unity ensures that contentious issues will rarely surface, but the representatives can and do make their feelings felt at fringe meetings and receptions where the cameras are absent. For the more fastidious party figures, conferences can be a trial: 'At our last party conference the audience would have been a credit to the zoo or wild regions of the globe,' wrote R.A. Butler, and Home Secretaries can usually expect rough treatment on the question of law and order and the reintroduction of capital punishment.

On this issue even the most popular senior Conservatives are not immune from criticism. In 1981 Home Secretary Willie Whitelaw was in the firing line:

I certainly both dreaded and disliked the prospect of the law and order debate, for the atmosphere was so strangely hostile and so different from that accorded to all one's colleagues . . . All seemed to be going quietly and therefore well, from my point of view, until one delegate made a fiery and brilliant speech in favour of capital punishment. He was applauded by Margaret Thatcher herself, who was sitting beside me on the platform. I certainly had no reason to complain about that because, bearing in mind her strong views, she was entirely entitled to do so. But naturally that in itself increased my isolation.

Worse was to follow. Another delegate spoke out against racism and was promptly booed by a large section of the audience. At this point even the normally placid and even-tempered Whitelaw had had enough and he proceeded to give the delegates a piece of his mind.

Generally the Party managers can prevent public dissension by discreet stage management. In his memoirs Cecil Parkinson shamelessly admits to introducing one now standard technique of manipulation: 'As chariman I had engineered standing ovations for speakers. This normally involved the platform rising as one as the speaker finished, and the audience taking the hint.'

There have been a handful of occasions when the conference has decided policy, most notably in 1950 when a debate on housing got out of party managers' control and the chanting delegates committed the Party to build 300,000 houses a year, a promise from which Harold Macmillan was able to extract maximum political mileage. In 1992, friction over Europe surfaced when Norman Tebbit whipped up some delegates into a vociferous anti-European mood.

In part this new aggressiveness was due to Mrs Thatcher's enthusiasm when leader in the 1980s for using the conference to browbeat Cabinet dissenters. As Kelly has observed:

During those years, she came to regard the conference not as an inconvenience, but as a chance to show doubting colleagues the extent of her support from the Party. When she felt under siege, particularly from what she saw as 'the establishment', she could rely on conference to boost her self-belief and renew her thirst for conflict. It played no small part in her eventual mastery of the Party.

Essentially the motions are selected for their timidity. They often congratulate the Conservative Government, but at times of trouble there are routine calls for better communication: the problem is never the message, simply the messenger. When a Labour Government is in power the motions crackle with condemnation, flaying socialist ineptitutude and lack of patriotism. A motion of 1949 is typical: 'That this Conference wholeheartedly deprecates the continual fostering and encouraging of bitter Class Hatred by Ministers of the present Socialist Government . . .'

Ultimately, the conference, like the Party generally, is more about display than policy. It is no coincidence that the motions passed at Labour Party conferences since the war have been three times as long as those passed at Conservative Party conferences. In addition, the Tory Party's structure makes it very difficult for factions to operate, unlike in the Labour Party, and thus the image of public unity is reinforced.

From time to time the television cameras at the annual conference will pan across the massed rows of Conservative delegates. At a glance, they seem to be just two sorts of people: either elderly ladies or else youngsters decked out with badges, frantically waving the Union Jack – hardly a representative cross-section of the British public.

Little academic research has been done on the composition and workings of the local associations. In part this demonstrates once again the success of the Conservative Party in deflecting interest away from its internal workings. It also indicates the difficulty of undertaking such research: each association traditionally regards itself as the best judge of its own interest and is always suspicious of Conservative Central Office. This jealously guarded autonomy even extends to keeping only scattered and fragmentary records. A minimum of information is held centrally.

Up to the Second World War, local associations were usually

dominated by the Member of Parliament and his, but rarely her, band of devoted supporters. In most safe constituencies there was an agent to keep an eye on things. The National Society of Conservative Agents might have been formed as long ago as 1891 but its existence has always been bedevilled by the issues of money and control. Who was to pay for the agent? If Central Office did so, then the agent was regarded with some suspicion by the local association. If it was the local association which stumped up the cash, then the agent was mistrusted by Central Office.

Typically, the minutes of the National Society of Conservative Agents only come to life when matters of professional standing are concerned. Meeting after meeting is devoted to the question of a professional examination for would-be agents, followed by the presentation of cutlery to retiring stalwarts. Virtually every motion is passed unanimously and political issues are rarely discussed.

These exclusively male agents were also perplexed by what their annual report of 1923–4 refers to as 'the somewhat difficult question of Women's Organization'. Continuing the tradition of the Primrose League, women were – numerically at least – a vital part of the Conservative Party. Throughout the 1930s the women's organisation claimed to have a membership of just below one million.

During the Second World War the Party's organisation fell into the doldrums and after the massive election defeat sustained in 1945 it was clear that an extensive overhaul was urgently needed. Churchill chose Lord Woolton to superintend the task. Formerly a businessman, Woolton had been a household name during the war as the Minister of Food; he was responsible for the unappetising 'Woolton Pie' which was meant to be nutritious yet sparing on vital rations – it was the first but not the last meat pie in history to contain no meat.

Woolton saw how vital it was that the Conservative Party after the war should be a mass-membership and fund-raising organisation. His business expertise prompted him to streamline and modernise the Party organisation, a striking example of the value of Conservative links with business. Trade union methods of organisation have served the Labour Party less successfully. Not only did Woolton launch a successful appeal for a sum of £1 million, he also tried to widen the social background of potential parliamentary candidates. He argued too that Conservatives 'must be capable of defeating Socialist theory with Conservative logic'. For the word 'logic', substitute 'organisation'.

Woolton's shake-up does seem to have transformed the Party, not just nationally – the number of party agents more than doubled between 1945 and 1950 – but also at grassroots level. Take St Marylebone Conservative Association in London. During the war its membership was no more than a few hundred and the association's records were scanty in the extreme. After the war the membership went up by leaps and bounds: 1,607 members in December 1946; 3,588 in December 1947; 4,629 in December 1948; 5,724 in December 1949; and in December 1950 it peaked at 6,860. In other words, membership quadrupled in just four years.

Even unpromising districts for Conservatives, such as the Labour stronghold of Islington in North London, were suddenly buzzing with fresh energy and new ideas. The association in East Islington, for example, published a well-produced bi-monthly magazine which covered political topics but also included pages on gardening, film and cooking, whilst South Islington Young Conservatives had their own journal called *Challenge*.

Outside of London, the story was the same. In Reading, for instance, membership of the association shot up to around 2,500 by the end of 1947 as local branches took on a new lease of life. But despite this seeming democratisation two particular families in Reading did continue to play a dominating role. As for membership activity, the emphasis was firmly on finance rather than political debate.

Overall, national membership of the Conservative Party peaked in 1952 at the remarkable figure of approximately 2,800,000 individuals. Women continued to carry out much of the more menial political work which needed to be done. According to Stuart Ball, 'Up to the 1940s this division of gender roles was generally accepted by Conservative women as the natural order, albeit with occasional grumbles as the men spent the money which the women had raised.'

In the last two decades, however, the traditional mass political party has been in steep decline. The Labour, Liberal and Conservative Parties have seen membership fall off dramatically. Neither Labour nor Conservative has ever kept totally reliable figures, but today the Labour Party has approximately 300,000 individual members, the Conservatives under half a million.

This decline in party membership has been most dramatically replicated in that of the Young Conservatives (YCs). The YCs grew out of the Primrose League, one of whose associated bodies was the grandly named Junior Imperial and Constitutional League (understandably known as the Jimps for short). Within eight years of its foundation in 1906, the Jimps claimed to have a membership of nearly 100,000.

It ceased to function during the Second World War and was reconstituted in 1945 as the Young Conservative and Unionist Organisation. By 1949 it had over 160,000 members and helped to promote the image of the Conservative Party as being comparatively youthful. As with the Primrose League, critics referred to it slightingly as the best marriage bureau in the country, but again the provision of social activities no doubt helped recruitment.

This was wonderfully brought out in the classic Tony Hancock episode *The Blood Donor*, written by Alan Galton and Ray Simpson and first transmitted in June 1961. Hancock solemnly tells the nurse that he has decided to do something for the benefit of the country as a whole: 'What should it be, I thought, become a blood donor or join the Young Conservatives? But as I'm not looking for a wife and I can't play table tennis, here I am. A body full of good British blood and raring to go.'

Many prominent senior Conservatives passed through the YCs but it was always a relatively quiescent body. Like the Conservative city associations, the YCs went into steep decline in the 1960s and 1970s, although there was a flurry of headlines in the Thatcherite era when the YCs swung heavily to the right. Delegates at the 1986 Conference sported badges with such charming logos as 'Kill Wets' and 'Hang Nelson Mandela'. According to the *Daily Telegraph*, total membership of the YCs is now around the 3,000 mark. In the 1950s, by comparison, membership of the Wimbledon branch of the Young Conservatives alone was 1,200.

The broad Conservative church is in danger of becoming more of a sect. The implications of this disintegrating basis of the Party are discussed at the end of the chapter.

What are the major characteristics of the Conservative Party away from Westminster? The dominating feature was, and still is, the independence of the local associations from centralised Party control. Relations between Conservative Central Office in London and the associations outside have always been uneasy. Each needs the other. Central Office relies upon the local activists and the money which the associations provide; the local associations need the propaganda skills and overall expertise of Central Office.

From time to time Central Office tries to win more centralising power. In recent years it has stipulated that associations now have to follow 'Model Rules' and may only choose 'approved' parliamentary candidates from the Central Office list, unless they are local; similarly the National Union, whose leadership works hand-in-hand with Central Office, now has the authority to disaffiliate dissident local associations. In particular, the centralising authorities within the Party would like to get their hands on the local associations' massive funds.

But the Conservative Party's instinctive preference for flexibility and informality means that no one part of the Party finds it easy to dictate to any other. In particular, Central Office has little patronage or influence which it can wield over association volunteers. Like the ideal model of the British Constitution, the Conservative Party is made up of a delicate series of checks and balances. Attempts, therefore, to encourage associations to widen their choice of parliamentary candidate and select more, any, working-class applicants have foundered on the rock of constituency autonomy.

A second characteristic is the prominent role which women have always played within the Conservative Party. This is, of course, a continuation of the Primrose League legacy and has given the Party access to a large, unpaid army of voluntary workers who have proved indispensable at election times. In 1965, the relatively unknown Margaret Thatcher told five thousand members of the National Union of Townswomen's Guilds at the Albert Hall: 'If you want something said, ask a man. If you want something done, ask a woman.'

A third feature is that most local Conservative associations in fact resolutely eschew political discussion and activity. One academic, Philip Tether, recently studied his own local Conservative association in Kingston-upon-Hull and found that the majority of the members were not in fact very interested in political activity. As Conservative MP Julian Critchley has put it, 'The Conservative Party is still in some ways the non-political political party.' Men and not measures are what count.

The value of 'presence', which is regarded as more important than political opinion or belief, was summed up by senior Conservative Walter Long as long ago as 1919: 'We owe our position in the country, and always have done, much more to local personal influence than to the popularity of our own political party.'

The great Victorian commentator Walter Bagehot observed in 1856 that 'The essence of Toryism is enjoyment', and it is not surprising that the social side of the Conservative Party has held up rather better than the more overtly political. Whilst party membership has slumped enormously, the number of Conservative clubs has declined only gently. There were about 1,500 clubs in 1948 and still around 1,350 at the end of the 1980s.

Labour Party members tend to place colleagues and opponents according to the colour of their political views. Within Conservative associations, the signifiers generally focus on appearance, accent or one's views about bloodsports or the BBC. Men wear a jacket and tie, women a dress or skirt rather than trousers.

Standard received pronunciation is essential. Sir Robert Peel was sometimes mocked by fellow MPs for the traces of a northern accent. Andrew Bonar Law was another Tory leader who was not out of the top drawer. One well-connected Tory, Lady Dawkins, recorded her impressions when hearing Bonar Law speak in public for the first time: 'I am bound to say that his personality and his voice with his Glasgow accent were a little disconcerting at first

(I felt rather as if I were being addressed by my highly educated carpenter).'

Similarly, Andrew Neil, former editor of the *Sunday Times*, has written of 'the length Edward Heath and Margaret Thatcher felt they had to go to adopt the speaking mannerisms of the traditional ruling classes'. Today, some Tories (and non-Tories) snobbishly mock John Major's voice.

Many local associations will have an ex-military man as one of their officers or as their agent; one observer of the 1950 election noted that 'the schedules of operations and voluntary workers' instructions read not infrequently like battle orders'. As for Conservative constituency chairmen, a survey conducted in 1969 found that 58 per cent of them were either in business or management. In other words they were members of what was once called the officer class and therefore accustomed to being in charge. Even the greater number of women association chairmen in position since the 1960s has, according to Stuart Ball, 'strengthened rather than loosened the middle-class hold on the leading positions, for whether career professionals or wives and mothers they nearly all come from the more affluent strata of local society'.

The informal unwritten codes which anyone who passes amongst Conservatives recognises as pervasive do not translate easily to paper. They are the kind of codes that prompted Central Office to canvass constitutency associations in 1952 to check that there would be no adverse reaction when the divorced Sir Anthony Eden, heir apparent to the Party leadership, planned to remarry. Similarly, Edward Heath's bachelor status was always a problem. Julian Critchley has written of how frequently people in his constituency would complain that he had no wife: 'The voters of Aldershot evidently much preferred dull wives to no wives at all.'

It is a mistake to think that the values of civility and niceness were random qualities. They emerged, as Ross McKibbin has shrewdly pointed out (in less than decorous prose), 'In the inter-war years when the Party was trying to incorporate fragments of the old Liberal Party and others who might have been offended by the robust style of the older Conservatism. Civility permitted an apolitical sociability and underpinned an associationalism which united hitherto disparate groups (particularly Nonconformist) into what was to become the modern Conservative Party.'

To argue that Conservatives are rarely political creatures is certainly not to claim that the Party and its members are strangers to passion and bitterness. Sir Geoffrey Howe's resignation in 1990 led to a leadership contest and the downfall of Mrs Thatcher. In his memoirs, Howe recalls that he was sent bags containing thirty pieces of silver – unsolicited gifts which he gave away to guide dogs for the blind.

A fourth characteristic was bluntly recognised by Philip Tether when he claimed that the 'closed environment' of Kingston-upon-Hull association was introspective and repelled new recruits: 'It [the Party] serves the function of a social club for a limited type of clientele – middle-aged to elderly, predominantly female but not exclusively so and completely middle-class in origin.'

Perhaps one should start by looking at some of the groups which the Conservative Party has never made very welcome. For instance, many associations in the past would never choose a Catholic to represent them. Lancashire in particular with its strong tradition of working-class Protestant Conservatism was one 'no go' area, but Lancashire was by no means unique. In 1924 Duff Cooper travelled to Stroud in Gloucestershire in order to meet the local officers, hoping to win the nomination but fearing that he would be asked all kinds of searching questions about agricultural matters: 'I was therefore relieved when the small party who received me, some six or seven ladies and gentlemen, only enquired concerning my health, my religion and the amount I was prepared to contribute to local expenses. When I say that they enquired concerning my religion I should make it plain that they wanted only to be assured that I was not a Roman Catholic.'

Until after the Second World War, Tory candidates were expected to state their religion on their Central Office form, which no doubt saved a lot of wasted journeys for would-be Catholic MPs. Today, the decline of the Church of England has undermined this orthodoxy.

Jews have also found it difficult to be accepted in party circles. Disraeli was subjected to a lengthy campaign of anti-Semitism by his colleagues and was routinely described at 'that damned Jew'. This century, it was Conservative MPs who led the campaign for an Aliens Bill which would restrict the immigration of Jews. As is often the case, the fiercest campaigners knew little of what they spoke. Sir Howard Vincent was the MP for Sheffield and warned of the tidal flood of illegal immigrants. In 1902, Sheffield had 21 'aliens'; by 1904 the number had swelled to 24. Birmingham's total of 121 in 1902 had gone down to 89 by 1904. And so on. An Aliens Act was eventually passed in 1906, but was not strictly enforced by the new Liberal govenment.

Anti-Semitism lived on. Tory backbencher Robert Sanders noted in his diary in June 1921 after a recent by-election: 'At St George's a number of people would not vote for Jessel because he is a Jew. Even in the Carlton one heard this said.' In his obsession with appeasement, Neville Chamberlain was prone to see Jewish-Communist plots everywhere; journalist James Margach has described how Chamberlain would respond to anyone who asked him a hostile question, saying that he was 'surprised that such an experienced journalist was susceptible to Jewish-Communist propaganda'.

Chamberlain's henchman Sir Joseph Ball ran a magazine called *Truth* which was vehemently anti-Semitic, whilst the Right Club was formed with the express purpose of ousting Jews from the Conservative Party. Sir Anthony Eden was another party leader who often indulged in anti-Semitic remarks.

The fall of Cabinet minister Leslie Hore-Belisha in 1940 was likewise applauded by some Conservatives on non-political grounds. Hore-Belisha had been a very successful Minister of Transport in the 1930s – responsible for introducing 'Belisha beacons', driving tests and the Highway Code – but his supposedly flashy and self-centred style brought accusations that he was a 'publicity-seeking Jew'. Scurrilous army marching songs ridiculed his Jewishness. He did not last long as Minister of War, but it is difficult to know whether his rapid downfall was due to anti-Semitism or because he lacked a political power-base having originally been a Liberal rather than a Conservative.

One notorious and more clear-cut example of party anti-Semitism came at the famous Orpington by-election in 1963 when the Conservative candidate Peter Goldman lost sensationally to the Liberal Eric Lubbock. On the face of it Goldman was an exceptionally promising candidate: a graduate of the high-powered Conservative Political Centre and the confidant of R.A. Butler whose memoirs he later helped to write. Although Goldman was energetic he was also arrogant and Jewish, soon managing to antagonise some of his voluntary workers.

It is impossible to say how much of this hostility was due to the difficult personality of Goldman himself, but after his defeat he blamed anti-Semitic elements in his own party for not giving him the support he thought he deserved. Goldman left politics and instead poured his formidable talents into the Consumer Association, turning *Which?* magazine from a scruffy pamphlet into the lynchpin of a large publishing empire.

On other occasions, Tory anti-Semitism is less overt. Harold Macmillan remarked in the 1980s that the Party was now dominated less by Etonians than Estonians and in his *Diaries* Alan Clark records various anti-Jewish observations. Sir Michael Latham, a Conservative MP for eighteen years, complained of 'the total silence from the Party hierarchy' about party anti-Semitism. Both Lord (Geoffrey) Howe and Julian Critchley in their memoirs have noted the anti-Semitic strain in the campaign which forced Leon Brittan out of office in January 1986. Critchley claimed that the vital meeting of the 1922 Committee 'resembled a pogrom'.

Fortunately Britain, unlike some other European countries, has no great tradition of anti-Semitism and in any case the bulk of the Jewish community seems to have shifted rightwards. This transition was exemplified by the Chief Rabbi Lord Jakobovits whose firm views on family values and self-reliance found a sympathetic listener in Mrs Thatcher, whereas she was clearly irritated by the liberal views of her Archbishop of Canterbury, Robert Runcie.

Some commentators noted that Mrs Thatcher appointed more Jews, five, to her Cabinets than any other Conservative Prime Minister. John Biffen's response was cautious:

It's difficult to talk about this: it puts people in a great tizz. But it just happens that the intellectual thrust of the new liberal economics substantially came from the Jewish intellectual elite. The Jews she had in Government were all very much of the new radical Right. They may not have been so identified with it as Keith Joseph, but Leon Brittan and David Young were part of the new, thrusting meritocracy. The Jewish community that she would have known in Finchley represented, I suspect, the Methodist values of Grantham to a very great extent.

It is not clear just how representative of grassroots opinion was this appointment of Jewish Cabinet ministers. Nigel Lawson felt impelled to note in his memoirs that 'it certainly demonstrated that there was not the faintest trace of anti-Semitism in her [Mrs Thatcher's] make-up: an unusual attribute'.

More usual seems to have been the resentment provoked amongst some sections of the Party, and Lord King, the former chairman of British Airways, once hinted obliquely to Mrs Thatcher that 'At the moment there is a feeling that you concentrate too much in selecting your advisers from north-west London.' This is the way in which discrimination manifests itself in the Conservative Party (and in many other organisations, for that matter), namely by hints and suggestions rather than by outright comment.

Very few delegates at the annual conference or in the higher echelons of the Party come from ethnic minorities. Once again, outright discrimination is rarely to be found. It is very rare for a Conservative candidate to campaign on an explicitly racist platform, as Peter Griffiths did at Smethwick in 1964 when he ousted senior Labour figure Patrick Gordon-Walker. For one thing, such an approach is usually electorally counterproductive, for another it breeches the Tory preference for civility and good manners.

One specific case arose when some activists at Cheltenham felt they were being bounced into accepting a favoured candidate, the black barrister John Taylor, to succeed the retiring MP, Sir Charles Irving. A handful of Conservative members were clearly appalled by the choice and volubly expressed racist sentiments. The Party leadership swiftly disowned their comments, but Taylor was defeated by the Liberal Democrat at the 1992 election. He has declined to stand again at Cheltenham, complaining that Conservative Central Office's idea of a race-relations policy was 'to have three or four receptions for Asian millionaires'.

Clearly there are racists on the fringes of the Conservative Party. The right-wing Monday Club, for instance, regularly called for repatriation in the 1960s and tried to organise their membership into country-wide branches. On the other hand, Edward Heath moved quickly to dismiss Enoch Powell from the Shadow Cabinet in 1968 after his 'rivers of blood' speech. Mrs Thatcher herself seems to have been ambivalent on matters of race and colour, rarely even genuflecting in the direction of racial equality – unlike her successor John Major.

Winning elections and retaining power are of paramount concern for Conservatives – and the Party is far too shrewd to risk throwing away votes by precipitous racist policies. That was the reason why, in the 1950s, successive Conservative governments did not oppose widescale immigration, fearing public disapproval if they did so. Today, it would be electorally short-sighted to let racism flourish.

To this end, in 1987 the Conservative Party laudably set up a body called 'One Nation Forum' to try and recruit support and membership from amongst ethnic communities, mainly in the inner cities. One senior figure in the Forum wrote that 'At heart, every ethnic community member is a Conservative . . . Living in inner cities, they are now a formidable force in the political sense. There are over 70 parliamentary seats where the ethnic votes are important if we were to win them.' An appeal to electoral advantage will generally prompt Conservatives to put their prejudices to one side.

On the Continent the rise of nationalism and unemployment have provoked a resurgence of the Far Right; here, although nothing could or should be taken for granted, the small but nasty British National Party is so obviously full of the intellectually challenged that it will make little headway.

'The great distinction of Britain is that for many centuries politics has not been the centre of life, not even for the handful of dignitaries who hold certain offices.' Shirley Robin Letwin was right: politics in Britain has always been a minority interest. Few people eagerly look forward to the prospect of addressing envelopes or sitting through dull meetings conducted in arcane language in draughty halls. Nor is doorstep canvassing with its polite and not so polite responses an attractive pastime.

But in the last two decades, political interest has declined even further. Membership of both the Conservative and Labour Parties is now less than a third of what it was at their peak in the 1950s. Typically, the Conservatives have always been vague about figures, preferring not to keep proper records. Membership seems to have peaked in 1952 at 2,800,000, declined to about 1,500,000 in the early 1970s and today is around the half a million mark – and dropping. Although the Conservative Party still has almost twice as many members as the Labour Party, as recently as 1973 it had nearly five times as many.

Even more striking is the profile of the typical Conservative member. The average age is a startlingly high sixty-three, and 77 per cent of members are aged fifty-five or over. For one thing, this elderly membership creates a problem in terms of political activity if nothing else: at the last general election in 1992, the Labour Party managed to field 160,000 canvassers in March and April 1992, the Tories – despite having more members – just 140,000 canvassers.

Three-quarters of members contribute no more to the Party than their membership fees, which, in the words of *The Economist*, 'they presumably regard as a sort of insurance premium against socialism'. As Stuart Ball has noted, 'Conservative Associations no longer play a central role in the social life of their communities, even in the most rural districts . . . In large swathes of contemporary Britain local Conservatism is no longer part of the rhythm of ordinary life.'

In particular, the available free time of middle-class women, a group on which the Conservative Party traditionally rested, has dwindled. This reflects a growing dissatisfaction amongst women generally with organised politics. A MORI poll in July 1993 found that 82 per cent of women between the ages of eighteen and twenty-four declared themselves uninterested in political activities, a damning indictment of the masculine bias of British politics, both Conservative and Labour.

It is not that people are no longer interested in the world around them: the membership of single issue groups and other voluntary organisations is phenomenal. For instance, the National Trust has over two million members, the Royal Society for the Protection of Birds has nearly a million, Greenpeace 350,000 members, Friends of the Earth 200,000 members and so on. In other words, 'politics' still matter but individuals are finding it more effective and worthwhile to bypass traditional political parties which remain wedded to old-style methods of politicking. Similarly the social side of political life which the Primrose League and then the Young Conservatives exemplified and profited from has been supplanted by the enormous growth of a vigorous entertainment and leisure industry shorn of direct political links.

The withering of the 'Conservative nation' with its local and provincial loyalties, as witnessed by the loss of the city associations and the decline of the Young Conservatives, underlines the problems facing the Tory Party. With its extensive social rather than political dimensions, the Conservative Party once offered members a set of defined and welcoming loyalties. It was as though the associations socialised and the big boys got on with the politics, yet there were enough people in the associations to suggest that the big boys were not simply playing a private game.

This is less straightforward today, as party officials clearly recognise. In October 1994 the Conservatives launched a national membership campaign to try and boost numbers. Its campaign pack stressed the ordinariness of Party members, claiming that the unemployed, immigrant groups and 'people like you join the Conservatives'. The pack recommended that local associations should levy a membership fee of £20 a year, a figure which seems unlikely to bring great numbers of the unemployed flocking to join the Party.

The implications of the decline of the Conservative Party as a mass political organisation will show themselves throughout the rest of this book. For one thing, it is sharpening the antagonism between associations and Central Office. A number of associations resent what they see as Central Office's lack of constructive help and have turned instead to outside political consultancies for help in fighting elections.

But perhaps the most important consequence is financial. Fewer members means less money – and the Conservative Party has always been an expensive organisation to maintain.

7

Money Matters

Financing the Conservative Party

'*Our one great advantage*: WEALTH. Let us use it. Its expenditure should be regarded as an insurance premium.'

Stanley Baldwin, 1927

'As Tory Party treasurer between 1975 and 1990, and one of the chief gatekeepers to Margaret Thatcher's inner circle, he [Lord Alistair McAlpine] raised more than £100 million for the cause, money that went a long way to ensuring that the 1980s were a decade of one-party rule.'

The Times, 19 June 1993

'To what extent a bigger budget buys more votes in an election is a matter for argument, but money certainly doesn't lose an election.'

Martin Linton, *Guardian*, 14 April 1994

The Conservative Party has always tried to ensure that its internal workings are kept well away from the public gaze. In particular, it has excelled at maintaining the secrecy which surrounds the most basic question of all, namely how is the Party financed?

From time to time there is a brief flurry of media interest. As long ago as August 1927, for instance, the *Daily Mail* argued that Conservative finances should be open for public scrutiny. To the relief of the Party's managers the furore quickly died away and to this day Conservative Central Office has never yet published a proper set of audited accounts. In fact, between 1979 and 1984 the Party issued no accounts whatsoever.

In the summer of 1993 the allegations of fugitive businessman Asil Nadir once again ignited press excitement about the topic. Nadir claimed that he had discreetly donated nearly £1.5 million to the Party in the expectation of receiving a knighthood, an honour which did not materialise. Prompted by Nadir's claims, newspapers and magazines turned their attentions to the Party's finances and soon revealed the huge sums of money involved. Since 1985 the Conservative Party has received over £70 million in unexplained and anonymous donations whilst Lord McAlpine, treasurer for much of Mrs Thatcher's period in office, was said to have raised £23 million solely for the crucial 1987 general election.

Central Office's reluctance to discuss the matter only fuelled the rumours. A series of offshore trusts supposedly laundered vast sums of money gifted by foreign supporters not even eligible to vote in British elections. Various tycoons – from Greek shipowner John Latsis to a bevy of Hong Kong businessmen – were alleged to be bankrolling the Party. There were even tales in the *Guardian* of suitcases containing millions of pounds being flown in from Saudi Arabia on private jets, stories which were subsequently retracted by the newspaper.

After a week or two, journalists moved on to fresh topics and different headlines. In April 1994 the House of Commons Home Affairs Committee issued a report on political funding which, predictably enough, split along party lines. The report issued by the Conservative majority on the committee gave the existing system a clean bill of health and recommended that there was no need for change. One of the great unmentionables of British politics was once again pushed firmly back into the closet

Despite this Conservative reticence, however, the importance of the issues ensure that they never stay in the closet for long. In late 1994 the owner of Harrods, Mohamed Al-Fayed, claimed that he had given huge donations to the Conservatives, amounting to a quarter of a million pounds in the election year of 1987 alone:

'They were delighted because they didn't have to disclose the money publicly because my company is a private one.'

The short-lived press campaigns invariably concentrate on possible Tory involvement with a number of shady and not-so-shady businessmen. Yet by honing in on this target, the equally important links between the Conservative Party and various sections of British industry – road construction, the banks, insurance companies, the tobacco industry and armaments firms – were and are almost completely ignored.

By focusing, too, on the resources of Conservative Central Office the substantial wealth of local Party organisations also gets overlooked: the associations in the Wessex Area alone, for instance, are estimated to have at least £3 million in various bank accounts which are kept well away from the clutches of the London headquarters.

So how exactly is the Conservative Party financed, by whom, why and with what results?

Money is at the heart of all political activity, simply because running a political organisation is expensive. Conservative Central Office in London eats up more than half a million pounds a week and the 1992 general election campaign alone cost the Party well over £20 million.

It was not always like this. In 1870 Central Office had a staff of just three full-time officials plus three secretaries. Thirty years later the Party was still financed largely by the Salisbury family who were based at Hatfield House. But in Britain general elections have never taken place at fixed intervals, unlike in the United States and many other countries, and political parties therefore needed to keep a bureaucracy permanently in existence. These bureaucracies have grown inexorably.

Towards the end of the nineteenth century it was becoming clear that the arrival of modern political parties complete with paid officials, election specialists, propaganda experts, agents and so on was an inevitable development. The Corrupt and Illegal Practices Act of 1883 had placed limits on candidates' expenditure at local level but it had said nothing about local spending between elections or, crucially, about restrictions at national level. Money, therefore, could make a political difference. How was this money to be raised?

The problem was not entirely new. English and Scottish kings had always been short of money in the past, particularly when Parliament started to demand a say in how revenue was raised. One way of circumventing parliamentary complaint was to sell honours to the wealthy and ambitious. On his coronation day in 1603, James I knighted no fewer than 432 individuals. In 1612 he introduced baronetcies which cost £1,000 a time and two years later he began selling off peerages, raising well over £600,000 in the process.

Early Conservative leaders frowned upon any underhand dealing: both Lord Liverpool and Sir Robert Peel were models of rectitude. Benjamin Disraeli, however, as one might expect from a politician who had been prepared to use his Young England group as a secret vehicle for French policy in return for funds, was rather more flexible. He was happy to exploit the honours system in order to keep his supporters in line. Essentially, however, the monetary needs of the Party were still limited because candidates either financed themselves at elections or were assisted by Tory peers who were expected to help candidates in their own counties.

The 1883 Act curtailing local election expenditure, together with the expansion in the size of the electorate, heralded the arrival of mass politics and the necessary creation of central party staff who had to be paid. Aristocratic money was no longer sufficient, particularly as many wealthy landowners had suffered during the agricultural depressions of the 1870s and 1880s and were now less generous donors.

The easiest way to raise money was by tapping the coffers of the new breed of Victorian businessmen desperately keen to advertise their arrival in society with the addition of a title. Only four business-men were ennobled between 1876 and 1886 but then eighteen followed in the next ten years. Many of the so-called parvenus were from industries eager for recognition, especially the 'beerage' as some critics sniffily described the newly titled brewers.

Perhaps the majority were worthy recipients and would have been honoured anyway. Surely, the argument went, it did not matter if these fabulously wealthy men contributed a little something to speed up the process. The Conservative Party also endeavoured to raise money from the beleagured rajas in India who hoped to enlist British power to defeat the growth of local nationalism, thus prefiguring more recent accusations about 'outsider' funding.

Not everyone was happy with these sorts of arrangements. In 1891, for instance, Lord Salisbury's Conservative Government preferred to lose a parliamentary seat rather than be pressured into granting a baronetcy to a Conservative backbench MP threatening to resign.

But of course it was much easier to promise future titles when in opposition; ironically the first time this happened was when the morally superior Gladstone was still leading the Liberal Party. In 1891, the year the Conservatives were frowning upon such practices, the Liberals agreed to sell peerages to two influential supporters called Stern and Williamson. After the Liberals were returned to office in 1894 the deals duly went through.

Another even more devious arrangement saw the Liberals awarding a baronetcy to a Conservative MP called Naylor-Leyland. In return, he was to resign his parliamentary seat, thus forcing a by-election which the Liberals were confident that they would win. This by-election success would provide a welcome fillip to party morale.

Such illicit activities soon became customary. Details are naturally hard to come by – no businessman wanted it known that his title owed more to the depth of his pockets than to the merits of himself. Identities had to be protected, but it is clear that the sums of money exchanged were enormous. Financier Ernest Hooley, later to end up at the Old Bailey on criminal charges, gave £50,000 to Conservative Party managers in the hope of a baronetcy, having already spent £40,000 just to purchase membership of the Carlton Club, the London club patronised by the Tory elite. Waldorf Astor, father-in-law of Nancy, shelled out over half a million pounds in 1900 in the expectancy of a title.

Even Lord Salisbury himself seems to have become rather more lavish when it came to doling out honours in the later years of his premiership. One contemporary claimed that Salisbury had created 'so many knights and baronets as to justify the saying that you cannot throw a stone at a dog without hitting a knight in London'.

Salisbury's nephew and successor as both Conservative Party leader and Prime Minister, A.J. Balfour, followed his uncle's example. Balfour's resignation honours list in 1905 contained no fewer than forty-five names, a number only to be equalled in Lloyd George's more infamous list of 1922. To give an idea of the tariff: a Mr S.W. Duncan paid over £20,000 to Central Office in 1905 for a baronetcy.

It is also clear that not just titles were on offer. The Balfour Papers in the British Library contain one fleeting example of the sort of transactions which took place. In 1899 an obscure Tory MP called Spencer threatened to resign his seat, which would have meant a worrying by-election for the government. Balfour persuaded him to relent, offering a knighthood as an inducement. Spencer accepted but then promptly changed his mind as to what reward he felt sufficient.

The exasperated Chief Whip Akers-Douglas had to write to Balfour, commenting that Spencer now wanted 'his pound of flesh in another shape', namely the Lunacy Commissionship. On reflection, Mr Spencer had clearly felt that the financial rewards of the commissionship outweighed the attractions of being a knight. Stray references such as this hint at the size of an issue which will never be uncovered in full because of the ease with which incriminating evidence can be destroyed. Why commit such indiscretions to paper?

Party managers were naturally careful to keep such matters hidden away. After the crushing election defeat in 1906, Akers-Douglas wrote to Balfour wholeheartedly supporting the appointment of a committee to examine the state of the Party. The committee should have the widest possible terms of reference, 'safeguarding only Finance or rather [the] Party Fund for obvious reasons'.

Of the major commercial interests that supported the Conservatives, many of which had fled the Liberal camp after the split over Home Rule in the 1880s, the most generous were the brewers. Several brewers were already Tory MPs who had been elected, as W.D. Rubinstein has pointed out, 'in constituencies where they were among the chief employers of labour'.

The brewers' financial assistance to the Tory Party was not of course philanthropic. Apart from the money itself, during election times pubs were traditionally regarded as Tory committee rooms. In return, the brewers expected the Party to protect their interests. In 1908, for instance, the Liberal government tried to introduce new licensing legislation which infuriated the brewers, especially when the bill made its successful way through the House of Commons. In the words of one historian:

> The brewers were determined to prevent any surrender by the Lords, and organised a costly and at times violent campaign against the measure. They poured money, propaganda and men into the by-elections, organised demonstrations, threatened to boycott charities and tradesmen, and even warned the Conservative Party that they would withdraw their funds if the measure passed.

It didn't. Many years later Lloyd George, himself no stranger to the more murky sides of political fund-raising, claimed that 'The attachment of the brewers to the Conservative Party was the closest approach to political corruption in this country.'

Although the Conservatives were out of power for nearly ten years before the First World War, they were none the less happy to accept money in return for the promise of future honours. Chief Whip Acland-Hood managed to establish a fund of no less than £300,000 and party chairman Sir Arthur Steel-Maitland continued such arrangements. And of course various arguments could always be made to validate the practice: if a political party was a force for good then surely giving money to it could be deemed a public service?

Sometimes assistance to the Conservatives took a non-monetary form but was very welcome none the less. In the Coventry area during the 1910 elections, for instance, the Rover, Swift and Daimler car companies supplied vehicles to party candidates which then helped transport supporters to the polls. The Conservatives' greater access to cars on election day was for decades a perennial Opposition complaint.

Finance was sometimes available on a personal basis: Max Aitken helped out his friend Andrew Bonar Law, leader of the Conservatives after 1911, with an annual gift of £10,000 and once paid the massive sum of £30,000 to get another fellow Conservative, the pugnacious and hard-living F.E. Smith, out of a scrape. Central Office also maintained – and still does – a discretionary fund to help out Tory MPs who got into financial difficulties.

It soon became clear that a new profession had been borne: that of the 'honours tout' who specialised in putting would-be recipients in touch with the powers that be. The most famous tout of them all was the extraordinary J. Maundy Gregory who, with a true lack of prejudice, flourished under all governments whatever their persuasion: Liberal, Conservative or coalition.

Maundy Gregory's early career was a sorry saga of failed business ventures: plays that crashed in the West End, surefire investments which collapsed and a seedy detective agency which spied on hotel guests. But like all conmen, Maundy Gregory knew the value of style. He was always driven around London not in a Rolls-Royce but in his own private taxi. Swathed in flashy jewellery, he ate at the finest restaurants and even set up his own club, The Ambassador, at 26 Conduit Street, Mayfair.

Naturally Maundy Gregory installed himself in an elegant set of offices opposite Big Ben and ran his own grandly named magazine *The Whitehall Gazette and St James's Review* which featured anyone wanting publicity – provided, that is, they paid for the privilege. As for Gregory's honours tariff, £100,000 in his direction purchased a peerage, £40,000 a baronetcy and £10,000 a knighthood.

The Maundy Gregory saga is embellished by his own unashamed boasting. Unsurprisingly he claimed to have links with the secret service, declaring proudly that 'in my work of counter-espionage I employed 1,000 agents'. Even if Gregory exaggerated the number of his 'operatives', it does seem probable that MI5 was happy to use the information picked up via his hotel detective agency.

It is clear, too, that Gregory did in fact have many high-level contacts – he was an usher at the wedding of the Duke of York, the future George VI – and his services were used both by Lloyd George, desperate after his split with the official Liberals to build up his own party fund, and also by the Conservatives. The Party leadership turned a Nelsonian blind eye to his activities.

Eventually, however, rather too many of the honours began to attract unwanted publicity. Lloyd George shamelessly invented the award of the Order of the British Empire (OBE) and had distributed over twenty-five thousand of them by the end of 1922. He also honoured no fewer than forty-nine journalists between 1918 and 1922 and created ninety-one peers in just six years. Such activity was bound to antagonise existing peers who felt that their titles were being devalued.

Questions were asked in both Houses – though not answered by Lloyd George. Finally, a Select Committee was set up which led to the creation of a scrutiny system that still operates today. Subsequently, names of possible recipients have been presented to a committee made up of senior politicians from all three parties.

Although individual Tories were happy enough to attack what they dubbed '£loyd George and the £iberals', their own party managers had not been entirely innocent. Conservative Party chairman Sir George Younger was happy enough to raise money via honours awarded by Lloyd George's coalition government. It was the Conservatives, for instance, who had nominated William Vestey for a peerage in 1922 which he duly received, even though it was public knowledge that during the First World War the Vestey dynasty had transferred their business empire abroad so that they would not have to pay tax. George V was furious at this award – but the Conservative Party was £20,000 better off.

Sir George Younger once wrote to party leader Stanley Baldwin in 1927 about the issue of raising money, and his letter is a masterpiece of ambiguity: 'I never, so to speak, sold an honour, nor did I ever make any bargains; but from time to time, I did raise a substantial contribution and I agree with old Lord Salisbury that no great Party can be run unless the Fund from time to time can be so strengthened.'

One feels, so to speak, that Sir George was being decidedly economical with the truth.

The system of selling honours relied upon absolute discretion and the more people involved the more chance there was of disclosure. The worst fears of the Party managers came true when the aged Conservative Party treasurer, Lord Farquhar, went senile in 1922. In his confused state, Farquhar refused to hand over the £1 million of party money which he had kept in his personal bank account, arguing that it was in fact coalition money. The money could not be touched without his approval.

Apart from Farquhar's mental condition, the problem was exacerbated by the fact that, despite the magnitude of the sums involved, nothing had ever put down in writing. The papers of Tory leader Andrew Bonar Law are full of frantic letters trying to ascertain exactly who had said what to whom. For example, the tycoon Viscount Astor had clearly handed over the monumental sum of £200,000 as a gift − but no one knew who it had been given to, and Astor himself was no help as he had since died. Some of the money was intended for charities nominated by King George V, some for the Conservatives and some for Lloyd George. But in what proportions?

Bonar Law himself interviewed Farquhar and found him 'so "gaga" that one does not know what to make of him', but the elderly peer still obstinately refused to hand over the money. The Conservatives had to make hurried efforts to raise finance from other sources. Bonar Law peremptorily dismissed Farquhar: 'As I told you to-day I think the time has come for making a change in the Treasurer of our Party and I therefore give you notice that from to-day you have ceased to occupy that position.'

Fortunately for the Party, Lord Farquhar died soon afterwards and Sir George Younger was then able to get his hands on the disputed riches. A new system was swiftly instituted. From then on, the money was to be kept in a trust account which had at least three trustees.

The new Conservative leader, Stanley Baldwin, was temperamentally hostile to the sleaziness that he felt Lloyd George had introduced into British politics and he tried to remedy the situation. His government introduced the Honours (Prevention of Abuses)

Act in 1925 which made it a criminal offence to obtain money by offering to procure honours.

Meanwhile, it seems clear that Baldwin's lieutenant, party chairman J.C.C. Davidson, had realised that the extraction of money from private individuals in the old way was now counterproductive and damaging. It was better to turn to more legitimate sources of funds, namely the City and businessmen who were becoming alarmed in the 1920s by the rise of the Labour Party.

Davidson understood that the 'haves' were more than happy to finance a party which would ensure that the 'have-nots' were kept in their place. At one fund-raising dinner he jotted down his targets: 'Oil. Newspapers. Prudential. Banks. Railways. Merchant [bankers] – London; – South American.'

The kind of people who helped the Conservative Party included the Rothschild family which regularly gave £12,000 a year and, it was remarked with relief, demanded nothing in return. £5,000 a year came from Sir John Ellerman, reputedly the wealthiest private individual Britain has ever seen. Originally trained as an accountant, Ellerman moved into shipping and then expanded his business empire to include newspapers, magazines and property in the West End of London. He owned huge chunks of Chelsea, South Kensington and the Oxford Street area.

Ellerman shrouded his affairs in the utmost secrecy, rarely leaving his huge Victorian mansion in Mayfair even to visit a church or a restaurant and never being photographed. Britain's answer to Citizen Kane, he planned his family's lonely and anti-social life down to the minutest detail, whispering at meal times in case the servants heard something they shouldn't. He prevailed upon his wife to give up her friends: 'He keeps me in a glass case,' she once remarked, 'but I keep him human.' It doesn't sound like most people's idea of humanity.

After Ellerman's death in 1933, at the depth of the Depression, his estate was still valued at over £36.5 million – in the region of £1,000 million at today's values. Understandably, Ellerman's son reacted against his father's material obsessions and instead established an international reputation as an animal specialist, publishing a three-volume work called *The Families and Genera of Living Rodents*.

However, this did not stop Sir John Ellerman junior from also giving donations to the Conservative Party, including the huge lump sum of £10,000 in the late 1930s in order to counter what he considered to be the pernicious influence of publisher Victor Gollancz's Left Book Club.

With the Rothschilds and Sir John Ellerman to hand, it is not to be wondered at that in the late 1920s Davidson managed to raise over £1 million in just three years. His trump card was always the alleged threat of revolutionary agitation and at one City lunch in November 1928 he secured no less than £130,000.

Doubts linger as to how thoroughly Davidson and Baldwin cleaned up the old sale of honours racket. It is odd, for example, that despite the passage of the 1925 Act, Maundy Gregory continued to flourish as a businessman and was not in fact prosecuted until February 1933. Gregory's Ambassador Club was still patronised by the Prince of Wales, the future Edward VIII, whilst his famous Derby Eve Dinners were attended by influential politicians; Davidson himself was present at the 1931 event.

Davidson might have clamped down on any explicit sale of honours but in the Conservative world where most matters of importance are settled behind closed doors, a word here and a handshake there proved more than sufficient. When the highflying civil servant Patrick Gower was enticed into joining Central Office in 1927, he demanded a suitable honour together with compensation for his lost pension rights. Gower was promptly knighted whilst the tobacco baron Sir Gilbert Wills was delighted to help out financially. Wills was soon raised to the peerage.

Another fleeting reference in Davidson's papers concerns the Independent MP J.M. Erskine who represented a traditionally Tory safe seat in Colchester which the Party badly wanted back: 'He is prepared to resign from St George's for a knighthood and £15,000', noted Davidson. The Conservative Party chairman's memo then went on to add, 'In 1922 Bonar Law offered him a Baronetcy and £10,000.' Clearly Mr Erskine's seat was much prized by the Party.

One specialist on the Conservative Party between the wars, Dr John Ramsden, has vividly concluded of Davidson's reforming efforts: 'The whole operation was rather less like the cleansing of an Augean stable than the periodic clearing out of a rabbit hutch.'

The eventual prosecution of Maundy Gregory under the 1925 Act was prompted by his attempt to obtain an honour for a retired Lieutenant Commander who was horrified when he realised that he was expected to pay for his title. The disgusted Lieutenant Commander went to the authorities who clearly had no alternative but to bring a prosecution. In February 1933 Maundy Gregory pleaded guilty at Bow Street Magistrates' Court to charges of illegally trying to secure an honour.

Gregory had hired the young up-and-coming barrister Norman Birkett to defend him, but his guilty plea meant that he never produced in court the damaging evidence which might well have implicated several influential political figures. The plea was almost certainly extracted from Gregory in return for the promise of a future pension. After two months in Wormwood Scrubs Maundy Gregory was released and departed for France. There he lived in exile under the name Sir Arthur Gregory on a quarterly pension of £2,000 a year.

Who paid for Gregory's pension? It is now known that this generous pay-off came via the Conservative Party. The money was provided by a Sir Julien Cahn in a deal brokered by Conservative leader Stanley Baldwin, which rather contradicts the image of squeaky-clean honesty propagated by Baldwin himself and faithfully repeated by historians.

Details of the arrangement only emerged in 1977 when David Marquand published his biography of Ramsay MacDonald who was then Prime Minister, and heading a national government in which the Conservatives played the dominating role. Apparently the matter was first raised in December 1933 when Baldwin told MacDonald that £30,000 would clear away Maundy Gregory, but that the sponsor Sir Julien Cahn expected his knighthood to be upgraded into a baronetcy. Cahn already paid Central Office £2,000 a year and clearly felt that any extra sum entitled him to demand something in return.

Five months later, MacDonald noted bitterly in a diary entry dated 19 May, 1934: 'Mr B . . . involves me in a scandal of honour by forcing me to give an honour because a man has paid £30,000 to get Tory headquarters and some Tories living and dead out of a mess.' Cahn duly became a baronet in June 1934. It is clear that Gregory could easily have produced evidence at any court hearing which would have discredited the Conservative Party.

Caught up in the German occupation of France at the outbreak of the Second World War, Maundy Gregory was to die in an internment camp in September 1941. Inevitably his papers were mislaid. For all his bombast and misbehaviour, he was one of the great characters of British political life and his career reveals more about the workings of the Conservative Party than that of many orthodox figures. Maundy Gregory's activities form part of the hidden history of the British Conservative Party.

Davidson was also involved in raising large sums of money from party supporters such as newspaper magnate Lord Beaverbrook, who enjoyed a sometimes tempestuous relationship with the Conservatives. Few people ever outwitted Beaverbrook but in 1929 Davidson seems to have managed it. He accepted a donation of £10,000 from him in the run-up to the election, ensuring that the *Daily Express* and his other publications were 'on side' throughout the campaign.

After the election was over, Davidson promptly returned the money with a curt note: 'As I have had no occasion to make use of the money I return it herewith.' Davidson had got what he wanted – newspaper support – but without being under any obligation to Beaverbrook.

Letters in the Davidson papers from Party accountant Sir Maxwell Hicks also show the existence of a secret chairman's account about which even Hicks knew little. To give some idea of the sums involved: the 1929 election cost the Conservative Party a little under £300,000, of which just over half was provided by donations. The shortage of £141,000 – a very large sum indeed – came from the secret account via money that Davidson had raised personally through individual and undisclosed sources. Six years later, in January 1936, Sir Maxwell was still in the dark about two trusts referred to as Y and Z, 'which are earmarked for special purposes'. The chairman's account also allowed payments to party figures in financial trouble: Lord Birkenhead received a gift of £3,500 in June 1926.

Important as this cloak-and-dagger element undoubtedly was to Tory Party finances, it should be remembered that much money at this time was not only raised locally by party associations but was spent by them too. Alfred Duff Cooper was the Tory MP for Oldham in the late 1920s and in his memoirs he noted, 'The strong attachment to the Conservative cause that exists among the working class surprised me. No appeal was made for funds, but at each election several hundred pounds were contributed in shillings, half-crowns and larger denominations from the electorate.'

The most fruitful source of revenue was the bazaar or fête at which the local MP and one national politician would speak. The walls of many constituency offices today still contain photographs showing the local Tory MP of the 1930s, sitting in the front row of a crowded platform, socks and a plentiful expanse of bare leg on display, gazing up at party leader Stanley Baldwin as he holds forth on the eternal verities of British Conservatism. Local associations were careful to safeguard their financial autonomy against Central Office encroachments or interference.

J.C.C. Davidson had been responsible for instituting a two-pronged approach to raising money. On the one hand there were the prosperous City and business interests; on the other, these small subscribers up and down the country were happy to contribute what they could. This second source of finance was in fact only really developed after the Second World War by the then party chairman, Lord Woolton. Although not a particularly well-known name today, Woolton was one of this century's most influential Conservative politicians.

Brought up in Liverpool before the First World War, Woolton was originally a Fabian socialist who was employed by the big department store of David Lewis. During the 1914–18 conflict he worked as the Civilian Boot Controller, an experience which convinced him of the dangers of bureaucracy and of stultifying controls imposed by civil servants who knew nothing about the industries they were supposed to be supervising. Churchill put Woolton in charge of the Ministry of Food during the Second

World War and then in July 1946 appointed him chairman of a dispirited and badly beaten Conservative Party still reeling from the crushing election loss the previous year.

Woolton set about trying to reinvigorate an almost moribund organisation by bringing his business skills to bear. He was determined to set the Party on a sound financial footing and launched an appeal for a fund of £1 million. Everyone said it would be impossible to raise such a massive sum in the straitened financial circumstances after the war, but Woolton understood full well the psychological impact of this almost mythical sum:

> Great enterprises are not furthered by trafficking with compromise or by the fear of failure. I realized that Conservatism was in peril and I remembered my experience years before, in Liverpool, when an appeal for four hundred pounds failed, whilst one for ten thousand – for the same object – succeeded. I rejected caution and decided to ask for a fund of one million pounds, thereby demonstrating my faith in the willingness of the Party to make sacrifices in order to convince the electors of the country of the rightness of the Conservative approach. These were shock tactics. I doubt very much whether I would have got the quarter of a million; it would have appeared so easy that nobody would have bothered working for it, but the demand for a million gave the Party the thrill of high endeavour. What was even more important was that they knew that we could not afford to fail.

In fact Woolton raised nearly £2 million and his campaign helped transform the Conservative Party into a mass-membership and fee-paying body. He also introduced a Central Board of Finance together with twelve area treasurers. Woolton's flair for publicity meant that anything good which happened to the Party was usually thought of as due to him. The egoism and arrogance of his memoirs duly magnified his own undoubtedly important role.

But if Woolton's public and acceptable activities await further examination, so too do the more dubious methods which he superintended. In 1948, for instance, the Conservative Party completed the reorganisation of its finances by setting up a network of eight so-called 'rivers companies' named after minor English waterways.

These seemingly innocuous companies in fact acted as intermediaries, allowing unidentified individual and business donors to make secret gifts to the Party without revealing their true destination in company accounts. The rivers companies also laundered money by getting around the legal provision that money from trusts was not to be left to political parties.

Woolton was full of admiration for the subtlety of this ruse and he wrote triumphantly to party leader Sir Winston Churchill in December 1948: 'Our lawyers have, in fact, given us a very ingenious solution to a problem that, up to now, has eluded those concerned with political funds.'

Details of these rivers companies only leaked out in 1988, additional testimony to the skill with which the Conservative Party has hidden its secret history. In large part, this concealment was successful because party officials knew when not to ask questions. In October 1953, director-general Sir Stephen Pierssene referred to donations from undisclosed and secret subscribers and wrote simply: 'I know nothing (and prefer to know nothing) of revenue from this source . . .' We know that at least one-third of the Party's total income between 1954 and 1963, for instance, was obtained through these rivers companies.

Another technique was devised to help companies sensitive about funding the Conservative Party directly. The Party set up a series of 'cut out' organisations which laundered funds through seemingly neutral sources. The most important of these bodies was formed in 1960 under the title British United Industrialists (BUI). BUI had a staff of just one person and received donations which were then, for a small handling fee, passed on to the Conservative Party. The accounts of the company involved therefore remained 'clean'. As the director-general of BUI, Alastair Forbes, emphasised in the run-up to the 1987 election:

> We believe that a donation to BUI is less emotive than a donation to the Conservative Party. Large donations from public companies must go through their boards for approval.

Even private companies, depending on their share structuring, may find it necessary to seek board approval. Donations through us are, however, not deemed to be political donations and a single telephone call from me will trigger an invoice plus VAT on which a payment can be made.

BUI was also adept at staying one step ahead of the law. A limited company until 1968, it was then dissolved and became instead an unincorporated association. This alteration in status meant that the BUI was not covered by the Companies Act passed in 1967 and therefore did not have to disclose in its annual accounts how much money had been contributed to the Conservative Party.

The one precondition essential to the BUI was that its workings remained hidden from public view. By 1992 excessive publicity meant that this was no longer the case and the organisation was closed down. In its forty-year existence the BUI is thought to have channelled at least £10 million into party funds.

Other intermediaries that do still exist include the Conservative Industrial Fund which was set up in 1948 and allows political donations not to bear the words Conservative Party, and also the organisation known as Aims. Formerly called Aims of Industry and founded in 1942, Aims concentrates on producing propaganda in favour of the free enterprise system, an objective which ensures that it is hostile towards the Labour Party. It is certainly well funded; in the mid-1960s it possessed a full-time staff of twenty together with twenty clerical staff. At the 1983 general election, for example, Aims spent nearly £250,000.

Aims is not explicitly a Conservative Party body but, as Sir Stephen Pierssene wrote in 1954, 'I know that there is quite a close liaison between them and our own Research Department.' Aims' propaganda material was circulated freely to Conservative candidates via Central Office, but the Party drew the line at joint funding.

Aims vigorously supports free enterprise, denouncing any measures which infringe the workings of the market system. In effect, therefore, it vigorously favours the Conservative Party, particularly the laissez-faire approach associated with Mrs Thatcher. Freed from the restraints of party politics, Aims' propaganda is often more virulent than anything to which the Conservative Party dare lend its own name.

This aggressive style has always characterised the activities of the private companies threatened by Labour's nationalisation plans. Understandably, private companies threatened with extinction by nationalisation since the end of the Second World War have fought tooth and nail against the Labour government's public ownership proposals. The Road Haulage Federation, for instance, conducted a bitter but unsuccessful battle against the Attlee administration's transport plans. Nothing, however, was as ferocious as the response of the private steel companies which had been nationalised by Labour in 1951 and promptly denationalised by the Churchill administration which came to office later that year.

In the early 1960s the prospect of another Labour government planning renationalisation goaded the steel companies into action. The sums of money involved were huge. The Iron and Steel Federation itself, the main spokesman for the private companies, spent £650,000 in 1963–4 on advertising that denounced Labour's plans. This figure represented more than double the amount spent by the Labour Party nationally on its propaganda efforts.

In addition, individual companies chipped in with their own campaigns. Stewarts and Lloyds spent £203,000, United Steel £100,000, Steel Company of Wales £98,000, Dorman Long £93,000 and so on. In all, in the run-up to the 1964 election, a total of £1.2 million was spent on electoral propaganda castigating the Labour Party's nationalisation programme; four times the budget of the national Labour Party. The companies argued that their expenditure was not party political yet their arguments explicitly favoured the Conservative Party rather than its opponents.

In fairness it must be said that some trade unions have also launched campaigns which indirectly benefit the Labour Party. The sums involved, however, are much smaller and the campaigns infrequent (and often poorly run). The point at issue is not whether such financial assistance is right or wrong in itself, but rather to assess the discrepancy between the financial clout of the two major parties.

⋆   ⋆   ⋆

Any analysis of Conservative Party finances reveals four areas of interest, two of which are not contentious. The first of these non-controversial topics concerns the amount of money which local Tory associations raise through their own efforts; the second, the sums which these same associations donate to central party funds.

In both these respects the Conservative Party has excelled, easily outpacing its political rivals. Conservative associations generate and spend three times as much as constituency Labour Parties. In 1992, for instance, local constituencies raised some £18 million. The historian of party finances, Michael Pinto-Duschinsky, justifiably comments: 'The story of British political finance since 1945 is mainly one of Conservative success and of Labour and Liberal failure in developing effective methods of collecting small political donations at the local level.'

The cumulative sums involved are massive: it has been estimated that the local parties have assets amounting to more than £8 million. Here the conflict between the constituency associations and Central Office is often acute; the associations begrudge handing over money to what is seen as a wasteful bureaucracy and as a result few of them meet the quotas laid down by Smith Square.

During the row in the summer of 1993 over political finance, Lord McAlpine wrote: 'It is high time that the Conservative Party explained that two-thirds of the money that is given comes from individuals who donate to constituency parties. Almost all that money is spent in the constituencies.' He then went on, 'Most Tory money is raised by the selling of jam, more often than not sold for less than it will cost the donor to make the stuff.'

Unlike most other political parties, the Conservatives do not have set membership fees. Although Party membership has been declining, Pinto-Duschinsky noted that the switch in the 1980s to computer-generated letters and reminders has brought about a striking increase in the average membership subscription to about £10. This means that today's half a million subscriptions raise twice as much in real terms as the one-and-a-half million subs of 1973.

The benefits of establishing deep roots within the community, an approach best exemplified by the Primrose League, have paid off a thousand times over for the Conservative Party.

The two other sources of Party finance are, however, rather more controversial. One concerns donations by companies and businesses to Central Office; the other centres on donations by private individuals. Both these sources of money have been the subject of much speculation, prompting both critics and supporters alike to bandy around massive sums.

In part these rumours and accusations are the Party's own fault because it does not issue properly audited accounts. The Conscrvative Party has no legal status. As an unincorporated association it is bound only by its own internal rules and is therefore under no legal obligation to publish financial accounts. But whatever the law may lay down, is this acceptable from a major political party which prides itself on accountability and honesty?

First there is the topic of corporate and business donations to the Conservative Party. The irony here is that Conservative governments of the 1980s legislated for the tighter control and accountability of trade union finance. Under the Trade Union Act of 1984, trade union members were given the right to inspect a union's financial accounts as well as a right of access to the accountants. In addition, all trade unionists must now be balloted every ten years as to whether their unions should maintain political funds. Many Conservatives hoped that this legislation would deprive the Labour Party of its main source of income.

And yet none of the above provisions apply to the Conservative Party itself. Companies are under no obligation to ask for shareholders' opinions before money is given to the Conservatives. Similarly, individual Conservative Party members have no right whatsoever to inspect the Party's financial accounts.

The only legal restriction stipulates that any sum of more than £200 used for political purposes must be declared in the company's accounts. Fine in theory, this requirement is in practice easily evaded, either by chanelling the money through intermediaries such as BUI and Aims or by using overseas trusts and associate companies to recycle the money. Companies can also declare donations but simply not specify where they are going.

In any case, the determined can easily massage the company accounts: the sum of £440,000 which Polly Peck's Asil Nadir donated to the Conservative Party was omitted from the company's books and was siphoned off via an offshore Jersey account. It only came to light because of the investigative work of accountants Touche Ross after Polly Peck had collapsed in 1990. The Manchester-based Sovereign Leasing gave £100,000 to the Party in 1990 – again, this was not disclosed as the law required and came out only when the company was the subject of a takeover.

Similarly it is clear that the Conservative Party was happy to accept substantial donations from Harrods' owner Mohamed Al-Fayed whose private company was under no legal obligation to declare political payments. Al-Fayed's contributions doubtless formed a part of the unexplained £70 million received by the Party since 1985, the figure mentioned at the beginning of this chapter.

Tiny Rowland, the former boss of Lonrho, now claims it was made clear to him in 1984 that a donation of up to £150,000 to the Conservative Party would help smooth his proposed takeover of the House of Fraser. No doubt if such a sum had indeed been paid it would have been massaged out of Lonrho's accounts.

So which companies do officially give money to the Party? According to the independent Labour Research Department – whose findings are accepted and regularly published by the *Daily Telegraph* and *Sunday Times* – the top ten declared donations in the run-up to the 1992 general election were headed by United Biscuits who gave £130,000, Taylor Woodrow £124,500, Hanson £115,000, Glaxo £102,000, P & O £100,000 and Rothmans £100,000. Of the ten top corporate donors between 1979 and January 1993, United Biscuits have given over £1 million, while Hanson, Taylor Woodrow, British and Commonwealth, and George Weston Holdings have donated over £800,000 each.

Traditional backers of the Conservative Party have always been the drinks trade, construction industries, property developers (in the past ones such as Slater Walker), and major multi-nationals like RTZ.

The oldest supporter of the Conservative Party, as we saw, has been the brewing industry. Not only have several wealthy

Conservative MPs derived their fortunes from the trade – such as right-wing die-hards John Gretton and Henry Page Croft who opposed virtually any and all social reform between the wars – but the drinks lobby has always signed up backbench MPs eager to protect its interests.

In one aside in his *Diaries* – the kind of detail spurned by much of the press in favour of revelations about the author's sexual habits – Alan Clark comments on just how many of his then fellow Conservative MPs were on the brewers' payroll. He also suggests that Lord (David) Young was undermined by that same lobby when he tried to cut the link between brewers and the pubs by reducing the number of tied-houses permitted.

Clark is referring to events in the mid-1980s when Young, then Mrs Thatcher's Trade Secretary, announced that he was 'minded to implement the recommendations' of the Monopolies and Mergers Commission to curb the powers of the six giant brewers and redistribute some pubs to smaller companies. As Jeremy Paxman has put it in his study of the British Establishment, Young was 'first abused and then humiliated by Conservative back-bench MPs in cahoots with the brewers. He capitulated. The brewers emerged from it all with their power and their profits substantially intact. It was an object lesson in how powerful businesses can bully government.'

Turn to Lord Young's memoirs for his full and frank version of events and you will find a complete and embarrassed silence – except for a throwaway aside in which he quotes the chairman of Grand Metropolitan as saying he (Young) had done a lot for the industry, and that is it.

Uncoincidentally, the brewing industry donated an estimated £250,000 to the Conservative Party in the election year of 1987. Industries can also provide payments in kind, just as we saw that car companies once provided transport. At the 1992 election most of the poster sites occupied by the Conservative Party were donated by the tobacco companies, whilst the *Sunday Times* has revealed that a senior executive from the disgraced Bank of Credit and Commerce International (BCCI) helped the Party by paying for money-raising banquets. Asian millionaire Nazmu Virani, serving a gaol sentence for his part in the BCCI scandal, also gave undisclosed sums to the Party.

This is the semi-official, semi-disclosed and semi-public relationship which exists between major companies and the Conservative Party. It is in the interests of neither that details should be made available: therefore only limited information about that relationship ever emerges.

Relying on impeccably orthodox sources (rather than the lurid accusations of left-wing conspiracy theorists), Ernest Saunders, once the chairman of Guinness, has alleged that during a fierce takeover bid he was tipped off by a Cabinet minister that a suitable donation to the Conservative Party would ensure the non-interference of the Monopolies and Mergers Commission. In his book about the affair, Saunders' son James claims that it was the then deputy chairman Jeffrey Archer who made indecent financial suggestions.

Alan Bristow, caught up in the acrimonious Westland helicopter row in 1986, alleges that he was offered a knighthood if he would agree to support the takeover bid by the American group Sikorsky-Fiat. The *Daily Telegraph* has reported that lunch at Mrs Thatcher's Downing Street cost around £50,000 for an aspiring captain of industry.

Researchers have detected links between honours and company donations. Since 1979 the Conservative government has awarded eighteen life peerages and eighty-two knighthoods to individuals connected with the seventy-six companies who have given £17 million to party funds. Industrialists are ten times more likely to be awarded peerages or knighthoods if their firms give money to the Conservative Party, according to the Labour Research Department's analysis of the honours lists since 1979. More than half the awards to so-called captains of industry have gone to Party contributors. Sir Hector Laing, chairman of the top Tory Party giver United Biscuits, was awarded a peerage in Mrs Thatcher's resignation honours list and his successor Robert Clarke a knighthood by John Major.

What do companies expect to get for their money? For one thing, it helps prevent the election of the Labour Party whose policies are seen as inimical to the interests of many Conservative sponsors. In May 1994, for instance, the Tobacco Manufacturers'

Association lobbied hard to defeat a private member's bill which proposed banning tobacco advertising. As the exective director of the association put it, 'The tobacco industry supports the Tory Party because Labour has . . . said it will ban advertising and do everything it can to destroy our industry. What can you expect us to do?'

More generally, they are also confident that the Conservative Party will take full note of their views. At the 1993 CBI annual conference, director-general Howard Davies specifically warned that the anti-European sentiments expressed at the recent Party conference were detrimental to business and he suggested that finance might be withdrawn. It was thought that the pharmaceutical firms in particular were concerned at the government's apparent outbreak of Europhobia.

Sometimes deeper relationships exist between the Party and its sponsors which, again, only come to light if things go wrong. The row over British aid to Malaysia and the Pergau dam project indicated the close ties between the construction industry, top civil servants and the Party. There is a regular dining club at the Savoy Hotel where senior civil servants and defence contractors meet.

The *Guardian* also reported that: 'Among the top construction firms, five companies [Balfour Beatty, GEC, Davy, Biwater and Amec] have taken 42.5 per cent of the entire £1.37 billion spent on aid linked to trade deals between 1978 and 1992. Most of the contracts are not put out to competitive bid.'

One of the companies involved in the Pergau dam episode, Trafalgar House, gave over half a million pounds to the Conservative Party between 1979 and 1993. Is it cynical to wonder why construction and road-building firms such as Wimpey, Tarmac, Mowlem and Costain are major disclosed supporters of the Conservative Party and why the Government is pushing ahead with road-building schemes and its plans to privatise the railways? It would be foolish and absurdly over-simplistic to categorise the Conservatives as just the bosses' party, but money can and does buy influence.

The sums involved here are as nothing compared with the 'Al-Yamamah' arms deals signed in 1985 and 1988 by Prime Minister Mrs Thatcher which were worth in total up to £100 billion. In November 1994 *Business Age* magazine detailed how a percentage of that agreement, perhaps up to £30 million in total, made its way to Conservative Central Office. Sums such as these helped to finance the 1987 and 1992 election victories, as well as explaining the holes in the Party's accounts. Mrs Thatcher's son Mark is alleged to have been one of the prime movers in these transactions. The size of the amounts involved would certainly have turned J.C.C. Davidson green with envy.

In the 1950s President Eisenhower spoke of the dangers of 'a military-industrial complex' so powerful that it could crucially influence the policies and actions of even the American government. What we seem to be looking at here is a similar mesh of interests, all of which further each other's concerns.

The fourth area of Conservative Party finance relates to individual donations to the Party. There is no obligation for any individual to declare these sums of money, but once again it is clear that massive amounts are involved. Since 1985 over £71 million has been donated to the Party via unknown individual sources.

In the election year of 1992 alone, for instance, the party received £19 million in gifts. £4 million of this sum was officially donated by companies and businesses – but no less than £15 million came from undisclosed and anonymous individual sources, perhaps from the Al-Yamamah deal. A former chairman of the Conservative Board of Finance, Major General Sir Brian Wyldebore-Smith, has confirmed that about £7 million were overseas contributions but that even he never knew where much of it came from. *Business Age* reported in May 1993:

> The one thing that links all the identified secret donors is a British tax loophole, scrupulously maintained by British governments for the past 14 years. This loophole allows anyone registering their UK assets abroad to avoid capital gains tax at 40 per cent – and to recover dividend withholding tax at 25 per cent . . . No other industrialised country permits such tax anomalies. In 1988 alone, Inland Revenue estimates indicate that the nation lost £10 billion

through this loophole – a sum sufficient to knock 4p in the pound off income tax.

The individual at the centre of this network of largesse was Lord McAlpine, treasurer of the Conservative Party from 1975 to 1990 and a staunch and undying supporter of Mrs Thatcher. In that time McAlpine raised more than £100 million, money which, in the words of a profile in *The Times*, 'went a long way to ensuring that the 1980s were a decade of one-party rule'. His methods were entirely private to himself: 'When I arrived at Smith Square [in 1975, the headquarters of Central Office] I had a lock put onto my office door and no one else was allowed in.' Only a handful of people at Central Office knew the identities of Lord McAlpine's donors and he himself has said that there are 'tons of off-shore accounts' which served to channel donations.

Who exactly are these individual donors? Some of the money came from foreign sources, such as the various groupings organised at Central Office since 1986 under the name Conservatives Abroad. This body was helped by the new government rules introduced three years later that allowed UK citizens living abroad to vote in the constituency in which they were last resident. Other beneficiaries of the Conservatives' fiscal measures include foreign businessmen who enjoy non-domicile status and therefore do not pay tax. In December 1991 Prime Minister John Major promised them that if the Conservatives won the next election the government would not change this arrangement.

It is only to be expected that the Conservative Party tries hard to woo such sources. *The Times* reported that John Major spent two days in Hong Kong in September 1991 with the express intention of raising money for the Party. He was successful; one of his dinner companions, Li Ka-Shing, is believed to have donated more than £1 million. The then governor of Hong Kong, Sir David Wilson, objected to this fund-raising expedition and was subsequently ousted from his post. According to the *Sunday Times*, Greek shipowner John Latsis contributed £2 million in March 1991 – thought to be the largest donation ever made to a British political party – whilst Octav Botnar, the disgraced former Nissan UK chief, gave £1 million over a period of some years.

The Conservative Party's recourse to rather less traditional sources of funds is not of course accidental but represents important changes in the nature of the Party. Up to the 1970s, for instance, any party treasurer could rely on 'blue chip' firms such as Barings, Kleinworts and Schroders to bring in donations. By the early 1980s the increasing cost of party political television broadcasts, associated with the firm of Saatchi & Saatchi, meant that such sources were no longer sufficient and the Party had to turn to what one former official in the Party's treasury deparment observed were representatives of a more enterpreneurial age: 'I'm not saying they were crooks and spivs, but they weren't from established firms which had been going for 300 years.'

In addition, companies hit by the prolonged recession of the early 1990s have been questioning their financial commitment to the Conservative Party. Several traditional business sponsors have recently cut back their contributions. In December 1994, *Labour Research* reported that in the year ending March 1994 no fewer than eleven major donors, which between them had given over £4 million to the Party since 1979, no longer contributed. Construction firm Taylor Woodrow, donors of over £840,000, now gave just a meagre £5,000 to the local Conservative Association in Ealing.

Another construction firm, Newarthill – one of whose directors is Lord McAlpine – cut its donation by 90 per cent to £6,000; similarly, United Biscuits reduced its contribution by nearly three quarters. Kenneth Clarke's 'mini budget' in December 1994, which raised alcohol duties, infuriated many of the Party's most stalwart supporters; as the *Daily Telegraph* reported on 10 December 1994, the Chancellor's decision is 'likely to prompt many of Britain's brewers and Scotch whisky producers to review their cash donations to the Conservative Party'.

Such a massive and accelerating fall in corporate donations means that an ever-increasing portion of party funds is coming from undisclosed sources.

And if that was not enough, Conservative associations are particularly wary of donating money to Central Office. In February 1993 it was revealed that local party funds now covered only one-tenth rather than one-third of national expenditure, and by the summer of 1994 donations from associations were down 20 per cent for the second year running. Instead of a projected contribution of £2.68 million, constituencies donated only £987,000. This shortfall reflects not just disenchantment with the current Conservative government, but also the long-term decline of the many local associations that was discussed in the previous chapter.

In terms of accountability, the Labour Party does indeed raise much money from its trade union allies. The difference is that union payments must be declared. They are transparent and open both to debate and criticism; several newspapers are full of little else at election times. But in fact union donations are much smaller than the sums discussed above: union sponsorship of MPs amounts at most to no more than a few thousand pounds.

By comparison, businesses can and do give donations to the Conservative Party without the knowledge or approval of their shareholders, simply by directing funds through overseas associate companies and then not declaring what they have done. The Party has a series of bank accounts maintained at Barclays in the off-shore haven of Jersey.

It is also important to stress that the fiercest campaigners against the secretive financial dealings of the Party have been Conservative ginger groups themselves, particularly the Charter Movement and the Party Reform Steering Group. Two former officials on the Conservative Board of Finance, Eric Chalker and John Strafford, have persistently advocated ending the secrecy which surrounds the Party's finances. Chalker has observed that in his four years on the board more than £67 million was spent at Central Office, but that nobody had to account for a penny to the board or to any other elected body.

Michael Pinto-Duschinsky has shown how the Liberal Party's dependence on a few wealthy individuals for money at the beginning of the century discouraged the Party from developing a mass membership. With virtually no income coming in from members, the Liberal Party swiftly fell apart in the 1930s when the prospect of power seemed remote. It is arguable, too, that the Labour Party's reliance on trade union backing has been limiting.

Similarly, Central Office's search for large, single donations has reduced the incentive to explore other avenues for raising money, notably through the process of direct mail which no British party has yet fully exploited. Contrast this with the situation in the United States where the Republican Party in 1984, for example, had a donor file of two million people and managed to raise no less than $215 million in all, 80 per cent of which resulted from mail and telephone shots. Making use of such methods might well help revive the Conservative Party outside Westminster.

A handful of Conservatives and rather more non-Conservatives argue in favour of another source of finance, namely state support for political parties. This already happens in several countries and is partly the case in Britain; the so-called 'Short' money helps to fund opposition parties in the Commons whilst large subsidies-in-kind are available for free postage and party political broadcasts.

The drawback to state funding is that it would in effect penalise the Conservatives for their efficiency and would further isolate the political parties from the population at large by reducing their need to involve people at grassroots level. Respected academic Vernon Bogdanor wrote that the majority report of the Houghton Committee in 1976 which called for state funding should have been renamed 'The Society for the Preservation of Old Parties'.

Different arguments surround the disclosure of large donations. Like it or not, in a democracy different parties compete for control of government. They are not charities and they do need resources. If money buys influence, then it is important the source of that money should be open to democratic scrutiny. The secrecy which cloaks the Party's finances inevitably encourages suspicion, not least from Conservatives themselves. Labour MP Robin Cook put it neatly: 'The danger to democracy of secret donations is that they put public government under private obligations.' Most other countries insist that donations above a certain level, usually in the region of £5,000, must be declared. They also ban contributions from abroad and insist on the publication of properly audited accounts.

In any democratic system, it is surely right that the finances of political parties should be above board. In November 1991, for instance, it was revealed that the Communist Party of Great Britain had been substantially financed by payments from the Soviet Union between at least 1958 and 1979. If such information about 'Moscow gold' had been available at the time, then the Communist Party's small membership would surely have been even smaller.

As for the possible sale of honours, one way to avoid any suggestion of impropriety would be to transfer their award to an independent body beholden to no one. Such a method would have thwarted Maundy Gregory.

At the end of the day the facts are relatively clear: between 1990 and 1993 the Conservative Party spent some £60 million on organisation and propaganda, double the amount which the Labour Party was able to afford. And if money does not necessarily win votes, it most certainly does not lose them.

In other words, the present system materially helps the Conservative Party in its quest for power. This explains why, to nobody's surprise, the Conservative majority on the House of Commons Home Affairs Committee, reporting in April 1994, recommended no change in the system, a system which was developed in the rather different circumstances of the nineteenth century, and called for a ceiling on local but not national election expenditure.

The Conservatives' financial advantage and their satisfaction with the present state of affairs mean that they possess an in-built – although not impregnable – advantage.

'The Bottom Line is Winning Elections'

How the Conservative Party wins elections

'The Bottom Line is Winning Elections'
The title of a seminar offered by
Conservative Central Office, 1994

'There is one thing you can be sure of with the Conservative Party, before anything else – they have a grand sense for where the votes are.'
Enoch Powell, 1981

'I think the big difference in marketing party political policies is that, of course, one has much less say about what goes into the product than one did then but, apart from that, I think it's more or less the same. It's communication. It's getting the message across.'
Christopher Lawson, Conservative Party Director of
marketing, on marketing Mars bars and the
Conservative Party (1983)

'The Conservative Party represents the toffs or them, the Labour Party speaks for the workers or us.' If this frequently expressed view was in fact correct then the Labour Party would be permanently in power, the Conservatives always out of office. Almost the exact opposite is true. Any simplistic assumption that each of the two, major political parties is purely a class party is wrong.

The British Conservative Party has largely refuted this class stereotype over the last one hundred years because it has excelled at winning elections. No other political party in a Western democracy can rival its electoral and campaigning record. As a result, the Party's election strategists are much in demand by right-wing parties all over the world eager to benefit from Conservative expertise and knowledge. Perhaps the most successful campaign ever fought by the Conservative Party came in 1983.

The general election of June 1983 gave the voters their first chance to pass a verdict on Mrs Thatcher's government after four years in office which had seen both the severest depression since the 1930s and the Falklands War. Unlike during several previous elections, the Conservative and Labour Parties were diametrically opposed on many key issues.

Mrs Thatcher's government wanted to continue 'rolling back' the policies of full employment, a mixed economy and the Welfare State, which had been virtually taken for granted since 1945. Michael Foot's Labour Party was committed to a massive programme of state intervention. On Europe, the Conservatives wanted to stay in and Labour wanted to pull out. On defence, the Conservatives advocated a strategy based on the nuclear deterrent whilst Labour called for unilateral nuclear disarmament. No one could have possibly confused the two parties.

The vast differences between the two major parties extended to their methods of campaigning. The Conservative Party used word processors, the most up-to-date computers and direct mail advertising to two million voters. They focused their resources on a hundred key marginals and installed a twenty-four-hour monitoring unit which meant they were able to react almost instantaneously to press stories.

The Conservatives also had over four hundred agents and ensured that Mrs Thatcher's meetings were ticket only in order to minimise the risk of disruption. They introduced audio-visual aids such as the 'sincerity' device which allowed speakers to read from notes but still appear as if they were looking the audience right in the eye.

A multitude of photo opportunities located by the campaign staff months beforehand were obligingly provided for the journalists and photographers following the Prime Minister in coaches. The new Conservative logo with its torch of freedom milked the association with the successful British film *Chariots of Fire*.

By contrast, the Labour Party had a malfunctioning computer, no special facilities for journalists and their polling organisation was given the funds to start work only three months before the election. Their advertising agency was continually criticised by members of the Left who distrusted all this glitzy paraphernalia. Michael Foot's campaign was directed solely at people who were already supporters or members of the Labour Party. At one point he ended up being jostled and heckled by farmers and blood-sports enthusiasts.

Party chairman Cecil Parkinson, who led the Conservative campaign, knew precisely who he was aiming for and when and how his targets should be achieved. The Conservatives actually distributed copies of the Labour manifesto in order to publicise its contents, knowing that its unilateralist sentiments and calls for widespread public ownership were unlikely to prove electorally popular. Labour's campaign committee was, in the damning words of its own chairman, 'a rag, tag and bobtail affair . . . people I had never seen before seemed to wander in and out giving advice and then vanishing'. Money, of course, helped: the Conservative Party's election expenditure of £8 million was twice that of the Labour Party.

Not surprisingly, the Conservatives won the 1983 election with a huge majority of 144 seats. It was a historic occasion: Mrs Thatcher's brand of Conservatism had secured not just a new mandate but also a fresh momentum which was to last throughout the 1980s.

The Conservative Party has always understood that the most effective way in Britain to secure power is to win general elections. And in an electoral system based on first past the post rather than any kind of proportional representation, it is vital that the Party projects an image of cohesion, unity and sense of purpose. Conservative Party leaders and managers strive to put the Party in the best possible light and their opponents in the worst.

How and why have the Conservatives been so formidable at winning elections? In the nineteenth century their record was poor; they were successful on just five occasions between 1832 and 1918. But ever since the emergence of mass democratic parties at the end of the Victorian era, the traditionally hidebound and reactionary Conservatives have consistently triumphed over their supposedly radical and iconoclastic opponents. Their success as a campaigning and electioneering body demonstrates the Party's skill in managing and reacting to change.

This chapter explores three areas of electoral significance. Firstly, it looks at the Conservative Party's electoral programmes and manifestos. Secondly, it examines how the Conservatives have developed their techniques of electioneering. Finally, it analyses how the electorate has responded to the Conservative message.

Benjamin Disraeli once admonished the editor of a new Tory magazine with the words, 'Above all no programme'. In other words, don't give any hostages to political fortune by specifying exactly what the Conservatives intend to do, when and how.

Disraeli's scepticism should be borne in mind when looking at the Conservative Party's manifestos and policy statements. In part he was reflecting the Tory devotion to 'circumstance' and the feeling that human life inevitably contradicts theories and systems – a constant theme in Conservative philosophy. Conservatives generally consider it foolish to give hostages to fortune in the shape of express commitments and pledges, preferring instead to present impressions rather than details.

Labour was, at least until recently, very different: their manifestos bristled with specific pledges and promises, from nationalisation to the level of child benefit. Kenneth Baker noted in his autobiography that 'The Labour Party could not resist the temptation to have a policy on everything, which was a sure way of alarming the maximum number of people.'

The one recent Conservative exception to this rule was the

methodical and intensely hard-working Edward Heath. In opposition between 1965 and 1970 he devoted enormous amounts of time to thirty different policy groups set up in order to provide the nuts and bolts of a new approach. Not only were the documents produced by these groups immensely dull – even Heath described his first reading of them as 'a terrible weekend's work' – but their profligacy confused voters.

Looking back at the lost 1966 election, senior Conservative Iain Macleod claimed that 'at the last election the Conservative Party Manifesto had contained 131 distinct specific promises. This was far too much to put across to the electorate, and the net result was that everybody thought we had no policy.'

When the Conservatives did regain power in 1970, events soon rendered the painstaking labours of the previous five years useless. People simply didn't behave as they should have done on paper. In particular, trade unions failed to register under the Industrial Relations Act of 1971, a ploy which had simply not occurred to the Party's thinkers.

Disraeli was only acknowledging the truth; that public interest in politics rarely extends to the reading of party manifestos. This may well be due to the fact that the manifestos themselves are generally so poorly written. The only good thing about the unreadable products issued by all three major parties in the 1983 general election was this marvellous dissection of them by John Carey:

> No one could read these publications without a pang. They look cheery and efficient on the outside, like hospitals. But once you open them you plunge straight into the knacker's yard of language. This is where clichés come to die. It's a pitiable sight. Arthritic old abstractions, bloodless metaphors, superannuated slurs, all dragging themselves along in a grim parody of animation. It seems callous to intrude on their terminal woes. But we should steel ourselves. For words portray their users, and if literary criticism has any public function it ought to help us assess the mental health of the three main parties by comparing their different ways of destroying the English language.

A number of themes are virtually ever-present in Conservative propaganda. The patriotic appeal, for instance, has served the Party well since the days of Disraeli. Electors, which do you prefer: the straight-talking John Bull jingoism of we Conservatives or the wishy-washy 'foreigner first' internationalism of the Liberals/Labour?

Other supposedly eternal values and verities – such indefinable concepts as monarchy, Church, family, and law and order which we encountered in the chapter on Tory ideas – are also duly emphasised: 'our hope lies in the preservation of Religion, the Monarchy and the Empire', declared a resolution at the 1947 annual conference, and for many Conservatives it seems as though it still does.

Alongside these affirmations goes the denigration of political opponents as a motley bunch of deviants. One striking leaflet of 1895 portrayed the Liberals as 'the present mongrel political combination of teetotallers, Irish revolutionists, Welsh demagogues, Small Englanders, English separatists, and general uprooters of all that is national and good' – a pretty comprehensive list of stereotypes to despise.

At other times, Conservative propagandists have warned electors that the other parties were financially irresponsible and dangerous: 'Guard Your Savings' and 'Your House to Go! Your Building Society Too! If Socialism Comes' were the two titles of two Conservative leaflets published during the 1935 election campaign. More recently, the 1992 election was dominated by Conservative-generated fears that a Labour administration would increase taxation.

Ultimately, however, it is almost impossible to know how important manifestos and policy statements were and are in influencing voters. It is generally thought that the Conservative manifesto of October 1974 was possibly the best written of them all – and yet the Conservatives lost. In the 1945 election they staked all on their trump card and simply called their manifesto *Mr Churchill's Declaration of Policy to the Electors*. Again, they lost. It is hardly to be wondered at that most Conservatives prefer to appeal to the Party's record rather than any detailed programmes for the uncertain future.

And yet the role of the manifesto has become increasingly important in recent years because of the influence of the academic and the business communities. Both have increasingly turned to management by objectives in which clear terms of reference are set at the start of a project and those responsible are held accountable for its outcome.

Each party's manifesto is now scrutinised by opponents because it is an overt statement of intent which they can gleefully criticise when the actual circumstances which confront those in office make the achievement of its aims impossible. Think of the political mileage which has been extracted from the issue of taxation, or the Conservative determination in 1994 not to mention the word 'federal' in their European Union manifesto.

Politically more significant than the actual manifesto, are the parties' respective campaigning methods, because they reach virtually every elector.

For much of the nineteenth century, general elections were essentially local affairs and in fact great numbers of seats went uncontested because of the expense of fighting them. Until the Corrupt and Illegal Practices Act of 1883 candidates endeavoured to buy the votes of the small electorate. The extension of the franchise in 1867 and 1884, the introduction of the secret ballot and the restrictions on election expenditure meant that by the end of the nineteenth century candidates had to devise other methods to woo voters.

Most effective was the public meeting which offered a form of bravura public entertainment. In an age without microphones, speakers were often judged by the size of the audience they could cope with: some were 'five thousand men', others 'ten thousand men'. The length of the speeches today seems extraordinary. Disraeli spoke for three and a half hours at the Crystal Palace in 1872. Public enthusiasm for political meetings knew no limits; take this eyewitness description of Conservative Prime Minister Lord Salisbury in Liverpool in 1893:

The meeting in the evening was a wonderful sight. The huge hall was packed; they said there were 8,000 people in it, and thousands more tried to force their way in. Forty policemen were fighting with the crowd and kept them out with great difficulty. Though noisy at first they kept as still as possible during Lord Salisbury's speech, and were most appreciative, seeing every point. They gave him a most enthusiastic reception.

It was virtually impossible for politicians to clamber up the greasy pole without possessing platform skills. The audience expected to listen to speeches with some substance in them which they then discussed after the event. In *My Early Life*, Churchill describes regularly speaking in front of audiences of five or six thousand. Open-air meetings also afforded the opportunity for a good fracas. Members of the Primrose League wanted to form a Punching Brigade in order to counter socialist heckling.

Many statesmen hated this whole paraphernalia of electioneering. It was the future Lord Salisbury who penned perhaps the most vitriolic damnation:

> The days and weeks of screwed-up smiles and laboured courtesy, the mock geniality, the hearty shake of the filthy hand, the chuckling reply that must be made to the coarse joke, the loathsome, choking compliment that must be paid to the grimy wife and sluttish daughter, the indispensable flattery of the vilest religious prejudices, the wholesale deglutition of hypocritical pledges . . .

Some politicians, on the other hand, loved the noise and excitement of the hustings and proved to be great showmen. F.E. Smith, for instance, once hired a wagon and paraded through his constituency sounding a bell. Even more spectacularly deployed were the highly visible charms of the Gaiety dancing girls hired by Brendan Bracken to accompany his friend Winston Churchill during the 1924 election.

When did politicians become aware of the power of image manipulation; of stage-managing events in order to try and produce an effect greater than the event itself? One early example was the Midlothian campaign launched by the 'Grand Old Man' William Gladstone in 1880 when his whistle-stop rail tour became a 'media event' – or the first photo opportunity, as Peter Clarke has called it. Queen Victoria declared herself horrified that one of her elder statesmen should stoop to the demeaning tactic of haranguing crowds at railway stations.

Joseph Chamberlain also realised the powerful possibilities offered by the railway. During the tariff reform campaign which split the Conservative Party in the first decade of the twentieth century, Chamberlain's arrivals at stations were carefully stage-managed – in fact one might say choreographed – to maximum effect. Often he would be accompanied from station to town hall by bands of musicians and dancing girls.

The man who masterminded many of these effects was Sir Arthur Pearson, the newspaper proprietor who had founded the *Daily Express* in 1900. Pearson continually pressed Chamberlain to adopt the most up-to-date techniques in order to reach the public, including the production of gramophone records of his speeches. (Chamberlain in fact turned this idea down.)

It is clear that the Conservatives swiftly learnt the importance of presentation from their business and manufacturing supporters such as Pearson whose well-being depended on keeping their customers happy. The advertising industry went from strength to strength during the late nineteenth century and many of its early clients such as Bovril, Hovis, Cadbury and Fry are still household names. Department stores like Selfridges and Harrods fully understood the importance of marketing an image and Shell introduced their striking posters and other graphic art forms as early as 1904.

Lord Northcliffe had started the *Daily Mail* in 1896. Investing half a million pounds in its launch he proceeded to sell copies of the paper at just ha'penny and within four years saw its circulation pass the million mark. Following Northcliffe's example, many newspapers began to rely on advertising for their income and developed a popular journalistic style which could appeal to all classes of reader.

Mass circulation newspapers such as the *Mail* and the *Express* reached many more people than could possibly attend even the most successful public meeting. The Conservative Party, buttressed by its links with the newspaper proprietors, saw that this was the shape of things to come. The question became, and remains, how to convey one's message in the most effective way, using the most up-to-date methods available?

By the end of the nineteenth century, for example, the Conservatives were already sending lecture vans equipped with magic lanterns to remote areas in order to put across their message, thereby anticipating the arrival of cinema, radio and television. Arguably the Labour Party, by contrast, has remained fixated by the public meeting, the march and the grubby leaflet. Attitude can be just as important as financial resources.

But effective propaganda is valueless without potent organisation. The Conservative Party is geared up to fight elections, win them and retain power. Conservatives this century are used to power – and when they lose it the effects are galvanising. 1906, 1910, 1945 and 1974 were all years of important election failures which provoked enormous change within the Party organisation. Nothing concentrates the Conservative mind so wonderfully as election defeat.

Under the leadership of Arthur Balfour, the Conservatives lost three elections in a row, one in 1906 and two in 1910. Unsurprisingly the defeats sparked off a power struggle between the Party in the country, which was led by the National Union, and the leadership at Westminster, which supervised Central Office. Who was to be master? Two different Party committees were set up in 1906 and 1911 to inquire into the state of the Party, but proceedings were dominated by friction between Conservatives at Westminster and Conservatives in the country at large.

It was the leadership that eventually outmanoeuvred the rank-and-file representatives by insisting on the precedence of Central Office. The country was divided up into twelve areas, each with its own office and area agent accountable to Central Office. A new post was introduced, that of the Party chairman who was appointed by the leader and was to be responsible for the running of Central Office. He was expected to liaise with the Party at large.

The first occupant of the post was Arthur Steel-Maitland and he took steps to run Central Office on the lines of business efficiency. On his arrival he had been horrified to discover the Party kept no accounts, there was no filing system in operation and members of staff had only a vague idea of punctuality. Fully supported in his efforts by the new party leader, Andrew Bonar Law – the Party's first businessman-leader – Steel-Maitland transformed the organisation.

As well as introducing business methods of work, he set up separate departments responsible for literature and speakers. The administration of election campaigns remained the prerogative of the London headquarters. The National Union was put firmly in its place as a body whose task was to educate and report on the feelings of the rank and file – but not much more than this. The chairman of the National Union noted that 'They hoped . . . to form . . . a businesslike organisation . . . like a railway company with a board of directors.' These changes turned Central Office into a highly efficient organisation adept at putting across the Conservative case.

By the 1920s, for instance, the magic lantern had been replaced by a fleet of cinema vans which was sent all over the country. Screens were erected in market squares and town halls and aggressively propagandist films were then shown. It has been estimated that more than two thousand people a day saw the films. Huge quantities of party material were also produced – nineteen million anti-union leaflets were printed in 1927 alone in the wake of the General Strike – whilst speakers were trained at the Party's residential college to present anti-socialist arguments.

One illuminating contrast between the supposedly hidebound Conservatives and the pioneering Labour Party can be seen in their respective use of the new medium of radio. Both parties were granted equal access at the general election in October 1924, the first occasion that the leaders addressed the public in this way.

Conservative leader Stanley Baldwin realised that radio called for very different techniques from those necessary at a public meeting. After much preparation he carefully recorded his speech at Broadcasting House in London. In contrast, the Labour leader Ramsay MacDonald relayed his broadcast live from the City Hall in Glasgow. He kept striding away from the microphone in order to harangue the live audience, with the result that listeners at home could barely hear him for much of the time.

By the time of the 1929 election MacDonald had improved his technique but it was still the two leading Conservatives, Baldwin and Churchill, who delivered the most powerful radio talks. At the 1931 election – by which time one family in three had a radio set – Baldwin again excelled; the *Manchester Guardian* remarked of his radio performances that 'with his feet on our fender, [he] was as successful as usual'; this was some years before President Roosevelt's 'fireside chats' became so famous.

The same difference applied when it came to the use of cinema. Here the Conservatives learnt from the big companies such as Cadburys and the tobacco companies which sponsored advertising films that were then shown free in lecture halls. Sound vans were introduced as early as 1928 and by the 1931 election they deployed eleven vans with sixteen operators. Their presentations even included cartoon films such as *The Right Spirit* and extracts from the successful film *Disraeli* (1929) in which the noted actor George Arliss, playing the Tory leader, had won Britain's first Oscar. By 1935 the Conservative effort was increased to twenty-two mobile film vans. Their displays are estimated to have reached over one-and-a-half million people.

Once again, Baldwin proved himself more adept at handling a new medium than his Labour counterpart. During the 1935 election, both Baldwin and the Labour leader Clement Attlee were filmed for newsreel use. Baldwin sat behind a desk, looking professional and in control; Attlee, on the other hand, chose to perch on the edge of a chair, reading out from notes which were precariously balanced on his knee.

The Conservative Party also tried to build up links with the mainstream film industry. Producer Sir Alexander Korda advised the Conservative and Unionist Films Association and plans were drawn up to acquire a financial interest in a major film company – bearing in mind of course that, as the leading figure Sir Albert Clavering observed, 'The question of disguising the activities of the Party would necessarily be an essential consideration.'

The arrival of both radio and cinema meant that political campaigning became increasingly national rather than local in character and throughout the 1930s Conservative Party managers pursued their quest for the latest methods of communication. They immersed themselves in the fledgling social sciences and in new American techniques such as market research. The *Conservative Agents' Journal* carried long articles on such topics as how to note and then make use of electors' views.

The most expensive and yet most secretive electioneering agency was set up by Joseph Ball, an ex-intelligence officer who handled both clean and dirty tricks at Central Office. Ball was unhappy with what he regarded as the Party's ponderous electioneering methods. In 1929 he was responsible for employing the advertising agency S.H. Benson, famous for their Guinness posters featuring a toucan and which had copy written by Dorothy L. Sayers. This was the first time a political party had used an outside body. Five years later Ball set up the innocuously named National Publicity Bureau. He made certain that the bureau's existence and activities never became public knowledge.

Although the bureau always claimed to be a temporary organisation, in fact senior officials had been engaged on five-year contracts right from its start in 1935. This suggests that, but for the intervention of the Second World War, it would have been a long-term project. It was financed, in Ball's own words, 'from a fund collected entirely from individuals and organisations who could not, or would not, subscribe to ordinary party funds'.

The bureau was chaired by Sir Kingsley Wood, the driving force behind the GPO Film Unit in the 1930s which had produced many important posters and films. Wood now put his expertise to use for Party purposes and the bureau pioneered several new campaigning techniques which are standard practice today, such as targeting 330 key constituencies and sending out direct mail to selected groups of voters. In the thirteen months leading up to the general election of November 1935, the bureau spent approximately £300,000 (some £6 million at 1990s' values).

Perhaps the bureau's most effective technique was to emblazon its slogans on huge posters all over Britain and to produce millions of broadsheets designed to look like ordinary newspapers. During the 1935 election the Bureau joined up with the Conservative and Unionist Films Association in order to put on film shows in virtually every important constituency. It had seventeen vans of its own which contained portable 16mm equipment. The bureau's self-confidence is shown by the way in which major London cinemas were hired in order to preview productions.

The bureau was in fact revived for the 1945 general election but had access to rather less generous funds than in 1935 – although it still spent £30,000 on posters and broadsheets. The bureau was closed down in 1946 because, as we shall see in Chapter 10, Sir Joseph Ball himself was now persona non grata within the Party itself.

The 1945 general election was the last of the old-style contests – that is, it took place pre-television. Throughout the campaign it was evident that the electorate was preoccupied with domestic issues and reforms; the Conservatives made the basic mistake of encouraging their candidates to appear in military uniform and to stress their military titles and exploits.

The voters were clearly not impressed by this, nor by Churchill's infamous 'Gestapo' remark about his Labour opponents, so recently his own colleagues in the coalition Cabinet. The Conservative campaign focused almost exclusively on Churchill; the candidate for Jarrow even sent a telegram to Churchill five days before polling which read, 'Tyneside would like to touch the hem of your garment on Monday, Tuesday, or Wednesday of next week.'

At the end of the day, it does not matter how potent an organisation's campaigning techniques are if it totally misjudges the audience. The shrewd observer Sir Robert Bruce Lockhart was clear about this in his diary entry for 26 July 1945:

> . . . the magnitude of Labour's victory was largely determined by the faulty election tactics of the Tories who turned what the vast majority of the public, and especially of the large class of new young voters, regarded as a most serious affair affecting their future lives into a kind of dog-fight of the last century in which abuse and slanging of the enemy takes the place of a constructive programme.

Four years later the Attlee government was damaged by a campaign which, although allegedly non–party political, had a great effect on the future of political campaigning. Having been scheduled for nationalisation by the Labour administration, the sugar company Tate & Lyle hired the public relations firm Aims of Industry to present their case for remaining in private ownership.

Aims responded by launching the highly successful 'Mr Cube' campaign. A memorable logo, namely a lump of sugar with human features, was devised and then printed on every packet of sugar. Inside was the slogan TATE NOT STATE. Mountains of printed material were distributed, cardboard cut-outs erected and schools visited by speakers. Six mobile propaganda vans toured Britain showing a film featuring the well-known television personality Richard Dimbleby – an early example of endorsement by a supposedly non-political celebrity.

The Mr Cube campaign took the Labour government unawares. Tate & Lyle had seized the initiative and eventually the government had to back down. Tate & Lyle remained in private hands. Aims' triumph confirmed the value of the links between the Conservative Party and business.

In 1948 Central Office was once again ahead of the game when it installed a Public Opinion Research Department, even though it was kept short of resources. Throughout the 1950s the Party continued to introduce new methods of political persuasion and the *Conservative Agents' Journal* contained articles on the value of opinion polls.

They were the first party to use the findings of opinion polls in order to design their policies and in June 1957 Harold Macmillan hired the advertising agency Colman, Prentis and Varley, which had been working for the Party on and off since 1948, to launch a new campaign. Costing nearly half a million pounds, their high-pressure initiative highlighting Conservative successes was a recognition that face-to-face electioneering was now of secondary importance. Labour politicians attacked what they sniffily called 'the worst sort of Americanisation'.

Nor were all Conservative MPs enamoured of such methods. Senior Tory Oliver Lyttelton preferred to remain well above the fray: 'I am very fond of my countrymen and I hate the squabbling and vulgarity and slogans of a popular contest.' But then Lyttelton did hold the safe seat of Aldershot.

Despite the old-school Edwardian image which he sometimes liked to convey, Harold Macmillan was quick to master the techniques of television, speaking to the camera and hence the viewer as if they were confidantes. Winston Churchill, accustomed to an earlier political world of public meetings and platform oratory, had hated the medium. He endured one secret screen test before deciding not to proceed – if television cameras got too close to him Churchill would simply put his hand over the lens.

Eden recognised the value of the medium, but was not long enough in office to utilise it effectively. Moreover his vanity in not wanting to wear glasses meant that during one crucial Suez broadcast he could not see properly. In his highly over-emotional state, Eden lambasted the BBC for allowing communists to shine lights in his eyes. Macmillan's cosy confidentiality, on the other hand, was well suited to the medium. He was inadvertently helped too by the image of Supermac, dreamt up by socialist cartoonist Vicky as a term of opprobrium. But in fact, in the words of Macmillan's biographer Alistair Horne, the image became 'one of affectionate admiration making the intended victim something of a folk hero'.

The one time when Labour actually managed to pull ahead of the Conservatives in terms of media professionalism was in the early 1960s under Harold Wilson's leadership. The Conservatives had already been worried by the expertise of Labour's political broadcasts during the 1959 election, masterminded by a young television producer Antony Wedgwood Benn. The Campaign for Nuclear Disarmament (CND) in the late 1950s and early 1960s also understood the value of image: stage designer Sean Kenny was asked for advice on 'dressing the Aldermaston march' in 1961 and the next year the Executive urged that delegates to an international conference should include 'a young and photogenic mother'.

But it was the transatlantic example of J.F. Kennedy and the influential book *The Making of the President* by Theodore H. White which captured the imagination of the Wilson entourage. Wilson's quick wits and talk of technological revolution were more than a match for the tweediness of Sir Alec Douglas-Home. For the first and only time, the Labour Party successfully identified itself with modernisation and the future – and won the 1964 and 1966 elections.

For once, the Conservative Party went backwards in its methods of campaigning. During the 1964 election, Sir Alec preferred to stump across the country, holding no fewer than eight open-air meetings a day and reaching a total audience of about twenty thousand people. When he arrived in London for *Election Forum* on television, which had an estimated audience of about seven-and-a-half million, he was understandably exhausted and unprepared.

But the Conservative Party in general and Central Office in particular have always been quick learners. Home's successor Edward Heath was more atuned to media demands, travelling throughout the 1970 election campaign with an advertising team and his own portable studio set in order to provide a photogenic backdrop. He was also responsible for introducing the television-style press conference. Such methods enabled Heath and the Conservatives to wrestle away the modernisation card which had been so effective for Harold Wilson's Labour Party in the mid-1960s.

Mrs Thatcher's leadership of the Conservative Party saw the wholesale introduction of American-style campaigning techniques. In 1978 a former television producer, Gordon Reece, was appointed director of publicity at Central Office and he, in turn, hired the advertising firm Saatchi & Saatchi. Their sharper Madison Avenue-style methods included the use of aggressive 'knocking' copy, the most famous example of which was the 'Labour Isn't Working' poster which had an enormous impact. Ironically, the sad-faced unemployed in the poster were volunteers from Hendon Young Conservatives.

Reece was keen to widen the appeal of the Conservative Party by targeting what the sociologists termed C1s and C2s, namely skilled manual labourers and council house occupants. This had importance for politicians: 'The consequences of Reece's way of looking at politics were that one appearance on the "Jimmy Young Programme" was considered to be worth several interviews on "Panorama". The *Sun* was regarded with more anxious concern than was *The Times*. An article in *Woman* was viewed as more important even than a feature in the *Sun*, because the latter (and other popular papers) would be bound to pick up what was said in *Woman*.' The usually turgid ten-minute party political broadcasts were transformed into crisp five-minute commercials.

Mrs Thatcher's appearance and style gradually altered. She took lessons from a teacher at the National Theatre and lowered the pitch of her voice. Her hair was flattened, her teeth straightened and crowned and she now wore more executive-style clothes. It is intriguing to compare photographs of Mrs Thatcher on her arrival in Downing Street in 1979 with those of her departure eleven years later.

Nor was Mrs Thatcher alone in using such means: François Mitterand had surgery on his jaw in 1981 to make it less prominent, Helmut Schmidt once had a face lift and a hair transplant, whilst Ronald Reagan resorted to just about every cosmetic device available. The meticulousness of Mrs Thatcher's approach to television was shown by the attention paid to every detail, down to the shape and colour of the chair she sat in for interviews. On one occasion a new chair had to be flown in from Sweden for a Thames Television programme.

Saatchi & Saatchi continued to be heavily involved in promoting the Conservative Party and in 1986 they helped plan, stage and design the annual conference. Working to the theme 'The Next Move Forward', ministers presented a carefully coordinated package of new policies in speeches whose outline had been drafted by Saatchis. Mrs Thatcher was happy to seek advice from executives of the *Sun* newspaper. Determined to stay in power, the Conservative Party had no qualms about dissolving the boundaries traditionally drawn between politics, advertising, PR and showbiz. One technique which has since become standard is the public endorsement of political parties by showbiz and media celebrities.

During the 1980s the Labour Party, in this area at least, learned quickly. Most commentators agree that theirs was the best campaign in the 1987 general election and at one point – 'Wobbly Thursday' – panic hit the Conservative ranks when it looked as if they might lose. Worried by the sharp image presented by the smart-suited Labour opposition, Mrs Thatcher stepped in and ordered Nigel Lawson to get his hair cut and Nicholas Ridley to discard a favourite old sweater.

In addition to these sartorial improvements, the Conservatives spent no less than £3 million in the last four days before polling day – which of course would have been impossible without access to the massive donations discussed in the previous chapter. The expert on British political finances, Michael Pinto-Duschinsky, estimated that 'The burst of spending by Conservative Central Office on press advertising during the week before the vote probably constituted the heaviest short-term, central campaign spending in British political history.'

Of course it was perfectly legal to do so. The 1883 Corrupt and Illegal Practices Act had restricted local election spending at a time when the absence of the mass media meant that elections were predominantly local in character. The Act had said nothing about national expenditure. The Labour Party's budget during the 1987 election was £6.5 million, the Conservatives spent nearly twice as much, £11.7 million. Individual candidates can spend no more than £8,000. It is not surprising that the Labour Party favours restrictions on national campaign spending and the Conservatives do not.

The 1992 election campaign saw a more sustained use of knocking copy, directed in particular at Labour leader Neil Kinnock. Again, this replicated similar tactics which had been used in the United States, particularly against the former Democratic presidential candidates Walter Mondale and Michael Dukakis. Roger Ailes, the media guru who helped George Bush win the presidency in 1988, observed that 'TV only covers three things – visuals, attacks and mistakes.' During that campaign Bush concentrated relentlessly on just three or four emotional issues which were known, after intensive market research, to resonate in the public consciousness. The 1992 presidential campaign degenerated into a war of the soundbites.

There is no reason to suppose that such techniques will not feature in British elections. Video tapes may well replace personal campaigning whilst direct mail will be targeted at individuals in their homes. The costs of this high-powered campaigning inevitably means that political parties will need to raise large sums of money.

It is certain too that election campaigns will increasingly be based around questions of personality rather than issues – and here the Labour Party's 'Kinnock' election broadcast in 1987 springs to mind. Election watcher David Butler has already noted that British general elections are becoming more presidential in their emphasis on the character and attributes of the leader. What will that mean for the future of political parties generally? After the death of Labour leader John Smith in May 1994, it was obvious that the photogenic qualities of Tony Blair gave him a head-start over rivals such as Margaret Beckett and Robin Cook.

One consolation is that our parliamentary system of rough and tumble, in which Prime Minister and minister alike are expected to handle regular parliamentary questions, does work against the appearance of completely synthetic, vacuous but good-looking politicians.

Since the eighteenth century the actual casting of votes in Britain has become increasingly less public. Originally the hustings were held in prominent places with both candidates and voters in full public view. For instance, the portico of St Paul's church in Covent Garden, London once hosted the Westminster elections which were spread out over two weeks. Heads were broken and blood spilt, and one observer was revolted by 'a scene only ridiculous and disgusting. The vulgar abuse of the candidates from the vilest rabble is not rendered endurable by either wit or good temper.'

The secret ballot in 1872 substituted the privacy and deliberation of the voting booth for the vigour of the public hustings. Radio and television contributed further to the decline of old-style campaigning whilst the prevalence of opinion polls can have a destabilising effect. Mrs Thatcher was in part brought down by them, when Tory backbenchers came to the conclusion that she would not win the next election, and similarly John Major's position was also weakened by the unending succession of polls showing how unpopular both he and his administration were.

In the future it may be possible to use cable television networks to hold frequent referenda; voters may well cast their vote at home. But it would be absurd to exaggerate the effect of American developments in Britain; here, voters elect political parties and not just individual politicians. Most academics agree that the personality of the individual MP in Britain counts for no more than 1,500 votes in his or her constituency.

On the other hand, the immediate and striking success of Silvio Berlusconi's Forza Italia party in the March 1994 elections in Italy offered a taster of media-led elections. In just three months, Forza Italia acquired more than 20 per cent of the national vote, immeasurably helped by the support of Berlusconi's television and newspaper outlets. As observer Martin Jacques pointed out, the traditional baggage of political parties – membership, fund-raising, democratic structures – was jettisoned in favour of the disciplines of market research, advertising and a voter-friendly image. Media glitz proved more effective than an army of door-to-door canvassers and envelope-lickers.

However, the difficulties which have since dogged Forza Italia suggest that substance can still be more important than show. An effective soundbite does not necessarily solve a country's economic and political problems.

The Conservative Party has excelled this century at winning elections. It has consistently outfought its opponents, helped no doubt by its greater financial resources and by an intense desire to exercise power. The Party's effectiveness has been derived too from its links with the business community which has always accepted that, in the continuous search for customers and markets, organisations must adapt or die. Many of those involved in Conservative Party communications since the Second World War have had a thorough grounding in business.

In addition, the Conservative Party has been materially assisted by what could once have been called Fleet Street. Few newspaper proprietors have ever been in favour of drastic political and social change, simply because they themselves are certain to be prospering under the present system. Of all the national newspapers, it is probably the *Daily Mail* which has provided the most unquestioning support for the Conservative Party. The *Mail*'s loyalty was exemplified by its front page of 26 April 1979, published in the middle of that year's election campaign, which read 'Labour's Dirty Dozen – 12 Big Lies They Hope Will Save Them'. Economising on both time and labour, the paper simply reproduced a handout from Conservative Central Office.

Yet it should also be remembered that, just as businesses ranging from the *Daily Mail* to British Airways have occasionally used dirty tricks in order to steal a march on competitors, so too has the British Conservative Party sometimes employed less than legitimate techniques in its pursuit of power. Later chapters will examine some of these underhand methods as well as analysing the significance of the Party's links with the press.

A famous passage in *The Times* newspaper on 18 April 1883, the second anniversary of Disraeli's death, claimed that 'In the inarticulate mass of the English populace, [Disraeli] discerned the Conservative workingman as the sculptor perceives the angel prisoned in a block of marble.' These angels form the base of the steep social pyramid which is the Conservative Party: voters at the bottom, then members, then officers, then MPs, then the Cabinet and at the apex the leader.

Without this crucial bottom layer – namely the one in three working-class voters who have traditionally voted Tory – the Conservative Party's claim to be a national party speaking for all interests and classes would be clearly fraudulent. And if there is one thing which unites all Conservatives, it is their determination to pose as a national and not a minority party: 'We, The Nation'.

The two most profound changes in terms of voting in British elections have been the gradual expansion of the electorate and the introduction of the secret ballot. Before the first Reform Act of 1832 only a quarter of a million people could vote; after it, approximately one in five adult males had the vote. After the 1867 Reform Act this had risen to one in three adult males. After the 1884 Reform Act the number was up to six in ten adult males.

The 1918 Act introduced a system of one man one vote, together with votes for some women. After the 1928 Act the arrival of one woman one vote meant that women were, and have remained ever since, in the majority – and the Conservative Party has excelled at attracting women's support.

Almost as important as the universal franchise was the introduction of the secret ballot in 1872. At the annual Conservative conference of that year there were some criticisms expressed of the Act for its 'likely promoting of secret political societies of revolutionary opinions', but such fears proved groundless.

It is illuminating that the Reform Acts of 1867 and 1928 were introduced by Conservative governments and there was much debate within the Party as to the merits of such a course. In the end, those Tories who preferred to trust in the electorate won out, but even they had qualms. As Stanley Baldwin put it in 1929: 'Democracy has come at a gallop in England. Can we educate them in time?'

The original strength of the Conservative Party was in the countryside and not in the big cities. But after the 1867 Reform Act, which gave the vote to the town voter, and the big increase in the number of urban seats after 1885, it was clear that unless the Party expanded it would rarely win elections. It grew most successfully in the North-West of England and in London, followed by Birmingham and the West Midlands. During the first decades of this century the Party strengthened its position too in Scotland. Two areas in particular remained stony ground for Tories – Wales and Yorkshire – but this was more than outweighed generally by the Party's appeal to women.

Since the Second World War both Labour and Conservative have been pushed back into their traditional heartlands: Labour to the cities, the Conservatives to southern England and the smaller towns. The Conservatives have been pushed out of the big cities, the North of England and Scotland. But always the Conservatives have attracted a significant proportion of the working-class vote to ensure their continuance as a national party: even in the sweeping defeat of 1945, for instance, 30 per cent of the working class voted Tory.

The comparative stability of the Conservative vote meant that the Party was well placed to benefit from the first past the post electoral system. Ever since the election of 1880, their share of the vote has usually been around the low 40 per cent mark. When it drops into the 30s, as it did in 1929, 1945 and twice in 1974, then electoral defeat is practically certain.

In several respects, Mrs Thatcher's brand of Conservatism was different from what had gone before. Unlike most socialist commentators and critics, she could see that the widespread changes transforming Britain since the end of the war were potentially detrimental to the Labour Party. The stereotypical council-house-dwelling, blue-collar trade unionist was becoming rarer. Social and geographical mobility was gradually destroying the collective blocks of support thought to favour the Labour Party.

'Class has faded as a political divider,' noted *The Economist* in September 1993. 'More complex patterns of allegiance now prevail. In the north, traditions of collective solidarity survive. In the south, individualism rules. Black people; women; environmentalists: each have agendas that do not fit the straitjacket of two competing class-based parties. Leadership now consists of constructing coalitions of interests rather than classes.'

Norman Tebbit and others were quick to recognise that Conservatism could reach a new set of people traditionally regarded as Labour sympathisers: 'I had long believed that . . . most of the values, ethos and policies of Conservatism were strongly supported by working-class voters. Those voters – especially the socio-economic groups C1 and C2 – I saw as natural Conservatives who nevertheless saw themselves for tribal reasons as Labour voters.'

One ardent Thatcherite, the former Labour MP Woodrow Wyatt, claimed quite correctly that the wider appeal of the new Conservatism, however much it might displease the traditional Tory grandees, made the Conservative Party more of a national party than it ever was before.

Paradoxically, opinion polls showed that the majority of the electorate was out of sympathy with the key tenets of Thatcherism, hoping for more money to be spent on welfare even if this meant an increase in taxes. On only one issue – the question of denationalisation – did the 1980s see a shift rightwards. Nevertheless, the Thatcher government was re-elected in 1983 and 1987.

In part this discrepancy between prediction and actuality reflected the inevitable failings of opinion polls: what people say to the pollster and what they do in the ballot box are not necessarily the same. But it also indicated that other factors such as leadership and strength of purpose might be more important to voters than actual programmes or policies.

Much of the Conservative electoral success since 1979 has been based on the promise of economic prosperity. Frantic attempts were made to massage the economy in the run-ups to the last three elections, as we shall see in Chapter 11. This is an explicit recognition that the electorate at large is now more calculating in its voting, swayed less by long-term traditional loyalties than by short-term personal interest.

Clearly this threatens the prospects of the Labour Party, which is still commonly associated with the non-achievers or failures in society. But it has implications for the Conservatives too.

Politicians of all parties face a common problem because disillusion with the political process is widespread and growing. The turnout in British general elections is dropping, that in local elections and European elections has been amongst the lowest of all member countries, and two million people no longer bother to register to vote at all.

In the short-term, some Conservatives might not see this as a problem. With their limited commitment to democracy and their suspicion of what the 'people' might come up with, this reversal of the nineteenth-century Reform Acts might even seem to be a blessing. After all, people who fail to register clearly feel they do not have much of a stake in the system and are therefore unlikely to be Conservatives anyway. Buttressing this argument, the noted liberal J.K. Galbraith in his book *The Culture of Contentment* has warned non-Conservatives to beware a situation in which people happy with their lot and fully prepared to make their voice heard can easily outgun a dispossessed and inarticulate remainder at the bottom of the system.

Thoughtful Conservatives recognise that there are long-term dangers here. For one thing, people's identification with political parties has dropped dramatically over the last few years, exposing even the Tory Party to the danger of traumatic electoral defeat.

More importantly, if people cease to express their approval or discontent through the existing political system then they will undoubtedly discover other channels of expression and these may well be violent ones. Robert Waller comments that the Conservative Party has always flourished 'because of their own continued ability to appeal to those from all walks of life and all levels of income'. If this ceases to be true, then the Party will no longer be able to boast that it is a national party – and then there will indeed be danger ahead.

———

Dirty Tricks

Conservative versus Labour

'If you look at the history of the Conservative Party, you will always find that it is when the country is scared of wild-cat schemes and wants safety that it turns to the Conservative Party.'

> Viscount Davidson, former chairman
> of the Party, speaking in 1961

'Conservatives do not worship democracy. For them majority rule is a device . . . And if it is leading to an end that is undesirable or inconsistent with itself, then there is a theoretical case for ending it.'

> Sir Ian Gilmour *Inside Right* (1977)

'In the Falklands, we had to fight the enemy without. Here the enemy is within, and it is more difficult to fight, and more dangerous to fight.'

> Prime Minister Margaret Thatcher, July 1984

In 1932 one of the leading lights at Conservative Central Office wrote a book called *The Game of Politics*. The title was in fact misleading, because Philip Cambray argued that politics was most certainly not a game but was more like military warfare. The 'General Staffs' of political parties should seek out and attack the enemy: 'Fraternisation with the enemy is as foolish a gesture in political warfare is in military warfare.'

Cambray had been deputy director of publicity at Conservative Central Office and in his book he singled out the so-called 'Zinoviev letter' episode of 1924, praising it as an example par excellence of effective surprise. Cambray particularly admired the skilful timing of the letter which made it impossible for the Labour Party to respond to Conservative accusations. He discreetly omitted any mention of his own involvement.

The Zinoviev letter was perhaps the most sensational of all bombshells to explode in the course of a British general election. There is still debate about its authenticity, but whatever its status the Conservatives made masterly use of it in order to undermine the Labour Party in the run-up to the 1924 general election.

The sequence of events was that on 10 October 1924 the Foreign Office intercepted a communication sent by the Moscow-based organisation Comintern, or Communist International. Dated 15 September 1924, it was signed by its head Grigori Zinoviev. This letter was addressed to the British Communist Party and urged its members to redouble their efforts to foment unrest and revolution. The Foreign Office spent some time trying to verify whether the letter was genuine or the work of anti-communist forgers.

Ramsay MacDonald, the first Labour Prime Minister, was informed of the letter and its contents but, caught up as he was in the middle of an election campaign, he had his mind on many other things and failed to recognise the possible importance of the document. Nothing further happened until suddenly, on the morning of Saturday 25 October, MacDonald and the rest of Britain woke up to read the bombshell headline on the front page of the *Daily Mail*: CIVIL WAR PLOT BY SOCIALISTS' MASTERS.

Elections then were fought in the absence of radio and television, so that press coverage took on enormous significance. As polling day was just four days later on Wednesday 29 October, the Labour Party had little time to respond to the specific allegation brought by Central Office and Fleet Street that MacDonald had tried to sit on the letter and that in general the Labour Party was a communist stooge.

The *Daily Mail*'s allegations were naturally taken up by the other newspapers. On polling day, 29 October 1924, the *Daily Mirror* made its preferences plain. Its front-page headline urged readers to 'Vote British, not Bolshie'. Underneath was the question 'Do You Wish to Vote for the Leaders of Law, Order, Peace and Prosperity?' – complete with pictures of the Conservative and Liberal leaders – or, as it continued remorselessly, 'to Vote for the Overthrow of Society and Pave the Way to Bolshevism?' The second option was accompanied by distinctly unflattering pictures of the Soviet leaders. At the election the Conservative Party under Baldwin regained power and the Labour Party lost forty seats.

How influential was the Zinoviev letter in altering the election result? The Labour Party was struggling for re-election and might well have lost anyway – and in any case its vote actually rose by one million. This is the kind of 'impossible to prove one way or the other' argument continually trotted out: who is to say that without the letter the Labour Party's vote might not have risen by two million, three million?

Rather more impressive is to let senior Conservative Party figures deliver their own verdicts. In 1929 party chairman Davidson wrote a memo about Philip Cambray: 'That we won the last General Election [in 1924] by the margin we did was due in no small measure to the way he directed matters in connection with the Zinovieff letter.'

Later, another senior Central Office figure, Percy Cohen, wrote an unpublished history of the Party which stated that the letter had 'enormous impact on the country'. Neither Davidson nor Cohen – drawing up internal party documents not intended for public consumption – bothered to claim that the Labour Party might well have lost the election anyway.

What the Zinoviev letter certainly did do was to play upon what Cambray himself called elemental prejudice, creating a climate of opinion which favoured the Conservatives as well as making MacDonald appear to be an inept bungler. And it was the Conservative Party itself which was largely instrumental in generating this prejudice.

Ever since 1924, much attention has been devoted to the question of whether the letter was a forgery or not. In the 1960s three journalists on the *Sunday Times* claimed to have interviewed the widow of one of the forgers, Alexis Bellegarde, but academic opinion remains divided. Many on the Left are convinced it was a forgery aimed at influencing the election result, whilst those on the Right stress the probity of the Foreign Office officials who thought the letter genuine. But not all: Hugh Trevor-Roper has poured scorn on the Foreign Office's feeble attempts to find out whether the letter was genuine.

It is more revealing to look at the role of Conservative Central Office in the Zinoviev letter affair. Here, the evidence is clearcut, even leaving aside the role of Philip Cambray. The three main figures involved were Admiral Sir Reginald 'Blinker' Hall, formerly the head of the Intelligence division of the Admiralty; J.C.C. Davidson, confidant of leader Stanley Baldwin; and Joseph Ball, another intelligence officer employed at Central Office.

Hall, Davidson and Ball agreed with Philip Cambray that the rise of the Labour Party and its alleged but unproven links with both the Communist Party and the Soviet Union threatened the entire basis of British society. The only solution was to meet fire with fire – and make sure one lived to boast about it afterwards in one's memoirs, as Davidson did:

> With Joseph Ball I ran a little intelligence service of our own, quite separate from the Party organization. We had agents in certain key centres and we also had agents actually in the Labour Party Headquarters, with the result that we got their reports on political feeling in the country as well as our own. We also got advance 'pulls' of their literature. This we arranged with Odhams Press, who did most of the Labour Party printing, with the result that we frequently received copies of their leaflets and pamphlets before they had reached Transport House. This was of enormous value to us because we were able to study the Labour Party policy in advance, and in the case of leaflets we could produce a reply to appear simultaneously with their production.

Even more blatant was a secret memo drawn up by Davidson in March 1927 in which he confirmed the intention of the 'Special Information Service to keep us informed of the enemy [Labour] and his plans'.

Clearly these activities of Davidson and Ball – which Conservative Party historian Lord (Robert) Blake intriguingly judges 'an achievement' – make the Watergate scandal in the United States look rather puny. Neither Davidson nor Ball would ever have needed to launch a Watergate-style burglary: they would have already had an agent safely inside the Democratic Party headquarters and very probably in charge of the Democratic campaign itself. And not even ex-President Nixon had the self-confidence to boast about Watergate in his memoirs, unlike Viscount Davidson.

The leading officials at Central Office did not flinch from a little matter such as exploiting a possibly forged letter. It was Hall and Ball who paid yet another former MI5 agent called Donald im Thurm £5,000 for a copy of the Zinoviev letter – although im Thurm was to receive the money at a later date – which was then deliberately leaked to the *Daily Mail*, knowing that the paper could be relied upon to use it to maximum effect. Their obliging headline on 25 October was timed for maximum political effect.

Not only was Conservative Central Office directly involved in exploiting the Zinoviev letter – and here the authenticity of the letter is immaterial – but so too were the secret services who helped plant this political bomb. Their respected historian Christopher Andrew has put it succinctly, 'The Zinoviev Letter was intended to bring down the Labour government.'

Perhaps the most masterly aspect of the whole affair was the way in which the Conservatives, and particularly J.C.C. Davidson, defused any leakages after the affair and ensured that the two parliamentary debates initiated by the Labour Party in December 1924 and March 1928 got nowhere. Virtually none of the commentators who have examined the Zinoviev letter episode actually seem to have read these debates. Several revealing points have therefore been ignored.

Speaking for the Labour Party in December 1924, J.H. Thomas managed to get the Conservatives to agree it was untrue that

MacDonald had sat on the letter. He was rather less successful in getting answers to his other two questions. How was it that the *Manchester Evening Chronicle* had published an article on 22 October, three days before the *Mail*'s revelations, which carried a photograph of Zinoviev and referred to a report that 'before polling day comes a bombshell will burst and it will be connected with Zinovieff'? Was the paper blessed with extraordinary predictive powers? And what had happened to the original copy of the letter?

Replying on behalf of the Conservative Government, Foreign Secretary Austen Chamberlain ignored the first question and claimed that in fact the government knew 'its [the letter's] whole course from its origin until it reached our hands'. This seemed unlikely, if only because he was unable to say what had happened to the original document, speculating that it had been destroyed by British communists.

A full-scale parliamentary debate was held in March 1928. Once again, the Labour Party wanted to know how and why Conservative Central Office had copies of the letter in the week beginning Sunday 19 October. Why were at least two provincial papers referring to a coming bombshell? And why, in particular, did Central Office warn journalists to keep themselves ready for something to happen that forthcoming weekend of 25 and 26 October?

By now, of course, Prime Minister Baldwin was able to take refuge in the argument of 'water under the bridge, impossible now to find out' and so on. Baldwin claimed that no one had been paid as regards the letter. No one had, at that time. Im Thurm was paid his £5,000 a few weeks later.

The full story of the Zinoviev letter will probably never be known – it forms another part of the hidden history of the British Conservative Party. But it is clear that the exploitation of the letter by Central Office and Fleet Street, together with the role of Party officials such as Philip Cambray, hint at the iron fist inside the velvet glove of British politics; as the phrase has it, politics is a dirty business. To be fair, it may not always have been as dirty in Britain as elsewhere, but that is no reason for complacency now or in the future.

This chapter examines how the state has safeguarded the status quo and seen off challenges to its well-being. It begins by looking at how various governments have coped with civil unrest and strikes. Then the special case of Ireland is explored. This is followed by an examination of the links between the Conservative Party and the intelligence services which discusses some of the dirty tricks that have been deployed. The chapter ends with a study of shadowy but powerful private bodies such as the Economic League.

Most other countries have a history spattered with revolution, riot and violent dissent. Since the civil war in the 1640s, however, Britain has experienced comparative stability apart from 'the Troubles' in Ireland.

There have of course been marches, unrest and demonstrations, but these have rarely been serious enough to worry those in power. On the rare occasions when the existing order has been threatened, the authorities have been swift to react and resort to a variety of methods in order to avert danger. There is almost a graduated response: first of all propaganda is directed against the proposed action and its leaders. This is followed by the enrolment of the public into special units, by enhanced powers for the police and mobilisation of the army; finally, the threat of force. Only in the last desperate resort is this measure used.

The Conservative Party has always been quick to oppose what it has seen as unconstitutional threats to the established order because, by and large, they are happy with that order. Conservatives have therefore always insisted on a 'strong state' and tried to ensure that there are a range of measures available to the Government in the event of civil unrest.

Much of the legislation underpinning this modern strong state was introduced just before and just after the First World War. Edwardian Britain had witnessed an extraordinary upsurge in civil unrest due to the suffragette movement, industrial disputes and likely civil war in Ireland, all of which threatened internal stability.

After the war, worries about the dire example of the Russian Revolution in 1917 were exacerbated by unrest amongst the troops clamouring for demobilisation and by a rapidly growing labour movement.

Between the summer of 1909 and winter 1920, therefore, the secret services MI5 and MI6 were created. The Official Secrets Act of 1911 was passed. The 'D notice' system to vet newspaper stories on sensitive topics was installed. The Special Branch was revamped as a domestic counter-subversive agency.

Finally, the passage of the Emergency Powers Act in October 1920 granted extensive powers to the authorities in the event of industrial disputes. Once a state of emergency had been declared by the Government, as historians Keith Jeffery and Peter Hennessy have put it, the 1920 Act 'was couched in such broad terms as to give the executive almost complete freedom to introduce what regulations it chose'.

This battery of legal powers was combined with additional expedient short-term action. In 1919, for instance, the Cabinet spent much time discussing the public furore over expensive and understrength beer. The Conservative leader Andrew Bonar Law, a prominent member of the coalition Government, informed his colleagues that 'There was no doubt that many people attributed the present industrial unrest to the lack and poor quality of beer.'

Bonar Law was anxious that continued discontent might spill over into political action. Six weeks later, the Cabinet papers reveal worries over the differing prices of beer and wine: 'The working man regarded the indifferent quality of beer as a typical case of class legislation, and complained that, whereas the labouring classes could only get a very poor quality of beer, the upper classes could still get wines of pre-war strength.'

But if the beer was indeed strengthened, what then of the Scottish teetotal movement, of which Bonar Law himself was a representative? In the interests of social stability, Bonar Law swallowed his principles. The Government duly scrapped the existing controls on the supply of beer.

The nearest that the country came to upheaval was in Glasgow on 31 January 1919 when a series of strikes concluded with a march through to George Square. Some members of the Cabinet counselled caution, the more pugnacious wanted it out once and for

all; as Winston Churchill put it, 'There would have to be
in order to clear the air.'

Pitched battles were indeed fought between the police
sections of the forty-thousand strong crowd but whatever sections
of the authorities might have thought, the demonstrators had no
intention of taking over the running of the city. At the end of the
day everyone simply went home. The next day the government
ostentatiously paraded six tanks through the streets of Glasgow.

Fears about social instability after the First World War prompted
the creation of yet more official bodies. The Supply and Transport
Committee was set up in October 1919 to deal with possible
unrest. Referred to simply as the STC, it displayed Whitehall's
talent for giving vitally important bodies the dullest of names. The
STC was introduced primarily because the army was reluctant to
get embroiled in civil matters unless absolutely necessary. It was
imperative therefore for the authorities to develop other means
of control. Jeffery and Hennessy have described the preparations:
'Stores of rifles and machine guns were stockpiled at Army depots
to provide rallying points for 'loyal' civilians, skeleton staff lists
were compiled and an emergency communications scheme was
drafted.'

The STC was continually upgraded and strengthened during the
early 1920s and J.C.C. Davidson, later to prove a very influential
figure within the Conservative Party, was appointed chief civil
commissioner in 1923.

The authorities feared that any future Labour government might
close down an organisation which was, after all, dedicated to
breaking strikes. They need not have worried. The first Labour
administration of 1924 proved pathetically eager not to rock the
boat; one Cabinet minister, Josiah Wedgwood, claimed later that
their slogan had been 'We must not annoy the Civil Service'.
Only a handful of ministers were actually informed of the STC's
existence and these chosen few were deliberately selected because
of their 'incapacity' to make a fuss.

The first major test for the STC came with the General Strike in
May 1926. The previous year the miners had threatened to strike
in pursuit of a pay claim. The Conservative Government under

to provide temporary subsidies, a seeming
labour movement duly dubbed 'Red Friday'.
nt had deliberately bought time and used the
g space to prepare for the coming struggle.
subsidy came to an end and was not renewed.
ed industrial action and were supported by the
ess and its constituent unions who promised to
bring out their members in sympathy with the miners. The 'nine
days in May' provoked much less alarm amongst the authorities
than did the events of 1919. This time they were prepared and
knew full well that the TUC was deeply embarrassed by the
turn of events. Virtually any excuse would suffice for them to
back down.

The STC worked efficiently. Most of the transport and power-
generating systems continued to function with the help of volunteers
whilst the controlled use of the army was dramatic and effective.
Major-General Lord Ruthven, in charge of the London region,
noted that the great lesson of the strike was the use of armoured
vehicles: 'They had a profound moral effect. Their influence was
always immediate and overwhelming.' Ruthven clearly appreciated
the theatrical dimension of power. The Coldstream Guards were
ordered to march through the East End with drums beating in
order to take over the Victoria and Albert Docks, whilst large
military camps were set up in highly visible fashion in some of
the capital's parks.

Ironically the major use of the Emergency Powers Act after 1926
was by Clement Attlee's post-war Labour government. Threatened
by a wave of unofficial strikes on the docks, the Government did not
hesitate to send the army in to move foodstuffs. A state of emergency
was declared twice, in 1948 and 1949. 'By 1948 strike-breaking had
become almost second nature to the Cabinet', observe Jeffery and
Hennessy. By contrast, the successive Conservative Governments in
the 1950s and 1960s were keen to keep in with the trade unions
and there were few major industrial disputes.

The one innovation introduced by Winston Churchill's Government was the system of 'positive vetting' of civil servants in order
to establish their political views. The Attlee Government had

supervised a discreet but limited purge of public servants with pronounced communist views, but as the Cold War got colder and McCarthyism took hold in the United States a handful of right-wing backbenchers badgered the Government for sterner measures. In January 1952 the Conservative Government conceded the system of positive vetting.

At no time did this system approach the virulence of McCarthyism, primarily because the senior civil servants ensured that they kept the process under their own control rather than that of hardline backbenchers. The civil servant in charge, Sir John Winnifrith, was determined to create no martyrs. In all, twenty-five civil servants were dismissed, twenty-five resigned and eighty-eight were transferred to other less sensitive posts.

There is, however, more to be found out. In December 1994 it was revealed that at the height of the Cold War, MI5 held files on a quarter of a million communist suspects in Britain. This figure represented 1 in 184 of the British population. We know too that some left-wingers, particularly academics, teachers and actors, were refused jobs because of their political opinions. The BBC, for example, employed a Security Liaison Officer who vetted potential employees and internal staff promotions.

In general, however, the 1950s and 1960s were a period of comparative political stability. Nevertheless there were enough official and unofficial stoppages for Edward Heath while in opposition to draw up plans to restrict trade union power. His attempts to implement these plans after 1970 provoked turmoil. The Industrial Relations Act set up a new court intended to arbitrate on disputes, but the trade union movement refused to recognise its jurisdiction. Friction with the trade union movement generally was exacerbated by a series of disputes with the miners, led by Joe Gormley.

The 1972 strike included one event which, even if it did not directly threaten the British state, caused great alarm amongst the authorities. The miners knew that to make any stoppage effective they had to picket the power stations and prevent supplies of coal getting through. By bussing pickets from site to site the strikers could, by sheer weight of numbers, close down the power stations.

In early February 1972 the miners and their supporters, led by a young Yorkshire NUM official Arthur Scargill, laid siege to the Saltley coke works in the Midlands. Gradually the pickets reduced the number of lorries which managed to get into the depot. The climax came on 10 February 1972 when Scargill assembled a crowd of between ten and fifteen thousand pickets complete with banners, bagpipes and much fervour. The numbers involved, together with the threat of serious violence, persuaded the Chief Constable to close Saltley. Influential members of Heath's government, such as Jim Prior, have since recounted how earthshattering this decision was.

Further disputes in 1973–4 led to a three-day week and power cuts. Throughout, Heath's government was ill-prepared for the seemingly endless series of disputes. One of his advisers, Douglas Hurd, has summed up the sense of chaos when he wrote in his diary for 11 February 1972: 'The Government now wandering vainly over battlefield looking for someone to surrender to – and being massacred all the time.'

Although she would perhaps be the last person to admit it, Mrs Thatcher learnt much from Edward Heath's mishaps. At first she was comparatively unworried by the threat of serious industrial action but she changed her mind after a threatened miners' strike in 1981. The Civil Contingencies Unit, which replaced the old STC in 1972, was overhauled and upgraded. In 1982 the Conservative government backed down over the question of pit closures because the time was not right for an all-out conflict, but as in 1926 it proceeded to prepare for future battles.

There are still many unanswered questions about the miners' strike which lasted from March 1984 to March 1985. Did Scargill intend to bring down the Government? Were the Government and the National Coal Board in cahoots? How much did the dispute cost? What would have happened if the miners had been balloted over industrial action?

Whatever the answers, it is evident that the Government was determined to win and was prepared to give the police their full support to take whatever measures they felt necessary. Mail was intercepted and the telephones of the miners' leaders were tapped

– at one point the system overloaded and the continuous
tape-recorders ground to a halt when the tapes ran out.
groups of pickets were turned back at road-blocks by t
In contravention of nearly 150 years of tradition, the police began
to move towards a coordinated national force. Within the police
itself it was clear that elite groups specialising in riot control had
been established, without parliamentary knowledge. MI5 seems to
have had a 'spy' in the NUM camp as well as being responsible for
the intensive and prolonged surveillance operations. The strike was
defeated – and that was what mattered to the Government.

With the exception of the Heath years, the government strategies
adopted during these disputes exhibit the subtlety and finesse which
characterises the British Establishment. Immeasurably helped by the
fact that few of the strikers had any intention of actually bringing
down the Government, the conflicts were never allowed to get
out of control. If the authorities often strayed close to breaking
the law, generally but not always they stayed within it because the
draconian powers granted by the Emergency Powers Act of 1920
were sufficient. A.J.P. Taylor claimed that the 1920 Act represented
'as big a blow against the constitution as any ever levelled'.

But what these episodes do suggest is the extent of the reserve
powers available to the state for moblisation if things get rough.

The Conservative Party has always tried to ensure that conflicts or
unrest are directed through the appropriate channels. This has the
effect of making them safe and more capable of control. As Professor
Dennis Kavanagh has pointed out, disputes in Britain are generally
settled at a low level of crisis before the system itself is brought into
question. The one exception to this rule is Ireland. Intriguingly, it
also offers one case where it was Conservatives themselves who
were actively fomenting insurrection.

The so-called Protestant Ascendancy imposed by Elizabeth I
was rooted in the subjection of the Catholic population. Wealthy
Protestants were given huge tracts of land or 'plantations' which they
occupied and controlled by force if necessary. It is not surprising that
this Ulster Protestant minority was therefore resolute that Ireland

should remain an integral part of the United Kingdom. Bloodshed and cruelty became habitual. Oliver Cromwell's bloody campaigns in the 1640s against Irish revolt halved the population to 750,000.

During the course of the nineteenth century the Irish nationalist movement, overwhelmingly Catholic, sought to break these alien ties with a foreign country and demanded Home Rule. Their sense of indignation was fuelled by the terrible famines in the 1840s when more than one-and-a-half million people died. Resentment was increased by the callousness of such newspapers as *The Times*: 'For our own part we regard the potato blight as a blessing. When the Celts cease to be potophagi, they must become carnivorous. With the taste of meats will grow an appetite for them; with the appetite, the readiness to earn them.'

Some of the Home Rulers, like the Fenians, were prepared to use violence to make their case and on the mainland there were occasional bomb explosions and murders. The British authorities responded by creating the Special Irish Branch in 1883, which concentrated on the surveillance of potential suspects. In 1888 its jurisdiction was extended and it was renamed the Special Branch.

The authorities also monitored moderate and law-abiding Home Rulers, most notably Charles Stewart Parnell. One particular episode aimed at smearing Parnell offered a foretaste of future tactics. In 1887 *The Times* newspaper printed a series of articles called 'Parnellism and Crime'. The series contained quotations from letters supposedly written by Parnell, implicating him in the Phoenix Park murders of 1882 when the new Chief Secretary and Under Secretary of Ireland were assassinated. As was to happen a century later over the supposed 'Hitler Diaries', the owner of the paper, John Walter, failed to inquire as to the authenticity of what he was publishing, even though the articles had been hawked about by a notorious con-man called Pigott to other papers (which had speedily rejected them). The articles were then widely distributed as pamphlets.

One of the other Home Rulers mentioned in the articles sued the paper for libel and promptly lost. At this point, Salisbury's Conservative Government, scenting the possible destruction of the hated Home Rule movement, gleefully set up a commission in the hope of extracting political capital. The Government did all it could to bolster *The Times*'s case, allowing the paper's solicitor access to files in Dublin in the hope of linking Parnell with the Phoenix Park murders.

Parnell was able to show that in fact the letters were not in his handwriting. Pigott was thoroughly discredited in the witness box and promptly fled to Spain where he committed suicide. The incompetent Pigott was a convenient fall guy but was unlikely to have been able to set up such an operation on his own because he lacked the expertise and contacts. Years later Robert Anderson, in charge of Special Branch and subsequently to be the head of the Criminal Investigation Department (CID), admitted his involvement in the forgeries.

Despite Parnell's subsequent downfall over the very public divorce of his mistress Kitty O'Shea, the Home Rule movement continued to grow and many within the Liberal Party were in favour of their demands. After the two general elections of 1910 it was the Irish MPs at Westminster who held the balance of power and the Liberal Government under Asquith pledged to introduce a Home Rule measure. In the past the Conservatives had been able to rely on their in-built majority in the House of Lords to frustrate such legislation. However, the Parliament Act of 1911 replaced this absolute veto with the power to delay unwelcome legislation for three years only. In other words, the Home Rule Bill of 1911 was certain to be enacted in 1914.

The Ulster Unionists and their Conservatives allies began to prepare to resist the law. They stockpiled arms, enrolled volunteers who underwent military training and prepared for insurrection. Die-hard Tory peer Lord Willoughby de Broke even organised the British League for the Support of Ulster and the Union in May 1913 which explicitly intended to 'arm all Unionists on this side of the water who wish to fight with the Ulstermen'.

Conservative leader Andrew Bonar Law, himself of Ulster descent, also gave the Ulster Unionists under Sir Edward Carson *carte blanche* for their actions and justified the use of force; during a speech delivered at Blenheim in July 1912, Bonar Law called the democratically elected Liberal Government 'a Revolutionary

Committee which has seized depostic power by fraud'. He went on: 'I can imagine no length of resistance to which Ulster can go in which I should not be prepared to support them . . .'

This represented a startling reversal of previous Conservative beliefs which had always placed so much emphasis on upholding the rule of law and on constitutional action. Bonar Law was even prepared to recommend that army officers should disobey their orders and not quell the Ulster rebels – in other words, to countenance mutiny. His biographer Robert Blake maintains that on this issue Law's views were moderate; it is surely difficult to know how much more illegal an extremist position might have been.

Civil war in Ireland would almost certainly have spilled over into cities such as Liverpool and Glasgow where religious antagonism between Catholics and Protestants was intense. In fact, the outbreak of the First World War caused the agitation to be postponed. After the war the Lloyd George coalition granted limited Home Rule to Ireland, keeping Ulster as a separate entity; this was enough to pacify majority opinion within the Conservative Party. However, the consequences of these decisions are tragically still with us today.

Another example of unscrupulous links between the government, the security services and the press is found in the Roger Casement affair. Casement was sentenced to death during the First World War for collaborating with the Germans in his fervent desire to promote a united Ireland. He was also gay and had committed to paper his various sexual experiences and fantasies. Worried that Casement's execution would arouse dissent, the authorities discreetly publicised the contents of his diaries by circulating them to various journalists and influential public figures, knowing that this would undermine any campaign on his behalf.

Two points are of particular interest. Firstly, although it was Asquith's Liberal government which was in power this did not hamper the intelligence services. Secondly, the handling of this affair was undertaken by Captain Reginald Hall, the chief of naval intelligence. Later, as Admiral Sir Reginald Hall, he was to be a key figure at Conservative Central Office and, as we have seen, played a part in the Zinoviev letter affair. He was also the organising manager on the *British Gazette*, the anti-union newspaper issued by the Conservative Government during the General Strike in May 1926.

Like his colleague Sir Joseph Ball, Hall is one of those elusive figures whose name is found in footnotes but who is clearly more important than many better-known and much-written about politicians. His biographer considered that 'No man has ever known better how to keep a secret when secrecy was necessary' but, as regards the Casement affair, it is now clear that Hall's role was to circulate extracts from the diaries, thus sealing Casement's fate.

The campaign for a united Ireland has been led by the Irish Republican Army (IRA), which has been prepared to resort to terrorism to attain its means. The British state has fought back against the IRA and not all its weapons have been legal; moreover, several have been counter productive because they have alienated the Catholic minority within Ulster.

The point here is not in any way to excuse the vile methods of the IRA and of various paramilitary Ulster Protestant groups, but rather to suggest the lengths to which the army, the police and the authorities are prepared to go if they are really threatened: internment, suspension of civil liberties, the use of agents provocateurs, torture and the condoning of assassination. It is probable that the British army, for instance, played a role in the Protestant workers' strike of May 1974 which brought down the so-called power-sharing Executive, originally set up by the Heath adminstration, which seemed to offer a promising solution to the Irish problem.

The distinguished journalist Robert Fisk was an eyewitness of those fifteen days when, in effect, a part of the realm was ungovernable. As had happened with the Curragh Mutiny in 1912, some army officers in Ulster were unwilling to deal with the Northern loyalists. The barricades were not removed and Protestant lawlessness was tolerated. The Ulster Workers' Council was permitted to set itself up as the de facto Government.

Further murky dealings came to light during the Colin Wallace affair. Wallace was an army information officer serving in Northern Ireland. He worked for the Information Policy Unit which targeted politicians both in Northern Ireland and on the mainland who were regarded as opponents of the security forces' hard-line approach.

Disgusted by the kind of smears or 'psyops' (psychological operations) which he was expected to initiate, he voiced his opposition
and was promptly removed from his post in December 1974. An
inquiry later found that he was unfairly dismissed. Wallace then
rapidly found himself on the receiving end of some frightening
developments. He was charged with murder, imprisoned and finally
released, but he continues to maintain his innocence.

John Stalker, former deputy chief constable of the Greater
Manchester police, was baulked when he held an inquiry into the
deaths of six men shot in the winter of 1982 by a specialist squad of
Northern Ireland policemen, carrying out an implicit 'shoot to kill'
policy. He too found himself obstructed at the highest levels in his
investigation and then smeared in the *Daily Mail*. It was yet another
dirty story in a dirty war, suggesting that in their understandable zeal
to combat terrorism, sections of the security services and the police
were themselves adopting the techniques of their foes.

This section examines the links between the Conservative Party and
the intelligence services and the way each has exploited the other.

There have always been overlaps in terms of personnel. Several
important officials at Central Office were once senior officials in
MI5 – Blinker Hall and Sir Joseph Ball were just two of the most
prominent – and a former co-director of the Conservative Research
Department once wrote that it was 'nothing new for intelligence
people to be at the Conservative Party'. Many Conservative MPs
served in intelligence between 1940 and 1945 and no doubt kept
up their contacts and friendships.

The espionage writer Nigel West, now himself a Conservative
MP under his real name of Rupert Allason, has commented that
'Numerous members of the Commons have served in MI5 and
SIS.' He listed several MPs – all Conservative – who wrote books
but preferred to omit mention of their undercover roles: Aubrey
Jones, Henry Kerby, Sir Stephen Hastings, Kenneth Younger,
Rex Fletcher and Jack Cordeaux. To this list can be added the
names of Douglas Dodds-Parker and John Baker White and no
doubt others.

Members of MI5 were recruited from the same narrow social circles familiar to most Conservatives and there were bound to be overlaps. Major-General Sir Vernon Kell ran MI5 for over thirty years until 1939 and he always handpicked his recruits. Refusing to employ Catholics on the grounds that he wanted to keep the Vatican well away from the British security service, Kell also insisted that recruits enjoyed private means, partly because the pay was so poor that no one could expect to survive on that alone.

Kell established good contacts with the press barons and MI5 always retained the services of several journalists – it would have been foolish from their point of view not to have made use of Fleet Street's information-gathering potential. As a result there existed, and still does, a network of individuals with interests in the Conservative Party, the security services and the press. The Labour Party has never enjoyed such a relationship with either press or the security services because it represents, for at least some members of these institutions, the enemy.

The very earliest Conservative dirty tricks were at best cack-handed. In 1885, for example, working on the principle of divide and rule, the Conservatives funded the election campaigns of several Marxist Social Democrat candidates in the hope that they would draw off Liberal votes and allow the Conservative to win. This was fine in theory, but in practice the Social Democracts were so unpopular that they attracted no more than a handful of votes and therefore this early use of 'Tory Gold' made no difference whatsoever to any result.

The real links between the intelligence community and the Party were established after the First World War when the example of the Russian Revolution and a rash of post-war strikes seemed to threaten revolution in Britain. The heads of MI5 and MI6 exploited the 'Red Scare' for all it was worth, having a vested interest in its existence. After all, if there was no threat then there was no need for a security system and in turn no jobs for security officers.

In reality it was clear that Sir Basil Thomson, the head of Special Branch, knew full well that the 'red menace' was not in fact all that threatening. Recognising the apathy of the British public and the steadying influences of royalty and sport, Thomson wrote in

January 1920 that 'The minority who would like to see a sudden and violent revolution is ridiculously small.'

The views of some intelligence officers show just how dramatically they saw the world in polarised terms of black and white. Standing at a by-election in 1919, Admiral Blinker Hall claimed that anyone who was not a Tory must be 'either a German, a Sinn Feiner or a Bolshevist'. The memoirs of Sir Wyndham Childs, head of the Special Branch in the 1920s, contain much in similar vein. Men such as Hall and Childs found it impossible to discriminate between the miniscule British Communist Party – which did indeed accept Soviet financial help – and the constitutional and moderate Labour Party. In fact, the Labour Party had expelled communists from its ranks in 1924 and proscribed any organisation which had any association whatsoever with the Communist Party. The implications of this seem to have been lost on British intelligence.

Several of the most powerful offensives involving some or all of the Conservative Party, national press and the intelligence services have been launched at election times. In 1910, for instance, rumours were spread to the effect that 'Asquith killed the King' by pressing on with the Liberal Government's demand for constitutional reform. In 1923 the Conservatives spread rumours that the socialists were planning to introduce 'compulsory free love' (!) and the next year there was the Zinoviev letter itself. The 1931 election was dominated by allegations that the Labour Party intended to confiscate people's Post Office savings. More recently, the 1992 general election saw both Central Office and the press continually reiterating the claim that if the Labour Party won power it would increase taxes – ironically enough, of course, it was the victorious Tories who put up taxes.

Sometimes concerted campaigns are launched against individuals regarded as threatening by the Establishment. Three particular cases spring to mind, namely those of Ramsay MacDonald, Harold Wilson and Tony Benn.

As a young man Ramsay MacDonald had belonged to a Marxist Party and although he soon dropped such revolutionary ideas he courageously spoke out against the conduct of the First World War. For his pains he found that his birth certificate – showing that he was illegitimate – was published in the press, his public meetings were broken up by stone-throwing mobs and he was subject to government surveillance.

MacDonald was always a bête noire to the secret services because he had voted against the passage of the Official Secrets Act in 1911 and one of his first acts on becoming Prime Minister in January 1924 was to ask to see his own Special Branch file. He was refused. Although MacDonald soon demonstrated that his moderate views were hardly a threat to the existing order, he was smeared in the press over his acceptance of a private car from his friend, Sir Alexander Grant, chairman of the biscuit manufacturer McVitie.

At first the relatively poor MacDonald travelled to Chequers, the Prime Minister's weekend residence, by public transport; he went by underground and then hired a taxi at the neighbouring station. Then he suddenly acquired the use of a chauffeur-driven Daimler. The press hunt, which was led by the *Daily Mail*, called this a bribe and noted that Grant had recently been knighted. This smear campaign conveniently ignored the fact that Grant had initially been nominated for an honour by the previous Conservative administration and that a recent Tory Prime Minister, Andrew Bonar Law, was for many years subsidised by his friend Lord Beaverbrook. Nor did it seem totally unreasonably for the Prime Minister to have an official car rather than having to rely on public transport.

During the Second World War Aneurin Bevan was regularly shadowed by an MI5 agent who even wormed himself into the family household as a friend. The surveillance seems to have been toned down when the agent was caught out in a lie. The furious Bevan cornered the man in a washroom, seized him by the throat and extorted a confession. However, the most sustained campaign of vilification directed against a Labour politician was aimed at Harold Wilson.

It is hard now to understand the anxiety with which Harold Wilson was regarded by the Establishment during the 1960s. Yet on his election as Prime Minister in 1964 he was not only the first socialist in Downing Street since Attlee, but, unlike Attlee who had always been firmly in the mainstream of the moderate

Labour Party and had spent five years as Deputy Prime Minister to Churchill, Wilson had a left-wing past. Anti-American and opposed to rearmament, he was in favour of stronger East-West trade links and was the commercial adviser to the timber firm of Montague Meyer, which traded with various Eastern European countries.

Wilson's intellectual and financial acumen meant that he was a formidable threat to the City and other established interests, particularly when he succeeded in greatly increasing the Labour Party's majority at the March 1966 election. He also seemed to favour parliamentary supervision of the intelligence services themselves.

It is commonplace to dismiss the campaign of smears and innu-endo against Wilson and his entourage as paranoia on a grand scale; the overheated left-wing imagination seeing enemies everywhere. But if most people were to have their homes burgled eight times during which papers were disturbed and stolen but no valuables taken, or to have found smears against them and their associates continually apearing on the front pages of hostile newspapers, then they would surely think it more than coincidental.

The homes and offices of Wilson's advisers were also regularly broken into. For example, the offices of Lord Goodman, Wilson's legal adviser, were burgled twice in 1974. Goodman, a pillar of Establishment rectitude and not given to fantasy, said that he had no notion why he was burgled: 'until much later, when I discovered that they had been searching for documents that might in some way incriminate Harold Wilson. We had no such documents. I don't think any such documents existed.'

The extent of the secret state's activities were confirmed by Peter Wright's memoirs *Spycatcher*: 'For five years we bugged and burgled our way across London at the State's behest, while pompous bowler-hatted civil servants in Whitehall pretended to look the other way.' Transport House, for instance, the headquarters of the national Labour Party, was a recipient of Wright and his colleagues' attentions. Sir Michael Hanley, head of MI5, subsequently admitted that there had indeed been problems with 'a small group of disaffected members' of the security service – and by the nature of their work such a group was potentially very powerful.

The Conservative Party also initiated a full-scale press campaign against Wilson whilst their associates in Special Branch regularly tailed both him and his deputy George Brown. The magazine *Private Eye* was used by the intelligence services as a channel for 'disinformation' – the allegation that Labour's deputy leader Edward Short had an illegal bank account in Switzerland first surfaced in the magazine in July 1974. Scotland Yard soon established that the documents were forged, but proved less successful in probing the source of the forgeries. Short's flat was also burgled.

It is not a pretty story, and the Conservative Party does not have clean hands. The Party was apparently involved, too, in the campaign against Tony Benn in the mid-1970s when his telephone was tapped, his house bugged, his family harassed and he received death threats. At the same time large sections of the press conducted a merciless campaign of sustained vilification against Benn: the *Daily Express*, for instance, published a photograph which compared him with Adolf Hitler, whilst the *Sun* of 22 May 1981 headlined an article: 'Mr Benn – Is He Mad or a Killer?' Ironically, the *Sun* and other Fleet Street papers were at this time campaigning, quite rightly, against the Soviet practice of incarcerating political prisoners in psychiatric hospitals.

A more recent example of dirty tricks may be seen in the attempt to smear the Liberal Democrat leader Paddy Ashdown during the 1992 election over an extra-marital liaison. He effectively countered this by coming clean over the episode. The run-up to that same election witnessed a more overt threat being utilised by Ian Lang, the Conservative Secretary of State for Scotland. Worried about the campaign for Home Rule, 'On 3 February he wrote to 50,000 businessmen warning of the dangers of independence. Pressure was put on the chairmen and chief executives of life-assurance companies, banks, investment houses and industrial companies to come out publicly and warn their workers against the consequences of Home Rule.'

Sometimes one or other of the three bodies, the Conservatives, the secret services and the press, acts independently. During the general election of 1945 the chairman of the Labour Party, Harold Laski, speaking at a public meeting in Newark, was needled by a heckler who claimed that Laski was the 'sort of bloodthirsty little man who had never smelled a bullet, but was always the first to stir up violence in peace'. Laski snapped back: 'Judging by the temper you display, you would be naturally one of the objects of violence when it does come.' On the face of it, one might think, a fairly innocuous sequence of events.

Not so. The *Daily Express* promptly seized on Laski's remark and headlined the claim that he was advocating 'Socialism even if it means violence'. The editor of the *Express*, Arthur Christiansen, later admitted that he was convinced he had given the Conservatives a weapon as good as the Zinoviev letter and which would likewise help them win the election by portraying the Labour Party as communist dupes. Funnily enough, it turned out that the Newark heckler, James Wentworth Day, had once been a publicity manager and feature writer for Lord Beaverbrook's *Express* newspapers. In fact the Laski affair proved to be much less effective then Christiansen hoped because in the 1945 election such smear tactics were ignored by a politically-aware electorate radicalised by the recent war.

The memoirs of Sir John Junor, the long-time editor of the *Sunday Express*, confirm how he happily followed in Christiansen's footsteps, searching around at election times for slip-ups or off-hand remarks by Labour politicians which could then be used to damn their party. In 1970, for example, after a tip-off from another Conservative MP, Junor headlined a comment from Labour's Richard Crossman that the economy was in a fragile state. According to Junor, Conservative Party leader Edward Heath later phoned him and said quite simply, 'Thank you, that may have turned the tide.'

The campaigns explored above are doubtless only part of the story. As with Robert Anderson's involvement in the Pigott forgeries, more evidence will certainly emerge later when we are safely dead and buried and it is all history. But at present, much of the illegal activity arises because the secret services are not accountable to Parliament and therefore exist as a kind of secret state inside Britain. Of all the established democracies, only Britain does not insist that applications for telephone taps, bugging or burglary must be scrutinised by the courts. The Official Secrets Act passed by Mrs Thatcher's government in 1989 narrowed the scope of the criminal law but made no concessions to critics calling for interest defence', amongst them Sir Edward Heath.

John Major has a more relaxed stance towards secrecy under its new director-general Stella Rimington – who played a large part in the surveillance of the NUM during the miners' strike in 1984–5 – is endeavouring to be a more law-abiding and accountable organisation. A new Intelligence and Security Committee was set up in December 1994. Chaired by Tom King, it will introduce a very general, but still welcome, parliamentary scrutiny of the security and intelligence services. These reforms should not, however, be allowed to whitewash or cover up their past activities.

It must be emphasised that these dirty tricks were planned and perpetrated only by certain groups within the intelligence services and the Conservative Party – even if others must have been prepared to turn a blind eye. Many decent and honest Conservatives would have been horrified at what was being done. Edward Heath, for instance, was one party leader who was never taken in by the grandiose claims of 'intelligence'.

In January 1988 Heath told the House of Commons that during his time as Prime Minister, 'I met people in the Security Services who talked the most ridiculous nonsense and whose whole philosophy was ridiculous nonsense' – the kind of people who got agitated if they saw somone reading the *Daily Mirror* on the tube. Similarly Lord Carrington, when he was chairman of the Party between 1972 and 1974, actively discouraged underhand dealings and as Foreign Secretary under Mrs Thatcher he scorned the lurid right-wing theories of men such as Brian Crozier, of whom more later.

But like any political party the Conservative Party is a coalition of interests, and some of those interests were and are prepared to resort to illegal methods to get their way. How ironic that these Conservatives would apparently agree with Lenin that the end justifies the means. It was a far cry from Benjamin Disraeli's vow to resign as party leader if any Conservative attempted to exploit rumours that Palmerston had given a job to the husband of one of his mistresses.

★   ★   ★

Much of the dirty work has traditionally been farmed out to semi-private bodies, which lessens the risk of the Government or the Conservative Party being too directly implicated. As one might expect, the greatest upsurge in such groups took place in the aftermath of the post-1918 unrest when employers and businessmen banded themselves into groups.

One of them was run by the shadowy figure of Sidney Walton, a former undercover agent who in 1919 was entrusted with funds of £100,000 – multiply this by fifty to get today's values – and placed in charge of propaganda against trade unions and socialism. By 1922 those on his payroll included MPs, journalists and even the Lord Chancellor, Lord Birkenhead, and Walton claimed to be able to place 'authoritative signed articles' in over 1,200 newspapers. Almost needless to say, Admiral Sir Reginald Hall was also involved.

Dr Keith Middlemas has written of the work of Walton and his associates: 'The octopus they created may, not unfairly, be compared with the Nixon apparatus at the time of Watergate, without the denouement of exposure.' Walton's funds came not from government but from industrial sources, particularly the Engineering Employers' Federation. He also used the money to bribe editors to print his articles.

Although the Conservatives did try to crack down on corruption after the downfall of Lloyd George in 1922, their efforts were chiefly directed at J. Maundy Gregory and the sale of honours. They pulled their punches when it came to Sidney Walton; in Middlemas's words, party leader Bonar Law 'had been far too close to the secret propaganda machine since 1916 for him not to have known, or for them to dare uncover the whole appalling truth'. Walton later worked specifically for the Conservative Party and handled their campaign against the General Strike in 1926.

Other motley right-wing groups, often dedicated one-man bands, came and went with bewildering speed. Several of them received a helping hand from the authorities. J. McGuirk Hughes of Liverpool had a long history of anti-socialist activity and in 1924 he set up a new anonymous organisation which was in part funded by Scotland Yard. Hughes's activities encompassed forgery, break-ins and theft as he manfully strove to accumulate information on potential 'subversives' which he then handed over to Scotland Yard and the intelligence services.

Another active organisation was the Anti-Socialist Union, founded as long ago as 1908, whose sole object was to oppose 'socialism, communism, and other subversive movements'. The Union lasted until 1949 when it was wound up and handed over its assets to the most important of these groupings, and one which is still going strong today, the Economic League.

Originally called National Propaganda, the league had been initiated, yet again, by Admiral Blinker Hall. His extensive range of contacts was backed up by the financial muscle of wealthy businessman Sir George McGill: the league had the then massive budget of a quarter of a million pounds. It stood for the support of free enterprise, which was reasonable enough, but rather more menacingly it promised to 'expose and counter subversive elements'.

The Economic League campaigned in support of capitalism and there was sometimes a foolhardy bravery to its actions, as in 1926 when its mobile vans or Flying Squads toured the mining areas urging the miners to return to work. It was formidably active as a propaganda agency: in one period from January 1930 to December 1931 it held over twenty thousand meetings which were attended by nearly three million people. In all, some twenty-nine million leaflets were distributed between 1919 and 1938. The league also offered a blacklisting service which warned employers about 'dangerous subversives' and it became evident that some of its information was derived from police files.

Its director from 1926 to 1945 was John Baker White, later to be Conservative MP for Canterbury. His two autobiographies barely mention the league, although clearly his involvement with it took up much of his time and energy. Baker White had decided from an early age that he wanted to dedicate his life to fighting communism. At a time when many young men were playing cricket or train-spotting, Baker White was hanging around 'frowsty little cafés', studying possible subversives.

In the late 1930s Baker White was ardently pro-Hitler but, like many others, he changed his opinions just in time to save himself from being labelled a traitor. During the Cold War, the virulence of his anti-communist views sought to make up for his former Nazi sympathies.

The Economic League was not, and is not, some tin-pot bunch of amateurs. In 1955 it employed two hundred people and one commentator noted that the views and background of its staff resembled that of the Conservative Party. This is hardly surprising when it is known that, in 1957, Conservative Party chairman Lord Poole replied to backbench MP Edward du Cann (himself to be party chairman in the 1970s), asking if his firm should subscribe to the league: 'We realise that it is not always possible for firms to give open financial support to our Party and in such cases we would say that help to the Economic League is sound.'

In 1978 a study of the league concluded that it could still afford six area offices and up to a hundred and fifty full-time staff. This means that it had about as much organisational clout as the Liberals, one of the three major political parties in Britain. The previous year the league claimed to have distributed seventeen million leaflets. Its funds were provided by major companies such as Tate & Lyle, Imperial and Shell as well as the four major clearing banks, whilst it also enjoyed a close relationship with the police.

Today in the 1990s it is estimated that the Economic League keeps files on more than 250,000 people in Britain. In the past twenty years approximately four-and-a-half million people have been screened by the league on behalf of the two thousand companies which make use of its services. By keeping its information on filing cards it is able to ignore the legal requirements imposed by the Data Protection Act which only apply to information held on computers. A strike at an engineering factory near Southampton in 1973 revealed that the Special Branch, the firm's management and the Economic League were regularly passing information from one to the other. Much of the information hoarded away is incorrect and defamatory.

If the Economic League is the most notorious of such bodies, it is by no means the only one. Other agencies such as Iris (a charming acronym for Industrial Research and Information Services) and Common Cause also operated blacklisting services. Private companies sometimes set up their own internal system: car manufacturers Rover, for instance, had its own secret vetting unit called – innocuously enough – B.G. Research Service.

Several of these shadowy groups received a welcome shot in the arm during the Cold War. Funds were indirectly provided by the informal Information Research Department (IRD), set up at the end of 1947 by the Attlee Government to counter communist subversion. Funded by the secret vote or subsidy available to government – a vote which allows governments of all persuasions to finance projects without informing Parliament – the IRD's very existence, let alone its work, was never made known to MPs. Information about the IRD only trickled out after its closure in May 1977.

The IRD's funding and range of activities grew rapidly during the peak of the Cold War era in the 1950s. Its satellite companies published a wide range of books, sometimes in collaboration with the respected publishing firm of Bodley Head, whilst news items and briefings were sent out to over a hundred journalists and a wide range of newspapers and magazines. A magazine called *Freedom First* was also circulated amongst trade unionists.

IRD was not some hole-in-the-wall affair: it occupied a twelve storey tower block in South London and its Soviet section alone had more than sixty members. At its height, the IRD had over two hundred and fifty employees. In the 1970s the IRD set up a counter subversion unit to wage a propaganda war against the IRA.

Money from the United States was also available too, and not just to the monthly magazine *Encounter* which was embarrassingly exposed as a CIA conduit in 1967: a case not so much of 'Moscow gold' but 'Washington dollars'. Other organisations which were secretly subsidised included Keep Britain In [Europe], the European Youth Campaign and the International Student Conference – successive American administrations wanted a united Europe to act as a bulwark against the Soviet Union and its satellite states.

Details about the extent of this illicit funding are still coming to light. In October 1993, for instance, the *Daily Telegraph* reported that Winston Churchill had been given American money in order to help finance a campaign for a united Europe. Up to £3.5 million was channelled by the CIA to this new front organisation called

The American Committee on United Europe. As Dr Richard Aldrich has noted, 'Overtly, the committee's role was to educate the American people about Europe. But its real purpose was to serve as a conduit for covert CIA funds.' The committee was finally wound up in 1960.

Yet another recipient of CIA funds was Brian Crozier who set up his innocent sounding Institute for the Study of Conflict (ISC) in 1970 under the aegis of the Information Research Department. The author of two admiring studies of the dictator-generals Franco of Spain and Pinochet of Chile, Crozier has recently published his memoirs which show that he spent much of the late 1970s and early 1980s desperately trying to persuade Mrs Thatcher of the dangers of the communist threat, hoping to establish a body with the sinister name of the Counter-Subversion Executive.

Just as Sir Wyndham Childs and others whipped themselves into a frenzy in the 1920s over the dangers of communist subversion, so in the 1980s were Crozier and his colleagues preoccupied with what they saw as the communist takeover of Labour – this at a time when the Communist Party had virtually disappeared and Neil Kinnock's Labour Party was heading sharply to the right.

One of the spin offs from the ISC was called Forum World Features (FWF). In 1983 it was revealed that FWF had been funded for several years by the South African apartheid government. In the years to come, as the South African archives are opened up to researchers, more information will undoubtedly come to light – just as the archives in what was once the Soviet Union indicate the number of gullible and misguided individuals 'on the take' from the communist bloc.

Even less savoury than the pocketing of foreign money were the antics of the private armies which sprang up in the middle of the 1970s during and after the collapse of the Heath government. Some of the ventures were clearly loopy, the work of loners. Others were more significant. George K. Young, a former deputy head of MI6, was a leading figure behind the proposed setting up of several civil defence militias, as too was General Sir Walter Walker, a retired NATO commander-in-chief.

Another participant was Sir David Stirling, the legendary founder of the SAS (Special Air Service) during the Second World War. Although none of these initiatives came to anything, it was later confirmed by Field Marshall Lord Carver, the former Chief of Defence Staff, that 'fairly senior' army officers had been talking about the possibility of military intervention at the time of the miners' strike in February 1974.

Organisations such as the Economic League were funded by business and private sources. The funds which these sources made available were substantial and enabled a variety of ad hoc groups to intervene in a variety of settings. One example of this was seen in the constituency of Newham North-East, east London, where the then Labour MP Reg Prentice had fallen out with virtually all his constituency activists and members.

A small group of Prentice supporters, which included Dr Julian Lewis (now employed at Conservative Central Office), fought a series of High Court actions in the mid-1970s to try and retain their control of the constituency. Despite never revealing where their funds came from, Lewis's colleague Paul McCormick wrote a book called *Enemies of Democracy* (1978) which excoriated the anti-Prentice majority.

It was later established that the efforts of the Prentice camp had in fact been funded by the far-right group called the Freedom Association which, in turn, was sponsored by construction firms McAlpine and Taylor Woodrow. That Reg Prentice was to be a member of Mrs Thatcher's Conservative Government in 1979 suggested that the accusations of the constituency party had in fact been correct all along.

It is inevitable that big organisations will strive to protect their interests – one is not joining the conspiracy theorists by pointing this out. Look at the dirty tricks employed by British Airways against Richard Branson's Virgin Atlantic: hacking into computers, libel, the use of private detectives to try and dig up dirt. Business schools and gurus in the 1980s endlessly preached the doctrine of ruthlessness.

It is unlikely that political parties, for whom rather more is at stake, should be more scrupulous – and of course the Conservative

Party has, as we have seen, traditionally enjoyed strong links with business.

Exploration of this subject is hindered by official secrecy. Twelve general D notices stipulate which subjects should not be explored by newspapers; notice number ten contains the sweeping demand: 'You are requested not to publish anything about: a) secret activities of the British intelligence or counter-intelligence services undertaken inside or outside the UK for purposes of national security.'

Censorship of sensitive material is today often carried out by means of Britain's stringent libel laws. It is relatively easy for any prominent figure to prevent public exposure of their wrongdoings simply by issuing a barrage of writs, and the lottery of our libel laws discourage exposure. Robert Maxwell was the foremost exponent of this strategy. After his death and subsequent revelations about his massive frauds which harmed many innocent people, the question asked was how had he got away with it for so long? Tom Bower, Maxwell's unofficial biographer – the recipient himself of no fewer than twelve writs – ruefully told the story in print, when it was too late.

Watergate in America remains the classic case of political wrong-doing, but this chapter alone has indicated that, in British terms, Watergate was a comparatively minor affair. Our Watergates, however, slumber undisturbed. As one leading investigative journalist summed up: 'It has rightly been said many times that the US Watergate exposures, difficult enough as they were in Washington, could never have happened in Britain where there is little formal right to knowledge and an arsenal of potential legal restraints.'

Lack of material also hampers research; unsurprisingly, many records have been destroyed. The records of the Special Branch, for instance, have been shredded or at least are no longer available. Likewise the papers of the Information Research Department (IRD) have also been destroyed. The Lord Chancellor's department justified this act of vandalism by saying that the records were 'in the main ephemeral and not considered to be of sufficient historical importance to be selected for permanent preservation'. We will, therefore, never know how significant the work of the IRD was from the late 1940s until its demise in May 1977.

In any case, the intelligence services tend to commit as little as possible to paper, always operating on the 'plausible deniability' factor so that, should operations go wrong, their involvement cannot be traced. It is also true, however, that most academics and researchers have generally ignored the topic of dirty tricks. In the academic world the subject is regarded as rather unworthy and unlikely to lead to professional advancement, even though a study of, say, Admiral Blinker Hall, Sidney Walton or Sir Joseph Ball would be infinitely more revealing than another volume devoted to Sir Winston Churchill and his circle.

The one serious study of the intelligence services, *Secret Service* (1985) by Christopher Andrew, is so full of good stories, many of them involving pigeons, that the political dimension disappears in laughter and headshaking that such buffoons could be placed in positions of authority and power. But, of course, the cultivation of the image of buffoonery has always been a most effective disguise.

In the last decade television companies, newspapers and magazines have cut back on their investigative work – partly because of expense but also because the consequences of offending recent Conservative administrations have proved to be very damaging. Similarly, academics often prefer to avert their eyes from such topics. The recent collection of essays, *Conservative Century* (1994), fails even to glance at the issues raised in this chapter. It would be reassuring to believe that politics in Britain is indeed innocent, pure and comprehensively covered in the official documents, but this is fairy-tale stuff.

What about the Labour Party? Have they too been perpetrating dirty tricks? Apart from the fact that this book is about the Conservative Party and not Labour (see my *To Build A New Jerusalem* [1992]), it is certainly true that Labour is rather more innocent – or some would have it, naive – over such matters. There is an illuminating passage in Tony Benn's diaries for September 1965 when he tells how the new Lord Chancellor, Lord Gardiner, and the Home Secretary, Frank Soskice, tried but failed to see their personal files. They were either fobbed off with excuses that the relevant file had been destroyed the day before or, at best, allowed to see the odd photocopied page. Who was the elected master and who the unaccountable servant?

There are one or two indications that the Labour Party is beginning to recognise that politics and power in Britain is more complex than a cross in the ballot box every five years or so. Speaking to the parliamentary Labour Party in October 1994, the new Labour leader Tony Blair warned his colleagues that they were facing 'a ruthless and unprincipled party'.

This ruthlessness shows every sign of continuing. A strategy paper by John Maples, Conservative Party deputy chairman, was leaked in November 1994 by the *Financial Times*. One proposal hit the headlines: the suggestion that Blair should be roughed up in parliamentary debate by some Tory backbenchers: 'maybe a few yobbos of our own to try and knock him about a bit'.

Similarly the *Observer* newspaper had carried a report in October 1994 that Conservative Central Office was drawing up 'oppo' – opposition research – aimed at their Labour opponents. This follows the trend of recent American elections during which politicians dredge up a mass of marital, personal and financial detail on their opponents. One of the leading researchers at Central Office is Dr Julian Lewis.

To write about this subject is, of course, to attract accusations that one is a conspiracy theorist and it is certainly true that much of the work in this area suffers from the explicitly anti-Conservative bias of its authors. A sense of proportion is essential – a sense lost both by the eminent left-wing scientist Professor J.B.S. Haldane who emigrated to India in 1957 because he thought that, in the wake of Suez, Britain had become a police state, and by playwright Harold Pinter who once compared critics of Mrs Thatcher's Conservative governments with the Czech dissidents fighting against the rather more oppressive communist regime.

Most of the material for this chapter has, however, been deliberately taken from Establishment sources, details of which are given in the notes and bibliography at the end of the book.

It may also be difficult to believe that the British governing class is capable of such conduct. Of course this is understandable, if only because on mainland Britain there has never been any serious threat of revolution. Acts of violence are never overtly publicised in British textbooks: during the Crofters' War in the Highlands of Scotland in the 1880s, for example, gunboats and marines were regularly sent in to quell the unrest; the enduring image of the General Strike in May 1926 is of strikers and policemen playing football together, which is a charming but rather incomplete picture.

However, if one turns to, say, Ireland or the empire, then a less comforting story emerges. Take the attitude of Lord Salisbury, Conservative Prime Minister at the end of the nineteenth century. On the face of it, one could hardly imagine a more decent and law-abiding citizen, a politician whom historians today routinely refer to as 'the great Lord Salisbury'. During the Boer War Salisbury advocated the branding of captured Boer soldiers in order to assist their identification by the authorities and he had no qualms whatsoever about burning the farms of the native population. As he told his Secretary of State for War: 'You will not conquer these people until you have starved them out.'

To take a more modern example, MI6 plotted to assassinate Colonel Nasser of Egypt in 1956 at the time of the Suez crisis. 'I want him murdered,' Prime Minister Eden is alleged to have said. Contact had been made with disaffected Egyptian army officers, but the plan was never carried out. Only then did Prime Minister Sir Anthony Eden proceed with military action.

It might well be said that foreign and domestic affairs are different matters entirely. But it is at least arguable that here in Britain the authorities have never been seriously threatened with insurrection or revolutionary upheaval but, if they were, then there is no reason to believe that they would not fight to the last ditch. The strength of their response to powerful threats – such as the Chartists in the 1840s, post-1918 agitation and the General Strike – hint at the determination and force with which the established order will defend its position.

Our knowledge in this area may well be limited and sketchy, but we know enough to realise that here is one major reason why the Conservative Party has exercised such power over the last century:

it has been prepared to use various decidedly shady and sometimes even illegal methods to ensure success.

This chapter began with Philip Cambray's book *The Game of Politics*. Cambray himself had a great deal of experience of working on the edge of legitimate politics. Before the First World War he had been the energetic secretary of the Union Defence League which flirted with the idea of armed resistance to the Liberal's proposed Home Rule bill.

During the war Cambray worked at Crewe House for Lord Northcliffe's propaganda outfit, before moving on to join the Conservative Party. At Central Office he supervised the systematic writing of letters to the press; one correspondent managed to get up to ten letters a week published under a variety of pseudonyms: 'Everyone knows that the correspondence columns of these papers are most carefully read. Connection with the [Central] office is absolutely concealed.' Cambray also ran a 'front' organisation called the Industrial Press Service which planted material in non-Conservative newspapers.

In 1927 Cambray was sacked from Central Office – ironically enough for intriguing – but was then promptly re-engaged by his only equal when it came to the black arts of politics, namely Sir Joseph Ball. Whereas Cambray's skills were directed against the external enemy, Ball seems to have spent just as much time undermining internal party opponents, which leads on to the fascinating topic of Conservative versus Conservative.

Conservative Versus Conservative

Internal dirty tricks

'On the benches opposite are your political opponents. Your enemies are on this side.'

> Advice of senior Conservative John Boyd-Carpenter, quoted in Douglas Dodds-Parker *Political Eunuch* (1986)

'Shortly afterwards Alec Dunglass [later Sir Alec Douglas-Home] and Jock Colville arrived, and told us that the PM [Neville Chamberlain] had just come back from the Palace, Winston had kissed hands and was now Premier ... We were all sad, angry and felt cheated and out-witted. Alec, who more than any other, has been with the Prime Minister these past few weeks, and knows his words and actions by heart, let himself go. I opened a bottle of Champagne and we four loyal adherents of Mr Chamberlain drank "To the King over the water".'

> Chips Channon, entry in diary for 10 May 1940

'Politics has always been a dirty business.'

> Lady Thatcher, October 1993

Professional politicians are naturally ambitious. Only a fervent desire to scale the greasy pole of political preferment explains why individuals are prepared to sacrifice so much – such as normal working hours or a conventional family life – for the grinding career of full-time politics. Consequently, only the most naive would expect political life to be a tale of enduring sweetness and light.

This ambition is rarely a pleasant characteristic: memoirs and autobiographies contain their full share of politicians cheerfully stabbing each other in the front and the back. Take one example from the autobiography of Lord (Peter) Rawlinson, a senior Tory in the Heath regime. In October 1969 Conservative leader Edward Heath was speaking at a dinner on the eve of that year's Party conference. He was in sparkling form, witty, charming and perfectly attuned to his audience.

Rawlinson looked around at Heath's senior colleagues and 'friends', expecting to see that they too were enjoying their leader's performance. They weren't. Instead, Rawlinson noted that their minds were concentrated on themselves: 'I could see that each of the "senior colleagues", if the opportunity ever presented itself, would readily unsheath the dagger – in the interests, of course, of the Party and the Country.'

Naturally such conduct is not exclusive to the Conservative Party. The future Labour leader Hugh Gaitskell once confided sadly in his diary: 'Ambition certainly does seem to kill the pleasanter aspects of human nature.'

This chapter is not about the kind of legitimate manoeuvering or cut and thrust familiar to devotees of *Yes, Minister* or to anyone who has read Cabinet ministers' accounts of the Wilson or Thatcher Cabinets. Instead it explores actions which veer into the underhand, if not always illegal; the kind of behaviour which most of the population – and most Conservatives too for that matter – would censure or reject.

This intriguing topic, largely ignored by historians and commentators, forms a significant part of the hidden history of the British Conservative Party. It forcefully contradicts the bland and united public face which the Party deploys as part of its formidable armoury. No doubt there is much more to be found out. No history is ever finished or complete, no matter how extensive the footnotes or ostentatious the display of research. But this chapter does at least offer a preliminary account.

★   ★   ★

The use of dirty tricks is much more likely to occur at a time of bitter internal strife – and few battles have provoked so much anger as the dissension within the Conservative Party at the beginning of this century over the question of tariff reform.

Launched by the dynamic figure of Joseph Chamberlain, the Birmingham industrialist, once a Liberal but now the leader of the Liberal Unionists who were allied with the Conservatives (or Unionists), the tariff reformers argued that the policy of free trade should be ditched in favour of measures of protection which would allow the British economy to rebuild behind tariffs.

But if Chamberlain and his supporters were vehement in their views, no less so were their Conservative opponents insistent that free trade was vital to the Party's electoral appeal. Some Conservatives were so opposed to the 'fair traders' that they left the Party and joined the Liberals, the most notable of these 'traitors' being the young Winston Churchill. Most Tory free traders, however, stayed within the Party and fought their corner.

The battle of ideas – for hearts and minds – soon degenerated into the struggle for parliamentary seats. Chamberlain's Tariff Reform League systematically undermined Conservative colleagues who favoured free trade. Joseph's son Austen tried to get party leader Arthur Balfour to excommunicate all Unionist free traders. Historian Neal Blewett has described the bitterness of the struggle: 'Consumed by ideological passion, the Unionist Party, the great exemplar of political pragmatism, degenerated into a set of squabbling factions venting their invective on each other rather than on the Liberals.'

The league even put up rival candidates at the general election of January 1906 when eleven Tory free traders were opposed by tariff reform candidates. A so-called confederacy – described by one historian as 'a secret society with all the trappings of oaths, threats and codes' – worked to oust free trade Conservatives by stirring up trouble in their constituencies. Seeing itself as 'the inquisitorial arm' of tariff reform, members of the confederacy were sworn to secrecy. One leading confederate boasted that local associations were now so overawed by the Tariff Reform League that they dare not adopt free trade candidates.

In January 1909 the *Morning Post* newspaper went so far as to publish a list of free trade 'heretics', claiming that the list itself had been sanctioned by Percival Hughes, the Party's chief agent. This move confirmed that Chamberlain and his supporters had captured Central Office, just as they had won over the National Union or voluntary side of the Party. The *Morning Post* also encouraged local associations to deselect Unionist free trade MPs.

The success of the tariff reformers was demonstrated by their liquidation of internal opponents inside Parliament. There had been sixty-five Free Trade Unionist MPs before the election of 1906, and thirty after it. But only one (Lord Hugh Cecil, a member of the Salisbury family) remained after the January 1910 election. In four years, therefore, an important and well-represented body of opinion within the parliamentary party had been almost completely wiped out. It was a ruthless and controlled campaign which has yet to be emulated by either the pro- or anti-European factions within the Conservative Party today.

Winning internal battles, however, was one thing; persuading the country at large was another – as the Labour Left under Tony Benn was to discover in the 1980s. The electorate was never to support outright protectionism.

It is hardly surprising that, in an organisation dedicated to the pursuit of power, internal rebels and dissenters who seem to threaten this objective are sometimes subjected to the same kind of unscrupulous methods deployed against external opponents. But, crucially, the unorthodox are often protected by the Tory tradition of local independence: that each association is lord and master in its own patch. Heavy-handed interference from Central Office is resented.

This means that much of the skulduggery takes place at grassroots level. We have already met Alderman Salvidge of Liverpool in Chapter 6. Salvidge ruled the formidable Tory machine in Liverpool with iron determination and he seems to have spent as much time ensuring that Party colleagues were kept firmly in place as in fighting his nominal opponents, the Liberals.

Salvidge's methods were so blatant that even J.C.C. Davidson, chairman of the Party and himself no stranger to the underhand, referred to Salvidge as 'nothing more than a Tammany Boss'. Davidson even claimed that Salvidge embezzled Party funds. Secure in his own fiefdom, however, Salvidge was virtually untouchable.

It is when Conservative MPs go out on a limb for their beliefs that they become vulnerable, particularly if they spurn Party orthodoxy by arguing their case in public. One straightforward instance concerned the maverick Conservative MP, the Duchess of Atholl. Elected MP for Kinross and West Perthshire in 1923, Katharine Atholl had been Scotland's first woman MP and notched up another first the next year when she was appointed to a post in the Board of Education and so became the first Conservative woman to hold ministerial office.

The duchess had suitably right-wing views, condemning Soviet Russia in her two books *The Conscription of a People* (1931) and *The Truth about Forced Labour in Russia*, published the next year. No one could accuse her of being 'pink', and in fact in the 1950s she was to sit on the committee of a distinctly far-right group called Common Cause.

As a good old-fashioned patriot, the duchess was concerned above all with what she saw as the protection of Britain's interests, and during the 1930s she came to the conclusion that Fascism posed more of a threat than did Soviet communism (in hindsight, of course, she was right). In 1936 she helped publish an unexpurgated English version of Adolf Hitler's *Mein Kampf*, ensuring that anyone who cared to look or read would know exactly where the German dictator's policies were leading.

When the Spanish Civil War broke out in the summer of 1936, the duchess felt that Britain would be better served if the Republicans rather than Franco's Nationalists, aided by the Italians, won. Her forthright opinions led the press to dub her 'The Red Duchess' and at one stage she resigned the Party whip in protest at the foreign policy of the new Chamberlain Government.

Constituency opposition to the duchess steadily grew. Some members felt that their MP should be devoting more time to local rather than international affairs; others supported Franco's

Nationalists. Relations between MP and Party officers deteriorated to such an extent that the association resolved to fight fire with fire and select another Conservative candidate to contest the seat at the next election.

The duchess decided to take the bull by the horns, resign and fight a by-election. The Party machine naturally moved into action against her, sending batches of loyalist MPs to Perthshire to speak against their former colleague. Other Party rebels of the time who were also opposed to the Chamberlain administration's foreign policy kept their heads down; only Winston Churchill dared to send a letter of support. He also phoned her every evening to find out how the campaign was going. The duchess went down to defeat by just over 1,300 votes in December 1938 to the official Tory candidate, a Mr Snadden, who was strongly pro-Chamberlain – proving how difficult it is to buck the Party when its full resources are mobilised.

Where, it might be said, were the dirty tricks? Surely what we had here was a straightforward case of an MP being legitimately replaced by the officers of the local association, as they were entitled to do. The duchess's biographer has made much of the fact that the Scottish whips' office advised the association on how best to get rid of their rebellious MP and that Central Office fought all-out on behalf of Snadden. But this was only to be expected. If the duchess had won the by-election, it would have been seen as a major defeat for the leadership of the Party.

The duchess was indeed the victim of underhand tactics. During the campaign, two leading landowners who were opposed to her notified their tenants of an abatement in rent; the notices were accompanied by cards bearing the slogan 'Vote for Snadden'. Political pressure can be and has been exerted in subtle and clandestine ways, particularly when the personal touch can be applied. Katharine Atholl lacked the political skills – she was by all accounts a poor speaker – to get away with her rebellion.

Others, however, were more fortunate. When Sir Anthony Eden controversially resigned as Foreign Secretary in February 1938, he determined to counter the possibility of local opposition. Seizing the first opportunity, Eden hired the biggest meeting place in his constituency in order to explain and defend his actions. His resignation was greeted with acclamation by a crowd which, according to his biographer Robert Rhodes James, numbered one thousand in the main hall, five hundred in the overflow meeting and a further four thousand in the streets outside.

Viscount Cranborne had also resigned alongside Eden: 'My people seem quiet for the moment, except for an occasional snarl.' In his case, however, the association members were no doubt careful as to exactly how they snarled at a future marquess. Ronnie Cartland, backbench MP and brother of novelist Barbara, was also a fierce anti-Chamberlain campaigner. He found himself frozen out of his local Birmingham district of the Party. After one attack on the Prime Minister in August 1939, Chamberlain decided to take steps to 'stimulate local opposition' to him. It was too late. Cartland enlisted when war broke out and was killed at Dunkirk in 1940.

The most formidable and persistent thorn in the flesh of the Party hierarchy was Winston Churchill, whose force of character and weight of experience meant that he was always a dangerous opponent. Winston's son Randolph was fond of declaring in a loud voice that 'We [Churchills] were never Tories and never will be. We just make use of the Tory Party.' Many influential Conservatives were fully aware of these Churchillian sentiments, duly confirmed by Winston's restless switching from party to party early in his career. He left the Tory Party over tariff reform in the early 1900s and only rejoined some twenty years later.

After the Second World War, Conservative memoirs tact-fully omitted the degree of opposition and bitterness levied at Churchill over many decades. The *Daily Telegraph*, for instance, had celebrated Churchill's defeat when standing as a Liberal in a by-election in 1908 with the headline: 'Winston Churchill is out – out – OUT!' Although he was Baldwin's Chancellor of the Exchequer between 1924 and 1929, Churchill's falling out with the Party in the early 1930s led to his 'wilderness years' when he fought tooth and nail against the official Tory Party policies on India, the abdication and, most importantly, appeasement.

In January 1931 Churchill spoke out publicly against the

Conservative leadership's stance on self-government for India; in particular he criticised the Viceroy's decision to release Gandhi from prison. He resigned from the Shadow Cabinet and proceeded to tour the country making his views known. Churchill's biographer Martin Gilbert describes what followed: 'In an attempt to undermine his criticisms, Conservative Central Office, under the guidance of J.C.C. Davidson, worked to destroy Churchill's credibility rather than to rebut his arguments.'

Churchill set up an organisation called the India Defence League; Davidson and Central Office replied with a movement called the Union of Britain and India. In May 1933 Churchill decided to launch a nationwide campaign via the league – Central Office replied with co-ordinated efforts. At one meeting, Churchill was barely able to finish his sentences because of the sustained interruptions and barracking.

The Party hierarchy also used its formidable contacts with the press to marginalise Churchill's views whilst a hand-picked band of young Tory MPs were briefed to hammer away at his arguments. Even the Party's film vans were deployed to show weekly 'talkie' films pushing the official viewpoint.

It cannot be said, however, that the vehemence of his opinions did Churchill much good or gained him credit; for instance, he called Gandhi 'this malignant and subversive fanatic' and urged that the leaders of Gandhi's Congress Party be deported. Conservative MPs warmly applauded Labour attacks on Churchill but he knew full well that so long as his constituency association remained on his side, then the Party managers could not silence him. He drew up elaborate plans to ensure that, on India, local opposition to his stance was neutralised by public meetings and votes of confidence. He also tried not to burn too many national bridges; as soon as the India bill was passed and therefore his campaign had failed, Churchill tried to make peace with the Party.

The fragile truce was disturbed once more in 1936 during the abdication crisis when Churchill took Edward VIII's side, another misjudgement which increased his reputation for waywardness. But nothing so provoked the leadership as Churchill's views on the threat posed by Germany and Italy which, once again, were opposed to the Party's official stance of appeasement.

Churchill gave careful if measured support to fellow rebels, sending a message of support to the Duchess of Atholl and writing in support of her actions: 'It is the course which I have always proposed myself.' But then he adds the rider which distinguishes the really ardent seeker of power from the dilettante, 'should circumstances require it'.

Party pressure on potential 'Churchillian' sympathisers was often crude. One Tory MP, who had abstained when Eden resigned, was bluntly told by Chief Whip Margesson that even to talk to Churchill would compromise his potentially bright political future. But more concerted steps needed to be taken, and the only way to try and get rid of Churchill was by means of his local Epping association.

The first alert came in the *Sunday Express* in November 1938 which carried an item: 'Trouble is being made for Churchill in Epping. The campaign is strong, the campaigners determined.' Within weeks, Churchill himself was referring to 'these dirty Tory hacks, who would like to drive me out of the Party'. He was describing the co-ordinated efforts launched by the Party hierarchy in an attempt to rid themselves of what they regarded as a squalid nuisance.

Central Office, together with Margesson and his deputy James Stuart, worked hand-in-hand with one leading Epping Tory, Colin Thornton-Kemsley. The plan was to staff branches with anti-Churchill supporters and then pass a motion of no confidence in their MP, forcing him to stand at the next election (due in 1940) as an independent Conservative and almost certainly go down to defeat like the Duchess of Atholl.

In his autobiography *Through Winds and Tides* (1974), Thornton-Kemsley gives a typically guarded version of events: 'From my contacts outside the esoteric confines of the Epping Division it was clear to me that the insurrection in Mr Churchill's constituency was not unwelcome in high places.' Anti-Churchill branches were carefully built up and Conservatives hostile to the MP were elected to the constituency General Council. An association dinner was held on 4 March 1939 at which all the Party officials present condemned Churchill's criticisms of Chamberlain and his foreign policy. Churchill was attacked for denigrating 'our great Prime Minister' and told that 'he ought not to shelter under the goodwill and name which attaches to a great Party'. Churchill's opponents began to cast around for a suitable replacement candidate.

As one might expect, Churchill counter-attacked fiercely, resorting to a favourite argument of MPs in trouble: 'How can our Parliamentary doctrines survive if constituencies return only tame, docile, and subservient members who try to stamp out every form of independent judgement?'

Churchill narrowly survived a motion of no confidence in the spring of 1939, but his constituency critics and Central Office enemies were consolidating their forces and preparing for the resumption of hostilities in the autumn of that year when war of a different kind broke out in September 1939. Churchill was returned to the Government, became Prime Minister in May 1940 and of course nothing more was heard about deselection.

Churchill had the good grace to write to Thornton-Kemsley in September 1939 that 'I certainly think that Englishmen ought to start fair with one another from the outset in so grievous a struggle, and so far as I am concerned the past is dead.' When he bumped into Thornton-Kemsley on Euston Station, he went out of his way to be friendly. Churchill's magnanimity never quite extended to Conservative Central Office. Legend has it that in all his years as Party leader, he never once visited the building.

Churchill's generosity was not reciprocated by the loyal followers of former Prime Minister, Neville Chamberlain. On 13 May 1940, when Churchill entered the House of Commons as Prime Minister, he found himself cheered by Labour and Liberal MPs. Conservatives reserved their cheers for Chamberlain. The announcement that Churchill was to be Prime Minister was received in dead silence in the House of Lords.

In his book *Eminent Churchillians* (1994), Andrew Roberts has shown that the 'Chamberlainites' took some time to accept that 'the King over the water' would not return. Roberts ends his essay 'The Tories Versus Churchill' in the summer of 1941, but in fact it seems that intriguing against Churchill continued for another year at least. In the unpublished diary of Lord Woolton, a senior Cabinet minister during the war, there are a number of fascinating entries.

Whenever the progress of the war went badly and battles were lost, a substantial section within the Conservative Party was prompted to search around for a replacement for Churchill. On 12 May 1941, for example, Alexander Erskine-Hill, chairman of the powerful backbench 1922 Committee, had a meeting with Woolton to see if he had any thoughts on who would make an acceptable alternative leader.

The next year, on 13 July 1942, Woolton (who was not at this time a member of the Conservative Party) recorded another meeting with the energetic Erskine-Hill: 'The Conservative Party is becoming uneasy about the value and strength of Winston as P.M. Things are not going well in the war and they are wondering how long he will last. Erskine-Hill came to see whether I had any views about succeeding him. The Party wouldn't mind having me, if I would take it on, because they know I don't want to hang on after the war is over.'

A month later, Woolton had lunch with a rising Tory star, Oliver Stanley, who was 'full of gossip about the Conservative Party and the fact that it thinks Winston has had his day. They are looking for a new leader.'

An upturn in military fortune seems to have saved Churchill's bacon, but this constant intriguing against the Prime Minister sheds new and illuminating light on the unanimity of the war effort, or at least of the true feelings of many outwardly loyal Conservative MPs.

Churchill's rebellious early career meant that he was never, despite his record during the Second World War, persona grata with the Tory hierarchy. His doctor, Lord Moran, recorded how quickly after the election defeat of 1945 he got on the nerves of the Party hierarchy: 'They would have liked to get rid of him, I fancy, if they had known how.' In late 1949, it was Party chairman Lord Woolton – who else? – who commissioned a confidential Gallup poll which showed that if Churchill was no longer party leader, the Tory share of the vote would not be affected.

Who else within the Party was behind the anti-Churchill campaign? In the 1930s, J.C.C. Davidson was certainly involved and so too was his formidable chief lieutenant, Sir Joseph Ball. Ball's name recurs throughout this book, whether it be in connection with the Zinoviev letter in 1924 or party electioneering in the 1930s. He also featured in the spate of books devoted to the activities of the spies Burgess, Philby and Blunt. In the late 1930s, when Guy Burgess managed to obtain confidential information about the deliberations of the French Cabinet, the information was passed on to Neville Chamberlain via Ball, thereby cutting out the Foreign Office which Chamberlain distrusted.

Ball has justifiably been described by Lord (Robert) Blake as the 'quintessential eminence grise'. He was discreet even in death, making sure not only that his own personal papers were burnt, but also the papers of all the various organisations with which he had been involved, including the Conservative Research Department and the National Publicity Bureau.

A brief outline of Ball's career demonstrates how certain personnel have always moved freely between important institutions. Originally a barrister, Ball worked at Scotland Yard before being recruited into MI5 in 1914. He swiftly rose to become head of the Investigation Branch.

In 1927 Ball left MI5 and joined the Conservative Party, nominally as director of publicity, and from 1930 to 1939 was director of the Conservative Research Department. Ball was knighted in 1936. During the Second World War he was deputy chairman of the Security Executive which handled potential German threats. After the war he was heavily involved in businessman Tiny Rowland's Lonrho company. He died in 1961.

That, at any rate, is the skeleton outline which appeared in publications such as *Who's Who*. In reality, Ball was the Conservative Party's dirty tricks specialist par excellence. As J.C.C. Davidson, himself no shrinking violet when it came to tough measures, once explained, Ball 'is steeped in the Service tradition, and has had as much experience as anyone I know in the seamy side of life and the handling of crooks'.

Ball was a central figure in the affair of the Zinoviev letter and its cover-up, discussed in Chapter 9. With Davidson's assistance, he also set up a Special Information Service 'to keep us informed of the enemy and his plans'; the enemy being the Labour Party. And, as we have also seen, Ball clandestinely ran the National Publicity Bureau which spent hundreds of thousands of pounds gathered from unknown sources in the run-up to the 1935 election.

In the 1930s Ball's devotion to Neville Chamberlain meant that he handled the telephone tapping of anti-appeasement Conservative MPs such as Ronald Tree and Harold Macmillan. In his autobiography *When the Moon was High* (1975), Tree reveals how he had his suspicions confirmed from the horse's mouth: 'Some time later, during the war, I came across Sir Joseph Ball at the Ministry of Information, a dislikeable man with an unenviable reputation for doing some of Chamberlain's 'behind-the-scenes' work. We got into conversation and he had the gall to tell me that he himself had been responsible for having my telephone tapped.'

Ball's links with the press were invaluable. When Eden and Lord Cranborne resigned from the Government in February 1938 in protest at Chamberlain's policies, he took 'certain steps privately' to make sure that their reasons received little publicity. The *Manchester Guardian* noted that 'For the most part the Government press has preserved a unity of silence that could hardly be bettered in a totalitarian state.'

One example of these private steps concerns an interview which Labour Party leader Clement Attlee gave to the newsreel company Paramount. Attlee argued at length that Eden's resignation demonstrated the bankruptcy of Chamberlain's foreign policy. A cinema manager in Cheshire, complaining that the other newsreel companies had made no attempt whatsoever to cover Eden's resignation, noted of the Paramount material that 'Within a couple of hours of delivery of this reel to the exhibitors, urgent orders were issued that the item must be deleted.'

Smear stories about Eden's mental and physical condition were discreetly circulated; *The Times* of 22 February 1938, for instance, referred to the rumour that Eden's health had completely broken down: 'He [Eden] is particularly anxious to refute the suggestion, which is still being circulated in some quarters, that his resignation was due to ill-health.' A report such as this cunningly exploits the widespread assumption that there can be no smoke without fire.

Ball's usefulness did not end here. Chamberlain also employed him to go on unofficial and shady missions to the Italian Embassy in London, bypassing the Foreign Office, and he frequently addressed hand-picked members of the press lobby so that he could reiterate the official Chamberlain line.

It is unlikely that Ball ever retired from MI5. His political views were decidedly reactionary and anti-Semitic. With Chamberlain's approval, he took over the magazine *Truth* in 1936 and systematically blackened the reputations of any Conservative who disagreed with Chamberlain's policies. *Truth* regularly inveighed against 'the Jew-infested sink of Fleet Street'.

During the war, Ball's association with Chamberlain meant that his career stalled. He was appointed head designate of the films division of the embryonic Ministry of Information, but pressure exerted by his enemies, the anti-appeasers now prospering under Churchill, forced him to be transferred.

In view of Ball's anti-Churchill activities in the 1930s it is hardly surprising that he left the Party organisation after the war and instead moved into the City. However, he still stepped in from time to time to ensure that his pre-war activities remained a closed book. In 1956 a former Conservative MP Sir Guy Kindersley planned to publish his version of how the Zinoviev letter had reached Conservative Central Office in 1924. Ball and J.C.C. Davidson summoned Kindersley to a meeting at Ball's Lonrho office – and Kindersley was persuaded not to publish his story.

It would be wrong merely to characterise Ball as some kind of primitive hatchet man. For one thing, he made many detailed contributions to a wide range of Conservative policies in the 1930s when he ran the Research Department. The department's papers are full of Ball's detailed suggestions on agricultural and industrial matters. But he was certainly one of those fixers invaluable to less scrupulous political bosses.

One of those subjected to Ball's methods was of course Anthony Eden. Yet in 1956 Eden himself employed dirty tricks over the Suez campaign. When one Conservative critic of the Government's military action, Anthony Nutting, resigned both from the administration and his parliamentary seat, Eden briefed the newspapers against Nutting. The pro-Eden *Sunday Express* printed a piece on 11 November 1956 which highlighted Nutting's separation from his wife and his friendship with another woman. To his credit, Eden's press secretary William Clark later resigned in disgust over such tactics.

Enoch Powell was another dissenting voice who met obstruction and opposition. According to his biographer Patrick Cosgrave, Central Office used to ensure that Powell addressed the annual Party conference at a time when the BBC was transmitting the popular children's programme *Play School*, thereby limiting public exposure to Powell's views.

'In Defeat, Malice – in Victory, Revenge!' – according to Jim Hacker, this was the attitude of his Prime Minister in an early episode of *Yes, Minister* called 'The Writing on the Wall'.

Mrs Thatcher was a Conservative leader who understood full well that politics was about power, and she and her advisers were never over-sensitive as to how she acquired or retained it. She knew what was best for Britain and therefore those who disagreed with her were not simply wrong – they were potential traitors to the cause. Both Mrs Thatcher's critics and supporters recognise that she was adept in her handling of the media, particularly as regards her use of the lobby and of selective 'leaks'. Once, over Westland, it nearly brought her down.

In 1986 the crisis over Westland helicopters suddenly erupted into public view. Westland planned to accept a financial rescue package put forward by an American company, Sikorsky. Defence Secretary Michael Heseltine wanted a European consortium to step in and he lobbied strongly that this was the better option. Passages from a letter written by the solicitor-general to Heseltine, complaining of 'material inaccuracies' in the Defence Secretary's statements, were leaked to the press in a bid to undermine his position. Heseltine dramatically resigned from the Cabinet, followed later by trade minister Leon Brittan whose department carried the can for the leakage.

The truth of what really happened has never been disclosed. It did become clear that the Prime Minister's press officer, her private office and the Cabinet secretary had all been involved in the leak. Mrs Thatcher stretched credulity to the limit by stoutly maintaining that she knew nothing – and Labour leader Neil Kinnock muffed his opportunity to find out more – and the Prime Minister successfully managed to wash her hands of the affair. Lord Howe has recently brought his legal skills to bear on the matter in his memoirs *Conflict of Loyalty* (1994) and Mrs Thatcher's role in the affair does look, at best, shaky.

Howe also remarked on the unpleasantly anti-Semitic mood amongst Tory backbenchers which sealed Leon Brittan's fate. According to Paul Foot, anti-Semitic propaganda directed against the number of Jews in Mrs Thatcher's circle was at this time often circulated amongst journalists and politicians.

Critics of Mrs Thatcher, notably Labour MP Tam Dalyell, have contrasted the fate of her inner circle leakers, Charles Powell and Bernard Ingham, with the public prosecution of other Civil Service leakers such as Sarah Tisdall and Clive Ponting.

At the heart of the Prime Minister's team of advisers was her press secretary, the pugnacious Bernard Ingham. Once a civil servant who had served under Tony Benn, Ingham saw his job as being to offer complete and unquestioning support to Mrs Thatcher. Between them, they were adept at briefing the lobby against difficult or recalcitrant Cabinet colleagues.

Prime Ministers have always made full use of the lobby system, but there is evidence that under Mrs Thatcher it was played with greater determination and malignance than ever before. Colleagues who later fell out with Mrs Thatcher, such as Nigel Lawson, can barely contain their anger when recollecting various episodes. It has even been suggested that when Mrs Thatcher and Lawson were engaged in acrimonious conflict over economic policy in general and the European Exchange Rate Mechanism in particular, Lawson's office at No. 11 Downing Street was bugged. Although

Lawson himself has discounted this suggestion, he does note in his memoirs that Mrs Thatcher was 'positively besotted' with the security services. A book published in Canada by Michael Gratton, press secretary to former premier Brian Mulroney, claims that Mrs Thatcher employed Canadian intelligence agents to spy on two unnamed members of her Cabinet.

A further murky episode came in 1990 when Michael Heseltine was mounting his leadership challenge to Mrs Thatcher. The *Sun* newspaper published a headline story on 13 November titled 'The Adulterer, The Bungler and The Joker' which smeared Heseltine and his two most prominent lieutenants Michael Mates and Keith Hampson. It has been suggested by one well-informed observer that the headline was orchestrated by Central Office.

Yet another recent example of internal dirty tricks concerned the internecine warfare waged amongst Scottish Conservatives. Mrs Thatcher always expressed herself disappointed that Scotland, the home of free market economist and philosopher Adam Smith, had not taken to Thatcherism with rather more gusto. Instead, she felt, the Scots had become too used to subsidy and Government feather-bedding.

Her anger was directed towards the Scottish Conservative Party hierarchy which she felt was not only insufficiently supportive of her policies, but was failing by some way to raise its quota of money. Her ire focused on the most influential Scottish Tory, Malcolm Rifkind, Secretary of State for Scotland. Mrs Thatcher appointed one of her more ardent supporters, Michael Forsyth, as chairman in July 1989 with the aim of 'Thatcherising' the Party.

The internal battle was bitter. Not only were most of the old guard or senior staff sacked by Forsyth, but other, rather more sinister activities also took place: filing Cabinets were broken into and material unfavourable to Thatcherite candidates was removed. The press was conscripted by both sides. Eventually Mrs Thatcher had to back down and Forsyth was moved to another post in September 1990. A few weeks later Mrs Thatcher herself was ousted; in her memoirs she herself makes the connection between these two events.

The same kind of bitterness was engendered by the very public rows over the passage of the Maastricht bill. The small Government majority made the leadership vulnerable to the determined efforts of a small but well-organised group of backbench rebels. The whips' activities extended to a little bit of discreet blackmail. One Conservative MP, Sir Nicholas Fairbairn, wrote to *The Times*: 'I am appalled at numerous reports that the whips saw fit to threaten to expose extra-marital conduct by backbench colleagues, in order to persuade them to abandon their consciences. There has been, as far as I am aware, no denial of these reports.' One Euro-sceptic MP did indeed find that details of his private life were leaked to the press.

The willingness of the whips to resort to shabby methods of blackmail was confirmed in May 1995. Michael Cockerell's documentary *Westminster's Secret Service*, shown on BBC2, revealed that the Tory whips kept a 'Dirt Book' recording details of MPs' private lives. One former whip, Tim Fortescue, admitted that the scandalous details were not always accurate, based as they were on gossip and hearsay. Fortescue went on to claim that in his day, as a Conservative whip in the 1970s, 'We were a very efficient organisation. When you were trying to persuade a member that he should vote the way he didn't want to vote, it was possible to suggest that perhaps it would not be in his interest if people knew something about him.'

Despite such techniques, the rows over Europe still continue. Andrew Roberts has compared the treatment of Chamberlain's opponents before the war with that of the Euro-sceptics today: 'The Conservative anti-appeasers of the 1930s comprised between 20 and 40 MPs, an almost identical number to today's Euro-sceptics. They, too, were subjected to abuse, anger and arm-twisting; their motives were ridiculed and their arguments deliberately misrepresented.'

Such activities simply confirm that the Conservative Party, whatever the moderation and good manners it prefers to display in public, is in fact an institution capable of more than its fair share of Machiavellian behaviour.

The discrepancy is best demonstrated by comparing Lord Woolton's unpublished diary with his sanitised memoirs. In the former, as we saw, he recorded the manoeuvrings which were taking place against Churchill at the height of the Second World

War. In his *Memoirs* (1959), Woolton includes an oblique reference to his doubts about Churchill's appointment as Prime Minister: 'At that time, I had doubts about the new Prime Minister. I had no doubt about his tremendous driving energy and about his passionate belief in Britain, or of the hold he could have on the country, but I had some doubt about his judgment and, with recollections of the First World War in my mind, I wondered what forces he would gather round him to carry on the executive job of winning the war.'

Woolton naturally never tells his public that these doubts led to prolonged intriguing against Churchill, which he himself did nothing to stop and tacitly encouraged. The gap between the public image and the private reality is often huge.

———

'The Economy is Safe in Our Hands'

The Conservative Party
and the British economy

'I have thought it consistent with true Conservative policy to promote so much of happiness and contentment among the people that the voice of disaffection should no longer be heard, and that thought of the dissolution of our institutions should be forgotten in the midst of physical enjoyment.'

Sir Robert Peel, 1846

'Toryism has always been a form of paternal Socialism.'

Harold Macmillan, 1936

'The Prime Minister should state, as boldly as he can, that it is his government's intention to turn Britain into the Hong Kong of Western Europe by the end of the decade – a low-cost, high-productivity, low-tax, high-tech offshore island whose growth and dynamism would be in marked contrast to the recession and sclerosis of the other major European economies.'

Editorial in the *Sunday Times*, 6 June 1993

'Everyone said that I was the worst Chancellor of the Exchequer that ever was. And now I'm inclined to agree with them. So now the world's unanimous.' Not even the most devoted Churchillian has

Sir Robert Peel, founder of the modern Conservative Party and Prime Minister 1834-5 and 1841-6. His icy public face contradicted his private warmness. *[Popperfoto]*

Benjamin Disraeli came to prominence when he clashed fiercely with Peel over the repeal of the Corn Laws. A master of PR, Disraeli's two terms as Prime Minister (1868 and 1874-80) were characterised chiefly by social reform at home and consolidation of the Empire abroad. *[Hulton Deutsch]*

The 3rd Marquess of Salisbury, who served three separate terms as Prime Minister. For much of his premiership he also functioned as Foreign Secretary, presiding over massive colonial expansion. *[Camera Press]*

Arthur James Balfour, photographed in 1903, a year after he succeeded his uncle, Lord Salisbury, as Prime Minister and Tory leader. Perhaps the most overtly intellectual of British premiers, Balfour's philosophical nature lent itself more readily to the abstractions of foreign policy than to domestic politicking. *[Hulton Deutsch]*

Andrew Bonar Law at the Party Conference in 1923. Leader of the Party since 1911, his tenure as the 'Unknown Prime Minister' was brief but influential, establishing a leadership style which continued throughout the inter-war period. *[Hulton Deutsch]*

Stanley Baldwin in the garden at Chequers in 1925, embodying the virtues of common sense and decency. The following year saw the General Strike which dominated his second period of office. [*Popperfoto*]

The General Strike, May 1926. Police charge a crowd in Walworth, South London. [*Hulton Deutsch*]

An armed escort for a food convoy - Holborn, 1926. The iron fist inside the velvet glove. *[Hulton Deutsch]*

J.C.C. Davidson, the influential Party Chairman in the 1920s who was determined to win at all costs. It was Davidson who worked closely with the Party's leading *eminence grise*, Sir Joseph Ball. *[Topham]*

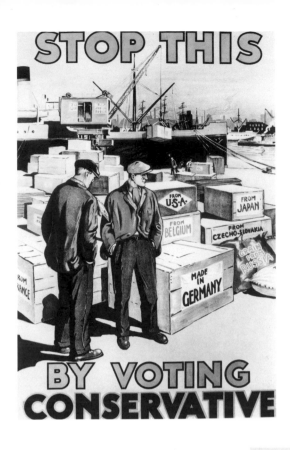

Campaign posters for the 1931 General Election. Although former Labour leader Ramsay MacDonald led the so-called National Government, it was the Conservatives who dominated this administration.
[Hulton Deutsch]

The poisoned chalice of appeasement: Neville Chamberlain proclaims 'peace in our time' at Heston aerodrome in September 1938, waving the Anglo-German agreement he had signed with Adolf Hitler in Munich. *[Topham]*

Cartoon by David Low for the London *Evening Standard*, October 1938. *[Courtesy of the University of Kent]*

Winston Churchill inspecting bomb damage in Manchester, April 1941.
[Hulton Deutsch]

Churchill in familiar pose -
but he himself noted his
poor record at winning
elections. *[Camera Press]*

The canvassing war, 1948: party activists take a mobile bookshop to Bexley Heath, Kent, in their drive to woo voters during Attlee's Labour government. *[Popperfoto]*

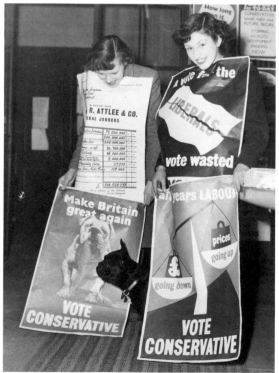

Activists at Abbey House, Party headquarters before the move to Smith Square, displaying campaign posters in 1950. *[Popperfoto]*

'An act of plunder': Sir Anthony Eden speaks to the world about the Suez crisis in August 1956. The overwrought Eden accused 'Communists' at the BBC of shining lights in his eyes. He would resign five months later. [Popperfoto]

Lords Hailsham (left) and Woolton, shortly after Hailsham had been appointed Party Chairman in 1957. Woolton had been a highly effective Chairman from 1946 to 1955. [Camera Press]

Harold Macmillan with Indian Prime Minister Jawaharlal Nehru in New Delhi.
Macmillan's liberal Toryism - a 'winds of change' foreign policy and expansionism
at home - remains highly contentious. *[Camera Press]*

" VOILA, THIS IS WHAT YOU CALL 'HIT FOR SIX', NON ..?"

Cartoon by Vicky (Victor Weisz) for the London *Evening Standard*, which first appeared two weeks before de Gaulle, on 29 January 1963, formally vetoed Macmillan's application to take Britain into the EEC. *[Courtesy of the University of Kent]*

Edward Heath signing the Treaty of Accession in Brussels, 22 January 1972, confirming Britain's belated entry into the EEC. Heath is watched by Foreign Secretary Sir Alec Douglas-Home (left), who had briefly served as Prime Minister after Macmillan, and Britain's chief negotiator Geoffrey Rippon (right). *[Topham]*

Margaret Thatcher with husband Denis on the steps of Number Ten after her first General Election victory in May 1979. She was just about to quote the soothing words of St Francis of Assisi. *[Hulton Deutsch]*

Thatcher with Sir Geoffrey Howe. For years her most loyal minister as Chancellor and Foreign Secretary, Howe would, in November 1990, make a mockery of his 'dead sheep' tag and deliver the devastating Commons speech which precipitated her downfall. *[Lionel Cherruault, Camera Press]*

John Major, Tory candidate for St Pancras North at the General Election of 1974. He lost, and few could possibly have predicted that 16 years later he would become Prime Minister. *[Hulton Deutsch]*

Major triumphant after the 1992 General Election, with wife Norma and Party Chairman Chris Patten, who had, however, just lost his Bath seat to the Liberal Democrats. What the electorate giveth, it can also take away. *[Mark Stewart, Camera Press]*

been able to make much of Winston Churchill's spell as Chancellor of the Exchequer in the Conservative administration of 1924 to 1929. He himself was amazed when Baldwin appointed him to the post after the 1924 election – Baldwin himself had been an unsuccessful chancellor between 1922 and 1923 – knowing full well that economics was not his speciality.

It never had been a family forte. His father Lord Randolph Churchill had briefly been chancellor in 1886, struggling to come to grips with 'those damned dots' as he called decimal points. In his turn Winston struggled too, lamenting to his parliamentary private secretary, Robert Boothby, about the mysterious devices of treasury economists: 'I wish they were admirals or generals. I speak their language, and can beat them. But after a while these fellows start speaking Persian. And then I am sunk.'

Churchill's cardinal mistake was to return to the Gold Standard in 1925 at the wrong, pre-war rate of parity, a decision which hamstrung the British economy between the wars. It was a material factor in the prolonged depression and slump of the 1930s.

With its strong links to business, industry and the City of London, the Conservative Party has always claimed that it alone, of all the political parties, possesses the expertise to guarantee economic strength. In turn these bodies faithfully support the Party and issue dire warnings about the consequences of a Labour election victory: a run on the pound, an international lack of confidence, business closures, higher taxes and so on. These warnings are of particular importance because most commentators maintain that it is the condition of the economy which crucially influences the results of general elections.

Yet the British economy has in fact been in comparative decline since the early years of this century – and the Conservative Party has largely been in power since the early years of this century. Nor is it immediately obvious that the six Labour chancellors since the war – Healey, Jenkins, Callaghan, Gaitskell, Cripps and Dalton – have been inferior to their Conservative counterparts. There have only been two Labour Governments with adequate working majorities and on both occasions, in 1951 and in 1970, they left office with the economy in relatively good shape.

Look at the post-war indictments which can be levelled at Tory administrations: there was the failure to float the pound in the early 1950s; Macmillan's preference for a huge inflationary government sector and the resignation of his treasury team in 1958; the inept pay pause of Selwyn Lloyd in the early 1960s; the artificial Maudling boom of 1963–4; the Barber boom and hyper-inflation of the early 1970s; the Heath Government's departure from office with a record rate of inflation, record budget deficit and record balance of payments deficit; the two prolonged recessions under Mrs Thatcher, the second of which, as *The Times* pointed out in May 1993, undid all the economic good of the 1980s; the squandering of North Sea oil assets worth billions of pounds; the continuing recession under John Major and the debacle over membership of the Exchange Rate Mechanism (ERM).

What does their handling of the British economy tell us about the Conservative Party and Conservative policies generally?

The Conservative Party is made up of a mixture of different interests and opinions which are sometimes in conflict with each other. This is never more true than when it comes to the question of the economy. All Conservatives would emphasise the priority of wealth creation over wealth distribution; you can't divide up what isn't there, they say. All agree that the only way to turn the have-nots into haves is by providing sustained economic growth, by creating – to use the phrase popularised by Sir Anthony Eden – a nation-wide property-owning democracy. All believe that capitalism is superior to socialism.

Yet when one moves beyond this rather vague and limited consensus, the arguments begin. There are disagreements over the role of the state and of markets, over economic growth, over taxation, employment and inflation, over the role of trade unions. It is a debate which has grown much fiercer in the last twenty years because the economic philosophy associated with Thatcherism explicitly challenged many fundamental, if unspoken, Conservative tenets.

Consider Mrs Thatcher's eulogy in her memoirs to pure undiluted capitalism: 'The free market was like a vast nervous system, responding to events and signals all over the world to meet the ever-challenging needs of people in different countries, from different classes, of different religions, with a kind of benign indifference to their status.'

For many Conservatives, past and present, the last phrase about 'indifference to their status' will have set alarm bells ringing. Status for them traditionally offered a sense of permanence in an unsettled world – it was something that had been acquired and built up over a period of time and was not easily to be discarded. The indifference of the free market to hierarchy could be dangerous and many Tories therefore baulked at the consequences of an unbridled free market economy or of undue emphasis on the material things of life.

Many Christian Conservatives remember too well some of the striking phrases in the Gospel according to St Luke: 'How hard it is for those who have riches to enter the Kingdom of God'; 'Blessed are the poor'; 'Woe to you that are rich'; 'A man's life does not consist in the abundance of his possessions'.

More recently, Quintin Hogg (later Lord Hailsham), claimed in his *The Case for Conservatism*, published in 1947, that the Conservative Party could boast the longest tradition of criticising capitalism as 'an ungodly and rapacious scramble for ill-gotten gains, in the course of which the richer appeared to get richer and the poor poorer'.

Nor is it Christians and Party intellectuals alone who have had worries about the emphasis placed on economic growth. The affluent 'never had it so good' days associated with Harold Macmillan's administrations also prompted unease at the grassroots, as a motion passed at the 1962 party conference shows: 'That this Conference, while appreciating that successive Conservative Governments have caused the material standard of living to rise faster during the past eleven years than ever before in our history, calls upon Ministers to emphasise that this is but one side of a policy founded on the true Tory principles of duty and service.'

Since the 1970s, arguments have centred upon various conflicting analyses of the Victorian age when Britain enjoyed unparalleled economic growth. Was this because, as some partisans maintain, pure and undiluted capitalism flourished free from government interference? In fact the state was materially involved during the early decades of the nineteenth century in creating the framework within which the entrepreneurial spirit could prosper. Government legislation was needed for the passage of the Enclosure Acts just as it was for the Rail, Bank and Company Acts. Later the Joint Stock Company Acts permitted limited liability for businessmen and stimulated further expansion.

Conservative Governments were also prepared to intervene in the free market in order to prevent chaos. The history of the provision of gas in London exemplifies this pragmatic approach. At one stage over two hundred different companies were competing fiercely with each other but, in their need to cut corners, they offered a poor service. In 1830 the Conservative government stepped in and awarded monopoly powers to certain statutory companies 'for the better protection of the public from the evils of unregulated competition'. Ironically, it looks today as if the tape is running backwards.

But if it is true that the Government's role throughout much of the nineteenth century was limited – in the 1860s the Chancellor of the Exchequer, William Gladstone, managed to reduce total government spending to just £66 million a year (multiply this sum by even a hundred and you still get a figure which is small change to today's chancellors) – it was not altogether obvious that this was a good thing. Tory radicals demanded measures of state intervention in order to improve social conditions and, as we shall see in the next chapter, Conservatives claim that under Disraeli it was they, rather than the Liberals, who were prepared to introduce welfare legislation which interfered with the workings of the free market.

The British economy was, of course, shaped by its overseas empire. These international trading interests meant that the requirements of the City of London prevailed over those of manufacturing industry. By the end of the nineteenth century the economic rivalry of the United States and Germany together with the second phase of industrialisation centring on the steel, chemical and electrical industries, meant that the old hands-off approach was now a liability. The demand for social services and the rise of the labour movement also posed difficult new questions for the Conservative Party. Political, social and economic considerations were now inextricably entwined.

Furthermore, as an amalgam of interests and groups the Conservative Party itself was pulled one way and then the other so that no clear and definite approach to economic management could or would ever be formulated. It was impossible to reduce the argument to a simple choice: either for government intervention or against it, and so it has remained. Some businessmen have always argued that a measure of government intervention is needed in order to stimulate economic growth, others maintain that the Government should keep its nose out of matters about which it knows little. All agreed, however, that the state of the economy would henceforward dominate the political agenda.

This conflict over the best way forward was vividly demonstrated by the fierce arguments over the tariff reform programme launched by Joseph Chamberlain in the early 1900s. He and his supporters wanted to ditch the traditional policies of laissez-faire and free trade in favour of a more dynamic and interventionist approach. They claimed that protection would shield the British economy from overseas competition and provide a breathing space during which industry and business could be reorganised on more modern and efficient lines. The obvious drawback, as the free traders insistently pointed out, was that the price of food would almost certainly rise.

In the 1906 election the protectionist Conservative Party was heavily defeated by the free trade Liberals. That same year Chamberlain was incapacitated by a stroke, but still the protectionist wing in the Party held the upper hand. In 1923 the new leader Stanley Baldwin fought another general election explicitly on this issue and again the Conservatives lost.

The attempt by Chamberlain, Baldwin and the protectionists to give the Conservative Party a definite set of economic policies failed and would never – until the 1970s and 1980s at least – be tried again. The best thing was to muddle through, emphasising first one set of measures and then another depending on the current circumstances. Pragmatism, not planning, was paramount.

This lack of a cohesive approach demonstrated that the Party was a coalition made up of various, often conflicting, interests – but it also showed the disdain which many leading Conservatives, often with a landed background, displayed towards those colleagues who had had to work for a living. One can hear the condescension in Arthur Balfour's voice when he referred to a colleague as 'that *rara avis*, a successful manufacturer who is fit for something besides manufacturing'.

Pragmatism was certainly evident in Conservative behaviour between the wars. On the one hand certain industries clearly needed Government assistance either financially or in terms of their reorganisation. Agricultural Marketing Acts, Cotton Industry Acts, protection of the steel industry, the setting up of the Central Electricity Board, the British Broadcasting Corporation and the London Transport Passenger Board – these were all important Conservative initiatives which interfered with the workings of the free market.

On the other hand, Montagu Norman, Governor of the Bank of England, ensured that the demands of the City remained paramount. Hence both the disastrous return to the Gold Standard in 1925 when Norman's dogmatism easily outweighed the warnings of outside economists like John Maynard Keynes, and the depression which blighted the 1930s because the Government insisted that a balanced budget was preferable to Government stimulation of the economy.

Nevertheless, one group within the Conservative Party did put forward a cogent and thoughtful new programme. It was led by Harold Macmillan, one of four young Conservative MPs who in 1927 published a book called *Industry and the State*; the other authors were Oliver Stanley, whose early death in 1950 probably robbed him of the succession after Eden, Robert Boothby and John Loder.

These four – 'the YMCA' as they were dubbed – maintained that laissez-faire had never been an integral part of Conservative policy and pointed out that, like it or not, governments were being inexorably drawn into intervention. They sketched out a blueprint which called for 'economic democracy', 'Labour Co-Partnership' and a National Wages Board in every important industry. Such ideas later became commonplace but at the time they were almost revolutionary, certainly within the context of the inter-war Conservative Party. The *Daily Mail* wondered why 'these gentlemen still figure in the Conservative Party'.

Interestingly enough, Macmillan and his colleagues stressed that their suggestions 'cannot possibly raise any issue of party politics'. This claim offered a preview of the so-called 'Butskellism' practised in the 1950s when both Conservative and Labour's economic policies were almost identical.

Macmillan sat for the deeply deprived constituency of Stockton-on-Tees. In the winter of 1932–3, for instance, unemployment on Teesside reached 27 per cent; the medical officer of health examined one set of schoolchildren in Stockton and found that 80 per cent of them were suffering from under-nourishment. In his memoirs *Winds of Change* (1966), Macmillan recalled the massive impact of the Great Depression, of the collapse of the Labour Government in 1931 and of mass unemployment:

> Up to 1931 there was no reason to suppose that [changes] would not, or could not, follow the same evolutionary pattern which had resulted from the increased creation and distribution of wealth throughout the nineteenth century . . . Now, after 1931, many of us felt that the disease was more deep-rooted. It had become evident that the structure of capitalist society in its old form had broken down, not only in Britain but all over Europe and even in the United States. The whole system had to be reassessed. Perhaps it could not survive at all; it certainly could not survive without radical change . . .

Essentially, Macmillan and his colleagues were trying to find ways of saving the structure of capitalist society and the summation of Macmillan's thinking was contained in his book *The Middle Way*, published in 1938. Its title was entirely appropriate because it charted a course between the Scylla of capitalism and the Charybdis of socialism.

The radical departure from Tory orthodoxy that this book represented is apparent even today when the young Conservative MP David Willetts, a wholehearted supporter of Mrs Thatcher, berates Macmillan's book as constituting the 'most vivid and depressing evidence of how much conservatism had shifted since Salisbury's day'; it 'hardly counts as a conservative text at all'.

Macmillan could not have imagined that he would ever have a chance to implement his ideas. He resigned the Conservative Party whip in 1938 and at one point nearly joined the Labour Party. During the war, however, 'middle way' ideas came to the fore when the manifest failings of the private enterprise system had to be rectified by widening the scope of the public. The breakdown of the system of free trade in 1932 and the measures of industrial concentration tacitly promoted by national governments throughout the 1930s might well have represented the first faltering steps for the new approach, but it took the war to bring them to fruition.

So dramatic was the transformation of the political landscape that during the general election of 1945 the Westminster Conservative Association actually republished *The Middle Way*. They hoped to persuade voters that it was in fact the Conservatives who had really been the progenitors of the Beveridge Report advocating a comprehensive system of welfare for all citizens.

The policies followed both by the Attlee Government after the war and by the Churchill, Eden and then Macmillan Governments were based on the desirability of full employment, a decent Welfare State and the public ownership of certain key services such as transport and education. They were very much in the line of the *Industrial Charter*, the manifesto issued by the Conservative Party in 1947 under the guidance of R.A. Butler in an attempt to show that the Conservative Party had indeed changed its spots from the inter-war years and was now happy to pursue a middle way. As Butler himself put it, the series of charters 'attempted to give capitalism a human look'.

Such policies were not to the liking of all Conservatives. The

Party leader himself, Winston Churchill, preoccupied as he was with writing his memoirs of the Second World War, was not altogether happy. Reginald Maudling, a future Chancellor of the Exchequer, has provided an evocative description of Churchill's attitude:

> I was working for Winston on his concluding speech to the [1947 Conservative] Conference and we came to the topic of the Industrial Charter. 'Give me five lines, Maudling,' he said, 'explaining what the Industrial Charter says.' This I did. He read it with care, and then said, 'But I do not agree with a word of this.' 'Well, sir,' I said, 'this is what the Conference adopted.' 'Oh well,' he said, 'leave it in,' and he duly read it out in the course of his speech, with the calculated coolness which he always accorded to those passages in his speeches, rare as they were, which had been drafted by other people, before he went back to the real meat of his own dictation.

Others in Churchill's circle were equally disapproving of the new stance. Lord Beaverbrook and Brendan Bracken exchanged many letters over several post-war years in which their disgust with the Butler-influenced Conservative Party was patently obvious. A handful of dissenters led by A.G. Erskine-Hill set up the Progress Trust which published the Signpost booklets attacking the charters. But, in the aftermath of the war, the political tide was running all one way in favour of government intervention.

In 1951 a new Conservative Government took office. But instead of embarking on a wholesale reversal of previous Labour policies, the Churchill administration was only too happy to continue in their general direction. One detailed study of the 1951 to 1955 period concluded that 'Only minor shifts of emphasis were to be seen on defence, the colonies and foreign policy. More remarkable is the continuity in economic and social matters.' Perhaps the startling change from the inter-war Conservative policies can be seen most clearly in the attitude towards organised labour.

Trade unions have always represented a problem for the Party because they exist primarily to interfere with the rigours of the capitalist system. They try to represent the low-paid and the less powerful members of society, arguing that the employers have a responsibility to make provision for their workforce – provisions which are often, from the employers' viewpoint, expensive and a hindrance to the way in which they want to run their firms.

As Andrew Taylor has put it, 'It is not surprising that Conservatives were wary of organizations embodying a class approach to politics, especially when committed to a socialist objective via affiliation to the Labour Party.' On the other hand, as Taylor continues, 'Conservatives simply could not afford to write off millions of trade-union votes.' In the pursuit of power, it is foolish and counterproductive to alienate important sections of British society.

During the 1950s successive Conservative Governments were determined to stay on friendly terms with the trade union movement. In part, no doubt, this reflected guilt, whether justified or not, at memories of the 1930s. It was also intended to make sure that the Party was never saddled with pre-war associations of unemployment and the means test.

This approach is illustrated by a typical Churchill story. He once telephoned his Chancellor of the Exchequer, R.A. Butler, at 2.30 a.m. and said, '"I thought you'd like to know we've settled with the miners." "Oh, really, Prime Minister," I said. "On what terms?" "On theirs, of course," he said. "Dammit, you've got to have electric light."'

Churchill deliberately chose the generous and emollient Walter Monckton to be the Minister of Labour in 1951 precisely because he was likely to get on well with the unions: 'He [Churchill] looked to me to do my best to preserve industrial peace. I said that I should seek to do that by trying to do justice . . . without worrying about party politics.' Trade union leaders such as Arthur Deakin, general secretary of the mammoth Transport and General Workers' Union, had access to Monckton whenever they wanted and their meetings included a full measure of beer and sandwiches.

In recent years, enthusiasts for Mrs Thatcher have looked back on post-war British history and claimed that the 'liberal Toryism' of charters and government intervention was largely responsible for the country's decline. Andrew Roberts, for example, has argued very powerfully that Conservatives overestimated the significance of the 1945 general election:

> Instead of treating it as the freak result it was, an entire generation of Tory politicians was emasculated by the 1945 election result, especially over the issues of nationalization, the growth of the state and trade union reform. They failed to learn the lesson of what an extra two and a half million Conservative voters between the 1945 and the 1951 elections meant, and instead ceded the intellectual high-ground to the collectivists for a quarter of a century and settled down to manage imperial and commercial decline. This allowed the 'ratchet effect' to pertain throughout the 1950s, 1960s and 1970s, whereby each incoming Tory Government merely preserved the shifts to the left made by the previous Labour one.

Walter Monckton in particular, Minister of Labour until 1955, has been singled out as one of the key villains of this particular piece, appeasing the unions at the cost of economic growth.

It seems unfair to pick on Monckton because not only did Churchill himself fully endorse Monckton's approach – in fact, he went further on several occasions – but it was an approach supported by all the senior members of the Cabinet; as Anthony Seldon has commented, 'to a considerable extent it was a collective policy'.

Essentially these 1950s Conservative administrations were indeed corporatist in character, seeking to involve government, employers and trade unions in a grand alliance. Their policies were the subject of much sustained debate – but, needless to say, this debate took place behind closed doors. It forms yet another part of the hidden history of the Tory Party.

The Cabinet papers reveal, for instance, that soon after the Churchill Government came to office in 1951, Chancellor of the Exchequer R.A. Butler was full of dire predictions: 'we are facing a balance of payments crisis of major dimensions'. He went on to warn his Cabinet colleagues in a secret memorandum that soon Britain would no longer be able 'to buy the basic food and raw materials on which this island depends . . . We still have time to organise ourselves to deal with this emergency . . . But there is not much time.'

In fact the Conservative goose was saved by an upturn in the world economy in the early 1950s – to such an extent that Chancellor Butler then went to the other extreme in his budget of April 1955. He introduced a so-called give-away budget, cutting both purchase tax and income tax, measures which stoked up inflation. As it happened, a general election was to be held the next month, in May 1955, which the Conservatives won handsomely. After the election, Butler had to claw back the extra spending power which he had unleashed in his budget, producing stagnation in 1956. The economy did not fully recover from Butler's April 1955 budget until 1958.

Not surprisingly, some sections of the Party began to argue that government expenditure was injecting a potentially dangerous bout of 'live now, pay later' inflation into the economy, storing up problems for the future. Exponents of this view included Peter Thorneycroft, Harold Macmillan's Chancellor of the Exchequer. He once said of his old boss that he 'loved spending – he almost invented it!' In 1958 Thorneycroft and his treasury team, Nigel Birch and Enoch Powell, resigned over an item of expenditure worth £50 million which they wanted to cut and Macmillan did not.

With characteristic insouciance Macmillan dismissed their resignations as 'a little, local difficulty'. He could afford to adopt this relaxed attitude, knowing as he did that his party chairman, Lord Hailsham, had already acted quickly to snuff out any possible grassroots revolt by sending off simultaneous telegrams explaining the leader's position to 'anyone in the Party network who could put "chairman" after his name'.

In July 1962, during the 'Night of the Long Knives', Macmillan sacked his Chancellor of the Exchequer, Selwyn Lloyd. Nigel Birch was swift to write to *The Times* and his letter was short and to the point: 'For the second time the Prime Minister has got rid of a Chancellor of the Exchequer who tried to get expenditure under control. Once is more than enough.'

Many commentators have since portrayed these episodes as

being the great schism. In the 1970s and 1980s the advocates of Thatcherism enthusiastically took Thorneycroft's side – Mrs Thatcher brought him out of retirement to be her party chairman – and Macmillan and his policies were denigrated. The attackers' case is helped by the fact that Macmillan himself seems to have had doubts about the turn of events. When de Gaulle turned down Britain's application to join the Common Market in 1963, Macmillan confided miserably to his diary that his Government's policies were in shreds.

On the other hand, there are those who review the Macmillan years and do not find them so unsuccessful after all. There was virtually full employment, low inflation, an expanding Welfare State and economic growth averaging over 4 per cent a year. Would it were so today.

But was full employment bought at the cost of continuing long-term decline? Politicians such as Macmillan and Butler, who had seen all too clearly the deprivations of the 'hungry thirties', were bound to regard the provision of jobs as paramount. Butler once rounded on his free market critics and told them that 'those who talked about creating pools of unemployment should be thrown into them and made to swim'. It remained to be seen whether those less solicitous of full employment would produce greater economic success.

In the late 1960s Edward Heath, whilst in opposition, looked set to jettison the middle way in favour of laissez-faire and free market policies. This approach was dubbed that of 'Selsdon Man' after the hotel in Croydon at which Heath's Shadow Cabinet had finalised its 1970 election manifesto. It was his Government's declared intention no longer to featherbed industry with financial assistance nor to support lame ducks. But Heath was essentially a pragmatic administrator and when it became clear in government that those policies would generate an unprecedented storm he backed down.

Heath was also frustrated by what he regarded as the inadequacies of British industry and business. Instead of the long-term planning and development which he had hoped to promote, he saw commercial energies being poured into an unsustainable spurt of property speculation. This 'short-termism' was typified by the activities of the company Slater Walker which became synonymous with greed and avarice. Heath also criticised Lonrho as representing 'the unacceptable face of capitalism' because of the massive perks and tax-free secret payments made to its managing director, Tiny Rowland.

The Heath Government tried to regularise the power of the trade union movement by cutting down on unofficial strikes and reducing the power of shop stewards. This was not purely a party political measure. Harold Wilson and Barbara Castle's *In Place of Strife* proposals had attempted something similar but in the face of union opposition they had had to retreat; Heath did likewise.

One of Heath's loyal lieutenants, Jim Prior, candidly admits in his memoirs that the administration rushed precipitously into trade union reform, even though 'apart from Robert Carr, our Secretary of State for Employment, scarcely anyone in the Party understood industrial relations or knew industrialists, let alone any trade unionists'.

The downfall of the Heath Government in 1974 and the collapse of his economic and industrial policies left a vacuum in the Conservative Party which was filled by a much sterner and more austere free market approach. These ideas were not new: they expressed the laissez-faire and free market voice of Conservatism dominant between the wars but submerged in the Macmillan years. The Institute of Economic Affairs (IEA), for instance, had been founded in 1957 and its small but growing band of enthusiasts had steadfastly argued their case.

The IEA and its supporters insisted on clarity of language in their publications – rather different from the turgid prose which left-wingers deemed mandatory – and in essence they argued that Macmillan and his middle way followers were trying to have their cake as well as eat it. The bloated public sector stifled competition and wealth creation and inevitably led to inflation. In turn this inflation diminished productivity.

Above all, the IEA maintained that the Government was not a very intelligent participant in economic affairs because it was inevitably pulled this way and that by competing special interests.

Its decisions were therefore made less on economic than on political grounds. This new hands-off approach was neatly summed up in the Conservative Party manifesto of 1977 called *The Right Approach to the Economy*: 'We believe that Government knows less about business than businessmen, less about investment than investors, and less about pay bargaining than trade union negotiators and employers. We think we understand the limitations on what a government alone can do. This is surely the beginning of wisdom and common sense.'

There was much that was appealing in these arguments. They seemed to explain the comparative decline of the British economy. They also provided a number of useful scapegoats, particularly the unions, who were deeply unpopular because of their antics during the Callaghan Government.

And finally they exalted the processes of untrammelled wealth creation, riding roughshod over the hesitancies which some Conservatives, as we have seen, had always felt about materialism. One American commentator, Martin J. Weiner, argued that Thatcherism actually represented a turning back of one hundred years of British history. The traditional non-materialism of the British was neatly summed up in a survey published in 1977:

> Very few [British people] sincerely want to be rich. Most people in Britain neither want nor expect a great deal of money. Even if they could get it, the vast majority do not seem prepared to work harder for it: most of our respondents thought we should work only as much as we need to live a pleasant life . . . It seems clear that the British today prefer economic stability to rapid economic growth.

Such views were anathema both to Mrs Thatcher and her supporters and their mission to overturn these attitudes was proclaimed with evangelical fervour. In some respects, as opponents like Denis Healey pointed out, this revulsion felt against the role of government intervention was a generational phenomenon. Mrs Thatcher was the first post-war party leader who retained no clear memories of the effects of the depression in the 1930s or of the inadequacies of private enterprise during the Second World War. Joseph Chamberlain had advocated sweeping measures of tariff reform in the early twentieth century in order to reinvigorate the British economy, but he was never in a position to implement his ideas. Mrs Thatcher was.

Her brand of market-led Conservatism was neither unique nor original, but did in fact represent a reversion to older party values submerged in middle way days. Take this quotation: 'Without a growing trade there can be no money for social reform. This purse of the State, into which the Socialist thinks he can go on dipping his hand for ever, is filled only by industry. The State spends: it does not earn.' Surely this is a passage from one of Mrs Thatcher's speeches? In fact they are the words of Neville Chamberlain, son of Joe, who led the Party at the end of the 1930s.

The economic policies applied by Conservative Governments during the 1980s sought to take the brakes off the market economy, to minimise restraint and to let the ensuing outburst of energy run wild. As her supporter Norman Tebbit put it, 'The Thatcher revolution has come a long way but most of its work has been devoted to the destruction of the restraints which had brought our economy to its knees.'

In pursuance of this, tax rates for the wealthy were lowered dramatically and companies were urged to go after a 'big bang'. This was undoubtedly in tune with most Conservatives' feelings – virtually every annual conference since the war had passed a resolution condemning the high rates of taxation. Self-made enterpreneurs and City dealers were encouraged to think of themselves as swashbuckling buccaneers championing British interests by hook or by crook.

It was inevitable that the trade union movement would come under severe attack. This would probably have happened anyway: all over Europe trade union membership was shrinking as the heavy manual industries such as coal, iron, steel and shipbuilding contracted. Soaring rates of unemployment naturally took their toll too, making people fearful of losing their jobs. Strikes diminished and Government legislation insisted that the workforce should be balloted before an industrial stoppage.

Interestingly enough, this was a change which had often been mooted in the past. Early in May 1926, with the General Strike looming into view, Cabinet papers record that 'Suggestions were made that in the event of a general strike, legislation should at once be introduced . . . to make a secret ballot necessary.' The suggestion surfaced once more in 1957 but was summarily dismissed by the Cabinet minister involved, Iain Macleod. As Minister of Labour, Macleod believed that a majority of Conservatives and probably the population too favoured reform of trade union law, but that this 'could only be forced through in the teeth of extensive trade union opposition'.

Secret ballots were not, therefore, an original idea of the Thatcher government – but it did take her political will to push it through 'in the teeth of extensive trade union opposition'. This welcome reform was one that the hidebound trade union movement should have introduced itself, but had not. Union hostility to the changes has now changed to one of grudging acceptance.

To reduce the fetters on wealth creation, much safety and industrial legislation protecting the workforce was dismantled and the wages councils safeguarding the low paid were abolished. The theory was that as the wealth creators got wealthier then some of that prosperity would trickle down to the low paid and unemployed. That, at least, was the theory.

Mrs Thatcher was extremely fortunate in the hand that fate dealt her. Whereas the Heath Government had been forced to cope with the quadrupling of oil prices in the autumn of 1973, the Thatcher Governments had the massive windfall of North Sea oil which proved to be worth some £100 billion. Even though North Sea oil is barely mentioned in Mrs Thatcher's memoirs of the period, it provided her Governments with much-needed revenue and in many ways acted as the scaffolding for Thatcherism.

In addition, Government coffers were swelled by the proceeds resulting from the privatisation of certain public companies such as Telecom and electricity. This policy was something the Government actually developed when in office, demonstrating yet again the Conservative ability to manage change. 'Privatisation', for example, was absent from the 1979 manifesto. The breakthrough came with the sale of British Telecom in November 1984.

The Government made full use of the electioneering and public relations techniques explored in Chapter 8. The advertising campaign in the press and on television cost £7.6 million but was regarded as a success because two million people bought shares. The subsequent sale of British Gas was launched by an advertising campaign costing £20 million – which was a pittance when it is remembered that privatisation in the 1980s generated some £90 billion for the Conservative Government.

Privatisation had the additional benefit for the Conservative Government of pleasing all its supporters. As John Redwood, one of Mrs Thatcher's key advisers and later himself a Cabinet minister, pointed out: 'It became something all wings of the Conservative Party could agree on, left and right, as it made available more money both for spending programmes and for the tax cuts dear to the hearts of both sections of the Party.'

No British Government in history ever possessed two such generous golden geese as North Sea oil and privatisation.

There was an outburst of activity in some areas: the number of small and medium-size businesses grew by one million during the 1980s, although many of these were perforce set up by individuals who had lost their jobs. These small businesses were never likely to generate more than a fraction of the employment lost in other industries: the 1.3 million jobs created in the 1980s were mainly part-time and did not replace the three million full-time jobs lost in manufacturing industries.

In the City, Big Bang and deregulation created a breed of conspicuous high-earners, dubbed Yuppies whose consumption of luxury items was most unlikely to trickle down to the poorest. Mrs Thatcher's sense of adventure meant that she admired the modern merchant adventurer. Individuals such as Sir Clive Sinclair, Gerald Ronson, Asil Nadir, Gerald Ratner and firms such as the Sock Shop, Saatchi & Saatchi, Next and so on were extolled for their entrepreneurial qualities, but in fact many of the individuals involved ended up bankrupt or in prison. Few were able to sustain their initial success. Similarly, many home-owners, having taken out huge mortgages in the anticipation of ever-rising house prices, found themselves unable to meet their payments and burdened with negative equity when boom turned to bust.

Some critics called Mrs Thatcher's approach 'growth through greed', but the Prime Minister herself was apparently unconcerned: for Mrs Thatcher, capitalism has no unacceptable faces.

The only sure way of judging the Thatcher Governments' economic record is by examination of results – and the results can only be described as patchy. It is perhaps significant that in her memoirs of these years Lady Thatcher herself eschews any such summary. From 1979 to 1993 (which includes the years of the Major administration when the government was dealing with the Thatcher-supervised recession) economic growth in Britain amounted to an average of just 1.6 per cent a year. This was distinctly worse than the much-derided Wilson years, for example, and was the lowest achieved by any industrial country in the world since 1945. In other words, the record appears to be one of failure even in Mrs Thatcher's terms.

It was unclear whether the introduction of flexible labour markets had any beneficial effect. Whilst the casualisation of labour and the growth of short-term contracts may well have increased, the uncertainty had a detrimental effect on overall morale. The brutal managerial language which became the norm exalted the balance sheet before human beings. If it wasn't profitable then it must be rationalised: in other words, eliminated.

One certainty was that shifting the tax burden from direct taxation to indirect taxes had increased the gap between those on high and those on low incomes. This discrepancy was confirmed in a report published by the independent Institute for Fiscal Studies in February 1994. As *The Times* commented on 9 February 1994, 'Since 1979, the poorest fifth of the population have seen their real incomes decline by 3 per cent while the real incomes of the top fifth have risen by up to 50 per cent.'

It was also evident that Mrs Thatcher had been trapped by her own rhetoric. If everything private was good, then anything public was bad: public transport, public education, public health care were by definition inefficient and financially detrimental to the tax-payer.

With such a black and white approach, her Governments never accepted that the short-term interests of the market neglected long-term investment in training or research and development. Successive Conservative Governments felt compelled to push on with such policies as rail privatisation, even though it was difficult to see what the advantages would be of such a measure.

There were no fewer than twelve different Ministers of State at the Department of Trade and Industry during Mrs Thatcher's time in office, which suggests yet again that within the Conservative Party the interests of the City generally come before those of manufacturing industry. Few Tory MPs have any industrial experience; many, however, come from a City and banking background.

Not that this is necessarily a guarantee of competence. In their respective memoirs, Lord Lawson and Lady Thatcher offer diametrically opposed views on whether the Prime Minister had known that, crucially, the pound was shadowing the Deutschmark. Thatcher claims that from March 1987 her chancellor had in fact been following a new policy unknown to her, and that she only found out about it via an interview with journalists from the *Financial Times* in November 1987. No matter who is telling the truth, the disagreement does not exactly enhance one's faith in the wisdom of our governors.

Hands off meant too that the Government shied away from trying to remedy Britain's chronic problem of under-investment. In large part this resulted from the inadequate provision of capital by banks and pension fund managers who were concerned above all with short-term dividends and financial gain. Laissez-faire can sometimes mean simply the substitution of private monopolies for public ones. The much-heralded partnership between the private and public sectors remained unconsummated. In London's Docklands, for instance, the failure to install an underground link meant that the entire project was hamstrung from the start. Everyone blamed everyone else for not providing this vital public access.

The *reductio ad adsurdum* of this policy was that the Thatcher Government resolutely failed to provide the funds to improve the railway system in Britain or to support the Channel link, but was prepared to grant £234 million in aid to Malaysia in order to help the defence industry – a transaction which in November 1994 the courts ruled to be illegal. Commentator Simon Jenkins was blunt:

> Defenders of the deal will of course say that this was a 'good deal for Britain'. In which case, why did the Government not forget the dam and simply give an export subsidy to the arms contractors? The answer is that the aid budget is not meant to be linked to weapons. Besides, the Thatcher Government did not believe in subsidising British industry. In 1988 the Prime Minister was fiercely denying public support for the Channel tunnel high-speed links, in which many of the companies fighting for Malaysian contracts might have had a hand. Bluntly, the taxpayer built a dam in northern Malaysia rather than a railway in southern Britain because railways do not sell arms. It is British hypocrisy, not Dr Mahathir's Asian values, that makes Pergau a story.

Perhaps the major reason for the ambiguity at the heart of Mrs Thatcher's economic policies was that she was trying to face several ways at the same time. According to John Redwood, popular capitalism is 'anarchic and democratic in its style. It does not matter who you are, who your parents were, where you came from: it is who *you* are and what you can contribute that matters.'

Fine in principle; but in practice, Mrs Thatcher had to win elections – in Britain, political power does not grow out of the barrel of a gun but depends on success at the ballot box. It was important not to alienate too many vote-casting supporters by unleashing too much anarchy. In spite of the rhetoric about updating and meeting new challenges – it was vital to try and avoid the word 'modernisation' which was too reminiscent of Harold Wilson's 1960s – Mrs Thatcher was careful to reward and succour her allies even if they were part of the problem.

The traditional Tory bias towards the City at the expense of manufacturing was maintained: one of her Government's first actions in 1979 was to abolish exchange rate controls, much to City delight. Interest rates averaged more than 12 per cent between May 1979 and mid-1991, hardly an enticing prospect for businesses wishing either to expand or to set up in the first place.

It was a similar situation with mortgage interest relief, which most economists insisted was damaging to the economy. Mrs Thatcher, despite her stated determination to take on and defeat all vested and special interests, steered well away from this topic: abolition of the tax relief would have upset the middle-class house-owning supporters who formed her electoral backbone in the South of England.

Despite the rhetoric of the Thatcher and then Major administrations, the free economy was in fact rarely free at all – or, at least, rarely free of political considerations. Some uneconomic industries simply had to be shored up for electoral not economic reasons. For instance, the maintenance of the Rosyth shipyard in Scotland was dictated by fears that its closure might well precipitate a Conservative electoral 'melt down' at a general election.

At heart Mrs Thatcher's primary concern, and that of her successor John Major, was less the economic future of Britain than the short-term electoral prospects of the Conservative Party. In 1955, R.A. Butler had helped manipulate the economy for electoral ends, as did Reginald Maudling in 1963–4. In 1986–7, Nigel Lawson proved happy to follow in their footsteps by presiding over a pre-election boom which stoked up consumer credit to reckless and unsustainable levels, a policy which he foolishly continued in the 1988 budget.

Five years later the Major Government emulated its predecessor's example by letting spending get out of control in the run-up to the 1992 election; putting off unpopular but economically sound decisions which might have lost votes. As David Smith, economics editor of the *Sunday Times*, neatly put it: 'Public spending rose by more than £20 billion in 1991–92 and by £25 billion in 1992–93. The combined rise of £45 billion was bigger than over the entire five-year period from 1985 to 1990.' It is not surprising that Britain amassed a public sector deficit of £50 billion.

Much of this is the result of the money which has had to be spent on supporting the mass of unemployed people about which the Thatcher and Major administrations, unlike those of their predecessors Churchill, Eden and Macmillan, seemed relatively unconcerned. And yet revenue from taxes is lost when people are out of work. This £50 billion deficit has been run up by an economy which had the inestimable advantage of North Sea oil.

The Conservatives have also found themselves hemmed in by their pledge to be the low taxation party and by their virulent assault on the Labour Party's proposed tax plans during the 1992 general election. Once again, electoral considerations outweighed the country's long-term economic health. Policy was reduced to a simplistic equation of low tax = good; high tax = bad. That the Conservative Government has now raised taxes, despite previous seemingly heart-felt promises, adds to the widespread public scepticism felt about politicians and politics.

Perhaps even more damaging to the overall reputation of the Conservative Party for financial competence was the debacle over membership of the European Exchange Rate Mechanism (ERM) in the autumn of 1992. The Prime Minister John Major and his Chancellor Norman Lamont staked their reputations on keeping the pound within the ERM, whatever the markets themselves might think. Enormous sums of money were spent shoring up the over-valued pound, but to no avail. The pound was forced out of the ERM in September 1992.

The Government's failed efforts not only cost the country some £5 billion but also severely damaged Conservative claims to be economically more expert than their political opponents. David Smith called it 'the biggest policy climbdown by any British Government since the 1967 devaluation'.

The bitter internal arguments over Europe spilled out into the open, underlining once again that the Party is a coalition of interests. Many of its most powerful supporters in industry favoured a single European currency – other important sections within the Party are resolutely opposed to such a move. There is no halfway house on such an either/or issue. Chapter 14 covers this question in more detail.

But one thing was for sure: the economy was beginning to look rather unsafe in Conservative hands. Protesting that the recession of the early 1990s was due not to Government policies but rather to international events outside their control, it was not surprising that the public seemed unwilling to attribute an economic upturn from 1994 to the policies of that same administration.

The Conservative dedication to wealth creation is rooted in the Party's belief that if you give people a stake in the system, then they are less likely to challenge that system. As Sir Robert Peel observed, disaffection would be 'forgotten in the midst of physical enjoyment'.

There is nothing sinister or wrong with this approach: it is a course of action practised by most established regimes. Clearly it is easier to buy off discontent when the cake is growing for everyone – easier too to sidestep questions about the share out of that same cake.

But, of course, the fundamental difficulty is to ensure that the economy does actually grow and here differing views are apparent. Some fundamentalist Marxists still thunder on about 'the ruling class this' and 'the ruling class that' but as we have seen no such single entity exists. Within the Conservative Party itself, the interests of big business and small business, of its leaders and its grassroots members, are often at odds. The Confederation of British Industry sometimes disagrees with the Institute of Directors, and trade associations often fall out with local chambers of commerce. Some Conservatives favour incomes policies, others argue passionately for free collective bargaining. The Conservative Party is, and always has been, a collection of interests.

But in the morass of conflicting views and arguments which have influenced Conservative approaches to the economy, one characteristic does stand out: the use of the economy to retain power. Competence in government has always been preferred to the luxuries of ideological debate.

The Conservative Party has been prepared to adopt short-term policies in order to ensure that the feel good factor predominates when voters casts their votes. It has shied away from implementing vitally needed policies of modernisation lest they upset the vested interests which make up the Party and provide its financial backing. In the 1980s, in particular, the Conservatives thought of the elector as being above all else a consumer and tried to ensure that nothing should thwart the growth of consumption. Appropriately enough, this was the decade in which the credit card came into general use.

This short-termism has sometimes had enormously deleterious results for the economy, leading to cutbacks and recession. This happened before and after the 1955 election, before the 1964 election which was lost, before and after the 1983 election when hire-purchase controls were abolished, and before and after the 1987 and the 1992 elections. Short-termism shuns hard and unpopular decisions in order to maintain unity and electoral success. The Conservatives have been preoccupied less with the long-term health of the British economy than with making sure that the electoral and financial cycles are in synch.

In many ways the Conservative Party has been able to get away with this because of public ignorance and apathy about the system of taxation and finances generally. Such is the opinion of the shrewd political commentator Noel Malcolm writing in the *Daily Telegraph* – in other words not the view of some jaundiced socialist. Throughout the 1980s and 1990s, successive Conservative administrations distracted attention from the overall increase in taxation by shifting the burden to indirect taxes: the doubling of VAT, eroding personal allowances and increasing National Insurance contributions.

But at some point the harsh realities are likely to penetrate the public consciousness and then the conflict between the interventionist and free market wings of the Conservative Party will intensify – as is already happening over the European issue. For instance, in its purest form Rupert Murdoch's *Sunday Times* advocates a low-wage, high-tech economy on the lines of that in Hong Kong. This ideal represents the complete antithesis of that middle way strand within the Conservative Party which has always depreciated the money-grubbing and materialist side of capitalism.

It is also unclear what the growing globalisation of the economy will mean. Countries in Western European have always had higher wage costs than the developing world and the consequences can be seen by comparing the living standards in, say, France and India. At present, however, the West is trying through a revised GATT

(General Agreement on Trade and Tariffs) to speed up the movement towards global free trade, which means that our industries will be competing directly against less costly ones from abroad.

The consequences could well be unimaginable, as Sir James Goldsmith and others warn, and it is highly unlikely that a Hong Kong-style economy here in Britain will leave our political system untouched.

Yet whatever criticisms can be made of the Conservative Party's economic record, it still remains one of their strongest electoral cards. David Willetts claims that 'Success in economic management is the most important single measure of the effectiveness and coherence of a party's political programme.'

Rightly or wrongly, the electorate still mistrusts the Labour Party as being advocates of big spending and high taxation. It is quite possible that the Conservative Government will prove able to continue to massage the economy, ensuring a feel good factor by the time of the next election – and, of course, because Britain has no system of fixed-term elections, they are able to call an election when it suits them best.

There is no doubt too that, in general, economic trends favour the parties of the Right. Vincent Cable of the Royal Institute of International Affairs put it best in December 1994:

> . . . the central economic ideas for the foreseeable future will be those of the right: markets, competition, private ownership, entrepreneurship. The momentum created by communications technology and global business competition is immense and irresistible. It will sweep away many of the remaining structures of state control, as it has in the UK and the US. There is hardly a socialist or former Communist Party anywhere which will fight for re-nationalisation, and few have any illusions that they can control prices or foreign exchange flows, or preserve job security or plan the future structure of the economy. The argument is about different types of capitalism and competition between them.

Of course, this does not mean that parties of the Left are doomed to electoral defeat, but it does point up the difficulties of the challenge facing them. The British Conservatives may well succeed in reducing the question of the economy to one of taxation: do *you* want to pay more taxes or less taxes? Whatever the moral issues or the replies given to pollsters, most voters when in the seclusion of the polling booth are still likely to answer less and therefore vote Conservative. On the other hand, the debacle in the House of Commons in December 1994 over doubling VAT on fuel once again questioned the Government's economic competence.

The Major Government is hoping to ride to another election victory on the back of the recovery, and the Chancellor of the Exchequer, Kenneth Clarke, is carefully preparing the way for substantial tax cuts in 1995 and 1996. In which case, the Conservative Party may well continue in power for another four or five years. Whether that will be beneficial for the long-term condition of the British economy as a whole is less clearcut.

12

One Nation and Two

The Conservative Party and the 'Condition of the People'

'What ransom will property pay for the security which it enjoys?'

Joseph Chamberlain, 1885

'If you do not give the people social reform, they are going to give you social revolution.'

Quintin Hogg (later Lord Hailsham),
speaking in the House of Commons, 1944

Although today Neville Chamberlain's name is indissolubly linked with the policy of appeasement towards Nazi Germany, he originally made his reputation as a social reformer. His Housing Act of 1923 granted a subsidy to private enterprise for every new house built and within just seven years over a million homes were completed. As Harold Macmillan was to realise three decades later, the provision of new housing is always popular with the electorate.

Much of his social reforming spirit was derived from his father Joseph, 'Radical Joe', who had transformed the city of Birmingham in the 1870s by introducing schemes of municipalisation wherever private enterprise had failed. Neville Chamberlain was also responsible for the unglamorous but essential reform of the rating system between the wars. Unlike some of his colleagues, he seems to have been well aware of social conditions away from the comforts of Westminster. In 1927, for instance, he visited the mining areas in the aftermath of the General Strike and wrote that 'the devastation in the coalfields can only be compared with the war devastation of France'.

It might have been thought, therefore, that when Chamberlain became Prime Minister in May 1937 he would have led a concerted attack on the devastating social conditions which characterised parts of Britain during the depression years. In fact, he devoted his formidable energies to diplomatic matters even though, as one of his junior ministers R.A. Butler noted, 'Chamberlain knew almost nothing about foreign affairs.'

In May 1940 Chamberlain resigned as Prime Minister. That summer, children from deprived city areas were evacuated to the countryside; he and his prosperous neighbours, playing host to the billeted children, along with many others saw at first hand what life had been like for millions of Britons. Shocked, Chamberlain wrote to his sister: 'I never knew that such conditions existed and I am deeply ashamed of my ignorance.'

We have seen that Chamberlain did know of such conditions as long ago as 1927 – but he had conveniently pushed to one side what he had witnessed then. The problem was less one of knowledge than of political will and determination.

The case of Neville Chamberlain highlights the Conservative Party's dilemma over social reform. On the one hand there is the genuine compassion felt at the difficult living conditions experienced by many of their fellow men and women; on the other hand there is the conviction that the present system, whatever its faults, offers the best prospect of improvement, albeit slow and gradual, and therefore radical reform is invariably counterproductive.

To complicate the issue further, it is vital that the Conservative Party be seen by the electorate as concerned about the welfare of all sections of society, including the disadvantaged. The Party must be a national organisation speaking for all sections and classes of society – if ever it is perceived to be the representative of just one sectional interest, then electoral disaster looms.

Naturally there are differing views within the Party about the extent of welfare provision. Some Conservatives feel that wealth creation should take priority. Social measures must not be allowed to fetter economic growth – in any case private welfare schemes directed by the market are superior to the wasteful bureaucracy of public services. Other Conservatives are quite prepared to interfere with the market in the interests of justice and equity. For them, social reform is a better and more just alternative to socialism. Arthur Balfour, a future Conservative Prime Minister, expressed this viewpoint best in 1895:

Social legislation, as I conceive it, is not merely to be distinguished from Socialist legislation but it is its most direct opposite and its most effective antidote. Socialism will never get possession of the great body of public opinion . . . among the working class or any other class if those who wield the collective forces of the community show themselves desirous to ameliorate every legitimate grievance and to put Society upon a proper and more solid basis.

However heated the arguments between these two schools of Conservative thought, one thing unites members of both sides: no one is prepared to threaten the existing system itself. They will candidly admit its flaws but maintain that, at the end of the day, it offers the least worst state of affairs.

Another difficulty is that, as we saw when looking at the composition of the Conservative Party, most of its leading figures, be they constituency chairmen, members of Parliament or Cabinet ministers, come from relatively privileged and comfortable backgrounds. Their knowledge of life outside those confines was and is limited.

In many ways this central conflict between those who favour market forces and those who want government intervention mirrors the tensions discussed in the previous chapter on Conservative economics. To intervene or not to intervene is indeed the question: if not social reform, then social revolution? These conflicts and contradictions are clearly visible in the measures associated with three men often cited as examples of great Tory reformers, namely Benjamin Disraeli, Winston Churchill and R.A. Butler.

Benjamin Disraeli entered politics at a time of volatile social change. Huge numbers of people were moving from the countryside into new towns and cities whilst the arrival of factories introduced new forms of work. Several people did well out of the changes – the Peel family, for instance – but many others did not and it was clear to even the most casual observer that the living conditions of many were disgusting: no sanitation, no decent housing, no educational or medical facilities.

Some argued that the growth of industrialisation inevitably produced casualties. Many Liberals were loath to interfere with the workings of what was regarded as an immutable system whose laws had been sent by God. But other observers, especially the Tory radicals, were deeply hostile to the effects of what was taking place. Not all of them were armchair theorists: Tories Richard Oastler and M.T. Sadler led the fight to restrict the number of hours which children could be forced to work, arguing that if England's wealth really did rest on the slavery of little children, then 'sink your commerce and rise Humanity, Benevolence and Christianity'.

A sustained critique of events was offered by Benjamin Disraeli in his novel *Sybil* which contains many semi-documentary passages. But Disraeli wanted to do more than just write about the abuses he witnessed and with a group of friends he formed the 'Young England' movement. Two of Disraeli's colleagues were from titled families – George Smythe was the eldest son of Lord Stangford, Lord John Manners was the second son of the Duke of Rutland – which suggests there was some sense of *noblesse oblige*, making the movement none the worse for that.

The ideas of Young England were always vague, but essentially its members idealised the past, hated the present and hoped that the future could resemble what had gone before. They advocated an alliance between the upper classes and the working classes in order to beat back what they regarded as the grasping and materialistic middle classes. It could never have happened, not least because the working classes at this time had no vote and therefore little political power.

The movement soon collapsed, but its idealism does seem to have given a thread of continuity to Disraeli's career. His brief spells in office never produced anything substantial in the way of social reform, but in 1874 he finally became the Prime Minister of a majority Conservative Government. By then, however, he was seventy-two years old, his beloved wife Mary Anne had died and clearly the appeal of politics was beginning to wane.

Nevertheless, this Tory administration did push through several social reforms. The Public Health Act of 1875 dealt with sanitation, an Artisans' Dwellings Act with slum clearance, the Merchant Shipping Acts forced shipowners to install a Plimsoll line to prevent the overloading of their vessels and trade union reform legalised peaceful picketing.

The drawback to many of these measures was that essentially they were merely empowering acts allowing the local authorities to carry out reforms if they so wished. In practice, the powerful ratepayers' lobby would almost certainly veto any such action. The Public Health Act was, in John Vincent's words, 'a consolidation act: essentially a reprint'. The introduction of the Plimsoll line was a good idea, but the Government did not specify where the line had to go – the owners could put it around the funnel if they so wished. The trade union legislation was more innovatory, allowing peaceful picketing during an industrial dispute.

The fact that this legislation aroused little opposition testifies to its cautious and limited scope. (Compare the furore which greeted the more drastic Liberal reforms passed between 1868 and 1874 and 1906 and 1914.) Professor Richard Shannon has observed of these 'Disraelian' measures that: 'Never did a political party make, unwittingly, a more profitable investment for the future in half a dozen items of low-key legislation.'

Disraeli's actual role in the drafting and passage of the legislation seems to have been minimal. Most of the legislation was in fact pushed through by the energetic Home Secretary Richard Cross, with Disraeli's acquiescence but not participation. He used to go to sleep as the measures were debated at Cabinet. After his death in

1881, Conservative propagandists were keen to play up the image of the Party as a national body speaking for all and naturally emphasised Disraeli's contribution as a pioneering social reformer. The record contradicts the legend.

'Winston used to ring me up before a Budget and say, "Remember compassion!"' So recalls R.A. Butler of his period as Chancellor of the Exchequer under Winston Churchill in the early 1950s.

It is common knowledge that Winston Churchill was easily moved to tears, whether it was touring the bombed areas of the East End during the Blitz or watching a sentimental film. Despite his pugnacity and however vehemently political opponents might disagree with his views, no one ever doubted that Churchill's heart was absolutely in the right place.

Part of the eternal fascination of Winston Churchill as both human being and politician derives from the curiously two-sided nature of the Churchill identity. On the one hand there was the aristocratic face: the palace at Blenheim, the Marlborough name, the self-confidence and security of a place within the higher ranks of the landed English aristocracy. On the other there was the more flamboyant, crowd-pleasing and demagogic side, the willingness and ability to mix with 'the other ranks' – as an army officer, Winston Churchill was always liked and respected by the men under his command. But note the words, 'under his command': Churchill was a paternalist and never an egalitarian.

He always favoured what he graphically called 'the ambulances of state aid' and as a Liberal Cabinet minister before the First World War was responsible for several social reforms. He helped set up Labour (Employment) Exchanges and also introduced the Trade Boards Act which laid down minimum wage levels in certain 'sweated' trades such as tailoring and lace-making. These initiatives were, by Victorian standards, unwarrantable intrusions into the workings of the free market.

Between the wars, apart from his period as Chancellor of the Exchequer, he was excluded from office and during the Second World War his energies were understandably focused on foreign affairs. Some members of his wartime administration did, however, initiate domestic reforms, notably the president of the Board of Education, R.A. Butler.

Butler came from a traditional privileged background. His father was in the Indian Civil Service and the young Rab was sent home to be educated at public school and then Cambridge. Whole areas of life were therefore unknown to him and soon after his appointment as president in 1941 he was heard inquiring as to the difference between an elementary school and a secondary school.

Nevertheless, Butler's Education Act of 1944 was undoubtedly an important piece of legislation. It did, however, contain one clause which became the focus of controversy. Butler wanted both men and women teachers to be paid the same rate for the same job – hardly, one would have thought, a revolutionary idea. Churchill was adamantly opposed to this clause and had it removed. A group of young Conservative MPs, banded together as the Tory Reform Committee, were insistent that the clause should be reinstated.

Churchill was furious with their impertinence. He promptly made the issue one of confidence in his Coalition Government and, of course, in the circumstances he got his way. One of the young reformers, Quintin Hogg, now Lord Hailsham, has recalled the ferocity of Churchill's petulant reaction. Butler was distinctly feeble in fighting his corner and Hailsham claims it was an early indication of Butler's unfitness to be Conservative Party leader. The system of private education was left untouched: Butler himself sent his three sons to Eton.

Churchill also dragged his feet over the popular Beveridge Report, published in 1942, which advocated a comprehensive social security system, full employment and a decent public health service. One recent study has suggested that 90 per cent of the parliamentary Conservative Party responded negatively to the Beveridge system, the other 10 per cent was represented by the Tory Reform Committee.

When Churchill returned to office in 1951 he too, like Disraeli, was an ageing statesman whose interest in domestic affairs was limited. His government was indeed responsible, through his Minister of Housing, Harold Macmillan, for a crash course of house-building, fulfilling the pledge of 300,000 new homes a year. Churchill's part in this was, however, marginal. His most fruitful period as a social reformer, as Paul Addison has pointed out, was in the Edwardian period when he was a Liberal.

Thus it is clear that Disraeli, Churchill and Butler, whilst indeed honourable and generous politicians concerned about the condition of the people, were not responsible for startling or far-reaching measures but rather for gently tidying up the system whilst leaving its core workings untouched.

The record of all three men reflects the uncertainty of the Conservative attitude towards welfare. In the main the Party has traditionally espoused the voluntarist approach to welfare: in other words, the provision of welfare and security is best left to people themselves. In the Victorian period, for instance, Britain did indeed generate a remarkable range of self-help voluntary institutions, from co-ops and friendly societies to burial clubs and local medical societies.

Yet however admirable these bodies were, they only protected a small percentage of the population. For those who fell outside such agencies then the mishaps of life could have fearful consequences, as a series of social investigations towards the end of the century revealed. Charles Booth's study *Life and Labour of the People of London* (1889 to 1902) was followed by Seebohm Rowntree's *Poverty, a Study of Town Life* (1901) which concentrated on York.

Both these studies demolished the Victorian assumption that poverty was usually the result of individual character failings such as fecklessness or weakness for drink. Instead it was demonstrated that low wages were the commonest cause of poverty, followed by industrial accident and injury. Such charity as existed was praiseworthy but inadequate; as one academic has pithily described the impact of Booth's work, 'The notion of a submerged tenth which would be nursed through temporary difficulties by philanthropic individuals was replaced by one of a submerged third requiring massive state intervention.' The results of urban squalor became all too apparent when many would-be recruits for the Boer War had to be turned down on medical grounds.

It was also becoming clear to many industrialists and manufacturers that, with the rise of Germany and the United States as economic competitors, an uneducated and untrained workforce was commercially disastrous. This argument had been put most vividly in 1868 by an organisation calling for a system of public education that would instruct what it called 'wild young ostriches':

> The first need of society is order. If order is to be produced in men and women, what kind of preparation for it is that which leaves the children as wild as young ostriches in the desert? When for the first ten or twelve years of life there has been no discipline either in life or body – when cleanliness has been unknown – when no law of God or man has been considered sacred, and no power recognised but direct physical force – is it to be expected that they will quietly and industriously settle down in mills, workshops, warehouses or at any trade in the orderly routine of any family, to work continuously by day, morning and evening, from Monday till Saturday? The expectation is absurd. Continuous labour and sober thought are alike impossible to them.

Arguments such as these, couched in terms of commercial self-interest rather than the merits of welfare reform per se, were to become familiar over the next hundred years. Together with the findings of Charles Booth and his contemporaries, they strengthened the hand of the 'social interventionist' wing inside the Conservative Party.

Another early sign of a more active approach was the Education Act of 1870 which introduced a state-supplied system of elementary education. This was followed in turn by the Education Act of 1902, steered through Parliament by A.J. Balfour, which reorganised secondary education and established that its provision was now a duty of the state.

Yet such measures were the exception rather than the rule and in any case were fairly half-hearted. It is true that central government expenditure on education by 1914 amounted to £19.5 million a year – but this represented a third of the sum spent by Germany. Britain had nine thousand university students,

Germany more than sixty thousand. The traditional bias towards studying the classics remained, particularly at Oxbridge. By the outbreak of the First World War, Germany was producing three thousand graduate engineers a year; Britain's total in all branches of science, engineering, technology and mathematics was a miserly three hundred and fifty.

The continuing dominance of the laissez-faire wing of the Party reveals itself in the policies of inter-war Conservative Governments which still favoured the voluntarist ideal. The networks of self-support established by the middle and upper classes were still working satisfactorily in the 1920s and 1930s and any radical social legislation ran the danger of upsetting this equilibrium.

Not a single Government-commissioned study was made of the effects of unemployment in the 1930s. Similar complacency about the status quo is shown by the experiences of Sir John Boyd Orr, a world-famous nutrionist, as he attempted to draw attention to the nutritional deprivation suffered by many people. Boyd Orr's work *Food, Health and Income*, published in 1936, found that half the British population had a less than satisfactory nutritional level. In his autobiography he recounts what happened next: 'Mr Kingsley Wood, the Minister of Health, asked me to come and see him. He wanted to know why I was making such a fuss about poverty when, with old age pensions and unemployment insurance, there was no poverty in the country. He knew nothing about research on vitamins and protein requirements, and had never visited the slums to see things for himself.'

It might be thought that Kingsley Wood was another typical product of public school and Oxbridge. Far from it: his father was for many years minister in charge of the Wesley Chapel in London (where the Thatchers were to get married) and he went neither to public school nor to university. He qualified as a solicitor and sat for a relatively deprived constituency in south London – but despite this unusual background for a senior Tory, Kingsley Wood was clearly as ill-informed as most of his colleagues.

Most but not all. Harold Macmillan had been through Eton and Oxford, but his experiences representing the desperately poor constituency of Stockton had opened his eyes to the conditions in which some people lived. His book *The Middle Way*, published in 1938, emphasised, as he put it, 'the twin evils of poverty and insecurity among the people as a whole'.

The work of experts like Boyd Orr, together with privately funded studies such as *Men Without Work* issued by the Pilgrim Trust, had only so much influence on public opinion. Much more powerful were the massive shifts in social awareness triggered by the Second World War when mass evacuation meant for the first time that one half of Britain saw how the other half lived. In May 1943 *The Economist* magazine claimed that evacuation was 'the most important subject in the social history of the war because it revealed to the whole people the black spots in its social life'. The impact of 'total war' and its accompanying rhetoric of 'fair shares for all' also generated a shift towards the Left.

It soon became obvious that private enterprise was incapable of meeting the demands made of it in terms of social support. The patchwork of health provision could not cope with the effects of the German bombing and so the Emergency Medical Service was born. The system of private transport lacked national co-ordination, so that too was taken into public ownership.

So many developments at that time demonstrated what Asa Briggs has called the link between warfare and welfare. Thoughtful Conservatives were well aware of the seismic shifts taking place. In 1943 the Tory Reform Committee was set up in an attempt to give the Party a more caring and interventionist face. Its members were unable to influence the result of the 1945 election, but their approach was welcomed by many new younger MPs, some of whom formed the One Nation group in 1950. The beliefs of these individuals – amongst whom were to be found Iain Macleod, Edward Heath and Enoch Powell – and their co-operative publication titled *One Nation* helped to distance the Party from the doleful associations of the 1930s.

For the first time in the history of the British Conservative Party, its interventionist wing was in the ascendant. Where the market was shown to be inadequate then a judicious injection of public funds would be acceptable. This did not mean, however, that the system itself was ever challenged, rather that specific failings and abuses were to be rectified. No Conservative, for instance, ever considered closing down the public schools or imposing a wealth tax.

Electoral considerations played a part in this provision of social reform. Take the Conservative concession in 1955 that female civil servants should at last be paid the same as their male counterparts. One recent study suggests that the concession was due less to a principled stance by the Cabinet than a fear that this issue might well be exploited to their detriment by the opposition. Worried by the Labour Party's announcement that it was prepared to campaign on the issue at the next election, the Cabinet hurriedly reversed long-held Conservative opinions.

In similar fashion, successive Conservative Governments shied away from imposing immigration controls and other measures in the 1950s. They sometimes thought about it: the Cabinet papers for 1952, for instance, contain this directive; the Home Secretary was asked 'to arrange for officials of the Departments concerned to examine the possibilities of preventing any further increase in the number of coloured people seeking employment in this country.'

The directive then went on to invite the Chancellor of the Exchequer 'to arrange for concurrent examination of the possibility of restricting the number of coloured people obtaining admission to the Civil Service.' The Cabinet also discussed plans to deport coloured people who had been convicted of criminal offences or were deemed 'a charge on public funds'.

When it came down to it, however, Conservative administrations preferred to placate opinion in the African and West Indian colonies and to present an enlightened image. They were also careful to avoid the danger of the issue being exploited by the opposition Labour Party.

Post-war Conservative and Labour administrations alike agreed on the efficacy of government action in promoting social justice. The Welfare State could often be inefficient and fail to target the right groups of people, but in general it did alleviate hardship. Leading Conservatives such as Harold Macmillan displayed as much zeal in their determination to improve social conditions as did their Labour counterparts. Just read this extract from a Macmillan speech delivered in 1958 when he spoke about the unemployment of the

1930s: 'As long as I live I can never forget the impoverishment and demoralisation which all this brought with it. I am determined, as far as it is within human power, never to allow this shadow to fall again upon our country.'

The first cracks in this political consensus came in the early 1970s when the Heath Government tried to shift the emphasis away from welfare towards the market. It proved to be a brief flirtation: Heath himself was essentially a One Nation man who retained vivid memories of the deprivation in the 1930s. But he was succeeded in turn by a new and younger generation for whom such memories and the compassion they engendered meant nothing. Instead they had grown up with a massive state sector, unresponsive unions and the spectacle of private initiative being smothered under a plethora of rules and regulations.

Sometimes lumped together under the label the New Right, this new breed of Conservative tended to stress the inadequacies of state provision in terms of housing, health and education and argued that the problem could be solved by the virtues of the market and the private sector. The high levels of taxation levied in the 1970s ensured that their demands for value for money struck a sympathetic chord among many.

Evidence was also mounting that many people in the country, and not just the Conservative Party, wanted a tougher moral approach to British society. In 1974 Sir Keith Joseph delivered a controversial speech in Birmingham in which he seemed to argue for restricting the size of the families of the less well-off. He maintained that people misinterpreted what he was saying, but opponents claimed that the speech had an unhealthy whiff of Nazi-style eugenics about it, even though Joseph himself was Jewish. Party leader Edward Heath might have deprecated the speech, but Joseph received sack loads of supporting letters, exactly as Enoch Powell had done after his 'rivers of blood' speech in 1968.

The furore prompted Joseph to reject any idea of standing for the Party leadership against Heath and the main beneficiary of his speech proved to be Margaret Thatcher. Although Mrs Thatcher had been a high-spending Minister of Education under Heath, she had occasionally delivered coded messages that she was unhappy with Tory collectivism. One Nation rhetoric was conspicuously missing from her speeches. She was, however, enough of a politician to disguise her true sentiments – by being photographed sitting at Harold Macmillan's feet, for instance, and by quoting from St Francis of Assisi's prayer for compassion and understanding in Downing Street after winning the election in 1979.

Rarely did Mrs Thatcher's guard drop. During a television interview with David Dimbleby in the 1987 general election, she suddenly berated the people 'who drool and drivel about caring'. The remark was speedily withdrawn, but clearly Mrs Thatcher was determined to reject the middle way and to revert to an older Conservative tradition of economy and restraint.

She had a number of easy targets, particularly some of the public sector unions whose commitment seemed to be very much towards their own interests rather than those of the public whose needs they were supposed to be serving. The National Health Service, for instance, in 1979 was suffering from bloated inefficiency. Criticisms of other parts of the state sector, notably education and transport, gained public support although it could be and was argued that their inadequacies were the result of years of under-funding and therefore the responsibility of Government in any case.

The Government's reforms sought to break up the large state monopolies. By the late 1970s, just under a third of all British households lived in council housing. The Conservative Governments of the 1980s encouraged the sale of council houses, hoping to bring about a 'property-owning democracy'. They were working on a principle enunciated as long ago as 1926 by a local Tory leader talking to a Labour audience: 'It is a good thing for the people to buy their own houses. They turn Tory directly. We shall go on making Tories and you will be wiped out.' Over one million council houses were sold off in the 1980s, and although by no means all purchasers turned Tory directly, further inroads had been driven into what had traditionally been solid Labour support.

Within the Health Service, the creation of hospital trusts was an attempt to take control of budgets away from administrators and give power back to the doctors themselves. Internal markets sought to restore notions of competition and cut down on bureaucracy. The health unions, some of which had behaved so badly in the 1970s during a number of industrial disputes, found their wings clipped.

As regards education, the Conservative Government's reforms were less certain, tacking from one position to another. They were caught between two stools. On one hand, they were keen to lay down national standards and to centralise control of the budget; however, this conflicted with their publicly stated claim of widening choice and parental power at a local level. What was certain was that the teaching profession felt demoralised and undervalued. Furthermore, as commentator Anthony Sampson pointed out, Britain was falling behind its competitors:

Among major industrialised countries Britain has proportionately the lowest numbers of sixteen- to eighteen-year-olds in full-time education and training: only 35 per cent in 1987, compared to 49 per cent in Germany and 69 per cent in France, 77 per cent in Japan and 80 per cent in the US. In an age of electronics, computers and robots, the Japanese have shown that a well-educated workforce is the key to industrial success; while the British cannot produce enough trained people in critical areas, including computer technicians. 'It's the most terrifying thing about this country,' said David Sainsbury, now chairman of Sainsbury's, 'which puts us at a huge disadvantage in world markets in future.'

As a graphic example of this disadvantage, *The Economist* magazine reported in October 1992 that the Nissan company near Sunderland was so dissatisfied with the poor quality of its workforce that it had virtually had to rewrite the syllabuses at the local colleges.

Some reforms, such as the idea of league tables and targeted standards, were opposed by the Labour Party and the unions, but have since turned out to have much merit. In late 1994, for example, the Labour Party declared that if returned to power it would retain league tables. Similarly the Party now seems to accept that most people, where possible, prefer to own rather than rent their homes.

Other reforms turned out to be disastrous, particularly the

decision to scrap the old rating system and replace it with a community charge or poll tax. The idea was that everyone should be responsible for paying something – in theory. In practice it seemed to contradict the basic assumption which no government had ever challenged before: that the wealthy should pay more than the poorest. The result was upheaval, Conservative unpopularity and even riots.

Another target of the Conservative Government was that favourite flock of scapegoats, namely the 'scroungers' who cheated the Welfare State over social security payments. Yet it was never apparent that the scale of fraud – concerning approximately one in three thousand claimants – even approached the 1.3 million people who fail to take up the benefits to which they are entitled, let alone the levels of fraud in the City and other financial institutions.

Reforms which on paper seemed so clearcut, such as the idea of making absent fathers contribute to their former family's maintenance, proved to be less amenable in practice; the state, via the Child Support Agency, found itself becoming more involved in people's affairs rather than less.

Some of Mrs Thatcher's supporters were disappointed in her inability to create a new moral Right similar to that in the United States. This would undoubtedly have delighted those sections of the public who wanted the reintroduction of capital punishment and hankered after much harsher penalties for criminals.

The problem here was the unresolved conflict between those Thatcherites who were authoritarians, keen to institute a moral counter-revolution and to penalise private behaviour; and those Thatcherites who preferred to leave moral behaviour to the market. As Lord (Ralph) Harris, a leading force behind the IEA, approvingly put it, the market will supply what consumers want, 'from prayer books and communion wine to pornography and hard liquor'; any attempt to provide one rather than the other would be an unwarranted intrusion into market forces. Should man be set free or placed in chains for his or her own good? Retribution or rehabilitation? This tension was never resolved and thus there was no moral crusade, even though the crime rate and people's fear of crime climbed steadily upwards.

Events after Mrs Thatcher's departure suggest that she may have been wise to have avoided this battlefield. Her successor John Major launched a 'Back to Basics' campaign: no one quite knew what it meant and some took it to apply to morality, not least that of Conservative MPs. A subsequent spate of resignations suggests that this is dangerous terrain for any political party to try and exploit. Those preaching strict morals to society must surely be above reproach – as a number of American television evangelists have also found to their cost.

Several of the reforms initiated in the 1980s, although opposed at the time, came to be accepted as beneficial, such as those which introduced a measure of democracy into the running of the trade unions. But the Thatcherite revolution was a perpetual one: it had to keep seeking fresh opportunities for the supposedly invigorating application of private enterprise. We have had privatisation of electricity, water, gas and British Telecom, and now railway privatisation is on the agenda. Most ministers' knowledge of public transport was and is limited: famously, Mrs Thatcher never used British Rail at all. Starved of funds by successive administrations, the public transport system was bound to be an easy target for people who have no personal reason to preserve and improve it.

The measures taken by Conservative Governments in the 1980s and 1990s represented a return to an older Conservative approach which valued economy and restraint above state intervention. Means-testing and the targeting of benefits were seen as preferable to the principle of universal entitlement which had characterised the Welfare State since the Second World War. What is missing today, though, has been a renewal of voluntary organisations or of community spirit. In fact, the privatisation of former public bodies seems to have lessened accountability and increased the potential for fraud and mismanagement.

In January 1994, for example, the Conservative-dominated House of Commons Public Accounts Committee issued stern warnings that the standards of public life were slipping. After documenting twenty-one separate cases involving public waste and mismanagement, the Report went on: 'These failings represent a departure from the standards of public conduct which have been

established during the past 140 years.' The report was partic
concerned about the lack of policing of the 1,444 quangos and
trusts now running state services and the way in which short-term
contracts are tending to destroy the public service ethos.

Mrs Thatcher and her colleagues were keen to get away from
'airy-fairy theories' and to concentrate on the facts of any situation.
However, they were somewhat selective about which facts they
were prepared to consider. In 1980 Thatcher abolished the Royal
Commission on Wealth and Income which had inconveniently
embarrassed the last Labour administration by revealing the persistent inequalities that still characterised British society. She probably
thought it would embarrass her too eventually.

At the time of writing, the new Conservatives have been in power
for nearly fifteen years. It is arguable that in many ways Britain's
quality of life has deteriorated. Look at the figures uncovered by
the Commission on Social Justice, set up by the Labour Party: one
in five of Europe's poor live in the United Kingdom; the top 10
per cent of householders pay 32 per cent of their income in tax,
compared with 43 per cent for the bottom 10 per cent; the bottom
half of the population receives only a quarter of the total national
income, compared with a third in 1979.

There are 400,000 homeless in Britain, an enormous increase
since the 1970s. Some 5.7 million people rely on less than £100
per week; 61 per cent of pensioners have an annual income of
less than £5,000. A flood of reports showed, inter alia, that the
gap between the wages of top earners and the lowest paid is now
wider than at any time this century, that the living standards of
the poorest tenth of the population have barely risen over the
last twenty years. According to the independent Institute for
Fiscal Studies, the number of people with income below half
the national average (£15,000) has trebled from 3.3 million in
1977 to about 11.4 million today – around one in five of the
population.

Figures such as these eventually numb the mind and induce what
might be called sympathy fatigue. The consequences of such statistics
are more readily felt in terms of the everyday experiences known
to us all: the burglary, the mugging, the stolen car, the beggars and

the homeless, the filthy streets, the declining council services, the abused and drug-ridden teenagers.

Although Mrs Thatcher tried desperately to inculcate Victorian ideals of self-help and self-reliance into the British public, opinion polls suggest that she largely failed. Commenting on the results of a MORI poll in 1988, Professor Ivor Crewe noted that: 'After nine years of Thatcherism the public remained wedded to the collectivist, welfare ethic of social democracy . . . So far the doctrines of Samuel Smiles have fallen on deaf ears.'

Worries about growing inequalities are not confined to the so-called Left. In March 1994 the director-general of the Confederation of British Industry (CBI), Howard Davies, pointed out that during the 1980s the average income of a tenth of earners rose by 62 per cent whilst that of the bottom 10 per cent had fallen by 14 per cent. The numbers on income support had risen from three million to four million: 'It is clear that, for a combination of reasons, not by any means all under our control, British society is becoming more unequal.' In the end, we all pay for such blatant inequality.

These inequalities not only undermine the Conservative claim to be the Party which represents all the people, but they are also a threat to the future of the political system and a denial of human rights, notwithstanding John Major's commitment to the citizens' charters. As Professor J.K. Galbraith once said: 'Nothing, let us forget, sets a stronger limit on the liberty of the citizen than a total absence of money.'

In 1925 a debate was held in the House of Commons in which the Labour Party, and the Labour Left in particular led by the militant Clydeside MPs, demanded action to ameliorate the poverty and degradation rife in some deprived parts of the country. The Conservative Government and its supporters rejected out of hand any proposals for action, preferring to place their faith in inactivity and prayer that the economic system would right itself of its own accord.

After the debate a Conservative MP approached one of the Clydeside MPs, David Kirkwood, and expressed his genuine sorrow at the stories of injustice that he had just heard. He then gave Kirkwood a £5 note and asked him to use it to try and help some of those most in need.

This anecdote represents both the best and the worst in the Conservative Party's social policies: the refusal to do anything constructive for fear of endangering the system; the well-intentioned, though somewhat limited, compassion of individual members. Some Conservative apologists argue that it is their party which has been responsible for most social reform in Britain; this is simply not true. Critics hostile to the Party love to stereotype Tory Governments as grinding down the faces of the poor – also not true.

The Conservative Party can sometimes be responsible for important domestic reforms, because it is vital that the Party be seen to represent interests wider than those of its activists and financial supporters. In addition, the Party's emphasis on the importance of economic growth as a way of buying off discontent and ensuring stability means that it recognises the value of a competitive workforce. This inevitably requires resources to be devoted to health, education, housing and so on.

However, this Tory commitment to the welfare of the people extends only so far as is useful and no further. If any proposed legislation seriously threatens the interests represented by the Party and its hold on power, then it is fought tooth and nail – even if the young ostriches do remain wild.

In High Places

The Conservative Party and the Establishment

'The Party of resistance [the Conservative Party] rests upon the satisfaction which the nation feels, or is presumed to feel, with its present institutions.'

Lord Salisbury, 1871

'The true answer to why I am a Conservative is not political at all. All my life had been formed by the institutions of this country and, because I think them admirable, I believe they should be preserved and put to use. The English village, my father and grandmother, memories of giving Lady Baldwin a bouquet in Devizes in 1937, a love of the basic things in English life, that's why I go on when there are more kicks than ha'pence.'

Douglas Hurd, 1993

'. . . our Establishment has presided over economic decline and bequeathed a culture of mediocrity. Why join a bunch of losers?'

Andrew Neil, editor of the *Sunday Times*, 1993

The child of a pedlar, Robert Peel established a thriving Lancashire cotton business and eventually desperately wanted an heir. Finally, after several miscarriages, his wife produced a son, also to be named

Robert. The first Sir Robert was so overjoyed that he sank to his knees and in his joy dedicated his son to the public service.

A cynical age might well ridicule Peel's behaviour, but together with philanthropists such as Lord Shaftesbury he embodied a tradition of public duty and responsibility characteristic of Conservatism at its best. The high standards of these men typified an ideal of public service evident throughout much of the nineteenth century and which found expression in the institutions created at that time.

Commentators often stress the continuity and stability of British life – we have not been invaded since 1066; there has been no major civil war or unrest since the 1640s. Political life has remained unbroken for centuries. But this superficial stability has been maintained because the British governing class has always been prepared to create and reinvigorate institutions and methods of government without needing to see them destroyed first. The upheavals of industrialisation and the creation of an urban society posed many new challenges and threats, but they were successfully contained and shaped by such nineteenth-century creations as a constitutional monarchy, a modern Civil Service, political parties and a reformed Church of England.

British Conservatives have, at least until recently, been staunch defenders of these major institutions. They supported them because they embodied certain values and assumptions which seemed to lie at the heart of British life. Benjamin Disraeli once claimed that the first great object of the Tory Party was 'to maintain the institutions of the country – not from any sentiment of political superstition, but because we believe that they embody the principles upon which a community like England can alone safely rest'.

For one thing the apparently non-ideological nature of these institutions meant that they were seen as being above the fray of party politics; for another they proved able to channel and defuse radical demands for change. Above all, perhaps, this establishment was Conservative, allowing Party members and supporters to create powerful networks of patronage and influence. Before the concept was even thought of, Conservatives had been 'networking' away like mad through the centuries and it is therefore impossible to explore the Party in isolation from this myriad of almost masonic links and recognitions.

There was something deeply perceptive about George VI's response when, after the sweeping Labour victory in the 1945 general election and Churchill's ejection from office, President Truman remarked to him 'I hear you've had a revolution.' 'Oh no,' replied the King, 'We don't have those here.'

The skill with which the Establishment and the Conservative Party have managed, behind a façade of continuity and order, continually to recreate and adapt to new circumstances was particularly apparent in the Victorian age. For instance, the new public schools were regulated and the older ones cleaned up. The purchase of commissions in the army was abolished. Corruption in the Civil Service was attacked by the Northcote Trevelyan Report which recommended that independent civil servants should work on a non-partisan basis.

Trade unions were legalised and their funds protected from misappropriation, whilst both the Conservative and Liberal Parties themselves grew up during the Victorian period. The conduct of elections was transformed by the introduction of the secret ballot in 1872 and the restrictions on candidates' expenses from 1883, whilst the new police forces were supervised by elected local watch committees.

In his fine study *The English Town* (1990), historian Mark Girouard offers a fitting tribute to the Victorian spirit of public duty:

If this book has heroes, they are the corporations of Victorian towns, especially of northern industrial towns. It has been a pleasure to find out about them, and savour their activities, in a climate so different from that of the present day. With unfailing energy and resourcefulness they took over services from inefficient private enterprise, and made them prosperous and fruitful, leaving behind them a rich harvest of town halls, court-houses, market halls, schools, viaducts, bridges, reservoirs, and pumping stations, all proudly flaunting the corporation coat-of-arms from ripely ebullient architecture.

The tradition of eighteenth-century patronage and corruption was therefore replaced with a more democratic and accountable system. Three major institutions overhauled at that time are still intimately connected with the Conservative Party: the monarchy, the Church of England and the press.

The reputation of the monarchy, tarnished by the self-serving behaviour of the later Hanoverians, was partly retrieved by the evident probity of Queen Victoria and Prince Albert. But Albert's early death in 1861 and Victoria's subsequent retreat into seclusion provoked much public disquiet about the very existence of monarchy. Was it really necessary to maintain this expensive institution? In the early 1870s the republican movement increased dramatically in size: eighty-four Republican Clubs were founded between 1871 and 1874 alone.

What saved the British monarchy was one fortuitous event which was effectively exploited to generate national rejoicing and solidarity, and a long-term and strategic plan. The first was the recovery of Prince Edward from serious illness in 1871; the public celebration, which included a thanksgiving service in St Paul's Cathedral, was deliberately encouraged by the authorities as a counter to republicanism. In the long-term, successful moves were undertaken to make Queen Victoria and the monarchy a national symbol with which the population could identify.

Two statesmen who in a different life might well have been impresarios or showmen were behind this stage-management of the monarchy. Benjamin Disraeli, newly ennobled as the Earl of Beaconsfield, thought up the title 'The Empress of India' which was conferred on Queen Victoria via the Royal Titles Act of 1876 and so initiated the link in popular consciousness between royalty and Britannia. Subsequently, Lord Esher exploited the theatrical possibilities of Victoria's Golden Jubilee in 1887 and her Diamond Jubilee in 1897 for all they were worth.

This groundswell of support for the monarchy effectively buried British republicanism, even within the labour movement. Despite the fiercely anti-royal sentiments of the Labour Party's founder Keir Hardie, whenever his party has attained office it has invariably shown itself to be as deferential and loyal as the Conservatives. Labour Cabinet ministers might mutter in their diaries about the absurd flummery of the whole exercise, but they always fall into line, adopting the rituals of convention and dress and eager to accept honours.

The monarchy itself, like the Conservative Party, seems to have been fully aware that new times meant new demands. The royal flair for public relations was evident at Christmas 1914 when each soldier in the trenches was sent a cigarette box with a photograph of Queen Mary inside. At the same time her husband George V was being encouraged to shake hands with members of the public. It was crucial, too, that the monarchy accept the electorate's verdict at general elections. Famously, George V wondered what his grandmother, Queen Victoria, would have felt after the election of the first Labour government in 1924, but he himself was resigned to its existence.

Central to the respect felt for the British monarchy was the sense of public duty and service displayed by the royal family. It is said that a minor royal figure being shown around yet another hospital muttered 'I'm tired and I hate hospitals.' Queen Mary snapped: 'You are a member of the British Royal Family. We are *never* tired, and we all *love* hospitals!'

During the bombing of London in the Second World War, it was imperative for the sake of their public reputation that the royal family remain in the capital.

The Church of England has always been regarded as the Conservative Party at prayer. Generally, in the words of one ecclesiastical historian, it did indeed embrace 'an organic vision of English society that traditional Conservatives found congenial'. To put it rather more pithily, the Church existed 'to keep men in their proper stations and bless the squire and his relations'.

During the first decades of the nineteenth century the Church of England opposed all political and social reform. Its bishops, for instance, played a considerable part in rejecting the Reform Bill of 1831 and its clergy were regarded, in the descriptive phrase of one opponent, as constituting 'a black recruiting sergeant in every village'. More far-sighted elements within the Church realised, as too did sections within the Conservative Party, that it was counterproductive and ultimately calamitous to remain a purely reactionary bulwark. That way disaster lay.

The Church of England's monopoly on religious truth in Britain was beginning to fragment by the 1820s when many Anglicans recognised that it was foolish and unjust to exclude Catholics from the mainstream of national life: they were currently unable to vote or obtain degrees from Oxford or Cambridge and were barred from holding most positions of authority. The passage of the Catholic Emancipation Act in 1829 removed these hindrances and introduced a religious toleration enjoyed in few other countries.

Doctrinal reform was followed by an administrative overhaul. The appointment of the Ecclesiastical Commission in 1836 helped rectify some of the most obvious abuses within the Church by redistributing the bishops' incomes, increasing the stipends of the poorer clergy and restricting the numbers of parishes which clergymen could represent.

The links between the Church and the Conservative Party continued to be underpinned by the religious affiliation of the vast majority of Tory MPs. Until just after the Second World War aspiring Conservative parliamentary candidates had to state their religion on Central Office's application forms, and we have already seen that Catholics and Jews never stood much chance of selection. The Church of England's hierarchy tended to mirror that of the Conservative Party generally: those at the top were from well-connected and privileged backgrounds and, with the odd exception such as the short-lived tenure of Archbishop of Canterbury William Temple during the last war, most senior Church figures were staunchly traditionalist if not necessarily Conservative in their outlook. By and large, the bishops tried not to be too identified with the Party.

The national press also developed during the nineteenth century. *The Times* had begun life as the *Universal Daily Register* in 1785.

The coming of the railways, the steam press, the telegraph and the growth of literacy provided new opportunities for journalism. Stamp duty and the advertisement tax were also abolished in the 1850s, leading to cheaper papers. National newspapers were now financed by advertising revenue and could achieve huge circulations. In 1896 Alfred Harmsworth spent half a million pounds on setting up the *Daily Mail*. The paper was a massive success and was soon followed by the *Daily Express* and later the *Daily Mirror*.

This new Fleet Street press was fully aware of the impact of headlines and the selling power of stories about the monarchy, empire, crime and sport. The *Daily Mail* of 22 February 1896 declared robustly that 'A little bloodletting is good for the nation that tends to excess of luxury' and Harmsworth told his staff to find 'one murder a day'. Politics was of interest only in so far as it could be presented in stark black and white terms. Harmsworth also ensured that the paper paid attention to 'women's interests', just as the Primrose League was at the same time drawing upon women's efforts to extend its influence.

Harmsworth himself had once been a Conservative parliamentary candidate and he and his fellow proprietors quickly became the pillars of a new establishment which overtly supplemented the declining landed aristocracy: Harmsworth became Lord Northcliffe, Aitken Lord Beaverbrook, whilst there were also Lords Rothermere, Camrose, Kelmsley and Sir Arthur Pearson. Even Julius Elias of the Labour-leaning *Daily Herald* ended up as Viscount Southwood. It was highly unlikely that such men would permit their publications to challenge the established system.

In order to make absolutely sure that the Conservative voice was well-represented, funds from Central Office were channelled to a whole range of newspapers. Proprietor Gardner Sinclair was helped in his efforts to buy the *Observer* and *Pall Mall* newspapers before the First World War by a guarantee of £45,000 from party funds. Max Aitken was assisted in purchasing the *Daily Express*, and the Party was also, in the words of Dr John Ramsden, 'propping up the *Globe*, the *Standard*, and a wide range of provincial dailies. All these transactions were secret, for there would be little use in keeping a paper alive if it were known to be owned by a political party. The papers were therefore bought through nominees or bank loans backed with party capital.' As late as 1927, Central Office was helping out no fewer than two hundred and thirty different papers.

Perhaps the most impish of these Conservative-backed proprietors was a man who exercised a long-standing influence on British politics. Lord Beaverbrook had been born in Canada in 1879. The son of a Church of Scotland minister, he started life as Max Aitken, making his fortune in business before migrating to Britain where he was soon elected Conservative MP for Ashton-under-Lyne in 1910. His friendship with Bonar Law, the leader of the Conservative Party, also born in Canada, ensured Aitken's steady rise. He headed the Ministry of Information during the First World War and slowly built up the circulation of his flagship newspaper, the *Daily Express*.

Beaverbrook liked to cultivate a reputation for being a radical outsider and to maintain friendships with people from all parts of the political spectrum. He was happy, therefore, to be associated with Winston Churchill and Lloyd George or Michael Foot and A.J.P. Taylor, but his ready acceptance of a peerage in 1916 suggests the limits of his iconoclasm. Above all, Beaverbrook loved interfering in politics and in 1930, together with Lord Rothermere, he founded the short-lived Empire Free Trade Party which advocated a programme of imperial protection.

Candidates were even run against the Conservative Party, but the new party was seen off by Baldwin after a famous by-election at St George's in London in 1931. Baldwin delivered a notable speech that attacked the two press lords for wanting to exercise power without responsibility. This, he declared, was 'the prerogative of the harlot through the ages', quoting words which were actually written by his cousin Rudyard Kipling.

Occasionally the press may have questioned aspects of various institutions, but it never challenged the institutions themselves. For example, its sense of restraint was apparent throughout the abdication crisis in 1936 when a self-imposed news blackout by the newspaper proprietors and their editors ensured that the public was kept completely in the dark about what was going on.

Thus there were severe limits to Fleet Street's independence. Perhaps the most ignominious period in its history came during the mid- and late-1930s. Several newspaper proprietors were enamoured of the rise of Fascism in Germany and not averse to seeing it in Britain either. The editorial in the *Daily Mail* of 8 January 1934 carried the explicit headline 'Hurrah for the Black Shirts'. A week later, the same paper described Sir Oswald Mosley's British Union of Fascists as 'a well-organised party of the Right ready to take over responsibility for national affairs with the same directness of purpose and energy of methods as Hitler and Mussolini have displayed'.

Neville Chamberlain's devotion to his policies of appeasement in the late 1930s led him to frantic attempts to ensure the press did not in any way jeopardise friendly relations with Hitler. By means of the lobby system through which the Government supplied the official viewpoint to journalists and also by means of threats and cajolement directed at journalists, editors and proprietors, Chamberlain and his press adviser George Steward made sure that the press printed nothing which would harm his plans. The director-general at Central Office, Sir Robert Topping, also briefed certain select true-blue correspondents.

In fact, most proprietors and editors needed little persuading, just as they had been happy to be absorbed into the war machine twenty years before during the 1914–18 conflict. On that occasion, as Phillip Knightley has shown, self-censorship was rewarded with knighthoods at the end of the war. Looking back on the thirties, *The Times* under Geoffrey Dawson is often singled out for being the most supine – Dawson admitted dropping little items into the paper with the aim of pleasing the Nazis – but the others were equally spineless. Lord Beaverbrook was a prime culprit; according to the recent authoritative study by Richard Cockett, he secretly placed his newspapers at the Government's disposal. In Cockett's words, 'The Lobby was merely an important and sophisticated part of contemporary Conservatism.'

The newsreel companies, several of which had strong links with the newspaper proprietors, proved to be just as servile and keen to practise self-censorship. Their reports all drew on the same Goebbels-approved film sources in Nazi Germany and when one vociferous critic of the Munich settlement, Wickham Steed, a former editor of *The Times*, was interviewed in September 1938, the item was quickly withdrawn.

The unreliability of the press in the 1930s prompted people to turn to the radio for less biased news from the BBC. Set up as a public corporation in 1926, the BBC had a limited but real independence. It remained neutral during the General Strike in 1926, successfully resisting Government attempts to commandeer it.

That, at least, is the orthodox version of what happened. In fact, the papers of J.C.C. Davidson, righthand man of Stanley Baldwin and one of the leading figures in charge of handling the strike, tell a rather different story. In a private and confidential memorandum, dated 14 May 1926, Davidson wrote: 'We did not take the BBC over, but as I happen to live next door to Reith, the Managing Director, and had installed two direct lines to 2 L.O. [BBC headquarters] in my room in the Admiralty my unofficial control was complete.'

This simply confirms that the BBC's independence operated within circumscribed limits; dissident voices – which in the 1930s included that of Winston Churchill who was at odds with his own party – were carefully monitored and rationed, not least by Central Office who built up a bulky file entitled simply 'Political Partisanship of BBC'.

In July 1931 Reith himself suggested an informal arrangement under which a representative of the Party would call on him from time to time with complaints – not a facility granted to the Labour Party. In addition, senior officials at Central Office such as Sir Patrick Gower, who was in charge of publicity, routinely put pressure on the Corporation over the membership of its board of governors. Such discreet lobbying was never enough to stop the backbench 1922 Committee indulging in a favourite party pastime, namely accusing the BBC of left-wing bias.

After the Second World War, however, several institutions traditionally immune from public criticism began to come under attack. These new challenges reflected the social and economic changes gusting through Britain. There was a dissolution of the social bonds which had once cemented society together, and a decline in the value formerly placed on hierarchy and deference;

people were no longer prepared to know their place and accept it. Jack was now as good as his master. Older collectives such as class, family, party, union and religion were also being undermined by growing affluence and more individualist attitudes.

In his essay on *The English People* published in 1947, George Orwell commented on the national tendency towards servility, noting in particular how often the word 'sir' was still used. This trait is rather less obvious today, particularly amongst the young. Another indication of this change is shown by the decline in the number of servants, of whom there were still well over a million in 1939.

Equally influential was Britain's gradual sense of comparative economic decline which was highlighted by the rapid recovery of the shattered European economies after the war. Germany, France and Italy all began to outstrip British rates of economic growth and Britain's uncertainty was all too apparent in its dithering over whether or not to join the European Economic Community. Economic difficulties sapped the confidence of the treasury and the Civil Service.

These challenges were compounded by the inevitable changes facing the three major institutions of monarchy, Church and press. The monarchy had continued to adapt to the demands of the media. In 1947 George VI turned down the idea of broadcasting Princess Elizabeth's wedding, but by 1969 the Prince of Wales's investiture was planned almost solely for the benefit of television: the throne was even given a laminated perspex canopy so that the view of the cameras would not be impeded.

But this complicity with the voracious demands of the media had its negative side when things went wrong: Princess Margaret's divorce and the marital problems of Prince Charles, Princess Anne and Prince Andrew all took place in the full glare of media attention. The great Victorian commentator Walter Bagehot once warned that 'We must not let in daylight upon the magic [of monarchy]' but as the press cameras flashed and supposedly intimate friends of the royals told all to the tabloids it was clearly too late to put the lid back on this particular Pandora's box.

The Church of England was also bound to come under stress

in an increasingly secular and multi-ethnic society. Fewer people went to church at all and much of the population only attended the traditional rites of birth, marriage and death. The social status of the clergy dwindled along with their incomes and clergymen now came from more varied backgrounds. An increasing number were prepared to speak out on social and political issues.

As for the press, this potentially loose cannon had always been disciplined by its integration into the Establishment. The radicalism of a Lord Beaverbrook had never amounted to very much. But as the Establishment itself began to lose its confidence and cohesiveness so too did its disciplinary powers fade. Several newspaper owners proved to be more interested in maintaining or increasing their circulation than in observing Establishment proprieties and began to publish stories their predecessors would have spiked. Just compare the press silence surrounding the abdication crisis of 1936 with the blanket coverage given to the intimate private lives of the modern royals.

A vivid demonstration of the struggle between the old and the new was seen in the battles within the Conservative Party over the introduction of commercial television in the 1950s. One section of the Party feared that it would be a destabilising force – Lord Reith, for example, the former director-general of the BBC, warned that commercial television would be an unmitigated disaster, 'like dog-racing, smallpox and bubonic plague'.

The opposing camp was led by Lord Woolton who had reinvigorated the Party after the election defeat of 1945. Arguing that the arrival of commercial television based on advertising would widen popular choice as well as challenge the BBC's monopoly of the airwaves, this group, as James Curran and Jean Seaton have pointed out, 'represented industry and advertising rather than law or hereditary wealth'. The modernisers and free marketeers were taking on the old guard or Tory grandees. Significantly, the modernisers won and the Act setting up commercial television was passed in 1954.

This clash offered an early glimpse of the kind of arguments and conflicts which were to be fought out in the Conservative Party during the Thatcherite era of the 1980s.

Mrs Thatcher herself was something of an intruder into the male club-like culture of the Conservative Party and she always retained a lasting suspicion of the old Tory establishment. Her media adviser Tim Bell claims that she thought 'all the problems of Britain were the direct consequence of two things. One was socialism. The other was the Tory grandees.'

For her, the great and the good, particularly those who were nominally Conservatives, were in fact a part of the difficulty and represented a soggy post-war consensus which had always preferred to take the easy way out. To put it more bluntly, as maverick Tory MP Julian Critchley once did, Mrs Thatcher could not resist handbagging British institutions. Her combativeness was evidenced by her willingness during the miners' strike of 1984 to 1985 to talk of 'the enemy within', a choice of words which One Nation Tories deplored.

There was always something paradoxical about Mrs Thatcher's assault on the Establishment: after all she herself was a representative of three powerful British institutions – Oxbridge, the bar, the Conservative Party – but she was not prepared to take them at their face value. Iconoclastic right-wing think-tanks asked embarrassing questions about British institutions: were they providing a decent service for the public? Were they efficient and competitive? Were they cost-effective? Were they obstacles to economic growth? In the past, even to have asked such questions would have been regarded as heresy. Now, however, market forces and business efficiency were conspicuously valued above tradition and continuity.

This challenge to Britain's major institutions, many of them Victorian in origin, marked a sharp break from traditional, old-style Conservatism which had always been wary of any call to set the people free, fearing what the people might actually do with their freedom. Although the new radicalism was a far more dynamic force than anything produced by the Labour Party, it did not seek to overthrow anything which clearly benefited the party. For instance, virtually no Conservative showed any interest in constitutional reforms such as the introduction of proportional representation or fixed-term elections.

Thatcherism's lack of deference was echoed too by the impact of media magnate Rupert Murdoch, an outsider who resisted the embrace of the British Establishment. He was not the first non-British newspaper proprietor, but he had a very different attitude from Lord Beaverbrook who had soon been ennobled and welcomed into the Establishment. As an undergraduate at Worcester College, Oxford in the early 1950s, Murdoch had kept a bust of Lenin prominently displayed on his mantelpiece. Although he quickly shed such overt radicalism his views retained an edge to them which was disconcerting – the *Sun*, for instance, once called for the abolition of the honours system, a sentiment which would have been anathema to the old-time, ennobled newspaper proprietors.

Murdoch was simply not interested in the British power game and, in fact, he despised the English ruling class because of their distaste for making money. Both the range of his interests and his restless energy meant that he simply lacked the time to be cultivated by the Establishment. In any case, Murdoch viewed his media empire in global terms so his horizons were much wider than the London scene.

Mrs Thatcher and Rupert Murdoch were united by their disdain for many traditional institutions, not least of them being the trade unions. A Faustian bargain was struck. The Thatcher Government eased up on legal regulation and allowed cross-media holdings between television and the press which benefited Murdoch. His acquisition of new titles such as *The Times* and *Today* were not referred to the Monopolies and Mergers Commission. He was also allowed to own 50 per cent of British Sky Broadcasting because the Government classified it as 'non-domestic', rather than the maximum of 20 per cent permissible to other newspaper proprietors in terrestial television channels.

In return, Murdoch's publications, particularly the *Sun*, were enthusiastically pro-Thatcher. According to one senior official at Central Office, Michael Dobbs, Mrs Thatcher in turn went to the *Sun* for advice. Murdoch's biographer, William Shawcross, has observed of the 1980s that 'The Thatcher revolution and the Murdoch revolution strode hand in hand across the decade.'

Many on the Left could barely contain their hatred for Murdoch, and not just the print unions who found their closed shop and restrictive practices smashed overnight in 1986 when Murdoch suddenly shifted his papers to new printing presses in Wapping. For example, journalist Francis Wheen once wrote that Murdoch 'has made a fortune from selling excrement and, in the process, has debauched our culture and corrupted our youth, producing a generation of lager louts, sex maniacs and morons', whilst Labour peer Lord Donoughue thought that Murdoch had done more damage to British society than Hitler's bombs.

Criticism of the *Sun* was not confined to the Left. When MacKenzie resigned as its editor in January 1994, an article in the *Daily Telegraph* called the *Sun* 'a newspaper which sums up all that is wrong with the popular press in Britain today'.

It is difficult to measure the importance of the Murdoch press in sustaining the Conservative Party in power during the 1980s and 1990s. The *Sun* itself had no doubts: after the unexpected Conservative victory in the 1992 general election, the headline in the paper claimed 'It Was The Sun Wot Won It'. In any case, Mrs Thatcher had been careful to hand out honours to her other press supporters such as Lord Matthews, Sir Nicholas Lloyd, Sir David English, Sir John Junor and so on and most of the press has always favoured Conservative administrations. The *Sunday Times* itself was later to comment that: 'Too many newspapers during the Thatcher years were in the pockets of the government.'

Certainly the *Sun* did no favours for the Labour Party under Michael Foot or Neil Kinnock. But the *Sun*'s allegiance was more to Mrs Thatcher and the ideal of strong leadership than to the Conservative Party per se. John Major's rather different approach, combined with the debacle of 'Black Wednesday' when Britain was forced to leave the European Exchange Rate Mechanism, provoked much of the press to turn on him.

What was undeniable was that a combination of Mrs Thatcher and the *Sun* meant that many British institutions suddenly found themselves under fierce attack – ironically, these two launched a much stronger assault on the Establishment than ever the Labour Party had done. Mrs Thatcher's substantial majorities combined with the growth in power of the executive meant that she could normally expect to get her own way. She was adept, too, at manipulating older forms of power, notably the lobby system, briefing journalists through her pugnacious press secretary Bernard Ingham so that her point of view was fully known and reported.

The BBC, of course, had always been a favourite target for some Conservatives because of its alleged bias. During the Falklands War in 1982 Norman Tebbit and others attacked the Corporation's apparent lack of patriotism: 'For me the British Broadcasting Corporation might have better called itself the Stateless Persons Broadcasting Corporation for it certainly did not reflect the mood of the British people who finance it.'

Likewise Bernard Ingham claimed that most damage to govern-ment – BBC relations was done in the early morning by the *Today* programme on Radio 4, hosted by Brian Redhead. Inevitably, the BBC was also a target for Rupert Murdoch's newspapers, keen to promote their proprietor's satellite television interests and to destroy the system of licence fee funding on which the BBC's independence had traditionally rested.

Commercial television was not safe either. Angered by Thames Television's programme *Death on the Rock* which criticised the role of the SAS in shooting suspected terrorists, Mrs Thatcher completely upended the commercial stations, awarding the new franchises by auction to the highest bidder. The late addition of a quality threshold saved some companies from extinction, but the sorrowful reaction of Mrs Thatcher to TV-AM's loss of its franchise after it was outbid by another station suggested that she had not thought out the implications of the changes.

The new franchise system ensured that the government now took a much larger share of commercial television's advertising revenue, leaving less money for actual programme making. One of the most respected figures within British television, Greg Dyke, considered that 'Never has government done so much damage to one industry in such a short period of time as the Conservatives have done to broadcasting over the past 6–7 years.'

The *Sun* and the other tabloids remained fixated by the British monarchy and that venerable institution now found itself caught in the crossfire of a circulation war. Even upmarket papers such as the

Sunday Times joined the circus, publishing lengthy extracts from biographies of the Prince and Princess of Wales which left very little private. The Queen's tax arrangements came under scrutiny and the antics of the Duchess of York became a national joke.

The Church of England came under attack too. The Church leaders' enthusiasm for speaking out on public issues irritated successive Conservative Governments. The Archbishop of Canterbury, Dr Runcie, was deemed to have delivered too forgiving a sermon in St Paul's Cathedral at the end of the Falklands War and the Church report *Faith in the City* appeared to damn the Government's market forces approach to social problems. In November 1993 the General Synod voted by 190 votes to nil (with two abstentions) condemning the Government's pit closure programme under John Major.

The Church Commissioners compounded the crisis by squandering some £800 million through ill-advised investments, a sum which represents the loss of perhaps one third of the Church's total assets and will lead to a further squeeze on clerical incomes. The ordination of women priests caused internal acrimony and feuding. Perhaps most ominously of all, Church of England attendance has declined by 30 per cent since 1968 and today only 2.4 per cent of the adult population go to Sunday services held by the supposedly national Church of England. This is fewer than attend Roman Catholic services.

Local government was yet another institution which found itself under prolonged assault during the 1980s. Press campaigns against the 'Loony Left' – and the ability of certain Labour councils to play up to that image – meant that there was little sustained public protest when Mrs Thatcher's government abolished the Greater London Council (GLC) and other metropolitan councils. Ironically, the GLC had in fact been created by Harold Macmillan's Conservative government in 1963. It clearly galled Mrs Thatcher that Ken Livingstone's GLC, based just across the river from Westminster in County Hall, was pursuing diametrically opposed policies to her Government. In Liverpool, the council dominated by Derek Hatton and other supporters of Labour's Militant Tendency emulated the tactics pioneered by Alderman Salvidge at the beginning of this century: one-party rule, 'jobs for the boys', a disdain for normal electoral procedures. Such well-publicised antics helped shore up support for the Conservative administration.

Gradually, central government took away many of the powers of local councils. Schools were encouraged to opt out from local government control and to be run instead by self-appointed government bodies; housing associations diminished the role of public-sector housing; and health trusts reduced the local accountability of the NHS. In particular, the ability to raise money was drastically cut. *The Economist* magazine estimated in the summer of 1993 that local government now received 84 per cent of its finances from central government.

Whereas other European countries were systematically devolving power to the regions, Britain alone was centralising. The splendid Victorian town hall, standing proudly in many city centres, increasing seemed like a dinosaur from a very distant past.

Other British institutions began to seem less than admirable. The trade unions suffered grievously from their excesses in the 1970s and rapidly lost both membership and influence. The legal system was expensive, cumbersome and slow, whilst the police were tarnished by a persistently rising crime rate and by a worrying spate of cases of corruption and miscarriages of justice. Parliament too, dominated by a powerful executive, seemed increasingly powerless to monitor the activities of the Government. The arms trade, for instance, was outside public control, as *The Economist* pointed out in an article entitled 'Ask me no questions, I'll tell you no lies': 'In theory government ministers are accountable to Parliament for anything and everything. But when it comes to the arms trade, the routine of parliamentary questions and select-committee investigations has proved to be little more than a charade.'

Another cynical example of the power of Government surfaced in May 1994 when a series of backbench amendments blocked the passage of a bill intended to help the disabled. The minister in charge, Nicholas Scott, initially denied that his officials had drawn up the amendments in collusion with the backbenchers involved. The MPs involved also claimed that the amendments were their own. This turned out to be untrue. Yet in spite of the fact that Prime Minister John Major had decreed just the month before that ministers who failed to give accurate and truthful information to Parliament should resign their posts unless there were overriding reasons of national interest, Nicholas Scott stayed in office.

Also under attack was Whitehall itself. Conservative think-tanks argued that power should be devolved away from Whitehall towards outside agencies. This contracting out of services was meant to reduce bureaucracy and lead to improvements in efficiency. Commentators such as Vernon Bogdanor were unimpressed by this dilution of the public service ethos: 'To introduce the commercial ethic into the Civil Service, as the Thatcher and Major administrations have done, is to call into question one of the most fundamental of our "tacit understandings", the understanding that government is not a business.'

By reducing accountability and opening up the possibility of fraud, these changes seemed to repudiate the Victorian ideals represented by the public corporations extolled earlier by Mark Girouard. For instance, many new appointments ranging from membership of hospital trusts and urban development corporations to those of training and enterprise councils were now exclusively in the hands of government ministers.

Trade and industry minister Baroness Denton once admitted in the House of Lords that she had never 'knowingly appointed a Labour supporter' to the hundreds of posts in her gift. Of the twelve peers appointed to positions in health authorities, eleven were Conservatives. Conservative nominee Duke Hussey was appointed to an unprecedented second term as chairman of the BBC.

Such conduct represented a return to the corruption and 'placemen' characteristic of the eighteenth century rather than the accountability of the Victorians. Privatisation simply encouraged secrecy – by definition, privatisation means making something private which was once public. In the summer of 1994 the independent Democratic Audit reported that Britain now had at least six-and-a-half thousand quangos, and of these more than five thousand possess executive power to affect people's lives – but are in no way democratically accountable. There is also persistent disquiet that too many appointments smack of jobs for the boys and girls. Being married to a Conservative MP seems to be better than any CV.

The first comprehensive investigation into the boards of National Health Service Trusts was published in December 1994. Like private companies, these trusts are run by a board of directors and are almost entirely unaccountable bodies who are required to hold just one public meeting a year. Their annual reports are often meaningless. It is therefore all the more disquieting to read the investigation's findings: 'The survey examined the political and occupational backgrounds of 2,629 chairs and non-executive directors in 482 NHS trusts – 419 in England, 39 in Scotland and 24 in Wales. It revealed that Tories on the boards outnumber Labour supporters by six to one.'

Away from the NHS, the Welsh Development Agency in particular has come under fire; the *Daily Telegraph* reported that 'In 1988–93 Welsh officials made hundreds of millions of pounds of incorrect or uncertified payments' and spoke of 'the impression of a patronage system at work.' Lord Bancroft, former head of the home Civil Service, was scathing:

> We are reverting to the situation in the early nineteenth century, when individuals were in effect given lump sums once a year, and told to hire and fire and get on with the job. How they spent the money was never inquired into: some of it was pocketed . . . It's a repulsive development. You have an agency responsible for some area of public expenditure, and there is also somewhere a Minister who regards the agency to be at arm's length from him. That is not accountability to Parliament.'

Not only did the new approach denigrate any notion of civic duty or public service – of course, anything public was naturally suspect – but it entailed, too, a substantial growth in the power of the executive, virtually unhampered by parliamentary scrutiny or by the existence of a written constitution. The results have been seen in the so-called Iraqgate and Pergau dam scandals. Seemingly guided by no morality other than that of the balance sheet, the Conservative Party was inevitably led into shady deals because such transactions would safeguard British jobs.

In November 1994 the courts ruled that the Pergau dam project had involved the illegal use of Government money. After several delays the Scott report delving into the sale of arms to Iraq is still awaited, but enough evidence emerged at the hearings and during the collapse of the Matrix-Churchill case to present a less than pretty picture of ministers shuffling off responsibility to civil servants. No one, it seemed, ever knew what either their right or left hand was doing, even when this meant signing Public Interest Immunity Certificates which might well have sent innocent men to gaol. Linguistic quibbles or 'elasticity' proved more important than principle or individual judgement.

In some ways the policies of successive Conservative Governments since 1979 have let the genie of individualism out of the bottle. In the past, the Conservative Party understood and valued the disciplining powers of many British institutions. Certainly they kept people in their place, but traditional Tories maintained that these institutions gave everyone a compensating sense of identity and security. This is no longer the case. The bonfire of the institutions since the early 1980s has destroyed but not created.

Ironically enough, words and concepts such as public duty, service, honour and obligation – once condemned by critics on the Left as being central to the Conservative mission of 'social control' – are now changing their significance. Because it has been Conservatives who seem to denigrate such values as all too reminiscent of the Tory grandee, some Labour politicians and commentators have began to argue that perhaps they were not so pernicious after all.

Continuing allegations that some MPs are prepared to accept money for tabling questions in the House of Commons as well as enjoy freebies have led to a decline in confidence in Parliament generally and in the integrity of MPs specifically. In 1952, senior Tory Party agent Frederick Walker looked back over fifty years of political activity and observed of his youth: 'To be in Parliament was a high honour and the Member was held in a respect amounting at times to adulation.' No more. The Select Committee on Members'

Interests, the body responsible for monitoring the financial dealings of MPs, has proved to be singularly ineffective. As for Parliament, a body unable to reform its own archaic system of working hours, which mitigate in particular against women MPs, seems unlikely to be able to reform anything else.

A general sense of malaise has spread to other institutions and events. There have been miscarriages of justice perpetrated by the police and exacerbated by the judiciary; delays over the completion of the Channel Tunnel and the new British Library; the losses at Lloyd's; the Bank of England's unsure handling of the BCCI scandal; Maxwell's raiding of pension funds; and the collapse of Baring's Bank.

The decline in so many institutions which were formerly taken for granted – only the armed forces appeared to have retained their self-confidence and this is ultimately being sapped by the effect of defence cuts closing down divisions in the army – has important long-term implications for the Conservative Party. These same institutions buttressed the Conservative Party; not always explicitly or overtly, but their permanence and longevity gave some substance to the status quo. Without their weight in society, the modern Conservative Party lacks much of its traditional ballast. Its increasingly fractious and undisciplined nature testifies that here is yet another British institution facing a crisis of identity.

Senior Conservatives have increasingly begun to realise the enormity of the changes that they so blithely sponsored. Norman Tebbit, for instance, has called for 'the rebuilding of the social restraints which have been greatly weakened by the doctrines of the permissive society' – naturally preferring to blame the 1960s rather than the individualism of the 1980s.

John Major's Back to Basics, whatever it did or did not mean, was an attempt to fill this very same vacuum. A much-noted speech by Michael Portillo in February 1994 criticised all those who attacked British institutions, even though it was his wing of the Party which had spent much of the previous fourteen years doing the attacking.

Growing public apathy with the entire political process threatens us all. Turnout at the 1950 general election was 84 per cent; more recently, the turnout has been in the low 70s. At local elections, three in four people do not bother to vote. Many young people and members of the ethnic communities do not even bother to register to vote. Polls and surveys show that few people know or even wish to know who wields power on their behalf. One survey of May 1987 revealed that 'One third of people who were asked to which party their MP belonged got it wrong.' Not many people know the names of their local councillors or Euro-MPs.

It is fashionable to argue that this apathy represents the terminal decline of an older political process which was underpinned by traditional mass parties. Instead, future political activity will supposedly revolve around direct democracy, the extensive use of referenda and so on. The independent think-tank Demos spoke enthusiastically of 'de-alignment' and such like, but their proposals are invariably long on abstraction and short on detail.

It is clear that Britain's constitutional arrangements – which were after all a response to the very different circumstances of Victorian Britain – do need drastic overhaul. And yet the Conservative Party, which has done so well out of the old arrangements, is unwilling to countenance such talk.

Some commentators would be happy to see the present political parties themselves disappear, but it is not at all certain that they will become relics of the past. For all its faults, our party system does offer two useful things. Firstly, the various parties provide the electorate with fairly clear alternatives from which to choose; and secondly, they make it possible to create popular majorities.

As admirable as most pressure groups are, the notion of rule by pressure group is intimidating. They are inevitably focused around single issues and, however important these issues might be, such groups are not necessarily equally informed or even concerned about the everyday 'housekeeping' which must be done for the nation, such as agreeing the level of spending on, say, schools, hospitals, public transport or defence.

But the prevailing uncertainty over the British political system naturally shows up within the Conservative Party itself and is evidenced by the sharply conflicting opinions of Douglas Hurd and Andrew Neil quoted at the head of this chapter. These contrasting viewpoints, both of which have substantial followings within the Party, show the dilemmas facing Conservatives.

It is tempting, but incorrect, to characterise the Hurd view as backward and outdated or Neil's as progressive and modern. Or to say that Hurd's remarks represent solid, traditional old-fashioned Toryism and Neil's flash, heartless Thatcherism. The modern Conservative Party defies such easy generalisations.

But the evident tensions between these two viewpoints are symptomatic of the serious disagreements which characterise today's Conservative Party. These conflicts are to be found on many other political, social and economic issues, particularly the question of Europe.

— ◆ —

Dangerous Liaisons

The Conservative Party and the outside world

'The Conservative Party, by long tradition and settled belief, is the Party of the Empire.'
>> From the Conservative Party manifesto
>> for the 1951 general election

'Being Conservative is only another way of being British.'
>> Quintin Hogg (Lord Hailsham), 1967

'We are the European Party in the British Parliament and among the British people and we want to cooperate wholeheartedly with our partners in this joint venture.'
>> Mrs Thatcher in *Europe As I See It*, August 1977

Conservatives have always possessed a strong sense of national identity, of knowing who they are and where they come from. At the Party conference, representatives unselfconsciously bellow out *Rule Britannia*. Socialists, on the other hand, have tended to appeal to a vague sort of internationalism which often evokes little widespread loyalty. At their annual conferences embarrassed Labour leaders can be seen mouthing revolutionary words about keeping the red flag flying – whereas Tory leaders relish *Land of Hope and Glory*.

Analysing socialism's lack of emotional appeal, George Orwell once put it bluntly: 'Men will not die for it [socialism] in anything like the numbers that they will die for King and Country.'

This sense of belonging and of nationhood – 'We, the Nation' – has always given a backbone to British Conservatism and once again it was first understood and then utilised by Benjamin Disraeli. He recognised the intense passions generated by a bellicose patriotism even though initially this trump card was held by the Whig Party whose leader Lord Palmerston was the archetypal jingoist.

After Palmerston's death in October 1865, Disraeli lost little time in transferring this card to the Tory hand. By October 1867 he was robustly declaring that: 'the national party is supported by the fervour of patriotism . . . I have always considered that the Tory Party was the national party of England.' The inclusive nature of patriotism was infinitely preferable to the divisive issue of class.

Ironically enough the patriotic party had originally been identified with the radicals and the Left. At the beginning of the nineteenth century radicals lambasted the Tories for being unpatriotic; but by the second half of the century it was the Conservatives who happily wrapped themselves in the Union Jack. The Liberals, in contrast, were identified with internationalism and peace.

In his Crystal Palace speech of 1872, Disraeli felt able to rewrite history and claim that 'since the advent of Liberalism – forty years ago – you will find that there has been no effort so continuous, so subtle, supported by so much energy, and carried on with so much ability and acumen, as the attempts of Liberalism to effect the disintegration of the Empire of England'.

In order to underpin this identification, leading Conservatives helped finance the Patriotic Association set up in 1878 by Ellis Ashmead Bartlett whose penny weekly newspaper *England* was aimed particularly at 'the Working Class and the Lower Middle Class'. Bartlett's efforts were rewarded with a safe parliamentary seat at the 1880 election.

The Primrose League likewise had no doubts about Britain's fitness to rule the waves. The potent concoction of king, country and God is uncompromisingly present in the *Hymn of the Primrose Buds*, sung by the members of the Junior Imperial and Constitutional League. The second verse goes:

We a pledge have taken
    Ever to be true
To our King and Country,
    And the Empire too –
True to our religion
    Ever serving Him
Who is loved by angels
    And the Seraphim.

Study of Conservative Party propaganda reveals how massively important has been this repeated claim to be the patriotic party. It has allowed Conservatives to denigrate their political opponents as unpatriotic or as motivated by alien and foreign creeds like communism. The belligerent side of this nationalism is evident in the pugnacity of jingoist mobs, in mindless xenophobia and in the aggressive flag-waving behaviour of football hooligans abroad and the fascist British National Party at home.

It is also found in tabloid newspapers. On 25 March 1994, for instance, the *Daily Star*'s front-page spread, signed by editor Brian Hitchens who was soon to be promoted to the chair of the *Sunday Express*, described Britain's European partners as 'Twopenny ha'-penny countries who, until they joined the Euro gravy train, were dung-shovelling peasants with their backsides hanging out'. To categorise the inhabitants of countries such as France, Italy and Germany, renowned for their exceptional artists, musicians, writers and poets, as 'dung-shovelling peasants' is taking bigotry to its furthest extremes.

Nationalism's more gentle side is displayed in what might be termed the Stanley Baldwin strand of Conservatism which dwells contentedly on certain tranquil and apparently timeless aspects of English life: the village green, the parish church, royal occasions, great sporting events, pageantry and ritual. Listen to Baldwin's evocation of what England meant to him, delivered to the Annual Dinner of the Royal Society of St George in 1924:

The sounds of England, the tinkle of the hammer on the anvil in the country smithy, the corncrake on a dewy morning, the sound of the scythe against the whetstone, and the sight of a plough team coming over the brow of a hill, the sight that has been seen in England since England was a land, and may be seen in England long after the Empire has perished, and every works in England has ceased to function. For centuries, the one eternal sight of England.

And so on and so forth.

But there are several problems with both versions of this nationalism, not least of which is the slippage between the words 'British' and 'English'. During her robust Bruges speech in September 1988 assailing the ambitions of the European Community, Mrs Thatcher mentioned the words British or Britain seventeen times in just nine pages. And yet Mrs Thatcher was never terribly interested in Scotland or in Wales – in her memoirs of her eleven years in power, Wales is mentioned just once (in connection with a proposed housing scheme).

For many Conservatives, an English way of life means something definite; the British way of life is less clearcut. It is no coincidence that the Conservative Party once drew its electoral strength from English seats, whilst the Liberal Party was powerful in Scotland, Wales and Ireland.

The strident version of English nationalism – the jingoism and 'Britain Rules the Waves' frenzy – has always been unattractive to Liberals and to many of the electorate who occupy the crucial centre ground. The more astute Conservative Party managers have discreetly acknowledged this. As Hugh Cunningham has pointed out, it is noticeable that the bellicose Ellis Ashmead Bartlett, for instance, was fobbed off with minor office and a knighthood. Men like Bartlett had their uses but, notwithstanding their very vocal huffing and puffing, they were expendable.

A further reason for this Conservative unease with being British is that Britain as a nation is a comparatively recent notion, despite the appeals to timelessness and eternity. As Linda Colley emphasised in her fine book *Britons: Forging the Nation 1707–1837* (1992), Britain has only existed as an entity since the Act of Union of 1707 which joined Scotland to England and Wales. As a nation, therefore, Great Britain is not much older than the United States of America.

Yet another difficulty with notions of both 'Britishness' and 'Englishness' is that they are being undermined by the changing world economy. The growth of multinationals which operate across national borders together with increasing global trade, the rise of world religions and media developments in television and satellite mean that we are all increasingly subject to the same kind of cultural influences. These changes threaten to obliterate many national characteristics and patterns: indeed, the 'nation state' itself is becoming obsolete.

Finally, there is of course the crucial question of Europe. Are we in fact all Europeans now? Could the downgrading of the Westminster Parliament by Brussels lead to the disintegration of nationally based political parties, replacing them instead by Europe-wide parties with European policies?

In Disraeli's day it was all so much more simple: Britain was an island with its own distinctive way of life, defended by its navy. As Winston Churchill put it so eloquently in *My Early Life*, first published in 1930: 'I was a child of the Victorian era, when the structure of our country seemed firmly set, when its position in trade and on the seas was unrivalled, and when the realization of the greatness of our Empire and of our duty to preserve it was ever growing stronger. In those days the dominant forces in Great Britain were very sure of themselves and of their doctrines.'

My Early Life was republished in 1947. Four years later, Prime Minister Sir Winston Churchill offered junior Tory MP Selwyn Lloyd a post at the Foreign Office. Lloyd protested: 'But sir, I think there must be some mistake, I've never been to a foreign country, I don't speak any foreign languages, I don't like foreigners.' 'Young man,' replied Churchill, 'these all seem to me to be positive advantages.'

Granted that this is one of those wonderful stories that happily attach themselves to Churchill – the kind of anecdote at which Conservatives with their love of character excel – there is more than an iota of truth here.

But, despite the exertions of Churchill and many others, Britain no longer rules the waves – and the implications are profound indeed for the British Conservative Party.

In the past, the Conservative Party dealt with the problems of Ireland, the Empire and the Commonwealth strictly on the grounds of *realpolitik*. In each case the status quo was defended to the bitter end but when, finally, the position became indefensible then the Party retreated and made the best of the new situation. A few Tory die-hards were always prepared to perish in the last ditch upholding their beliefs, but the bulk of the Party could see that such fanaticism was finally self-defeating. Dedication to power has always triumphed over devotion to principle.

The Conservative Party's habit of going to the brink but then pulling back from it can be seen very clearly on the question of Ireland. From the days of Elizabeth I and Oliver Cromwell, Ireland was a vital element within British Conservatism if only because the wealthy Protestant minority in Ulster supplied both resources and numerous influential figures to the Party. The 'Protestant Ascendancy' stiffened the backbone of the Conservative Party.

As for the Catholic majority, without a vote or political influence, they were stereotyped in ways designed to justify the inequalities. Benjamin Disraeli, for instance, was capable of this breathtaking generalisation in 1868: 'The Irishman is a very imaginative being living in a damp climate and contiguous to a melancholy ocean. With extraordinary talent he has no variety of pursuit open to him, there is no nation in the world leading such monotonous lives as the Irish. All men are discontented when they are not amused.'

The importance of Ireland to Conservatives was shown by the Party's willingness to change its name after Gladstone's conversion to Home Rule in the 1880s had split the Liberal Party. A large section of the Liberals, led by Joseph Chamberlain, had broken off and now called themselves the Liberal Unionists. In order to make their own allegiance clear, the Conservatives began to describe themselves as the Unionist Party.

In cities such as Liverpool and Glasgow it was the Unionist movement in the shape of the Orange Lodges which gave local

Conservatism a sense of muscle and will-power. Similarly the Primrose League drew upon its full resources to battle against Home Rule: in one year alone three million leaflets were distributed, backed up by posters, lantern slides and cartoons. Skits were performed under the title 'The Pig, the Paddy and the Patriot M.P.'.

Before the First World War, Unionist opposition to Home Rule for Ireland – the 'Ulster will fight, and Ulster will be right' campaign – took them, as we saw earlier, to the verge of insurrection. Zealots argued that Ulster should never surrender, that Home Rule had to be defeated by force if necessary, that the Union must be maintained at all costs. On the face of it, one would have thought that the vehemence of such slogans meant the Unionist Party would rather have died and dissolved itself than accept the partition of Ireland.

But, of course, one should never underestimate the factor of opportunism. It might be thought that Lord Randolph Churchill for example, the originator of the 'Ulster will fight' slogan, was indissolubly wedded to principle. Not so. In February 1886, he had written candidly to a friend: 'I decided some time ago that if the G.O.M. ['Grand Old Man', i.e. Gladstone] went for Home Rule, the Orange Card would be the one to play. Please God it may turn out the ace of trumps and not the two.'

Political principles reduced to a game of cards. The Churchill way was clearly catching. Less than sixty years later, Randolph's son Winston was to conclude a percentage agreement with Joseph Stalin which divided up Europe, allotting some countries to the 'West' and others to the 'East'.

Sure enough the Unionist Party, including its leaders such as Bonar Law and F.E. Smith who had seemingly been opposed to Irish nationalism to the death, happily endorsed the Treaty of December 1921 which divided Ireland into the Irish Free State and the six Protestant Ulster counties. Even the stalwarts of the Liverpool Conservatives, traditionally the experts at playing the Orange Card (no doubt helped by Lord Randolph's card-sharping skills), fell into line at the crucial Conservative Party conference in 1922. It was Alderman Archibald Salvidge no less, the man whose political career had been built on zealous anti-Catholicism, who personally masterminded the defeat of the die-hards.

Why this sea-change? Because it was clear by 1921 that the game was simply not worth the candle; the resources required to maintain the Union in its entirety were beyond the Party's command. And there were of course other considerations to be borne in mind, as more thoughtful Tories realised. The creation of the Irish Free State brought enormous electoral advantage to the Party: approximately seventy anti-Conservative Irish MPs were taken away from the House of Commons and replaced instead by a core of solidly Conservative Ulster Unionist MPs.

Even the most innumerate Conservative could calculate that this augured well for the Party's prospects of power. It was much better to control what you had than risk everything by being greedy. The Unionist Party therefore happily reverted to its more familiar 'Conservative' label.

As it turned out, the role of the Ulster Unionists proved vital. Attlee's Labour Government of 1950 was deprived of a decent working majority in the House of Commons by the ten Ulster Unionist MPs. The administration stumbled to electoral defeat the next year. Similarly, after the 1992 election when John Major's Government secured only a narrow working majority, the votes of the Ulster Unionists were crucial in sustaining the administration.

Again, the question of India and of the British Empire seemed to lie at the very heart of Conservative identity. The Party had always resolutely favoured the retention of links with the Empire, not least because many ex-Colonial service members retired to Britain and formed the backbone of scores of local constituency associations.

By the 1920s and 1930s, however, it was becoming obvious that India's demand for a measure of self-government could no longer be denied, even though the Empire itself was still expanding: according to James Morris, it carried on growing until 1933, by which time it covered no less than 13.9 million square miles and contained a population of 493 million.

The India die-hards were led by Winston Churchill. He managed to enlist the financial support of the dukes of Westminster, Salisbury and other party grandees. But in fact Churchill and his allies were comprehensively outmanoeuvred both by the leadership and by Conservative Central Office who succeeded in persuading the bulk of the Party that, once again – albeit with regret – this particular game was not worth the candle.

The Government laboriously pushed through Parliament the complicated Government of India Bill between 1933 and 1935. According to Rab Butler, one of the junior ministers involved in the legislation, 'The 1,951 speeches made on the subject of the Bill filled 4,000 pages of Hansard with 15½ million words ... Altogether the debates in Parliament on India lasted many years and added up to 20 books the size of the Bible.' No small group of rebels could possibly hold out against such determined armoury.

Imperialist sentiment remained strong, particularly when the Second World War demonstrated the extent of Britain's foreign commitments. Victory suggested to some Conservatives that Britain was now strong enough to resume its foreign mission: the 'white man's burden' could once again be taken up.

It was not to be, as one event in particular showed, namely the Suez venture. Even today, this episode is shrouded in uncertainty and mystery because of the authorities' extreme sensitivity on the matter. In 1967 Sir Anthony Nutting, who had resigned from the Government in protest at its actions, wrote a book about the affair, claiming that secrecy 'allowed a government to deceive Parliament and people and sheltering behind that deception to lead the nation into war'. The then Cabinet secretary tried to stop publication. According to Nutting, Sir Burke Trend 'went through the book with me page by page objecting to almost all'. Pressure was put on *The Times* to scrap serialisation of Nutting's book, but to no avail.

Thirteen years later, in 1980, the BBC planned to show six thirty-minute programmes called *Lord Mountbatten Remembers*. The six programmes were soon slimmed down to five: yet another Cabinet secretary had vetoed, successfully this time, the transmission of views that the Eden Government's actions had been mistaken. By contrast, Sir Anthony Eden's own official account of what happened was published in its entirety, but has since turned out to be mendacious.

It is true to say that in Britain – and no doubt elsewhere – the more sensitive the issue, the higher the degree of censorship.

At the heart of the matter of the Suez affair was the feeling amongst Britain's rulers that the country, so recently victorious in a world war, was still assured of a global role in world affairs. In a speech delivered in 1952, Sir Anthony Eden had dismissed moves towards a Common Market with the claim that 'Britain's story and interests lie far beyond the continent of Europe. Our thoughts move across the seas to the many communities in which our people play their part, in every corner of the world. These are our family ties.'

Britain's rulers were also haunted by their failure to stand up to Hitler in the 1930s, guilty of their part in appeasement. 'Never again' was the dominant feeling. And so when Colonel Nasser of Egypt unexpectedly nationalised the Suez canal in July 1956, arguing that he needed the revenue to pay for the building of the Aswan dam, here seemed yet another tin-pot dictator who needed to be taught a lesson.

International diplomacy produced an agreement in October 1956 between all the parties which appeared to secure a peaceful future for the canal, but Eden was in fact looking for a military solution. As he had said months before, 'It is either him or us, don't forget that.'

His pugnacity fuelled by the aggressive jingoism of delegates at the Conservative Party conference in Llandudno that October, Eden agreed to a French plan that would allow Israel to attack Egypt. Britain and France would intervene on the pretext of separating the two forces. Although the Government declared then and afterwards that there had been no collusion between the British, French and Israeli governments, this is now known to be untrue. Israel duly launched an offensive against Egypt on 30 October 1956 and the Anglo-French forces in their turn attacked Port Said on 6 November.

It all went horribly wrong. The Americans were shocked and horrified – President Eisenhower, up for re-election in November 1956, certainly did not want any boats to be rocked – delegates at the United Nations scarcely less so, and at home the Labour Party under

Hugh Gaitskell, after initial prevarication, also strongly opposed the Government.

The overwrought Eden, already suffering from health problems and accompanied everywhere by a huge chest of pills, looked upon dissent to his Government's actions as traitorous – just as Mrs Thatcher did in 1982 during the Falklands War. He even hatched plans to take over the BBC in order to ensure that the public received just one, officially sanctioned, viewpoint. It emerged in September 1994 that in any case British intelligence had for fifteen years been running an important Arabic radio station which, with the full co-operation of the BBC, pumped out anti-Nasser propaganda during the Suez affair.

People protested in different ways. Of the major newspapers, the *Manchester Guardian* alone came out strongly against the military action, promptly losing 40 per cent of its advertising revenue. On the other hand, senior civil servant William Armstrong, probably the most influential mandarin since the Second World War, felt called upon to make his views clear, but in his case dissent was restricted to the wearing of a black tie.

Senior members of the Cabinet rapidly began to lose their nerve. Most notoriously, the Chancellor of the Exchequer Harold Macmillan soon had second thoughts. Initially, his stomach for a fight was clear; senior Tory Brendan Bracken observed that 'Until a week ago, Macmillan, whose bellicosity was beyond description, was wanting to tear Nasser's scalp off with his own fingernails.'

But a week, as another politician was later to observe, is a long time in politics and Chancellor Macmillan had neglected to take financial precautions by withdrawing Britain's assets from the International Monetary Fund, as the French had done. The subsequent run on the pound was worrying if predictable. Today there are suggestions that he misrepresented the situation to his Cabinet colleagues, exaggerating the losses by some £70 million. Macmillan clearly advocated 'first in, first out' when it came to military action.

The troops were indeed pulled out, the job but half done, thus ensuring that Britain got the worst of every world: not having achieved its military target yet having upset virtually everyone.

Conservative MPs were deeply shaken by the sequence of events; one of them described the atmosphere within the Party in late 1956: 'It was rather like going on board a steamer at the end of a very rough crossing. There was a slight smell of sickness in the Smoking Room and almost everyone looked green.' The Chief Whip, Edward Heath, deployed his full artillery of persuasion, threat and appeals to loyalty. And as often proves to be the case in a Conservative crisis, the opposition scored an own goal when Labour leader Hugh Gaitskell broadcast an appeal to dissident Tories to overthrow Eden – thus prompting an immediate closing of Conservative ranks.

The Conservative commitment to party ahead of abstract principle was clearly displayed when the parliamentary Party, which had voted almost unanimously for tough action in the autumn of 1956, then voted almost unanimously in the spring of 1957 for the reversal of that policy.

'He was the last Prime Minister to believe Britain was a great power and the first to confront a crisis which proved she was not.' Robert Blake's succinct summary in his obituary notice of Sir Anthony Eden put the matter in a nutshell. Eden retired to writer Ian Fleming's home on Jamaica to recuperate, returned to London and insisted that there had been no collusion with Israel. Clearly a scapegoat was needed for the whole debacle and, as is invariably the case in the Conservative Party, it was the leader who had to carry the can. Eden resigned. His successor was, of course, Harold Macmillan who was in fact three years older than Eden. Keith Kyle has best summed up the vagaries of political fortune:

> If there had been one person more set on destroying Nasser than Eden it had been Macmillan; one person more responsible for the most serious misjudgement of all, that of Eisenhower's likely reaction to an Anglo-French ultimatum; one man whose abrupt change of front contributed most of all to the aborted nature of the campaign. Yet, two months after his talk of being ready for the morgue, Harold Macmillan's was the older blood to which Eden gave way.

However vocal the passions of the Tory die-hards, the Suez crisis confirmed that Britain could no longer roar and expect the rest of the world to cower. Nor could Britain's economy sustain the cost of her overseas commitments. These had to be slimmed down before they jeopardised living standards at home.

In February 1960 Harold Macmillan delivered his famous 'winds of change' speech which accepted that the sun was indeed beginning to set on the British Empire. He was astute enough to appoint the progressive Iain Macleod as his Colonial Secretary in order to bear the brunt of opposition to decolonialisation. Macleod had no hesitations, boldly declaring at the 1961 Conservative Party conference that he believed, 'quite simply, in the brotherhood of man – men of all races, of all colours, of all creeds'.

If Macleod ever proved insufficient as an air-raid shelter, Macmillan would simply sidetrack Party discontent by reverting to his masterly and time-honoured tactics of evasion. As one senior Conservative MP put it: 'The 1922 Committee was not very keen on the policy of retreat from Africa, but when Harold Macmillan was at the top of his powers, he would give us a lecture about Norman land-holdings in Saxon Britain and that would be that.'

There were indeed furious internal rows over the extent and speed of decolonialisation, arguments which rarely surfaced in public. Some dissidents felt impelled to form the very right-wing Monday Club in 1961 in order to press their views, but they remained a fringe element within the Party.

Which was not to say that this fringe did not command a voluble and substantial hearing within the Conservative Party. Lord Carrington was the Foreign Secretary supervising the negotiations in 1979 leading to free elections in Rhodesia/Zimbabwe. At that year's Party conference, a huge meeting organised by the Monday Club displayed 'Hang Carrington' banners. As he walked down the street, people even shook their fists at him.

At the 1992 general election, the Conservative leader John Major made several impassioned pleas for the retention of the Union with Scotland. On the face of it, therefore, one might have thought that here at last was a core principle which formed part of the

Conservative bedrock: namely, implacable opposition to devolution for Scotland and Wales.

In fact this is not so. During the hard-fought election campaign of 1950, Opposition leader Winston Churchill told an Edinburgh audience that Scotland had a right of secession and a need for 'further guarantees of national security and internal independence'.

Likewise when they were in opposition, both Edward Heath and Margaret Thatcher toyed with setting up some form of Scottish Assembly. Their idea was to undercut both Labour and the nationalist parties, which meant that it was the Conservatives themselves who appeared to be advocating the break-up of the Union. Both proposals were put forward not on the grounds of principle but for reasons of electoral expediency, namely as a means of maximising opposition to the Labour Governments of the time.

These flirtations showed how the changing electoral situation was undermining the Conservatives' much-cherished claim to be the national party. As recently as the 1955 general election the Conservatives had obtained a majority of the seats in Scotland – but within little more than a decade, at the 1966 election, the Labour Party reversed the majority. The Heath plans were drawn up in 1968 but were quietly dropped after the election of 1970 was won. Labour won both the 1974 elections and the Thatcher plans were drawn up in 1975. These were discreetly shelved after the election of 1979 was won. Both sets of proposals had helped the Conservative Party to defeat Labour, had outlived their usefulness, and were therefore now expendable.

Even bearing in mind this seeming triumph of expediency over principle, it is unlikely that the Conservatives will ever write off Scotland and Wales as they did most of Ireland. In large part this is because Scots and Welsh nationalism has, so far, been less vigorous than its Irish counterpart. As the political commentator Andrew Marr has put it, 'Scotland never rebelled. There has been virtually no violence and relatively few outbreaks of mass protest, merely a sullenness, an emptiness, at the centre of Scottish public life.' Demands were comparatively easily bought off, for example by setting up a Scottish Office in 1885. And of course, Scotland and Wales are physically joined to England.

*   *   *

In 1895 Cecil Rhodes, coloniser of Rhodesia, spoke out bluntly:

> In order to save the 40,000,000 inhabitants of the United
> Kingdom from a bloody civil war, we colonial statesmen must
> acquire new lands to settle the surplus population, to provide
> new markets for the goods produced by them in the factories
> and mines. The Empire, as I have always said, is a bread and
> butter question. If you want to avoid civil war, you must become
> imperialists.'

With difficulty, the Empire has been relinquished and civil war
avoided. The question of Europe poses problems of a similar
magnitude for the Conservative Party. Europe goes right to the
heart of that sense of identity which underpins the Conservatives,
a party rooted in a strong sense of national consciousness ever since
the days of Disraeli. Is Europe, in Cecil Rhodes's words, a bread and
butter question which offers the prospect of avoiding civil war? If
not, then what is it?

In the past, threats to the Conservative sense of identity,
for example over Ireland and India, have been bought off by
surrendering parts of the whole. As long ago as April 1892 Lord
Salisbury warned a Primrose League audience of the danger of
surrendering Ireland. He used a striking analogy: 'If you fail in this
trial, one by one the flowers will be plucked from the diadem of
Empire and you will be reduced to depend on the resources of this
small, over-peopled island.'

The flowers have indeed been plucked and the question now
is what lies ahead for this 'small, over-peopled island'. As regards
Europe, Britain is for the first time being invited to join a new
diadem, although it is not one of her own making. Will the
Conservative Party accept the dilution of national sovereignty in
a much bigger and wider entity? Can and should Britain leap from
being a nation state and merge into a larger and federal entity
where it is no longer master in its own house?

After 1945, the Cold War between West and East meant that

arguments about the future could easily be subsumed into a 'them' and 'us' approach: democratic us against totalitarian them. During the 1979 election campaign, for instance, Conservative supporters like Lord Chalfont stridently told readers of the *Sun* 'Why We Must Fight the Red Menace'. Since 1989 and the collapse of the Soviet bloc, this bloodcurdling approach has become obsolete and questions about the future cannot be glibly dismissed with rhetoric about the enemy within and without.

Equally threatening to the traditional Tory sense of identity is the fact that the European issue never stands still. In terms of its name alone, the Common Market became the European Economic Community, then the European Community and is now the European Union. Both its membership and its powers have expanded in tandem. At first the Common Market was intended to be purely an economic arrangement, but over the years it has developed a political dimension. The terrain is constantly shifting and its unfamiliarity poses problems of control for a Conservative Party accustomed to being in charge.

Worse still, the fresh demands and challenges mean that – unlike in the past when parts of Ireland or the Empire could be given up – there is no obvious place to which the Party can retreat. If withdrawal from the European Union in its entirety is ruled out, and only a few die-hards fail to accept that the trading patterns set up since the early 1970s now make this impossible, then the range of alternatives on offer are all perilous and uncertain. Even the Party's traditional powers of obfuscation are of little assistance.

The size of the threat is emphasised by the fact that since 1986 no fewer than seven Conservative Cabinet ministers have resigned or been forced out of office because of issues containing a European dimension – Leon Brittan and Michael Heseltine in 1986 over who should own Westland helicopters, Europe or America; Nicholas Ridley because of anti-German statements expressed in a magazine interview; Nigel Lawson over Europe and the economy; Howe over Mrs Thatcher's anti-Europeanism; and finally Norman Lamont over the question of the European Exchange Rate Mechanism (ERM).

As for the seventh resignation, it was the disastrous 1989 European election results, when the Conservatives warned electors of the dangers of 'a diet of Brussels', which started the serious slide in Mrs Thatcher's fortunes. Her anti-European views were crucial to her eventual downfall. Since Mrs Thatcher's departure, the bitterness of the internal Conservative debates over the Maastricht treaty has aggravated the Party's divisions. No issue has so divided Conservatives since the early years of this century when Joseph Chamberlain launched his tariff reform campaign.

The level of bitterness and acrimony between pro- and anti-Europeans is reminiscent of the Bevanite struggles inside the Labour Party in the 1950s which effectively torpedoed the Party's chances of electoral power. The electorate has shown time and time again that it does not approve of political parties torn apart by internal strife.

In November 1994 the internecine Party conflict moved into very public centre stage. John Major took the unprecedented step of depriving eight Conservative but Euro-sceptic MPs of the Party whip, resorting to the kind of strong-arm tactics never before employed by a Conservative Prime Minister no matter how irritated they had been by backbench dissent – not by Heath over the Common Market battles in 1971–2, not by Eden over Suez, not by Chamberlain over opposition to his foreign policy in the late 1930s. It was a move entirely at odds with the traditional Tory way of doing things.

The whole question of the Conservative Party and its uncertain relationship with Europe has always been complicated by a number of factors. Britain is an 'island race' whose security and impregnability has encouraged a strong sense of nationhood, which has in turn been buttressed by the continuity of the country's institutions. Britain has also regarded itself as a partner in other important non-European relationships, firstly with the Empire, then with the Commonwealth, and finally with the United States. Understandably, Britain has been little concerned in the past with continental relationships. Both geography and history seem to discourage 'foreign' liaisons.

It is not surprising that both the Conservative Party and its leaders' attitudes to Europe since the Second World War have been ambiguous and contradictory. Winston Churchill, for instance, is claimed by some pro-Europeans as almost a father figure of the movement. Anti-Europeans maintain that he did indeed favour European union, but purely for the Europeans and not for Britain. The verdict will almost certainly be that Churchill was not consistent; he changed his mind according to circumstance.

Churchill, Eden and some other Conservatives were at times beguiled by the possibilities of the 'special relationship' with the United States. These hopes caused successive Tory Governments to drag their feet over Europe, and to become embroiled in a massively expensive programme of nuclear defence. However it became increasingly clear that, whatever the historic ties of friendship between the two countries, for Britain at least they could never compensate for her declining international and economic position.

Political expediency and the search for power meant that the Conservative Party never had a consistent policy; nor did the Labour Party. A strong Europhile such as Robert Boothby thought that Sir Anthony Eden robbed Britain of its chance of leading Europe. Eden was not alone in his lukewarm attitude. Other leading Conservatives were equally tepid: Rab Butler was one, despite speaking fluent French, and Harold Macmillan sometimes another – although he later changed his mind and sanctioned the doomed application to join in 1963.

In his memoirs, Macmillan confirmed that his vacillation over Europe was largely conditioned by his fear that the issue might well split the Party. Files held at Conservative Central Office in the early 1960s show how anxiously Party officials scanned local constituencies for signs of anti-European revolt. 'Spies' attended meetings of the Anti-Common Market League and reports were sent in showing that some Tories feared the Common Market was yet another 'Popish plot', a plan by Catholic Europe to subvert Protestant England.

Several leading party figures, particularly Edward Heath, were Europeans through and through, fully prepared to resort to half-truths in order to support their case. A White Paper produced by Heath in 1971 explained that there would be 'no question of any erosion of essential national sovereignty'. This was simply not true.

In many ways, Europeans like Heath hoped that joining Europe would bring Britain the benefits of modernisation and access to a larger market without disturbing arrangements at home. In fact the issues of modernisation, reform at home and Europe all go hand in hand.

Chopping and changing inevitably meant that the Conservatives got the worst of both worlds. Unable to go it alone, Britain was seen as an unwilling participant in the European venture, constantly at war during Mrs Thatcher's lengthy period in office with the other members of the Community.

Mrs Thatcher was, in her own blunt words, 'an English nationalist and never you forget it'. Like many Conservatives, she had been deeply shocked by the Suez fiasco. It was Suez which, as Lord Beloff has pointed out, forced the Conservative Party to abandon its role as the imperial party and to adopt instead the ideal of European unity. To put it concisely, Suez led to Europe.

In Mrs Thatcher's eyes, success in the Falklands War in 1982 changed all that. Her memoirs emphasise that she saw the Falklands episode as reversing the verdict of Suez and in effect signalling the end of British retreat − just as her economic policies were overturning post-war domestic decline. Her English nationalism became more strident. By 1989, allies such as Nigel Lawson were horrified at how the Prime Minister planned to use that year's Euro-elections:

> I suddenly realized, with a shiver of apprehension, that she saw the Euro-campaign as a trial run for the next General Election campaign; and that, with the short-term economic outlook unpromising, she saw a crude populist anti-Europeanism as her winning strategy. It was a strategy that would undoubtedly have evoked a considerable response: xenophobia always does.

But whether Mrs Thatcher was exhibiting xenophobia or a healthy nationalist spirit, the passing years had already drawn Britain increasingly into Europe. In terms of business alone, Britain's companies now have over £5 billion invested in Europe and her business leaders are naturally enthusiasts for the Union. At the 1993 CBI conference, its director-general Howard Davies criticised the strident anti-European tone of that year's Conservative Party conference which had been held only a few weeks before. A CBI survey showed that an overwhelming majority of British companies favoured a single currency – a position which was and is anathema to the Conservative Government.

As the European Union develops, so understandably does it want to speak with its own voice and this voice will be immeasurably strengthened by having common policies backed up with a strong measure of unanimity. This objective lay behind the public disputes over the ERM and European Monetary Union. The collapse of the ERM may have stilled these arguments for a while but it is certain that, before long, the problem will return. Indeed Chancellor Kohl of Germany has stated that the timetable for European Monetary Union is unalterable.

Equally important is the matter of enlarging the Union, which the Conservative Government favours, and the expansion of majority voting allowing individual countries to be more easily overridden, which the Conservative Government most certainly does not. Ironically, it was the Single European Act of 1987, pushed through by Mrs Thatcher keen to have a single European market, which introduced qualified majority voting into most areas of European legislation. This replaced the single-nation veto that had formerly allowed Britain to block measures it did not like.

The position of the British Conservative Party is further complicated by the differing policies of its European colleagues, grouped together in the European People's Party (EPP). The EPP favours not just federal measures, consequently weakening British national sovereignty, but also the 'social chapter' which almost the entire British Conservative Party considers to be a smuggling-in by the back door of the kind of creeping socialism and corporatism whose defeat even Mrs Thatcher's Tory critics regarded as one of the achievements of the 1980s. As Mrs Thatcher put it at Bruges in 1988: 'We have not successfully rolled back the frontiers of the state in Britain, only to see them reimposed at a European level, with a European super-state exercising a new dominance from Brussels.'

The Conservative Members of the European Parliament (MEPs)

are clearly more pro-European in outlook than their colleagues in Westminster. The differences between even the most sceptical of Tory MEPs and their supposed allies back in Britain are striking. Bryan Cassidy, MEP for Dorset East and Hampshire West, stated that 'While I count myself as a Euro-sceptic, some MPs I will not name are xenophobic. They believe wogs, or should I say foreigners, begin at Calais. Some of their anti-European comments are frankly racist.'

It is symptomatic of the Party's divisions that, so far, few MEPs have been selected by local Conservative associations to stand in attractive election seats back in Britain. A survey by the *Sunday Telegraph* of the Party's eighty-five Euro-candidates standing in the June 1994 elections revealed very different views on the crucial question of a single currency whilst polls of Tory MPs testify to the large number of Euro-sceptics at Westminster.

Many of the Party's financial backers are keen to benefit from the spoils of the European venture, for example by ensuring that some of the new European federal institutions will be based here in Britain. But the Government's rhetoric hardly encourages Britain's partners to be accommodating over such matters. In terms of tackling unemployment and promoting economic growth, which virtually all economists recognise will require a European-wide strategy, Britain draws back from co-operative projects even though such initiatives would benefit her own economy.

Caught between the devil and the deep blue sea, John Major has veered between claiming that Britain must be 'at the heart of Europe' and abusing John Smith as 'Monsieur Oui, the poodle of Brussels'. He has craftily stilled the storm for the moment by talking about a multi-speed Europe, implying that Britain may choose to tootle along in the slow lane if she wishes.

But scanning the immediate horizon, one discerns a long stretch of storm clouds which are unlikely to disperse. For a start, the law lords are beginning to recognise the primacy of European law and regulations. In March 1994 they held that the rights of part-time workers were governed by European employment law. The implication here is that the Conservative Government's much-vaunted opt-out from the social chapter may ultimately be nibbled away.

The Conservative Government is trapped in a Catch-22 situation: either it pleases its European partners and infuriates vocal and important sections within the Party; or it pleases the Party with a series of difficult compromises, but alienates the rest of Europe. This inconsistency and negativity does not exactly reassure or impress Britain's European partners. Once again, a sensible, coherent and constructive approach towards Europe is being sabotaged by the pre-eminent demands of the Party itself.

And yet more problems loom. In 1996 the Inter-Government Conference will completely revise the voting system and it is certain that the upshot will be a further dilution of national sovereignty. European leaders such as Chancellor Kohl and President Mitterand are enthusiastically in favour of further European integration and it is unlikely that their successors will adopt a different approach. Thoughout, Conservative Euro-sceptics will ceaselessly call for a referendum and there are signs that John Major may, in order to head off further trouble, reluctantly acquiesce. This in turn would infuriate Cabinet Euro-enthusiasts such as Kenneth Clarke and Michael Heseltine. Not just Major but the Party as a whole seems to be trapped in a classic no-win situation.

The Conservative Party has always been a coalition of interests. In recognising this, Party managers have been careful not to push one interest too hard at the expense of others. Party unity is more important than anything else because disunity threatens the prospect of power. But the European issue leaves little room for manoeuvre and provides a constant reminder that two distinct sections, which on the Continent are often represented by two different parties, shelter under the Conservative banner.

One of these is the Christian Democratic wing, namely those One Nation Tories not scared of government intervention or even of the social chapter. The other is the free market strand which opposes anything that smacks of regulation, collectivism or federalism. It is becoming harder and harder for the two to co-exist within the same party; over the last few years co-existence has largely been achieved by the power of patronage. The whips have been able, by a variety of methods explored elsewhere, to enforce their will. One measure of their success is that the eighty-four backbench Conservative MPs who signed the implicitly anti-European 'Fresh Start' motion in June 1992 were reduced to a hard core of twenty by the time of the key Maastricht debates.

But what happens if the Party loses office at the next election? The power of the whips and the trammels of ministerial restraint will come to an end and it is not difficult to foresee a distinctly un-Conservative free-for-all taking place in public.

Some commentators think that the Conservative Party should indeed divide. Paul Johnson, for instance, suggests that the existing two-party system of Conservative and Labour should be dissolved and replaced by two groupings representing the European and nationalist parties.

Others think the Party will indeed split. Writing in the *Sunday Telegraph*, a house organ of the anti-Europe group which ensures that these party frictions cannot be conducted behind closed doors as invariably happened in the past, Niall Fergusson thought that Tory grassroots suspicion of Maastricht was growing and that the issue simply could not go away: 'Sooner or later some kind of split seems inevitable, with Messrs Cash and Co doing to the pro-Maastricht Tories what Joe Chamberlain did to the free-trading, Home-Ruling Gladstonian Liberals.'

Fergusson concluded that there was a real prospect of the twentieth-century Conservative Party following the same route to extinction as the nineteenth-century Liberals.

In the past, Conservative rebels and dissidents have eventually recognised that no point of principle is more important than the imperative need for party unity. The Party's rebels over Ireland or India may have fought tooth and nail for their cause, but they eventually pulled back from going over the precipice – this would entail actually standing against official Conservative Party candidates during elections. The eight Conservative MPs who lost the whip in November 1994, joined by another who voluntarily relinquished it, seem to have secured constituency backing for their stand.

In large part, this is because they feel that public opinion, certainly within the Party itself, is beginning to shift in their favour. A national survey of Conservative Party members in 1992 found that 68 per cent of the sample agreed with the statement that 'Britain's national sovereignty is being lost to Europe.' In 1994, the percentage had risen to 72 per cent. Commentators began to talk of the two Conservative Parties, the parliamentary enthusiasts and the constituency sceptics.

It might well be that on this issue of national sovereignty, which covers not just the powers of Parliament but also the supremacy of the English courts and the future of the monarchy, a series of unwelcome European Union decisions pushed through by qualified majority voting decisions might just be the straw that breaks the camel's back. Bill Cash, a leading Conservative Euro-sceptic, is careful to couch his arguments in terms of sovereignty, arguing that the proposed changes within the Council of Ministers would 'reduce the House of Commons to a cipher'. Can national sovereignty in fact be pooled without ceasing to be national sovereignty? This line of attack might well strike a chord amongst many people in Britain: in which case, principle might well come before power.

Critics love to write off the Tories. In the mid-1970s, for instance, after they had lost four out of the last five general elections, the respected academic Andrew Gamble wrote a book seemingly consigning the Conservatives to the dustbin of history. Whereupon they promptly won the next four elections in a row.

But the European issue does seem to present very serious and long-term problems for the Conservative Party, not least because it poses questions about the entire basis of British society and government on which its success has rested, questions which have profound implications for the continued success of Conservatism. For instance, the British parliamentary system precludes any notion of the power-sharing which is taken for granted on the Continent.

Thus Europe threatens the entire identity and existence of the Conservative Party. Lady Thatcher is typically forthright: 'The lesson of the century has been that people feel far more comfortable and more stable with a nation state. It is the nation state which is the unit of loyalty. Ours is the United Kingdom.'

Lady Thatcher may well be right but the nation state itself – like it or not – is being subjected to pressure both from below or at the grassroots level, where other countries except Britain are trying to decentralise, and from above via the European Union.

British Conservatism was, and still is, founded upon a particular conception of English national consciousness. As this changes and fragments, the potential effect on the Conservative Party is momentous.

And yet one should always bear in mind the ruthless pragmatism which forms the backbone of the British Conservative Party. In the early 1930s, Winston Churchill led a fierce campaign to try and thwart any moves leading to Indian independence. He told J.C.C. Davidson, one of the Party's most senior figures, that he felt sure that Empire and India was a good rallying cry. Davidson disagreed. 'I told him that I thought that the British public was much more interested in the size of their pay-packet on Friday than by great rhetorical appeals to their loyalty to the British Empire.'

The Conservative Party has always understood the relationship between politics and power. Rhetoric is fine as far as it goes, but should never endanger the unity on which electoral success ultimately depends. However bitter the arguments or fierce the passions, most Conservatives understand this only too well. Surely not even Europe will overturn this understanding.

Tory Mavericks, Rebels and Outsiders

'I love fame; I love public reputation; I love to live in the eye of the country; and it is a glorious thing for a man who has had my difficulties to contend against.'

Benjamin Disraeli, speaking at Shrewsbury in 1841

'Damn these Chamberlains – they are the curse of our party and of the country.'

The 17th Earl of Derby,
senior Tory Party grandee, writing in 1910

'. . . I fear I shall always be a bad Party man, being of a restless and somewhat obstinate disposition.'

Lord (Bob) Boothby, quoted in
Robert Rhodes James, *Bob Boothby* (1991)

Few politicians seemed so obviously destined for high office as Robert Boothby. Member of Parliament for East Aberdeenshire at twenty-four, he was handsome, intelligent, charming and full of self-confidence. In October 1926, aged just twenty-six, he was selected by the Chancellor of the Exchequer, Winston Churchill, to be his parliamentary private secretary. So different from the worthy but dull military types who formed the parliamentary party's backbone between the wars, Boothby was everyone's tip as the coming man.

The next year he confirmed his intellectual credentials when he co-authored a pioneering book *Industry and State* with Harold Macmillan and two other promising Conservative MPs, which pointed a way forward for the Party. It argued that governments should not be afraid of intervening in the economy in order to create economic growth and social justice. Boothby's popularity with his constituents rapidly turned East Aberdeenshire into a safe seat, ensuring that he never had to waste time looking over his shoulder.

But from then on, his career stalled. During the 1930s he was out of sympathy with both the domestic and foreign policies of his own party, whilst his personal life was complicated by a long-standing relationship with Dorothy Macmillan, Harold's wife, by whom he subsequently had a daughter. In 1940 Boothby was censured by the House of Commons for a murky episode involving the unprincipled use of Czech assets when he failed to declare a personal interest. This incident seemed to confirm the accuracy of Churchill's judgement that 'Boothby had much capacity and no virtue'. His political career never recovered.

Rather bizarrely, Boothby was proud to have been the only Conservative MP who accompanied the new Labour members when they sang the *Red Flag* in the House of Commons in 1945. He happily remained a thorn in the side of his own party, particularly over the Suez episode, but his parliamentary reputation was increasingly overshadowed by his television fame. Although he was created a life peer in 1958, his personal life began to dissolve into a morass of drink, alleged homosexuality and a notorious association with the Kray twins.

He was rescued from collapse by marriage to his second wife Wanda in 1967. His memoirs *Recollections of a Rebel*, lucid, bombastic and full of wit and wisdom, emphasised both Boothby's remarkable qualities and the extent to which they had never been fully used by the Conservative Party. He died in July 1986.

Why did Boothby's political career never fulfil its enormous promise? Was it because he lacked the stamina for ministerial office and had a tendency to self-destruct? Or was it because his fizz and sparkle − 'my religion is humour' he often remarked − were out of place in a political world of dull, grey men? Was it bad luck or bad judgement?

What is certain is that the political fate of mavericks, rebels and outsiders such as Robert Boothby often reveals more about the workings of the Conservative Party than does that of Tories who stick to the mainstream. Some on the Left would sniff at the claim that there can ever be Tory mavericks, asserting that all Conservatives, by definition, belong to the Establishment. But in fact, as Lord (Robert) Blake has pointed out, 'There is a buccaneering, adventurous, unconventional element on the Conservative side as well as on the Left.'

By daring to be unorthodox, and being punished for their daring, Conservative outsiders throw light upon the nature of Party orthodoxy. These mavericks reveal what is and what is not beyond the Tory pale, offering yet more perspectives on the hidden history of the British Conservative Party. They challenge the idea that any history of the Party can ever be presented as a seamless and dull web of unity.

These troublemakers will be remembered long after more safe and conventional politicians have been forgotten. Most back-benchers secure a minor and fleeting reputation only because of their unquestioning obedience to the Party whips. It is not the kind of epitaph which most human beings would care to have inscribed on their memorial.

'I wholly sympathize with you all because I was never "respectable" myself.' Benjamin Disraeli's message to a party dissident towards the end of his life remind us that he was the outsider who came inside. Although his father Isaac fell out with the local synagogue and subsequently brought Benjamin up within the Church of England, Disraeli's exotic looks and his flamboyance were distinctly non-English. His Jewish origins would always set him apart.

Disraeli deliberately cultivated these origins rather than hiding them. In his novel *Coningsby* he lauds the purity of Jewish blood – 'The Hebrew is an unmixed race' – which he contrasts with that of the hybrid and mixed European races. Throughout this book he eulogises an omniscient Jewish character called Sidonia, who had 'exhausted all the sources of human knowledge; was master of the learning of every nation, of all tongues dead and living, of every literature, Western and Oriental'. He was unapologetic about his Jewishness and saw it in heroic terms.

Throughout his career Disraeli was faced with anti-Semitic slurs and abuse, not least from his own colleagues who referred to him as 'that damned Jew'. But his lack of respectability also included financial misadventures as a young man. When he stood for the seat of Shrewsbury in the general election of 1841, he found the town placarded with lists of his unpaid debts amounting in all to the massive sum of £22,000. That he still won the election and eventually became leader and Prime Minister demonstrates how prodigious talent can surmount virtually every obstacle.

But the sneers never ceased. In his unfinished reminiscences, Disraeli describes attending the marriage of the Prince of Wales in 1863 together with his wife:

> There is no language, which can describe the rage, envy, and indignation of the great world. The Duchess of Marlborough went into hysterics of mortification at the sight of my wife, who was on terms of considerable intimacy with her, and said it was really shameful after the reception which the Duke had given the Prince of Wales at Blenheim, and as for the Duchess of Manchester, who had been Mistress of Robes in Lord Derby's administration, she positively passed me for the season without recognition.

Disraeli was later offered a dukedom by Queen Victoria. Clearly it was as well for the temper and blood pressure of various aristocratic ladies that he turned down the Queen's offer.

As his biographer Lord Blake has noted, Disraeli above all else scorned a 'moderate reputation'. For him, life was boom or bust – and it turned out to be boom. Many aspiring individuals no doubt made the same choice and went bust, but we do not know about them: history books always tend to record the names of winners and not losers. In his first novel *Vivian Grey* (1827), the young Disraeli had claimed that in order to enter high society a man needed breeding, money or a genius. Disraeli clearly had the third.

The same might also be said of Winston Churchill who survived in spite of his constantly changing political allegiance, from Conservative to Liberal and back again. But Churchill was always careful to retain his personal friendships which crossed political barriers and to make sure that he would always be welcome inside the governing circles. The same could not be said of his father or of his son, the two Randolphs.

Lord Randolph Churchill was perhaps the first modern demagogue because he was happy to use any slogan or cry in order to get his way; in the words of one of his admirers, he was 'unembarrassed by scruple'. Lord Randolph's volatile temperament was displayed early in his career when in 1876 he was caught up in the Aylesford divorce scandal. Trying to keep his elder brother the Marquess of Blandford out of the courts, Randolph blackmailed the Prince of Wales (later Edward VII) by threatening to reveal incriminating letters that the Prince had written to Lady Aylesford. The Prince was so angry that he challenged Randolph to a duel in France. In the end the Aylesfords separated rather than divorced and the letters never came to public light.

According to one biographer, this affair only encouraged Lord Randolph's liking for confrontation and histrionic gestures. On one occasion he theatrically trampled on a republican pamphlet in the House of Commons with which he vehemently disagreed. He was also a master of the art of publicity, embarking on national speaking tours and ensuring that his speeches and writings were continually in the public eye. If necessary, violent methods were adopted: delivering a series of inflammatory speeches in Joseph Chamberlain's Liberal fiefdom of Birmingham, Lord Randolph happily encouraged the young guard of Birmingham Conservatives to break up Liberal meetings. He was even burnt in effigy at a Coventry meeting – and was no doubt delighted to be so unpopular with his political enemies.

Randolph Churchill rose quickly within the Conservative Party but found his way to the very top barred by the existing leadership. No matter, he would enlist the help of the Party in the country. By dint of much critical talk which characterised the leadership as 'the Old Gang' and by his appeals to Tory democracy – which he himself described as chiefly opportunism – he secured a power base away from Westminster. In many ways his assault on the metropolitan party grandees presaged the impact made by Mrs Thatcher and 'Essex man' a century later.

But Churchill's tightrope tactics always carried an element of risk and eventually this led to his downfall. As Chancellor of the Exchequer under Lord Salisbury, aged just thirty-seven, he frequently threatened resignation in order to get his way. He made the mistake of threatening once too often. Salisbury called his bluff, accepted the offer and Churchill was out in the political cold from which he never returned. One academic commentator has likened the speed of his fall to that of Lucifer. Lord Randolph died of syphilis in January 1895, aged forty-six, leaving debts of well over £65,000.

Another politician who caused ructions within the Conservative Party leadership was Joseph Chamberlain, but in his case it was something of a repeat performance of what he had already done within the Liberal Party. Chamberlain, along with Winston Churchill, probably holds the record for changing political allegiance. He began as a Liberal, became a Liberal Unionist and ended up a Conservative. As one commentator has noted: 'One factor which did as much as any other to damage Chamberlain's reputation was his failure to place party loyalty at the heart of his political creed.'

Although Chamberlain was born and brought up in London, he moved to Birmingham where his dynamic energy built up the family screw-making business. He turned his attention to local affairs and was elected mayor in 1873, whereupon he initiated a highly effective programme of slum clearance, sanitary reform and civic improvement. In many ways this 'gas-and-water socialism', as some critics dubbed it, represented the first creative use of public enterprise and can be seen as a forerunner of government intervention and the Welfare State.

Chamberlain was a man of immense force; he once proposed marriage to Beatrice Potter (later Webb), who turned him down. But she remained fascinated by him, admiring his 'energy and personal magnetism, in a word, masculine force, to an almost superlative degree'. Inevitably Chamberlain's restless talents caused him to look towards national politics. Elected an MP in 1876, the next year he set up the National Liberal Federation which heralded the advent of the modern political party in terms of its organisation, membership lists and canvassing.

With his monocle and an orchid in his lapel, Chamberlain was one of the first politicians to cultivate an image which he knew the press would publicise. He was, as Stephen Koss has noted, 'Obsessively concerned with the press'.

Party leaders were less impressed by Chamberlain's radicalism. He once denounced Conservative Prime Minister Lord Salisbury as leading 'those who toil not neither do they spin', whilst his ambition soon meant that he clashed with his own leader William Gladstone, the 'Grand Old Man' of the Liberal Party who was not used to rivals. Gladstone's conversion to Home Rule for Ireland propelled Chamberlain out of the Liberals in 1886 into the eventual embrace of the Conservative Party.

His ability to attract and retain powerful loyalties was illustrated by the fact that Birmingham and the West Midlands both changed allegiance accordingly. And yet despite his undoubted charisma, Chamberlain never quite fitted in to the Tory Party. Salisbury's nephew Arthur Balfour was happy to claim that 'Joe, though we all love him dearly, does not form a chemical combination with us.' For the word chemical, read 'not one of us'. To the Cecil family, the Chamberlains would always be upstarts.

In many ways Chamberlain was the first modern professional politician. Quite apart from his preoccupation with image, there was also his willingness to employ what we would now call dirty tricks. As one contemporary journalist commented, 'The Chamberlain tradition is that you must give no quarter in politics and that the spoils are to the victors.' There is some suspicion, for instance, that Chamberlain deliberately gave bad advice to his friend and rival Sir Charles Dilke who had got embroiled in a messy divorce case, and he certainly lied when denying that he had ever met the woman centrally involved in the case.

Chamberlain was also happy to speculate in public as to the

private life of his political opponent Lord Randolph Churchill. He was probably involved too in the Charles Stewart Parnell affair, helping to persuade Captain O'Shea to name Parnell in the divorce suit which ended the Irish leader's political career.

Chamberlain's maverick qualities were evidenced by his disregard for the Party system; he caused major upheaval not just in one party but in two. In 1903 he launched a tariff reform campaign aimed at overturning the Conservative Party's economic policies and called for measures of protection behind which the British economy could be rebuilt. Free traders and other influential figures in the Party such as the 17th Earl of Derby and, naturally, the Cecil family were furious. Once again Joseph Chamberlain, helped by his son Austen, was prepared to resort to underhand tactics. A mysterious 'Confederacy' was founded which subsidised tariff reform Conservatives at elections, ignoring the free traders.

Joseph's flair for publicity was fully in evidence as he sought to convert his own party. Indeed, some of the tariff reform meetings had all the trappings and razzmatazz more usually associated with party conventions in the United States. With his energy and force of character Chamberlain might well have succeeded in seizing the leadership but for an incapacitating stroke in 1906. No matter how ostentatious his public successes, Chamberlain's private life had always been full of pain: his first two wives both died in childbirth before the age of thirty. He lingered on, tragically disabled, until his death in 1914.

Perhaps the saddest and most enduring image of 'Radical Joe' was supplied by his son Neville, who did indeed become Prime Minister, occupying the job which Joe had coveted above all. Neville once described his father as he was in 1914, just before his death: 'His only real pleasure was in watching his grandchildren. He could not even talk to them. He could only make uncouth noises which often frightened them, and it was touching to watch his efforts to attract them.'

This is one of those images which linger in the memory long after any number of dull placemen have been forgotten. The fact that Joseph Chamberlain almost managed to lead both the Liberal and the Conservative Parties gives his career an air of disappointment and failure. By contrast his less gifted sons, Austen and Neville, rose higher in the political firmament than their father: Austen as Chancellor of the Exchequer and Foreign Secretary, Neville as Prime Minister.

Yet there was always something rather driven and off-putting about Joseph Chamberlain. As Lord Salisbury once said: 'Mr Gladstone was greatly hated, but he was also greatly loved. Who loves Mr Chamberlain?' Was Chamberlain perhaps aware of this sentiment as he sat there after his stroke, disabled, unable to speak, and frightening his grandchildren?

If Lord Randolph Churchill's career was frustrated by poor judgement and Joseph Chamberlain's by the hierarchy of both Liberal and Conservative establishments suspicious of the volcanic energies and ambitions of this *nouveau* outsider, then F.E. Smith's demise was largely self-inflicted.

Like Lord Randolph Churchill, 'F.E.' was a wonderful orator at a time when political meetings were a form of public entertainment. After carefully cultivating a friendship with the 'boss' of Liverpool, Archibald Salvidge, F.E. was elected MP for Walton in 1906. Unlike virtually all maiden speeches in the House of Commons which are deliberately non-controversial, F.E.'s was a fireworks display of audacity which poured ridicule on the new Liberal administration and instantly made his name.

Even today F.E.'s quips and retorts, whether as barrister, politician or after-dinner speaker, still spring from the page. Two examples of his wit were at the expense of the Labour MP and trade unionist J.H. Thomas who would have enjoyed the jokes as much as anyone. One night Thomas was complaining about a hard night before: 'Ooh, Fred, I've got an 'ell of an 'eadache.' F.E.'s remedy was instantaneous: 'Try a couple of aspirates.' And once, after the newly elected Thomas was still trying to find his way around Parliament, he asked Smith the way to the lavatory. 'Down the corridor, first right, first left and down the stairs,' F.E. told him. 'You'll see a door marked "Gentlemen", but don't let that deter you.'

On the face of it, F.E.'s vehement support for the Ulster Unionists before the First World War, when his bellicose sentiments acquired for him the nickname of 'Galloper' Smith, suggest that he was a die-hard Tory. He once publicly assured Sir Edward Carson, leader of the Ulster Unionists, that if it came to civil war in Ireland, then 'we will undertake to give you three ships that will take over 10,000 young men of Liverpool'.

In fact, his political views were less predictable than this seeming bigotry suggests; and he was a staunch supporter of proportional representation. Always alive to the need for social reform, Smith helped found the Unionist and Social Reform Committee and in his book *Unionist Policy* (1913) he was scathing about those politicians who advocated a hands-off approach: 'The wrongs under which so many poor persons labour are so cruel and so undeniable that it is astounding that any school of political thought should conceive a policy of inactivity to be possible.'

Lloyd George, Winston Churchill and F.E. made a formidable team. In January 1919 Lloyd George appointed Smith Lord Chancellor, the youngest holder of the post since Judge Jeffreys over two hundred years before. Thereafter he played a full part in the passage of the Irish Treaty in December 1921 which temporarily halted the bloodshed in Ireland. But as the fortunes of the wartime Coalition Government led by Lloyd George inexorably declined in the years of peace, so too did those of the new Earl of Birkenhead. Unlike most other Conservatives, he had wanted the coalition to continue after 1922 because his restless energies were always uncomfortable with party orthodoxies and hierarchies.

After the coalition finally ended he never held senior office under Baldwin who heartily disapproved of the excesses of his rackety personal life. In his resentment, Birkenhead mercilessly pilloried what he regarded as the stupid and unimaginative bulk of the Conservative Party. His self-regard, never modest, now grew to immense proportions and the cartoonist David Low accurately portayed him as 'Lord Burstinghead'.

Extravagance and mounting debts – he had to support two houses, six cars, eight horses, three grooms and a yacht – led him into the clutches of the blackmailer and honours tout Maundy Gregory, whom he dubbed 'the Cheerful Giver'. He fell in love with a much younger woman, Mona Dunn, who had originally been a friend of his daughter. Such was Birkenhead's obsession with her that he actually paid a man to marry her in order to provide a cover under which their relationship could continue. Sadly Mona died of peritonitis in December 1928, aged just twenty-six.

Not even Birkenhead's constitution could withstand the sheer quantity of alcohol which he consumed every day. Baldwin dared not reappoint him Chancellor of the Exchequer in 1928 for fear of his being seen drunk in the street – Party chairman J.C.C. Davidson contrasted the sparkling talents of a sober Birkenhead with 'the one which I have seen so often, fuddled, reeling, dragging his dignity and his manhood into the dirt'. One famous after-dinner speech ended with Birkenhead gently sliding under the table with a drink in one hand, a cigar in the other and his beloved cairn terrier Jane tucked under one arm. He died of cirrhosis of the liver in September 1930, leaving his family only debts.

In one of his most famous speeches he had coined the phrase 'the glittering prizes'. F.E. Smith could have had them all but, unlike his great friend Winston Churchill, he lacked the final ingredient of self-discipline to achieve this gaol.

If in some respects F.E.'s behaviour and views were thoroughly repulsive – epitomising the anti-feminist strand within Conservatism, he regarded women as 'mere conduit pipes' – there was also something more which prompted Churchill to write: 'Some men when they die after busy, toilsome, successful lives leave a great stock of scrip and securities, of acres or factories or the goodwill of large undertakings. F.E. banked his treasure in the hearts of his friends, and they will cherish his memory till their time is come.'

Other mavericks within the Conservative ranks included those Tory reactionaries who disapproved of virtually everything in modern life and harked back to a vanished world of master and servant. Take Sir Frederick Banbury, stockbroker and MP for the City of London, who always wore a frock coat and top hat to the House of Commons. He thought social reform pampered the lower classes and never quite recovered from the introduction of women MPs, particularly as the first to take up her seat, Nancy Astor, was there on behalf of his own party.

Then there was the wonderfully named Sir Waldron Smithers.

After the Second World War, Smithers deplored the remodelling of the Conservative Party by R.A. Butler and others. Despite the vociferousness of his views, he mustered just three votes against Butler's proposals at the 1947 annual conference and only eight at the 1949 conference. He was handicapped by his buffoonish manner – in his diaries Chips Channon calls him 'an ass of a man' – and by the preposterousness of his views. Take his submission to the Beveridge Committee on Broadcasting in 1949: 'One of the main weapons of Communism is to demoralise the people. *Morning Music* and *Bright and Early* are designed to this end. All crooning and much of the jazz and rhythm should be forbidden; public taste should not be pandered to if it demands these things.'

Nancy Astor can also be classified as a maverick, simply because she was the first woman to be elected as a Conservative MP when she won at Plymouth in 1918. She always attracted extreme opinions: Chips Channon was consistently rude about her in his diaries but, as Martin Pugh has pointed out, 'Her correspondence shows that she rapidly came to be regarded by many women in Britain as their Member of Parliament.'

Like Joe Chamberlain, Nancy Astor does not seem to have been easy to love, if only because of her vehement anti-Catholic prejudice. But perhaps the last word on Nancy Astor should be left to Chips Channon, who loathed her. In his diaries, Channon describes the elderly Waldorf Astor making his way into the House of Lords in March 1944: 'She had barged in, with the usual jangle of bracelets, and I happened to see Lord Astor's tired face light up, as he smiled at her with infinite tenderness: and I realised that that mad witch is still loved by her husband, after nearly forty years of marriage.'

The joys of such a relationship are surely far more important than the transient successes of any politicking.

Another woman who was undoubtedly loved by her husband was Clementine Churchill. This did not mean, however, that she necessarily approved of Winston's friends. In particular she deprecated the influence on him of what she called the three Bs. One B was Birkenhead, another B was Beaverbrook, the Canadian press magnate who built up the *Express* empire. The last B was

Brendan Bracken, a mysterious backstage wire-puller who delighted in concealing his origins and allowing it to be thought that he was Winston's illegitimate son.

In fact Bracken was born in Ireland in February 1901 and his father Joseph was a founder of the Gaelic games. His mother's death and father's remarriage prompted Bracken to emigrate to Australia. On his return he bizarrely paid his way through Sedbergh public school, pretending to be several years younger than he was.

Bracken went into journalism where his range of contacts, mostly acquired and cultivated through an assiduous study of *Who's Who*, brought him success. On meeting Churchill he seems to have realised that here indeed was a man of destiny and for the rest of his life Bracken dedicated his career to helping his friend. One biographer has speculated that the friendship flourished because Bracken's zest and vitality could sometimes lift the dreaded 'black dog' of deep depression off Churchill's shoulders. It is certainly true that Bracken was one of the very few who dared to stand up to Churchill and contradict him.

Bracken excelled at the rough and tumble of electioneering. When Churchill was campaigning at a London by-election in 1924, Bracken had the Churchill children driven through the constituency in a cart which sported the placard 'Vote for my Daddy'. For his own election in North Paddington in 1929 he toured the constituency in a caravan emblazoned with the slogan 'Stop me and Ask one'.

With his thick glasses, ungainly manner and wayward mop of red hair, Bracken was perhaps not the most prepossessing of individuals. He sometimes tried to make up for his appearance by adopting the persona of a tough guy. His close friend and fellow Conservative MP Ronald Tree once observed: 'Above everything, he [Bracken] wanted to be considered a tough guy, and taking Damon Runyan as his model, was for ever telling stories to illustrate how tough he was. This was very largely a pose and underneath it was a gentleness he tried to hide.'

During the war Bracken was appointed Minister of Information. Afterwards he continued to expand the *Financial Times* newspaper, of which he became chairman in 1945, and built a new set of offices in the City of London. The pale pink brick of Sir Albert

Richardson's building matched the colour of the paper and a clock face still bears the pudgy image of Winston Churchill.

Bracken lived in a lovely house in Lord North Street, close to the Houses of Parliament. His personal life always remained a mystery to inquisitive outsiders and on his death in August 1958 he ensured that all his private papers were immediately destroyed. It took his chauffeur several days to dispose of them in the fireplace. Whether this concealment was due to Bracken's abiding love of mystery or his wish to cover up the more murky aspects of the Churchill circle will never be known, but his career illustrates that loyalty can sometimes pay off.

Years later, it was revealed that even on his deathbed when he was painfully dying from cancer of the throat, Bracken was concerned above all with the future of a soon-to-be-orphaned young boy.

Another loyal devotee of Winston Churchill was his only son Randolph, who possessed all the defects of his father and grandfather but few of their virtues. Brought up within the mystique of the Churchill dynasty, he was spoilt and petted from birth. His charm and talent for publicity were marred by his self-indulgence and violent temper. Randolph only won a seat in the House in 1940 because the wartime electoral truce meant he was unopposed.

He fought a spirited campaign during the 1945 election, although his plan to ride through Preston on two elephants hired from Manchester Zoo at the rate of £20 a day and draped in Tory colours was rejected by a horrified committee. Randolph consoled himself by making gramophone records of his campaign song, but still lost the seat during the Labour landslide.

Churchill's fearsome temper, which he seems to have inherited from his equally short-fused grandfather Lord Randolph, unerringly led him from one scrape to another: after losing another election in 1950 to his opponent Michael Foot, he launched into a tirade damning the local Devonport Conservatives without realising that the microphone was still switched on. If ever he was booed at a political meeting, he simply booed back.

Inevitably, Churchill's pugnacity led him to the law courts. His success in libel cases was rather better than that at elections. He lost in 1935 when he accused the then Liverpool city boss, Sir Thomas

White, of improperly influencing the election of the Lord Mayor. He won in 1956 after the *People* newspaper had referred to him as one of the 'paid hacks [who] write biased accounts of the [1955] campaign'.

Churchill won another libel action after Conservative MP Sir Gerald Nabarro had called him a coward during a speech in December 1958. He lost in 1961 when he foolishly described another journalist as a hack whose opinions were dictated by his employees. And finally he won in March 1963 when *Private Eye* in turn called him a hack.

Churchill's appalling treatment of his wives and servants showed him to be a bully and his career dissolved in a welter of drink and recrimination. He died in June 1968, barely three years after his father but with nothing to match his achievements. He had never been able to escape from Winston's shadow and his last years were spent beginning the monumental, authorised biography of his father which was eventually completed years after his death by Martin Gilbert.

Winston Churchill had likewise idolised his father, Lord Randolph, but he had been fortunate that Lord Randolph died at an early age so that he could carve out his own political career in freedom. Randolph junior could never escape the all-too-living presence of his father Winston. Perhaps the most accurate assessment of Randolph was provided by an American journalist who noted in his diary: 'Poor Randolph died today, as always, a footnote.'

Perhaps the most notable Tory maverick since the Second World War is the one who actually urged his supporters to vote for the Labour Party in 1974. That Enoch Powell still manages to retain a considerable body of admirers within the Conservative Party and elsewhere – journalist Simon Heffer has called him the most 'morally immense' politician since the Second World War – testifies to the power of the man and his ideas.

As a young man at Cambridge, Powell displayed a formidable energy and sense of determination, working phenomenally long hours from 5.30 a.m. to 9.30 p.m.; he exercised by walking to the railway station and back, perhaps the least interesting walk the city can offer. He was a professor at twenty-five, but academic life was interrupted by war service after which he joined the Conservative Research Department. He was elected MP for Wolverhampton South-West in 1950.

Powell's increasing dissatisfaction with the drift of Party policy and what he regarded as its dangerously inflationary tendencies came to a head in 1958 when the entire treasury team of Chancellor Thorneycroft, Birch and Powell resigned from the Macmillan government over the sum of £50 million. This was the overt cause of their departure. At root, however, the problem was that the three did not trust Macmillan – Powell in particular was always a free marketeer: 'Often, when I am kneeling down in church, I think to myself how much we should thank God, the Holy Ghost, for the gift of capitalism.' Nevertheless, Macmillan later brought Powell back into the Cabinet in July 1960 as Minister of Health.

There are still doubts about the extent of Powell's ambitions under Heath. He had, after all, stood against Heath at the leadership contest in 1965, attracting just fifteen votes or 5 per cent of the total. Was he staking out a position so that he could take over from Heath if, as seemed likely, Heath was defeated by Wilson in the next election due after 1966?

On 20 April 1968 Powell delivered his notorious 'rivers of blood' speech at Birmingham in front of an audience of just eighty-five people. He prophesied a future of racial conflict brought about by mass immigration. The reaction from some sections of the public was overwhelming: within a few days Powell had received more than forty-five thousand letters at his home in London with another four sacks delivered to Westminster – in all, his speech prompted over a hundred thousand letters. Hastily taken opinion polls showed much sympathy for his views.

Powell's speech effectively put him out of the mainstream of the Conservative Party. He was sacked from the Shadow Cabinet by Heath, and colleagues such as Hailsham and Whitelaw never forgave what they saw as a betrayal of trust: during a Shadow Cabinet meeting a few days before his speech at which immigration had been discussed, Powell had said nothing.

In the run up to the 1970 election Powell issued what was virtually a separate manifesto to that of the Conservative Party and during the campaign itself his press coverage equalled or outdid that of each of the three major party leaders. But if he was anxious to displace Heath then his hopes were dashed by the Conservative election victory. There was never any 'Powellite' organisation within the Conservative constituency associations and his grim and unsmiling personality prevented him building up a body of supporters.

Powell's vehement opposition to Britain's entry into the Common Market in 1973 further marginalised him. At the February 1974 election he urged Conservatives to vote Labour and actually did so himself. When a heckler at one meeting shouted that he was a Judas, Powell replied, 'Judas was paid. I am sacrificing my whole political career.'

At the October 1974 election he was elected Ulster Unionist MP for Down South, a seat which he held until 1987, but he was now regarded as a lone and almost eccentric voice within Parliament. On the face of it, the Thatcher years should have brought preferment and recognition but he was antipathetic to Mrs Thatcher herself: 'that dreadful voice, and those frightful hats'. Like Sir Frederick Banbury, Powell has never been happy with the notion of women MPs.

As a loner and intellectual maverick who prided himself on the relentless logic of his thinking, it is doubtful if Powell could ever have been a comfortable Conservative politician. Some people thought Powell was the future which the Tory Party should have embraced but gutlessly shied away from; others thought it was a pity that he ever left academic life. The touch of melancholia which surrounds the man and his career sometimes surfaces in interviews: 'I don't like things which interfere with one's heart strings. It doesn't do to awaken longings that can't be fulfilled.'

Another Tory maverick was undoubtedly Sir Keith Joseph. The son of a former Lord Mayor of London, Joseph was educated conventionally at Harrow and Oxford but his pronounced social conscience prompted him to enter politics specifically to try and relieve poverty.

His intellectual gifts ensured that he quickly became a Cabinet minister, but his record was not entirely happy. As Lord Annan has observed, Joseph was the Minister of Housing under Macmillan who helped introduce high-rise flats; the Minister of Local Government who wiped out local and regional affinities; the Minister of Health who introduced another layer of bureaucracy. Ironically enough in view of what was to come, in the Heath Cabinet of 1970 to 1974 it was Joseph and Mrs Thatcher who were the two big spenders.

The collapse of the Heath Government caused Joseph to experience a Damascan conversion: 'It was only in April 1974 that I was converted to Conservatism. I had thought that I was a Conservative but now I can see that I was not one at all.' What he meant was that he had now begun to identify monetarism and the free market philosophy as the proper path forward. Together with Mrs Thatcher, he helped set up the Centre for Policy Studies in 1975 in order to provide justification for this intellectual revolution and to 'think the unthinkable'.

In a series of characteristically tortured and anguished speeches – the intellect of the man visibly struggling with his human instincts, the resulting anguish causing critics to dub him the 'The Mad Monk' – Joseph helped challenge the entire basis of Conservatism since the Second World War. He was tipped as a leadership contender but destroyed his chances during a speech in Birmingham in October 1974 which, with its talk of 'human stock', seemed to call for restrictions on working-class breeding.

Even Conservative critics of Joseph were blunt and to the point. 'Keith Joseph?' Reginald Maudling used to remark. 'He's as nutty as a fruit cake.' To begin with, Joseph and his small band of enthusiasts were operating well outside the political orthodoxy and it was no coincidence that several of them possessed the zeal of converts: Alfred Sherman, the director of CPS, had been a communist whilst Paul Johnson, Woodrow Wyatt and Hugh Thomas had been socialists. Peter Jay was the son-in-law of Jim Callaghan and had been appointed ambassador in Washington by Callaghan's Labour Government.

What might justifiably have been labelled 'Josephism' became instead Thatcherism, mainly because he lacked Mrs Thatcher's surer political instincts. Whereas she ensured that she remained within the Party mainstream, keeping her head down if necessary, Joseph allowed himself to become isolated and marginalised.

He was appointed Secretary of State for Industry in Mrs Thatcher's Government in 1979, specifically to implement his ideas of Government non-intervention. He was not successful, as fellow Cabinet minister James Prior noted: 'He simply was not the right choice as he was constantly regaled with tales of woe from industrialists and pleas to be baled out from the state-owned industries. Being a decent, soft-hearted man, he found this unbearably difficult.'

Joseph was moved to the Department of Education and then retired to the House of Lords. Whatever his failings as a minister, few mavericks have the satisfaction, as he had done, of seeing their heresies become orthodoxies. Yet it is surely this hope which drives mavericks on in the face of their colleagues' indifference and hostility.

Similarly Humphry Berkeley was a Tory backbencher who never attained ministerial office but had more influence on British politics than many who did. It was Berkeley who in the early 1960s led the campaign to introduce properly contested leadership elections, which bore fruit in 1965 when Edward Heath became leader; Berkeley who seconded the bill which suspended hanging; and Berkeley who initiated the legalisation of homosexuality between consenting adults.

The last was the kind of measure guaranteed to go down badly with many of the electorate. During the 1966 election campaign, Berkeley later recalled, 'I had 40 meetings in the constituency [of Lancaster], and I had to talk about sex all the time. That was all they asked me about.' Berkeley duly lost his seat.

He then changed parties with bewildering regularity – his autobiography was accurately called *Crossing The Floor* (1972) – but, like Joseph, he had seen heresies become accepted. Berkeley died in November 1994.

It takes personal courage to be an outsider; there was, for example, the sort of bravery which Boothby exhibited in visiting his personal but not political friend Sir Oswald Mosley when the latter was interned during the Second World War.

Such strength of character does not necessarily make for easy or likeable individuals. Some people found F.E. Smith arrogant and offensive, Astor a perpetual irritant, Boothby a braggart, Powell distant and unfriendly and Randolph Churchill vile – Evelyn Waugh once said of him after a successful hospital operation: 'Trust the doctors to find the only part of Randolph which wasn't malignant and remove that.' In particular, their families seem to have borne the brunt of their egocentricity and personal obsessions.

The rise of the career politician and the increasing power of the whips' office and the executive have meant that fewer characters now enter politics, let alone prosper there. Eccentricity is no longer regarded as admirable or even tolerable, but rather as evidence of potential unreliability. It also makes individuals vulnerable to the attentions of the tabloid press.

Even to possess independent views can sometimes be disastrous for any Conservative MP wishing to be more than a backbencher. Baronet Sir Anthony Meyer, Eton, Oxford and the Foreign Office, was and is a One Nation Tory. Naturally he did not prosper in the Thatcherite years of the 1980s. Finally in 1989, disgusted by his own party's negative campaign for that year's European elections, Meyer challenged Mrs Thatcher for the leadership.

Meyer knew that he stood no chance of victory, but was determined to make his point. In the event, no fewer than thirty-three Conservative MPs voted for Meyer and another twenty-seven abstained. Some of Mrs Thatcher's fiercest supporters, including the then party chairman Kenneth Baker and former Chief Whip Lord (John) Wakeham, have commented on how damaging the contest was to the Prime Minister. Chris Patten likened Meyer to 'the little boy [who] had run out of the crowd and asked what clothes the Empress was wearing' – one of the maverick's main aims in life. Meyer was promptly deselected by his constituency in Wales. His political career might have been at an end, but here is a case of the foolhardy maverick who, knowingly or not, sets momentous events in train.

In order to carve out a successful political career today, aspirants have to start young. Few of them have time to amass the range of experiences or interests displayed in the past. Fifty years ago Iain Macleod, briefly to become Chancellor of the Exchequer under

Edward Heath before his early death in July 1970, earned a living as a professional bridge player. Today such a raffish pursuit would be frowned upon; it is better to be a political researcher or in PR if you want to get on. Television journalist Jeremy Paxman attended a series of Conservative selection board meetings for his book *Friends In High Places* (1990). He was not impressed:

> With parliamentary life now dominated by machines rather than individuals, the back benches are packed with men and women whose only hope is to be offered a job in the Whips' Office or a junior ministerial brief. Even those who have long since abandoned hope of winning Downing Street's favour have increasingly won their places after passing through a selection process which prevents the eccentric and the too-individualistic getting a look-in. Small wonder the back benches look so dull.

There is certainly no place here for the Lord Randolphs, the F.E.s, the Boothbys, the Waldron Smithers or the Powells. In the 1940s and 1950s, three successive party leaders – Churchill, Eden and Macmillan – had at some point in their careers rebelled noisily and publicly against the Tory Party hierarchy. By contrast, the last three leaders of the Party – Heath, Thatcher and Major – have all risen to the top by closely hugging the inside track.

Further evidence of this change is the decline in the art of oratory. Politicians in the past had to master the skills of public speaking, learning how to deal with hecklers whilst inspiring huge numbers of people without the assistance of microphones. Virtually all the individuals discussed above were masters of the art. Perhaps two things strike one most today. One is the extraordinary length of their speeches. Disraeli's speech at the Free Trade Hall, Manchester in April 1872 lasted no less than three and a quarter hours. The sixty-seven-year-old statesman sustained himself by drinking white brandy, getting through two bottles by the end.

The second is the size of the audiences. One Conservative MP at the end of the nineteenth century, Ellis Ashmead Bartlett, was described as a 'five-thousand audience man'. In an age without microphones, clearly one requirement for any politician was to possess a powerful speaking voice – one reason why so few women were politically effective.

Lord Randolph Churchill, for instance, was a formidable speaker whilst F.E. Smith liked nothing better than a mass meeting at which he could display his quick wit. On one occasion he declared: 'And now I shall tell you exactly what the Government has done for all of you.' A woman in the gallery shouted out, 'Nothing!' Birkenhead's response was immediate:

> My dear lady, the light in this hall is so dim as to prevent a clear sight of your undoubted charms, so that I am unable to say with certainty whether you are a virgin, a widow, or a matron, but in any case I will guarantee to prove that you are wrong. If you are a virgin flapper, we have given you the vote; if you are a wife, we have increased employment and reduced the cost of living; if you are a widow, we have given you a pension – and if you are none of these, but are foolish enough to be a tea drinker, we have reduced the tax on sugar.

As his friend Winston Churchill noted, it is the spontaneity of the response which is so staggering. Of course some observers have always distrusted the flamboyant word-smith: in Anthony Trollope's novel *Phineas Finn* (1869), there is the character of Turnbull who, 'being an orator, was not called upon either to study detail or master fact'. Today Turnbull would be an endangered species: speeches are the polished and bland result of a battery of speech writers, and are most carefully rehearsed, as the pedestrian performances at the annual conferences demonstrate. Much care is lavished on the soundbite, the telling phrase or sentence suitable for television transmission.

Of recent Conservative politicians only Michael Heseltine possesses a streak of demagoguery and it has come to something when Cabinet minister John Redwood has to practise his smile in front of a television monitor.

Not only will political life be duller without its share of mavericks, but their disappearance will also deprive the Conservative Party of much potential. Dedicated to the pursuit of power, the Conservative

Party has never worried about appropriating people and ideas from any background if they are the means to that end.

One thing is certain: if the Party managers between the wars had managed to eliminate all but orthodox professional career politicians then Winston Churchill would never have survived and the world may have looked very different.

Less Than Meets The Eye

Official faces of the Conservative Party

'Nothing was in the shop-window; everything was in store.'

> Stanley Baldwin's son on his father, 1955

'. . . the old trick of the British upper classes; charm through self-denigration.'

> Paul Foot, 1989

'Really? They weren't meant to be interesting.'

> Alleged response of Viscount (Willie) Whitelaw
> when someone told him that they had found his
> memoirs interesting

Once, when he was asked a difficult question, Winston Churchill replied: 'Only history can relate the full story.' He then paused, before continuing: 'And I shall write the history.'

This typically Churchillian story is a reminder that what we think of as history is created by historians and, like it or not, the ways in which Conservatives and the Conservative Party have been portrayed in the past undoubtedly influence our perception of them.

This image has been largely created in one of two ways: either by the writings of insiders, namely the memoirs, autobiographies and diaries of active Conservatives who have played some part in what they are describing. Or, secondly, by the work of outsiders, namely commentators, journalists and historians who are on the outside looking in.

The heart of even the most assiduous political commentator sinks when surveying the library shelves which groan with the weight of Conservative memoirs and autobiographies. It seems hard to believe that there is room for yet another account of, say, 'My Part in the Thatcher Years' – but no, here comes a further batch. So far, no fewer than fifteen former members of Mrs Thatcher's Cabinets have published books which contain material on Conservative Governments of the 1980s: Lords Prior, Carrington, Pym, Hailsham, Gilmour, Young, Walker, Ridley, Whitelaw, Tebbit, Lawson, Sir Norman Fowler and Kenneth Baker. Lord Howe's account has just swelled the ranks. And, of course, there is Lady Thatcher herself.

If one feels a need for yet more, these accounts can be supplemented by the views of Mrs Thatcher's junior ministers such as Alan Clark, or the memoirs of her press secretary Sir Bernard Ingham, or the autobiography of backbencher Julian Critchley, or daughter Carol Thatcher's diary of the 1983 election, or insiders' versions of the 1987 election campaign . . . And on and on it goes.

This outpouring is a comparatively recent phenomenon. In the past, most Conservative leaders scrupulously observed the doctrines of collective responsibility and official secrecy, resisting the temptation to write their memoirs. In fact, they probably did not even consider doing so. Of the Tory leaders up to the Second World War, none wrote formal accounts, although Arthur Balfour left behind some unfinished and uncontroversial autobiographical jottings.

Things changed with the advent of Sir Winston Churchill who had always relied upon his pen to supplement his income – to such effect that he was awarded the Nobel Prize for Literature in 1953. In 1962, three years before his death, a study of Churchill's literary output found that he had published 143 different books and 524 newspaper and magazine articles from which he had earned in the region of £4 million. A hundred and five books had already been written about the man. 'Churchilliana,' claimed the article, 'is now a minor publishing industry comparable to gardening, cookery, and algebra as a money-spinner.' In the intervening thirty years, this minor industry has become a major one.

Churchill's example opened the floodgates and it now seems to be accepted that Conservative leaders (plus Liberals and Labour) are entitled to earn a little something in retirement. Anthony Eden's three-volume opus was followed by Harold Macmillan's six. Lord Home has published his memoirs which are typically modest and brief. Sir Edward Heath is under contract to publish his version of events, a book which has so far been a long time in the making. Lady Thatcher's *The Downing Street Years* (1993) covered just her eleven years in office, but a subsequent 'prequel', *The Path to Power*, appeared in 1995 to elaborate on her early years, and further instalments are a possibility.

Lady Thatcher's high-pressure marketing of her memoirs, complete with book signings, publicity fanfares and endless radio, press and television interviews, took the technique of the hard sell to unprecedented heights and would have amazed her predecessors. It also confirmed the changing character of the modern Conservative Party. In the past, many Tory MPs saw their political careers in terms of public duty and not personal advancement. Unwritten rules decreed that internal party dissensions should on no account be paraded in public for fear of damaging the image of unity on which the Party has always relied so heavily. By contrast, everyone even remotely involved in the downfall of Mrs Thatcher in 1990 has had their published say.

Perhaps encouraged by the voluble example of their leaders, more and more senior Conservatives have also published books about themselves and their political careers. Few can resist justifying their actions, hoping to nudge posterity along the right lines. The public is often less interested. Most secondhand bookshops contain their full quota of, say, the Earl of Woolton's *Memoirs* or *Political Adventure* by the Earl of Kilmuir.

Some Conservatives even have two stabs at writing their mem-oirs: Robert Boothby, John Baker White and Lord Hailsham, for example. Indeed, the back-bench MP and journalist Julian Critchley has mastered the art of recycling the same stories through a number of books. Clearly it is difficult to resist one final chance to appear before the public eye.

What generalisations can be made about this avalanche of print? First of all, few of these books could ever be described as an exciting read. Their authors all seem to feel that no detail of their political career is too trivial for inclusion. They invariably start off well with either elegiac or horrific memories of childhood, make their way through public school and Oxbridge, contain a sprinkling of wartime reminiscences, and then dwindle into a dull and pompous plod through a succession of appointments and ministerial posts. We are privileged to see the gallant author grapple heroically with administrative problems at the Milk Marketing Board or, say, road traffic policy in Sheffield in 1971.

Most memoirs are naturally produced by politicians in the twi-light of their careers, fully aware of their own gravitas and weight of years. Well buttoned up, they eschew the personal in favour of the official and pompous. Even a sparkling conversationalist like Harold Macmillan, still capable of minting fresh and pithy comments on the Thatcher administration well into his eighties, was responsible for six volumes which his sympathetic biographer Alistair Horne remarks are notable for their 'blandness'.

It is perhaps too much to ask of any politician that, after a career spent wading through the contents of red boxes or drawing up manifestos and policy documents, they should still retain any literary skills. Some politicians, for example, excel at communicating in one media but not others. Dr Charles Hill, the well-known 'radio doctor', was superb at delivering party broadcasts after the Second World War. His autobiography *Both Sides of the Hill* (1964) is rather less compelling. Similarly, Cecil Parkinson was renowned for his communication skills, but one would never have guessed it from his *Right at the Centre* (1992).

Another drawback is the desire not to give too much away: one may settle a few old personal scores, perhaps, but not breach too blatantly the longstanding Tory belief that disagreements should be kept out of the public domain. The demands of publishers and press eager for titbits sit uneasily with traditional codes of Party conduct, producing a curiously flat style of writing.

These faults seem especially pertinent when one trawls through memoirs of the Thatcher years, most of which are ponderous and wooden. Few moments of passion are permitted to intrude, except when the author strenuously denies responsibility for dreaming up the ill-fated poll tax. In the past, many Tory politicians reviewing their careers made copious use of public school and military metaphors; this has now gone, replaced instead by a colourless managerial lanaguage.

One exception to this bland façade is Lord (Nigel) Lawson's *The View from No. 11*, which might have been subtitled 'God protect me from my friends'. Apart from being nearly a thousand pages long and taking the palm for personal vanity – the book contains endless photographs of his less than photogenic self – Lawson offers a distinctly unflattering portrait of former colleagues: Sir Ian Gilmour is 'sour'; Nicholas Ridley 'a political liability'; 'not even his greatest friends would describe him [Kenneth Baker] as either a profound thinker or a man with a mastery of detail'; Peter Walker is 'unsound'. And these are individuals supposedly on the same side of the Party divide.

Jim Prior's account of the 1980s likewise testifies to the hostility which Mrs Thatcher and her supporters aroused in the old guard of the Party. Her early treasury teams, for instance, had never run a whelk stall and clearly Prior feels that even this would have been beyond their capabilities: 'Their attitude to manufacturing industry bordered on the contemptuous.' Both the Prime Minister and Prior relentlessly leaked to the press in order to advance their position – the official Labour opposition, on the other hand, is barely mentioned.

Television programmes featuring individual Conservatives have been more revealing (and mercifully shorter) than the politician's considered and formal account. Margaret Thatcher's *The Downing Street Years* is long on detail – she helpfully lists the acronyms of scores of long-forgotten committees featured in her pages

– but is short of any sense of the former Prime Minister's style or convictions. Rather more illuminating was a four-part television documentary which was screened on BBC1 in October to November 1993 at the same time as the publication of her memoirs. These programmes showed Margaret Thatcher in full eye-blazing flow, taking no prisoners and sparing no opponent from her lash.

The same could be said of the television programmes devoted to Norman Tebbit and Kenneth Baker which were both more revealing than their memoirs. At one point, full of barely concealed anger, Tebbit told a story of Macmillan attending a debate at the House of Commons and commenting in his best patrician and disdainful way on Tebbit's cockney accent – an episode which reveals much about the changing character of the Tory Party in the 1980s. One looks in vain for this story in Tebbit's *Upwardly Mobile*.

These personal touches make politicians' reminiscences come to life, but it is precisely these touches which seem to be most rigorously eschewed in case the author gives too much away. Take Lord David Young's *The Enterprise Years* (1990) which carries the less than riveting subtitle 'A Businessman in the Cabinet'.

Young himself seems rather bored by the book, admitting at one point that 'When I read what I have written, I find it curiously one-dimensional.' And so it is, except for two stories. When Young was brought into the Cabinet by Margaret Thatcher, he found that sacked minister Arthur Cockfield refused to surrender his official car or office: 'I had no office, no private secretary, no staff, no job description and nothing to do.' It sounds like the complaint of *Yes, Minister*'s Jim Hacker, newly appointed to the Ministry of Administrative Affairs.

Similarly, Young describes sitting on the platform at the Tory Party conference the morning after the Brighton bomb in 1984. He noticed that many of his colleagues were wearing brand new suits and shoes which still had the price tickets stuck to the soles – the police hadn't allowed them back into the Grand Hotel to pick up their clothes, and outfitters in Brighton had enjoyed a sudden surge of early-morning patronage.

One enduring feature of all Tory memoirs without exception is that even the dullest perk up whenever Winston Churchill makes an entrance. Suddenly the book crackles into life as he effortlessly occupies centre stage and the good stories begin to flow. Former Chief Whip James Stuart describes Churchill working in bed, surrounded by official papers. Churchill's cat was asleep on one of the official red boxes and discussion of an important issue had to be suspended because the relevant paper was in that precise box and on no account was the cat to be disturbed. In 1947 Stuart was deputed by his colleagues gently to inform Churchill that it was possibly time for him to retire as leader. Incandescent with rage, Churchill banged the floor vigorously with his stick.

The Earl of Kilmuir (Sir David Maxwell-Fyfe) tells of Churchill, who enjoyed a drink or three, comparing his appearance with that of the teetotal Sir Stafford Cripps: 'I get the drink. Stafford Cripps gets the blue nose. That's life, David.' Once Churchill was in a bad mood and started shouting away at the top of his voice. His poodle Rufus, shut up in the next room, also began to make a commotion. Churchill called one of his staff: 'Take that dog away. We cannot both be barking at once.'

No other politician has had quite such an invigorating effect on colleagues, acquaintances and foe alike.

If one had to pick a shortlist of the most rewarding of these Conservative memoirs and autobiographies, which titles would appear? One entrant would certainly be Churchill's own *My Early Life* (1930). Although it is best remembered for his schoolboy stories, the book has much on British politics at the turn of the century. There is Gladstone in his eighties, piloting a Home Rule bill: 'The Grand Old Man looked like a great white eagle at once fierce and splendid. His sentences rolled forth majestically and everyone hung upon his lips and gestures, eager to cheer or deride.' There are also splendid descriptions of vigorous electioneering when crowds of five or six thousand were the norm at political meetings.

Churchill knew how to write. The same is true of two other Conservative politicians, namely John Buchan and Duff Cooper. Buchan is discussed more fully in the next chapter, but it is fair to say that his political career – eight years in the House of Commons as MP for the Scottish Universities – was not terribly memorable. In *Memory Hold-The-Door* (1940), he disposes of a period that covered the Great Crash, the onset of the depression, the collapse of a Labour Government in 1931 and the rise of Hitler, with the sentence: 'In my time, as I have said, there were no great political storms brewing.'

Duff Cooper was a more prominent political figure and *Old Men Forget* (1953) charts the ups and downs of a career which ended at the British Embassy in Paris. A glance at the index shows how wide-ranging were the enthusiasms and friendships of this urbane individual. Published just months before Duff Cooper's death, the book ends: 'I love the sunlight but I cannot fear the coming of the dark.'

Perhaps the main reason why these books are so thoroughly alive is that Churchill, Buchan and Cooper had many other interests. Politics was certainly important to them, particularly to Churchill, but they also revelled in books, wrote biographies, loved history and had many non-political friends.

Another contender for the recommended shortlist is, surprisingly perhaps, the memoir of Sir David Maxwell-Fyfe, who became Lord Chancellor and ended up as the Earl of Kilmuir. On the face of it, Maxwell-Fyfe's story is one of a talented and hard-working lawyer who hugged the inside track and studiously edged along the path of political advancement. But Kilmuir clearly had a pretty tart tongue and couldn't stand his Labour opponents. His hostile portraits of Hugh Gaitskell and Aneurin Bevan in the 1950s shed a rather different light on a time when both major political parties were supposedly as alike as two peas in a pod.

Kilmuir also recorded one memorable episode in *Political Adventure* (1964). After Eden's sudden resignation in 1957, senior party grandee Lord Salisbury was in charge of finding his successor: either Rab Butler or Harold Macmillan. Kilmuir describes the vocally challenged Salisbury calling in Cabinet ministers one by one and demanding: 'Wab or Hawold?'

Some autobiographies are immensely revealing about the Conservative Party itself, amongst them Reginald Bevins' *The Greasy*

Pole. Bevins was a working-class Conservative from Liverpool who never really fitted into Harold Macmillan's Tory Party. He noted that when Macmillan sacked one-third of his Cabinet in July 1962, the axe fell disproportionately on those from relatively humble backgrounds, even though he himself survived. The next year Bevins attended a high-powered Government meeting at Chequers and observed that of those present only he and Ernest Marples did not possess landed estates.

In many ways *The Greasy Pole*, published in 1965, anticipated the changes which took place a generation later under Mrs Thatcher; in particular, Bevins called both for the denationalisation of certain public monopolies and for rank and file Conservatives to assert themselves against the Old Etonians who dominated the existing party hierarchy.

Valuable, too, is Robert Boothby's *Recollections of a Rebel* which offers a fine reflection of the author: pompous, egocentric, vain but with a magnificent sweep illustrating all too clearly that he was no conventional party man or professional career politician. Another entrant is Lord Hailsham's very readable *The Sparrow's Flight* (1990). The 'cheeky chappie' of the British Conservative Party, Hailsham's memoirs are full of interest once again because of the range of the author's political career which includes the Oxford by-election of 1938 and the experience of being Lord Chancellor under Mrs Thatcher.

Also worth reading is Sir Ian (now Lord) Gilmour's *Dancing with Dogma*. Gilmour was always a notable Tory exponent of the One Nation philosophy – or a 'wet' as such individuals were called in the 1980s. His hatchet job on the Thatcher years could not have been bettered by any Labour opponent of Mrs Thatcher. Gilmour records elegantly but with passion his ire and frustration at what he saw as the minority takeover of the Conservative Party.

Another non-Thatcherite Tory who provided a witty and irreverent look at the events of the 1980s was MP Julian Critchley. In February 1980 he published an anonymous article in the *Observer* newspaper which was critical of Mrs Thatcher. The identity of the writer was soon discovered, ensuring that Critchley failed to progress beyond the backbenches. In his book *Westminster Blues*

(1985), later reworked as *Palace of Varieties* (1989), he offered a cheeky portrait of the changing Conservative Party in the 1980s. Previously, claimed Critchley, 'Gentlemen went into politics as an extension of their social obligation', but Mrs Thatcher's Party was now full of businessmen, small-town surveyors and estate agents.

In 1994 Critchley published his autobiography *A Bag of Boiled Sweets* – sweets being the only safe pleasure for any politician – which contains a full measure of witticisms. Canvassing in Aldershot in the 1970 election, for instance, Critchley describes being driven around the constituency in the back of an open Land Rover, 'beribboned like a bullock'.

He notes the changing nature of the parliamentary party – 'Thirty-five years ago you could tell a Tory just by looking at him ... A Tory MP was well suited' – and laments too the disappearance of the knights of the Shires. Critchley tells a marvellous story of his return to Parliament in 1970:

> Gone were such luminaries as Sir Walter Bromley-Davenport whose brief sojourn at the whips' office has passed into legend. In those days the whips were posted at the various exits to discourage MPs from sneaking off home after the ten o'clock vote. Walter pursued an errant Member, caught up with him and booted him up the arse. The arse belonged to the Belgian ambassador. War was averted, but Bromley-Davenport was promptly replaced as a whip by the young Ted Heath. Such are the vagaries of fate.

Churchill, Buchan, Cooper, Kilmuir, Bevins, Boothby, Hailsham, Gilmour, Critchley: these seem to me to be the pick of a pretty mixed bunch. Others have their moments or even chapters, but find it difficult to keep going from start to finish.

Having handed out plaudits, perhaps there should be brickbats as well. If all memoirs are selective, then some are rather more selective than others. Of numerous choice specimens in this category, pride of place goes to the mendacious versions which retired statesmen peddled about the Suez episode in 1956.

We now know for certain that, despite vehement assertions at the time, the British, French and Israeli Governments were working hand in hand. This did not stop Sir Anthony Eden from the bland assertion in *Full Circle* (1960): 'On October 25th a report came that Israel was about to mobilize. She did so on the 27th and moved against Egypt on the evening of the 29th.' This statement was brazenly economical with the truth. The Earl of Kilmuir went further, flatly denying there had been any collusion and that, in fact, the British had striven to prevent military action.

Rab Butler was another eminent statesman whose memory proved fallible in retirement. In his short and elegant *The Art of the Possible* (1971), he skated unconvincingly over his pro-appeasement views of the late 1930s which embarrassingly lasted well into 1940. Less distinguished examples are provided by the numerous Conservative MPs such as John Baker White and Douglas Dodds-Parker who omit from their memoirs any mention of their links with the intelligence services, generally the only thing of interest in their political careers.

A more recent contender in this genre of half-truth and omission is Margaret Thatcher's *The Downing Street Years*. If recent revelations about 'Iraqgate' or the Pergau dam affair in Malaysia tempt readers to scurry in search of what the former Prime Minister says about both episodes, they should save themselves the trouble: neither are mentioned.

If it is the personal voice which makes some political memoirs so much more interesting than others, then the reader turns to diaries and letters with greater expectancy – and, by and large, these expectations are met.

It has been said that there is nothing more boring than a discreet diary – and surely nothing more unpublishable. The Bodleian in Oxford holds the three-volume diary of Harry Crookshank, a senior Conservative who witnessed at first-hand many events of the 1930s, 1940s and 1950s under a series of Prime Ministers.

Mounting excitement as one tries to decipher Crookshank's difficult handwriting soon subsides. Virtually every entry begins with an account of the weather. If you want to know whether it rained on 18 September 1949, then Crookshank is your man. There are indeed passages of interest (most of which are referred to elsewhere in this book): at one point Crookshank shows how petty politics can be. A minister in Neville Chamberlain's Government up to 1940, Crookshank was miffed that the Prime Minister failed to take more interest in his work. When Chamberlain departs at a moment crucial in European history – the Germans rampant in Europe, Britain tottering – Crookshank pettishly notes on 10 May 1940: 'I find it hard to forgive his never mentioning coal to me in two years.'

The Bodleian also contains another unpublished diary of much greater interest, namely the jottings of the Earl of Woolton, Cabinet minister during the war, Conservative Party chairman after it, and a man whose enormous talents were matched only by the size of his ego.

Once again, the interesting parts of Woolton's account are mentioned elsewhere in this book – especially the plotting against Churchill during the war – but his diary does contain several hostile portraits of political colleagues, unlike his formal memoirs which are much more guarded. It is also valuable because Woolton covers a twenty-year period, from 1940 to 1960, although in the latter years he seems to have written his diary only intermittently.

Somewhat ironically in view of Woolton's own devotion to self-image, he notes how Churchill couldn't resist playing to the crowd. In June 1942, for instance, Woolton travels in the Prime Minister's car: 'It was interesting to see the way in which he always had his eye on the public whilst we were talking in his car; he was waving his hat and showing the V sign to the people as we passed. I was very surprised that so great a man should have this sense of public showmanship on a journey which he must have taken thousands of times.'

Woolton's diary deserves to be published. The Historians' Press has published the diaries of other Conservatives such as Sir Robert Sanders and tetchy Cuthbert Headlam, and the letters exchanged by Beaverbrook and Bracken. Unfortunately, the cost of such scholarly productions means they are unlikely to penetrate far outside acadamic circles.

This limited appeal is certainly not the case with Chips Channon's diaries. Socialite, gossip and art connoisseur, Channon was also Conservative MP for Southend-on-Sea from 1935 until his death in 1958. He portrays a lost world of private houses in Belgrave Square and hobnobbing with the royals, but there is much about Parliament and the Conservative Party. There is Prime Minister Baldwin being amiable to new MPs, the ups and downs of Churchill's career in the 1930s and an unflattering portrait of Sir Anthony Eden: 'He is, always has been, and ever will be, a lightweight.'

What makes Channon's diary, indeed any diary, special is the intermingling of high and low, of farce and tragedy. At one point – sandwiched between the Abyssinian crisis and his own election as an MP – Channon finds a lost dog. He manages to track down the owner and returns the dog in his Rolls-Royce: 'He was a lean little man of fifty and he cried when he saw his dog – burst into tears as he hugged the animal to his bosom.'

Another diarist is Douglas Hurd, and no doubt in time his account of the Thatcher years will shed much light on what really happened. His sketch of the Heath Government of 1970 to 1974, *An End to Promises* has already been published. It is a perceptive combination of the personal and political. There are snapshots of the Prime Minister himself – 'Instead of speaking to people, Mr Heath would too often speak at them' – and a powerful account of an administration collapsing in slow motion.

Hurd also includes reflections which emphasise how scholar-politicians can bring their unique combination of gifts to bear: 'Because historians tend to analyse one subject at a time they sometimes lose sight of the pell-mell of politics. Problems crowd in on top of each other, competing for scarce time.'

One of Hurd's ministerial colleagues in the 1980s was Alan Clark, and he of course has published his writings. The *Diaries* leave the more considered and stuffy memoirs of his Conservative colleagues in government far behind. This is not just because they were produced by someone who actually knows how to write. Like Samuel Pepys, he is an inveterate opponent of 'political correctness' and happily jots down what most diarists carefully and discreetly omit.

There is the lusting after unavailable young women; the irritation at a bad train journey probably caused by one of British Rail's statutory quota of disabled employees having an epileptic fit; the admission that he can't answer Robin Day's direct questions and often doesn't know what he's voting on in the House of Commons; the unflattering picture of his local Plymouth association. As with Channon, there is the mixture of high and low. Clark recalls once being phoned up by the *Western Evening Herald* who urgently wanted to know his reaction to being blacklisted by the Esperanto Society.

As befits a historian, Clark also has a sense of the past. The Tory Party, he observes, 'knows it is an old whore that has been around for 400 years'. Even though he was a devoted admirer of 'The Lady', his diaries vividly reveal both the virtues and vices of the old patrician wing of the Tory Party as it gently expires: he found it snobbish, arrogant, humorous, honest.

The candour of the diarist means that the book is full of cutting sketches of internal party politics, revealing the dissensions and conflicts rarely on public display. Taking tea at the Brighton Metropole during the 1984 party conference, Clark reflects: 'So much traffic of "notables", so much peeping, prying and listening to do. The egos flare and fade and flare again like a stubble fire.' Later he observes even more caustically, 'There are no true friends in politics. We are all sharks circling, and waiting, for traces of blood to appear in the water.'

Most compelling of all in Clark's *Diaries* is the way he records the gradual disintegration of Mrs Thatcher's position as Prime Minister during the course of 1990. After eleven years, he notes, the parliamentary Party is sick of her. Members of the Cabinet begin to leak information to the press: 'We're almost getting to the point where they are no longer afraid of her.' Mrs Thatcher suffers from 'bunker syndrome' and her army begins to fragment: 'Whole units are mutinous and in flight.' And a few days later, 'The Party is virtually out of control . . .'

The mishandled leadership contest at the end of 1990 leads to disaster for Mrs Thatcher at the first ballot and soon she is brutally and ignominiously shuffled off the political stage.

Exit Mrs Thatcher, and with her our diarist's hopes of Cabinet office.

In conclusion, how should one rate the quality of the insiders' perspective on the Conservative Party? From such an outpouring, one can recommend only the memoirs and autobiographies mentioned here, together with the writings of Chips Channon, Douglas Hurd and Alan Clark. There is little gold but much dross – when these works are good they are very very good, but when they are bad they are awful.

How have the outsiders, namely historians and commentators, fared?

'Celts are still apt to be unwashed.' It is hard to believe that this is the considered opinion of one of Britain's leading historians, Dr A.L. Rowse. If prejudice is in the eye of the beholder, then clearly some beholders have worse eyesight than others.

In the previous section, we saw that Conservative insiders and activists had, through the means of memoirs, autobiography and diary, offered at best partial and incomplete accounts. Surely the non-partisan authors have done better?

The obvious starting point is the political biography. The British are well known for their apparent fondness for biographies and indeed most eminent Conservatives have been studied, many more than once. The Victorian approach was that statesmen could only be dealt with in reverential multi-volume tomes; size alone would testify to the subject's eminence.

Messrs Moneypenny and Buckle, for instance, devoted six volumes to Benjamin Disraeli whilst Lady Gwendolen Cecil wrote four volumes about her brother Lord Salisbury and was still going strong when death, perhaps mercifully for her readership, intervened. This century it is Joseph Chamberlain who has received the full treatment, his life being covered in six volumes by journalist J.L. Garvin and Conservative MP Julian Amery.

Today, however, the economics of publishing mitigate against such projects – with one exception. Martin Gilbert has meticulously covered the life of Sir Winston Churchill in eight volumes, a massive project which has been supplemented by hefty companion volumes containing documentation and records, as well as by one-volume condensations, by pictorial accounts and so on.

There are several difficulties with such a comprehensive approach. Gilbert's thirty-year quest for Churchill – itself the subject of another recent Gilbert volume entitled *In Search of Churchill* – together with the sheer weight of information presented means that the author inevitably struggles to convey any sense of Churchill as a human being. The man himself is continually submerged beneath a torrent of encycylopaedic detail. As historian Sir Robert Rhodes James, himself once a Conservative MP, rather tartly commented: 'To have made Churchill boring was, in its way, a remarkable achievement.'

The second problem is that although Gilbert claims to give the reader all the information he or she needs in order to reach an opinion on Churchill, in fact Gilbert only includes the detail which he himself thinks is relevant or interesting. For example, some volumes cover just two years in Churchill's life and yet the last twenty years between 1945 and 1965 – when he was after all Prime Minister for four more years – is dispensed with in just one volume.

Many important facets of Churchill's career are simply omitted by the author. To give just two examples: earlier we saw that in 1948 Churchill helped set up a series of semi-legal rivers companies (see Chapter 7) in order to assist the Conservative Party get around certain tax requirements regarding wills and legacies. Turn to the relevant Gilbert volume and you will find that this episode is not mentioned. Nor is there anything relating to Churchill's secret acceptance of American money after the war to help finance a United Europe. Even in a project totalling millions of words, Gilbert is unable to spare a paragraph for either topic.

It is, of course, impossible to include everything – any biographer is faced with the problem of choice but not, it seems, Martin Gilbert. The amassing of detailed information in order to present a 'complete' narrative account is a worthy ambition, but a more selective method inevitably becomes an act of interpretation, and the reader deserves to be told how this has been done.

Other studies of Churchill which narrow the focus are often more revealing. For instance, Rhodes James published an account with the provocative subtitle 'A Study in Failure 1900–1939' that examined the decidedly patchy political career of Churchill between the wars, and Paul Addison's *Churchill on the Home Front 1900–1955* reviewed his achievements in terms of domestic policy.

In their constant search to sell books and to find a good new angle, publishers sometimes commission books which rather self-consciously pry into corners and are faintly scandalous: ordeal by revisionist. Churchill in particular is now undergoing this process. John Pearson's *Citadel of the Heart*, for instance, looks at the decidedly tempestuous and not always very happy marriage of Churchill and his wife Clemmie.

The statesman's alleged racism is analysed in Norman Rose's excellent one-volume study and also appears as part of a sustained indictment of Churchill by Clive Ponting. Ponting's book is an example of overkill: eight hundred pages of rancid sourness in which Churchill can do no right.

Sometimes the unofficial study is an understandable counter to the reverential biography: Richard Davenport-Hines's *The Macmillans*, exploring the trials and tribulations of the Macmillan family as a group, was a valuable supplement to Alistair Horne's two-volume study of Harold Macmillan.

Occasionally the publicity hype can backfire. Stanley Weintraub's biography of Disraeli explored several newish angles, particularly the anti-Semitism which Disraeli routinely encountered. But in fact Weintraub's publishers chose to highlight his speculations that Disraeli had fathered two illegitimate children. The evidence for this was at best tenuous and the understandable disappointment of reviewers at having been conned caused them to underestimate the merits of the rest of the book. As a result, the excellent standard biography by Robert Blake and the very readable shorter studies by André Maurois and Bradford retain possession of the field.

Another ploy adopted by publishers and authors is to claim that their books offer a life of their subject whereas in reality they present no such thing. David Carlton's study of Sir Anthony Eden is subtitled 'A Life' but contains virtually nothing about Eden the man, concentrating rather on Eden the politician as revealed in official publications. Similarly Andrew Roberts' biography of Lord Halifax is also called 'a life' but focuses almost exclusively on Halifax's role in appeasement between 1937 and 1940. Halifax is Viceroy of India after just fifteen pages and vital parts of his life, such as his Anglo–Catholicism, are simply ignored.

The weight of attention devoted to Disraeli and Churchill looks set to be matched by that given to Margaret Thatcher. Already she has been the subject of at least ten biographies which range from the hagiographical to the more considered and critical, such as the excellent *One of Us* by Hugo Young. Her colleagues, as we saw earlier, can barely contain themselves or their recollections and there are several volumes of essays edited by distinguished academics such as Professors Skidelsky, Kavanagh and Minogue.

Reading the above, one might think that the Conservative Party is a much-analysed phenomenon. Yet this is not so: the books mentioned have been devoted to individual Conservatives rather than to the Party itself. In fact there have been only two general histories of the Party; the standard volume by Robert Blake and the dull and out–of–print book by T.F. Lindsay and Michael Harrington.

A multi-volume academic series edited by John Barnes has recently been joined by *Conservative Century*, a well-produced volume edited by Anthony Seldon and Stuart Ball which contains a series of essays by various specialists analysing aspects of the Party over the last hundred years. The eight hundred-plus pages are bursting with important information, detail and statistics.

Conservative Century is also interesting because of what is left out: there is nothing, for example, on party finance – the heart of any political party – or on dirty tricks or on images of the Party. The essays give virtually no sense or feel of the Party or of the individuals who actually comprise it; not just the well-known names but also the rank and file. Why they joined the Party, what makes them tick and so on. Neglected, too, is an assessment of the less obvious signals – dress, accent, humour, background – which carry so much meaning in Tory circles.

Considering that we are talking about the world's most successful political party, the published material doesn't add up to very much. So why has the British Conservative Party been allowed to slumber relatively undisturbed?

First of all, as we have seen throughout this book, Conservatives pride themselves on being non-political. They have successfully confined the definition of politics to the goings-on at Westminster. In his monumental study of the British aristocracy, David Cannadine noted aristocrats' success in 'restricting the agenda of political discussion, largely to their own advantage'.

Exactly the same might be said of the Conservative Party at large. This pose of being above the political fray is perhaps best displayed by individual Conservatives. Stanley Baldwin, Harold Macmillan and Willie Whitelaw, for example, shrewd operators all, liked to cultivate the gentleman-amateur pose. It is worth remembering Bence-Jones and Montgomery-Massingberd's comment on the British aristocracy: 'Behind the aristocrat's vague, bumbling or cosy exterior lies a filament of steel; something which those unfamiliar with the aristocracy are apt not to realize.' Substitute the word 'Conservative' for 'aristocrat'.

This pose has been reinforced by the way in which the Conservative Party has excelled at representing politics as being of marginal interest to the majority of the public. 'Let the politicians get on with it' is the typical cry, which of course suits the defenders of the status quo very nicely. Sixty per cent of young people between the ages of sixteen and thirty-five now watch no news at all on the television. In Britain, as has often been pointed out, there is inexhaustible public interest in sexual scandal: but when it comes to anything scandalous about how our lives are run, then concern is minimal.

Secondly, Britain lacks any great tradition of investigative reporting – unlike the United States where five thousand journalists belong to the American Society of Investigative Reporters and Editors. The search for ratings means that few television companies are prepared to devote resources to programmes other than game shows, chat show or sitcoms. Controversial programmes are cut, delayed or shelved such as the *Panorama* investigations into

Conservative Party funding (cut) and Dame Shirley Porter and Westminster Council's gerrymandering activities (eventually shown) or Central Television's investigation of parliamentary lobbying (scrapped).

Television companies, newspapers and magazines often shy away from anything which might upset the authorities, partly because of the resources which can be brought to bear against them: look at the trouble and expense to which the Government went in its attempt to prevent publication of Peter Wright's *Spycatcher*. There are other instances of pressure being applied noted in this book, particularly in Chapters 9 and 10. The restrictive libel laws and high cost of litigation understandably put off all but the most determined. The British cult of official secrecy does not encourage anyone to ask awkward questions.

The lobby system also furthers the complicity between politicians and press. In the published version of one of the *Yes, Minister* scripts, Anthony Jay and Jonathan Lynn note that:

> The Lobby was a uniquely British system, the best way yet devised in any democracy for taming and muzzling the press. This is because it is hard to censor the press when it wants to be free, but easy if it gives up its freedom voluntarily . . . The politicians loved the Lobby system because they could leak any old rubbish, which the Lobby would generally swallow whole. As they heard it in confidence, they believed it must be true.

Perhaps it should be mentioned that Anthony Jay was a recent adviser to the Conservative Party on communications.

That the Conservative Party has successfully projected a public image of unanimity and agreement which has helped it to exercise enormous power and influence over decades, is not of course the result of a deliberate conspiracy. There are no Party managers beavering away in Central Office censoring and expurgating. It is simply that the Party's strong links with the Establishment discourage too pertinent or probing scrutiny.

Thirdly, most studies of British political parties have been written by partisans and sympathisers. Socialists write about the Labour Party and Conservatives write about the Tory Party. 'Men of the Left' such as Ralph Miliband, John Saville and Ben Pimlott analyse the Left; 'men of the Right' such as Lord (Robert) Blake, John Charmley, Patrick Cosgrave and Andrew Roberts study the Right. And of course much excellent work results – but the feeling lingers that it is all rather a closed shop. Sir Hugh Trevor-Roper (Lord Dacre) once remarked in 1980 that 'historians are great toadies of power'.

Recently, much attention has been devoted to what one newspaper called 'The Dons of War', a loose grouping of right-wing historians who appear to challenge the criticial consensus. The best known are John Charmley and Andrew Roberts. Charmley's revisionist study of Churchill – yet another – argued that Churchill could and should have saved the British Empire by making peace with Adolf Hitler in 1940. His book had the inestimable advantage of being 'puffed' by Alan Clark, which ensured headlines and coverage in the national press. However, neither Charmley nor Clark were convincing that the British Empire had a future in any case, world war or not, nor that Hitler would have respected any such deal.

Written with verve and panache, Andrew Roberts' *Eminent Churchillians* (1994) slaughters a number of sacred cows with great gusto. Mountbatten, the royal family, the 'Chamberlainites' and historian Sir Arthur Bryant all feel the weight of his lash. Seeking to explain why Britain has been reduced to her present stature of 'Italy with rockets' – the book is full of such telling phrases and good jokes, not a feature of most political writing – Roberts points the finger: 'The British ruling class – relieved, perhaps, that they had not suffered the same fate as their European counterparts – appeased the working-class movement, with ultimately disastrous consequences for Britain's competitiveness.'

Reread this quotation and note the calculated use of the word 'appeased' which tars the working-class movement with the Fascist brush. Admitting that this is Thatcherite history, Roberts clearly follows in his heroine's footsteps by regarding opponents as the enemy within. If A. L. Rowse thought of Celts as unwashed, Roberts still seems to think that the working class keep coal in the bath, when, that is, they can spare the time from engaging in more treasonable activities. Here he is giving readers of the *Daily Mail* a potted catalogue of 'Lenin's legacy of shame': 'Bearded revolutionary academics: Generations of Left-wing polytechnic lecturers have secretly taken this brilliant if pedantic monster as their aesthetic mentor. The repulsive results are still widely to be seen – particularly on late-night television chat shows and in the Open University.'

This is very familiar stuff. Perhaps it should be mentioned that some writers on the Left offer mirror images which likewise deal in bigotry. The respected commentator and novelist Robert Harris actually likened Margaret Thatcher's *The Downing Street Years* to Hitler's *Mein Kampf*. Such silly hyperbole only cheapens politics, to no one's benefit.

At first glance, it might appear that the work of Charmley, Roberts and others rather undermines the argument that the Conservative Party has got off lightly in terms of critical scrutiny. But in fact it is noticeable that their work again concentrates on the aberrations of individuals and leaves the Party itself untouched.

It is no coincidence that several of the most illuminating recent studies which throw light on the workings of the Conservative Party in and out of government did not focus entirely on individuals. Peter Hennessy, for instance, has produced several studies, such as *Cabinet* (1986), which probe beneath the official surface. Likewise, Richard Cockett's *Twilight of Truth* (1989) memorably analyses, in the words of the book's subtitle, 'Chamberlain, Appeasement and the Manipulation of the Press'. Cockett demonstrated the insidious relationship between the Chamberlain Government and Fleet Street in the late 1930s whereby unwelcome news about Hitler was 'self-censored'.

Also revealing was Stephen Dorril and Robin Ramsay's *Smear!* (1992) which documents the campaign against Harold Wilson launched by Conservative Central Office and their allies in the press and secret services. Not surprisingly in view of its contents, *Smear!* was produced by two independents working outside academia. Unfortunately the impact of the book was diminished by its tortuous style.

The work of Hennessy, Cockett, Dorril, Ramsay and others was and is important in challenging some of the unexamined generalisations often complacently trotted out regarding the nature of British politics. By shifting the focus away from individual studies, these authors have begun to reveal patterns and parallels, to go behind the shop-window and see what is in store – to adapt Baldwin junior's phrase. Obviously I hope that *We, The Nation* does likewise.

Unofficial Faces

Conservatives and the Conservative Party in novels, plays, films, caricatures and on television

'At that time we had not thoroughly learnt by experience, as we now have, that no reform, no innovation – experience almost justifies us in saying, no revolution – stinks so foully in the nostrils of an English Tory as to be absolutely irreconcilable to him. When taken in the refreshing waters of office any such pill can be swallowed.'

Anthony Trollope, *The Bertrams* (1859)

'Growing older, I have lost the need to be political, which means, in this country, the need to be Left. I am driven into grudging toleration of the Conservative Party because it is the Party of non-politics, of resistance to politics.'

Kingsley Amis, 1967

'. . . that nasal whinny peculiar to the Conservative front benches'

John le Carré, *The Night Manager* (1993)

In the previous chapter we saw that the official face of the British Conservative Party is at best a partial view – but one might well say 'so what'? Few people buy memoirs, even fewer still academic studies of aspects of the Party. But it is not of course historians alone who mould our attitudes towards politics and politicians. Powerful representations also reach us through the media of plays, novels, films, cartoons and television.

To take a number of cases: for many people the image of the selfish and amoral Conservative MP associated with Mrs Thatcher's Conservative Party became embodied in the character of Alan B'Stard, played by comedian Rik Mayall in the series *The New Statesman*.

Throughout the series, B'Stard is presented as thoroughly selfish, corrupt and callous and it is no surprise to find that *The New Statesman*'s writers, Laurence Marks and Maurice Gran, are both Labour Party supporters. They freely admitted that B'Stard was 'a deliberate attempt to offend Tories'. At one point B'Stard gleefully kicks away the stick of a handicapped person, as if demonstrating the alleged Thatcherite devotion to 'each to their own'.

As for the figures of 'Essex Man' and 'Essex Girl', supposedly encapsulating the type of new voter which Mrs Thatcher was thought to have won for the Conservative Party in the 1980s, these stereotypes have become part of the national consciousness via jokes told in pubs, bars and offices, but rarely committed to paper. They will therefore be unintelligible to any historian in a century's time who is fixated by official publications and printed words.

Similarly the image which many people have of Prime Minister John Major as a weak and schoolboyish figure derives in large part from the work of *Guardian* cartoonist Steve Bell who always shows Major with his underpants worn outside his trousers. Readers of *Private Eye* magazine, on the other hand, are privileged to read John Major's diary with its wondering and disingenuous style which owes much to Sue Townsend's creation Adrian Mole: a profoundly well-meaning but absolutely hopeless individual. This is comparatively gentle satire, but influential nevertheless. In *Spitting Image*, on the other hand, John Major is portrayed as a thoroughly grey man, dull, uninspired and tedious.

Whether academics like it or not, Alan B'Stard, Essex Man and John Major's underpants are images familiar to many more people than will ever wade through a weighty piece of political analysis. It is impossible to say how significantly these stereotypes influence voters, but we can be sure that they matter. Take the depiction by Conservatives and their allies in the press in the early 1980s of Labour leader Michael Foot as a daft and shabby 'Wurzel Gummidge': this image more than cancelled out any number of anti-Conservative pieces in the *Daily Mirror* or *Guardian*.

Such images certainly affect politicians themselves: former Liberal leader David Steel has admitted that one reason why he ended the pact with David Owen's Social Democrats was his irritation at seeing himself portrayed as Owen's lapdog by the *Spitting Image* programme. It is worth bearing such matters in mind when reading histories devoted exclusively to the 'high' politics of Cabinet meetings, Civil Service briefings and editorials in *The Times*.

What then are the stereotypical images of Conservatives and the Conservative Party? How have they been represented in the media and elsewhere: fiction, plays, films, television and caricature? Why does there seem to have been a watershed in the 1960s? Before then, much was glossed over. Afterwards, the gloves came off.

Benjamin Disraeli is sometimes referred to as the father of the political novel. Having realised that this would be a sure way of attracting attention and publicity, Disraeli was not afraid to people his novels with characters clearly based on contemporaries or to use them as mouthpieces for his own opinions.

Yet despite his remark in *Coningsby* that 'It is the personal that interests mankind, that fires their imagination, and wins their hearts', at times both this novel and the more famous *Sybil* are little more than turgid political tracts. In particular, Disraeli loses no opportunity to lambast Peel's Conservative Party and to engage in abstruse historical argument about the Party's lineage – not, it must be thought, a question of great interest to most novel readers.

As a result, these books are read today less as literature than for their historical information. *Sybil*, for example, has vivid descriptions of women working down the pits, of rapacious employers and the initiation rites of some early trade unions. It portrays Westminster as a village and London as a 'great prison'. *Coningsby* also offers us the two minor characters of Tadpole and Taper, representatives of the new wheelers and dealers associated with the rise of the modern party system.

The work of Charles Dickens is full of political material, all the more effective for being integrated into gripping narrative. His devastating portrayal of injustice and greed still makes the blood boil. He is profoundly critical of the new commercial and industrial society which he had seen grow up in his lifetime, but neither the Conservative Party nor the Liberals are indicted by name. Instead Dickens offers a more generalised critique of Victorian society.

Dickens's stance of 'a plague on all your political houses' was vividly demonstrated in *Bleak House* by his reduction of Cabinet-making to the level of farce: 'Then, giving the Home Department and the Leadership of the House of Commons to Joodle, the Exchequer to Koodle, the Colonies to Loodle, and the Foreign Office to Moodle, what are you to do with Noodle? You can't offer him the Presidency of the Council; that is reserved for Poodle . . .'

Away from his novels, Dickens was a fervent anti-Tory. In the summer of 1841, for instance, he published a series of lampoons in the *Examiner* magazine. One of them, 'to be said or sung at all Conservative Dinners', contains this verse:

> The bright old day dawns again; the cry runs through the
>   land,
> In England there shall be − dear bread! in Ireland − sword
>   and brand!
> And poverty, and ignorance, shall swell the rich and grand,
> So, rally round the rulers with the gentle iron hand,
>   Of the fine old English Tory days;
>   Hail to the coming time!

It was sentiments such as these which encouraged the Chartists to try and woo Dickens for the radical movement. He, however, would have none of it; indeed one of his most repellent characters is the trade union organiser Slackbridge in *Hard Times*, shifty, unprincipled and out for himself.

Dickens also turned down the offer of standing for the constituency of Reading in 1841 as a Whig because he did not want to compromise his independence or be wedded to one party label. He knew full well that such identification would possibly alienate half of his potential readership.

Anthony Trollope was less afraid of wearing party colours; he supported the Liberals. His autobiography tells of how he was struck 'with awe and horror at the misery of many of our brethren'. He made one unhappy attempt to enter Parliament, standing for the notoriously corrupt seat of Beverley in Yorkshire in 1868. Not only did he fail, the time he spent canvassing represented 'the most wretched fortnight of my manhood'. Still, at least he was able to recycle his experiences in his novel *Ralph the Heir*.

The six novels in Trollope's Palliser series explore the nature of British politics, but the artistic requirements of plot and characterisation take priority over political point-scoring. Throughout, however, Trollope's shrewd perception of human beings as politicians is always to the fore. Take this passage from *Phineas Finn* (1869):

'I always observe', said Madame Max Goesler, 'that when any of you gentlemen resign, which you usually do on some very trivial matter, the resigning gentlemen becomes of all foes the bitterest. Somebody goes on very well with his friends, agreeing most cordially about everything, till he finds that his public virtue cannot swallow some little detail, and then he resigns. Or someone, perhaps, on the other side has attacked him, and in the mêlée he is hurt, and so he resigns. But when he has resigned, and made his parting speech full of love and gratitude, I know well where to look for the bitterest hostility to his late friends. Yes, I am beginning to understand the way in which politics are done in England.'

Undoubtedly one or two recent former Conservative ministers will recognise this particular scenario.

What is today regarded as perhaps Trollope's masterpiece, *The Way We Live Now* (1875), is a magnificently sustained indictment of the greed which he saw around him on his return to Britain after a spell abroad. At the heart of the novel is the figure of Augustus Melmotte, the grasping tycoon and financier all too reminiscent of Robert Maxwell, who eventually comes to a messy end under a railway train. Contemporary reviewers deplored Trollope's onslaught on Victorian society.

Trollope's most recent biographer, Victoria Glendinning, claims that he is 'very rude about the Tories', but such sentiments have not stopped Trollope's works from being much admired by many Conservatives, particularly Prime Ministers Macmillan and Major.

Today we expect our political parties to have very clearly defined identities and contrasting policies. In the nineteenth century, however, it was often difficult to see any great differences between the Conservative and Liberal Parties, except on the question of Empire. As we have seen, this was very much a Tory Party card and the wave of imperialist fiction was implicitly pro-Conservative. The glorification of the 'white man's burden', exemplified by a breed of fearless Englishmen venturing into the unknown and taming the savages, quickly became a stereotype, but was none the less powerful for all that.

Two of the most effective exponents of this strain of fiction were, unsurprisingly, Conservative parliamentary candidates: John Buchan was successful, Rider Haggard was not. Many of their novels remain in print more than half a century after both men's deaths, and their heroes Richard Hannay and Allan Quartermain are still of interest to film-makers. No fewer than twenty-eight films have so far been made from Rider Haggard's novels and they clearly inspired Steven Spielberg's *Indiana Jones* trilogy.

The sixth son of a Norfolk squire, Rider Haggard was sent out by his father to join the colonial service in South Africa. The whirlwind of experiences inspired the energetic and thoughtful young man to start writing. By the age of thirty-one he had produced his three masterpieces: *King Solomon's Mines* in 1885, followed by *She* and then *Allan Quartermain*.

Haggard believed in the progressive character of imperialism: 'The strong aggressive hand of England has grasped some fresh portion of the earth's surface [and] there is a spirit of justice in her heart and head which prompts the question . . . as to how best and most fairly to deal with the natives of the newly-acquired land.' It is impossible to ignore the anti-Semitic and racist sentiments of his works, yet he should not be dismissed as some blinkered blimp – for instance, he idolised the Zulus for their strength and intelligence.

Nevertheless, Rider Haggard's involvement with active politics was as brief and unhappy as that of Anthony Trollope. In 1895 he stood as the Conservative candidate in East Norfolk but found local passions so stirred that stone-throwing gangs disrupted his meetings – at one point he and his supporters were besieged in a local hotel. The 'Battle of Stalham Bridge' only came to an end when police reinforcements arrived with cutlasses. Losing the contest by just 198 votes he understandably decided that he was not a party man.

At that same 1895 election, however, Rider Haggard campaigned publicly for national insurance, for the provision of old age pensions and for heavy subsidies for the railways; policies which were poles apart from the official Conservative position. For the last years of his life he strongly advocated that church lands should be confiscated and given to bankrupt farmers.

John Buchan was another popular novelist often scorned today for his supposedly reactionary views. Yet he too possessed much broader sympathies than the stereotype of the Tory jingoist allows for, both as a politician and a novelist.

Take, for instance, his novel *Mr Standfast*, one of the Richard Hannay series. Published in 1919, its events centre around the anti-war and pacifist movement. One would expect to find a stereotypical gallery of cranky, wishy-washy pacifists and traitors, but in fact these characters are presented in human and understandable terms: not as dupes but as courageous and principled, if misguided, individuals. At one point Buchan praises a conscientious objector for his bravery in enduring abuse on so many public platforms and the Fabian, Launcelot Wake, turns out to be something of a hero when he dies taking a message through the German lines. Buchan himself campaigned hard to get conscientious objectors released from prison.

Buchan's novel about post-war unrest, *The Three Hostages* (1924), reflects fears that the traditional social order would not survive the post-war upheaval. In fact he is more concerned with the general shattering of certainties resulting from the First World War than with the red menace. Likewise the anti-Semitic remarks of some of his characters are less expressions of Buchan's own sentiments than his conception of how those characters would have thought and behaved.

In reality, as a Conservative MP for the Scottish Universities from 1927 to 1935, Buchan always spoke in favour of Zionist and Jewish causes. In April 1932, for instance, he called for the setting up of a Jewish homeland. Speaking at a rally two years later, Buchan declared that 'When I think of Zionism, I think of it in the first place as a great act of justice. It is a reparation for the centuries of cruelty and wrong which have stained the record of nearly every Gentile people.'

Opponents of Buchan always quote the anti-Semitic outburst of the American, Scudder, in *The Thirty-Nine Steps* as damning evidence. Apart from the fact that it is foolish to mix up the views of fictional characters with those of the author, Scudder is clearly presented as deranged and with a paranoia about Jews. Even more tellingly, critic and historian Christopher Harvie possesses a copy of a Nazi 'Who's Who in Britain', published in 1938. One entry refers to Buchan, or Lord Tweedsmuir as he had become: 'Tweedsmuir, Lord: Pro-Jewish activity'.

Perhaps Buchan's finest novel was his last, *Sick Heart River* (1941), written when he was governor-general of Canada. The main character, Sir Edward Leithen, is a lawyer and politician at the end of his life who realises that he has squandered much of his resources on a futile struggle to achieve fame and fortune: 'He had made a niche for himself in the world, but it had been a chilly niche.' But after helping a group of Indians in the far north of Canada to cope with disease and illness, Leithen is reconciled to himself and his fellow human beings and he dies relatively content.

The writer associated above all others with the Empire was Rudyard Kipling. He has suffered from the tendency of some modern critics to judge the past by contemporary standards; also perhaps from a spate of films often very loosely based on the books and others which made the most of stereotyping. Yet Kipling was 'politically correct' enough for the Soviet authorities to allow him to become enormously popular in the USSR.

As a young man Kipling was distinguished by his insatiable curiosity about other people's customs and habits. When in India he was noted for his love of the Indian people and even made the effort to learn Hindustani, hardly the mark of an out-and-out racist. Certainly Kipling wrote about the 'white man's burden', but he was perceptive enough to see both the flaws and virtues of the imperial adventure – and he was conscious that sooner or later that adventure would come to an end, as his fine poem *Recessional*, published at the time of the Diamond Jubilee in 1897, makes clear.

James Morris has pointed out that probably only Kipling could have expressed such views at that moment and still have commanded respectful attention; 'Though the hysteria of the New Imperialism shrilled on its way unabashed, still the publication of *Recessional* was a watershed in the imperial progress – the moment when the true laureate of Empire saw, apparently for the first time, something ugly beneath the canopy.'

Less defensible is the anti-Semitism which often shows up in Kipling's writings, though again, in contrast, there is a portrait of an admirable and praiseworthy Jew in *The Treasure and the Land*. It would also be foolish to underplay the anti-Bolshevik sentiments of Kipling and Rider Haggard who were both involved in the Liberty League which was financed by newspaper proprietor Lord Northcliffe. As one contemporary lampoon had it:

> 'Every Bolsh is a blackguard,'
> Says Kipling to Haggard.
> 'And given to tippling,'
> Said Haggard to Kipling . . .

Other writers who dealt with imperial themes included G.A. Henty – 'probably nobody more profoundly influenced the late Victorian generation of young Britons' – and even Winston Churchill who published a single novel called *Savrola* in 1900. In *My Early Life* he declared, 'I have consistently urged my friends to abstain from reading it.' He was in fact too modest about this entertaining read, even though the inexperienced author had to ask advice from a fellow army officer on how best to write the book's obligatory love scene.

Set in a mythical European state of Laurania ruled by a dictator called Molara, the novel tells how the charismatic figure of Savrola – clearly Churchill himself – sets out to win power. He fails and goes into exile: a foretaste of 'the wilderness years', perhaps? At one point President Molara remarks: 'I think that the English Government also have to keep the electorate amused. It is a conservative ministry; they keep things going abroad to divert the public mind from advanced legislation.'

The worst aspects of the writings of Rider Haggard, Kipling, Churchill and Buchan are fully on display in popular spy fiction and thrillers unleashed on the British public after the First World War. Those individuals writing in the aftermath of the Russian Revolution and the unrest in Britain during 1919–20 created an army of red revolutionaries busily subverting law and order. They seem quite clear that since the Labour Party and the communists are virtually identical, then the only hope of all decent men and women must lie in the forces of law and order (otherwise known as the Conservative Party and its allies). The foremost exponent of this sensationalist genre was Leutenant Colonel Herman Cyril McNeile who wrote under the pseudonym of 'Sapper'.

His hero was Captain Hugh 'Bulldog' Drummond, massive in size and certain of outlook, who disguises his native shrewdness behind a frivolous manner. Fortunately he does not need brains in order to spot the 'Red men', because conveniently enough they always have pointed beards and unfortunate personal habits. The first novel in the series concerns a conspiracy, backed by Moscow gold, to overthrow the Government by means of a general strike.

In the second, *The Black Gang*, first published in 1922, Drummond foils the dastardly reds who plan to launch a series of explosions. Central to this book is the theme of innocents being misled by

the politically corrupt, as Drummond tells the villainous MP
Charles Latter:

> Ever since the war you poisonous reptiles have been at work
> stirring up internal trouble in this country. Not one in ten of
> you believe what you preach: your driving force is money and
> your own advancement. And as for your miserable dupes –
> those priceless fellows who follow you blindly because – God
> help them, they're hungry and their wives are hungry – what
> do you care for them, Mr Latter? You just laugh in your sleeve
> and pocket the cash.

In Bulldog Drummond's eyes this justifies his actions when he
ties up Charles Latter and then sends him mad by strapping a
bomb to the end of his bed. Sapper clearly endorses the activities
of Drummond and his Black Gang 'which aimed merely at the
repression of terrorism by terrorism'.

It is perhaps easy to snigger at such stuff and dismiss it out
of hand, but *The Black Gang* went through fifty-one impressions
by 1950 and was doubtless read by hundreds of thousands more
people than ever waded through a political manifesto. Nor are
the sentiments, particularly the obsession with 'red revolution', so
different from the opinions expressed by many newspapers or the
political views of many in the intelligence services, that home of
would-be Bulldog Drummonds.

Likewise the aversion to foreigners for being irredeemably
shifty and dishonest, characteristic of this entire genre of popular
fiction, is not far removed from the views of some Conservative
anti-Europeans quoted in Chapter 14. The historian of this literary
genre, Richard Usborne, has summed up the attitude of Sapper and
others: 'The dago, the Teuton, the Jew, the Russian – scratch a
foreigner and you find an enemy of England.' However, another
commentator, Colin Watson, has stressed that Sapper only mirrored
existing views: 'The connection . . . was not one of cause and effect.
Popular fiction is not evangelistic; it implants no new ideas.'

The sub-genre of 'what if the socialists take over Britain' scare
novels contains such gems as Agatha Christie's *The Secret Adversary*

which was published in 1922 and is another example of the post-war anxiety already noted in earlier chapters. In Christie's novel, gullible trade union leaders are being exploited by a 'Mr Big': 'Bolshevist gold is pouring into this country for the specific purposes of procuring a Revolution . . . The Boshevists are behind the labour unrest – but this man is behind the Bolshevists.'

At one point hero Tommy observes a meeting comprised of an Irish Sinn Feiner, a common criminal, a pale Russian and 'the efficient German master of the ceremonies'. 'Truly a strange and sinister gathering!' adds the author helpfully.

Another much later example of this dishonourable genre is Frederick Forsyth's inaccurate *The Fourth Protocol* (1984) which blithely misrepresents the process under which Labour leaders are elected to office: needless to say, a moderate is elbowed aside by a 'red'. A novel such as this one, with its overheated plot involving Soviet occupation of Britain, is explicitly anti-Left and it is perhaps unsurprising that Mrs Thatcher once told an interviewer that she had read *The Fourth Protocol* not once but twice (a feat in itself).

Did Conservatives have the novel all to themselves? No, there was a school of socialist writers who explicity attacked the Establishment, but their wooden characters and unbelievable plots explain their small sales. Yet one powerful denunciation of the entire political system has stood the test of time.

Robert Tressell's *The Ragged Trousered Philanthropists*, published posthumously just before the First World War, remains very much in print. As a Marxist, Tressell was not impressed by either the Conservative or Liberal Parties and he wrote a savage description of an election in which the two candidates, called Adam Sweater and Sir Graball D'Encloseland, try to woo a gullible and stupid electorate. The novel is a powerful anti–Establishment tract and it is intriguing that John Major, according to biographer Edward Pearce, regularly rereads *Philanthropists*.

Some memorable fictional Conservatives created by less partisan writers include Evelyn Waugh's Arthur Box-Bender, the Tory MP in the *Sword of Honour* trilogy whose support for the war effort during the Second World War does not extend to making any personal sacrifices himself. Box-Bender in *Men At Arms* (1952) has his country house listed as a repository for 'National Art Treasures' so that he will not have to billet evacuees. Also contemptible is Rex Mottram in *Brideshead Revisited*, a politician on the make with a liking for loud suits. Mottram was supposedly based on the politician Brendan Bracken, a friend of Winston Churchill.

Another unattractive Tory is P.G. Wodehouse's incomparable Aubrey Upjohn, the prep school headmaster who on several occasions made life distinctly hot for the young Bertie Wooster. In retirement, Upjohn proposes to stand for the Conservatives in the Market Snodsbury by-election. The story revolves around his inability to make a speech without notes − a failing common to most of today's politicians who rely on the auto-cue.

In a later Wodehouse novel, *Much Obliged, Jeeves* (1971), Market Snodsbury is once again the scene of a by-election. Bertie is asked to go and help out a friend, Ginger Worsnip, who is standing as the Conservative candidate:

> 'What does it involve?' I asked guardedly. 'I shan't have to kiss babies, shall I?'
> 'Of course you won't, you abysmal chump.' [Aunt Dahlia replies]
> 'I've always heard that kissing babies entered largely into these things.'
> 'Yes, but it's the candidate who does it, poor blighter. All you have to do is to go from house to house urging the inmates to vote for Ginger.'

Later, Ginger complains about the sacrifices a candidate such as himself is called upon to make: 'What blighters babies are, Bertie, dribbling, as they do, at the side of the mouth. Still, it has to be done.'

Look back at Chapter 8 on electioneering and you will see that Ginger's attitude is wonderfully reminiscent of that of Lord Salisbury in the nineteenth century and more recently of Oliver Lyttelton in Aldershot.

Another splendid Wodehouse creation is the would-be dictator Roderick Spode, clearly modelled on the figure of Oswald Mosley.

At one point in *The Code of the Woosters* (the date of publication, 1938, confirms Wodehouse's target), even the usually gentle and mild Bertie Wooster loses his temper at Spode's swaggering arrogance:

> The trouble with you, Spode, is that just because you have succeeded in inducing a handful of half-wits to disfigure the London scene by going about in black shorts, you think you're someone. You hear them shouting 'Heil, Spode!' and you imagine it is the Voice of the People. That is where you make your bloomer. What the Voice of the People is saying is: 'Look at the frightful ass Spode swanking about in footer bags! Did you ever in your puff see such a perfect perisher?'

Perhaps the most sustained work of anti-socialist vituperation in novel form was the series of books produced by Angela Thirkell in the late 1940s. In *Peace Breaks Out* (1946) she laments the election defeat of Winston Churchill, swept from power 'by the millions of tired, impatient and most irresponsible people whom he had served'. Thirkell berates what she dubbed the 'Brave and Revolting New World'. In *Private Enterprise* (1947), socialist traitors 'give away' the Empire and she seems to have felt a special animus for the National Health Service. Clearly Thirkell must have struck a chord because her novels sold tens of thousands of copies.

Another bestseller, except that his books are still very much in print, was Ian Fleming, creator of James Bond. Fleming was perhaps the only elector in history to cast his vote on the issue of politicians' buttocks: 'I vote Conservative rather than Labour mainly because the Conservatives have bigger bottoms, and I believe that big bottoms make for better government than scrawny ones.'

The sophistication of such views prepares one for the Bond books with their full quota of Sapper-style bigotry; negroes are 'clumsy black apes' whilst America is only a 'civilised country. More or less.' In *Thunderball* (1961), Bond lets rip at a working-class taxi driver: 'It was typical of the cheap, self-assertiveness of young labour since the war. This youth, thought Bond, makes about twenty pounds a week, despises his parents, and would like to be

Tommy Steele. It's not his fault. He was born into the buyers' market of the Welfare State.'

As for women, there is no namby-pamby stuff about equality for Commander Bond: 'These blithering women, who thought they could do a man's work. Why the hell couldn't they sit at home and mind their pots and pans and stick to their frocks and their gossip, and leave men's work for the men.'

Fleming's Bond, given a new lease of life by the enormously successful films made from the books, is a convenient point at which to pause. It is clear that up to the 1960s most writers and novelists portrayed the Conservatives, and in particular Empire and Establishment, in a broadly favourable light – if that is, they wrote about them at all.

This is equally true of the theatre, except that virtually no political comment appeared on stage because of the activities of the theatre censor. The Lord Chamberlain had the right to vet and cut out anything which he deemed unsuitable without having to explain or justify his decisions. Traditionally, each and every Lord Chamberlain since 1737 banned anything which trespassed on the unholy trinity of religion, politics and sex – which doesn't seem to leave much for the audience to watch.

Nevertheless, Victorian stage melodrama was full of stereotypical grasping squires and wicked factory-owners menacing virtuous but abnormally naive factory girls. Some of the plays are vehement in their portrayal of dire social conditions but the dramatists never explicitly suggest that any particular political party is responsible for them. Take John Walker's *The Factory Lad*, which was staged in 1832 and is often held up as an example of radical melodrama. The play contains a stony-hearted squire, Westwood, who is 'rationalising' his factory by introducing new steam looms. The legal system is portrayed as unjust – the magistrate is inevitably called Judge Bias.

Yet it is clear that the oppression and injustice shown in *The Factory Lad* and other such plays is of a personalised nature. They do not set out to portray, let alone condemn, the structures of society. In other words, individuals are singled out for blame rather than the social order itself, nor is there any evidence that the audience was much interested in the plays' political content anyway. Usually they have happy endings, similar to so many 'industrial novels' of the 1840s and 1850s. Plays and novels were simply not regarded as suitable vehicles for political propaganda.

More subtle and therefore more effective were productions which applied the stiletto rather than the bludgeon. And here, Gilbert and Sullivan were the masters, reintroducing to the stage a tradition of political satire which had been castrated by the Lord Chamberlain.

W.S. Gilbert was a typical example of an old-fashioned 'plague on both your houses' Tory – like Ian Fleming, he too probably thought that bottoms were a good test of political reliability. The Savoy Operas were, in David Cannadine's words, 'a paean of praise to national pride and to the established order' and Gilbert tended to lambast organised politics in general: in *HMS Pinafore* he has one Admiral say of his time as an MP, 'I always voted at my party's call,/ And I never thought of thinking for myself at all'. Similarly in *Iolanthe*, a character remarks:

> 'When in that House MPs divide,
> If they've a brain and cerebellum, too,
> They've got to leave that brain outside,
> And vote just as their leaders tell 'em to.'

In 1873, however, Gilbert did level his fire specifically at Gladstone and the current Liberal Government in the burlesque *The Happy Land*. The Liberal administration was depicted as living in a never-never land and the Prime Minister was portrayed as a fairy. Such explicit references prompted the Lord Chamberlain to step in and demand changes. Needless to say, the consequent publicity ensured that the censored production ran for more than seven months.

Did the play have any political effect? Gladstone himself seems to have pioneered the most effective strategy adopted by all intended victims. He attended a production in person and was seen to rock with laughter (admittedly, not easy to visualise) – rather as Denis Thatcher happily attended a performance of *Anyone for Denis?* in the 1980s.

In general, however, the West End theatre steered clear of political issues. Managers knew full well that their audiences, decked out in evening dress, had most certainly not come to their theatres to discuss political issues. Left-wing agitprop groups and the more permanent Unity Theatres staged plays dealing with contemporary issues in which capitalism was always the villain of the piece and Stalin's communism the hero, but such productions preached only to the very small number of converted.

The pervasive power of censorship was even more in evidence when it came to cinema. The British Board of Film Censors was in fact set up by the industry itself before the First World War in its determination to keep to the straight and narrow. Like their theatrical counterparts, cinema audiences clearly preferred entertainment to politics when they went out for the evening. As Leslie Halliwell once put it, 'Politics, as any exhibitor will tell you, is the kiss of death to a film as far as box office is concerned.'

One partial exception was the film *Disraeli* (1929) in which George Arliss, playing the Prime Minister, won Britain's first Oscar. As we saw in Chapter 8, Conservative Central Office was happy to arrange screenings of extracts. Arliss's Disraeli was presented as the 'great impresario of Empire', shrewdly outwitting foreign rivals in order to acquire the Suez canal for Queen Victoria.

One should also mention much-praised productions such as the Korda brothers' film *Sanders of the River* (1935) in which Paul Robeson, playing the part of the native Bosambo, is used by the white district commissioner to keep the African tribes under British control. Adapted from Edgar Wallace's story, it was the distribution of 'Empire' films like these, generally much cruder than the original novels, which tarred writers such as Rider Haggard, Buchan and Kipling with an uncritical adulation of imperial power.

At one point in *Sanders*, the British commissioner delivers a homily on the benefits of white rule. George MacDonald Fraser has speculated exactly how well this speech must have gone down with Jomo Kenyatta who was one of the film's extras and later to be president of Kenya.

Similarly, radio and then television generally avoided contentious topics and speakers. It was not just a simple matter of censorship, although the Conservative Government had kept a tight rein during the General Strike and mavericks such as Churchill were denied broadcasting access in the 1930s. There was little evidence that listeners and viewers demanded anything different.

During the Second World War, however, J.B. Priestley broadcast a series of Saturday night radio talks called *Postscripts* which were designed to have 'a very broad and classless appeal' and proved immensely popular. When Priestley added more of an edge to the talks, he was taken off the air. 'I received two letters . . . and one was from the Ministry of Information, telling me that the B.B.C. was responsible for the decision to take me off the air, and the other was from the B.B.C. saying that a directive had come from the Ministry of Information to end my broadcasts.'

Turning from the novel, stage, film and radio to the medium of caricature, one might well expect a much greater degree of political comment. And that is certainly the case. Artists such as William Hogarth and James Gillray often depicted contemporary events and politicians, but rarely in a flattering light.

Nevertheless it is noticeable that Hogarth, the father of English caricature, was careful not to get embroiled in party politics for fear of losing sections of his audience. Like Dickens, he seems to have thought that discretion could sometimes be the better part of valour. Similarly Gillray's more ferocious creations were directed at the French and Napoleon, asserting that potent and confident John Bull could see off any foreigner any time.

The rise of party politics in the Victorian period coincided with a new gentility in British caricature, symbolised by the founding of *Punch* magazine in 1841. No one could call *Punch* in any way subversive let alone party political. The magazine favoured the established order and regarded anyone who threatened it – Irish Fenians, radicals, foreigners – as stock figures of fun or menace. In particular, the arrival of the first gorilla at London Zoo in 1860 prompted legions of Victorian illustrators to portray the Irish as apes.

This century has seen the appearance of well-known newspaper cartoonists. The most famous, David Low, worked for Lord Beaverbrook and his cartoons often adopted a stance at odds with the proprietor's Conservatism. Low was protected by an agreement which he had signed in 1927 with Beaverbrook: 'It is agreed that you are to have complete freedom in the selection and treatment of subject-matter for your cartoons and in the expression therein of the policies in which you believe.' Even so, the force of Low's work, particularly when he was critical of appeasement in the late 1930s, meant that pressure was brought to bear.

Low was generally regarded as a man sympathetic to the Left and it is ironic that one of his two enduring images – the TUC as a carthorse (the other being Colonel Blimp) – should have been much exploited by Conservatives. A similar experience happened to Vicky (Victor Weisz), an out-and-out socialist who depicted Harold Macmillan as Supermac, intending to poke fun at him. The image backfired and the Tory press happily adopted Vicky's image as boosting the Prime Minister's standing.

Vicky, like Low, knew full well that Beaverbrook was being rather crafty in employing two political opponents in prominent positions. When it was put to him that he was merely a left-wing fig leaf concealing Beaverbrook's imperial public parts, Vicky used to shrug and reply: 'Of course, and I make use of it.'

So what can one conclude of representations of Conservatives and the Conservative Party up to the 1960s? By and large, the media preferred to stay well clear of partisan party politics, but the overall tendency was to support the status quo and to be suspicious and hostile towards individuals or groups who challenged it. Critics happily refer to 'socialist novels' or 'left-wing cinema'; that no one ever talks of 'the Conservative novel', for example, shows how taken for granted is our habit of looking at the world in certain traditional ways. 'We' are the nation.

Since the 1960s, however, the media generally have adopted rather more robust and challenging viewpoints.

Throughout this book we have noted some of the widespread political and social changes which have transformed Britain since the 1950s. In a nutshell, ever greater individualism has brought a more challenging and less deferential attitude towards society and authority. In the 1950s the class structure in Britain was still fairly rigid: most people were manual workers or married to a manual worker, living in council property in stable family units.

Now, of course, such certainties appear less permanent and their fragmentation has spawned a media industry less respectful of hierarchy and the Establishment. The arrival of commercial television in the mid-1950s was one manifestation, the 'satire boom' of the early 1960s – the era of *That Was The Week That Was* and the introduction of the magazine *Private Eye* – another. Censorship was less restrictive and, as regards the theatre, the sway of the Lord Chamberlain was abolished outright in 1968.

The political novel as produced by more literate Members of Parliament has in part exemplified these changes. From Disraeli onwards, backbenchers with time on their hands have used their inside knowledge as the basis for novels. Perhaps the best post-war writer was the Labour MP Maurice Edelman, closely followed by Wilfred Fienburgh whose *No Love for Johnnie* charted the work and loves of a Labour MP; it was made into an excellent film starring Peter Finch. Sadly Fienburgh was killed in a car accident in 1958 aged only thirty-seven. Another MP and novelist who died early was the Conservative David Walder, whilst C.P. Snow, responsible for the enormous *Strangers and Brothers* sequence, was briefly a Labour minister in the 1960s.

The best current example of politician-authorship is undoubtedly Douglas Hurd, now a very eminent Foreign Secretary. In the early 1970s, however, he was a Heath man and clearly recognised that, given the vagaries of political fortune, another string to his bow might well be advisable. Therefore, often in conjunction with co-authors such as Andrew Osmond and Stephen Lamport, Hurd produced a string of thrillers which have never received the recognition they deserve.

Not only are they are well-researched and full of accurate detail, the novels are also highly topical. *Send Him Victorious* was published in 1968 at the time of the Wilson Government's problems with Ian Smith's breakaway regime in Rhodesia. It concerns a Tory administration's similar difficulties with internal unrest and racial civil war. Actually it is very much like the

Conservative-inspired Ulster revolt against possible Home Rule before the First World War.

Vote to Kill (1975) was indeed about recalling the troops from Northern Ireland and *Scotch on the Rocks* (1971) tackled the issue of Home Rule for Scotland and depicted the use of street violence by the fictional Scottish Liberation Army. The real-life Scottish National Party was so upset that they protested loud, long and effectively after the BBC had filmed this novel. The film was subsequently destroyed.

The Palace of Enchantments (1985) features a Tory Foreign Office minister struggling with the conflict between his own conscience and the dictates of party government. Hero Edward Dunsford is blunt about the opportunism and expediency of political life: 'Men lost their seats or floundered in debate. They were discovered in brothels or with guardsmen. Or they failed even with the civil service prop to achieve the low minimum of competence required in office. Others conversely did well. Often it was a matter of luck, sometimes of skill. But none of this had anything to do with beliefs or principles.'

Hurd and his co-writers manage to create a vivid feel of British political life. The same is true, to a lesser extent, of Jeffrey Archer's Westminster novel, *First Among Equals* (1984), which follows the careers of four politicians as they jockey and jostle their way to the top. Archer does not shy away from including real events in his novel. There is even a sly reference to his own election as an MP when he notes that both parties were surprised by the swing to the Tories at the Louth by-election at the end of 1969. The author is uncharacteristically modest in failing to mention that he was the Conservative candidate involved. The perils which await the writers of fictional history are demonstrated by the novel's prophecy that Gary Hart would become president of the United States in 1988.

Archer's portrayal of the Conservative politician, Simon Kerslake, is no more nor less flattering than that of his three rivals. Like Douglas Hurd, Archer is shrewd enough to know that novels rarely prove to be suitable conduits for party propaganda – it is foolish to alienate possible readers.

First Among Equals was made into a television series, as were two novels by Michael Dobbs. Having worked at Conservative Central Office from 1975, Dobbs fell foul of Mrs Thatcher during the 1987 election campaign. Mrs Thatcher was critical of the performance of Central Office under her party chairman Norman Tebbit, and he sided with his boss.

Looking for a new career after the 1987 election, Dobbs decided to make use of his inside knowledge in his books, *House of Cards* and *To Play the King*. Most memorable was the character of the scheming, duplicitous Francis Urquhart, a Chief Whip determined to reach the top of the greasy pole. He was played with sharp malice on television by the actor Ian Richardson. Two early chapters in this book on Conservative dirty tricks have suggested that the Party is not above reproach. Nevertheless, it stretches credibility to breaking point to imagine a Chief Whip engaged in such criminal activities as blackmail and murder.

If Dobbs's often far-fetched novels have less of the feel of political life than those of Douglas Hurd, then they are at least better than the latest raft of books by Conservative backbench MPs eager to exploit their parliamentary connections. Amongst them are Rupert Allason, also known as Nigel West the spy writer, who was responsible for *Murder in the Commons*, and Julian Critchley, author of *Hung Parliament* and *Floating Voter*. Another backbencher Conservative MP-cum-novelist is Michael Spicer, author of *The Cotswold Murders*.

Neither Allason, Critchley nor Spicer have quite so brazenly leapt aboard the sex 'n' shopping cycle of blockbusters as has Edwina Currie, whose novel *A Parliamentary Affair* is full of unzippings and couplings in uncomfortable places inside the Houses of Parliament. The political content of these novels is rather less prominent than the sexual. It is intriguing to wonder what Benjamin Disraeli would have made of Currie's bestseller.

None, perhaps, of the recent writers mentioned above would make much claim for their literary prowess, which accounts for the two-dimensional characters and the flat dialogue. Rather different is John Mortimer, barrister, playwright and novelist whose *Paradise* series, again televised, contains the memorable creation Leslie Titmuss, the aspiring MP meant to be symbolic of Mrs Thatcher's Conservative Party. He was played with creepy conviction by David Threlfall.

Describing himself as 'an old fashioned socialist', Mortimer clearly loathes Mrs Thatcher's brand of populist Conservatism and yet his portrayal of Titmuss, the touchy, sensitive 'upstart' from the wrong side of the tracks is not unsympathetic. At one point, attempting to win nomination as a Conservative parliamentary candidate, Titmuss makes an impassioned speech extolling the virtues of his working-class parents:

> You know what my parents are? They're the true Conservatives! And I can tell you this. They're tired of being represented by people from the City or folks from up at the Manor. They want one of themselves! You can forget the county families and the city gents and the riverside commuters. They'll vote for you anyway. What you need to win is my people. The people who know the value of money because they've never had it. The people who say the same thing every night because it makes them feel safe. The people who've worked hard and don't want to see scroungers rewarded or laziness paying off. Put it this way, ladies and gentlemen. You need the voters I can bring you! They are the backbone of our country.

If Mrs Thatcher had been able to call upon such brilliant speech writers, perhaps she would still have been in office.

The figure of Titmuss was clearly meant to symbolise the changes which were indeed taking place within the Conservative Party of the 1980s. Titmuss was a very different creature from the superior Richard Bellamy MP who featured in the long-running television series *Upstairs, Downstairs*. Bellamy lived in Eaton Square and was an 'Old School Tie' Tory.

Also to be seen on television were the nauseating MP Alan B'Stard – played with demonic energy by comedian Rik Mayall – who recognises no interest beyond his own; and the greedy Sir Giles in Malcolm Bradbury's adaption of Tom Sharpe's *Blott on the Landscape*. Sir Giles is into shady property development, as too was

Leslie Titmuss. Clearly this is what Thatcherite MPs were supposed to be up to in their spare time.

Sir Giles was played by actor George Cole who also created the archetypal figure of Arthur Daley in the television series *Minder*. Small-time entrepreneur Daley, ducking and diving as he tries to earn a living, is descended from a long line of spiv characters who first saw the light of day during rationing under the post-war Labour Government. Critics of the Conservative Party in the 1980s used Arthur Daley as a convenient stick with which to beat Thatcherism.

Others dispensed with the stick and simply went all out for the jugular: Salman Rushdie in *The Satanic Verses* called Mrs Thatcher 'Mrs Torture' and 'Maggie the Bitch' – not much nuance or subtlety there. Rushdie is still experiencing at first-hand the differences between a parliamentary democracy which allows the expression of such sentiments and more fundamentalist regimes.

Normally novelists and script writers reject the dull minutiae of government as being undramatic. Exceptions to this general rule, however, were the enormously successful *Yes, Minister* and *Yes, Prime Minister*. The series follow the progress of Cabinet minister Jim Hacker, played by Paul Eddington, as he progresses up the greasy pole via the Department for Administrative Affairs and into 10 Downing Street. The stories themselves, however, are carefully non party political.

Co-writer Anthony Jay once explained that 'the fun of the series comes from showing civil servants as politicians see them and politicians as civil servants see them'. Based on meticulous research and interviews with senior civil servants and politicians, the episodes capture the feel of Whitehall and government and are all the more powerful for being carefully non-specific.

The political party to which Hacker belongs is not revealed and the early series discreetly avoided political topics by putting him in charge of Administrative Affairs. When Hacker became Prime Minister however, Jay and Lynn were careful to construct a defence policy, for instance, which did not coincide with the Conservative, Labour or Alliance platforms: 'We did it by deciding that if Hacker abolished Trident and Cruise,

kept Polaris, spent the money on conventional forces and introduced conscription, we shouldn't get into trouble from the
politicians.'

Their humorous view of the relationship between government,
Whitehall and 'the secret state' was rather different from that
presented in another novel which was memorably televised. *A Very
British Coup* by Labour MP Chris Mullin features a left-wing Labour
Prime Minister, Harry Perkins (superbly played by Ray McAnally)
who comes to office determined to implement his party's radical
policies. His administration is subjected to a systematic campaign
of dirty tricks not unlike some of those examined earlier. Book
and series end with an army coup reminiscent of events in Chile
in 1973.

That *Coup* was made for and shown on television shows that,
on occasion, companies were prepared to broadcast plays with
political substance. The early work of Dennis Potter, particularly
his Nigel Barton trilogy featuring a Labour MP, comes into this
category as do controversial features such as *Cathy Come Home* and
the work of Trevor Griffiths. The advent of Channel Four also
generated a range of plays and documentaries which would have
had Sir John Reith spinning in his grave. One of Channel Four's
co-productions, *The Ploughman's Lunch* starring Jonathan Pryce as
an unprincipled journalist, offered a unflattering portrayal of 1980s
Thatcherism.

The biggest change in terms of politics on television has
been in interviewing styles. In the 1930s and 1940s, politicians
were statesmen and accorded all due respect by the obsequious
interviewer. By the middle of the 1950s, however, the arrival of
commercial television and the appearance of younger journalists
such as Robin Day eager to penetrate the air of remoteness which
once hid politicians, undermined this deference.

One of this new breed of television interviewer was former
Labour MP Woodrow Wyatt, who claims to have pioneered a
'different type of questioning to the hitherto deferential "Yes,
Sir/No, Sir" approach to the important by the BBC interviewer.
None of the people I interviewed seemed to me more awesome
than many I had been used to dealing with on level terms for eleven

years. I asked firm questions, central to the issues, and would not let the interviewee dodge them . . .'

ITN's more personalised style of news reporting led to the creation of programmes such as *That Was The Week That Was* in 1962 which was soon attracting audiences of ten million. A Conservative Government was then in power and naturally they bore the brunt of the satire. Home Secretary Henry Brooke in particular was mercilessly lampooned as an upper-class bungler. Sir Alec Douglas-Home remains convinced that *TW3* harmed him politically.

But even though television is less respectful than it was – and the name Jeremy Paxman has become a by-word for aggressive interviewing – politicians in turn have been quick to learn the new tricks of this particular trade. Television needs them just as much as they need television.

In 1968 the power of the Lord Chamberlain to censor stage plays was abolished by a private member's bill sponsored by Michael Foot. It might have led to more nudity and swearing on stage but politics remained firmly in the wings. A few playwrights such as David Hare and Caryl Churchill wrote plays with political themes, but they were the exception to the rule.

Alan Bennett delved into the past for a convenient stereotype. In his play *Forty Years On*, he depicted Neville Chamberlain as a pathetic dupe with a silly umbrella. The advent of Mrs Thatcher generated near apoplexy in several left-wing writers and playwrights. Agitprop plays tediously castigated the failings of the yuppies and depicted Mrs Thatcher as a cross between Satan and Adolf Hitler.

Greater licence was enjoyed by the army of stand-up comics who adopted a relentlessly hostile attitude towards the Conservative Government. There was nothing surprising about this: satire is generally directed at those in power. Most of the comedy was relentlessly ephemeral, but Ben Elton made his anti-Tory views clear and Harry Enfield did create a character fond of 'loadsamoney', who brandished five-pound notes in the face of the audience, a comment on the supposedly materialistic obsession of Mrs Thatcher's supporters.

Perhaps the biggest changes took place in the realm of caricature. Since the 1960s many cartoonists have introduced a new edge or bite to their work: Ralph Steadman and Gerald Scarfe positively seem to glory in any perceived oddities or quirks in their victims. Cartoonists working for right-wing newspapers – Cummings on the *Express*, Franklin on the *Sun* and Jak on the *Evening Standard* – have happily lampooned left-wingers such as Michael Foot, Tony Benn, Arthur Scargill and Ken Livingstone, whilst Steve Bell of the *Guardian* retaliated against the Conservatives. Nicholas Garland of the *Independent* and *Telegraph* and Peter Brookes of *The Times* have eschewed explicit partisanship, and have often been the better for it. As for the puppets of *Spitting Image*, no politician or public figure is safe.

But politicians soon learn to take it: just as Gladstone went and laughed at a satirical portrait of himself, so today do politicians such as Sir Edward Heath and Kenneth Baker collect caricatures and most make a point of buying their *Spitting Image* puppet. Perhaps Winston Churchill put it best in an essay he once wrote called 'Cartoons and Cartoonists':

> Just as eels are supposed to get used to skinning, so politicians get used to being caricatured. In fact, by a strange trait in human nature they even get to like it. If we must confess it, they are quite offended and downcast when the cartoons stop. They wonder what has gone amiss. They fear old age and obsolescence are creeping upon them. They murmur: 'We are not mauled and maltreated as we used to be. The great days are ended.'

It is arguable, though, that the new cynicism towards organised politics is in part a result of the much greater licence with which the media has portrayed politicians generally since the 1960s.

In the past, the Conservative Party fully exploited its traditional air of authority and command. Conservatives liked to argue that they embodied the natural order of things. Today, there is no such order and the Party has to accept its fair share of satire and public criticism and in the process has lost some of the self-confidence on which it once so unerringly drew.

It does not make the task of pursuing power any easier.

18

Conclusions
The pursuit of power

'All the pleasing illusions, which made power gentle and obedience liberal . . .'

Edmund Burke, 1790

'The Party! What is the meaning of a Party if they don't follow their Leaders? Damn 'em, let 'em go.'

The first Duke of Wellington, 1829

'I reminded him [John Profumo] that the Conservative Party was in the business of winning and keeping power; it had no scruple in sacrificing any of its servants should interest demand it.'

Solicitor-general Sir Peter Rawlinson
speaking to John Profumo, 1963

So, finally, to return to the question with which this book began: why has the British Conservative Party been so successful? Or more accurately, why has it been so successful this century after being rather less so for most of the nineteenth century? Why has it outlasted all the other 'throne and altar' parties created in Europe?

The answer is to be found in the Conservative Party's recognition that the overriding purpose of political activity is the achievement of power. This appetite for power is the Conservative Party's governing idea. Without power, as the Party knows full well from its long spell out of office in the middle of the nineteenth century, virtually nothing can be achieved or safeguarded.

This relentless pursuit of power explains so much of the history and development of the Conservative Party explored in the previous chapters. It explains why, for example, the Conservative Party has never had a consistent body of ideas or a clearcut ideology, in case these should get in the way of power: hence the famed flexibility of the Party. It explains why the Party is so ruthless towards its leaders – having a loser as leader is the swiftest way to electoral defeat. The view first advanced by Lord Kilmuir that loyalty is the Tories' secret weapon is only a half truth, as the loyal Kilmuir himself found out when summarily dismissed by Macmillan in 1962. But if Kilmuir had been referring to loyalty to power, then he would indeed have been correct.

It explains why the Conservative Party is not terribly bothered how, why and from whom it obtains finance. It explains too why the Conservative Party is so adept at electioneering – because that is the simplest and easiest way to achieve political power in Britain. It also explains why, if necessary, the Party will resort to dirty tricks: power rather than legality is the final arbiter.

This formidable Conservative desire for power also explains why the Party has to pose as a national party in order to attract crucial working-class electoral support, even though most of its leading figures have come from privileged backgrounds. Its success has been so overwhelming that for most of this century the much-vaunted two-party political system has, in practice, barely existed. Since the 1880s we have had a continuous series of Conservative administrations with the odd exception. After 1918, for example, the Conservative Party has only been totally excluded from office in 1924 and between 1929 and 1931, 1945 and 1951, 1964 and 1970 and 1974 and 1979.

In addition, the Conservatives' links with other major institutions in this country mean that even when nominally out of office the Party is certainly no impotent and passive being. The Labour Party was in opposition for virtually all of the 1950s and 1980s and its impact on national life then was, bar only a handful of cases, minimal. The same could not be said of the Conservative Party and its allies when out of office.

Its pursuit of power explains why the supposedly hidebound Conservative Party is often more radical than the Labour Party because sometimes the attainment of power demands risk – it was the Conservatives after all who supplied the first Jewish Prime Minister, the first bachelor Prime Minister and the first woman Prime Minister. The Labour Party, on the other hand, as well as many European conservative parties, has demonstrated a rather less marked devotion to power; doctrinal disputes and ideological squabbling, in public if needs be, often take priority.

In particular, the Party learnt the traumatic lessons of 1846 and has never split because no principle, personality or promise is worth the upheaval and the inevitable loss of power. Consistency is therefore ranked low in the list of Tory virtues. It was the Conservatives who introduced and then abolished the Corn Laws; the Conservatives who vowed to retain a united Ireland, but accepted partition; the Conservatives who built the Empire and then helped dismantle it; the Conservatives who frowned on the Common Market and then took Britain into it. But, of course, 'circumstances' are indeed continually changing. The Party is driven by what might be called lethal pragmatism. This flexibility means that it soon recovers from seemingly crushing election defeats, whereas the Labour Party seems to find it much harder to accommodate seismic shifts in public opinion and the Liberal Party disintegrated in the 1920s.

The Conservative Party's lust for power ensures that it strenuously maintains a public image of unity and loyalty, however untrue this may be in private; disunity is fatal to any party seeking power within the British political system. In any case, a national party cannot afford to be riven by dissension; as Lord Salisbury once said of Disraeli, his 'only fixed political principle was that the Party must on no account be broken up'.

It explains why the composition of the parliamentary Party was, until recently, so uniform because the shared background of its members made it much easier to enforce unwritten codes and customs. It explains, too, why the Conservative Party's preoccupation with power is more important even than the efficient running of the economy; tough economic policies will always be relaxed if they threaten electoral success.

It also illustrates why it is so important to see the Conservative Party as a *party* and not merely as a random collection of individuals or interests. This attention to the Party as an institution is one reason why it has been so careful to root itself in the country, whether locally or as a crucial part of the British Establishment. It explains why, contrary to the received myth of immobility and stagnation, the British Conservative Party excels as a body which is continually making and remaking itself. Like the Catholic Church and most successful businesses, the Party has learnt how to manage change: the art is to undertake this change beneath a mask of continuity and tradition.

Finally, it is this hidden agenda, this often unacknowledged search for power, that explains why there is such a large discrepancy between the official and sanitised story of the British Conservatives and the hidden history of the Party which as far as possible is left undisclosed.

And yet this pursuit of power has rarely been a cold-eyed and ruthless affair: Conservatives have always appreciated the importance of humour and charm, which are invariably more effective than graceless zealotry. Tyrants never tend to last long, unlike the Conservative Party. By and large, British people are moderate and tolerant and Conservatives would be foolish – which they most certainly are not – to offend these widely held sentiments. But one shouldn't be blinded to the fact that the Tory voice has always been one of command and of authority.

It would be stupid to denigrate the achievements of the Conservative way: Britain's history is remarkably free of bloodshed and mayhem, whilst the continuity and stability of its institutions – which includes the Conservative Party itself – have given a sense of permanence to most people's lives which is valued by all but the most ardent revolutionary. Only the rigid and unbending pro- or anti-Conservative can view the development of the Party in stark black and white terms.

We, The Nation has tried to bring out the good things in the history of the Conservative Party. It is a multi-layered and rich story which continually refutes glib generalisations: the image pushed by Conservative partisans that they are living embodiments of sweetness and light versus the claims of opponents that the Party exists purely to grind down the poor and helpless. I hope that the fascination which I have felt as I have worked on and written this book is clear. It is an endlessly changing story because Conservatives understand full well that the world itself never stands still.

But it must finally be recognised that the Party exists to protect and nurture a particular existing order. And whether one agrees with this position or not, that order is changing and in turn causing enormous problems to the Party.

Several chapters in this book have sounded warning bells: for instance, the growing fractiousness within the parliamentary Party; the decline of the Party as a mass political organisation; financial problems; its increasing inability to halt economic decline; problems of dealing with growing social inequality; and the decline of public confidence in many British institutions which traditionally buttressed the Party.

Above all, perhaps, the Party is becoming less and less of a national body. As Anthony Seldon has rightly pointed out, 'In 1900 the Conservatives were a national party with support (if not always seats) spread across the country. They have ended the century the party of the south, weak in the Midlands, Wales, and the north of England and facing extinction in Scotland.'

This shrinkage in turn relates to the increasingly fraught relationship between the Party and the English nationalism which has always been its core. The bitter disputes over Europe reflect a weakening of Conservative identity in a global economy of multinationals and mass media which leap effortlessly over national boundaries.

The key question is whether the Conservative Party can once again re-create itself in its pursuit of power or whether, after nearly two centuries, its leaders and party managers will finally be unable to square the circle. It might well be that just as the twentieth century was indeed the Conservative century, the next century will bring about a drastic recasting of the British political system and of the British political parties themselves.

But no one should ever underestimate the resilience or the determination of the British Conservative Party in its pursuit of power.

Short Chronology

1832 March: the Carlton Club is founded in London.

1834 December: Peel issues the 'Tamworth Manifesto'; copies also sent to the press.

1846 June: downfall of Sir Robert Peel. The split in the Conservative Party deprives them of majority office for decades.

1867 August: Disraeli pushes through the Second Reform Act extending the franchise.

1867 December: the first conference of the National Union of Conservative and Constitutional Associations is held.

1872 May: Disraeli's speech at Manchester outlines his conception of Conservatism; followed up by his speech at Crystal Palace in June.

1874 February: Disraeli becomes Prime Minister.

1883 November: the formation of the Primrose League.

1885 June: the Third Marquess of Salisbury becomes Party leader.

1891 November: creation of the National Society of Conservative and Unionist Agents.

1902 July: Arthur Balfour succeeds his uncle, Lord Salisbury, as Prime Minister and Party leader.

1906 January: crushing Conservative defeat in general election.

1911 June: Arthur Steel-Maitland appointed Party Chairman.

1912 July: Bonar Law at Blenheim commits Party to unconstitutional means in defence of Ulster.

1923 April: establishment of 'the 1922 Committee' of backbenchers.

1924 October: general election muddied by the *Daily Mail*'s publication of the Zinoviev Letter on October 25th. Baldwin's Conservatives return to power.

1926 October: J.C.C. Davidson is appointed Party Chairman.

1929 November: setting up of the Conservative Research Department; Joseph Ball appointed its first director.

1935 March: secret formation of the 'National Publicity Bureau'.

1945 July: Churchill's Conservatives heavily defeated by Attlee's Labour Party in the general election.

1946 July: Churchill appoints Lord Woolton as Party Chairman.

1947 October: the annual Party Conference overwhelmingly endorses the 'Industrial Charter'.

1948 December: Lord Woolton supervises the setting of illegal 'rivers companies' to launder money.

1956 October: Suez invasion begins.

1957 January: Harold Macmillan succeeds Sir Anthony Eden as Prime Minister and Party leader.

1957 January: the Conservative Party launches an expensive advertising campaign devised by the agency Colman, Prentis and Varley.

1958 January: Chancellor of the Exchequer Peter Thorneycroft and colleagues Nigel Birch and Enoch Powell resign over the

Cabinet's decision not to support their deflationary economic policies.

1963 January: General de Gaulle blocks Britain's application to join the EEC.

1963 June: John Profumo resigns from the Government.

1963 October: Macmillan's unexpected resignation as Prime Minister and leader leads to the 'emergence' of Lord Home.

1964 October: the Conservatives lose office after thirteen years in power.

1965 July: Edward Heath defeats Reginald Maudling and Enoch Powell in the Party's first contested leadership election.

1970 June: Heath's Conservative Party defeats Harold Wilson's Labour Party.

1973 January: the Heath Government takes Britain into Europe.

1975 February: Margaret Thatcher elected leader in place of Edward Heath.

1975 August: Alistair McAlpine is appointed Party Treasurer, a post which he holds until 1990.

1978 Summer: advertising agency Saatchi & Saatchi begin work on behalf of the Conservative Party, producing the slogan 'Labour Isn't Working'.

1982 June: Argentinian surrender in the Falklands.

1983 June: Mrs Thatcher's Conservatives crush the Labour Party led by Michael Foot in that month's general election.

1984 July: Mrs Thatcher speaks of the striking miners as 'the enemy within'.

1985 March: end of the miners' strike.

1990 November: Margaret Thatcher steps down as leader and is replaced by John Major.

1992 April: John Major's Conservative Party unexpectedly wins the general election.

1992 September: the Government is forced to withdraw from the Exchange Rate Mechanism (ERM).

Notes

These notes give the source of quotations and other important details mentioned in the text. They provide an opportunity for acknowledging the academics, commentators and politicians themselves on whose work I have drawn.

The place of publication is London unless otherwise specified.

The full titles of the most important books are given in the Select Guide to Further Reading.

CHAPTER ONE
The Tory Story

p. 1 *Sobered by inactivity*: George Peel (ed) *The Private Letters of Sir Robert Peel* (John Murray, 1920) p. 18

p. 2 *Not natural party of government*: Jim Bulpitt 'The Discipline of the New Democracy: Mrs Thatcher's Domestic Statecraft' in *Political Studies*, volume XXXIV, no.1, March 1986, p. 39

p. 2 *Not trusting human reason*: Sir Keith Feiling *Toryism* (G. Bell, 1913) p. 37

p. 2 *Man to adore*: Disraeli quoted in Harvey Glickman 'The Toryness of English Conservatism' in *Journal of British Studies*, volume 1, no.1, November 1961, p. 127

p. 3 *Cosy lunches*: Sir John Junor *Listening for a Midnight Tram* (Chapmans, 1990), *passim*

p. 3 *Gastronomic pimping*: Bevan quoted in Alan Doig *Westminster Babylon* (Allison & Busby, 1990) p. 307

p. 3 *Broadcasters*: Greg Dyke delivering the annual MacTaggart Lecture, quoted in *The Times*, 27 August 1994

p. 4 *Middle-aged historians*: Brian Harrison *Separate Spheres* (Croom

Helm, 1978) p. 16

p. 4   *Half a ton*: Kenneth Young *Arthur James Balfour* (G. Bell, 1963) xxi

p. 4   *495 boxes*: D. R. Thorpe *Selwyn Lloyd* (Cape, 1989) xvi–xvii

p. 4   *Meet Conservatives*: John Vincent 'Tory Intellectuals' in *Encounter*, March 1990, volume LXXIV, no.2, p. 70

p. 5   *ICVCs*: Philip Norton and David M. Wood *Back from Westminster: British Members of Parliament and their Constituents* (Lexington, USA: University Press of Kentucky, 1993) p. 139

p. 5   *Politics about power*: James Margach *The Anatomy of Power* (W. H. Allen, 1979) vii

CHAPTER TWO
Old Dog, New Tricks

p. 9   *True blue moments*: Ian Gilmour *The Body Politic* (Hutchinson, 1971) p. 81

p. 9   *Dedicated to office*: Norman Tebbit 'Silver spoons and chips on the shoulder' in the *Sunday Telegraph*, 16 May 1993

p. 9   *1895 Cabinet*: Barbara Tuchman *The Proud Tower* (Papermac, 1980) pp. 3–4

p. 10   *Not knowing place*: Penny Junor *The Major Enigma* (Michael Joseph, 1993) p. 53

p. 11   *New remedies*: Bacon quoted by Lord Rayner in Basil Watson (ed) *The Morality of the Creation of Wealth* (St Lawrence Jewry talks, 1985) p. 14

p. 12   *Changing name*: e.g. John Campbell *F. E. Smith* (Cape, 1983) p. 535; Anthony Sampson *Macmillan* (Pelican, 1968) p. 83

p. 12   *1923 posters*: *National Society of Conservative Agents*, Minutes of Council Meeting, 15 June, 1923 (in Minute book kept at Westminster Central Library, London): Ref. 485/4

p. 14   *Peel's accent*: Eric Evans 'Sir Robert Peel: A Suitable Case for Reassessment?' in *History Review*, 18, p. 25

p. 15   *Sending out manifesto*: Sheila Smith in her introduction to Benjamin Disraeli *Coningsby* (Oxford: University Press, 1982) xi

p. 15   *Duke pointing to blinds*: W. Thornbury and E. Walford *Old and New London* (Cassell, n.d.) volume IV, p. 363

p. 16   *Relieved for ever*: George Peel (ed) *The Private Letters of Sir Robert Peel* (John Murray, 1920) p. 281

p. 17   *Mackintosh and loyalty*: Robert Stewart *Party and Politics, 1830–1852* (Macmillan, 1989) p. 6

p. 20   *Times and amenities*: R. B. McDowell *British Conservatism 1832–1914* (Faber, 1959) p. 10

p. 20   *Alternating Cabinets*: Balfour quoted in James Harvey and Katharine Hood *The British State* (Lawrence & Wishart, 1958) p. 36

p. 23   *Middle-class tact*: Balfour quoted in J. P. Cornford 'The Parliamentary Foundations of the Hotel Cecil' in R. Robson (ed) *Ideas and Institutions of Victorian Britain* (G. Bell, 1967) p. 296

p. 23   *Role of women*: Joni Lovenduski, Pippa Norris and Catriona Burness in Anthony Seldon and Stuart Ball (eds) *Conservative Century* (Oxford: University Press, 1994) p. 619

p. 24   *Educate in time*: Baldwin in Philip Williamson '"Safety First": Baldwin, the Conservative Party and the 1929 General Election' in the *Historical Journal*, volume 25, no.2, p. 387

p. 24   *Daily Mail*: Noreen Branson *Britain in the Nineteen Twenties* (Weidenfeld & Nicolson, 1975) p. 204

p. 24   *Carlton recruits*: Sir Charles Petrie *The Carlton Club* (White Lion, 1972 ed) p. 208

p. 25   *Churchill's photograph*: Virginia Cowles *No Cause For Alarm* (Hamish Hamilton, 1949) p. 72

p. 25   *Churchill losing elections*: Robert Rhodes James (ed) *Memoirs Of A Conservative* (Weidenfeld & Nicolson, 1969) p. 171

p. 26   *National press/share of votes*: Roger Eatwell *The 1945–1951 Labour Governments* (Batsford, 1979) pp. 41–2, 42–3

p. 27   *Charter stage managed*: Anthony Howard *RAB* (Papermac, 1988) pp. 156–7

p. 27   *Ruins*: Peter Hennessy 'Harold Macmillan' in *The Economist*, 20 April 1991, p. 24

p. 29   *Enlisting talent*: Norman Tebbit in the *Sunday Telegraph*, 16 May 1993

p. 31   *Leader must lead*: Mrs Thatcher interviewed in the *Daily Express*, 28 October 1989

p. 32   *Suburban rump*: Macmillan quoted in Richard Davenport-Hines *The Macmillans* (Mandarin, 1993) p. 3

p. 34   *Punchbag*: Nigel Lawson *The View From No. 11* (Bantam, 1992) p. 653

p. 35   *Instinct to survive*: Mathew Parris quoted in Nicholas Baldwin *The Conservative Party* (Oxfordshire: Wroxton College, 1990) p. 13

p. 36   *1950 postal voting*: H. G. Nicholas *The British Election of 1950* (Macmillan, 1951) p. 9

p. 36   *Expat vote*: Stuart Ball 'Local Conservatism and Party Organisation' in Anthony Seldon and Stuart Ball (eds), p. 307

p. 38   *Leave tactics to generals*: John Ramsden (ed) *Real Old Tory Politics* (Historians' Press, 1984) p. 10

p. 38   *Not splitting*: Sir Ian Gilmour *The Body Politic*, p. 90

CHAPTER THREE
Why Are We Here?

p. 40   *Length of chain*: John Vincent 'Toryism and democracy' in the *Spectator*, 24 October 1970

p. 40   *Leave talking*: obituary notice in the *Daily Telegraph*, 21 December 1990

p. 40   *Guide to Classics*: *Daily Telegraph*, 21 December 1990

p. 41   *Contempt for politics*: Bernard Crick 'The World of Michael Oakeshott' in *Encounter*, volume xx, June 1963, pp. 70–71

p. 41   *Great decisions*: Eugen Weber 'Ambiguous Victories' in the *Journal of Contemporary History*, volume 13, no.4, October 1978, p. 827

p. 41   *Oakeshott and Europe*: Noel Annan *Our Age* (Weidenfeld & Nicolson, 1990) p. 400

p. 42   *Sin of intellectualism*: Lord Butler *The Art of the Possible* (Penguin, 1973 ed.) p. 16

p. 42   *Clever people wrong*: Macmillan's speech of 1946 quoted in Harvey Glickmann 'The Toryness of English Conservatism' in *Journal of British Studies*, volume 1, i, November 1961, p. 122

p. 42   *Personal relationships*: Eustace Percy *Some Memories* (Eyre & Spottiswoode, 1958) p. 18

p. 42   *Very breath*: Harold Begbie *The Conservative Mind* (Mills & Boon, 1924) p. 9

p. 42   *Human experience*: F. A. Pottle (ed) *Boswell's London Journal 1762–1763* (Heinemann, 1950) p. 314

p. 43   *Why be a Conservative?*: Roger Scruton *The Meaning of Conservatism* (Macmillan, 1984 ed.) p. 204

p. 43   *Johnson on Burke*: Christopher Hibbert *The Personal History of Samuel Johnson* (Penguin, 1984) p. 157

p. 46   *Burke not knowing*: John Morley *Burke* (Macmillan, 1988) p. 235

p. 46   *Intellectual resistance*: Conor Cruise O'Brien *The Great Melody* (Sinclair-Stevenson, 1992) p. 596

p. 47   *Worthless bauble*: quoted in Conor Cruise O'Brien, p. 510

p. 48   *Salisbury rather than Disraeli*: Maurice Cowling in M. Cowling (ed) *Conservative Essays* (Cassell, 1978) p. 22

p. 48   *Party of movement*: A. L. Kennedy *Salisbury 1830–1903* (John Murray, 1953) p. 74

p. 49   *Don't trust experts*: quoted in Martin Kettle 'Common sense of the absurdly unfunny' in the *Guardian*, 19 February 1994

p. 49   *Principles of common sense*: Balfour quoted by David Dilks in 'Baldwin and Chamberlain' in Lord Butler (ed) *The Conservatives* (Allen & Unwin, 1977) p. 273

p. 50   *Why change?*: Lord Hugh Cecil *Conservatism* (Williams and Norgate, 1912) p. 11

p. 50   *Intellectuals intermarrying*: N. G. Annan 'The Intellectual Aristocracy' in J. H. Plumb (ed) *Studies in Social History* (Longmans, Green, 1955) pp. 284–5

p. 50   *National Review*: R. B. McDowell *British Conservatism 1832–1914* (Faber, 1959) p. 93

p. 50   *Mallock and the few*: Robert Eccleshall *English Conservatism Since the Restoration* (Unwin Hyman, 1990) p. 171

p. 51   *Baldwin's place*: Martin J. Weiner *English Culture and the Decline of the Industrial Spirit 1850–1980* (Cambridge: University Press, 1981) pp. 101–2

p. 51　*Wilden semi-feudal*: Robert Blake 'Baldwin and the Right' in John Raymond (ed) *The Baldwin Age* (Eyre & Spottiswoode, 1960) p. 27

p. 51　*Halifax's spinning wheel*: Martin J. Weiner 'Conservatism, Economic Growth and English Culture' in *Parliamentary Affairs*, volume xxxiv, no.4, p. 415

p. 52　*Macmillan and green lawns*: Hugh Thomas *The Suez Affair* (Weidenfeld & Nicolson, 1986 ed.) p. 163

p. 52　*Rapacious scramble*: Quintin Hogg *The Case For Conservatism* (Penguin, 1947 ed) p. 52

p. 52　*Championship of religion*: Lord Hugh Cecil, p. 116

p. 52　*Original sin*: Nigel Lawson 'The New Conservatism' (London: Centre for Policy Studies, 1980) quoted by Ian Aitken in the *Guardian*, 6 August 1980

p. 53　*Crusade*: Anthony Sampson *Macmillan* (Pelican, 1968) p. 85

p. 53　*1963 Cabinet*: Matthew D'Ancona 'Red threat raised hopes of Vatican link' in *The Times*, 1 January 1994

p. 53　*Imperfection*: Ian Gilmour 'Foreword' in Zig Layton-Henry (ed) *Conservative Party Politics* (Macmillan, 1980) xii

p. 54　*Gray on Gilmour*: 'Thatcherism is as British as Gaullism is French' in the *Sunday Telegraph*, 18 October 1992

p. 54　*Own ideology*: Hugo Young *One of Us* (Macmillan, 1989) p. 406

p. 55　*Banging table*: Richard Cockett *Thinking the Unthinkable* (Harper-Collins, 1994) p. 174

p. 55　*Process*: Shirley Robin Letwin *The Anatomy of Thatcherism* (Fontana, 1992) pp. 25–31

p. 55　*Believers fell away*: Lady Thatcher in *Thatcher: The Downing Street Years*, 4, 'Wielding the Knife', BBC1, 10 November 1993

p. 55　*Economic Dining Club*: Nicholas Ridley *My Style of Government* (Hutchinson, 1991) p. 20

p. 56　*IEA and language*: Michael Davie 'Men who told Thatcher there was an alternative' in the *Observer*, 24 March 1985

p. 57　*Too few revolutionaries*: Margaret Thatcher *The Downing Street Years* (HarperCollins, 1993) p. 306

p. 57　*Vast cars*: Butler quoted in the *New Statesman*, 20 February 1976, p. 225

p. 58　*Mother wonderful*: John Ranelagh *Thatcher's People* (HarperCollins, 1991) p. 211 fn.3

p. 58　*Major's long shadows*: speech in the *Daily Telegraph*, 23 April 1993

p. 60　*Eve's misbehaviour*: F. J. C. Hearnshaw *Conservatism in England* (Macmillan, 1933) p. 20

p. 61　*Manfully resist*: Edmund Burke 'Thoughts and Details on Scarcity' in Robert Eccleshall, p. 77

p. 62　*Liberty of citizen*: J. K. Galbraith *The Good Society Considered* (Cardiff: Law School, 1994) no pagination

p. 62   *Ruling class/needs of strong*: Anthony Arblaster 'Intellectual by Appointment' in the *New Socialist*, November 1985, p. 17

p. 62   *Common sense*: David Willetts *Modern Conservatism* (Penguin, 1992) p. 6

p. 63   *Vote Conservative*: Morley quoted in Christopher Hollis 'The Conservative Party In History' in *Political Quarterly*, volume 32, no.3, July–September 1961, p. 227

p. 64   *Promiscuity*: Kenneth Baker (ed) *The Faber Book of Conservatism* (Faber, 1993)

p. 64   *Varied repertoire*: G. W. Jones 'Conservative Characters' in *Parliamentary Affairs*, volume 43, no.2, 1990, p. 236

CHAPTER FOUR
All Power To The Leader?

p. 65   *Pigs to market*: Keith Middlemas and John Barnes *Baldwin* (Weidenfeld & Nicolson, 1969) p. 263

p. 65   *Private lives*: Robert Rhodes James *Bob Boothby* (Headline, 1992) p. 111

p. 66   *Leader leads*: R. T. McKenzie *British Political Parties* (Heinemann, 1963) p. 145

p. 66   *Abandonment of the Lady*: Alan Clark *Diaries* (Weidenfeld & Nicolson, 1993) p. 361; *Praetorian Guard*, p. 289

p. 69   *Great man now*: Robert Blake *The Unknown Prime Minister* (Eyre and Spottiswoode, 1955) p. 85

p. 69   *Degradation of secret ballot*: John Ramsden (ed) *Real Old Tory Politics* (Historians' Press, 1984) pp. 35–6

p. 69   *Pretyman in 1921*: R. T. McKenzie *British Political Parties* p. 21

p. 71   *Macmillan at 1922*: Philip Goodhart *The 1922* (Macmillan, 1973) p. 175

p. 72   *Q badges*: Martin Gilbert *In Search of Churchill* (HarperCollins, 1994) p. 237

p. 72   *Artificially boosting Hailsham*: John Junor *Listening for a Midnight Tram* (Chapmans, 1990) p. 133

p. 72   *Dilhorne's arithmetic*: Nigel Fisher *The Tory Leaders* (Weidenfeld & Nicolson, 1977) p. 107

p. 73   *Loaded revolver*: Patrick Cosgrave *The Lives of Enoch Powell* (Bodley Head, 1989) p. 188

p. 73   *Macleod's article*: printed in full in George Hutchinson *The Last Edwardian At No. 10* (Quartet, 1980) pp. 123–141

p. 73   *Macleod cut*: Humphry Berkeley *Crossing the Floor* (Allen & Unwin, 1972) p. 96

p. 73   *Eton and disdain*: Anthony Sampson *Anatomy of Britain* (Hodder & Stoughton, 1962) p. 89

p. 73   *Berkeley's letter*: Humphry Berkeley, p. 29

p. 74   *Home and emergence*: Lord Home *The Way the Wind Blows* (Collins, 1976) p. 218

p. 77   *Being Prime Minister*: Lady Thatcher quoted in *The Times*, 4 October 1993

p. 78   *Splitting Party*: Butler quoted in Vernon Bogdanor 'The Selection of the Party Leader' in Anthony Seldon and Stuart Ball (eds) *Conservative Century* (Oxford: University Press, 1994) p. 95

p. 80   *Scared groom*: this is the kind of story which often attaches itself to an unpopular man like Peel; according to his biographer, the coachman told him not to ride the horse but was overruled: Norman Gash *Sir Robert Peel* (Longman, 1972) p. 697

p. 81   *Another deanery*: Richard Shannon *The Age of Disraeli, 1868–1881* (Longman, 1992) p. 53

p. 82   *Paper knife*: A. L. Kennedy *Salisbury 1830–1903* (John Murray, 1953) pp. 251–2

p. 82   *Hang nobody*: J. P. Cornford 'The Parliamentary Foundations of the Hotel Cecil' in R. Robson (ed) *Ideas and Institutions of Victorian Britain* (G. Bell, 1967) p. 295

p. 82   *Bishops dying*: A. L. Kennedy, p. 302

p. 83   *What closes today*: Barbara Tuchman *The Proud Tower* (Macmillan, 1980) p. 59

p. 83   *Eel and soap*: David Dutton *Austen Chamberlain* (Bolton: Ross Anderson, 1985) p. 63

p. 84   *Game of bridge*: Lord Boothby *Recollections of a Rebel* (Hutchinson, 1978) p. 159

p. 84   *Wanting a little of this*: Robert Blake, p. 412

p. 84   *Law ambitious*: Sir Austen Chamberlain *Down The Years* (Cassell, 1935) p. 225

p. 85   *Week-ends free*: letter of 12 June 1923 in *The Papers of J. C. C. Davidson*, House of Lords, Box 155, June 1923–January 1924

p. 85   *Blowing greenfly*: Douglas Hurd *An End To Promises* (Collins, 1979) p. 87

p. 85   *Dirt*: Iain Macleod *Neville Chamberlain* (Muller, 1961) p. 203; *are dirt*: David Dilks *Neville Chamberlain* volume one (Cambridge: University Press, 1984) p. 519

p. 86   *Rigid competency*: Lloyd George quoted in Peter Clarke *A Question of Leadership* (Penguin, 1992 ed.) p. 114

p. 86   *Shuttle diplomacy*: John Campbell in *The Times*, 25 October 1993

p. 87   *Autocrat*: Amery quoted in Richard Cockett 'Appeasement' in *Modern History Review*, volume 1, no.3, p. 16

p. 88   *Macmillan and Labour*: James Margach *The Abuse of Power* (W. H. Allen, 1978) p. 115

p. 89   *Deliberation*: reproduced in Peter Hennessy 'Harold Macmillan' in *The Economist*, 20 April 1991, p. 19

p. 89   *Totting up majorities*: Alistair Horne *Macmillan 1857–1986* (Macmillan, 1989) pp. 254–5

p. 89 *Sit in pavilion*: Douglas Dodds-Parker *Political Eunuch* (Ascot: Springwood Books, 1986) p. 118

p. 90 *Superiority of mind*: Lord Hill *Both Sides of the Hill* (Heinemann, 1964) p. 235

p. 90 *Double crosser*: Simon Heffer 'Centenary of a Double-Crosser' in the *Spectator*, 5 February 1994

p. 90 *Please not me*: James Margach *The Abuse of Power*, p. 128

p. 90 *Butler would have been better*: Alistair Horne, p. 582

p. 91 *Social life difficult*: Peter Rawlinson *A Price Too High* (Weidenfeld & Nicolson, 1989) p. 244

p. 91 *Dreadful voice*: Patrick Cosgrave *The Lives of Enoch Powell* (Bodley Head, 1989) p. 443

p. 92 *Quislings*: Sir Anthony Parsons quoting Mrs Thatcher in the television series *Thatcher: The Downing Street Years*, BBC1, 20 October 1993

p. 92 *Swamping and polls*: George Brock 'Mrs Thatcher's Arithmetic' in the *Spectator*, 15 June 1985

p. 94 *Major unidentified*: Bruce Anderson *John Major* (Headline, 1991) p. 122

p. 95 *Love and power*: Reginald Bevins *The Greasy Pole* (Hodder & Stoughton, 1965) p. 5

p. 95 *No friendship at top*: Lloyd George quoted in Anthony Howard *RAB* (Papermac, 1988) p. 322

p. 96 *What are politics*: David Dutton, p. 335

p. 96 *Butler's father*: Lord Butler *The Art of the Possible* (Penguin, 1973) p. 21

p. 96 *Churchill thumping ground*: James Stuart *Within the Fringe* (Bodley Head, 1967), p. 147

p. 97 *Battle of Omdurman*: Philip Goodhart *The 1922* (Macmillan, 1973) p. 167

p. 98 *Tea-lady*: Theresa Gorman *The Bastards* (Pan, 1993) p. 5

p. 100 *Political lives in failure*: Patrick Cosgrave, p. 425

CHAPTER FIVE
The Led

p. 101 *Male paradise*: Robert Rhodes James *'Chips'* (Weidenfeld & Nicolson, 1993) p. 128

p. 101 *Don't appear clever*: Julian Critchley *Westminster Blues* (Hamish Hamilton, 1985) p. 29

p. 102 *Hard-faced type*: Willie Gallacher *The Chosen Few* (Lawrence & Wishart, 1940) p. 169

p. 102 *Upstarts*: John Mortimer interviewed by Beatrix Campbell, 'A Decent Chap', in *City Limits*, 10 June 1983

p. 102 *Tax avoidance*: Alan Clark *Diaries* (Weidenfeld & Nicolson, 1993) p. 159

p. 102   *300 seats not fought*: Martin Pugh *The Evolution of the British Electoral System 1832–1987* (Historical Association, 1988) p. 16

p. 102   *5,000 and political career*: Robert Stewart *Party and Politics, 1830–1852* (Macmillan, 1989) p. 35

p. 102   *3/4 patricians*: David Cannadine *The Decline and Fall of the British Aristocracy* (Picador, 1992 ed.) p. 14

p. 103   *Winterton's nomination*: Earl Winterton *Pre-War* (Macmillan, 1932) p. 1

p. 104   *J. H. Pettifer*: Martin Pugh *The Tories and the People 1880–1935* (Oxford: Blackwell, 1985) p. 168

p. 104   *Astor, politics and Cliveden*: Christopher Sykes *Nancy* (Collins, 1972) pp. 107–8, 169

p. 105   *On way to Lords*: Nigel Fisher *The Tory Leaders* (Weidenfeld & Nicolson, 1977) p. 10

p. 105   *Casino capitalism*: Macmillan quoted in Harvey Glickman 'The Toryness of English Conservatism' in *Journal of British Studies*, volume 1, no.1, November 1961, p. 137

p. 105   *Cousinhood*: Simon Haxey *Tory M. P.* (Gollancz, 1939) p. 125

p. 106   *1930 seats on sale*: Stuart Ball *Baldwin and the Conservative Party* (Yale: University Press, 1988) p. 20

p. 106   *How much money*: Simon Haxey, p. 30

p. 106   *Butler's election fund*: Anthony Howard *RAB* (Papermac, 1988) p. 51

p. 106   *Hogg and £400*: Lord Hailsham *A Sparrow's Flight* (Collins, 1990) p. 112

p. 106   *Harvey's complaint*: J. F. S. Ross *Parliamentary Representation* (Eyre and Spottiswoode, 1948 ed.) pp. 297–9

p. 106   *Cartland's novels*: *Daily Telegraph Magazine*, 23 April 1994; Barbara Cartland *Ronald Cartland* (Collins, 1942) pp. 139, 169

p. 107   *Camel and needle*: Duff Cooper quoted in Simon Haxey, pp. 178–9

p. 107   *Absence of working class*: David Butler and Michael Pinto-Duschinsky 'The Conservative Elite, 1918–78: Does Unrepresentativeness Matter?' in Zig Layton-Henry (ed) *Conservative Party Politics* (Macmillan, 1980) pp. 187, 191

p. 109   *Social prejudice*: Michael Pinto-Duschinsky *British Political Finance 1830–1980* (USA, Washington: American Enterprise Institute, 1981) p. 130 fn.8

p. 109   *Whitelaw's nomination*: William Whitelaw *The Whitelaw Memoirs* (Aurum, 1989) p. 49

p. 109   *Prior and tractor*: Jim Prior *A Balance of Power* (Hamish Hamilton, 1986) p. 17

p. 109   *Tebbit at Epping*: Norman Tebbit *Upwardly Mobile* (Futura, 1990 ed.) pp. 97, 103, 106–7

p. 109   *City stockbroker in morning*: James Stuart *Within the Fringe* (Bodley Head, 1967) p. 77

p. 110 *Heavy drinking*: Robert Rhodes James 'Sick and tired of politics', *The Times*, 23 June 1993

p. 110 *A cad*: Robert Rhodes James 'Serving the country right or left?', *The Times*, 7 November 1992

p. 110 *Thatcher and Etonians*: Alfred Sherman quoted in John Ranelagh *Thatcher's People* (HarperCollins, 1991), p. 180

p. 110 *Public school decrease*: Philip Norton and D. M. Wood *Back from Westminster*. (Lexington, USA: University Press of Kentucky) pp. 18–19

p. 110 *Middle-class*: Hugh Montgomery-Massingberd 'Top and Bottom of the Tory Class' in the *Spectator*, 3 May 1986

p. 111 *'Real Tories don't read books'* Steve Platt and Julia Gallagher in the *New Statesman*, 7 October 1994

p. 111 *Prior on knights*: Jim Prior, pp. 22–3

p. 111 *False squires*: Margaret Thatcher *The Downing Street Years* (HarperCollins, 1993) p. 104

p. 111 *Tenth to a third*: Peter Riddell *Honest Opportunism* (Faber, 1994) p. 22

p. 111 *12 letters a year*: Sir Gervaise Rentoul *Sometimes I Think* (Hodder & Stoughton, 1940) p. 15

p. 111 *33 letters a day*: Philip Norton and David Wood 'Constituency Service by Members of Parliament' in *Parliamentary Affairs*, volume 43, no.2, April 1990, p. 198

p. 111 *Technical replies*: Norton and Wood *Back from Westminster* p. 43

p. 112 *60 hours a week*: Lisanne Radice, Elazabeth Vallance and Virginia Willis *Member of Parliament* (Macmillan, 1987) xiii

p. 112 *Churchill on politics*: Lord Moran *Winston Churchill* (Constable, 1966) p. 327

p. 113 *Drink Champagne*: Sir Charles Petrie *The Carlton Club* (White Lion, 1972 ed) p. 172

p. 113 *Married, unmarried*: Beatrix Campbell *The Iron Ladies* (Virago, 1987) p. 252

p. 113 *Revolutionary change*: Earl of Woolton *Memoirs* (Cassell, 1959) p. 346

p. 114 *Denis's money*: Penny Junor *Margaret Thatcher* (Sidgwick & Jackson, 1983) p. 35

p. 114 *Major needing £500*: Edward Pearce *The Quiet Rise of John Major* (Weidenfeld & Nicolson, 1991) p. 15

p. 114 *£5,000 a year*: Beatrix Campbell, pp. 248–9

p. 114 *522 directorships*: Mark Hollingsworth *MPs for Hire* (Bloomsbury, 1991) p. 1

p. 114 *Elected public servants*: Mark Hollingsworth, p. 22

p. 115 *Serpents*: Martyn Harris 'Oiling wheels over here' in the *Daily Telegraph*, 26 February 1987

p. 116 *170 MPs paid*: Andrew Boyle *Poor, Dear Brendan* (Hutchinson, 1974) p. 242

p. 116 *Crookshank*: diary entries dated 22 February 1938; 24 February 1938; 4 October 1938; 6 October 1938 (unpublished diary held at Bodleian Library, Oxford)

p. 117 *Only 3 survived*: Leon D. Epstein 'British MPs and their Local Parties: the Suez Crisis' in *American Political Science Review* volume LIV, no.2, pp. 374–88

p. 117 *Suez adventure*: Christopher Hollis 'Parliament and the Establishment' in Hugh Thomas (ed) *The Establishment* (Blond, 1959) p. 164

p. 118 *Flushed with triumph*: Sir Gervaise Rentoul, p. 231

p. 118 *Platform for moderates*: Stuart Ball 'The 1922 Committee: the Formative Years, 1922–45' in *Parliamentary History*, vol 9, 1990, p. 153

p. 119 *MPs' pay*: Philip Goodhart *The 1922* (Macmillan, 1973) p. 7

p. 119 *Not politics first*: Viscount Hailsham *The Conservative Case* (Penguin, 1959) p. 13

p. 119 *Chaps won't have you*: Goodhart, p. 161

p. 120 *Shop stewards*: Sir Anthony Meyer *Stand Up and Be Counted* (Heinemann, 1990) pp. 116, 123

p. 121 *Akers-Douglas marriage*: Peter Marsh *The Discipline of Popular Government* (Hassocks: Harvester, 1978) pp. 154–5

p. 121 *Disagree in private*: William Whitelaw, pp. 64–5

p. 121 *Retaining seat*: Noel Malcolm 'Leadership means more than getting the balance right' in the *Daily Telegraph*, 12 May 1994

p. 122 *'Party Faithful'*: Philip Norton '"The Lady's Not For Turning". But What About The Rest? Margaret Thatcher And The Conservative Party 1979–1989' in *Parliamentary Affairs*, volume 43, no.1, January 1990

p. 122 *Loss of ballast*: Peter Rawlinson *A Price Too High* (Weidenfeld & Nicolson, 1989) p. 132

p. 122 *Levin, 1985*: quoted in Lisanne Radice *et al*, p. 35

p. 123 *Lowlier*: Alan Watkins *A Conservative Coup* (Duckworth, 1991) p. 198

p. 124 *Baldwin and Harrow*: Simon Haxey, p. 180

p. 124 *Baldwin at Harrow*: Robert Blake 'Baldwin and the Right' in John Raymond (ed) *The Baldwin Age* (Eyre & Spottiswoode, 1960) p. 28

p. 124 *Macmillan 35/85*: Christopher Hollis 'The Conservative Party in History' in *Political Quarterly*, volume 32, no.3, July–September 1961, p. 220

p. 124 *Little choice*: 'The Economy Drive' in Anthony Jay and Jonathan Lynn *Yes Minister* (BBC, 1981) p. 57

p. 125 *Thatcher at Cabinet*: Kenneth Baker *The Turbulent Years* (Faber, 1993) p. 255

p. 125 *Announce policy in interviews*: Margaret Thatcher *The Downing Street Years* (HarperCollins, 1993) p. 579

p. 125   *Not collegiate*: Lord Hailsham *A Sparrow's Flight* (Collins, 1990) p. 300

p. 126   *Thorneycroft at art class*: obituary of Lord Thorneycroft in the *Daily Telegraph*, 6 June 1994

p. 127   *250,000 letters*: Philip Norton and David M. Wood *Back From Westminster*, p. 44

p. 127   *24 tons*: Geoffrey Howe *Conflict of Loyalty* (Macmillan, 1994) p. 568

p. 127   *Form of madness*: Peter Rawlinson, p. 252

p. 129   *In office or out*: Balfour in David Cannadine *The Decline and Fall of the British Aristocracy* (Picador, 1992 cd.) p. 46

p. 129   *60% Old Etonians*: J. F. S. Ross *Parliamentary Representation*, p. 52 fn

p. 129   *9 Cecils*: David Cannadine, p. 203

p. 130   *Titles on councils*: Jeremy Paxman *Friends in High Places* (Penguin, 1991) p. 45

p. 130   *Lordships*: Peter Riddell 'Cabinet and Parliament' in Dennis Kavanagh and Anthony Seldon (eds) *The Thatcher Effect* (Oxford: University Press, 1989) pp. 107–8

p. 130   *Eye tests*: K. D. Ewing and C. A. Gearty *Freedom Under Thatcher* (Oxford: University Press, 1990) p. 6

CHAPTER SIX
Now Is The Time For All Good Men (and Women) . . .

p. 132   *Blain*: Council meeting of *National Society of Conservative Agents*, 29 July 1925: Minutes held at Westminster Library, Ref. 485/4

p. 132   *Well turned out*: Rupert Morris *Tories* (Edinburgh: Mainstream, 1991) p. 129

p. 134   *Battle of constitution*: Eric Evans 'Sir Robert Peel: A Suitable Case for Reassessment' in *History Review*, 18, p. 27

p. 135   *Only six turning up*: Robert Blake *The Conservative Party from Peel to Thatcher* (Fontana, 1985) p. 114

p. 135   *Horsham 1847*: W. L. Burns 'Electoral Corruption in the Nineteenth Century' in *Parliamentary Affairs*, volume IV, 1950–51, pp. 437–8

p. 135   *Blackburn*: Donald Richter 'The Role of Mob Riot in Victorian Elections, 1865–1885' in *Victorian Studies*, volume XV, 1971–72, pp. 20–21

p. 136   *Sir Henry James*: W. L. Burns, p. 441

p. 137   *Music hall*: Martin Pugh *The Tories and the People., 1880–1935* (Oxford: Blackwell, 1985) p. 29

p. 137   *Habitations in Scotland*: Gerald Warner *The Scottish Tory Party* (Weidenfeld & Nicolson, 1988) pp. 168–9

p. 138   *Occult depths*: Roy Foster *Lord Randolph Churchill* (Oxford: University Press, 1988 ed.) p. 134

p. 138   *Vulgar:* Janet Robb *The Primrose League* (USA, New York: AMS Press, 1968 ed.) p. 87

p. 139   *Cycling clubs:* Peter Marsh *The Discipline of Popular Government* (Hassocks: Harvester 1978) p. 205

p. 140   *Balfour and valet:* R. T. McKenzie *British Political Parties* (Heinemann, 1963 ed.) p. 82

p. 141   *Solicitors and expenses:* Arthur Fawcett *Conservative Agent* (National Society of Conservative and Unionist Agents, 1967) p. 9

p. 141   *National Association and no. of agents:* Peter Marsh, p. 194; *exams* p. 197

p. 141   *Girls and ribbons:* Earl of Woolton *Memoirs* (Cassell, 1959) pp. 30–31

p. 142   *Patrick Murphy:* Bernard Porter *Plots and Paranoia* (Unwin Hyman, 1989) p. 85

p. 142   *Alcohol-free:* Stanley Salvidge *Salvidge of Liverpool* (Hodder & Stoughton, 1934) p. 16

p. 143   *Tammany Boss:* Robert Rhodes James (ed) *Memoirs of a Conservative* (Weidenfeld & Nicolson, 1969) p. 117

p. 143   *Deals before ideals:* P. J. Waller *Democracy and Sectarianism* (Liverpool: University Press, 1981) p. 211

p. 144   *All patronage:* Randolph S. Churchill *Lord Derby* (Heinemann, 1959) p. 244

p. 144   *Genial Judas:* Robert Rhodes James (ed) *'Chips'* (Weidenfeld & Nicolson, 1993) p. 30

p. 144   *Al Capone:* W. F. Deedes in the *Daily Telegraph*, 1 July 1991

p. 144   *Birmingham:* H. G. Nicholas *The British General Election of 1950* (Macmillan, 1951) p. 26

p. 145   *Last feudal fief:* Anthony Howard 'Cook County, U. K.' in the *New Statesman*, 31 July 1964

p. 147   *No ballots 1950–67:* Richard Kelly 'The Party Conference' in Anthony Seldon and Stuart Ball (eds) *Conservative Century* (Oxford: University Press, 1994) p. 258

p. 147   *Listening leadership:* Richard N. Kelly *Conservative Party Conferences* (Manchester: University Press, 1989) p. 188

p. 147   *Zoo:* Lord Butler *The Art of the Possible* (Penguin, 1973) p. 53

p. 147   *Whitelaw at 1981 conference:* William Whitelaw *The Whitelaw Memoirs* (Aurum, 1989) p. 256

p. 148   *Standing ovations:* Cecil Parkinson *Right at the Centre* (Weidenfeld & Nicolson, 1992) p. 252

p. 148   *Thatcher and Conference:* Richard Kelly 'So much more than showbiz' in the *Independent*, 10 October 1994

p. 150   *One million women:* Martin Pugh 'Popular Conservatism in Britain: Continuity and Change, 1880–1987' in the *Journal of British Studies*, volume 27, 1988, p. 262

p. 151   *Conservative logic:* Woolton's foreword to the *Islington Conservative and Unionist Association Year Book 1948*, held at Islington Central Library: Ref. Yp L251.7 p. 5

p. 151 *Marylebone*: figures taken from records of subscriptions of the St Marylebone Conservative association, 1946–1954, held at Westminster Library, Marylebone Road, London: Ref. 1322/8

p. 151 *Reading families*: Jean Blondel 'The Conservative Association and the Labour Party in Reading' in *Political Studies*, volume VI, no.2, p. 108

p. 151 *Gender roles*: Stuart Ball 'Local Conservatism and Party Organisation' in Seldon and Ball (eds), p. 270

p. 152 *YC decline*: Zig Layton-Henry 'The Young Conservatives 1945–70' in the *Journal of Contemporary History*, volume 8, no.2, pp. 143–156

p. 152 *YCs today*: *Daily Telegraph*, 16 June 1994

p. 153 *Little patronage*: Michael Pinto-Duschinsky 'Central Office and "Power" in the Conservative Party' in *Political Studies*, volume xx, no.1, p. 8

p. 154 *Ask a woman*: Penny Junor *Margaret Thatcher* (Sidgwick & Jackson, 1983) p. 69

p. 154 *Versus politics*: Philip Tether *Kingston-upon-Hull Conservative Party* (Hull University: Hull Papers in Politics 19, 1980) p. 5

p. 154 *Non-political party*: Julian Critchley *Westminster Blues* (Hamish Hamilton, 1985) p. 45

p. 154 *Our position*: Walter Long in David Cannadine *The Decline and Fall of the British Aristocracy* (Picador, 1992 ed.) p. 150

p. 154 *Bagehot*: Kenneth Baker (ed) *The Faber Book of Conservatism* (Faber, 1993) p. 263

p. 154 *1,350 clubs*: Philip Tether *Clubs: A Neglected Aspect Of Conservative Organisation* (Hull University: Hull Papers in Politics, 42) p. 2

p. 154 *Dawkins on Law*: John Ramsden *The Age of Balfour and Baldwin 1902–1940* (Longman, 1978) p. 91

p. 155 *Heath and Thatcher*: Andrew Neil 'Snobbocracy and me' in the *Evening Standard*, 26 June 1993

p. 155 *Chairmen in 1969*: John Ross *Thatcher and Friends* (Pluto, 1983) p. 19

p. 155 *Women chairmen*: Stuart Ball 'Local Conservatism', p. 270

p. 155 *Eden remarrying*: Alan Doig *Westminster Babylon* (Allison & Busby, 1990) p. 48

p. 155 *Civility*: Ross McKibbin 'Skimming along' in the *London Review of Books*, 20 October 1994, p. 20

p. 156 *Bags of silver*: Geoffrey Howe *Conflict of Loyalty* (Macmillan, 1994) p. 677

p. 156 *Repels recruits*: Philip Tether *Kingston-upon-Hull*, p. 8

p. 156 *Stroud and Catholics*: Duff Cooper *Old Men Forget* (Hart-Davis, 1953) p. 128

p. 157 *Aliens*: Paul Foot *Immigration and Race in British Politics* (Penguin, 1965) pp. 87,99

p. 157 *Not voting for Jessel*: John Ramsden (ed) *Real Old Tory Politics* (Historians' Press, 1984) p. 157

p. 157   *Experienced journalist*: James Margach *The Abuse of Power* (W. H. Allen, 1978) p. 53

p. 157   *Hore-Belisha's downfall*: see Major-General A. J. Trythall 'The Downfall of Leslie Hore-Belisha' in the *Journal of Contemporary History*, volume 16, 1981, pp. 391–2, 396, 398, 408

p. 157   *Marching song*: Andrew Roberts *Eminent Churchillians* (Weidenfeld & Nicolson, 1994) pp. 27–8

p. 158   *Estonians*: Richard Davenport-Hines *The Macmillans* (Mandarin ed, 1993) p. 3

p. 158   *Total silence*: *Evening Standard*, 11 June 1993, reporting remarks made in the *Jewish Chronicle*

p. 158   *Leon Brittan*: Geoffrey Howe, p. 469

p. 158   *Pogrom*: Julian Critchley p. 199; also p. 180

p. 158   *Difficult to talk*: John Biffen quoted in John Ranelagh *Thatcher's People* (HarperCollins, 1991) p. 56

p. 159   *Unusual attribute*: Nigel Lawson *The View From No. 11* (Bantam, 1992) p. 256

p. 159   *King's hint*: John Junor *Listening for a Midnight Tram* (Chapmans, 1990) p. 315

p. 160   *3 or 4 receptions*: John Taylor quoted in the *Daily Telegraph*, 15 October 1993

p. 160   *One Nation Forum*: see Dr Ray Chaudran 'Natural Conservatives' in *Conservative Newsline*, October 1992

p. 160   *Politics not central*: Shirley Robin Letwin 'The battle for Britain is not over yet' in the *Sunday Telegraph*, 27 June 1993

p. 161   *Party membership*: Stuart Ball 'Local Conservatism', pp. 291–3

p. 161   *Less than a third*: Michael Pinto-Duschinsky 'Tory chiefs in danger of losing their troops' in *The Times*, 10 October 1993

p. 161   *Average age 63*: Patrick Seyd referred to in 'Seaside beggars every one' in *The Economist*, 25 September 1993

p. 161   *Rural districts*: Stuart Ball 'Vanishing Tories' in the *Guardian*, 10 October 1994

p. 161   *82% v politics*: Jonathan Prynn 'After 75 voting years women shun politics' in *The Times*, 12 July 1993

p. 162   *RSPB*: 'A nation of groupies' in *The Economist*, 13 August 1994

p. 162   *1994 campaign pack*: Patrick Wintour 'Hanley launches drive for members' in the *Guardian*, 15 October 1994

p. 163   *Turning to outsiders*: 'Associations scrape barrel as Tory cash crisis deepens' in *The Times*, 6 June 1994

CHAPTER SEVEN
Money Matters

p. 164   *Great advantage*: memo of Conservative Party strategy meeting, 9 March 1927, in *The Papers of J. C . C. Davidson*, House of Lords, Box 180, January–December 1927, document 404

p. 164 *Daily Mail, 1927*: G. R. Searle *Corruption in British Politics* (Oxford: Clarendon Press, 1987) pp. 403, 409

p. 165 *Over £70 million*: 'Tory Money: deals, donors and deceit' in *Business Age*, July 1993, p. 40

p. 166 *Private company*: Al-Fayed quoted in Peter Preston 'The anatomy of a scandal' in the *Guardian*, 21 October 1994

p. 166 *Wessex area*: Simon Heffer 'A very expensive party' in the *Spectator*, 15 June 1991

p. 166 *Hatfield House finance*: R. B. Jones 'Balfour's Reform of Party Organization' in *Bulletin of the Institute of Historical Research*, volume XXXVIII, no.97, p. 94

p. 167 *Disraeli prepared to accept French money*: John Vincent *Disraeli* (Oxford: University Press, 1990) p. 4

p. 167 *Tory peers' help*: Robert Blake *The Conservative Party from Peel to Thatcher* (Fontana, 1985) p. 143

p. 168 *Raj finance*: Michael Pinto-Duschinsky *British Political Finance 1830–1980* (USA, Washington: American Enterprise Institute, 1981) p. 36

p. 168 *Naylor-Leyland case*: H. J. Hanham 'The Sale of Honours in Late Victorian England' in *Victorian Studies*, March 1960, pp. 286–7

p. 169 *Throwing stone*: Peter Marsh *The Discipline of Popular Government* (Hassocks: Harvester, 1978) p. 192

p. 169 *S. W. Duncan*: G. R. Searle, p. 92

p. 169 *Balfour Papers*: Balfour Papers at the British Library, Add MS 49772/15; Add MS49772/26

p. 170 *Chief employers*: W. D. Rubinstein *Men Of Property* (Croom Helm, 1981) p. 90

p. 170 *Brewers determined*: Neal Blewett *The Peers, the Parties and the People* (Macmillan, 1972) p. 50

p. 170 *Lloyd George on brewers*: *The Papers of J. C. C. Davidson*, House of Lords Library, Box 112, document 373

p. 170 *Loan of cars*: Neal Blewett, p. 50

p. 171 *Discretionary payments*: John Ramsden *The Age of Balfour and Baldwin 1902–1940* (Longman, 1978) p. 219

p. 171 *Gregory's tariff*: Richard Lane 'Coronets for Sale' in *Lilliput*, volume 26, no.2, p. 99

p. 171 *MI5 and agency*: Richard Deacon *A History of the British Secret Service* (Granada, 1980 ed.) pp. 212–3

p. 172 *Lloyd George's honours*: Gerald Macmillan *Honours For Sale* (Richards Press, 1954) pp. 19, 84

p. 172 *Vestey and George V*: Phillip Knightley *The Rise and Fall of the House of Vestey* (Warner, 1993) pp. 48–52

p. 172 *Younger's letter*: Robert Rhodes James (ed) *Memoirs of a Conservative* (Weidenfeld & Nicolson, 1969) p. 290

p. 173 *Farquhar saga*: John Ramsden *Balfour and Baldwin*, pp. 170, 219

p. 173 *Law and Farquhar*: Bonar Law Papers at House of Lords, Box 108, Folder 4, 15/1/1923; 26/1/1923; 15/3/1923; 24/1/1923

p. 173 *Trust account*: John Ramsden (ed) *Real Old Tory Politics* (Historians' Press, 1984) p. 211

p. 174 *JCC's jottings*: J. C. C. Davidson Papers, Box 180, January–December 1927, no date

p. 174 *Ellerman and Conservatives*: W. D. Rubinstein, p. 45

p. 174 *Ellerman's lifestyle*: Robert E. Knoll *McAlmon and the Lost Generation* (USA: University of Nebraska, 1962) pp. 153–4

p. 175 *Left Book Club*: James Taylor *Ellermans* (Wilton House, 1976) p. 108

p. 175 *£130,000 lunch*: Michael Pinto-Duschinsky, p. 109

p. 175 *Ambassador Club*: Tom Cullen *Maundy Gregory* (Bodley Head, 1974) pp. 121–2

p. 175 *Erskine*: J. C. C. Davidson Papers, Box 186, memo dated 1 May 1929

p. 176 *Rabbit hutch*: John Ramsden *Balfour and Baldwin*, p. 224

p. 176 *Cahn's £2,000*: J. C. C. Davidson Papers, Box 191, dated 27 January 1931 and 31 January 1931

p. 176 *Scandal of honour*: David Marquand *Ramsay MacDonald* (Cape, 1977) pp. 745–7

p. 177 *Beaverbrook episode*: J. C. C. Davidson Papers, Box 188, letter dated 12 June 1929

p. 177 *Secret accounts*: J. C. C. Davidson Papers, Box 190, letters dated 14 January 1930; Box 191, letters dated 15 January 1936 and 28 October 1936

p. 178 *Oldham*: Duff Cooper *Old Men Forget* (Hart-Davis, 1953) p. 167

p. 179 *Great enterprises*: Earl of Woolton *Memoirs* (Cassell, 1959) p. 336

p. 180 *Rivers companies*: see *Business Age*, July 1993; also the *Sunday Times*, 27 June 1993

p. 180 *Woolton to Churchill*: MS Woolton 21, Document 13, 28 December 1948 (*Woolton Papers* at Bodleian, Oxford)

p. 180 *Pierssene not knowing*: Conservative Party Archive, Bodleian: Folder 'Constituency Finance', CCO 4/5/100; letter dated 28 October 1953

p. 180 *Forbes of BUI*: quoted in *Private Eye*, 2 July 1993

p. 181 *BUI as unincorporated association*: John Walker *The Queen Has Been Pleased* (Secker & Warburg, 1986) p. 169

p. 181 *BUI's £10 million*: *Daily Telegraph*, 26 June 1993

p. 181 *Aims staff of 20*: Richard Rose *Influencing Voters* (Faber, 1967) p. 97

p. 181 *Aims 1983*: Michael Pinto-Duschinsky 'Trends in British Political Funding 1979–1983' in *Parliamentary Affairs*, volume 38, no. 3, summer 1985, p. 339

p. 181 *Close liaison*: Conservative Party Archive: 'Aims of Industry', CCO 3/4/27

p. 181 *Circulating material*: Conservative Party Archive: CCO 3/4/27; 11/5/55; funding 9/55; letter 24 November 1954

p. 182 *Steel companies' campaign*: Richard Rose, pp. 114–30

p. 183   *Story of British political finance*: Michael Pinto-Duschinsky *British Political Finance*, p. 127

p. 183   *£8 million local assets*: 'Tory reformers at war with Fowler over party democracy' in the *Guardian*, 29 April 1993

p. 183   *McAlpine and jam*: Alistair McAlpine 'The self-restraint of the Saudis' in the *Spectator*, 26 June 1993

p. 183   *Average subs up*: Michael Pinto-Duschinsky 'MPs funding local parties with up to £1,000 a year' in *The Times*, 11 October 1994

p. 184   *No legal status*: Justin Fisher 'Political donations to the Conservative Party' in *Parliamentary Affairs*, volume 47, no. 1, January 1994, p. 62

p. 185   *Asil Nadir undeclared*: Justin Fisher p. 65

p. 185   *Sovereign Leasing*: *Daily Telegraph*, 16 June 1993

p. 185   *Rowland*: *Guardian*, 5 November 1994

p. 185   *Die-hard brewers*: W. D. Rubinstein, p. 90

p. 186   *Brewers' payroll*: Alan Clark *Diaries* (Weidenfeld & Nicolson, 1993) p. 340

p. 186   *Humiliation of Young*: Jeremy Paxman *Friends in High Places* (Penguin, 1991 ed.) p. 258

p. 186   *Young's silence*: Lord Young *The Enterprise Years* (Headline, 1990) p. 326

p. 186   *Brewers' donation*: L. Allen and E. Arthur *Drink* (1990) p. 6, referred to in Justin Fisher, p. 69

p. 186   *BCCI*: 'Tory connection with disgraced bank' in the *Sunday Times*, 30 October 1994 and 'BBCI cheat gave cash to Tories' in the *Sunday Times*, 13 November 1994

p. 187   *Ernest Saunders*: James Saunders *Nightmare* (Hutchinson, 1989) pp. 165–6

p. 187   *Bristow*: *The Times*, 19 June 1993

p. 187   *£50,000 lunch*: *Business Age*, May 1993

p. 187   *Donations and honours*: Paul Johnson 'When rich men come to the aid of the party' in the *Daily Telegraph*, 17 June 1993; also Martin Linton in the *Guardian*, 16 June 1993; 'How Tory donors pick up titles' in the *Sunday Times*, 27 September 1992

p. 187   *Tobacco manufacturers*: 'Lobby firm "helped block tobacco bill"' in the *Independent*, 14 May 1994

p. 188   *Savoy dining club*: 'Oiled palms, arms and the woman' in the *Guardian*, 19 February 1994

p. 188   *Five companies*: *Guardian*, 19 February 1994

p. 188   *Al-Yamamah*: 'Dirty Money' in *Business Age*, November 1994, pp. 52–7

p. 189   *£15 million undisclosed*: Martin Linton 'Bid decline in income' in the *Guardian*, 19 June 1993; see also the *Daily Telegraph*, 26 June 1993

p. 189   *Wyldebore-Smith*: 'Paying the piper' in *The Economist*, 16 April 1994

p. 189   *Tax loophole*: 'Tory Money' in *Business Age*, May 1993, p. 48

p. 190   *Lock on door*: 'Tory Money', p. 41

p. 190   *Off-shore accounts*: Lord McAlpine on ITN, quoted in the *Guardian*, 18 June 1993

p. 190   *Objections of Sir David Wilson*: *The Times*, 19 June 1993

p. 190   *Latsis £2 million*: *Sunday Times*, 27 June 1993

p. 191   *Crooks and spivs*: 'Funny Money' in the *Sunday Times*, 27 June 1993

p. 191   *Labour Research*: 'Earth Slips Under Tories' Feet' in *Labour Research*, volume 82, no.12, December 1994, pp. 9–11

p. 191   *Business cuts*: *Daily Telegraph*, 15 August 1994

p. 191   *Brewers*: 'Brewers may turn off tap on Tory cash' in the *Daily Telegraph*, 10 December 1994

p. 192   *Local funds down 20%*: *The Times*, 6 June 1994

p. 192   *Chalker on board*: Sheila Gunn 'Conservatives call for end to secrecy over party funds' in *The Times*, 19 June 1993

p. 193   *Little use of direct mail*: Michael Pinto-Duschinsky 'Funding of Political Parties Since 1945' in Anthony Seldon (ed) *UK Political Parties Since 1945* (Hemel Hempstead: Phillip Allan 1990) p. 97

p. 193   *Republican Party*: Torin Douglas 'Letter From . . .' *Observer*, 17 May 1987

p. 193   *Preservation of Old Parties*: Vernon Bogdanor 'Reflections on British Political Finance' in *Parliamentary Affairs*, volume XXV, no 4, Autumn 1982, p. 368

p. 193   *Danger to democracy*: Cook quoted in the *Guardian*, 17 June 1993

p. 194   *Moscow gold*: see special issue of *Changes*, 28, 16–29 November 1991; 'Kremlin cash bankrolled British strikes' in the *Sunday Times*, 17 November 1991

p. 194   *Money not losing votes*: Martin Linton 'The Mad Hatter's Tory Party' in the *Guardian*, 14 April, 1994

CHAPTER EIGHT
'The Bottom Line is Winning Elections'

p. 195   *Bottom Line*: Conservative Central Office, 'National Training Initiative '94', no.3

p. 195   *Votes*: Enoch Powell in the *Listener*, 28 May 1981

p. 195   *Marketing policies*: Christopher Lawson quoted in Michael Cockerell 'The marketing of Margaret' in the *Listener*, 16 June 1983

p. 196   *1983 campaigns*: Martin Linton 'Disaster snatched from the jaws of defeat' in the *Guardian*, 30 June 1983

p. 197   *Labour's ad agency*: Johnny Wright 'Advertising for Change' in *Marxism Today*, January 1985, pp. 30–1

p. 197   *Buying up Labour manifesto*: David Butler and Dennis Kavanagh *The British General Election of 1983* (Macmillan, 1984) p. 91

p. 197 *Rag, tag and bobtail*: see Sam McCluskie quoted in the *Guardian*, 30 June 1983

p. 198 *Disraeli and no programme*: R. B. McDowell *British Conservatism 1832–1914* (Faber, 1959) p. 9

p. 198 *Alarming people*: Kenneth Baker *The Turbulent Years* (Faber, 1993) p. 293

p. 199 *Heath's policy groups*: Anthony King 'How the Conservatives evolve policies' in *New Society*, 20 July 1972, p. 122

p. 199 *Macleod's 131 promises*: John Ramsden *The Making of Conservative Party Policy* (Longman, 1980) p. 252

p. 199 *Not registering 1971*: John Barnes and Richard Cockett 'The Making of Party Policy' in Anthony Seldon and Stuart Ball (eds) *Conservative Century* (Oxford: University Press, 1994) p. 382

p. 199 *Carey on 1983 manifestos*: John Carey 'The strange death of political language' in the *Sunday Times*, 5 June 1983

p. 200 *1895 leaflet*: Robert McKenzie and Allan Silver *Angels in Marble* (Heinemann, 1968) p. 55

p. 200 *Guard Your Savings*: D. E. McHenry *The Labour Party in Transition 1931–1938* (Routledge, 1938) p. 186

p. 201 *Salisbury*: Randolph S. Churchill *Lord Derby* (Heinemann, 1959) p. 42

p. 202 *Meetings of 5–6,000*: Winston Churchill *My Early Life* (Odhams, 1947) p. 355

p. 202 *Punching Brigade*: Martin Pugh *The Tories and the People 1880–1935* (Oxford: Blackwell, 1985) p. 191

p. 202 *Screwed up smiles*: Kenneth Rose *The Later Cecils* (Weidenfeld & Nicolson, 1975) p. 22

p. 203 *Midlothian photo opportunity*: Peter Clarke *A Question of Leadership* (Penguin, 1992 ed.) p. 30

p. 203 *Chamberlain choreography*: Sidney Dark *The Life of Sir Arthur Pearson* (Hodder & Stoughton, 1922) p. 104; gramophone records, pp. 106–7

p. 203 *Bolsheviks*: Roger Pethybridge *The Spread of the Russian Revolution* (Macmillan, 1972) p. 76

p. 205 *Steel-Maitland's impact*: J. A. Ramsden *The Organisation of the Conservative and Unionist Party in Great Britain, 1910–1930* (Oxford DPhil., 1974) pp. 38, 283

p. 205 *Railway company*: Keith Middlemas *Politics in Industrial Society* (Deutsch, 1979) p. 39

p. 205 *Magic lantern*: Peter Marsh *The Discipline of Popular Government* (Hassocks: Harvester, 1978) p. 204

p. 205 *2,000 a day*: John Ramsden *The Age of Balfour and Baldwin, 1902–1940* (Longman, 1978) p. 235

p. 205 *1927 and 19 million leaflets*: see Keith Middlemas, pp. 354–5

p. 205 *1924 radio broadcasts*: John Antcliffe 'Politics of the Airwaves' in *History Today*, March 1984, pp. 5–6

p. 206 *Sound vans*: T. J. Hollins 'The conservative party and film propaganda between the wars' in the *English Historical Review*, volume XCVI, 1981, p. 9

p. 206 *1931 vans*: *Sight and Sound*, Summer 1974, p. 146

p. 206 *1½ million*: *World Film News*, December 1936, p. 29

p. 206 *Clavering*: T. J. Hollins, pp. 368–9

p. 207 *S. H. Benson*: Michael Pinto-Duschinsky *British Political Finance 1830–1980* (USA, Washington: American Enterprise Institute, 1981) p. 98

p. 207 *NPB activities*: Don Macpherson *Traditions of Independence* (British Film Institute, 1980) pp. 143–4

p. 208 *Hiring London cinemas*: *Educational Film Review*, July 1935, p. 101

p. 208 *NPB's role*: *Papers of the 1st Earl of Woolton*, held at Bodleian, Oxford: Ref. MS 21

p. 208 *1945 military uniform*: Ian Harvey *To Fall Like Lucifer* (Sidgwick & Jackson, 1971) p. 55

p. 208 *Hem of garment*: quoted in Anthony Howard 'We Are the Masters Now' in Michael Sissons and Philip French (eds) *The Age of Austerity 1945–1951* (Hodder & Stoughton, 1963) p. 17

p. 208 *Dog-fight*: Kenneth Young (ed) *The Diaries of Sir Robert Bruce Lockhart* (Macmillan, 1989) p. 474

p. 209 *Aims and Mr Cube*: A. A. Rogow with Peter Shore *The Labour Government and British Industry* (Oxford: Blackwell, 1955) pp. 142–5; Richard Dimbleby's role is not mentioned in Jonathan Dimbleby *Richard Dimbleby* (Hodder & Stoughton, 1975)

p. 209 *Public Opinion Department*: John Ramsden *The Making of Conservative Party Policy*, p. 144

p. 209 *Opinion polls*: e.g. *Conservative Agents Journal*, August–September 1954, no 402, pp. 206–8

p. 209 *Colman, Prentis and Varley*: Richard Rose *Influencing Voters* (Faber, 1967) p. 21

p. 210 *Fond of countrymen*: Viscount Chandos *The Memoirs of Lord Chandos* (Bodley Head, 1962) p. 327

p. 210 *Hand over lens*: Michael Cockerell *Live From Number Ten* (Faber, 1989 ed.) pp. 22–3

p. 210 *Supermac*: Alistair Horne *Macmillan 1957–1986* (Macmillan, 1989) p. 149

p. 210 *CND dressing march*: Christopher Driver *The Disarmers* (Hodder & Stoughton, 1964) p. 135

p. 211 *Home 1964 and open-air*: Grace Wyndham Goldie *Facing the Nation* (Bodley Head, 1977) p. 270

p. 211 *Heath's studio set*: Michael Cockerell, p. 158

p. 211 *Reece and Woman*: 'Image maker to the PM' in the *Observer*, 13 June 1986

p. 212 *5-minute commercials*: Sir Tim Bell speaking on 'There Now Follows . . .', BBC2, 8 October 1993

p. 212   *Mrs T's appearance*: 'Why Maggie looks so good at sixty' in the *Sunday Times*, 13 October 1985

p. 212   *Chair from Sweden*: Penny Junor *Margaret Thatcher* (Sidgwick & Jackson, 1983) p. 171

p. 212   *Saatchis at 1986 Conference*: Robin Oakley 'Saatchis claims it drafted crucial conference speeches' in *The Times*, 26 October 1987

p. 212   *Advice from Sun*: William Shawcross *Murdoch* (Pan, 1993 ed.) p. 211

p. 213   *Lawson's hair*: Rodney Tyler *Campaign!* (Grafton, 1987) pp. 187–8

p. 213   *1987 burst of spending*: Michael Pinto-Duschinsky 'Trends in British Party Funding 1983–1987' in *Parliamentary Affairs*, volume 42, no. 2, April 1989, p. 199

p. 213   *TV and 3 things*: Charles Bremner 'TV Chiefs "used by campaign"' in *The Times*, 9 November 1988

p. 213   *Cost of elections*: Frank I. Luntz *Candidates, Consultants and Campaigns* (Oxford: Blackwell, 1988) pp. 217, 222, 224

p. 214   *Elections more Presidential*: David Butler in Robert Skidelsky (ed) *Thatcherism* (Chatto & Windus, 1988) p. 70

p. 214   *Polls undermining Mrs T*: Peter Kellner quoted in John Ranelagh *Thatcher's People* (HarperCollins, 1991) p. 37

p. 215   *Candidates worth no more than 1,500 votes*: Lisanne Radice, Elizabeth Vallance and Virginia Willis *Member of Parliament* (Macmillan, 1987) p. 103

p. 215   *Berlusconi episode*: Martin Jacques 'Big Brother' in the *Sunday Times*, 3 April 1994 and Chris Endean 'The selling of a Prime Minister' in *The European*, 1–7 April, 1994

p. 216   *Voting figures*: Martin Pugh *The Evolution of the British Electoral System 1832–1987* (Historical Association, 1988) pp. 7–9

p. 217   *Secret societies*: Richard Shannon *The Age of Disraeli, 1868–1881* (Longman, 1992) p. 142

p. 217   *Stable vote and figures*: Martin Pugh 'Popular Conservatism in Britain: Continuity and Change, 1880–1987' in *Journal of British Studies*, volume 27, July 1988, pp. 254–5

p. 218   *Class fading*: 'Wanted, leadership' in *The Economist*, 25 September 1993

p. 218   *C1s*: Norman Tebbit *Upwardly Mobile* (Futura, 1989 ed.) p. 172

p. 218   *Policies unpopular*: Ivor Crewe and Donald Searing 'Ideological Change in the British Conservative Party' in *American Political Science Review*, volume 82, no.2, 1988, p. 375

p. 219   *Lack of identification*: Peter Kellner in the *Sunday Times*, 1 August 1993

p. 220   *All walks of life*: Robert Waller 'Conservative Electoral Support And Social Class' in Anthony Seldon and Stuart Ball (eds) *Conservative Century* (Oxford: University Press, 1994) p. 608

CHAPTER NINE
Dirty Tricks

p. 221   *Country scared*: Robert Rhodes James (ed) *Memoirs of a Conservative* (Weidenfeld & Nicolson, 1969) p. 199

p. 221   *Not worshipping democracy*: Sir Ian Gilmour *Inside Right* (Hutchinson, 1977) p. 211

p. 221   *Enemy within*: quoted in John Osmond *The Divided Kingdom* (Constable, 1988) p. 39

p. 222   *Fraternisation*: Philip G. Cambray *The Game of Politics* (John Murray, 1932) p. 12

p. 222   *Timing of Zinoviev letter*: Cambray, pp. 26, 27, 83

p. 223   *Daily Mirror*: quoted in James Curran and Jean Seaton *Power Without Responsibility* (Fontana, 1981) p. 77

p. 223   *Davidson on Cambray*: *The Papers of J. C. C. Davidson*, House of Lords; Ref: Box 188, document 426

p. 223   *Enormous impact*: Percy Cohen *Disraeli's Child* (unpublished history of the Conservative Party held at Conservative Party Archive, Bodleian) chapter 25, p. 6

p. 223   *Elemental prejudice*: Cambray, p. 67

p. 224   *Bellegarde as forger*: Lewis Chester, Stephen Fay and Hugo Young *The Zinoviev Letter* (Heinemann, 1967) p. 51

p. 224   *Trevor-Roper*: Tony Bunyan *The History and Practice of the Political Police in Britain* (Quartet, 1977) pp. 160–1

p. 224   *With Joseph Ball*: Robert Rhodes James, p. 272

p. 225   *1927 memo*: *The Papers of J. C. C. Davidson*, held at the House of Lords; Ref: Box 180, document 404, 9 March 1927

p. 225   *Achievement*: Robert Blake 'Tory Achates' in the *Spectator*, 13 September 1969

p. 225   *£5,000 payment*: Lewis Chester et al., p. 178

p. 225   *Bring down government*: Christopher Andrew 'The British Secret Service and Anglo-Soviet Relations in the 1920s' in the *Historical Journal*, volume 20, no.3, p. 706

p. 225–6 *No delay*: *Parliamentary Debates*: Commons, volume 179, 1924–5, 15 December 1924, column 740; *Manchester Evening Chronicle*, column 745; destroyed by Communists, column 689

p. 228   *Strong state 1909–20*: Bernard Porter *Plots and Paranoia* (Unwin Hyman, 1989) p. 120

p. 228   *Broad 1920 Act*: Keith Jeffery and Peter Hennessy *States of Emergency* (Routledge & Kegan Paul, 1983) p. 58

p. 228   *Quality of beer*: Chanie Rosenberg *1919* (Bookmarks, 1987) pp. 78–9

p. 228   *Wine*: PRO CAB 23/9 WC 544 13/3/19

p. 229   *Churchill clear*: PRO CAB 23/9 War Cabinet 522 30/1/19

p. 229   *Stores of rifles*: Peter Hennessy and Keith Jeffery in *The Times*, 15 January 1980

p. 229   *Not annoying Civil Service*: Jeffery and Hennessy, pp. 77–8

p. 230   *Armoured vehicles*: Keith Jeffery 'The British Army and Internal Security 1919–1939' in the *Historical Journal*, volume 24, no.2, p. 391

p. 230   *Strikebreaking second nature*: Peter Hennessy and Keith Jeffery 'How Attlee stood up to strikes' in *The Times*, 20 November 1979

p. 231   *BBC vetting*: Mark Hollingsworth and Richard Norton-Taylor *Blacklist* (Hogarth Press, 1988) p. 99

p. 231   *1/4 million files*: Stephen Ward in the *Independent*, 1 December 1994 and Channel Four *What Has Become Of Us?*, December 1994

p. 232   *Looking to surrender*: Douglas Hurd *An End to Promises* (Collins, 1979) p. 103

p. 233   *Tapes running out*: Stephen Dorril *The Silent Conspiracy* (Heinemann, 1993) p. 38

p. 233   *1984–5 roadblocks*: K. D. Ewing and C. A. Gearty *Freedom Under Thatcher* (Oxford: University Press, 1990) pp. 103–12

p. 233   *NUM spy*: see Seumas Milne *The Enemy Within: MI5, Maxwell and the Scargill Affair* (Verso, 1994)

p. 233   *Taylor*: Christopher Andrew *Secret Service* (Sceptre, 1986 ed.) p. 389

p. 233   *Settling disputes*: Dennis Kavanagh *Crisis, Charisma and British Political Leadership: Winston Churchill as the Outsider* (Sage, 1974) p. 28

p. 234   *Population ½* : Liz Curtis *Nothing But The Same Old Story* (Information on Ireland, 1984) p. 28

p. 234   *Potato blight*: Liz Curtis, p. 51

p. 234   *Parnell smears*: Bernard Porter, p. 111

p. 234   *Times*: L. P. Curtis *Coercion and Conciliation in Ireland 1880–1892* (USA, Princeton: University Press, 1963) pp. 285–6, 298–9

p. 235   *Political capital*: Viscount Chilston 'The Tories and Parnell 1885–1891' in *Parliamentary Affairs*, volume XIV, no.1, pp. 64, 68

p. 235   *Anderson authorship*: Bernard Porter, p. 112

p. 235   *Blenheim speech*: A. T. Q. Stewart *The Ulster Crisis* (Faber, 1967) pp. 56–7

p. 236   *Countenance mutiny*: Robert Blake *The Unknown Prime Minister* (Eyre & Spottiswoode, 1955) pp. 156–7

p. 236   *Circulating diaries*: Admiral Sir William James *The Eyes Of The Navy* (Methuen, 1955) p. 114; David Pallister 'Sex, lies and red tape' in the *Guardian*, 29 March 1994

p. 237   *Keeping a secret*: Admiral Sir William James, xxiii

p. 237   *Eyewitness*: Robert Fisk *The Point of No Return* (Deutsch, 1975) pp. 13, 91, 92–3, 96

p. 237   *Colin Wallace affair*: Paul Foot *Who Framed Colin Wallace?* (Macmillan, 1989)

p. 238   *Daily Mail and Stalker*: John Stalker *Stalker* (Penguin, 1988) pp. 121–3

p. 238   *Intelligence people at Conservative Party*: Percy Cohen quoted in Arnold Beichmann 'Hugger-Mugger in Old Queen Street: The Origins of the Conservative Research Department' in the *Journal of Contemporary History*, volume 13, 1978, p. 688, fn. 29

p. 238   *Aubrey Jones et al*: Nigel West 'Library Agents' in the *Sunday Times*, 19 September 1993

p. 239   *Kell v Catholics*: Nigel West *MI5* (Grafton, 1983) p. 424; *private means*, p. 41

p. 239   *Steadying influences*: Christopher Andrew *Secret Service*, p. 346

p. 240   *Small minority*: Jeffery and Hennessy *States of Emergency* p. 9

p. 240   *Hall's 1919 views*: P. J. Waller *Democracy and Sectarianism* (Liverpool: University Press, 1981) p. 283

p. 240   *Childs' memoirs*: Sir Wyndham Childs *Episodes and Reflections* (Carnell, 1930) p. 221; *brains and money*, p. 212

p. 240   *Asquith killed king*: Amber Blanco White *The New Propaganda* (Gollancz, 1939) p. 300

p. 240   *Free love*: C. L. Mowat *Britain Between the Wars* (Methuen, 1968) p. 169

p. 241   *Smears v MacDonald*: James Margach *The Abuse of Power* (W. H. Allen, 1978) pp. 38–9

p. 241   *Bevan and MI5*: Jennie Lee *My Life With Nye* (Penguin, 1981) p. 152; Michael Foot *Aneurin Bevan 1897–1945* (Paladin, 1975) p. 339

p. 242   *Wilson and Goodman burglaries*: Stephen Dorril and Robin Ramsay *Smear!* (Grafton, 1992) p. 292

p. 242   *Bugging and burgling*: Peter Wright *Spycatcher* (Viking, 1987) p. 54

p. 242   *Hanley's handful*: David Leigh *The Wilson Plot* (Heinemann, 1988) pp. 250–51

p. 243   *Tailing of Brown*: Dorril and Ramsay, p. 46

p. 243   *Role of Private Eye*: Ben Pimlott *Harold Wilson* (HarperCollins, 1992) p. 712

p. 243   *Short*: Tam Dalyell *Misrule* (Hamish Hamilton, 1987) pp. 125–6, 140–41

p. 243   *Campaign versus Benn*: Mark Hollingsworth *The Press and Political Dissent* (Pluto, 1986) – chapter on Benn, pp. 37–76

p. 243   *Lang's letter*: Andrew Marr *The Battle for Scotland* (Penguin, 1992) p. 255

p. 244   *Laski and heckler*: David Hooper *Political Scandal, Odium and Contempt* (Coronet, 1986 ed.) pp. 84–6

p. 244   *Christiansen and Laski*: William Harrington and Peter Young *The 1945 Revolution* (Davis-Poynter, 1978) p. 165

p. 244   *Crossman's slip*: John Junor *Listening for a Midnight Tram* (Chapmans, 1990) p. 177

p. 245   *Applications not scrutinised*: Richard Norton-Taylor 'The slick spy master' in the *Guardian*, 20 June 1994

p. 245   *Heath and nonsense*: Mark Hollingsworth and Richard Norton-Taylor *Blacklist* (Hogarth Press, 1988) p. 128

p. 245   *Disraeli to resign*: Sir Charles Petrie *The Powers Behind the Prime Minister* (Macgibbon and Kee, 1958) p. 18

p. 246   *Walton*: all the information on Walton from Keith Middlemas *Politics in Industrial Society* (Deutsch, 1979) pp. 132, 352–4

p. 246   *J. M. Hughes*: Ron Bean 'Liverpool Shipping Employers and the Anti-Communist Activities of J. M. Hughes, 1920–25' in *Bulletin of the Society for the Study of Labour History*, 34, Spring 1977, pp. 22–4

p. 247   *Economic League budget*: Arthur McIvor '"A Crusade for Capitalism": The Economic League, 1919–39' in the *Journal of Contemporary History*, volume 23, 1988, p. 635

p. 247   *'Flying Squads'*: John Baker White *True Blue* (Muller, 1970) p. 150

p. 247   *Hanging around cafés*: John Baker White *It's Gone For Good* (Vacher, 1941) p. 115

p. 247   *Baker White's views*: Mark Hollingsworth and Charles Tremayne *The Economic League* (NCCL, 1988) pp. 9–10

p. 248   *1955 and Conservative Party*: Allen Potter *Organized Groups in British National Politics* (Faber, 1961) p. 147

p. 248   *Poole to du Cann*: *Conservative Party Archive*, Bodleian Library, Oxford; Ref: CCO 3/5/62: Economic League, letter dated 28 February 1957

p. 248   *1978 study*: 'The Economic League' in *State Research Bulletin*, no.7, 1978, pp. 135–45

p. 248   *1973 strike*: Tony Bunyan *The Political Police in Britain*, p. 249

p. 249   *Rover vetting*: Stephen Dorril, p. 158

p. 249   *Size of IRD*: David Leigh *The Frontiers of Secrecy* (Junction, 1980) p. 220; also see Paul Lashmar 'Covert in glory' in the *New Statesman*, 3 March 1995

p. 249   *Over 250 employees*: Richard Fletcher 'How the secret service shaped the news' in the *Guardian*, 18 December 1981

p. 249   *Washington dollars*: Richard Fletcher 'Who Were They Travelling With?' in Fred Hirsch and Richard Fletcher (eds) *The CIA and the Labour Movement* (Nottingham: Spokesman Books, 1977)

p. 249   *Churchill and CIA*: Michael Smith 'Churchill sought US cash for united Europe' in the *Daily Telegraph*, 3 October 1993

p. 250   *Counter-subversion Executive*: Brian Crozier *Free Agent* (Harper-Collins, 1993) p. 146; Communist takeover p. 278

p. 250   *South African funding*: Nick Toczek *The Bigger Tory Vote* (Stirling: AK Press, 1991) p. 26

p. 251   *1974 army intervention*: David Pallister 'Ex-Army chief confirms takeover talks rumour' in the *Guardian*, 5 March 1980

p. 251   *Prentice affair*: 'Light on Prentice cash backing' in *The Times*, 13 October 1979

p. 251   *Freedom Association and Taylor Woodrow*: Dorril and Ramsay, p. 292

p. 251   *British Airways*: Martyn Gregory *Dirty Tricks* (Little, Brown, 1994)

p. 252   *Maxwell and law*: Tom Bower 'Maxwell and the strong-arm of the law' in the *Guardian*, 9 December 1991; also Tom Bower *Maxwell The Outsider* (Mandarin, 1991 ed.) *passim*

p. 252   *Watergate*: David Leigh, p. 79

p. 252   *IRD suppression*: David Leigh 'Secret cold war files are scrapped by Foreign Office' in the *Observer*, 28 February 1982

p. 253   *Lord Gardiner*: Tony Benn *Out of the Wilderness: Diaries 1963–67* (Arrow, 1988 ed.) p. 328

p. 254   *Ruthless*: Tony Blair quoted on *The World At One*, Radio Four, 19 October 1994

p. 254   *Maples leak*: *Financial Times*, 21 November 1994

p. 254   *Oppo*: Chris Blackhurst 'Dirty tricks file on Labour' in the *Observer*, 23 October 1994

p. 255   *Crofters' war*: David Cannadine *The Decline and Fall of the British Aristocracy* (Paladin, 1992 ed) p. 59

p. 255   *Salisbury and Boers*: Peter Marsh *The Discipline of Popular Government* (Hassocks: Harvester, 1978) p. 297

p. 255   *Eden*: Keith Kyle *Suez* (Weidenfeld & Nicolson, 1991) pp. 99, 150–51

p. 256   *Union Defence League*: A. T. Q. Stewart, p. 135

p. 256   *Cambray*: John Ramsden *The Age of Balfour and Baldwin 1902–1940* (Longman, 1978) p. 231

CHAPTER TEN
Conservative Versus Conservative

p. 257   *Benches opposite*: Boyd-Carpenter quoted in Douglas Dodds-Parker *Political Eunuch* (Ascot: Springwood Books, 1986) p. 122

p. 257   *King over water*: Robert Rhodes James (ed) '*Chips*' (Weidenfeld, 1993 ed.) p. 250

p. 257   *Dirty business*: Lady Thatcher interviewed in the *Radio Times*, 16–22 October 1993

p. 258   *Unsheath dagger*: Peter Rawlinson *A Price Too High* (Weidenfeld & Nicolson, 1989) p. 139

p. 258   *Ambition*: Philip M. Williams (ed) *The Diary of Hugh Gaitskell 1945–1956* (Cape, 1983) p. 46

p. 259   *Ideological passion*: Neal Blewett *The Peers, the Parties and the People* (Macmillan, 1972) p. 35

p. 259   *Secret society*: Richard A. Rempel *Unionists Divided* (Newton Abbot: David & Charles, 1972) p. 176

p. 260   *Blacklist*: Alan Sykes 'The Confederacy and the Purge of the

Unionist Free Traders, 1906–1910' in the *Historical Journal*, volume XVIII, no.2, pp. 360–61

p. 260 *Fight for Central Office*: Neal Blewett 'Free Fooders, Balfourites, Whole Hoggers: Factionalism Within The Unionist Party, 1906–10' in the *Historical Journal*, volume XI, no.1, p. 113

p. 261 *Tammany*: Robert Rhodes James (ed) *Memoirs of a Conservative* (Weidenfeld & Nicolson, 1969) p. 117

p. 262 *Churchill phoning*: Sheila Hetherington *Katharine Atholl* (Aberdeen: University Press, 1991 ed.) p. 212

p. 262 *Rent and cards*: Stuart Ball 'The Politics of Appeasement: the Fall of the Duchess of Atholl and the Kinross and West Perth By-election, December 1938' in *Scottish Historical Review*, volume LXIX, April 1990, p. 79

p. 262 *Eden meeting*: Robert Rhodes James *Anthony Eden* (Papermac, 1987) p. 200

p. 263 *Snarl*: Robert Rhodes James, p. 201

p. 263 *Frozen out*: Barbara Cartland *Ronald Cartland* (Collins, 1942) pp. 216–7, 246

p. 263 *Churchills not Tories*: Woodrow Wyatt *Confessions of an Optimist* (Collins, 1985) p. 173

p. 263 *OUT!*: John Ramsden 'From Churchill to Heath' in Lord Butler (ed) *The Conservatives* (Allen and Unwin, 1977) p. 408

p. 264 *Davidson v Churchill*: Martin Gilbert *Churchill: A Life* (Minerva: 1991 ed.) p. 499

p. 264 *MPs and film vans*: Robert Rhodes James (ed) *Memoirs of a Conservative* p. 384

p. 265 *Churchill to Atholl*: Sheila Hetherington, p. 212

p. 265 *Trouble*: William Manchester *The Caged Lion* (Michael Joseph, 1988) p. 376

p. 265 *Margesson*: Jorgen S. Rasmussen 'Government and Intra-Party Opposition: Dissent Within the Conservative Parliamentary Party in the 1930s' in *Political Studies*, volume XIX, no.2, p. 183

p. 265 *Esoteric confines*: Colin Thornton-Kemsley *Through Winds and Tides* (Montrose: Standard Press, 1974) p. 93

p. 266 *Subservient members*: Martin Gilbert *Winston S. Churchill volume V, 1922–1939* (Heinemann, 1976) p. 1043

p. 266 *Start fair*: Colin Thornton-Kemsley, p. 114

p. 267 *Woolton and Erskine-Hill*: *Unpublished diary of 1st Earl of Woolton* held at Bodleian, Oxford: Ref. MS Woolton 2, entries dated 12 May 1942 and 13 July 1942

p. 267 *Oliver Stanley*: *Woolton diary* at Bodleian, entry dated 18 August 1942

p. 267 *Get rid of him*: Lord Moran *Winston Churchill: The struggle for survival 1940–1965* (Constable, 1966) p. 308

p. 267 *1949 poll*: *Private Papers of 1st Earl of Woolton* kept at the Bodleian, Oxford; Ref. MS Woolton 21, 'Chairman's Confidential Report' dated 5 October 1949

p. 268   *Ball and Burgess*: Barrie Penrose and Simon Freeman *Conspiracy of Silence* (Grafton, 1987) p. 221; Bruce Page, David Leitch and Phillip Knightley *Philby, The Spy Who Betrayed A Generation* (Sphere, 1977 ed.) p. 96

p. 268   *Eminence grise*: Robert Blake's entry on Ball in the *Dictionary of National Biography 1961–1970* (Oxford: University Press, 1981), p. 68

p. 268   *Seamy side of life*: Robert Rhodes James *Memoirs of a Conservative*, p. 212

p. 269   *SIS v Labour*: Michael Pinto-Duschinsky *British Political Finance 1830–1980* (USA, Washington: American Enterprise Institute, 1981) p. 97

p. 269   *Tree and Ball*: Ronald Tree *When the Moon was High* (Macmillan, 1975) p. 76

p. 269   *Private steps*: Stephen Koss *The Rise and Fall of the Political Press in Britain* (Fontana, 1990 ed.) p. 108

p. 269   *Unity of silence*: Richard Cockett 'Ball, Chamberlain and *Truth*' in the *Historical Journal*, volume 33, no.1, p. 133

p. 269   *Eden and newsreel*: Jonathan Lewis 'Before Hindsight' in *Sight and Sound*, volume 46, no.2, Spring 1977, p. 72

p. 269   *Eden's health*: Amber Blanco White *The New Propaganda* (Victor Gollancz, 1939) p. 21

p. 270   *Hand-picked lobby*: James Margach *The Abuse of Power* (W. H. Allen, 1978) p. 103

p. 270   *Jew-infested*: Richard Cockett *Twilight of Truth* (Weidenfeld & Nicolson, 1989) p. 162

p. 270   *Persuading Kindersley*: Robert Rhodes James (ed) *Memoirs of a Conservative*, pp. 199, 203–4

p. 271   *Nutting's separation*: Leon D. Epstein 'British MPs and their Local Parties: the Suez Crisis' in *American Political Science Review*, volume LIV, no.2, June 1960, p. 378

p. 271   *Play School*: Patrick Cosgrave *The Lives of Enoch Powell* (Bodley Head, 1989) p. 329

p. 271   *Westland*: Geoffrey Howe *Conflict of Loyalty* (Macmillan, 1994) pp. 462–75

p. 272   *Anti-Semitic propaganda*: Paul Foot *Who Framed Colin Wallace?* (Macmillan, 1989) p. 274

p. 272   *Leakers*: Tam Dalyell *Misrule* (Hamish Hamilton, 1987) p. 49

p. 273   *Positively besotted*: Nigel Lawson *The View From No.11* (Bantam, 1992) p. 314

p. 273   *Smear v Heseltine*: R. K. Alderman and Neil Carter 'A Very Tory Coup: The Ousting of Mrs Thatcher' in *Parliamentary Affairs*, volume 44, no.2, April 1991, p. 131

p. 273   *Filing Cabinets*: Arnold Kemp *The Hollow Drum* (Edinburgh: Mainstream, 1993)

p. 273   *Connection*: Margaret Thatcher *The Downing Street Years* (Harper-Collins, 1993) p. 623

p. 274   *Appalled*: Fairbairn letter in *The Times*, 10 November 1992

p. 274   *Anti-appeasers*: Andrew Roberts 'Echoes of Munich' in the *Sunday Telegraph*, 27 November 1994

CHAPTER ELEVEN
'The Economy is Safe in Our Hands'

p. 276   *Physical enjoyment*: Peel quoted in Robert Stewart *A Dictionary of Political Quotations* (Europa, 1984) pp. 129–30

p. 276   *Paternal socialism*: Macmillan in Harvey Glickman 'The Toryness of English Conservatism' in the *Journal of British studies*, volume 1, no.1, 1961, p. 137

p. 276   *Unanimous*: John Pearson *Citadel of the Heart* (Pan, 1993 ed.) p. 200

p. 277   *Damned dots*: A. L. Rowse *The Later Churchills* (Penguin, 1971 ed.) p. 321

p. 277   *Persian*: Lord Boothby *Reflections of a Rebel* (Hutchinson, 1978) p. 46

p. 278   *Heath Government*: David Willetts *Modern Conservatism* (Penguin, 1992) p. 43

p. 278   *Property-owning democracy*: Robert Rhodes James *Anthony Eden* (1987) p. 328

p. 279   *Vast nervous system*: Margaret Thatcher *The Downing Street Years* (HarperCollins, 1993) p. 11

p. 279   *St Luke quotations*: Brian Griffiths *The Creation of Wealth* (Hodder & Stoughton, 1984) p. 40

p. 279   *Rapacious scramble*: Viscount Hailsham *The Case for Conservatism* (Penguin, 1947 ed.) p. 52

p. 279   *1962 motion*: F. W. S. Craig (ed) *Conservative and Labour Party Conference Decisions 1945–1981* (Chichester: Parliamentary Research Service, 1982) p. 24

p. 282   *Rara avis*: Jamie Camplin *The Rise of the Plutocrats* (Constable, 1978) p. 128

p. 283   *Why in Conservative Party*: Harold Macmillan *Winds of Change 1914–1939* (Macmillan, 1966) p. 224

p. 283   *Not raising party politics*: Robert Boothby et al *Industry and State* (Macmillan, 1927) p. 37: Alistair Horne in his biography of Macmillan calls this weighty tome a 'pamphlet'

p. 283   *Stockton 1932–33*: Alistair Horne *Macmillan 1894–1956* (Macmillan, 1988) p. 102

p. 283   *Up to 1931*: Harold Macmillan *Winds of Change*, p. 283

p. 284   *Willetts v Macmillan*: Willetts, pp. 30, 34

p. 284   *Republishing Middle Way*: Paul Foot *The Politics of Harold Wilson* (Penguin, 1968) p. 341 fn.1

p. 284   *Human look*: Butler in Lord Butler (ed) *The Conservatives* (Allen & Unwin, 1977) p. 14

p. 285   *Working for Churchill*: Reginald Maudling *Memoirs* (Sidgwick & Jackson, 1978) pp. 45–6

p. 285   *Signpost*: Andrew Gamble *The Conservative Nation* (Routledge, 1974) pp. 35–6, 44–5; Shirley Robin Letwin *The Anatomy Of Thatcherism* (Fontana, 1992) pp. 56–7

p. 285   *Only minor shift*: Anthony Seldon *Churchill's Indian Summer* (Hodder & Stoughton, 1981) p. 421

p. 286   *Conservatives wary*: Andrew Taylor 'The Party And The Trade Unions' in Anthony Seldon and Stuart Ball (eds) *Conservative Century* (Oxford: University Press, 1994) p. 540

p. 286   *Miners' terms*: Churchill quoted in John Mortimer *In Character* (Allen Lane, 1983) p. 128

p. 286   *Preserving peace*: Lord Birkenhead *Walter Monckton* (Weidenfeld & Nicolson, 1969) p. 274

p. 286   *Deakin's access*: V. L. Allen *Trade Union Leadership* (Longmans, Green, 1957) p. 150

p. 287   *Freak result*: Andrew Roberts *Eminent Churchillians* (Weidenfeld & Nicolson, 1994) pp. 253–4

p. 287   *Collective policy*: Anthony Seldon, p. 207

p. 287   *Butler secret Cabinet memo*: PRO CAB/128/49: C52(8); C52(10)

p. 288   *Butler's budgets*: Michael Pinto-Duschinsky 'Bread and Circuses? The Conservatives in Office, 1951–1964' in Vernon Bogdanor and Robert Skidelsky (eds) *The Age of Affluence 1951–1964* (Papermac, 1970) pp. 64–9

p. 288   *Loved spending*: Thorneycroft quoted in Alistair Horne 'What went wrong for Supermac?' in *The Times*, 9 February 1994

p. 288   *Hailsham and telegrams*: Lord Hailsham *A Sparrow's Flight* (Collins, 1990) p. 317

p. 288   *Birch in The Times*: quoted in Anthony Sampson *Macmillan* (Pelican, 1968) p. 203

p. 289   *Pools of unemployment*: Lord Butler *The Art of the Possible* (Penguin, 1973) p. 61

p. 290   *Rushed into reform*: Jim Prior *A Balance of Power* (Hamish Hamilton, 1986) p. 72

p. 290   *IEA language*: see remarks of John Wood, deputy head of the IEA, in Michael Davie 'Men who told Thatcher there was an alternative' in the *Observer*, 24 March 1983

p. 291   *Right Approach*: quoted by Andrew Gamble 'Economic Policy' in Zig Layton-Henry (ed) *Conservative Party Politics* (Macmillan, 1980) p. 26

p. 291   *Few want to be rich*: Martin J. Weiner *English Culture and the Decline of the Industrial Spirit, 1850–1980* (Cambridge: University Press, 1981) p. 163

p. 292   *Chamberlain*: Harold Begbie *The Conservative Mind* (Mills & Boon, 1924) p. 66

p. 292   *Thatcher revolution*: Norman Tebbit *Upwardly Mobile* (Futura, 1989 ed.) p. 340

p. 293   *Macleod*: Andrew Taylor, p. 520

p. 293   *Secret ballot*: PRO CAB 23/52 (C21/26), 2 May 1926

p. 294   *All could agree*: John Redwood *Popular Capitalism* (Routledge, 1988) p. 147

p. 295   *Low growth*: Peter Kellner in the *Sunday Times*, 20 February 1994

p. 296   *FT journalist*: Margaret Thatcher, p. 701

p. 297   *Defenders of deal*: Simon Jenkins 'Why did we give a dam?' in *The Times*, 2 March 1994

p. 297   *Anarchic*: John Redwood, p. 44

p. 297   *Interest rates 12%*: David Smith *From Boom To Bust* (Penguin, 1993 ed.) p. 214

p. 298   *Rise in public spending*: David Smith 'Broken Promises' in the *Sunday Times* 10 April 1994

p. 299   *Climbdown*: David Smith *From Boom To Bust*, p. 245

p. 301   *Credit card decade*: David Smith, pp. 34–5

p. 302   *Economic management*: David Willetts, p. 124

p. 302   *Central economic ideas*: Vincent Cable 'Freeing the market in ideas' in the *Independent*, 2 December 1994

CHAPTER TWELVE
One Nation and Two

p. 304   *Chamberlain*: quoted in Derek Fraser *The Evolution of the British Welfare State* (Macmillan, 1973), p. 130

p. 304   *Give people social reform*: Hogg quoted in William Harrington and Peter Young *The 1945 Revolution* (Davis-Poynter, 1978) p. 124

p. 305   *Chamberlain in mining areas*: Noreen Branson and Margot Heinemann *Britain in the Nineteen Thirties* (Weidenfeld & Nicolson, 1971) p. 62

p. 305   *Chamberlain and foreign policy*: interview with Butler in John Mortimer *In Character* (Allen Lane, 1983) p. 128

p. 305   *Never knew*: Paul Addison *The Road to 1945* (Quartet, 1977) p. 72

p. 306   *Balfour, 1895*: Derek Fraser, p. 129

p. 307   *Sink commerce*: Derek Fraser, p. 18

p. 308   *Consolidation*: John Vincent *Disraeli* (Oxford: University Press, 1990) p. 11; Plimsoll line, p. 11

p. 308   *Profitable investment*: Richard Shannon *The Age of Disraeli, 1868–1881* (Longman, 1992) p. 212

p. 308   *Disraeli sleeping*: John Vincent, p. 12

p. 309   *Disraeli and social reform*: Paul Smith *Disraelian Conservatism and Social Reform* (Routledge, 1967) p. 322

p. 309   *Remember compassion*: Butler in John Mortimer, p. 128

p. 310   *Butler and elementary/secondary*: Anthony Howard *RAB* (Papermac, 1988) p. 113 fn

p. 310   *Churchill and equal pay*: Lord Hailsham *A Sparrow's Flight* (Collins, 1990) pp. 217–21

p. 310   *90% unenthusiastic*: Kevin Jeffery 'British Politics and Social Policy during the Second World War' in the *Historical Journal*, volume 30, no.1, 1977, pp. 129–30

p. 311   *Edwardian Churchill*: Paul Addison 'Churchill and Social Reform' in Robert Blake and W. R. Louis (eds) *Churchill* (Oxford: University Press, 1993) p. 76

p. 311   *Submerged tenth*: Derek Fraser, p. 127

p. 312   *Wild young ostriches*: quoted by Brian Simon *The Two Nations and the Educational Structure 1780–1870* (Lawrence & Wishart, 1974) p. 359

p. 312   *Figures re university students*: E. J. Hobsbawm *Industry and Empire* (Weidenfeld & Nicolson, 1968) p. 192

p. 313   *Kingsley Wood's isolation*: Lord Boyd-Orr *As I Recall* (Margitton and Kee, 1966) p. 115

p. 314   *Middle Way*: Harold Macmillan *Winds of Change 1914–1939* (Macmillan, 1966) p. 501

p. 314   *Evacuation and Economist*: quoted by Richard M. Titmuss *Problems of Social Policy* (HMSO, 1950) p. 516

p. 314   *Warfare/welfare*: Asa Briggs 'The Welfare State in Historical Perspective' in *Archives Européennes De Sociologie*, 1961, no 2, p. 227

p. 315   *Equal pay in 1950s*: Harold L. Smith 'The Politics of Conservative Reform: The Equal Pay for Equal Work Issue, 1945–1955' in the *Historical Journal*, volume 35, no.2, 1992, pp. 401–15

p. 315   *1952 Cab*: PRO CAB 128/25 CC 52, dated 18 December 1952

p. 315   *Restricting immigration*: D. W. Dean 'Conservative Governments and the Restraints of Commonwealth Immigration in the 1950s' in the *Historical Journal*, volume 35, no. 1, 1992, pp. 171–94

p. 315   *Plans to deport*: David Walker 'Churchill sought ways of keeping blacks out of Civil Service' in *The Times*, 2 January 1985

p. 316   *Impoverishment*: Macmillan quoted in John Ramsden 'From Churchill to Heath' in Lord Butler (ed) *The Conservatives* (Allen & Unwin, 1977) pp. 448–9

p. 316   *Sacks of support*: John Ranelagh *Thatcher's People* (HarperCollins, 1991) p. 134

p. 317   *Turn Tory*: quoted in John Ramsden 'A Party For Owners Or A Party For Earners?' in *Transactions of the Historical Society*, volume 37, 1987, p. 57

p. 318   *Figures re further education*: Anthony Sampson *The Essential Anatomy of Britain* (Hodder & Stoughton, 1992) pp. 64–5

p. 318   *Nissan and syllabuses*: 'A Survey of Britain' in *The Economist*, 24 October 1992, p. 14

p. 319   *Scroungers*: John Pilger in the *New Statesman*, 17 December 1993

p. 319   *Harris and prayer books*: Joan Isaac 'The New Right And The Moral Society' in *Parliamentary Affairs*, volume 43, no. 2, April 1990, p. 212

p. 320 *PAC Report, January 1994*: David Hencke 'Millions lost in waste and fraud' in the *Guardian*, 28 January 1994

p. 321 *Poverty in Britain*: for example, the report of the Institute for Fiscal Studies in the *Independent*, 3 June 1994

p. 322 *S. Smiles*: Ivor Crewe 'Values: The Crusade that Failed' in Dennis Kavanagh and Anthony Seldon (eds) *The Thatcher Effect* (Oxford: University Press, 1989) pp. 243–4

p. 322 *British society less equal*: Howard Davies' speech in 'CBI leader deplores Britain's new poverty' in the *Guardian*, 11 March 1994

p. 322 *Total absence of money*: J. K. Galbraith *The Good Society Considered: the economic dimension* (Cardiff: Law School, 1994) no pagination

p. 323 *Conservative's £5*: David Kirkwood *My Life of Revolt* (Harrap, 1935) p. 206

CHAPTER THIRTEEN
In High Places

p. 324 *Party of resistance*: A. L. Kennedy *Salisbury 1830–1903* (John Murray, 1953) p. 74

p. 324 *True answer*: Douglas Hurd interviewed by Graham Turner in the *Sunday Telegraph*, 17 October 1993

p. 324 *Our Establishment*: Andrew Neil 'Snobbocracy and me' in the *Evening Standard*, 26 May 1993

p. 325 *Maintain institutions*: Robert Eccleshall *English Conservatism since the Restoration* (Unwin Hyman, 1990) p. 136

p. 326 *George VI, 1945*: Peter Young and William Harrington *The 1945 Revolution* (Davis-Poynter, 1978) p. 207

p. 326 *Heroes*: Mark Girouard *The English Town* (Yale: University Press, 1990) p. 8

p. 327 *1871 service*: Richard Shannon *The Age of Disraeli, 1868–1881* (Longman, 1992) p. 134

p. 328 *Cigarette box, 1914*: John Pearson *The Ultimate Family* (Michael Joseph, 1986) p. 19

p. 328 *George V shaking hands*: James Harvey and Katharine Hood *The British State* (Lawrence & Wishart, 1958) p. 69

p. 328 *Queen Mary and hospitals*: John Pearson, p. 20

p. 328 *Organic vision*: Kenneth Medhurst 'Reflections on the Church of England and Politics at a Moment of Transition' in *Parliamentary Affairs*, 44, 2, April 1991, p. 241

p. 329 *Black recruiting sergeant*: *Dictionary of English Church History* (Cassell, 1912) p. 429

p. 330 *Bloodletting and murder*: James Curran and Jean Seaton *Power Without Responsibility* (Fontana, 1981) pp. 60, 69

p. 330 *Central Office funds*: Curran and Seaton, p. 73

p. 330 *Party buying newspapers*: John Ramsden *The Age of Balfour and Baldwin 1902–1940* (Longman, 1978) p. 70; 230 papers, pp. 234–5

p. 331   *Abdication*: Stephen Koss *The Rise and Fall of the Political Press in Britain* (Fontana, 1990 ed) p. 1105

p. 332   *Hurrah for Blackshirts*: Koss, p. 971

p. 332   *Topping's briefings*: Richard Cockett *Twilight of Truth* (Weidenfeld & Nicolson, 1989) p. 8

p. 332   *Self-censorship and knighthoods*: Phillip Knightley *The First Casualty* (Quartet, 1978) p. 80–81, 98

p. 332   *Beaverbrook and lobby*: Richard Cockett, pp. 56, 187

p. 332   *Newsreels*: Jonathan Lewis 'Before Hindsight' in *Sight and Sound*, Spring 1977, pp. 66–73; Tony Aldgate '1930s Newsreels: Censorship and Controversy' in *Sight and Sound*, Summer 1977, pp. 154–7

p. 333   *Party and BBC, 1926*: The Papers of J. C. C. Davidson, Box 173 'Report on the General Strike'; Box 1/3, doc U5, Memo dated 14 June 1926; also see *Conservative Party Archive*, CCO 4/1/23 'Political Partisanship of BBC' e.g. letter from Reith, July 1931

p. 333   *Left-wing bias*: Philip Goodhart *The 1922* (Macmillan, 1973) p. 82

p. 334   *Servility*: George Orwell *The English People* (Collins, 1947) p. 29

p. 334   *One million servants*: David Cannadine *The Decline and Fall of the British Aristocracy* (Picador, 1992 ed.) p. 629

p. 334   *Perspex canopy*: John Pearson, p. 194

p. 335   *Reith and dog-racing*: Michael Cockerell *Live From Number Ten* (Faber, 1989 ed.) p. 25

p. 335   *Representing industry*: James Curran and Jean Seaton, p. 208

p. 336   *Tim Bell on Mrs T*: quoted by Jeremy Paxman in *Friends in High Places* (Penguin, 1991 ed.) p. 125

p. 336   *Handbagging*: Julian Critchley *A Bag of Boiled Sweets* (Faber, 1994) p. 125

p. 337   *Went to the Sun*: Michael Dobbs in *Thatcher: The Downing Street Years*, BBC1, 20 October 1993

p. 337   *Hand in hand*: William Shawcross Murdoch (Pan, 1993 ed.) p. 210

p. 338   *Selling excrement*: Francis Wheen quoted in William Shawcross 'Does it make sense to hate Murdoch?' in the *Evening Standard*, 8 September 1992

p. 338   *All that is wrong*: Paul Vallely 'The code of Kelvin: jolly japes and base instincts' in the *Daily Telegraph*, 22 January 1994

p. 338   *Honours to press supporters*: William Shawcross *Murdoch* p. 154

p. 338   *Papers in government pockets*: editorial in the *Sunday Times*, 23 January 1994

p. 339   *Thatcher and lobby system*: see Michael Cockerell, Peter Hennessy and David Walker *Sources Close to the Prime Minister* (Macmillan, 1984)

p. 339   *Tebbit versus BBC*: Norman Tebbit *Upwardly Mobile* (Futura, 1989 ed.) p. 248

p. 339   *Redhead*: Bernard Ingham *Kill the messenger* (HarperCollins 1991) p. 354

p. 339   Greg Dyke 'How to save British TV' in the *Guardian*, 14 March 1994

p. 340   *Decline in church attendance*: 'Nave gazing' in *The Economist*, 12 March 1994

p. 341   *In theory*: 'Ask me no questions' in *The Economist*, 12 February 1994

p. 342   *Commercial ethic*: Vernon Bogdanor 'This isn't the place to build a market' in the *Daily Telegraph*, 17 November 1993

p. 342   *6,500 quangos*: the *Guardian*, 28 January 1994

p. 342   *Over 5,000 with executive power*: see Hugo Young on the findings of Democratic Audit in the *Guardian*, 28 July 1994

p. 343   *NHS trusts*: 'The NHS: Unelected Tory Quangos' in *Labour Research*, volume 83, no.12, December 1994, pp. 12–14

p. 343   *Welsh Development Agency*: Sonia Purnell 'Redwood fails to stem the tide of scandal' in the *Daily Telegraph*, 31 May 1994

p. 343   *Lord Bancroft*: David Rose 'A dangerous state of irresponsibility' in the *Observer*, 30 January 1994

p. 344   *High honour*: Frederick Walker 'Half a Century of Political Battle' in *Conservative Agents' Journal*, no.377, May 1952, p. 118

p. 345   *Social restraints*: Norman Tebbit, p. 340

p. 346   *1/3 not knowing*: *Daily Telegraph*, 14 May 1987

FOURTEEN
Dangerous Liaisons

p. 348   *European party*: Mrs Thatcher quoted in Nigel Ashford 'The European Economic Community' in Zig Layton-Henry (ed) *Conservative Party Politics* (Macmillan, 1980) p. 113

p. 349   *Not dying for socialism*: George Orwell 'Fascism and Democracy' in Victor Gollancz (ed) *The Betrayal Of The Left* (Gollancz, 1941) p. 213

p. 349   *Fervour of patriotism*: Hugh Cunningham 'The Language of Patriotism, 1750–1914' in *History Workshop Journal*, no.12, Autumn 1981, p. 21

p. 349   *Advent of Liberalism*: Disraeli quoted in Robert Eccleshall English Conservatism since the Restoration (Unwin Hyman, 1990) p. 137

p. 349   *Ashmead Bartlett*: Hugh Cunningham, p. 23

p. 350   *Hymn of Primrose Buds*: Martin Pugh *The Tories and the People* (Oxford: Blackwell, 1985) p. 215

p. 351   *Sounds of England*: Stanley Baldwin *On England* (Hodder & Stoughton, 1939) p. 5

p. 351   *Bruges speech*: Shirley Robin Letwin *The Anatomy of Thatcherism* (Fontana, 1992) p. 304

p. 351 *Bartlett*: Hugh Cunningham 'The Conservative Party and Patriotism' in Robert Colls and Hugh Cunningham (eds) *Englishness, Politics and Culture 1880–1920* (Croom Helm, 1986) pp. 289–90

p. 352 *The Nation*: Linda Colley *Britons* (Yale University Press, 1992); also 'Britain 1994: nation in search of an identity' in *The Times*, 31 January 1994

p. 352 *Child of Victorian era*: Winston Churchill *My Early Life* (Odhams, 1947) ix

p. 352 *Positive advantages*: D. R. Thorpe *Selwyn Lloyd* (Cape, 1989) p. 153

p. 353 *Irishman imaginative*: Disraeli quoted in R. B. McDowell *British Conservatism 1832–1914* (Faber, 1959) p. 109

p. 354 *Primrose League and Ireland*: Janet Robb *The Primrose League 1883–1906* (USA, New York: AMS Press, 1968 ed.) pp. 188–92

p. 354 *Lord Randolph*: A. T. Q. Stewart *The Ulster Crisis* (Faber, 1967) p. 21

p. 354 *Salvidge v diehards*: Stanley Salvidge *Salvidge of Liverpool* (Hodder & Stoughton, 1934) pp. 213–15

p. 355 *Attlee 1950*: Ross McKibbin *The Ideologies Of Class* (Oxford: Clarendon Press, 1990) p. 263 fn

p. 356 *India Bill*: Lord Butler *The Art of the Possible* (1973 ed.) p. 55

p. 356 *Nutting*: David Leigh *The Frontiers of Secrecy* (Junction, 1980) p. 52

p. 356 *Mountbatten programmes censored*: see Bernard Levin's two articles in *The Times*, 5 November 1980 and 11 November 1980

p. 357 *Britain's story*: David Carlton *Anthony Eden* (Allen & Unwin, 1986 ed.) p. 311

p. 357 *Him or us*: Keith Kyle *Suez* (Weidenfeld & Nicolson, 1991) p. 86

p. 357 *Eisenhower and re-election*: Daniel Yergin *The Prize* (Simon & Schuster, 1993 ed.) p. 484

p. 358 *Radio station*: Richard Norton-Taylor 'BBC connived with MI6 to oust Nasser' in the *Guardian*, 16 September 1994

p. 358 *40% advertising*: Francis Beckett 'Press and Prejudice' in Peter Beharrell and Greg Philo (eds) *Trade Unions and the Media* (Macmillan, 1977) p. 47

p. 358 *Armstrong's black tie*: Hugo Young 'Arch-mandarin who went public' in the *Sunday Times*, 13 July 1980

p. 358 *Macmillan and Nasser*: Richard Cockett (ed) *My Dear Max* (Historians' Press, 1990) p. 196

p. 358 *Macmillan mishandling*: Simon Heffer 'Centenary Of A Double-Crosser' in the *Spectator*, 5 February 1994; also see Keith Kyle, p. 228

p. 358 *Macmillan exaggerating*: Simon Heffer 'Century of a Double-Crosser' in the *Spectator*, 5 February 1994

p. 359 *On board steamer*: Philip Goodhart *The 1922* (Macmillan, 1973) p. 175

p. 359   *Gaitskell*: Robert Rhodes James 'Political Echoes' in Anthony Moncrieff (ed) *Suez Ten Years After* (BBC, 1967) p. 111

p. 359   *Blake on Eden*: Blake quoted in James Margach *The Abuse of Power* (W. H. Allen, 1978) p. 100

p. 359   *More set*: Keith Kyle, p. 534

p. 360   *Brotherhood of man*: Macleod quoted in Anthony Howard 'Iain Macleod' in the *Listener*, 9 October 1980

p. 360   *Norman land-holdings*: Philip Goodhart *The 1922*, p. 211

p. 360   *Shaking fists*: Lord Carrington *Reflect on Things Past* (Collins, 1988) p. 298

p. 361   *Churchill and Scotland*: Bill Miller, Jack Brand and Maggie Jordan 'Government Without A Mandate: Its Causes and Consequences for the Conservative Party in Scotland' in *Political Quarterly*, volume 52, 1981, p. 205

p. 361   *Scotland not rebelling*: Andrew Marr *The Battle for Scotland* (Penguin, 1992) p. 2

p. 362   *Rhodes and civil war*: Bernard Porter *The Lion's Share* (Longman, 1975) p. 132

p. 362   *Salisbury and diadem*: Donald Southgate 'From Disraeli to Law' in Lord Butler (ed) *The Conservatives* (Allen & Unwin, 1977) p. 215

p. 363   *Chalfont in Sun, 1979*: quoted in Anthony Howard 'Not many Don't knows left in Fleet Street' in the *Observer*, 22 April 1979

p. 364   *Churchill's views*: Max Beloff 'Churchill and Europe' in Robert Blake and Wm. Roger Louis (eds) *Churchill* (Oxford: University Press, 1993) pp. 443–55

p. 365   *Boothby on Eden*: Lord Boothby *Recollections of a Rebel* (Hutchinson, 1978) pp. 222–3

p. 365   *Macmillan's fears*: *At the End of the Day* (Macmillan, 1973) p. 31

p. 365   *Popish plot*: *Conservative Party Archive* at Bodleian, Oxford: see file 'Anti-Common Market' CCO 500/51/3

p. 366   *English nationalist*: John Osmond *The Divided Kingdom* (Constable, 1988) p. 38

p. 366   *Suez-Empire*: Lord Beloff 'The Crisis and its Consequences for the British Conservative Party' in W. R. Louis and R. Owen (eds) *Suez 1956* (Oxford: University Press, 1989) p. 334

p. 366   *Falklands reversal*: Margaret Thatcher *The Downing Street Years* (HarperCollins, 1993) p. 173

p. 366   *Shiver of apprehension*: Nigel Lawson *The View From No. 11* (Bantam, 1992) p. 992

p. 367   *CBI survey*: Philip Bassett 'Business leaders oppose Major on single currency' in *The Times*, 15 November 1993

p. 367   *Rolling back frontiers*: Shirley Robin Letwin, p. 303

p. 368   *Wogs at Calais*: Bryan Cassidy quoted in Peter Hetherington 'A hard row to hoe for Euro MPs' in the *Guardian*, 21 May 1994

p. 368   *Euro-candidates split*: 'Tories in Euro-vote disarray' in the *Sunday Telegraph*, 29 May 1994

p. 370   *Two groupings*: Paul Johnson 'Let the Nationalists face the Federalists' in the *Sunday Telegraph*, 14 March 1993

p. 370   *Some kind of split*: Niall Fergusson in the *Sunday Telegraph*, 25 July 1993

p. 371   *68/72*: Paul Whiteley and Patrick Seyd 'Tory party faces mutiny of rank-and-file Conservatives' in the *Independent on Sunday* 4 December 1994

p. 371   *Sovereignty arguments*: Bill Cash in the *Sunday Times*, 13 March 1994

p. 371   *Dustbin of history*: Andrew Gamble *The Conservative Nation* (Routledge, 1974) p. 234

p. 371   *Nation state*: Lady Thatcher in the *Sunday Telegraph*, 13 December 1992

p. 372   *Implications of dissolution of nation state*: Nigel Harris *Competition and the Corporate State* (Methuen, 1972) p. 273

p. 372   *Size of pay-packets*: Robert Rhodes James (ed) *Memoirs of a Conservative* (Weidenfeld & Nicolson, 1969) p. 385

CHAPTER FIFTEEN
Tory Mavericks, Rebels and Outsiders

p. 373   *I love fame*: Disraeli quoted in Robert Rhodes James 'Where did all the idealists go?' in *The Times*, 21 October 1993

p. 373   *Damn Chamberlains*: Randolph S. Churchill *Lord Derby* (Heinemann, 1959) p. 160

p. 373   *Bad Party man*: Robert Rhodes James *Bob Boothby* (Headline, 1992) p. 88

p. 374   *Churchill on Boothby*: Unpublished Diary of 1st Earl of Woolton held at Bodleian, Oxford: Ref. MS Woolton 2, entry dated 17 October, 1940

p. 374   *Red Flag*: Kenneth Young (ed) *The Diaries of Sir Robert Bruce Lockhart*, volume two (Macmillan, 1980) p. 477

p. 375   *Buccaneering*: R. Blake 'Baldwin and the Right' in John Raymond (ed) *The Baldwin Age* (Eyre & Spottiswoode, 1960) p. 42

p. 375   *Never respectable*: John Gorst *The Fourth Party* (Smith 1906) p. 148

p. 376   *Damned Jew*: Michael Foot 'The Good Tory' in M. Foot *Debts of Honour* (Paladin, 1980) p. 59

p. 376   *Shrewsbury placarded*: Robert Blake *Disraeli* (Methuen, 1969) p. 163

p. 376   *No language*: H. M. and M. Swartz *Disraeli's Reminiscences* (Hamish Hamilton, 1975) p. 78

p. 376   *Immoderate reputation*: Robert Blake, p. 54

p. 377   *Unembarrassed by scruple*: Lord Rosebery's biography, quoted in A. L. Rowse *The Later Churchills* (Penguin, 1971 ed.) p. 297

p. 377   *Confrontation*: Roy Foster *Lord Randolph Churchill* (Oxford: University Press, 1988) p. 32; pamphlet, p. 65

p. 377   *Birmingham*: Roy Foster, pp. 162–3; opportunism, p. 107

p. 378   *Falling like Lucifer*: Peter Marsh *The Discipline of Popular Government* (Hassocks: Harvester, 1978) p. 102

p. 378   *Chamberlain not party man*: David Dutton 'Joseph Chamberlain and the Liberal Unionist Party' in *History Review*, 18, p. 31

p. 379   *Masculine force*: Potter quoted in Duncan Watts 'Juggler Joe' in *Modern History Review*, volume 5, no.1, September 1993, p. 20

p. 379   *Image*: Stephen Koss, p. 219

p. 379   *Chemical*: Jan Morris *Pax Britannica: The Climax of an Empire* (Penguin, 1979) p. 249

p. 379   *Give no quarter*: journalist J. St Loe Strachey quoted in David Dutton *Austen Chamberlain* (Bolton: Ross Anderson, 1985) p. 49

p. 379   *Chamberlain and Dilke*: John Juxon *Lewis and Lewis* (Collins, 1983) p. 219

p. 380   *Making noises*: H. Montgomery Hyde *Neville Chamberlain* (Weidenfeld & Nicolson, 1976) p. 20

p. 381   *Who loves Chamberlain*: Robert Blake 'Confessions of a tough operator' in the *Evening Standard*, 6 June 1994 – charmingly, Lord Blake says himself that he can't find the reference

p. 381   *FE on Thomas*: John Campbell *F. E. Smith* (Pimlico, 1991 ed.) p. 258

p. 382   *Three ships*: William Camp *The Glittering Prizes* (Macgibbon & Kee, 1960) p. 78

p. 382   *Lord Burstinghead*: John Campbell, p. 683

p. 382   *Six cars*: William Camp p. 129

p. 382   *Mona Dunn*: John Campbell, pp. 688–9

p. 383   *In dirt*: *The Papers of J. C. C. Davidson*, House of Lords: Box 180, document 408

p. 383   *Drunk in streets*: John Campbell, p. 804; sliding under table, p. 705

p. 383   *Conduit pipes*: David Cannadine 'Lord Birkenhead' in *The Pleasures Of The Past* (Collins, 1989) p. 304

p. 383   *Treasure in heart*: Winston Churchill *Great Contemporaries* (Collins, 1937) p. 151

p. 383   *Banbury and social reform*: Christopher Sykes *Nancy* (Panther, 1979) p. 265

p. 384   *Ass of man*: Robert Rhodes James (ed) *'Chips'* (Weidenfeld, 1993) p. 312

p. 384   *3 and 8 votes*: Anthony Howard *RAB* (Papermac, 1988) pp. 156,165

p. 384   *Smithers on music*: Peter Hennessy and Gail Brownfeld 'Britain's Cold War Security Purge: The Origins Of Positive Vetting' in the *Historical Journal*, volume 25, no.4, 1982, p. 974

p. 384   *Astor as women's MP*: Martin Pugh 'Popular Conservatism in Britain: Continuity and Change, 1880–1967' in the *Journal of British Studies*, volume 27, July 1988, p. 267

p. 384   *Mad witch*: Robert Rhodes James *'Chips'*, p. 390

p. 385   *Black Dog*: C. E. Lysaght *Brendan Bracken* (Allen Lane, 1979) p. 58; Vote for Daddy, p. 66

p. 385   *Stop me and Ask one*: Andrew Boyle *Poor, Dear Brendan* (Hutchinson, 1974) p. 169

p. 385   *Tough guy*: Ronald Tree *When the Moon was High* (Macmillan, 1975) p. 111

p. 386   *Death bed*: Robert Rhodes James *Anthony Eden* (Papermac, 1987) p. 607 fn.

p. 386   *Randolph and elephants*: Brian Roberts *Randolph* (Hamish Hamilton, 1984) p. 284

p. 386   *Gramophone*: Julian Amery in Kay Halle (ed) *Randolph Churchill* (Heinemann, 1971) pp. 194–5

p. 386   *Devonport*: Brian Roberts, p. 302

p. 386   *Randolph and libel cases*: David Hooper *Public Scandal, Odium and Contempt* (Coronet, 1984) pp. 93–101

p. 387   *Randolph as footnote*: C. L. Sulzberger quoted in Brian Roberts, p. 364

p. 387   *Morally immense*: Simon Heffer in the *Evening Standard*, 26 October 1993

p. 387   *Powell at Cambridge*: Patrick Cosgrave *The Lives of Enoch Powell* (Bodley Head, 1989) pp. 43,45

p. 388   *Kneeling in church*: Powell quoted in Robert Eccleshall *English Conservatism since the Restoration* (Unwin Hyman, 1990) p. 225

p. 388   *45,000 letters*: Diana Spearman 'Enoch Powell's Postbag' in *New Society*, 9 May 1968 and 27 June 1968

p. 389   *No Powellite organisation*: Douglas E. Schoen *Enoch Powell and the Powellites* (Macmillan, 1977) p. 277

p. 389   *Judas paid*: Patrick Cosgrave p. 347

p. 389   *Heart strings*: Powell interview in John Mortimer *In Character* (Allen Lane, 1983) p. 50

p. 389   *Joseph and poverty*: John Campbell *Edward Heath* (Cape, 1993) p. 381

p. 389   *Annan on Joseph*: Lord Annan *Our Age* (London: Weidenfeld & Nicolson, 1990) p. 346

p. 390   *Maudling on Joseph*: Simon Hoggart 'Mrs Thatcher's man-in-waiting' in the *Guardian*, 31 July 1980

p. 391   *Not right choice*: Jim Prior *A Balance of Power* (Hamish Hamilton, 1986) p. 125

p. 391   *Berkeley and Lancaster*: obituary in the *Daily Telegraph*, 16 November 1994; Humphry Berkeley *Crossing the Floor* (Allen & Unwin, 1972) p. 129

p. 392   *Baker, Wakeham and Patten*: Kenneth Baker *Maggie's Minder*, BBC2, 18 September 1993

p. 393   *Parliamentary life and machines*: Jeremy Paxman *Friends in High Places* (Penguin, 1991 ed.) p. 90

p. 393   *Manchester, 1872*: Robert Blake *Disraeli*, p. 522

p. 393   *5,000 man*: Gervaise Rentoul *Sometimes I Think* (Hodder & Stoughton, 1940) p. 17

p. 394   *My dear lady*: Winston Churchill *Great Contemporaries* (Fontana, 1959) pp. 145–6

p. 394   *Redwood practising smile*: 'There is Left, Right and Redwood' in the *Daily Telegraph*, 19 January 1994

CHAPTER SIXTEEN
Less Than Meets The Eye

p. 396   *Shop window*: A. W. Baldwin *My Father: The True Story* (Allen & Unwin, 1955) p. 105

p. 396   *Self-denigration*: Paul Foot *Words as Weapons* (Verso, 1990) p. 251

p. 396   *Full story*: James Stuart *Within the Fringe* (Bodley Head, 1967) p. 96

p. 398   *Churchilliana*: Peter Lewis 'Staggering Churchill' in the *Daily Mail*, 12 November 1962

p. 399   *Blandness*: Alistair Horne *Macmillan 1894–1956* (Macmillan, 1988) p. 300

p. 400   *Whelk stall*: Jim Prior *A Balance of Power* (Hamish Hamilton, 1986) p. 122

p. 401   *Cockney*: *Norman Tebbit: A Loner in Politics*, BBC2, 7 March 1993

p. 401   *One-dimensional*: Lord Young *The Enterprise Years* (Headline, 1990) p. 323

p. 401   *No office*: Young, p. 118; *Brighton*, pp. 124–5

p. 402   *Blue nose*: Earl of Kilmuir *Political Adventure* (Weidenfeld & Nicolson, 1964) p. 166; *Rufus*, p. 166

p. 403   *Wab*: Earl of Kilmuir, p. 285

p. 404   *Axe*: Reginald Bevins *The Greasy Pole* (Hodder & Stoughton, 1965) p. 136; *landed estates*, p. 102

p. 405   *Gentlemen into politics*: Julian Critchley *Westminster Blues* (Hamish Hamilton, 1985) p. 16

p. 405   *Bullock*: Julian Critchley *A Bag of Boiled Sweets* (Faber, 1994) p. 112

p. 406   *Israel to mobilise*: Sir Anthony Eden *Full Circle* (Cassell, 1960) pp. 522–3

p. 406   *No collusion*: Earl of Kilmuir, p. 278

p. 406   *Crookshank*: *Unpublished Diary of Viscount Crookshank*, held at Bodleian, Oxford; Ref: MS Eng Hist d 359, vol. 2

p. 407   *Churchill in car*: *Unpublished Diary of the 1st Earl of Woolton*, held at Bodleian, Oxford; Ref: MS Woolton 3, entry dated 29 June 1942

p. 408   *Lightweight*: Robert Rhodes James (ed) *'Chips'* (Weidenfeld, 1993) p. 452; *lost dog*, p. 40

p. 408   *Historians*: Douglas Hurd *An End to Promises* (Collins, 1979) p. 113

p. 409   *Old whore*: Alan Clark *Diaries* (Weidenfeld & Nicolson, 1993) p. 360; *sharks*, p. 373

p. 410   *Celts unwashed*: A. L. Rowse *The Expansion of Elizabethan England*, quoted in Liz Curtis *Nothing But The Same Old Story* (Information on Ireland, 1984) p. 75

p. 411   *Churchill boring*: Robert Rhodes James 'Blood, toil, tears and biography' in *The Times*, 11 March 1993

p. 414   *Restricting agenda*: David Cannadine *The Decline and Fall of the British Aristocracy* (Picador, 1992 ed.) p. 14

p. 414   *Filament of steel*: Mark Bence-Jones and Hugh Montgomery-Massingberd *The British Aristocracy* (Constable, 1979) p. 184

p. 414   *5,000 journalists*: Stephen Dorril *The Silent Conspiracy* (Heinemann, 1993) p. 67

p. 415   *Lobby*: 'The Death List' in *The Complete Yes Minister* (BBC, 1984) p. 209

p. 416   *Dons of War*: Peter Bradshaw in the *Evening Standard*, 11 January 1993

p. 416   *Italy with rockets*: Andrew Roberts *Eminent Churchillians* (Weidenfeld, 1994) p. 3; *ruling class*, pp. 3–4

p. 417   *Bearded*: Andrew Roberts 'Lenin's legacy of shame' in the *Daily Mail*, 22 January 1994

SEVENTEEN
Unofficial Faces

p. 419   *Thoroughly learnt*: quoted in Andrew Gamble *The Conservative Nation* (Routledge, 1974) p. 16

p. 419   *Growing older*: Kingsley Amis in Robert Stewart *A Dictionary of Political Quotations* (Europa, 1984) p. 3

p. 420   *Deliberate attempt*: see 'Funny Business' in the *Guardian Weekend*, 30 October 1993

p. 422   *Dickens lampoons*: Edgar Johnson *Charles Dickens* (Allen Lane, 1977 ed.) p. 185

p. 422   *Dickens and Chartists*: N. C. Peyrouton 'Dickens and the Chartists' in *The Dickensian*, Spring 1964 and Autumn 1964

p. 423   *Dickens and Reading*: Edgar Johnson, p. 187

p. 423   *Awe and horror*: Anthony Trollope *An Autobiography* (Oxford: University Press, 1980 ed.) p. 292; *wretched fortnight*, p. 300

p. 424   *Reviewers and Live Now*: see James Pope-Hennessy *Anthony Trollope* (Cape, 1971) pp. 311–13

p. 424   *Rude about Tories*: Glendinning quoted in the *Guardian*, 6 October 1993

p. 424   *28 films*: Tom Pocock *Rider Haggard and the Lost Empire* (Weidenfeld & Nicolson, 1993) p. 244

p. 425   *Battle of Stalham Bridge*: Tom Pocock, p. 99

p. 426   *Buchan and Zionism*: Janet Adam Smith *John Buchan* (Oxford: University Press, 1985 ed.) p. 317

p. 426   *Nazi Who's Who*: Christopher Harvie *The Centre of Things* (Unwin Hyman, 1991) p. 170 fn.13

p. 427   *Kipling in USSR*: see Jack Dunman 'Rudyard Kipling Re-visited' in *Marxism Today*, August 1965

p. 427   *Recessional*: James Morris *Pax Britannica. The Climax of an Empire* (Penguin, 1979 ed.) pp. 347–8

p. 427   *Kipling to Haggard*: Tom Pocock, p. 225

p. 428   *Abstain*: Winston Churchill *My Early Life* (Odhams, 1947) p. 153

p. 428   *Savrola*: W. D. Norwood 'Sir Winston Churchill as Novelist' in *Bulletin of the New York Public Library*, volume 66, 1962; also Sir Compton Mackenzie 'Churchill The Novelist' in Charles Eade (ed) *Churchill By His Contemporaries* (Hutchinson, 1953)

p. 429   *Dago*: Richard Usborne *Clubland Heroes* (Barrie & Jenkins, 1974) p. 147

p. 429   *Not evangelistic*: Colin Watson *Snobbery With Violence* (Eyre & Spottiswoode, 1971) p. 71

p. 430   *Major and Philanthropists*: Edward Pearce *The Quiet Rise Of John Major* (Weidenfeld & Nicolson, 1991) p. 13

p. 432   *Thirkell's sales*: David Pryce-Jones 'Towards the Cocktail Party' in Michael Sissons and Philip French (eds) *The Age of Austerity* (Hodder & Stoughton, 1963) pp. 214–15

p. 432   *James Bond*: see the excellent discussion by David Cannadine 'James Bond and the Decline of England' in *Encounter*, volume VIII, no. 5, September 1979

p. 433   *Stage melodrama*: Andrew Davies *Other Theatres* (Macmillan, 1987) pp. 16–17

p. 434   *Gilbert and Sullivan*: David Cannadine 'Gilbert and Sullivan: The Making And Unmaking Of A British "Tradition"' in Roy Porter (ed) *Myths of the English* (Cambridge: Polity Press, 1992) pp. 12–32

p. 434   *The Happy Land*: Elwood P. Lawrence '"The Happy Land": W. S. Gilbert As Political Satirist' in *Victorian Studies*, volume XV, no.2, pp. 161–83

p. 435   *Kiss of death*: Leslie Halliwell *Halliwell's Filmgoer's and Video Viewer's Companion* (Paladin, 1989 ed.) p. 882

p. 435   *'Empire' films and attitudes*: John Ramsden 'The Changing Base of British Conservatism' in Chris Cook and John Ramsden (eds) *Trends in British Politics since 1945* (Macmillan, 1978) p. 36

p. 435   *Kenyatta*: George MacDonald Fraser *The Hollywood History of the World* (Michael Joseph, 1988) p. 142

p. 436   *Postscripts*: J. B. Priestley *Margin Released* (Heinemann, 1962) p. 221

p. 436   *First gorilla*: Liz Curtis *Nothing But The Same Old Story* (Information on Ireland, 1984) p. 60

p. 437   *Low*: Adrian Smith 'Low and Lord Beaverbrook' in *Encounter*, volume LXV, no.5, December 1985, p. 9

p. 437   *Supermac*: Alistair Horne *Macmillan 1957–1986* (Macmillan, 1989) p. 149

p. 437   *Fig leaf*: James Cameron *Vicky: A Memorial Volume* (Allen Lane, 1967) p. 12

p. 439   *Scotch on the Rocks*: Graham Lord 'The thrilling side of Mr Hurd' in the *Daily Telegraph*, 29 July 1993

p. 441   *Old-fashioned socialist*: Mortimer interviewed in *City Limits*, 10 June 1983

p. 442   *Civil servants as politicians*: Peter Fiddick 'The makings of a Prime Minister' in the *Guardian*, 6 June 1986

p. 442   *Hacker and Trident*: Graham Turner 'The makers of Jim Hacker' in the *Sunday Telegraph*, 11 January 1987

p. 443   *Yes, Sir*: Woodrow Wyatt *Confessions of an Optimist* (Collins, 1985) p. 239

p. 444   *TW3*: Michael Cockerell *Live from Number 10* (Faber, 1988 ed.) pp. 86, 98

p. 445   *Eels skinned*: 'Cartoons and Cartoonists' in Winston Churchill *Thoughts and Adventures* (Odhams, 1932 ed.) p. 13

Conclusions

p. 447   *Pleasing illusions*: Burke in Robert Eccleshall 'English Conservatism as Ideology' in *Political Studies*, volume XXV, no.1, 1977, p. 66

p. 447   *The Party*: Wellington in Harvey Glickmann 'The Toryness of English Conservatism' in *Journal of British Studies*, volume 1, no.1, 1961, p. 134

p. 447   *Reminded him*: Peter Rawlinson *A Price Too High* (Weidenfeld & Nicolson, 1989) p. 93

p. 448   *Loyalty*: Earl of Kilmuir *Political Adventure* (Weidenfeld & Nicolson, 1964) p. 324

p. 449   *Fixed principle*: James Cornford 'The Transformation of Conservatism in the Nineteenth Century' in *Victorian Studies*, volume VII, 1963–4, p. 43

p. 451   *Ending century*: Anthony Seldon 'Conservative Century' in Anthony Seldon and Stuart Ball (eds) *Conservative Century* (Oxford: University Press, 1994) p. 63

Select Guide to Further Reading

Long lists of titles have always seemed to me to be incredibly unhelpful. Usually they are intended not to benefit the reader but to show off the author's diligence. I have included only those books (and a handful of articles) which I found most valuable, arranging them thematically like the chapters.

No title is mentioned more than once. Another 250 books and articles which I used for just one or two points can be found in the notes. The place of publication is London unless specified. The dates refer to the edition which I used, which in virtually every case is the edition most readily available to the general reader. An asterisk marks the titles I particularly recommend.

General

*Noel Annan *Our Age: Portrait of a Generation* (Weidenfeld & Nicolson, 1990)

Robert Blake *The Conservative Party from Peel to Thatcher* (Fontana, 1985)

Lord Butler (ed) *The Conservatives: A History from their Origins to 1965* (Allen & Unwin, 1977)

*Peter Clarke *A Question of Leadership: From Gladstone to Thatcher* (Penguin, 1991)

Journal of Contemporary History, special issue 'A Century of Conservatism', volume 13, no.4, 1978

Andrew Gamble *The Conservative Nation* (Routledge & Kegan

Paul, 1974)

Zig Layton-Henry (ed) *Conservative Party Politics* (Macmillan, 1980)

Zig Layton-Henry (ed) *Conservative Politics in Western Europe* (Macmillan, 1982)

T. F. Lindsay and Michael Harrington *The Conservative Party 1918–1979* (Macmillan, 1979)

Ross McKibbin *The Ideologies Of Class: Social Relations in Britain 1880–1950* (Oxford: Clarendon Press, 1990)

James Margach *The Anatomy of Power* (W. H. Allen, 1979)

Rupert Morris *Tories: From Village Hall to Westminster* (Edinburgh: Mainstream, 1991)

Philip Norton and Arthur Aughey *Conservatives and Conservatism* (Temple Smith, 1981)

Political Quarterly, Special Number on 'The Conservative Party', volume 32, no. 3, July–September 1961

John Ross *Thatcher And Friends: The Anatomy of the Tory Party* (Pluto Press, 1983)

Trevor Russel *The Tory Party* (Penguin, 1978)

Anthony Seldon and Stuart Ball (eds) *Conservative Century: The Conservative Party since 1900* (Oxford: University Press, 1994)

Old Dog, New Tricks

Stuart Ball *Baldwin and the Conservative Party: The Crisis of 1929–1931* (Yale: University Press, 1988)

*Jim Bulpitt 'The Discipline of the New Democracy: Mrs Thatcher's Domestic Statecraft' in *Political Studies*, volume xxxiv, no.1, 1986

James Cornford 'The Transformation of Conservatism in the late Nineteenth Century' in *Victorian Studies*, volume vii, 1963–64

*Douglas Hurd *An End to Promises: Sketches of a Government 1970–74* (Collins, 1979)

Dennis Kavanagh and Anthony Seldon (eds) *The Thatcher Effect* (Oxford: University Press, 1989)

Wm. Roger Louis and Roger Owen (eds) *Suez 1956: The Crisis and its Consequences* (Oxford: Clarendon Press, 1989)

R. B. McDowell *British Conservatism 1832–1914* (Faber, 1959)

Peter Marsh *The Discipline of Popular Government: Lord Salisbury's domestic statecraft, 1881–1902* (Hassocks: Harvester Press, 1978)

John Ramsden *The Age of Balfour and Baldwin 1902–1940* (Longman, 1978)

John Ramsden *The Making of Conservative Party Policy: The Conservative Research Department since 1929* (Longman, 1980)

John Ramsden 'A Party For Owners Or A Party For Earners?' How Far Did The British Conservative Party Really Change After 1945?' in *Transactions of the Royal Historical Society*, 5th series, 37, 1987

John Raymond (ed) *The Baldwin Age* (Eyre & Spottiswoode, 1960)

Richard Shannon *The Age of Disraeli, 1868–1881: The Rise of Tory Democracy* (Longman, 1992)

R. M. Stewart *The Foundation of the Conservative Party 1830–1867* (Longman, 1978)

Why Are We Here?

Kenneth Baker (ed) *The Faber Book of Conservatism* (Faber, 1993)

Harold Begbie *The Conservative Mind* (Mills & Boon, 1924)

Arthur Bryant *The Spirit of Conservatism* (Methuen, 1929)

Lord Hugh Cecil *Conservatism* (Williams & Norgate, 1912)

Maurice Cowling (ed) *Conservative Essays* (Cassell, 1978)

Robert Eccleshall *English Conservatism Since the Restoration* (Unwin Hyman, 1990)

Keith Feiling *Toryism* (G. Bell, 1913)

Ian Gilmour *The Body Politic* (Hutchinson, 1971); *Inside Right: A Study of Conservatism* (Hutchinson, 1977)

Harvey Glickman 'The Toryness of English Conservatism' in the *Journal of British Studies*, volume 1, number 1

Brian Griffiths *The Creation of Wealth* (Hodder & Stoughton, 1984)

F. J. C. Hearnshaw *Conservatism in England* (Macmillan, 1933)

Quintin Hogg *The Case For Conservatism* (Penguin, 1947); later revised as Lord Hailsham *The Conservative Case* (Penguin, 1959)

Shirley Robin Letwin *The Anatomy of Thatcherism* (Fontana, 1992)

Charles Moore and Simon Heffer (eds) *A Tory Seer: The selected journalism of T. E. Utley* (Hamish Hamilton, 1989)

Conor Cruise O'Brien *The Great Melody: A Thematic Biography and Commented Anthology of Edmund Burke* (Sinclair-Stevenson, 1992)

Noel O'Sullivan *Conservatism* (Dent, 1976)

Roger Scruton *The Meaning of Conservatism* (Macmillan, 1984)

John Vincent *Disraeli* (Oxford: University Press, 1990)

David Willetts *Modern Conservatism* (Penguin, 1992)

All Power To The Leader?

Bruce Anderson *John Major* (Headline, 1992)

Robert Blake *The Unknown Prime Minister: The Life And Times of Andrew Bonar Law* (Eyre & Spottiswoode, 1955)

Robert Blake and Wm. Roger Louis (eds) *Churchill* (Oxford: University Press, 1993)

John Campbell *Edward Heath: A Biography* (Cape, 1993)

David Carlton *Anthony Eden* (Allen & Unwin, 1986)

J. P. Cornford 'The Parliamentary Foundations of the Hotel Cecil' in R. Robson (ed) *Ideas and Institutions of Victorian Britain* (G. Bell, 1967)

Julian Critchley *Some of Us: People who did well under Thatcher* (John Murray, 1992)

Richard Davenport-Hines *The Macmillans* (Mandarin, 1993)

David Dilks *Neville Chamberlain, volume one: Pioneering and reform, 1869–1929* (Cambridge: University Press, 1984)

David Dutton *Austen Chamberlain: Gentleman in Politics* (Bolton: Ross Anderson, 1985)

Nigel Fisher *The Tory Leaders: Their Struggle For Power* (Weidenfeld & Nicolson, 1977)

Norman Gash *Sir Robert Peel* (Longman, 1972)

Martin Gilbert *Winston S. Churchill* (8 volumes plus accompanying volumes)

Alistair Horne *Harold Macmillan, volume 1, 1894–1956; volume 2, 1957–1986* (Macmillan, 1988, 1989)

Robert Rhodes James *Churchill: A Study in Failure 1900–1939*

(Pelican, 1973)

Robert Rhodes James *Anthony Eden* (Papermac, 1987)

Penny Junor *Margaret Thatcher: Wife, Mother, Politician* (Sidgwick & Jackson, 1983)

A. L. Kennedy *Salisbury 1830–1903* (John Murray, 1953)

Iain Macleod *Neville Chamberlain* (Muller, 1961)

Keith Middlemas and John Barnes *Baldwin: A Biography* (Weidenfeld & Nicolson, 1969)

Lord Moran *Winston Churchill: The Struggle for Survival 1940–1965* (Constable, 1966)

Charles Petrie *The Powers Behind the Prime Ministers* (Macgibbon and Kee, 1958)

*John Ranelagh *Thatcher's People: An insider's account of the politics, the power and the personalities* (HarperCollins, 1991)

Robert Shepherd *The Power Brokers: The Tory Party and its Leaders* (Hutchinson, 1991)

Donald Southgate (ed) *The Conservative Leadership 1832–1932* (Macmillan, 1974)

H. M. and M. Swartz *Disraeli's Reminiscences* (Hamish Hamilton, 1975)

Margaret Thatcher *The Downing Street Years* (HarperCollins, 1993)

Alan Watkins *A Conservative Coup: The Fall of Margaret Thatcher* (Duckworth, 1991)

Stanley Weintraub *Disraeli: A Biography* (Hamish Hamilton, 1993)

*Hugo Young *One of Us: A Biography of Margaret Thatcher* (Macmillan, 1989)

Kenneth Young *Arthur James Balfour* (G. Bell and Sons, 1963)

The Led

Stuart Ball 'The 1922 Committe: The Formative Years, 1922–1945' in *Parliamentary History*, volume 9, 1990

David Cannadine *The Rise and Fall of the British Aristocracy* (Picador, 1992)

Ivor Crewe and Donald Searing 'Ideological Change in the British Conservative Party' in *American Political Science Review*, volume 82, no.2, 1988

Julian Critchley *Westminster Blues* (Hamish Hamilton, 1985); *Palace of Varieties* (John Murray, 1989)

Philip Goodhart with Ursula Branson *The 1922: The Story of the Conservative Backbencher's Parliamentary Committee* (Macmillan, 1973)

Simon Haxey *Tory M. P.* (Victor Gollancz, 1939)

Anthony King 'The Rise of the Career Politician in Britain – And Its Consequences' in *British Journal of Political Science*, volume 11, July 1981

*Philip Norton '"The Lady's Not For Turning" But What About The Rest: Margaret Thatcher And The Conservative Party' in *Parliamentary Affairs*, volume 43, no.1, 1990

Charles Petrie *The Carlton Club* (White Lion, 1972)

Lisanne Radice, Elizabeth Vallance and Virginia Willis *Member of Parliament* (Macmillan, 1987)

John Ramsden 'The Changing Basis of British Conservatism' in Chris Cook and John Ramsden (eds) *Trends in British Politics Since 1945* (Macmillan, 1978)

*Peter Riddell *Honest Opportunism: The Rise of the Career Politician* (Faber, 1994)

Now Is The Time For All Good Men (and Women) . . .

Beatrix Campbell *The Iron Ladies: Why do Women vote Tory?* (Virago, 1987)

Randolph S. Churchill *Lord Derby: 'King of Lancashire'* (Heinemann, 1959)

Arthur Fawcett *Conservative Agent: A study of the National Society of Conservative and Unionist Agents and its members* (National Society of Conservative and Unionist Agents, 1967)

Richard N. Kelly *Conservative Party Conferences* (Manchester: University Press, 1989)

Robert McKenzie and Allan Silver *Angels in Marble* (Heinemann, 1968)

*Martin Pugh 'Popular Conservatism in Britain: Continuity and Change 1880–1987', *Journal of British Studies*, volume 27 (1988)

Martin Pugh *The Tories and the People 1880–1935* (Oxford: Blackwell, 1985)

Janet Robb *The Primrose League 1883–1906* (New York: AMS Press, 1968 ed.)

Stanley Salvidge *Salvidge of Liverpool: Behind the Political Scene 1890–1928* (Hodder & Stoughton, 1934)

*P. J. Waller *Democracy and Sectarianism: A political and social history of Liverpool 1868–1939* (Liverpool: University Press, 1981)

Gerald Warner *The Scottish Tory Party: A History* (Weidenfeld & Nicolson, 1988)

Paul Whiteley, Patrick Seyd and Jeremy Richardson *True Blues* (Oxford: University Press, 1994)

Money Matters

Tom Cullen *Maundy Gregory: Purveyor of Honours* (Bodley Head, 1972)

Michael De-la-Noy *The Honours System* (Virgin, 1992)

Justin Fisher 'Political Donations to the Conservative Party' in *Parliamentary Affairs*, volume 47, no.1, 1994

Mark Hollingsworth *MPs for Hire: The Secret World of Political Lobbying* (Bloomsbury, 1991)

Phillip Knightley *The Rise and Fall of the House of Vestey* (Warner, 1993)

Barry McGill 'Glittering Prizes and Party Funds in Perspective, 1882–1931' in *Bulletin of the Institute of Historical Research*, volume LV, number 131, May 1982

Gerald Macmillan *Honours For Sale: The Strange Case of Maundy Gregory* (Richards Press, 1954)

*Michael Pinto-Duschinsky *British Political Finance 1830–1980* (USA, Washington: American Enterprise Institute, 1981)

W. D. Rubinstein *Men Of Property: The Very Wealthy In Britain Since The Industrial Revolution* (Croom Helm, 1981)

G. R. Searle *Corruption in British Politics 1895–1930* (Oxford: Clarendon Press, 1987)

James Taylor *Ellermans: A Wealth of Shipping* (Wilton House Gentry, 1976)

John Walker *The Queen Has Been Pleased: The British Honours System at Work* (Secker & Warburg, 1986)

'The Bottom Line is Winning Elections'

*Michael Cockerell *Live From Number 10: The Inside Story of Prime Ministers and Television* (Faber, 1989)

Grace Wyndham Goldie *Facing the Nation: Television and Politics 1936–1976* (Bodley Head, 1977)

Frank I. Luntz *Candidates, Consultants, and Campaigns: The Style and Substance of American Electioneering* (Oxford: Blackwell, 1988)

Richard Rose *Influencing Voters* (Faber, 1967)

Rodney Tyler *Campaign! The Selling of the Prime Minister* (Grafton, 1987)

Dirty Tricks

Christopher Andrew *Secret Service: The Making of the British Intelligence Community* (Sceptre, 1986)

Tony Bunyan *The History and Practice of the Political Police in Britain* (Quartet, 1977)

Sir Wyndham Childs *Episodes and Reflections* (Cassell, 1930)

Philip G. Cambray *The Game of Politics: A Study of the Principles of British Political Strategy* (John Murray, 1932)

Lewis Chester, Stephen Fay and Hugo Young *The Zinoviev Letter* (Heinemann, 1967)

Tam Dalyell *Misrule: How Mrs Thatcher has Misled Parliament from the Sinking of the Belgrano to the Wright Affair* (Hamish Hamilton, 1987)

Stephen Dorril *The Silent Conspiracy: Inside the Intelligence Services in the 1990s* (Mandarin, 1994)

Stephen Dorril and Robin Ramsay *Smear! Wilson and the Secret State* (Grafton, 1992)

Mark Hollingsworth and Richard Norton-Taylor *Blacklist: The Inside Story of Political Vetting* (Hogarth Press, 1988)

Keith Jeffery and Peter Hennessy *States Of Emergency: British Governments and Strikebreaking since 1919* (Routledge & Kegan Paul, 1983)

David Leigh *The Wilson Plot: The Intelligence Services and the Discrediting of a Prime Minister* (Heinemann, 1988)

Seumas Milne *The Enemy Within: MI5, Scargill and the Maxwell Affair* (Verso, 1994)

Barrie Penrose and Roger Courtiour *The Pencourt File* (Secker & Warburg, 1978)

Ben Pimlott *Harold Wilson* (HarperCollins, 1992)

★Bernard Porter *Plots and Paranoia: A history of political espionage in Britain 1790–1988* (Unwin Hyman, 1989)

A. T. Q. Stewart *The Ulster Crisis* (Faber, 1967)

Peter Wright *Spycatcher: The Candid Autobiography of a Senior Intelligence Officer* (Viking, 1987)

Conservative Versus Conservative

Neal Blewett *The Peers, the Parties and the People: The General Elections of 1910* (Macmillan, 1972)

Richard Cockett 'Ball, Chamberlain and "Truth"' in the *Historical Journal*, volume 33, no.1, 1990

Alan Doig *Westminster Babylon* (Allison & Busby, 1990)

Theresa Gorman with Heather Kirby *The Bastards: Dirty Tricks and The Challenge to Europe* (Pan, 1993)

Sheila Hetherington *Katharine Atholl 1874–1960: Against the Tide* (Aberdeen: University Press, 1981 ed.)

William Manchester *The Caged Lion: Winston Spencer Churchill 1932–1940* (Michael Joseph, 1988)

Philip Norton *Conservative Dissidents: Dissent within the Parliamentary Conservative Party 1970–74* (Temple Smith, 1978)

'The Economy is Safe in Our Hands'

Richard Cockett *Thinking The Unthinkable: Think-Tanks and the Economic Counter-Revolution 1931–1983* (HarperCollins, 1994)

Andrew Gamble *The Free Economy and the Strong State: the Politics of Thatcherism* (Macmillan, 1988)

★Nigel Harris *Competition and the Corporate Society: British Conservatism, the State and Industry 1945–1964* (Methuen, 1972)

Peter Jenkins *Mrs Thatcher's Revolution: The Ending of the Socialist Era* (Pan, 1989)

Nigel Lawson *The View From No.11: Memoirs of a Tory Radical (Bantam Press, 1992)*

Keith Middlemas *Politics in Industrial Society: The experience of the British system since 1911* (Deutsch, 1979)

John Redwood *Popular Capitalism* (Routledge, 1989)

Anthony Seldon *Churchill's Indian Summer: The Conservative Government, 1951–1955* (Hodder & Stoughton, 1981)

David Smith *From Boom to Bust* (Penguin, 1993)

Martin J. Weiner *English Culture and the Decline of the Industrial Spirit 1850–1980* (Cambridge: University Press, 1981)

One Nation and Two

★Paul Addison *Churchill on the Home Front, 1900–1955* (Pimlico, 1993)

Paul Addison *The Road to 1945: British Politics and The Second World War* (Quartet, 1977)

Vernon Bodganor and Robert Skidelsky (eds) *The Age of Affluence 1951–64* (Macmillan, 1970)

Noreen Branson *Britain in the Nineteen Twenties* (Weidenfeld & Nicolson, 1975)

K. D. Ewing and C. A. Gearty *Freedom Under Thatcher: Civil Liberties in Modern Britain* (Oxford: University Press, 1990)

Paul Foot *Immigration and Race in British Politics* (Penguin, 1965)

Peter Fraser *The Evolution of the British Welfare State* (Macmillan, 1973)

★Peter Hennessy *Never Again: Britain 1945–1951* (Vintage, 1993)

Kevin Jefferys *The Churchill Coalition and Wartime Politics 1940–1945* (Manchester: University Press, 1991)

Paul Smith *Disraelian Conservatism and Social Reform* (Routledge and Kegan Paul, 1967)

Richard M. Titmuss *Problems of Social Policy* (HMSO, 1950)

In High Places

Anne Chisholm and Michael Davie *Beaverbrook: A Life* (Hutchinson, 1992)

Michael Cockerell, Peter Hennessy and David Walker *Sources Close* to *The Prime Minister: Inside the hidden world of the news manipulators* (Macmillan, 1984)

★Richard Cockett *Twilight of Truth: Chamberlain, Appeasement and the Manipulation of the Press* (Weidenfeld & Nicolson, 1989)

James Curran and Jean Seaton *Power without Responsibility: The Press and Broadcasting in Britain* (Fontana, 1981)

Mark Hollingsworth *The Press and Political Dissent* (Pluto Press, 1986)

John Junor *Listening for a Midnight Tram* (Chapmans, 1990)

Phillip Knightley *The First Casualty: From the Crimea to Vietnam: The War Correspondent as Hero, Propagandist, and Myth Maker* (Quartet, 1978)

Stephen Koss *The Rise and Fall of the Political Press in Britain* (Fontana, 1990)

James Margach *The Abuse of Power: The War between Downing Street and The Media* (W. H. Allen, 1978)

★Jeremy Paxman *Friends in High Places: Who Runs Britain?* (Penguin, 1991)

Andrew Roberts *The Holy Fox: A Biography of Lord Halifax* (Weidenfeld & Nicolson, 1991)

William Shawcross *Rupert Murdoch: Ringmaster of the Information Circus* (Pan, 1993)

Dangerous Liaisons

★David Baker, Andrew Gamble and Steve Ludlam '1846 . . . 1906 . . . 1996? Conservative Splits and European Integration' in *Political Quarterly*, volume 64, no.4, 1993

★Linda Colley *Britons* (Yale: University Press, 1992)

Hugh Cunningham 'The Language of Patriotism' in *History Workshop Journal*, xii, 1981

Hugh Cunningham 'The Conservative Party and Patriotism' in Robert Colls and Philip Dodd (eds) *Englishness: Politics and Culture 1880–1920* (Croom Helm, 1986)

Liz Curtis *Nothing But The Same Old Story* (Information on Ireland, 1984)

★Arnold Kemp *The Hollow Drum: Scotland Since The War* (Edinburgh: Mainstream, 1993)

*Keith Kyle *Suez* (Weidenfeld & Nicolson, 1989)

*Andrew Marr *The Battle For Scotland* (Penguin, 1992)

James Mitchell *Conservatives and the Union: A Study of Conservative Party Attitudes to Scotland* (Edinburgh: Mainstream, 1990)

John Osmond *The Divided Kingdom* (Constable, 1988)

Hugh Thomas *The Suez Affair* (Weidenfeld & Nicolson, 1986)

Tory Mavericks, Rebels and Outsiders

*Robert Blake *Disraeli* (Methuen, 1969)

*Lord Boothby *Recollections of a Rebel* (Hutchinson, 1978)

Andrew Boyle *Poor, Dear Brendan: The Quest for Brendan Bracken* (Hutchinson, 1974)

William Camp *The Glittering Prizes* (Macgibbon and Kee, 1960)

John Campbell *F. E. Smith: First Earl of Birkenhead* (Pimlico, 1991)

Richard Cockett *My Dear Max: The Letters of Brendan Bracken to Lord Beaverbrook 1925–1958* (Historians' Press, 1990)

Patrick Cosgrave *The Lives of Enoch Powell* (Bodley Head: 1989)

Kay Halle (ed) *Randolph Churchill: The Young Unpretender* (Heinemann, 1971)

Robert Rhodes James *Bob Boothby: A Portrait* (Headline, 1992)

C. E. Lysaght *Brendan Bracken* (Allen Lane, 1979)

Sir Anthony Meyer *Stand Up And Be Counted* (Heineman, 1990)

Philip Norton *Conservative Dissidents: Dissent within the Parliamentary Conservative Party 1970–74* (Temple Smith, 1978)

Brian Roberts *Randolph: A Study of Churchill's Son* (Hamish Hamilton, 1984)

Norman Rose *Churchill: An Unruly Life* (Simon and Schuster, 1994)

Douglas E. Schoen *Enoch Powell and the Powellites* (Macmillan, 1987)

Christopher Sykes *Nancy: The Life of Lady Astor* (Panther, 1979)

Less Than Meets The Eye

Biographies, Memoirs and Autobiographies
Up to 1945
Barbara Cartland *Ronald Cartland* (Collins, 1942)

Sir Austen Chamberlain *Down the Years* (Cassell, 1935)

John Charmley *Duff Cooper* (Weidenfeld & Nicolson, 1986)

Duff Cooper *Old Men Forget* (Hart–Davis, 1953)

*Robert Rhodes James (ed) *'Chips': The Diaries of Sir Henry Channon* (Weidenfeld, 1993)

Robert Rhodes James (ed) *Memoirs of a Conservative: J. C. C. Davidson's Memoirs and Papers 1910–1937* (Weidenfeld & Nicolson, 1939)

R. F. Foster *Lord Randolph Churchill: A Political Life* (Oxford: University Press, 1986)

Eustace Percy *Some Memories* (Eyre & Spottiswoode, 1958)

John Ramsden (ed) *Real Old Tory Politics: The Political Diaries of Sir Robert Sanders, Lord Bayford, 1910–35* (Historians' Press, 1984)

Gervaise Rentoul *Sometimes I Think* (Hodder & Stoughton, 1940)

Colin Thornton-Kemsley *Through Winds and Tide* (Montrose: Standard Press, 1974)

Ronald Tree *When the Moon was High: Memoirs of Peace and War 1897–1942* (Macmillan, 1975)

John Baker White *True Blue: An Autobiography 1902–1939* (Muller, 1970)

After 1945
Maurice Ashley *Churchill as Historian* (Secker & Warburg, 1968)

Reginald Bevins *The Greasy Pole* (Hodder & Stoughton, 1965)

Lord Butler *The Art of the Possible* (Penguin, 1973)

Viscount Chandos *The Memoirs of Lord Chandos* (Bodley Head, 1962)

Patrick Cosgrave *R. A. Butler: An English Life* (Quartet, 1981)

Douglas Dodds-Parker *Political Eunuch* (Ascot: Springwood Books, 1986)

Martin Gilbert *In Search of Churchill: A historian's journey* (HarperCollins, 1994)

Ian Harvey *To Fall Like Lucifer* (Sidgwick & Jackson, 1971)

Lord Home *The Way the Wind Blows* (Collins, 1976)

Anthony Howard *RAB: The Life of R. A. Butler* (Papermac, 1988)

Lord Hill *Both Sides of the Hill* (Heinemann, 1964)

Earl of Kilmuir *Political Adventure* (Weidenfeld & Nicolson, 1964)

Reginald Maudling *Memoirs* (Sidgwick & Jackson, 1978)

Andrew Roberts *Eminent Churchillians* (Weidenfeld & Nicolson, 1994)

D. R. Thorpe *Selwyn Lloyd* (Cape, 1989)

James Stuart *Within the Fringe* (Bodley Head, 1967)

Earl of Woolton *Memoirs* (Cassell, 1959)

Woodrow Wyatt *Confessions of an Optimist* (Collins, 1985)

1970 onwards

Kenneth Baker *The Turbulent Years: My Life in Politics* (Faber, 1993)

Humphry Berkeley *Crossing the Floor* (Allen & Unwin, 1972)

Lord Carrington *Reflect On Things Past* (Collins, 1988)

*Alan Clark *Diaries* (Weidenfeld & Nicolson, 1993)

Julian Critchley *A Bag of Boiled Sweets* (Faber, 1994)

*Ian Gilmour *Dancing with Dogma* (Simon & Schuster, 1992)

Lord Hailsham *The Door Wherein I Went* (Collins, 1975); *A Sparrow's Flight* (Collins, 1990)

Morrison Halcrow *Keith Joseph: A Single Mind* (Macmillan, 1989)

Geoffrey Howe *Conflict of Loyalty* (Macmillan, 1994)

Cecil Parkinson *Right at the Centre: An Autobiography* (Weidenfeld & Nicolson, 1992)

James Prior *A Balance of Power* (Hamish Hamilton, 1986)

Peter Rawlinson *A Price Too High* (Weidenfeld & Nicolson, 1989)

Nicholas Ridley *My Style of Government: The Thatcher Years* (Hutchinson, 1992)

Norman Tebbit *Upwardly Mobile* (Futura, 1989)

William Whitelaw *The Whitelaw Memoirs* (Headline, 1990)

Lord Young *The Enterprise Years: A Businessman in the Cabinet* (Headline, 1990)

Unofficial Faces

I have omitted the novels and plays mentioned in this chapter.

Janet Adam Smith *John Buchan* (Oxford: University Press, 1985)

David Cannadine 'Gilbert And Sullivan: The Making And Unmaking of a British 'Tradition' in Roy Porter (ed) *Myths of the English* (Cambridge: Polity Press, 1992)

David Cannadine 'James Bond and the Decline of England' in *Encounter*, volume xxviii, no.5, September 1979

Christopher Harvie *The Centre of Things: Political Fiction in Britain from Disraeli to the Present* (Unwin Hyman, 1991)

Andrew Lownie *John Buchan: Presbyterian Cavalier* (Constable, 1995)

Tom Pocock *Rider Haggard and the Last Empire: A Biography* (Weidenfeld & Nicolson, 1993)

Joan Smith 'Who's afraid of Frederick Forsyth?' in the *New Statesman*, 15 January 1988

Richard Usborne *Clubland Heroes* (Barrie & Jenkins, 1974)

Colin Watson *Snobbery with Violence: Crime Stories and their Audience* (Eyre & Spottiswoode, 1971)

However invaluable the above sources are, nothing rivals the mixture of tedium and excitement of trawling through the Conservative Party Archive at the Bodleian Library in Oxford, the Public Records Office or the collections of unpublished material held at various institutions up and down the country.

Index

Page numbers in **bold** denote chapter/major section
devoted to subject.